LETTERS OF
LEONARD
WOOLF

LETTERS OF
LEONARD
WOOLF,

EDITED BY
FREDERIC
SPOTTS

HARCOURT

BRACE

JOVANOVICH

SAN DIEGO   NEW YORK   LONDON

Library of Congress Cataloging-in-Publication Data
Woolf, Leonard, 1880–1969.
[Correspondence. Selections]
Letters of Leonard Woolf/edited by Frederic Spotts.—1st ed.
p. cm.
Includes index.
ISBN 0-15-150915-8
1. Woolf, Leonard, 1880–1969—Correspondence. 2. Political
scientists—Great Britain—Correspondence. I. Spotts, Frederic.
II. Title.
JA94.W6A4 1989
320'.092'4—dc19 89-2027

Designed by Michael Farmer
Printed in the United States of America
First edition
A B C D E

CONTENTS

ILLUSTRATIONS

PREFACE

LEONARD WOOLF had a life whose scope and variety of accomplishments were equaled by few other Englishmen of the century. He was a precocious colonial administrator who became one of the earliest and most persistent advocates of dismantling the Empire. As a literary critic and publisher of some of the most important books of our era, he exercised a significant intellectual and cultural influence in the interwar period and beyond. Through his political writings, the various journals he edited and his advisory role in the Labour Party and the Fabian Society, he was a leading proponent of democratic socialism. He wrote one of the earliest blueprints for the League of Nations and devoted the remainder of his life to advocating ways of deterring international aggression. His marriage to a literary genius and his close friendship with many other eminent writers placed him at the center of the most remarkable intellectual coterie of our time. That he never achieved great fame or high political position—neither of which he aspired to—in no way detracts from his fascination. "What a life he has led," said E. M. Forster, "and how well he has led it!"

These letters are the epistolary shards of that life. They are a fraction of the roughly 8,000 letters that have been found, which are in turn only a small portion of the total number Leonard wrote. Fortunately, correspondence survives from every period except adolescence, and on every aspect of his personal and professional life. If the letters became briefer in his late years, up to the end he preferred his typewriter to his telephone.

Letter writing is a mark of a highly civilized person in a highly civilized society. It presupposes a common culture, a pleasure in sharing thoughts and a desire for intellectual and emotional intimacy. The good correspondent is the person who knows how to be a good friend. Leonard Woolf grew up in an era and a society and a class in which writing letters was as natural and important as reading and conversation. He and his friends treasured their correspondence, carefully preserving it and treating it like a well-loved book. That their letters might be published would never have crossed their minds.

What would Leonard, then, have thought of this volume? In a letter written near the end of his life to Lord Annan, he seems almost to address the point from beyond the grave, decrying

> . . . the fog which seems to spread over masses of letters and juvenilia just laid out on a table or in a book. It is partly the deadness of the dead. All these things dashed off in half a minute by a living hand and mind are served up to us as if they were carved in stone, and the more there are of them the more marmoreal they become. But the main thing is the obvious fact that in letters and diaries people tend (1) much more often to write when they are miserable than when they are happy. Virginia noticed this somewhere in her diaries. (2) to exaggerate and dramatize their miseries. Not only our sweetest songs are those which tell of saddest thoughts, but they are also the sweetest to the singer.

Despite these strictures he felt no inhibition in publishing various letter collections, including a small volume of correspondence between his wife and Lytton Strachey. So it seems fair to follow his example, while bearing in mind his caveat.

If Leonard's comment to Lord Annan makes a valid point, it also contains much inadvertent self-revelation—and that is part of the enjoyment in reading someone's letters. Correspondence is unwitting autobiography. "Unwitting" is especially relevant in Leonard's case, since he has to his credit one of the best autobiographies of his time. For all its scope and honesty, however, the memoir is an account filtered through the discretions of a stoic and the perceptions of a man in the twilight of a long life. These letters are to his autobiography what a photograph is to a self-portrait: one does not belie the other; each leaves its own impression. The appeal of gaining direct access to another person's thoughts as they occurred and emotions as they were felt was explained by Freud in a comment on biography that applies equally well to correspondence. *We* are raised to the level of the subject by observing his strengths, while *he* comes down to us by revealing his weaknesses. As a result we come closer as human beings.

From the surviving letters, some 600 have been selected from the various phases of Leonard's life and career. Since the letters are of remarkably even quality and interest, choosing among them was difficult. The letters included are, above all, those that best give a sense of the flow of Leonard's everyday life and the evolution of his professional activities. Letters were also selected that offer insight into the sort of man he was—his character, emotions and interests, his relations with others and the credo that drove and guided his life. And ample space was allowed for correspondence to and about his wife. A few writers have attempted, against all the evidence, to turn Leonard into a villain who misunderstood and even mistreated her. Others contend that if there were a Nobel Prize for marriage, Leonard would deserve to be its laureate. None of the letters were specifically selected to address either point of view. But in light of the interest in the couple's relationship, all of Leonard's letters to Virginia—save one insubstantial and largely illegible postcard—are included, along with correspondence to him about her health.

General principles, however, are not conclusive guidelines. A very detailed letter written in 1914 about his research into women's wages in industry well illustrates Leonard's feminist sympathies, his nascent concern for social justice and his work for better minimum wages for women. The letter, scarcely one that many readers would find gripping, has been omitted, along with other correspondence of this sort. If all Leonard's letters on Virginia's illnesses had been included, this volume would have been a medical case history; to avoid tedium, just enough were included to give an impression of the problem he faced. Any number of letters to famous persons were left out because they did not reveal much about Leonard. Most social correspondence as well as the multitude of letters offering advice and help to friends and strangers were omitted for the same reason. However, to pass over everything of this sort would distort his life. So a few notes, to such friends as Sylvia Townsend Warner, Dame Peggy Ashcroft and William Plomer, are included in the final chapter, though they can only hint at the atmosphere of civility and quiet humor that surrounded his life, particularly in its later years. In all, it proved necessary to omit four out of five of the letters written at Cambridge, over half of those sent from Ceylon, around five out of six regarding publishing and editing, half the letters and almost all the memoranda on political matters and uncounted correspondence regarding his everyday life from 1912 to the time of his death.

To allow space for as many letters as possible, some were abridged. This is not a happy compromise. A letter has an innate integrity that normally should not be tampered with. In the long political letters, in particular, nuances in a line of argument can be lost. Moreover, ellipsis inevitably leaves the reader feeling short-changed, if not suspicious about what has been deleted. Still, omitting portions of some letters has definite advantages. It not only removes repetitive and extraneous material but helps to maintain focus on the main subject. A short note to Margaret Llewelyn Davies in 1920 about developments in the Soviet Union begins: "We return [to London] Wednesday & I hope it wont be quite so long an interval before we meet. It is amazingly pleasant leading the simple life here [in Sussex], though we both get through 100% more work than in London. And all the afternoon we plant potatoes, sow seeds, hang curtains, paper walls." In most cases eliminating this sort of domestic atmosphere would mar the nature of a letter; doing so in a note selected for its political content avoids digression. No letter was abridged or excluded for any other reason.

A word on the postal service may be helpful in understanding some early letters. Prior to the First World War there were eight deliveries a day in London and six in provincial cities, running from 8:15 in the morning to 9:15 at night; there was one delivery on Sundays and public holidays, including Christmas. A letter posted during daylight hours would normally be delivered about three hours later; one sent at midnight would reach its destination by breakfasttime the next morning. Although Sunday deliveries were stopped after 1914 and daily deliveries were further curtailed after 1940, for most of Leonard's lifetime letter exchanges could normally be accomplished within twenty-four hours. Of course, when staying at an isolated house in the countryside, deliveries were slower. And when Leonard was at an outstation in Ceylon, mail generally took around three weeks for delivery.

As is evident in the original texts and as he remarked in a 1967 radio interview about his writing in general, Leonard wrote with great spontaneity, never changing and rarely adding a word or punctuation. His letters consequently have the matter-of-fact, almost rough quality that puts one in mind of Orwell's writing. They come straight from the heart and head, with no frills or artifice or weasel words, and little or no desire to entertain or amuse, but simply to convey feelings, ideas and information.

That said, a significant difference can be detected between the early letters and all the others. Leonard's character underwent a significant change around 1909, after he had been given his own district to govern in Ceylon. Before then the letters were often long, gossipy conversations. But when the Cambridge undergraduate matured into a tough colonial administrator, they avoided gossip about people and took on a serious tone they never again lost.

Another trait is their detachment, which is not to be mistaken for dispassion. Leonard was in fact quite passionate and easily moved to tears and laughter. And he could be very prickly when angered. But he viewed life from a considerable emotional distance and when he felt something deeply he controlled or repressed his feelings. Friends visiting him when France fell to the Germans in 1940 found him so distraught they seriously thought he might collapse. Yet he said nothing at the time and his correspondence makes no mention of the event. Similarly, it is difficult to detect from the letters how profoundly he suffered from Virginia's breakdowns and suicide. He was someone whose deepest feelings were expressed in silence.

The presentation of this correspondence differs from convention in two respects. To allow the various strands of Leonard's life to emerge clearly, the letters have been arranged in part thematically. The book begins with a chapter of letters from his undergraduate years at Cambridge, between 1899 and 1904, followed by a selection of those written while a colonial civil servant in Ceylon, from 1904 to 1911, and continues with letters about his life with Virginia, from 1911 to 1941. The next chapter goes back to 1912 and takes up his career as a publisher and editor, and the following one comprises letters in the same period about his political activities. The final chapter resumes his personal life after Virginia's death, in 1941, and continues until his own death, in 1969. Despite its clear drawbacks, this arrangement reflects the remarkable compartmentalization of his various activities and gives them a coherence that would otherwise be lost. Also it usually permits consecutive letters on a single topic to run without interruption.

Another unorthodox feature of this volume is the inclusion of some letters *to* Leonard, either in the text or in footnotes, which proved to be a more economical and interesting way of explaining his corresponding letter than straightforward annotation. Occasionally it was a means of replacing a letter of Leonard's that has not survived but whose content can easily be construed from the reply. These letters also have the incidental benefit of lending the collection some of the quality of true correspondence—an exchange—and leave an impression of the people and ideas to which Leonard was responding.

To reduce the need for footnotes, each chapter begins with a brief introduction. These alembicized commentaries make no attempt to sum up, much less assess, Leonard Woolf's life and career. Their purpose is merely to explain the background of the letters and to highlight some of the important points that arise. The reader who wishes to encounter the correspondence directly, without any explanatory veil, is encouraged to ignore them.

SOURCES AND
ACKNOWLEDGMENTS

THE SEARCH for correspondence is not unlike the search for archeological remains. In this case some portions were found almost entirely intact, some in fragments; some could be surmised to have existed; some have vanished without a trace. Some came to light easily; some resisted remorseless search. The whim of the recipient and the vagary of fate ordained what has survived; the effort and luck of the editor determined what has been found.

Leonard Woolf's 8,000 surviving letters and the much larger number to him are but a fraction of the total he wrote and received. The handwritten letters—all those before 1914 and a small portion of those thereafter—are obviously only those retained by the recipient. Significant batches of them—to Lytton Strachey, Saxon Sydney-Turner, Margaret Llewelyn Davies, Virginia Woolf, R. C. Trevelyan and Trekkie Parsons—have survived apparently intact. The existing typed letters are either the originals retained by the addressee or carbon copies which Leonard made. As a publisher, he retained copies of the Hogarth Press correspondence once the firm had become a serious business, around 1923. Otherwise he made relatively few copies; in any event, only a small number survive. But many friends—T. S. Eliot, Vita Sackville-West, Kingsley Martin, William Plomer, Sylvia Townsend Warner and Dame Peggy Ashcroft, to mention a few—kept all or nearly all he sent them. Lytton Strachey was the single most important correspondent, the two having exchanged nearly 500 letters from 1900 until 1931. Since Leonard and Virginia were seldom apart after marriage, there are relatively few letters between them.

What is known to have been lost or destroyed? There are no letters to family members apart from a few written in childhood and late in life. Those to his mother, along with all her photographs, were destroyed in the blitz in 1940; correspondence held by his sister Bella is said to have been burned after her death. Fortunately Leonard retained all or most of the family correspondence he received between 1896 and 1912—over 900 such letters—and these give some idea of the content of his own to them. The war was responsible for other losses; for instance, some files of the Independent Labour Party and those of the *Nation* and the *New Statesman*, which no doubt contained some letters, were destroyed by bombs. Most Fabian Society correspondence was surrendered to a paper scrap drive in 1942.

Other losses can also be identified. Leonard retained about 40,000 of the letters he received; relatively few of his corresponding ones have survived or could be traced. Only a small portion of the letters listed in Sigmund Freud's correspondence log came to light. None of the voluminous correspondence between 1915 and 1918 about the Ceylon riots could be found in the National Archives of Sri Lanka or the Public Record Office. There are enough hints in the Labour Party files, the Public Record Office and a number of private collections to suggest that great quantities of letters on political affairs between 1914 and 1946 have been lost. Almost no record remains of his quarrels with the BBC over its "under-housemaid snobbery," nor could any relics be found of his messianic crusade for better classical-music broadcasts. And, alas, there is no trace of the response to Vita Sackville-West's letter in 1942 about a seer who had received messages for him from Virginia.

Although the bombs that fell on and around Mecklenburgh Square in September 1940 wrecked the walls and ceilings and broke water pipes in the Woolfs' house, they destroyed none of their belongings. Most of these were eventually transported to Sussex; but the movers confused their instructions and left some things behind. After the war, when Leonard vacated Mecklenburgh Square, the remaining effects were transferred to his new house in Victoria Square, along with what had been stored in Sussex. In this melee—Leonard lost track of what papers had survived and their whereabouts—letters may well have been lost. Certainly some were misplaced; one trunk of miscellaneous correspondence came to light only twenty-five years later, under circumstances that have never been fully clarified. More mysterious are the Hogarth Press files. John Lehmann was of the impression that all but the working files were completely destroyed, and Leonard believed that few had survived. Presumably they were moved, with the printing press, to Sussex in 1940, and following the war and the Press's affiliation with Chatto & Windus, were deposited in the new offices on William IV Street, where they were lost sight of.

The most important holdings of Leonard Woolf's papers are two collections at the University of Sussex. The Monk's House Papers comprise manuscripts and letters that Leonard made available to Quentin Bell for use in writing his biography of Virginia Woolf. They were sorted and listed by Anne Olivier Bell; though primarily relating to Virginia, they include some of Leonard's letters as well. The Leonard Woolf Papers comprise the remaining bulk of his files of correspondence, documents, pocket diaries and financial account books, totaling some 60,000 items, of which roughly 4,000 are the originals or copies of his own letters. Both collections were left by Leonard to Trekkie Parsons, who donated them to the university shortly after his death. She also deposited correspondence between herself and Leonard from 1943 to 1969. Although this correspondence is closed until her death, she permitted me to select letters for publication. The Woolf Papers were sorted, catalogued and indexed in 1976–77 by George Spater with the assistance of Elizabeth Inglis. Also at Sussex are the papers of Kingsley Martin, the longtime editor of the *New Statesman*, which include several dozen exchanges between himself and Leonard.

Two other collections are of exceptional importance. Reading University holds the surviving files of the Hogarth Press. These were transferred there in 1985–86 from the firm's London office and have been meticulously catalogued by Michael Bott. Although the individual dossiers on some books and some authors are missing and many are only partly intact, the collection comprises thousands of letters between Leonard and his authors from 1924 on. The other rich collection is at the Harry Ransom Humanities Research Center, The University of Texas at Austin. Here are all Leonard's letters to Lytton Strachey from 1900 to 1904 and most of those from 1912 to 1931, along with much of his correspondence with John Lehmann and a vast array of others.

Additional letters were found, singly or in the dozens, in the files of libraries, archives and institutions around the world. In the United Kingdom these include the Bodleian Library; the BBC Written Records Collection; the British Library; Cambridge University Library; Churchill College, Cambridge; City of London Polytechnic; Clare College, Cambridge; the Dorset County Museum; Durham University;

Hatfield House; the House of Lords Record Office; the India Office Library; the Institute of Psycho-Analysis; King's College, Cambridge; the Labour Party; the London School of Economics and Political Science; the Marshall Library, Cambridge; the National Library of Scotland; Nuffield College, Oxford; the Public Record Office; Rhodes House Library, Oxford; the Royal Economic Society; Ruskin College, Oxford; the John Rylands University Library, Manchester University; Trinity College, Cambridge; and Warwick University. In the United States and Canada letters are held by Alfred University; Ball State University; the Beinecke Library at Yale University; Boston University; Bryn Mawr College; Columbia University; the Houghton Library at Harvard University; the Huntington Library; the Lilly Library at Indiana University; McMaster University; the Henry W. and Albert A. Berg Collection, The New York Public Library, Astor, Lenox and Tilden Foundations; Northwestern University; Princeton University; Southern Illinois University; Temple University; the University of California at Los Angeles; the University of Illinois; the University of Victoria and Washington State University. The Department of National Archives of Sri Lanka has a few private letters, Leonard's official diaries as Assistant Government Agent and correspondence while he was an official of the government of Ceylon. A copy of the Reichssicherheitshauptamt's *Sonderfahndungsliste*, listing Leonard and Virginia Woolf, is at the Hoover Institution at Stanford.

The following individuals and publishers also provided letters, though unfortunately not all of them could be included: Lord Annan; Edward Arnold, Publishers; Dame Peggy Ashcroft; Quentin Bell; the Cecil family; Chatto & Windus, Publishers; Leon Edel; Mrs. T. S. Eliot; John Graham; Harcourt Brace Jovanovich; Mitchell Leaska; Jill Day-Lewis; Sir Henry Lintott; Little, Brown and Co.; Victor Lowe; Malcolm Muggeridge; the *New Statesman*; Nigel Nicolson; Vanessa Nicolson; Frances Partridge; Peter Parker; S. P. Rosenbaum; Roberta Rubenstein; Lucio Ruotolo; Clare Sack; Daphne Sanger and Ina Wolf.

A good many of the photographs are published for the first time, though for the sake of continuity some are included that have appeared elsewhere. Credit for these illustrations is due the Anthony d'Offay Gallery; Gisèle Freund; the BBC Hulton Picture Collection; Barbara Strachey Halpern; the Harvard Theatre Collection; Richard Kennedy; the National Portrait Gallery, London; Trekkie Parsons; Clare Sack; the University of Sussex; and the Tate Gallery. Permission to include photographs of several portraits of Leonard Woolf was generously granted by their copyright holders: Angelica Garnett for Vanessa Bell;

Henrietta Garnett for Duncan Grant; Lady Pansy Lamb for Henry Lamb; and Trekkie Parsons. Thanks to her unrivaled knowledge of photographs of the Woolfs, Elizabeth Richardson provided much helpful advice.

Those who have helped in one way or another probably number in the hundreds; some have in the meantime become friends. My primary debt is to Trekkie Parsons, Leonard Woolf's literary executor, who gave permission to publish the letters. I should also like to express my appreciation to Chatto & Windus/The Hogarth Press for allowing me to use some fifty of Leonard Woolf's letters from their files; and to the *New Statesman* for permission to publish letters Leonard wrote as literary editor of the *Nation*. I am grateful to the estate of the author, The Hogarth Press and Harcourt Brace Jovanovich for permission to quote from Leonard Woolf's autobiography, and to Sir Laurens van der Post and The Hogarth Press for permission to quote a short extract from *In a Province*.

Obviously I am deeply indebted to all the individuals, archivists and librarians who conscientiously searched their files and permitted publication of what they held. In particular I am grateful to A. N. Peasgood, Librarian of the University of Sussex Library; Cathy Henderson, Research Librarian at the Harry Ransom Humanities Research Center; Michael Bott, Archivist at Reading University; Angela Raspin, Archivist at the London School of Economics; and Michael Halls, Modern Archivist at King's College, Cambridge. But I must single out Elizabeth Inglis, Assistant Librarian at Sussex, for special thanks. Her incomparable knowledge of the Sussex collections and her inexhaustible patience and helpfulness in countless ways over a period of several years were somehow fully equal to the exigence of my requests and inquiries.

In annotating the letters and in writing the chapter introductions, I was greatly aided by those who knew Leonard Woolf well—above all, by Trekkie Parsons and Anne Olivier Bell and Quentin Bell, but also by Lord Annan, Richard Kennedy, John Lehmann, Sir Henry Lintott, Mary Lyon Manson, Frances Partridge, George Rylands and Sir Stephen Spender. Leonard Woolf's niece Clare Sack provided photographs, family information and her valuable collection of family letters to Leonard. While a list of the names of everyone who answered letters and questions would be impossibly long, I should like to mention Dame Peggy Ashcroft, Sir Isaiah Berlin, Mrs. T. S. Eliot, A. W. Freud, Sir Rupert Hart-Davis, Lord Kahn, Jill Day-Lewis, Robert Robson and Robert Skidelsky. Patricia Pugh, Mona Harrington and Dr. Anthony

Storr read portions of the text, and Anne Olivier Bell and Quentin Bell read the entire manuscript. I am grateful to them all for their helpful comments.

My thanks also go to those copyright holders of letters *to* Leonard Woolf who could be traced: The Baksettown Trust for Octavia Wilberforce, Sally Belfrage for S. Henning Belfrage, Quentin Bell and Angelica Garnett for Clive and Vanessa Bell, D. M. M. Carey for Archbishop Lord Fisher of Lambeth, Eleanor Fish for Frank Fish, John Freeman for Kingsley Martin, Sigmund Freud Copyrights for Sigmund and Anna Freud, Livia Gollancz for Sir Victor Gollancz, Diana Harding for Sir Arthur Gaye, Lady Harrod for Sir Roy Harrod, Sir Nicolas Henderson for Sir Hubert Henderson, Miles Huddleston for John Lehmann, Mervyn Jones for Ernest Jones, the Provost and Scholars of King's College, Cambridge, for E. M. Forster, Alfred A. Knopf, Inc. for Blanche Knopf, A. K. S. Lambton for Lord and Lady Robert Cecil of Chelwood, Jill Day-Lewis and A. D. Peters & Co. for Cecil Day-Lewis, William Maxwell for Sylvia Townsend Warner, Dame Alix Meynell for Sir Francis Meynell, Timothy Moore for G. E. Moore, Nigel Nicolson for Vita Sackville-West, the Rhodes House Library for Dame Margery Perham, Mary Duchess of Roxburghe for the Marquess of Crewe, Philip Snow for Lord Snow, the Society of Authors as agents for the Strachey Trust for Lytton and James Strachey, John Sparrow for Sir Maurice Bowra, Rayner Unwin for Sir Stanley Unwin and A. P. Watt Ltd. for H. G. Wells. I am also grateful to Lord Annan, Quentin Bell, Sir Isaiah Berlin, Sir Moses Finley and Ann Stephen Synge for permission to quote their own letters to Leonard Woolf, as well as to Rosemary Dinnage and the Estate of Gerald Brenan for allowing me to use Gerald Brenan's letter to Ms. Dinnage.

For the use of Lytton Strachey's letters to Leonard Woolf, credit is due the Harry Ransom Humanities Research Center, The University of Texas at Austin; Princeton University; and the Henry W. and Albert A. Berg Collection, The New York Public Library, Astor, Lenox and Tilden Foundations.

Finally, though not least of all, I wish to express appreciation for expert editorial advice and support. John Ferrone of Harcourt Brace Jovanovich helped shape the book from the very start. Candida Brazil of Weidenfeld & Nicolson suggested improvements in the text. And Alan Bell, with his outstanding knowledge of British literature, read a draft of the text and provided helpful information and much useful counsel.

Words of appreciation inevitably sound perfunctory in cold print; these are deeply felt.

For academic hospitality during the preparation of the book I must thank Professor Carl Rosberg and the Institute of International Studies at Berkeley, where the work was begun, and the Warden and Fellows of St. Antony's College, Oxford, where it was largely done. I am also grateful to Professor Stanley Hoffmann and Abby Collins of the Center for European Studies at Harvard for support in various ways during my periodic sojourns in the other Cambridge.

NOTE ON EDITING

PREPARING THESE LETTERS for publication presented few problems. Despite his lifelong hand tremor, Leonard Woolf's calligraphy is neat and easy to read. Virtually all the letters carry the full date. Those with only the day and month could confidently be placed in the correct year and those lacking any date, within a fortnight of when they were written. The carbon copies Leonard retained of his typed correspondence show no sending address; this too could in most cases be established from diaries and is added in brackets.

The letters have been transcribed as closely as possible to the originals, with all their idiosyncracies of spelling, punctuation and style. "To-morrow" and "to-day" were common in letters before 1912 but might be written without the hyphen in the same letter. "Don't" was normally written without the apostrophe and sometimes the Victorian "do n't" appears. Leonard referred to Virginia as "V." and sometimes "V" and might write both in the same letter. He was careless at times with apostrophes; hence King's College and Clifford's Inn and even sometimes Monk's House were written without one. Accent marks on French words were at times overlooked. General affiliations—communist, socialist, liberal, jewish—were mostly not capitalized. When quoting, he usually, but not invariably, placed punctuation outside quotation marks. Handwritten letters were often not indented at the beginning of a paragraph, particularly at the outset of a letter. In a few cases there was no period at the end of a sentence. To make it easier to read an occasional awkward sentence—clearly written in haste—punctuation has sometimes been added or changed and in a very few cases syntax slightly altered. Several exceptionally long passages have been divided into paragraphs. Underlined words have been italicized, as have the titles of books, plays and operas.

Additions to the text and explanatory comments are enclosed in brackets. When a letter has been abridged, the ellipsis is marked in the conventional editorial fashion. Some insubstantial postscripts, however, have been dropped without indication. In those rare cases where Leonard ended a letter with spaced dots, this is indicated by "[*sic*]." Words that cannot be deciphered are indicated in brackets.

In the salutation, close and subscription of his letters, Leonard followed the conventions of his time. Before about 1910 this dictated using surnames only or, with close friends, a nickname; with extremely close friends the salutation might be dropped. By the end of the Edwardian era the use of first names was permitted among friends, though Leonard never broke the habit of addressing those who were his senior at Cambridge, such as Bertrand Russell and G. E. Moore, in the old way. When convention further relaxed after the Second World War, he easily fell in with the change and after the mid-1950s used first names with the abandon of an American. Throughout his life the close he used was "Yours" to intimates and "Yours sincerely" to everyone else, and he rarely placed a comma after either. He always signed himself "L." to a very few intimates; otherwise he used "Leonard Sidney Woolf" or "L. S. Woolf" prior to 1918 and "Leonard Woolf" after that, even to old friends like E. M. Forster. When no signature shows on carbon copies, the two names have been assumed and added. Only late in life and with friends did it become simply "Leonard." The absence of a signature on a holograph letter is so indicated.

Personal titles can be confusing. The rule followed here is to employ the name as it first appears in the correspondence. Thus Sidney Webb remains Sidney Webb after becoming Lord Passfield. The honorific for a person subsequently knighted is placed in parentheses. Bella Woolf remains Bella Woolf even after she became Bella Lock, later Bella Southorn and still later Lady Southorn.

Reference is made in the chapter introductions and footnotes to

Leonard Woolf's autobiography; this was published between 1960 and 1969 in five volumes: *Sowing*, 1880–1904; *Growing*, 1904–1911; *Beginning Again*, 1911–1918; *Downhill All the Way*, 1919–1939 and *The Journey Not the Arrival Matters*, 1939–1969.

All editorial work follows American spelling and punctuation.

FAMILY TREE

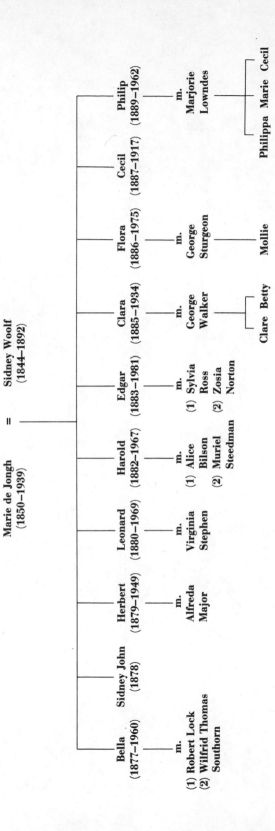

Marie de Jongh (1850–1939) = Sidney Woolf (1844–1892)

Bella (1877–1960)
m.
(1) Robert Lock
(2) Wilfrid Thomas Southorn

Sidney John (1878)

Herbert (1879–1949)
m.
Alfreda Major

Leonard (1880–1969)
m.
Virginia Stephen

Harold (1882–1967)
m.
(1) Alice Bilson
(2) Muriel Steedman

Edgar (1883–1981)
m.
(1) Sylvia Ross
(2) Zosia Norton

Clara (1885–1934)
m.
George Walker

Clare   Betty

Flora (1886–1975)
m.
George Sturgeon

Mollie

Cecil (1887–1917)

Philip (1889–1962)
m.
Marjorie Lowndes

Philippa   Marie   Cecil

CHRONOLOGY

1880
  25 November   Born at 72 West Cromwell Road, London

1889   St. Paul's Preparatory School

1890–1892   Tutored at home

1892   Father dies

1892–1894   Arlington House (school), Brighton

1894–1899   St. Paul's School

1899–1904   Trinity College, Cambridge

1902
  June   Receives First in Classical Tripos, Part I
  October   elected to Apostles

1903
  June   Receives Second in Classical Tripos, Part II

1904
  October   Appointed to Colonial Civil Service
  19 November   Sails for Ceylon
  16 December   Arrives in Colombo

1905
   5 January   Cadet in Jaffna

1906
   February–April   Koddu Superintendent at Pearl Fishery
   August   Acting Assistant Government Agent in
                           Mannar

1907
   August   Office Assistant in Kandy

1908
   August   Assistant Government Agent in Hambantota

1911
   20 May   Leaves Hambantota for London
   July–August   Visits Sweden and Denmark
   August   Begins *The Village in the Jungle*
   December   Moves to 38 Brunswick Square

1912
   2 May   Resigns from Colonial Civil Service
   29 May   Is engaged to Virginia Stephen
   Summer   Finishes *The Village in the Jungle*; works
                           briefly with Shoreditch Care Committee in
                           East End; joins suffrage movement; meets
                           Margaret Llewelyn Davies; begins writing for
                           Co-operative News
   10 August   Marries at St. Pancras Registry Office
   August–October   Honeymoon in France, Spain and Italy
   October   Begins *The Wise Virgins* and several short sto-
                           ries; Woolfs move to Clifford's Inn
   October–   Secretary to the Second Post-Impressionist
   December   Exhibition

1913
   February   *The Village in the Jungle* published
   March   Lectures to Women's Co-operative Guild
                           societies
   June   Finishes "The Two Brahmins"
   July   Meets Webbs; joins Fabian Society; begins
                           writing for *New Statesman*

July–September	Virginia has mental breakdown; attempts suicide
August	Finishes *The Wise Virgins* and "The Three Jews"
December	Woolfs leave Clifford's Inn and live at Asheham House

1914

	Spends much of year writing articles and reviews; active in Women's Co-operative Guild and Fabian Society
October	Woolfs move to 17 The Green, Richmond
December	Commissioned to write study on international order for Fabian Society
	The Wise Virgins, Education and the Co-operative Movement and *The Control of Industry by Co-operators and Trade Unionists* published

1915

February	Virginia has mental breakdown
March	Woolfs move to Hogarth House, Richmond
July	Report on international order published in *New Statesman*
	Co-operation and the War I: Effects of War on Commerce and Industry, Co-operation and the War II: Co-operative Action in National Crises and *The Control of Industry by the People Through the Co-operative Movement* published

1916

January	Joins editorial board of *War and Peace*
June	Rejected for military service
July	*International Government* published

1917

March	Woolfs purchase printing press
July	*Two Stories* published as first Hogarth Press publication
October	Helps organize 1917 Club
December	Acting editor of *War and Peace*
	The Future of Constantinople and *The Framework of a Lasting Peace* (ed.) published

1918
  January   Heads delegation to Colonial Office hearings
                     on Ceylon riots
  May   Appointed Secretary, Advisory Committee on
                     International Questions of Labour Party
  December   Appointed editor of *International Review*
                     After the War published

1919
  July   Woolfs purchase Monk's House
  December   *International Review* closes; appointed an ed-
                     itor of *Contemporary Review*
                     Co-operation and the Future of Industry and
                     International Economic Policy published

1920
  May   Adopted as candidate for Parliament
  July–October   Acting political editor of the *Nation*
                     Empire and Commerce in Africa, *Mandates
                     and Empire* and *Economic Imperialism* pub-
                     lished

1921
  December   Resigns from *Contemporary Review*
                     Stories of the East, *Socialism and Co-opera-
                     tion* and *Scope of the Mandates under the
                     League of Nations* published

1922
  September   Appointed political editor of the *Nation*
  November   Fails to win seat in Parliament in general
                     election
                     International Co-operative Trade published

1923
  March–April   Woolfs travel to Spain via Paris
  April   Appointed literary editor of the *Nation*
                     Fabian Essays on Co-operation (ed.) pub-
                     lished

1924
  February   Appointed Secretary, Advisory Committee on
                     Imperial Questions
  March   Woolfs move to 52 Tavistock Square

1925

March–April   Woolfs visit France
                   Fear and Politics: A Debate at the Zoo
                   published

1926

May   Supports General Strike

1927

March–April   Woolfs visit France and Sicily
                   Essays on Literature, History, Politics, Etc.
                   and *Hunting the Highbrow* published

1928

March–April   Woolfs visit France
                   The Way of Peace and *Imperialism and Civ-
                   ilization* published

1929

January   Woolfs visit Berlin
June   Woolfs visit France

1930

March   Resigns as literary editor of the *Nation*

1931

April   Woolfs visit France
                   Appointed co-editor of *Political Quarterly*;
                   appointed to Executive Committee of New Fa-
                   bian Research Bureau and head of Interna-
                   tional Section
                   After the Deluge, vol. 1, published

1932

April–May   Woolfs visit Sicily and Greece

1933

May   Woolfs visit France and Italy
                   The Intelligent Man's Way to Prevent War
                   (ed.) and *The Modern State* (co-author)
                   published

1934

April   Woolfs visit Ireland
                   Labour's Foreign Policy published

1935
  May   Woolfs visit Netherlands, Germany, Italy and France
                                Quack, Quack! published

1936
  May   Woolfs visit Cornwall
                                  Helps found Association For Intellectual Liberty
                                  The League and Abyssinia published

1937
  May   Woolfs visit France

1938
  June   Woolfs visit Scotland
                                  Appointed to Civil Service Arbitration Tribunal

1939
  June   Woolfs visit France
  July   Mother dies
  August   Woolfs move to 37 Mecklenburgh Square
                                  After the Deluge, vol. 2, *Barbarians at the Gate* and *The Hotel: A Play in Three Acts* published

1940
  September   37 Mecklenburgh Square damaged by bombs; Hogarth Press moved to Letchworth
                                  Becomes member of Fabian Society Colonial Bureau; becomes sole editor of *Political Quarterly*
                                  The War for Peace published

1941
  28 March   Virginia commits suicide
  September   Appointed to Executive Committee of Anglo-Soviet Public Relations Committee

1942   Elected a director of *New Stateman*
                                  The Death of a Moth and Other Essays (ed.) published

1943   Elected Chairman, International Bureau of Fabian Society Research Department
                                Moves to 24 Victoria Square

1944	The International Post-War Settlement and A Haunted House and Other Short Stories (ed.) published
1945	Resigns as Secretary, Advisory Committees on International and Imperial Questions
1946	Sells 50% share of Hogarth Press to Chatto & Windus; resumes position as co-editor of Political Quarterly
1947	Foreign Policy: The Labour Party's Dilemma and The Moment and Other Essays (ed.) published
1949 July	Visits France
1950	What is Politics and The Captain's Death Bed and Other Essays (ed.) published
1951 July	Visits France
1952 July	Visits Scotland
1953	Principia Politica and A Writer's Diary (ed.) published
1955 April–May	Visits France
1956	Virginia Woolf & Lytton Strachey: Letters (co-ed.) published
1957 April–May	Visits Greece and Israel
1958 April	Visits France
Granite and Rainbow: Essays (ed.) published
1959	Retires as co-editor of Political Quarterly
1960 February	Visits Ceylon
Sowing published

1961
  April–May   Visits Greece
                       Growing published

1962
                       Retires as literary editor of *Political Quarterly*
                       Diaries in Ceylon published

1964
  April–May   Visits France
  June   Awarded honorary doctorate by Sussex
                       University
                       Beginning Again published

1965   Resigns as a director of *New Statesman*

1966   Visits United States and Canada

1967   *Downhill All the Way* and *A Calendar of Con-
                       solation* published

1969
  14 August   Dies at Monk's House
  October   *The Journey Not the Arrival Matters* published

July 13. 1903.

It is very strange & dull up here & I wish
you would come. I thought my nerves would
give under the strain at first of only the
Yen & Greenwood. It started by my going
to see the Yen on Wednesday night; about 11
Russell appeared & they tried to define 'the present'
until 1. I was lost about a thousand times.
Then the Yen & Greenwood were to come to
me on Saturday & when I got back late from
a river supper I found them sitting to-gether
in the nervous gloom of one light. At first

PART ONE

———

CAMBRIDGE

Like the equivocal opening chords of *Tristan and Isolde*, a few ambivalent words at the outset of Leonard Woolf's autobiography hint at the essence of everything that follows. Looking across the eighty years of his life, he saw himself an entity that had arbitrarily appeared and would soon disappear in the stream of time, and wrote coolly: "This passage from non-existence to non-existence seems to me a strange and, on the whole, an enjoyable experience." Simple words, but they manifest the curious amalgam of detachment, stoicism and bemused wonder that characterized his passage through life. The paradoxical sense that whereas everything matters, in the end nothing matters was central to his outlook. Yet if he found the universe sometimes merciless and always incomprehensible, it is revealing that he changed the title of the final volume of his memoirs, completed just before his death at eighty-nine, from "The Weariest River"—alluding to the wistful Swinburne poem he knew in youth—to a phrase from Montaigne, *The Journey Not the Arrival Matters*.

The journey began in London in 1880 when Leonard was born the fourth of ten children in an assimilated Jewish family of considerable affluence. Both parents were from large and prosperous families and created in their ample Kensington home a warm, comfortable and typically late-Victorian environment. His mother, Marie de Jongh, came of a Dutch family that had settled in London in the mid-nineteenth century. Though Leonard admired her resourcefulness and good sense, he came to feel that she inhabited a "dream world of rosy sentimentality" and loved him least of her children. Sidney Woolf, Q.C., was a highly successful barrister; Leonard was his favorite child and heir to his intelligence, drive and instinctive morality. To his father Leonard also owed a nervous tremor in his hands; in later years friends noticed that his whole body seemed to pulsate with pent-up energy.

Frail all his life, Sidney died of tuberculosis and heart failure in 1892, when he was forty-eight. Although he had earned a great deal, he left Marie with almost no savings and nine children, of whom the eldest was fifteen and the youngest three. This emotionally and financially devastating blow was absorbed by the Woolfs with remarkably little overt change in their way of life, even if they now lived in a less fashionable part of London and had three servants instead of eight. There was never a shilling to spare, but the surviving family correspondence leaves the impression of a wonderfully close and cheerful family, with intelligent interests and boundless energy.

For Leonard at eleven, Sidney's death was a trauma that, judging by his early poems, gripped him for years in gloomy ruminations on death and dashed hopes. Even before then he had been a sensitive boy with precocious existential concerns. His autobiography records moments in very early childhood when he had been "overwhelmed in melancholy," afflicted with a "sense of profound, passive cosmic despair" and stricken with a feeling of being "powerless in face of a hostile universe." Now he had had a brutal lesson in the precariousness of existence and material security. It was no doubt at this critical age that there took root the "fatalistic and half-amused resignation" that he said was his deepest trait.

Formal education was the other influence that molded his life. After a period largely at home with tutors, he spent two years at Arlington House, a preparatory school in Brighton, where his performance earned him admission with a scholarship to St. Paul's School, scholastically among the best of the public schools and particularly strong in classics. There Leonard was quickly identified as a boy of promise, segregated with other outstanding scholars and force-fed Greek and Latin until he was, in his phrase, turned into "classical pâté de foie gras." None of his letters from this period survive, but school essays among his papers attest to his having been a very earnest student with an interest not just in classics but in some social and political issues of the day. From being fourth in his form on entry in 1894, he rose to be top boy

4

in his last years, won school prizes and was elected to a select debating society frequented at the time by an older Pauline, G. K. Chesterton.

Like many another public-school boy of the time, Leonard looked back on those years in some anger. Not that he was ostracized or bullied as a "swot"; he was too adept on the playing field for that. What he never forgave was the philistinism of both his schoolmasters and his schoolmates, who together deprived him of intellectual stimulation at an irretrievable moment of his life. St. Paul's was nonetheless a critical phase for him. His solid grounding in classics led to a familiarity with Greek philosophy that became a foundation of his beliefs. And there was one schoolmaster who did see into Leonard's secret world and encouraged him to write, to read widely and to develop a critical judgment, awakening in him a lifelong enthusiasm for literature. It also marked an important step in social acceptance. His academic career says as much about the times—the rapid changes in late-Victorian society—as about Leonard. A generation earlier a public-school education for a boy who was not only middle class but impecunious and Jewish at that would have been out of the question.

The beatific moment came in 1899, when he achieved one of the most coveted of scholastic honors, entry as a classics scholar to Trinity College, Cambridge. At neither of the ancient English universities could Leonard have found a more congenial intellectual home than in this citadel of Cambridge rationalism, and his five years there were in many ways the happiest of his life. It is nonetheless striking that when he and Bertrand Russell, eight years his senior, looked back in old age on their Cambridge days, they had point for point the same reactions. In his autobiography Leonard Woolf devoted more than a hundred pages to Cambridge; studies, he dismissed in three sentences, and his tutors were not so much as mentioned. What had counted for both men were the intellectual inspiration and the intimate friendships they had found.

Those years were the golden age of Trinity, and Leonard immediately fell in with some of the best minds there. It was the revelation of his life to find himself in what seemed a boundless universe of ideas, surrounded by a group of exciting friends anxious to explore it with him. His closest and most uninhibited friendship, presumably through the attraction of opposites, was with Lytton Strachey. Thoby Stephen, John Maynard Keynes, Desmond MacCarthy, Clive Bell, E. M. Forster and Saxon Sydney-Turner, with whom Woolf shared rooms, were other close friends. He also came to know some of the distinguished younger Fellows of the College—J. M. E. McTaggart, Russell, A. N. Whitehead and G. H. Hardy. But towering above them all was a man whom Russell labeled "a genius" and Leonard revered as "the only great man" he ever knew: G. E. Moore.

Moore's influence over his Cambridge generation was almost hypnotic. Only in part was this due to the appeal of his philosophy, great as that was. When Leonard arrived at Trinity, Moore was just becoming the great seminal influence in the Cambridge, indeed in the Anglo-American, philosophical world. He it was who expelled Kant and Hegel from the garden of British metaphysics and with his *Principia Ethica* in 1903 offered a radical new way of looking at philosophical questions. Russell said the effect was to liberate him from a mental prison. For Leonard it was as though "an obscuring accumulation of scales, cobwebs, and curtains" had suddenly been removed, "revealing for the first time . . . the nature of truth and reality, of good and evil and character and conduct." Keynes and Strachey used similarly dramatic metaphors. Leonard aptly said Moore "coloured" their minds. But whether he actually put new ideas into them is less certain. He may have demolished ethical philosophers from Aristotle and Christ to Kant and Herbert Spencer, as Strachey claimed, but they were not men whom Leonard or the others had ever esteemed. And the component of Moore's philosophy that most attracted Leonard—the central importance of ethics, of finding criteria to decide what one *ought* to do —was the part Keynes said he and his friends ignored. What Moore offered was "a scientific basis," in Leonard's phrase, for believing what they already subliminally believed—such as the ultimate value attached to the enjoyment of beauty and the pleasure of human companionship.

In any case, the correspondence between Leonard and his contemporaries offers no evidence that Moore, although he was invoked to justify what they said and did, either revolutionized their thinking or changed their lives. Rather, it shows that, however much they enjoyed philosophical discussion, literature was what excited and nourished them. Leonard's weltanschauung may well have been influenced—colored—by his conversations with Moore, but in many important respects it had taken shape before *Principia Ethica* was published and even before he met Moore the previous year.

During his first year or so at Cambridge, Leonard went through a deep spiritual crisis. The other Woolf children abandoned their Judaism at a fairly early age and easily slipped into a state of indifference. Leonard, however, was crushed by a sense of a human existence without reason or order, indeed an existence in which there was nothing worth believing. These were not perplexities he could take up with his

6

Cambridge friends, none of whom had ever had enough existential feeling to sense a void. But he did discuss them with his sister Bella in letters to which only her replies survive. "I admire the seeking spirit," she wrote in April 1900, "which wants to know you 'know' to put it vulgarly . . . but you have everything in you to make you one of the most delightful of companions as well as the most distinguished of men, and I am so afraid when I see you drifting about in shoals of depression and dissatisfaction." She returned to the subject again in a further letter, included in this chapter.

All that remains in Leonard's own hand is a long, bleak poem written in July 1901, one stanza of which reads in part:

> . . . For soon Doubt came upon me black as Hell,
> And everything seemed slipping from my grasp
> And the whole world was vanity—I saw
> For the first time into the heart of things,
> Beneath the shining surface of this pool . . . .

The remainder of the poem is an impassioned fugue around the theme of a universe without meaning. Eventually he surrendered to disbelief. "I at any rate," he told a group of friends in 1903, "have no philosophy beyond a broken down scepticism." Years later, in a book on human beliefs indicatively entitled *Quack, Quack!*, he expressed feelings that clearly went back to those Cambridge days:

It requires no little courage to stand up in the face of the universe and say: "I do not know. I do not know what you mean. I do not understand this circus of the heavens. I see no meaning in this procession of the stars, in the senseless motion of the sun, in the earth and the moon, in my life or in the life of the earth worm in my back garden. I can find no place for and no explanation of my life or my mind in this fantastic universe." To say this and to accept the consequences of it requires a courage which only the standards of intellectual integrity, derived from the Greeks, can give us.

It was this void that Moore helped to fill, not with a creed but with a moral code, a sense that there is something of value in the universe, that there is a right and wrong and a good and bad in the nature of things, rather than in arbitrary religious doctrines. And this conviction Leonard derived less from Moore's teaching than from his character— his purity and innocence, his passion and absolute detachment in the search for truth, indeed his conviction that *nothing* mattered but the

7

truth. Moore's personal example raised a moral and intellectual standard which unfolded in Leonard's life as dedication to duty and his highest sense of right, whatever the personal consequence.

Moore, friendship and intellectual stimulation came together in what Leonard found the most enjoyable feature of his Cambridge years: membership in the Cambridge Conversazione Society, better known as the Apostles. The Society went back to 1820, and Russell's claim that it had subsequently incorporated the brightest figures at the university was not much of an exaggeration. In tone it was Socratic. At meetings no subject was taboo, absolute candor was required and truth was pursued through the clash of differing opinions. Since everything was subject to question and reason was supreme, it was also Socratic in effect, being potentially subversive of all forms of orthodoxy. Indeed it was this "comprehensive irreverence," in Keynes's phrase, that was the Apostles' hallmark and, to many, their offense.

If friendship and intellectual challenge were, above all, what Leonard, like Russell, remembered about the years at Trinity, there was for him the additional stimulus of being an undergraduate at the beginning of a new era. "We were still Victorian," Russell commented, "they were Edwardian." Arbitrary as it is to break history into the conventional one-hundred-year blocks, the turn of the current century did in fact mark a rough watershed in British history. With the death of Queen Victoria the old order crumbled. For Leonard and his circle, most of whom hoped to be writers, the stage for this revolt was the arts, in particular literature and the theater. Ibsen, Shaw, Butler, Swinburne and even Hardy and Wells were regarded as leaders in a broad movement to demolish the self-deceptions, hyprocrisy and cant of the past. In effect Cambridge was the starting point from which Leonard and his friends traveled down a path that took them to the cultural avant-garde and the political left, that made them both inveterate debunkers and daring innovators.

The rarefied pleasures of Cambridge were not what produced brilliant examination results and, Keynes apart, Leonard and his circle were not stellar academics. When Leonard sat for Part I of the Classical Tripos in 1902, he received first-class honors but in the third division. This disappointed the Master of Trinity, who evidently discerned promising fellowship material, and he encouraged Leonard to study for Part II, Greek philosophy. But by then effortless superiority had given way to superior effortlessness; with his time devoted to literary interests, talks with Moore and picnics by the Cam, he had little time for the syllabus. To general dismay, he took only a second in the exam.

8

He cared, he wrote to Strachey, and at the same time he did not really care.

The Cambridge state of mind had by then become Leonard's way of life. The outlook was embodied in the old aphorism that someone who went to Oxford thought he owned the world, while someone who went to Cambridge did not care who owned it. It was what Forster had in mind in writing of that "fearless uninfluential Cambridge that sought for reality and cared for truth." Leonard had so deeply imbibed this ethos that he went so far as to write a poem in praise of failure, a tribute that included a line all too prophetic of his own future:

> *. . . May success*
> *Not lie in the soul's nest hid*
> *In the fight & the storm & the stress?*

If worldly success is the true measure of worth, Cambridge crippled Leonard for life, leaving him permanently bereft of a desire for power, success and wealth. Every succeeding stage of his subsequent life was marked by a subtle inhibition—the studies not pursued, the colonial governorship never sought, the political career spurned, the publishing venture kept small, the editorship resigned. Instead, the *summum bonum* was creative talent and a life spent exploring the world of ideas and turning them into the tangible form of books. Even then, the goal was not public esteem but a personal sense of having produced something innately worthwhile. The austere life he led in later years, the aristocratic contempt for money, the disdain for status and pedigree were the effect not of his socialism or even his periodic impecuniousness, but of the Cambridge spirit. When he wrote to Strachey, "poets, artists & musicians are the happiest," he was speaking both for himself and for his whole circle.

So as the time approached to leave the university, Leonard found himself adrift, as in fact did almost all his friends. In any event, their Apostolic ethos left them outsiders. Writing was the vocation that seemed natural, and most of them did just that, even though they went through years of torment in trying to find where their creative impulse and their talent intersected. Leonard, however, had to earn a living and was free neither to write nor to realize a vague notion of following his father's footsteps into the law.

The only remaining prospects were to teach in a school or to go into the Civil Service, which was attracting the best Oxbridge graduates. Without much conviction Leonard and Sydney-Turner decided on the latter and lingered in Cambridge for a fifth year desultorily preparing for the exams. Sydney-Turner did well and went into the Treasury; Leonard fell well below form and was faced with the invidious choice of going into the Colonial Civil Service or becoming a schoolmaster. As his letters make clear, he did not want to go overseas but was under pressure from his family—and the moral ethic of Moore—to do so for financial reasons. Schoolmastering was poorly paid, and also, as he wrote to Strachey, it was not clear that good Christian parents would want their sons taught by an atheistic Jew. Through his contacts with older Trinity Apostles in government, he tried to pull strings to get a position in the Home Civil Service. It was to no avail. Instead, he was offered an Eastern Cadetship and to his horror found himself in the fall of 1904 bound for Ceylon. He likened the unwelcome break from his friends to the trauma of birth.

From the period up to his departure for Ceylon, there survive about 150 letters, almost all to Strachey and Sydney-Turner, as well as an almost equal number to him from Cambridge friends and several hundred from his family. Notes written in childhood, apart from ominous references to his father's health, record normal youthful activities—vacations, outings and days in the classroom at home. Since essays alone remain from the years at St. Paul's, the letters begin after matriculation at Trinity.

We enter the correspondence, as it were, in the middle of the first act. Leonard had already made his closest friendships and charted his interests and activities. The earliest letters, concerning play and poetry readings, along with later ones about cricket and fives, plays and concerts in London as well as those dissecting abstruse problems of Greek literature and philosophy have been omitted. Passages referring to unidentifiable undergraduates and recondite matters that would require elaborate annotation have been abridged. Most letters here are to Strachey; not only are they more candid than those to Sydney-Turner but they record the development of a friendship that played an important part in Leonard's life. For obvious reasons, the letters were normally written away from Cambridge, during vacations, when the correspondents were at home or traveling.

In some ways Leonard and his friends emerge as typical of almost all Oxbridge students of the time. They loved to walk and loved to talk; they took for granted that they learned more from one another than from dons and lectures; they rarely mentioned studies and resented giving them much time. Otherwise they were decidedly atypical. Literature was their great passion; Leonard mentions reading about

120 books in an average year. He and his friends were arrogant and clannish; they scorned established institutions such as the Union, whose showy debates they considered vulgar, and organized their own groups, such as the Midnight Society and the 'X' Society, where plays and poetry by lesser-known writers and lesser-known writings of major writers were read. They were skeptical in general and antireligious in particular; Thoby Stephen led a campaign to abolish compulsory chapel attendance. And they were united by bonds that were almost familial in nature. Inevitably their exclusivity and unorthodoxy aroused antagonism. Leonard retained several letters—one is included—that record how he and his circle were regarded by others in college. Indeed, at one point they were evidently so unpopular that they lived, as Leonard wrote, "in mortal terror of attack." " 'The college' is really enraged with us," he warned Strachey.

Not surprisingly the letters of this period convey the aura of near sanctity surrounding the Society. But they do not make it easier to understand Moore himself, who appears irascible, ill-tempered, depressed, unpredictable. His silences were frequent and terrible, though not remarkable in a man who taught that one should speak only when one had something to say that is both true and important. Yet his hold was demonstrable. He was the one person whom Leonard, in his last frenetic days before leaving for Ceylon, had to see, even though it meant dashing off to Edinburgh.

Another topic arising in the correspondence is Strachey's homosexuality, for a time sublimated in pornographic essays and poems and then exuberantly breaking out just after Leonard went down from Cambridge. Strachey's letters on the subject left Leonard at times amused, sometimes exasperated, and often worried by the legal danger—it was only a few years since Oscar Wilde had been consigned to Reading Gaol. Strachey reacted by labeling Leonard a puritan, Keynes a rabbi. The sexual freedom that seems to have swept Cambridge after 1904 has sometimes been traced to the influence of Moore's teaching that behavior should be governed by reason not convention and inhibition. But excerpts from a few of Strachey's letters included here show that his views on the matter predated *Principia Ethica*.

One subject notable for *not* being mentioned is politics. In part this was because Leonard and his friends were products of Cambridge; in part it was because they were products of their time, an era when social progress seemed predestined, world order secure and public affairs irrelevant. It is nonetheless striking that one searches these letters in vain for even a passing reference to the Boer War, Home Rule, free trade or any other great political issue of the day. Symptomatically, in a paper to the Apostles in May 1903, Leonard commented, "I feel it would be no unfair charge if anyone summed me up as ignoring politics, dabbling in philosophy & taking an interest in Art & Literature."

The Cambridge letters employ a private vocabulary. Until the end of the Edwardian era, the use of first names in conversation and writing was proscribed outside the immediate family. So nicknames were invented for friends and close acquaintances. Some were affectionate and used openly: "the Goth" was Thoby Stephen—so known because of his height and physical and emotional solidity; the term was also used adjectivally, "Gothic"; "(the) Strache" was Lytton Strachey; "Trevy," Robert Calverly Trevelyan; "Goldie," Goldsworthy Lowes Dickinson; "Hom," Hugh Owen Meredith. Saxon Sydney-Turner, usually simply "Turner," was occasionally "Sachs." One name frequently used, though not face to face, was "the Yen," for G. E. Moore, which had as its adjectival form, "Yenistic." Some names were pejorative: "the taupe," for E. M. Forster—because of his timorousness and alleged resemblance to a mole (in French, *taupe*); and "the Corporal," for Walter Lamb—because of his earnestness and mediocrity.

Moreover, the Apostles had their own recondite and whimsical jargon. Someone being considered for membership in the Society was an "embryo"; a rejected embryo was, logically enough, an "abortion" and an accepted one a "new birth." Meetings of "the brethren" took place around a "hearthrug." An Apostle who left Cambridge and resigned from the Society was said to "take wings" and thereupon became an "angel." One pair of words appearing in these letters over many years is of the utmost conceptual significance: "phenomenal" and "phenomenon"—the shortest of shorthand terms for everything and everyone the Apostles rejected. The Apostolic notion that the world was divided into the "real" and the "phenomenal" was absolutely fundamental.

Even in their abridged form and with their occasional arcane references, the letters offer a memorable glimpse into the formative years not only of one undergraduate but also of a remarkable intellectual fraternity. What took shape at Cambridge in the early years of the century was to become one of the most interesting and creative groups of our time.

*   *   *

To Lytton Strachey[1]

Lexham
March 20th 1901   Colinette Road, Putney.

It is late, quite late & I have been sitting all the evening over an immense fire with a wind roaring round the house with that comfortable stormy rattle which makes one feel the cosiness of one's fire all the more. I have been sharing my chair with my dog & reading the Book of Job again & now I feel quite sunk in the drowsy dreaminess of brain-weariness.[2] Well there are two things my evening cries to me to tell you & the first is ever so many thanks for the book which is a perfection of delight to me. If there is one thing which spoils one's pleasure in reading Job & Ecclesiastes it is the horror of those two barbarous columns in the ordinary barbarously bound bible—& I have always prayed for a relief from those awful double columns, which are the hall-mark of religious respectability. The second thing I have to say to you is a prayer—that you will remove the slur from our Tripos list & give the book of Job its due—a Fellowship.[3] The more I read it the more certain I feel that it is above the first class, that it is absolute perfection & *can only* rank with Plato & Shakespeare. I may be wrong & probably am—perhaps there really is Eastern blood in my veins which answers the cry of an ancestor—how splendid if one discovered that one was descended from Job!—perhaps that makes me partial but really it does seem to me to 'dwell apart'.

I feel that this letter is wandering & getting out of my control but my mind is in a state of reaction & I should give anything for a talk with you & the King in the 'Watch-tower'.[4] I have been in a state of kicking against the pricks all day—do you often feel like that—as if you want to break through this hen-coop of an existence & do something inordinantly outrageous. And the worst of it all is that one *never*

1. For Lytton and other members of the Strachey family, see Biographical Appendix.
2. The dog was Charles (1900–1905), LW's fox terrier, whose reckless courage was extolled in *Growing*. The reading of Job was prompted by having received a handsome edition of the work from Strachey, who had found it the day before in a bookshop. The significance of Job in the history of Western thought was expressed with considerable feeling more than fifty years later, when LW wrote *Principia Politica*.
3. LW, Strachey and Saxon Sydney-Turner (see Biographical Appendix) had drawn up an elaborate list of writers through the ages, ranking them as they deserved to stand in a Cambridge tripos (examination) list. Plato and Shakespeare not only stood at the top but also had been awarded fellowships.
4. "The King," also known as "His Majesty" and "The Sublime Porte," was Sydney-Turner. The "Watch-tower" referred to Strachey's rooms in a turret on the Great Court of Trinity known as Mutton Hole Corner.

does. One only smokes another pipe & goes to bed & four days afterwards the same thing takes place all over again.

What a shame that you leave London so soon for now I suppose I shall not see you until next term![1] Give my regards to the King when you see him & tell him that I expected—though it was lèse-majesté I suppose—to see him here yesterday but as usual was disappointed.

My fire is going out & it will soon be getting light so once more thanks, thanks, thanks.

Farewell.

Yours
L.

I must confess to a partiality for Pater & for his style though I allow it often smacks too much of a hot-house & exotics, but the last paragraph of the Postscript (?) of the *Renaissance*—[2]

To Lytton Strachey

April 9th 1900 [1901].   Lexham,
                                Colinette Road, Putney.

Your letter was to me as an emanation: I saw your own soul image shine through the mist of incoherencies: it danced in the sunshine of abstractions, it made faces at the realities of the many. It was dancing the measure of Time hand in hand with the two Maidens Poetry & Laughter. It was naked & unashamed. And there passed by two Philistines & said one to the other 'Thank God we are not as this man is'. —The angels smiled.

You ask me—in the part of the letter which you tell me not to read— whether I do not agree that boredom is Life. To quibble with the word—I should rather say Life consisted of a few isolated flashes of existence, oases in a great wilderness of boredom. We live once perhaps in a week, sometimes perhaps in a year. I incline for the moment to the belief—it is in the *Symposium* almost—that Life is only a striving, to make two souls into one, to complete the bisected mystic circle.

1. Because of his delicate health, Strachey was periodically removed from Cambridge by his mother to undergo a "rest cure."
2. Strachey had written of his distaste for the works of Walter Pater (1839–1894).

Each soul is but a half circle, there is somewhere its complement &
we are all striving, searching to find the other half. Sometimes we find
one that is almost—but not quite—the complement, the soul of a man
or woman alive or the soul of a dead man living in music or poem—
& there is a flash of soul fire & for a moment we live. But the flame
dies down for the circle was not complete & then the old wandering
in the wilderness of Boredom begins again. If only one could really
complete the circle! Poets, artists & musicians are the happiest—for
they create another soul out of their own & these two half circles—
the old & the self-created souls—join & there is a flash that never dies
down & *they* always live. The only consolation of the wilderness I find
is to watch other people trying to find their particular halfcircles. Some
find them so easily: there is the man who only thinks of a good dinner
& could complete his circle—if he were not rather blind—with the
soul of any pig that has ever wallowed in a sty & I know hundreds of
people who have found what they sought in the soul of a clothes-prop.

I have been in the wilderness to-day but before I end I must tell
you that I did live last week an hour or two—which being interpreted
is that I read *The Column* by Charles Marriott which if you have not,
do. If I were a reviewer I should shout & scream 'A New Great Author'.
But I'm not. Farewell.[1]

Yours ever
L.

I bow unconvinced to the eloquence of my collegues, much as I respect
their judgment in the other glades of Parnassus.[2] But Job was always
badly treated, don't you think?

To Saxon Sydney-Turner

April 17th 1901

Trinity College
Cambridge

You send me a mood which I know always lives in you, mated with
song. I send you one back dead now & unmated with song, born of
the World (with a big W.)

1. Charles Marriott (1869–1957), a popular writer; *The Column* (1901) was his first novel.
2. Strachey and Sydney-Turner had rejected Job for a fellowship in the literary tripos list.

I've done with all philosophies
*   That tell how God this world has fled*
And bowed to Mephistopheles.

I heard thy song, Parmenides
*   With wings of thought envellopéd,—*
I've done with all philosophies.

Some glorious unrealities
*   Despairingly were Truth I said,*
And bound to Mephistopheles.

Then, Plato, often spurning these
*   I bound thy bough about my head—*
I've done with all philosophies.

On intricate inanities
*   Of quibbling Germans I have fed,*
And bowed to Mephistopheles.

But now with these I finishéd
And burned my books & gone to bed
*   And bowed to Mephistopheles.*
I've done with all philosophies.

L.

FROM BELLA WOOLF[1]

May 4th, 1901

My dearest Len,
    . . . I'm dreadfully sorry—I can't help saying so—that the "un-
answerables" of life take such hold of you that for the time being you
cannot see the sun because of the clouds. But I do believe you will
rise triumphant from the Valley of the Shadow of "Doubt"—as all
true "seekers after light" do. Only it's the transition which is a trial—
both to you & to others.
    . . . I have hours & days when like you I feel I must find the key to
the door, that I'm consoling myself with false hopes & buoying myself

---

1. For Bella, and other members of the Woolf family, see Biographical Appendix.

up with vain theories. I can't believe in those moments that there is a
personal God, for I see the wise man troubled & the evil prosper &
everything is wrongly adjusted. . . . And then there comes a reaction
& there's something—in me—which raises me out of the slough &
there seems so much good to counterbalance the bad, so much beauty
in the world, so much satisfaction to be extracted from the everyday
living of life. Don't you ever feel that?

. . . If that doesn't satisfy you, you will no doubt go on seeking &
will find at last. It's idle of course to tell anyone to "follow light & do
the right" if they have no light & don't know what is the right, but I
do so want you not to "faint by the wayside" & miss all the "joie de
vivre" which belongs of right to being young. . . .

Ever your loving
Belle

To Lytton Strachey

Lexham,
Colinette Road, Putney.

July 11th 1901.

My dear Strache,

On Monday night I lived for a few hours & now feel a desire to
communicate the fact to you. I saw Her in [Racine's] *Phèdre*—it was
simply one superb whirl of sensations & reduced one to an after Beethoven state—absolute collapse.[1] It is the first time that I have ever
found acting add to a play which is already on the heights. I thought
of you & wondered whether by any chance you were there—were you?

I am pining for an epistolary ray of light from you. I always feel in
a kind of twilight here, just on the borderland of night. I dabble with
work in the morning, take a dog—or relations(!)—for a walk, trot
people aimlessly round to other people or places. Next week I am going
to Cornwall I believe to walk or ride about. . . . Still I pray for one
beam from you to dispel the cobwebs—yours are always so much you.

The other day I was in Brighton & rushed off to see Sachs [Sydney-
Turner]. I found him playing Wagner. Unfortunately I could only see
him for a few minutes & a scheme to go to *Tristan* fell through.

I hope this heat has not had a bad effect on you. To-night I dissolve.
Ever yours

L.

1. "Her" was Sarah Bernhardt, then in London on one of her periodic triumphal tours.

King Arthur's Arms Hotel
Sept 1st 1901.   Tintagel, Cornwall

My dear Strache,

Your rapsody wiped it all away if it was ever there. It was in London
that I felt the silent contempt.[1] London in August!—alone in a sweltering house—except for a dog & a cook—I like it because I choose
it by refusing to fly London with the rest of the world & my own
people but it induces bile & the chewing of the chewed. I like wandering
through the deserted streets tawdry with painter's ladders & half
starved cats & soiled fluttering tags of newspapers. Have you ever tried
it? It fascinates me by its bare brutality of ugliness, & produces the
aesthetic titillation of a slum. During that season too I batten upon
Balzac & his hold remains on me for weeks afterwards so that I am
rereading *Le Père Goriot* out on the cliffs & rocks here.

My brother & I are here on tramp, 15 miles a day & next week 20.
We are going on up to Bideford in Devonshire with knapsacks on our
backs. We lead the lives of kine—except for Balzac & Meredith &
Sterne which hang about our belts—& sleep like logs from 10.30 P.M.-
9.30 A.M. The coast is superb—all rocks & I seem to have been bal-
ancing on the edge of rocky precipices from all eternity. It would be
the solution of many problems to fly it all & become a day labourer
& earn one's bread in the sweat of one's brow. But I suppose it's only
the novelty that charms.

I began a play but after writing half the first scene it suddenly struck
me that the plot was nearly the same—unconsciously or perhaps sub-
consciously—as the motif of *Paracelsus* so I subsided.[2] But you *must*
write one.

Salute the Goth for me.[3] I cannot write more as this room has become
invaded with all manner of loathsome insects.

Yrs
L.

1. In a prior letter LW accused Strachey of "silent contempt" for failing to write.
2. LW had undertaken to write a play for the 'X' Society, which had recently read Robert
Browning's *Paracelsus*.
3. The Strachey and Stephen families were vacationing nearby in Hampshire. See Biographical Appendix for Thoby (the Goth) and other members of the Stephen family.

From Arthur Gaye[1]

September 5: 1901

My dear Woolf,

   Your letter is a challenge, which I have expected for some time. I accept it, and try to explain my change towards you. The causes come under two distinct heads: First, I cannot endure the people I meet in your rooms. Either they or I had to go, and as I was the newest and alone I waived my claim to the older friends and the majority. Strachey, Campbell, Law, Pearsall, &c are to me in their several ways the most offensive people I have ever met, and if I had continued to meet them daily, I would not be answerable for anything I might do.[2]

   Secondly comes a more difficult point. The kind of conversation and habits, which I had with you, had a kind of fascination for me—call it mysticism, if you will—but it would have ended in ruin of health, physical, moral and intellectual. So I set myself against it and gave myself to healthier and less metaphysical, though perhaps less entertaining, pursuits. I cannot afford to fail; if such living gave Sydney-Turner a 1.3 and Strachey a 2nd, it would give me a 2nd. So I withdrew partly from consideration for my own ultimate good, partly also because to me a good deal of the conversation was very offensive. I am not what is known as religious, but I was not going to associate with people who scoffed and jeered at my religion; fair criticism given in a gentlemanly way I do not mind. But the tone of Strachey and even you on matters of religion was not gentlemanly to me. You spoke about these things to me or at any rate before me, as though I were one of yourselves, which I sincerely hope never to be. Apart from this I have no personal grievance against you, and I had not this one, till your adored Strachey appeared on the scene. You have him to thank in great measure that my feelings towards you are not what they were, and I can assure you that no one is more disappointed than myself. I am still, I hope, your friend, but not the friend I was once.

                  Yours ever
                  Arthur S. Gaye

1. (Sir) Arthur Gaye (1881–1960), a Trinity scholar.
2. Leopold C. H. Douglas Campbell (1881–1940), later 6th Baron Blythswood, became a High Church Anglican priest. (Alan) Rokeby Law (1880–1906) and his family were described in *Sowing* as "conservative, conventional, commonplace . . . the middle middle-class backbone of nineteenth-century England." C. W. Pearsall was a Trinity undergraduate.

Sept 12 1901   Lexham
                                          Colinette Rd., Putney.

My dear Strache,

Both your letters or rather your one & a half reached me here just after I have returned. I would I had had them before as I believe I *could* just have managed to look in on you on my way back. I passed through Basingstoke which seems as if it ought to be near you. I should so have liked to see you. Now all that is behind & I am trying to get up a work fever.

It was all very nice while it lasted though I feel with you that one's own bed is a thing divine—but sometimes I like to get rid of all anchors & just tramp on not knowing where I shall be by evening. Sometimes there are disadvantages—once, the day after I wrote to you, we got caught in the rain & had to put up in a lonely cottage right out on the coast. We got no sleep all night—there were fowls roosting just over our heads, a dog howling outside all night, & cows shuffling & kicking in a stall under our room while our beds housed if not as big at least as many animals. But then the sea & the cliffs & the colours make up for everything.

I don't think you are quite fair to me & ugliness. I do not mean to say that the brutal hideousness of London in August appeals to my sense of the Beautiful or aesthetic in that sense—but to mere morbidity which after all one can call aesthetic titillation. It is just the same with a slum & Zola. They both have rather to do with a human feeling than an artistic & give one—or me perhaps—a morbid pleasure. If you have never felt anything of the kind then you are absolutely a pagan & Lucian was not the last of the Greeks. Personally I feel I shall never get back to that, there is always a taint of the centuries that are passed which will never leave my blood. And I have never yet met anyone who has not got it somewhere & most people all through.

Poor Turner is worried by the *Timaeus* [of Plato]. I have done my best to help him but I am afraid 'tis a poor best.

                                          Yours ever,
                                          L.

Lexham,

Jan 4th 1902. Colinette Road, Putney.

I meant to make this arrive on what Turner calls the jour de l'an—[1]
you see the links I daresay—but have descended during the last week
into an utter grave of slothfullness. All which comes from the envi-
ronments: the rain it raineth every day here & when it doesn't it tries
to—so that it comes as somewhat of a relief to hear that there are
places somewhere where people have roses & sunshine.[2] Even you
would have a satiety of clouds if you were where I am, for the sky is
just one continuous cloud. From which meteorological discussion you
may also deduce the state of my temper.

The best news I have heard for a long time is about the play. Beppo
is an innovation is he not? Qua length if there are five acts of 500
lines each, it will not be the longest play on record as [Thomas Kyd's]
The Spanish Tragedy which I have just read has—counting the additions of Ben Jonson I believe—about 2970 lines. Of course that is a
four Act play & Act III has the enormous number of 1410 lines. *Hamlet*
runs to 3911 lines, which you will observe begins with a a 3 & a 9;
moreover $3 + 9 + 1 + 1 = 14 = 7 + 7$—so we have all the great
numbers represented. Are these the 'mystical mathematiks'?[3]

I sent the Goth a cutting from a newspaper entitled 'What is Sport?'
being a diatribe against the current idea. I got back six closely written
pages to prove that the writer was 'talking through his hat' in true
Gothic style. From the same paper[+] I cut out the enclosed which I
thought might interest you. I have spent most of the vac. it seems to
me cutting extracts out of newspapers.

On Monday I go up to Cambridge to that disgraceful exam.[4] I believe
it really begins on Monday although Turner assures me it is Tuesday.
Still I nurse a hope sub pectore that when I come up I shall find that
the horror has already begun in which case I shall have a peaceful
week up there.

Yours ever,

L.

([+] *The Pall Mall Gazette.*)

1. Strachey was having another period of rest cure, this time at Menton; to pass the time
he was writing a dramatic tragedy, "The Duke of Ferrato," for the 'X' Society.
2. From Menton, Strachey had ventured into Italy, where he reported finding sunshine,
roses and Roman arches.
3. LW was at this time writing an essay on mystics.
4. Presumably for a college prize, possibly in Greek or Latin.

Lexham,
April 1st 1902   Colinette Road, Putney.

My dear Strache,   This is the first letter I have written this vac.—I
have been meaning to write so many & not least to you—but have
been sunken in the depths of insidious vac.-coma (is that the way to
spell it?). I see you say you are sometimes demi-depressed, well I must
say that I have been not demi or quasi but up to the hilt in it for the
last two weeks thanks to surrounding circumstances & what you would
call the weakness of bowing to them. You must however allow that
sometimes one is simply entangled in the toils of them & for the time
there is no escape. . . .

I have read nothing except a book by the new—comparatively—
Russian, Gorki. It is called *Foma Gordyeeff* & is ultra-Russian, savage
& what is better pitiless to sentimentality, though not inhumanly pitiless. For all that I don't like it—he is too crude & unartistic & has
merely baldly told what a number of bored & rather brutal fools would
do with their lives. The book is often consequently baldly sordid. . . .

Adieu

Yours ever
Len.

I hope you look after yourself & drink that foul mess bread & milk
every night. I can smell it now.

Lexham,
April 8, 1902.   Colinette Road, Putney.

My dear Strache,   I was glad to hear you really had read it [*Le Père
Goriot*] & I agree with you—in the main—about it. Of course personally I never or try never to compare it with *Lear* because though it
challenges comparison all through on the face of it, I don't really think
it is fair to do so. Balzac never attempts to do what Shakespeare does
& *Le Père Goriot* never even shimmers on the transcendental. He never
really gets further than 'En ce moment je vois ma vie entière. Je suis
dupe! elles ne m'aiment pas, elles ne m'ont jamais aimé! Cela est

clair!' so that the resemblance is really very superficial, in fact only the instruments & setting. As regards the other people I must say they did not bore me but perhaps that was because I knew most of them from the other books where they come & they interested me before. Rather strangely too especially Madame de Beauséant for she is so delightful in *La Femme Abandonnée*.

As last time, it is now a day later than when I began this. I was so sleepy last night that I gave it up & went to bed. I had really done some work yesterday—in fact I have this vac.—& it has a soporific effect on me.

Yes, the Goth told me about Trevelyan & Webster.[1] Of course they *are* blind fools & are annoyed with people who won't be blind with their crew. They don't really know what literature is of course. They read a novel for the story & poetry for 'a criticism of life' & they only recognize what they call style when it shouts at them like in Milton—& even then they mix it up & think it's the same as in Macaulay. They know they don't understand it & that it bores them unless there's something indecent in it to tickle their pruriency or something 'good' to tickle their lickerish sense of moral respectability. Why *don't* they leave it all alone & go off to their Marie Corelli, Byron & Mrs Hemans?[2]

I hear violent sounds of the cat fighting with Charles, I hope he takes revenge for the last verse—but I suppose I had better separate them so farewell.

Yrs
L.

No murder was done.

1. George Macaulay Trevelyan (1876–1962), an Apostle and Fellow of Trinity, noted historian and Master of Trinity 1940–51. To LW, the philistinism of Trevelyan and his friends was epitomized by their dislike of the Elizabethan dramatist John Webster, whose *Duchess of Malfi* was read and admired by the 'X' Society.
2. Marie Corelli (1855–1924), the popular English novelist, and Felicia Hemans (1793–1835), a romantic poet, were, along with Byron, symbols to LW of vapid sentimentality and exaggerated emotions.

Lexham,

July 13th 1902.   Colinette Road, Putney.

If I didn't know you, I really should have thought from your letter that you were in love.[1] But I don't, because you see I know you could not be or at any rate would not—with women. I never am either with any individual of the species—yet—except perhaps for a moment with some face or form—only it is more than that—that I see in a carriage or bus or gutter. But at any rate I know I have the δύναμαι [ability] if not the ἐνεργεια [inclination]—I can't express it any other way, but you understand—but then I am not repelled by what 'is all the fiend's' & I am certain that there is a good deal of what is beneath the girdle in love, although certainly it is not everything. What I find is, that whenever my δύναμαι is on the point of becoming ἐνεργεια with anyone I really know, I am simply repelled by finding that there *is* nothing above the girdle; the gods never had a finger in it at all, & I am simply left with the bare feelings of sexuality, & very often not even those. Perhaps that is all that love really is—the desire to lie with your neighbour's wife or daughter—but somehow or other, I rather hope it is not, as otherwise my ideas on the subject are damned sentimentality.

I didn't go to *Phèdre* at all this time, I absolutely could not every night she gave it. I saw however *La Tosca* & thought her more superb than ever.[2] She looked hideous—I don't quite know why more than usual—when she first came on but after the first act one simply forgot all about that. Otherwise *I* dribble on among Aristotle, golf & Byron. The last is a stiff job—my God I've never read such trash as those Giaours & Corsairs.[3] I had never read them before & assumed that they were nauseous, but I never imagined such feeble banalité as they contain. The letters however make up for a great deal & on the whole there is some amusement in steadily plodding through a whole author & really for once getting to know about one. Still I don't see much chance of ever writing the essay. I have also at last read [Joris Karl

1. Strachey, on vacation in the company of several young women, had written to LW: "For me I dribble on among ladies, whom I *cannot* fall in love with. One of them is beautiful, young, charming—oughtn't I to be in love with her? We go for walks together, read each others sonnets, sit out together at nights, among moons, stars, & the whole romantic paraphernalia—oughtn't I to be in love? We talk about it. Oughtn't I—?"
2. Bernhardt was back in London; *La Tosca* had been written expressly for her by Victorien Sardou.
3. In a competition for a university essay prize, LW had begun a study of Byron; *The Giaour* (1813) and *The Corsair* (1814) are two of his works.

Huysmans'] *A Rebours* . . . it *is* diseased magnificence. The words simply dazzle me. I rather thought that that sentence in the colossal chapter on the flowers & des Essintes' nightmare was in a way an epitome of Huysmans if not of all France. 'Tout n'est que syphilis.' Pish! I suppose everything is.

Ever yours
L.

To Saxon Sydney-Turner

Lexham,
July 28 1902   Colinette Road, Putney.

. . . I have just finished the *Ethics* & as usual with Aristotle it seems to me an eminently futile work as a whole, but extraordinarily shrewd in isolated observations. Chapter XI of Book VI beats me completely, it seems to contradict & to be absolutely irreconcilable to what has gone before in that book & the commentators seem quite fuddled over it. For God's sake (if you don't believe in Him) & have some idea of what this chapter is driving at, let me know it as I have already spent an unconscionable time over this already.

Have you written anything? I don't think I ever shall again. My brain has already sunk I really believe into a swamp & miasma of middle-aged stupidity. I don't know whether this is the result of a plethora of Byron but it is a melancholy fact. I am ploughing steadily through 'the noble lord' (a prize essay is about all I *can* rise to) & don't find him quite as hopelessly *dull* as I imagined though for drivelling imbecility his verses defy imagination. But he interests me ἡ ἐστιν ἀνθρωποι [as a person] if not as a poet though whether I shall ever get up energy enough to write is very much on the Gods' knees. . . .

Yrs,
L.

July 31, 1902.   Lexham,
                                 Colinette Road, Putney.

My dear Strache, . . . I had a funny interview with a doctor the
other day. Owing to the persistent outcry of my whole family, I was
induced to go to see him about my delirium-trementic hand. He is an
old but I think very clever man, as doctors go. He asked me what
work I was doing & on my telling him Greek Philosophy, he suddenly
burst out into an invective against Plato & the Greeks in general. 'A
filthy beast! I call him', he said; 'You know they were all Paiderastics
& Plato's writings are corrupted with it. He was a shrewd man, a wise
& in many ways a good man but a filthy beast too & if Plato or any
other paiderastic came in at my door I'd kick him out again whoever
he was'. Then I had a lecture on paiderastia from the medical man's
point of view. Consequently my interview lasted over an hour with
him.

Thanks much for your Byronic information.[1] I don't know anything
about *La Pucelle*; & although I thought of reading Morley I have not
yet as he usually bores me & I think is rarely worth reading at all. I
can't stand his conscientious unoriginality.

You say you have or are going to have a crisis in your family. We
have had for the last two weeks & are having one here but it is too
long to relate & would only bore you. Anyway it adds one more to
our list of diseases. My brother has had one & had to be operated on
last week. He is allowed to go away to the sea to-morrow so we are
in hopes that he will get all right. I am growing a moustache & taking
many probably useless concoctions (the latter only) for the shaking
as to my hands.

                                         Yrs
                                         L.[2]

1. In an earlier letter Strachey had written of Byron: "Shelley was obviously in love with
him. But not he of course with Shelley. Though I daresay B. was a sodomite. . . . Don Juan
is without a doubt a lineal descendent of *La Pucelle* (Voltaire). John Morley (rather an old
early Victorian Liberal fool) has written something on Byron. . . ."
2. To this Strachey responded, "I trust your doctor knows more about Delirium Tremens
than Plato, & I hope you assured him that the dear good man was rather against all that
than otherwise. A little out-spoken perhaps, but at heart—oh, I must think it—one of the
earliest of the Puritans. I shall for ever fail to see what difference (medicine apart) a particular
act can make."

Grand Hôtel de la Poste
                                              Place Duguesclin, 21
le 22 Sept 1902   Dinan (Côtes-du-Nord).

I received your letter here many days after it was written which accounts for my not answering. I am keeping the [Greek] iambics to
spring on my brother [Edgar] when I come home if he is not at
Cambridge—he goes up at some unearthly date—I cannot say *I* find
some of the lines very easy to translate though I know what they are
about, but then I find I cannot even translate Sophocles any more.

I did become a Christian for a few days & damnably unpleasant it
was. Byron had something to do with it & I suppose the Father, the
Son & the Holy Ghost; anyway, though I wanted to be with one of
the Trinity, I 'chose the Path of Duty' (Amen) & found a Heaven in
the British Museum which was extraordinarily Hellish.

I am here with a (not the silent) brother [Harold] & sister [Bella]
& we have been stopping a day or two at various small towns in
Normandy & Brittany. This is much the most beautiful place we have
been in & would be absolutely perfect if it were not for the 72 stinks
& several stenches quite easy to count wherever one goes abroad. Mont
St Michel too is of an eminence but spoilt in the day time by the
accursed tripper. One night when everyone had gone to bed we
tramped up almost to the top of the abby—the sands stretch away for
miles & miles of desolation & with the moon shining on them & the
black patch of dark forest leagues away on the shore it looked like
the world's end.

I would write more but have no time now. I have begun Byron—
very feeble & thin.

Yrs
L.

To Lytton Strachey

Lexham
Sept 27, 1902   Colinette Road   Putney

My dear Strache,   I enclose as much—except a few sentences—as I
have done of Byron. Can you return it at once as I really want to
continually refer back to it. It is my only copy. I want you to tell me
the following. Is the part about the nature of poetry obscure or too

much spun out & irrelevant & also whether the whole thing is too much in detail? I feel somehow that it is dull & repeats itself & every morning I get up with the intention of not going on with it at all & begin again immediately after breakfast. Tell me plainly what you think as while I am actually writing a thing, I never feel I can trust myself to judge & there is too much sheer laboriousness in this for me to want to go on with it if you candidly do not think it is worthwhile. I don't feel a bit in the mood for writing anything. . . .[1]

I wish you would not spread a report that I am now a Christian, as however true—& I have bought a rosary—I only lived on the reputation of not being one.

Have you read Henry James' 600 new pages [*The Wings of the Dove*]? They are all about Lancaster Gate & Lexham Gardens which is quaint, as I lived in the latter for 15 years.[2]

Yrs
L.

To Lytton Strachey

Lexham
Putney.

Jan 2nd 1903

I don't know whether my 'poor old friend' has sunk completely into blitherdom or whether at last the police are really on his track—but you did not apparently enclose what you said you were, & the letter, when I received it, hadn't even the decency to be shut.[3] Now really— I don't think this could have harmed the morals EVEN of a postman— but I have known some which, well mildly, might, & what was there to prevent it being one of them? But perhaps it was after all the police, who of course blunderingly opened the one virgin of your whole correspondence. . . .

---

1. Strachey responded warmly: "Byron's claims to being a poet you seem to me to have quite satisfactorily shattered. . . . What I liked particularly about the Essay was that it seemed to bring out the magnificence of true poetry." On submission, the essay was awarded second prize. LW had already won the Trinity English Essay Prize by examination in 1901 and the Classical Tripos Prize for a study on mystics the following year.
2. The Strachey family lived in a capacious Victorian house at 69 Lancaster Gate.
3. Strachey had been writing and circulating erotic and homosexual satires and poems.

Qua the Goth I don't feel like Zeus.[1] There is much more in the magnificence scale than in the lack of interest one, & after all surely you & certainly I are pretty bored on the hearthrug. Of course we don't lie quite so obviously in chairs, but it is quite obvious for all that, & I can't see that it matters much if it is. He *must* be elected some time, & probably ought to have been a term ago. Are you going up on Monday 12th in order that by visiting all the angels & devils you can lay hands on you may make it before term begins into a really flaming crisis such as is the delight of your heart? I go up on the 14th, I think, so that I shall expect to find you already in blue flames by then.[2] But leave your present abode on Monday & then I shall see you in the evening as I shall be then turning reels at your house.[3]

I don't think my December list of books read equals yours. It includes however Bernard Shaw, Schopenhauer, Barry Pain, Browning, D'Aurevilly, Oscar Wilde, Flaubert, *A Manual of Ethics* & Shakespeare. I found on making up my accounts for the year that I had read 121 books, which beats all previous records by one book. I don't see how anyone, after reading *Madame Bovary*, can doubt which is the supremest of all novels—though I now remember writing the same to you about *Le Père Goriot*.

I have just been listening to a wretched woman make a violin simply screech out a splendid Brahms sonata, consequently my head & temper are the worse for it.

Your

L.

1. LW and Strachey were secretly vetting both John Maynard Keynes (see Biographical Appendix) and Thoby Stephen to be members of the Apostles. Though they did not like Keynes, they were certain of his intellectual suitability; while they respected Stephen's "magnificence," they were not certain of his interest in the Society. Trying to make up his mind, Strachey said he felt "like Zeus at the critical moment." To their later regret, they never proposed Stephen.
2. According to popular myth in Victorian times, humans might self-combust in blue flames.
3. Philippa Strachey was teaching a group of friends to dance Scottish reels.

To Saxon Sydney-Turner

June 20th 1903

Lexham
Colinette Rd., Putney.

Dear Turner, I ought to have thanked you before for the telegram at which I was enraged. Still it is a comfort that I can congratulate you out of the Trinity, though I don't think you deserve it. I shall take the first opportunity of talking to Jackson about the existence of green.[1]

Are you in London & are you going to bring your [cricket] team? I wish you would as I am in a raging temper, which I try to cure by reading Stout's *Psychology*.[2]

I am sending this to Cambridge.

Yrs
L.

To Lytton Strachey

June 22nd 1903.

Lexham,
Colinette Road, Putney.

I had, when I received your second letter, already got the tickets [to *A Doll's House*], but it is all right as I telephoned to the theatre & they agreed to take them back.

Damn Barnes & the Master & Rosie & the whole world of blithering jackasses.[3] That's just it, if one weren't bothered by their sickly remarks, one wouldn't care a damn. Although—I don't know whether or not it is they who drive me into the Greenwood vein—I *do* find myself enraged at seeing myself classed with Wordsworth & you with other nameless abortions, & I perhaps vilely say to myself that even the papers I did were as good as Greenwood's on knowledge, only they blatantly contradicted Jackson—& then I curse myself for thinking of

1. In Part II of the Classical Tripos, LW received a second and Sydney-Turner a first. Henry Jackson, Regius Professor of Greek, Fellow of Trinity and an Apostle, was one of the examiners. "The existence of green" may refer to one of the examination questions on the Aristotelian and Platonic concepts of sense perception.
2. George Stout (1860–1944), a seminal influence in British psychology. It is not clear whether LW was reading *Analytic Psychology* (1896) or *A Manual of Psychology* (1899).
3. E. W. Barnes was Head Examiner at Trinity; the Master of Trinity was H. Montagu Butler—a man who Bertrand Russell said "came straight out of Thackeray's *Book of Snobs*"—and Rosie Haigh was a Trinity bedder. All had evidently expected LW to achieve better examination results.

it at all.[1] The truth is I believe that I have been, ever since I came down, in a vague hell & I only wanted something like this to make it definite. I suppose in the end if you never get what you want, you even begin to care when you don't get what you didn't care whether you got or not. I am sure now it's all your 'infinity of desire'; I want to get out into the open, not to be penned in this swamp of trivialities, having to think twice about spending a penny on an evening paper because one bought a shilling book one hardly desired. Curse.

Goodnight.

L.

I wonder if selfishness is *bad*. I believe I am the most selfish person in the world & you I rather think are a good second.

To Lytton Strachey

Lexham
June 25th 1903.   Colinette Road, Putney.

. . . No, I don't think you are nearly dead yet, you always have some living reality in you. You have your crises & you feel them, your loves & your hates & your passions & you feel them, & though they may wash you up now & then a wreck high & dry, you soon get back again into it all—& after all to be in it is I believe the thing. I often envy you that, for I am, I feel it, so usually a mere spectator with my hands in my pockets. You can't live by desiring an extremely vague desire of a very vague moon; so that I am resigning myself to the lot of being merely an ever-embryonic Dickinson.[2]

I went on Tuesday to Réjane after all in the pit.[3] I was dead tired

1. L. H. G. Greenwood (1880–1965) took a First in both parts of the Classical Triposes and went on to become University Lecturer in Classics 1926–45; C. W. Wordsworth, another Trinity scholar, and Strachey received Seconds in the Historical Tripos, Part II.
2. Goldsworthy Lowes Dickinson (1862–1932), known as "Goldie," was a Fellow of King's and an Apostle; the man who coined the name "League of Nations," he was a long-standing proponent of international understanding. Though fond of him, LW thought his "gentleness and high-mindedness" produced "a weakness, a looseness of fibre" in the man and his work. Strachey once described him to LW as "a mummy, dreaming of eternities; silent, strange, dark, dead."
3. Gabrielle-Charlotte Réjane (1857–1920), famous French actress who frequently performed in London.

before it began, fearfully hot, the seats damnably uncomfortable & the people all round chattered French so continuously that it was impossible to hear what was said on the stage, so that the circumstances were not ideal. Still I thought her very wonderful & the play [*A Doll's House*] more so. The last act was quite tremendous, though I thought she made Nora rather too silly in the first. All the people round me thought the last Act supremely comic, & an Englishman near me when the front door shuts summed it up by 'That's a damned rum play'. Your mother I saw in the stalls.

Yrs,

L.

To Lytton Strachey

July 13, 1903.

Trinity College,
Cambridge.

It is very strange & dull up here & I wish you would come. I thought my nerves would give under the strain at first of only the Yen & Greenwood. It started by my going to see the Yen on Wednesday night; about 11 Russell appeared & they tried to define 'the present' until 1.[1] I was lost about a thousand times. Then the Yen & Greenwood were to come to me on Saturday & when I got back late from a river supper I found them sitting to-gether in the nervous gloom of one light. At first I thought death would creep upon me, but it was all right & practically no silences, while Greenwood was more or less suppressed. When he went at 12, it became perfect. The height was perhaps reached on Sunday when I went to the Yen & found him playing a duet with Greenwood. Later he played on the comb & nearly expired of laughter. All this is I suppose the strange part; in the intervals dullness hangs in the domination of Barwell. Keynes appeared for the first time today; his dullness is sublime over a tea of two hours.[2]

I was shaved by the dark youth at Richardson's today. He asked me if many people were up at Kings & I told him I was of Trinity. He apologised & then: 'Mr Straky is of Trinity, isn't he, sir?' I said he was. 'Mr Straky is very popular at Kings, isn't he, Sir?' I agreed again.

1. For G. E. Moore ("the Yen"), see Biographical Appendix. Bertrand Russell (1872–1970), the mathematician and philosopher.
2. Noel Barwell, a Trinity graduate and bon vivant, was one of LW's outer circle of friends.

'I thought so, Sir. I notice he comes here with a lot of different gentlemen from Kings & he seems very popular with them'. Then I had to
go.

Yr

L.

To Lytton Strachey

Trinity College,

Cambridge.

August the ninth, 1903.

. . . I like Fernaphilius; how *did* you evolve the name?[1] I don't
believe in the one about the good & the bad; it is only partially true.
Besides the good are so afraid of the bad. That reminds me that I have
had a fright & sport my door every night now in mortal terror of
attack.[2] It all came through a strangely ordinary man Barlow (a friend
by the way of Gerald). You must be careful next term for 'the college'
is really enraged with us. They think you are a witch & given up to
the most abandoned & horrible practices & are quite ready to burn
us alive at the slightest provocation. One of Barlow's acquaintances,
a scholar of the college, it is now a well-known fact, once went to tea
with you & came out white to the lips & trembling. 'The conversation',
he said, 'was too horrible! & the pictures & the atmosphere!'[3]

Your

L.

I went to chapel last Sunday. There was a guffaw from Barwell &
Gray[4] at the opening words of the psalm: 'The fool hath said in his
heart: there is no God.'

1. Strachey was spending the summer writing "Reflexions in the manner of the French" of
which Fernaphilius was the first—and only. According to one of his maxims, "The human
race is divided into two classes—the good and the bad: and the bad are afraid of the good."
2. To "sport a door" was university slang for shutting an outer door to prevent entry.
3. Strachey responded: "Your letter sent me into seventeen fits. What horrors you seem to
hint at! I shudder and turn pale. . . . Unreason is the most horrible of all evils. . . ." Barlow
was a Trinity undergraduate.
4. Harry Gray became a famous surgeon; LW's contact with him after Cambridge is related
in *Sowing*.

To Lady Strachey[1]

L. Lupus S.D. omnibus Strachientibus

Si vos omnes valetis, ego valeo. Quamquam Imperator ille Indicus celeberrimus, domus dominus, olim coniectavit (recte quidem, ego coniecto) me linguae Latinae satis ignarum esse, hoc modo solum Americanolatino hospitem Atlantidis vincere posse puto. Nam ad gentis antiquae et magnificae laudem aptior est antiqua et magnifica lingua. Itaque dominae nobilissimae, natorum matri nobilissimorum, gratias primum ago. Anglarum sane familiarum equidem non omnino sum ignarus, sed haec vestra familia super omnes ingenio candore hospitio pulchritudine crustulum capit: hic floret bellum, floret ars, florent litterae: quo numerosior, eo hilarior: uno verbo hoc illorum dierum qua monumentum aeternum scribo 'Velox Tempus in Loco Veloci.' Curate ut valeatis et intellegatis. A.D. XVI KAL. O

[TRANSLATION:

L. Woolf Sends Greetings to All the Stracheys

If you are well, I am well. Although that very famous Indian general, the master of the house,[2] once suggested (quite rightly, *I* suggest) that I am rather ignorant of the Latin language, I think that Americanized Latin[3] is the only way that the guest of the wife of Atlas[4] can win. For a venerable and grand language is more suitable for praising a venerable and grand people. And so, I first give thanks to you most noble lady, mother of most noble children. I am certainly not unacquainted with English families, but this family of yours, surpassing all others in talent, openness, hospitality, and beauty, takes the cake. Here war, art, literature flourish—the more, the merrier. In this single phrase I compose the eternal monument of those days: "A Swift Time on a Swift Occasion." Take care to be well—and to understand [these words]. 16 Sept.]

---

1. The Strachey family was spending the summer in Cranbrook, Kent, at a house known as Swift's Place. At Lady Strachey's invitation LW had spent the early part of August there.
2. Lytton's father, Lieutenant-General Sir Richard Strachey.
3. A reference to two American colloquialisms that follow.
4. General Strachey was a noted geographer.

To Lytton Strachey

Sept 20th 1903.

Lexham,
Colinette Road, Putney.

Of course I have wished many a time that I was back in Cranbrook, I did really enjoy it so much. On the other hand I have indeed done five hours work a day for two days in succession.

I had a strange journey back among drunken female & male hoppers. At Tonbridge (where by the bye I saw Gascoigne) the females burst into the Gentlemen's Lavatory while I was there & began using it passim. They then danced upon the platform; this led to a fight, & it all ended in one lady being forcibly ejected by five porters from the station & the wails & weepings of her comrades.

In the train I tried to write 'Thoughts'. I send you three, against which you may write as your ancient prototype did. They are certainly the most fascinating things to attempt, but failure as usual, I think, is in the complete absence of style. The two first are really 1a, 1b.

1. Death would lose for us most of its irksome persistence, if only our imaginations could really picture an utter annihilation, a blank nothingness of self. But to do this we should have first to die: & so that haunting horror of death comes upon us from looking forward to our dead selves as in a kind of conscious unconsciousness. In that strange land our half-dead souls are always peeping through the coffin-lids at their dead bodies.[1]

2. The brutes are not, as the theologians would have us believe, examples of what is lowest in man; they are in fact standing monuments of the monotony which he expects in death.

3. The Present is, for the most part, made up of the pain of desires & the ache of regrets.

I have suggested Bernard Shaw to Trevy.[2]

Your
L.

I promised to send your brother & sister the enclosed prescription for testing whether films & prints have been sufficiently cleaned.

[1]. "Our own death is unimaginable, and whenever we make the attempt to imagine it, we can perceive that we really survive as spectators" (Freud in *Thoughts for the Times on War and Death*, 1915).

[2]. R. C. Trevelyan (1872–1951), known as "Trevy," a classics scholar at Trinity and an Apostle, was G. M. Trevelyan's brother. "He became a very scholarly, but not very inspired, poet," Bertrand Russell wrote charitably of him in his autobiography.

11 Oct 1903

Christ! I have just written off a letter to the Yen.[1] It had to be done. The knot is now cut, the Rubicon crossed & the alia jacta. . . . If it doesn't come off, the doom is too frightful. . . . Have you read it? The last two chapters—glory alleluiah! And the wreakage! That indiscriminate heap of shattered rubbish among which one spies the utterly mangled remains of Aristotle, Jesus, Mr Bradley, Kant, Herbert Spencer, Sidgwick & McTaggart! Plato seems to be the only person who comes out even tolerably well. . . .

> *Your*
> *G L S*

TO LYTTON STRACHEY

Lexham
Oct 12, 1903.   Colinette Rd., Putney.

Well you've begun early enough. I see you have laid a long train of crises to last you out the whole term. And it is—everything is—*so* dangerous with the Yen, so I don't think I shall come up until everything's settled down or exploded up. I've just got his book, it *is* magnificent!

I don't know if I shall come up at all but if I do it will be I suppose Wednesday. I'm sunken & besotted.

> L.

TO THOBY STEPHEN

Trinity College,
Feb 23, 1904.   Cambridge.

My dear Goth,   I was so grieved to read in this morning's paper of the death of your father.[2] I thought I should like just to tell you how

1. Moore's *Principia Ethica* had been published on September 25.
2. Sir Leslie Stephen had died of cancer in his seventy-second year.

sorry I am that this loss has come to you & how I really sympathize with you & Adrian.

Yours ever
Leonard Woolf

To Lytton Strachey

April 12, 1904.   Lexham.

I have returned, as you see, with your razor, your sister's map & a rug which I imagine must be yours. I shall send them to Lancaster Gate. I forgot about your stockings.

I walked to Lynton on Saturday morning solus with the Yen.[1] He at last talked about his depression. The week he said had been like a very long night-mare, & his depression was due in great measure to his being with many people. According to him, he wants someone who will keep off his depression by acting as a perpetual stimulus without ever feeling a reaction from the depression. If he could only find a female stimulus of this kind, he would marry but he has given up hope, I think, of finding her. I saw him yesterday as you did last year, in the little bed with his head wrapped round in the sheet.

I had too a long conversation with Ainsworth on Friday.[2] We walked to Combe Martin & lost ourselves. He asked me about your state of mind & all about Sheppard.[3] He said he felt as if he had lost touch with you & that we had got beyond him, as if both you & he had been continually seeking an opening to talk about realities & had always been baffled back to drivel. *I think* I kept my head, though you won't believe that I did. He said the same things about Sheppard as he said two terms ago, except that he did not understand how at one moment you seemed to see through him & at the next were carried off your feet. 'I don't see what attracts him so much—but after all I was myself once'. He is coming up one Saturday next term to curse Sh[eppard]

1. During the spring vacations Moore held reading parties to which he invited a few close friends, and always included LW and Strachey. That year's event had been held at Hunter's Inn, near Lynton in Devon.
2. Alfred Richard Ainsworth (1879–1959), a brilliant King's scholar in both classics and moral sciences, had left Cambridge in 1902 to lecture, first at Manchester and then Edinburgh. "Ansell" in E. M. Forster's fictional account of the Society in *The Longest Journey*, Ainsworth was Moore's closest friend at this time and in 1908 married one of his sisters.
3. (Sir) John Tresidder Sheppard (1881–1968), a classicist, an Apostle and Provost of King's 1933–54. Strachey was then infatuated with him.

to his face & then I should think die. He gave me a long description of his quarrels with the Yen, the awfulness of the Yen's rage & a sketch of the Yen among his family. I suppose you had told him of the schema as he suddenly said that he thought the Yen ought to marry one of your sisters.[1]

Your
L.

To Lytton Strachey

May 1st 1904   Trin. Col. Camb

. . . I dined with the Yen last night. It was a little lugubrious at dinner. A[insworth] insisted upon arguing against me, the Yen took my side & A. went on for hours in a peevish & perpetual stream. The Society was rather good, a dull paper about beauty by K[eynes], but the Y[en] soared for nearly half an hour. I don't think he is quite so sunken as at Hunter's [Inn]—we have moved from fives to golf. Keynes, he & I journey to Royston where in extraordinarily uncomfortable attitudes & with immense vigour he hits at the ball—for quite a long time he missed it altogether.

I did Churton after all—in the last week of the vac.[2] Every night I began at 12.15 & ended at 1.15. It stopped almost in the middle of a sentence & read like a piece of badly stitched patchwork.

Where will you stay next Sat., there is some devil I believe in your rooms.

Your
L.

1. Strachey replied: "He *is* married—to Ainsworth. I believe he sometimes pines for a divorce. . . ." The schema was to arrange a marriage between Moore and Strachey's sister Philippa.
2. An unsigned review for the *Spectator* of John Churton Collins's *Studies in Shakespeare* and Richard Moulton's *The Moral System of Shakespeare*. This article, along with an earlier one in the *Independent Review*, marked LW's debut as a reviewer. He also contributed poetry to the *Cambridge Review*.

TO LYTTON STRACHEY

June 23, 1904.

Lexham
P.

Yes, do come Sat., though I shan't be able to talk to you—I am completely sunk.[1] I don't think Bradfield is really worth seeing—it certainly has not got what you want to see & what Keynes bewailed the absence of throughout, though he had brought an Eton 'creature' with him. Besides the whole thing is sordid & silly, the play is a miserable play & I could not remember Verrall.[2] There were King's men there who said the trip[os] lists had been full of surprises & when I absently asked them why, they told me Sheppard had got a second.

The only Roman law I can remember is that Justinian enacted by his 'sacred constitutions in the cause of that modesty granted by previous laws to women that for legal purposes puberty should for males be reckoned to commence at 12 & should no longer be decided for each individual case by personal examination'. Also dung is not counted as the fruits of animals. I wonder how many marks I shall score by this.

Yr
L.

TO LYTTON STRACHEY

July 25. 1904

Lexham,
Putney.

My aunt, I am sure, will be delighted to see your sister: they are not actually in Copenhagen at this moment, but have a country house quite near somewhere on the Sound, I believe. They are all damnably good & damnably kind, & consequently a little boring; they are of all nationalities mixed, Danish, Dutch & Swedish predominating; & my youngest sister [Flora] is among them at this moment.[3] I am told that the right way of doing this is to write a letter which I enclose & that it is the greatest insult in the world to lick it down. Whatever happens

1. LW had now returned home to cram in earnest for the Civil Service examination, which took place over three weeks in August.
2. The boys of Bradfield College, noted then as now for their performance of Greek dramas, had performed the *Alcestis* of Euripides. A. W. Verrall, Trinity Fellow and Professor of English literature, was a noted translator of Greek plays.
3. See Biographical Appendix for LW's foreign relatives.

don't let your sister go to the Ethnographical Museum—they always say you must see it & it's death.

I am not really dead now—having reached such a depth that I don't really much mind anything any more. I just read my books & go to bed, & as I don't remember anything I read, it does not much matter. Still I think I shall be glad when the 24th comes. As regards the exam., I find it is sheer death, there are practically no [Civil Service] vacancies &, what there are, are wretched. . . .

Yr
L.

Lyngebaeksgaard or Nivaa is I
believe almost in Copenhagen; you
go by train to it from the Osterbahn
station in Copenhagen.

To Lytton Strachey

Aug 7. 1904.

Lexham
Putney

> There is nothing for you to read in this letter,
> but my head is like wool.

I felt I could never write during the week—I hardly can now—as my hand is simply weary of holding a pen. It is a wonderful experience this—sheer hell the first days: the rooms were absolutely on fire & everyone, except Turner, without coats, waistcoats or collars writing for dear life. The most depressing thing is to look at the people's faces. They are ugly to a degree with a most appalling look of determination on them. In the luncheon interval & at tea we meet the whole of Cambridge. The Goth twice, once to his club which is very depressing; he looks horribly ill & has just had an operation, his nose being boned. Then "the taupe,"[1] in Slaters or the ABC [tearooms] I forget which; we went with him to the Green Park & sat on chairs surrounded by board school children & workmen on their faces; he was just as querulous & apologetic as usual.

1. E. M. Forster; see Biographical Appendix.

Turner was terribly depressing at first & of course would tell me scarcely anything of Cambridge & the Yen. . . .[1]

I wrote to my Aunt about your sister, & got a reply saying she will be delighted to see her.

I can't write any more as I have to prepare for tomorrow!

Yr,
L.

To Lytton Strachey

August 21, 1904

Lexham,
Colinette Road, Putney.

The Yen had just told me that Littlewood was rather nice & looked intelligent, when I returned to my rooms & found your letter.[2] I thought that the suspensive attitude was the wiser, & had adopted it. Cambridge annoyed me rather, covered with awnings & beer-gardens & Maclaren[3] & Greenwood. I couldn't speak to the Yen; I dined with him alone on Wednesday, I don't know whether he was more Turnerian than usual, but he seemed rather bleak & far away. He disappeared on Thursday & wrote to me from Exeter to say his father had died that day just after he arrived.

I very nearly rode over to see you on the Thursday, but had no energy with the wind against me & probable rain. I suppose you are bound to finish Hastings all right, the Yen seemed to regard it as a monumental work.[4] The only thing I thank God for is that we never worked when we were up, & if you've gone through anything like what I have in the last 8 weeks & shall until Thursday, I should think you do as well. I believe it would have been much better to have gone straight down [in 1903] & become clerks & ushers [assistant school-

1. Strachey had reported being in Moore's rooms the preceding weekend when Ainsworth had talked so much he left Moore "black with rage on the sofa. . . . Next day, of course, it all came out. Ainsworth complained of the Yen's harsh treatment of him, said that after I'd gone he was simply abused by the Yen for several hours."
2. John Littlewood, a new Trinity undergraduate, was considered by Strachey to be "hopeless." He in fact became a brilliant scholar and distinguished mathematician.
3. He was mentioned in Sowing as "a rather older scholar."
4. Strachey was now in the final stage of work on his Trinity fellowship dissertation on Warren Hastings, the controversial first Governor-General of India.

masters] at once, than sweat over dissertations & exams, until one positively dries up. I now have to return to Roman Law.

Your
L.

To Lytton Strachey

Aug. 27. 1904   Lexham,
                                    Colinette Road, Putney.

You must come—I don't guarantee Sanger either about you or me, but he can be damned.[1] Anyway you won't die of walking. Also I can't tell you where we shall be, because that ass Keynes is managing it all & won't tell me anything about it; all I know is that I am going to meet him at Chester or Denbigh either on Monday or Tuesday, but I have not the faintest idea what we do then. Still I shall write to you to Cambridge, where you could meet us on Thursday or Friday—so you must come. I don't think I shall be able to come up [to Cambridge] after Wales, as I am, & shall be more, bankrupt. . . .

Yr
L.

To Lytton Strachey

Sept 8. 1904.   Lexham,
                                    Colinette Road, Putney.

If I weren't very nearly a saint, I should have lost my temper long ago. Ever since Monday I have done nothing but write letters to you & to the stationmaster at Chester without getting any reply from either. I have lost all my luggage & all the clothes I ever possessed, except a pair of 'knickers' & a frayed shirt without a collar. . . .

I'll only say one thing, that I never realized how supreme we had

1. The Civil Service exam now over and Strachey's dissertation finished, LW wanted Strachey to join him, Keynes and Sanger on a walking tour in Wales. Charles Percy Sanger (1871–1930), a brilliant Trinity classicist and an Apostle, became a noted Chancery barrister. "He was a gnomelike man with . . . the character of a saint, but he was a very amusing, ribald, completely sceptical saint with a first-class mind and an extremely witty tongue. . . ." (*Sowing*). Fearing that Sanger would not welcome his company, Strachey declined.

been &, for all the 'reticence' & 'pessimism', are. Until that walk, I hadn't talked to a soul for months, & I simply longed to talk to you, & I nearly quarrelled with Keynes & hated him for his crass stupidity & his hideous face. I feel enormously optimistic—a little, I am afraid, like you in the early B[ritish] M[useum] days—& I'm sure I'm not a brute & that you're in a passing trough & that we were & are extraordinarily right. There's only one word in your letter that makes me a little afraid.

> Your
> L.

FROM LYTTON STRACHEY

Sept. 9th 1904

. . . Yes; our supremacy is very great, and you've raised my spirits vastly by saying so. I sometimes feel as if it were not only we ourselves who are concerned, but that the destinies of the whole world are somehow involved in ours. We are—oh! in more ways than one—like the Athenians of the Periclean Age. We are the mysterious priests of a new & amazing civilization. . . . We have abolished religion, we have founded ethics, we have established philosophy, we have sown our strange illumination in every province of thought, we have conquered art, we have liberated love. . . .

Your letter was wonderful, and I was particularly impressed by the curious masculinity of it. Why are you a man? We are females, nous autres, but your mind is singularly male. . . .

My misery was added to by Moore's departure—the thought of it, I mean. I really half cried when I had to see him for the last time in those rooms. . . .[1]

> *GLS*

1. Following the expiry of his Prize Fellowship at Trinity, Moore went to Edinburgh, where he lived with Ainsworth.

Sept 27, 1904   Lexham,
                                             Colinette Road, Putney.

I couldn't write to you yesterday I felt so depressed, & now—the crash
has come &, by God, it is a crash. It came just an hour ago. I'm 65th!
absolutely hopeless. I suppose one ought not to mind really, & in a
strange rather real way I don't, but I'm sunk under the weight of
solemn faces, of gloom, of what people don't say & what they will. I
wish, I do wish I could talk to you. I haven't really decided yet what
to do, though I think it will probably be a mastership & if you can
manage it, Holland House.[1] But then on the other hand, I found from
a talk with my brother [Herbert], that money affairs are much worse
than I thought, so that the bar is impossible, & from their point of
view—though they don't say it—I ought to take the colonies with its
certainty & its greater pay. Every now & then I almost give way. One
ought to be able to do exams I suppose. Does it show complete in-
competence? Am I to be an usher—a conceited one—all my life &
nothing else, with this eternal harass of no money? Can I write, or is
my brain sterile & dull? (I've just had to inform one more of my
family, & it will very soon drive me mad.)

   The interim has been dinner. I've got a wretched headache now, so I
shan't write any more. Do you see a battered usher of 50, among filthy
boys & people with whom he cannot talk, on £150 a year when he wants
150,000? Good God, what a farce, for it might, I feel, so easily be true.
Yet I shouldn't mind a damn, if the menage were possible: but the difficulties, I see, are enormous with the appalling state in which we may be
in another year or two, & perhaps the final crash.

                                                    Your
                                                    L.

                                                         Lexham,
Sept 29, 1904.   Colinette Road, Putney.

I am so sorry about my letter of yesterday—it was simply silly, I think,
& probably did nothing but depress you more. Still, I was in a state,
& longed to talk to you, as I do now. I don't think however that I had

1. Presumably a preparatory school.

better come to C[ambridge] tomorrow, as the complications here are growing. You see I have to decide so soon & the question of Jew or Christian is now the absorbing topic, & I have to rush about trying to find out whether people will allow their sons to be taught by Jews & Atheists. Then there is the whole financial crisis, & I find that I simply must make enough not only to support myself but to contribute [to the family]. Would the Yen say that I therefore *ought* to go to the colonies? I believe I *ought*, especially as I might have to wait months doing nothing before I became an usher. Could you play Dickinson to my Ferdy? —he went to Hong Kong didn't he?[1] I should come back every 6 years for a year, very yellow & silent—but I should be making £600 a year! I suppose I shall decide all this one day, & whether Hong Kong is better than Straits Settlements or Malaya better than both, & whether I shall die in the climate of all three. At present I know nothing, so if you can give me any information on these points, do.

This is a sordid letter, but I feel so. At any rate I have got over yesterday's mood, & recovered the courage you recommend. We shall need it much more, I think, if I go to H K. . . .

They are yelling for the letters. I shall go to Sanger's to-morrow on the chance of meeting Hawtrey![2]

Your
L.

I am summoned to decide by next Thursday.

FROM LYTTON STRACHEY

Sept. 30th 1904.

Oh no, no, no. Say what you feel at any & every moment. How could I bear anything else? As it is, I can bear everything; only I must cry out and groan. To all these horrors & Fates I send up my love as a sacrifice and a propitiation. It is all I have. If you settle for the Colonies,

---

1. Ferdinand Schiller, the great love of Dickinson's life, left Cambridge in 1888 for a successful business career in Calcutta. Dickinson, morose and lonely, had to keep in touch by mail.
2. (Sir) Ralph Hawtrey (1879–1975), known to LW at Trinity and as an Apostle, became a famous economist, serving in the Treasury from 1904 until 1945.

I'm sure Hong Kong would be best. . . . If you felt you'd be utterly miserable at H.K. nearly all the time, I'm sure you oughtn't *to go. . . .*

Your
GLS

To Saxon Sydney-Turner

Oct 3, 1904.

Lexham
Putney.

I am continually being congratulated on getting on the list, & I feel very like congratulating you in revenge. Are you coming up to make your choice. If you do, come out & see me & tell me what happens.[1]

Yr
L.

To Lytton Strachey

Oct 3, 1904

Lexham,
Colinette Road, Putney.

This place is in a complete uproar, as my sister has just returned from Denmark & everyone is talking at the same time. I am still in the same state of rushing wildly about seeing schoolmasters & doctors & agents & all manner of people. I went to Sanger on Friday & found a vast crowd there composed of American female philanthropists, women in wonderful trailing dresses, bearded anarchists, Hawtrey & Crompton. Hawtrey was rather consoling & thought I should get offered some rotten Home [Civil Service] thing, which of course I should take. Sanger told me to call on Marsh, who with Bernard Holland & Lyttelton

1. LW, like Sydney-Turner, was placed on a rank-ordered list of those examinees eligible for appointment to the Civil Service—but whether Home or Colonial was subject to some negotiation.

would get me into the Colonial Office.[1] I have decided that if there is the ghost of a chance of a Home [Civil Service] thing, I shall not go to H K & I rather think that in any case I shall risk the ushership. I don't think you are Dickinson or that I am Ferdy, really, but six years seems too appalling, & after all, as far as the damned money goes, I believe an usher gets £150 & I could live on 80.

The Babel here is too much, I can't write any more. I have begun the pseudonym scheme & will send you something I thought of sending to the *Independent*.[2] Tell me whether the Monism is too great. I think it would at most give me away, especially as the whole thing is two sentences out of one of my papers for the Society expanded.

Your letters have been the one comfort in this succession of silly crises; so if you can, write.

Your
L.

I have just had a letter from your mother, she recommends H.K....

To Lytton Strachey

Oct 11. 1904   Lexham

If anything could have made me feel more utterly miserable, it was your letter. I suppose this only adds truth to Montaigne.[3] I don't know why one doesn't commit suicide, except that one is dead & rotten

1. (Sir) Edward Marsh (1872–1953), a junior official in the Colonial Office responsible for vetting appointments to the Colonial Service, went on to become private secretary to (Sir) Winston Churchill, Joseph Chamberlain and Prime Ministers Herbert Asquith and Ramsay MacDonald. He was also an author and patron of the arts, whom LW consulted between 1912 and the early 1920s about publishing his short stories. The Hon. Alfred Lyttelton (1857–1913) was Colonial Secretary, and Bernard Holland (1856–1926) was his private secretary. For Crompton Llewelyn Davies, see Biographical Appendix. All four men had been at Trinity and in the Society.
2. The *Independent Review*, which ran from 1903 to 1907, was a left Liberal, essentially Cambridge, monthly journal about politics and culture. LW had already contributed a review of a biography of Voltaire to its January 1904 issue. The "pseudonym scheme" cannot be identified and no article appeared in the *Independent*.
3. From Cambridge, Strachey reported intimations that his fellowship dissertation would be rejected and quoted Montaigne, "Je ne pense point qu'il y ait tant de malheur en nous, comme il y a de vanité; ny tant de malice, comme de sottise; nous ne sommes pas si pleins de mal, comme d'inanité, nous ne sommes pas si misérables, comme nous sommes vils."

already. I have done nothing but sit in this accursed room since I saw you; nothing happens & I haven't the energy to begin to do anything myself. I feel that, in a way, you are lost to me already; you at any rate will be here, & there are other people, but I shall be rotting in Ceylon. I shall be out of date after 6 years.

I suppose you will answer truly with Montaigne.

Your
L.

To G. E. Moore

Lexham,
Colinette Road, Putney.

Oct 14. 1904

Dear Moore, I am in a horrible state of mind, & complete despair. I have taken an Eastern Cadetship, & shall get either Ceylon or Hong Kong. I shall have to leave about October 28th; there are of course millions of things to do, but I should like so much, if I have time, to rush up & see you before I go. I do hate the thought of it all, but I was simply overwhelmed by circumstances: if it had not been for *Principia Ethica*, I believe I should have become an usher.

Love to Ainsworth.

Yours
L. S. Woolf

To Lytton Strachey

Lexham,
Col. Rd. P.

Oct 21. 1904

I've literally not had a moment to write in, for as soon as you left & I had read Warren Hastings, the real rush began. I spend my days in the Army & Navy Stores; & I have at last heard that I am going to Ceylon. When, God knows. If I have time, I shall go to Edinburgh— I had a most Yenistic letter.[1]

I rushed to C[ambridge] on Sat. Melancholia was black upon it & they're going—they told me—to elect Furness. I took wings & so did

1. It does not survive.

Hom.[1] I dined at the High Table on Sun. & sat next to Jackson who was black with rage until I asked him whether he had ever read Mason's novels.[2]

W[arren] H[astings], I thought, was enthralling, but I believe I see what those asses mean. It's too enthralling, & not enough like a dissertation. It's a little too graceful for them: & if you made it all seem much more laborious & magnified all the points, they would have elected you. I shall deliver it at Lancaster G[ate].

I have n't sent the letters yet. It's too dangerous, & I think there's plenty of time?[3]

Yr
L.

To G. E. Moore

Lexham,
Colinette Road, Putney.

Oct 21, 1904

My dear Moore, I am definitely for Ceylon now, but I don't know when I shall have to go. I am rushing about buying mad things like riding breeches & cholera belts;[4] but if I have time, I shall let you know when I could come for a night or two to you. I only meant that if I had been an Egoistic Hedonist, I should n't have chosen Ceylon, but an ushership.

I went to Cambridge on Saturday & took wings. The gloom over the whole place was appalling.

Yours
L. S. Woolf

1. (Sir) Robert Furness (1883–1954), a classicist and Keynes's best friend at King's, was not elected to the Apostles. "Hom" was the nickname of Hugh Owen Meredith (1873–1963), Fellow of King's and later Professor of Economics at Queen's University, Belfast. Forster's first great love, Meredith was a model for the hero of *A Room with a View*; Forster celebrated their friendship in his posthumously published novel, *Maurice*.
2. A. E. W. Mason (1865–1948), author of popular historical novels.
3. Fearing their blunt talk about sex made them too risky to take along to Ceylon, LW proposed to return Strachey's letters. In reply, Strachey asked if it would not be prudent to "write on the outside of the packet 'Damned private. To await arrival'? You might say 'Explosives' with truth; but then people might be heroic & plunge them into the W.C., which would be a calamity at large."
4. LW had a crash course in riding at Knightsbridge Barracks; the belt was a flannel waistband, mandatory for imperial service, in the belief it prevented stomach disorders.

FROM BELLA WOOLF

Oct. 30th [1904]

My dearest Len,

Like Mama & Herbert, I am much exercised in my mind as to your choice of a profession, especially as the decision looms so near. . . . From your letter I can see that you have little preference, for I know you would far sooner cast in your lot with Literature with a capital L. . . . I wish you'd tell me honestly if you care for the Bar & if you feel you could throw yourself into it, if once you took it up. We should not like to see you go to India for good & all, unless you felt the East a-calling! Of course the money question hampers the Bar. But, if you would like the chance, I will pay the £40 required. I have a serial ordered by Cassell's for which they promise to pay me £60—& well, there's my offer. Don't be foolish and decline on sentimental grounds— it is too important a question. . . .

Your loving
Belle

Don't thank me—it's my ambition to have a finger in the making of the fortunes of some of you.

To Lytton Strachey

Lexham,
Nov 1, 1904   Colinette Road, Putney.

I don't know that I have anything to say except that we seem very far apart. Shall I ever see you; I can't believe that my last sight will be of your back upon the omnibus. I am going to Scotland on Thursday night: I really in the end should have broken through everything & come to you last Friday in a rush, but they insisted that I should stay here because my mother had a birthday on Saturday. I have gone mad, & spend my evenings in giving the wildest dinners. I have even gone as far as MacCarthy, the Goth & Turner for to-morrow (though there is still a hope thank God that only the Goth will come).[1] The

1. For Desmond MacCarthy, see Biographical Appendix. LW was also guest of the Stephens at a farewell dinner a fortnight later, when he met Virginia (VS) for the second time; they had previously met in Thoby's rooms at Trinity in 1903.

taupe asked if he could come & see me, so he lunched here to-day, & has absolutely depressed me. Then I met Bob Trevy on Sat. at *Doctor Faustus*, & his wife who is beautifully soothing. He said that he would 'have to get people to write to me' when I'm in C.[+] & he suggested you as one who would probably write good letters with plenty of news in them.

It is very depressing: my bottom is raw from riding & I am dressed completely in new clothes. My balls are in a suspensory bandage with four straps round my legs & hips, my calves in sock suspenders, & my belly in a cholera belt. . . .

I feel that you are either ill or dying. I have already become middle aged.

Yr
L.

[+] Ceylon

To Lytton Strachey

Lexham,
Colinette Road, Putney.

Nov. 10. 1904

There is only one book for you: *The Anatomy of Melancholy* Part III.[1] If I did not know you—I believe so well—I should hardly believe your letter. I suppose I ought to pity you, & yet, if it really has happened why shouldn't it be the best thing that could? I always believe you are happier really in the fever & the fret than in the British Museum. And yet I'm enraged. I shall come up, I suppose, & act your love surveyor & expert all over again for Sat & Sunday.

I shall not be up till about 7, as I want to hear the C Minor for the last time.[2] Will you get me a room? I promised to tell Turner, if I am going up—which I now regret, I suppose that's the last confession.

---

1. This was Robert Burton's three-volume work, first published in 1621, about the types, causes and cures of melancholy. The recommendation followed Strachey's news that his dissertation had been rejected.
2. Probably Beethoven's Fifth Symphony; at Cambridge LW wrote a poem called "The C Minor."

I stayed with the Yen: I could talk to him alone, but was speechless with & before Ainsworth, who therefore became black.

Your
L.

If you go to Hall now, sign me on.

To Lytton Strachey

Nov 18. 1904   Lexham,
Colinette Road, Putney.

I am after all taking your letters with me under lock & key in the old cigar box. Do you think it's dangerous? I am in the last mad rush, & shall [be thankful] when to-morrow evening is here, or there. The right way to address letters is:

Passenger per S.S. "Syria"
% the P. & O. S.N. Co's Agent
Marseilles (or Port Said or Aden
whichever you write to)

Farewell.

Your
L.[1]

---

1. In a letter that caught up with LW at Port Said, Strachey wrote: "Oh, I don't know, but as I watched your ship in the Channel last night, I thought that all was lost. You have vanished; and the kisses that I never gave you, your embraces that I have never felt, they are all that remain—nonexistent and disconsolate entities—the eternal ghosts of our desires and dreams."

Rangefontuini
Ceylon.

April 30. 1905

Dear Moore, I was very glad to get your letter, but really, if it is any worry at all for you to write, please do not do it. What I find is that I continually want to write to people, but hate it when I come to do it. It is so difficult to say what you mean, & one knows how different from what you meant it is from what it would be in conversation, it will all sound. And then I loathe the actual writing.

I am writing this on a wonderful glaring white beach, which is composed not of sand or stones, but solely of millions of minute shells. The sun is simply blazing down on me, & there is no shade for the only trees are palmyrahs & cocoanuts which are practically useless.

PART TWO

———

CEYLON

What Leonard Woolf termed his second birth occurred on December 16, 1904, when he landed in Colombo to take up his duties as a junior official in the government of Ceylon. From the first day he was attracted by the beauty of the country, the charm of the people and the exoticism of the Orient; in fact, he quickly formed an attachment to the island that he retained to the end of his life. But at the same time he was devastated by a sense of being cut off from everyone and everything that meant most to him. Not surprisingly, his letters reflect a deep ambivalence—fascination with the day-to-day life in a colony at the zenith of empire combined with a loneliness, depression and anger he could never escape.

Professionally Leonard was an immediate success. He was highly competent, drove himself remorselessly and made himself so indispensable that wherever he served he soon became the person who was really in charge. He also had the good fortune to be in right places at right times and was able to meet—and impress—the highest colonial officials. Although he rubbed some colleagues the wrong way on his rise up the bureaucratic ladder, the Ceylon government was flexible and tolerant enough to recognize exceptional ability and rewarded him with unusually rapid promotion. And so, while he had vague misgivings about British imperialism from the moment he got off the boat, he was a model imperialist.

The Ceylon in which Leonard worked was itself considered a model, the senior crown colony. Its administrative system had been established by Sir Thomas Maitland in 1802, when the island was ceded to Britain by the Dutch, who had taken it from the Portuguese in 1658. The Ceylon Civil Service, by far the oldest in the Empire, was incorruptible, able and dedicated to beneficent government under the rule of law. Although its powers were absolute, it interfered as little as possible with the lives of the people and left intact the local authority of the indigenous aristocratic structure of headmen. At the pinnacle of the Ceylon government was a governor appointed by the Crown; in Leonard's time they were men of little ability. In practice it was the colonial secretary, a senior career official with considerable experience in the area, who was chief executive. The island itself was divided into nine provinces, each headed by a government agent, and the provinces were subdivided into districts, headed by assistant government agents. Under an AGA was an office assistant. At the bottom of the structure was the newly arrived cadet, who had to learn his work as he went along.

Cadet Woolf started off in January 1905 in the northernmost province, Jaffna, a physically harsh area inhabited by Tamils—Hindus of Indian origin. Chafing at his routine duties, he bullied his superior into giving him more substantial work, and in no time he was appointed additional police magistrate and additional collector of customs. In less than a year he was raised to office assistant, and not long afterward was temporarily put in charge of Mannar, a godforsaken jungle district, where he thrived on the authority and solitude.

In the summer of 1907 he was suddenly promoted to office assistant at the island's ancient capital, Kandy, where he was captivated by the softer, Buddhist culture of the Sinhalese. There he came into contact not only with the Acting Governor but also such unlikely visitors as former Empress Eugénie, who had come to see one of Kandy's attractions, the tooth of Buddha. He handled them all with such aplomb that after a year he was again promoted out of order, and given a district of his own, Hambantota, on the south coast of the island. Working sixteen hours a day, despite chronic malaria and other maladies, he made his area the most efficiently governed in the colony. His rigid moral and administrative standards did not always make him popular. In 1910 the people of one village presented him with a list of all the evils that had befallen them as a result of the appearance of Halley's comet that year. Evil number six was "a strict Assistant Government Agent." In another village, one disgruntled person had

58

an explicit recommendation, which he advertised in a local newspaper: "Mr. L. S. Woolf deserves to be shot." However, respect for him was so deep that when he returned to Ceylon fifty years later, the government treated him almost as a visiting chief of state and further commemorated the event by publishing the official diaries he kept as district governor.

Leonard was never a typical anything and certainly not a typical imperialist. He was scrupulous in following Maitland's principles of colonial administration. He learned to speak, read and write both Tamil and Sinhalese. He studied law and accounting. He traveled constantly to get to know his district and its problems. He was enthralled by the sheer challenge of the work. In devoting himself completely to the welfare of his people, he was acting in the best tradition of British imperialism. What set him apart, then as in every phase of his life, was his independent judgment and his refusal to accept the established norms of the time and place. In Ceylon this attitude drove him to question—and finally to doubt—the sacred premises of British rule.

Although these letters contain anything but a ponderous discussion of imperialism, they do offer a memorable glimpse of the system in action. A striking feature is the remarkable delegation of authority. As London invested the Ceylon government with virtual autonomy, so the authorities in Colombo gave the provinces—and the provinces, the districts—nearly independent jurisdiction. Although originally a consequence of the sheer size of the Empire and the primitive communications, this arrangement was by Leonard's time deliberate British administrative practice. The average district officer therefore enjoyed responsibilities that his colleague in a London ministry would have assumed only after vastly more experience and seniority. Within two weeks of his arrival in Jaffna, Leonard was left temporarily in charge of the entire northern province. A few years later, at the age of twenty-seven, and with less than four years on the job, he was made entirely responsible for a thousand-square-mile chunk of the Empire that had a population of 100,000.

Perhaps being entrusted with such responsibility compensated for what emerges as another feature of imperial administration: the primitive life that the colonial official at times had to be prepared to endure. On call twenty-four hours a day, despite the debilitating climate and frequent illness, he might live in only a hut; he usually traveled by bullock cart, horse or bicycle; and, when on circuit, unless content with a remorseless diet of stringy chicken or canned sardines, his only food was what he shot with his own rifle.

A further notable trait of imperial administration was the extraordinary thinness of staffing—several dozen civil servants governed the entire colony of Ceylon. As a result, the range of duties was practically limitless. Even as a lowly trainee, Leonard served as administrator, policeman, customs authority, judge, veterinarian, agronomist and examining magistrate. A little later he was made responsible for revenue collection and expenditure, municipal and local government, and the sale and development of Crown lands. As if that were not enough, he also supervised prisons, schools, hospitals and irrigation works. He witnessed hangings, implemented divorce and marriage regulations and even arbitrated the personal disputes brought to him by local inhabitants. At one time or another he directed a famine-relief project, oversaw a religious pilgrimage of 4,000 Buddhists and helped direct a chaotic pearl-fishing operation of some 40,000 Arabs. When he eventually was put in charge of a district of his own, he carried out all his regular duties and at the same time managed to have an unprecedented amount of salt collected and the decennial census statistics compiled with record speed. He improved elementary education and introduced a new mode of plowing. At one moment he was combatting a devastating cattle disease; at another he was coddling Baron Blixen and other Danish relatives of Queen Alexandra, who had come to hunt big game.

Finally, what implicitly emerges from the letters is the pacific nature of British imperial authority. Whatever kept the structure of the Empire intact, it was not physical might. In Ceylon the few soldiers were in Colombo and Kandy and were essentially ornamental. Even policemen were rare; there were but two in the entire Jaffna province during Leonard's time there. At the pearl fishery and during the Buddhist pilgrimage, where real mayhem could easily have occurred, it was taken for granted that the mere presence of one or two British officials would be sufficient to maintain order.

This was literally Pax Britannica. And Leonard had no doubt that it both kept the peace and conferred material benefits. What troubled him was not the peace, but the fact that it was British. The conventional belief in the superiority of the "civilized races" and the need for an educated elite to govern backward people for their own good—which was the moral keystone of the British Empire—was difficult for him to accept. Instinctively he found it repugnant that people of one culture should impose their standards on those of another. In several letters, he wrote of certain Tamils who, because of their high caste, refused to carry dirt for construction projects. "And they are quite right, I think, don't you?" he wrote to Robert Trevelyan. He also put his finger on the fundamental fallacy in the imperial system: Its premises were directly contrary to the political values of Britain itself. "Theoretically everyone is told that he is equal with everyone else," he wrote to Strachey, "while practically we try to be paternal, despotic, to be what we were & refused to remain 50 years ago." And he was convinced that colonial rule could only succeed, as he commented to Strachey, "if the natives believe in us & it, & they don't. . . . They don't understand & they don't believe in our methods." Such is the extent of his few fugitive political comments. It is enough, however, to show that his misgivings cut to the core of the imperial ideal.

If the system was bad for the governed, in Leonard's view it was also bad for the governors, creating in them a sense of separation and superiority. Nothing was more ridiculous to him than what he referred to as the "circumambient air of a tropical suburbia" that his colleagues generated around themselves. This world of sahibs and memsahibs—their ruling-caste mentality and elaborate class system and racial assumptions—had such an aura of artificiality that he found it impossible to know, as he commented in a letter to Strachey, whether Kipling modeled his characters on them or they modeled themselves on Kipling's characters. The ineffable boredom of their social life and the unconscious comedy of their tea parties, tennis matches and drinking bouts are the subject of some of the most amusing letters. And the cast of characters—the mustachioed wife of the governor, the pathetic Dutton pounding away at Beethoven's Fifth Symphony on piano keys held together with string and General Sir Hector Macdonald, with his "reputation"—is what one expects of Edwardian colonials.

Not that Leonard's view of the native population was tainted by a naïve belief in the "noble savage." Reports of cruelty, superstition and ignorance abound in the correspondence. But beyond doubt what meant most to him during his six and a half years on the island was his contact with the Tamils and Sinhalese and the understanding, respect and affection he developed for them. Leonard was anything but unusual among British colonial officials in acquiring an expert knowledge of the country in which he served and in wanting to promote the interests of the native population. What made him unique was his ability to see and feel almost as though he were one of them.

So remarkable was this empathy that when he came to write his novel about Ceylon, *The Village in the Jungle*, it had an authenticity that was unequaled even in works by Conrad and Forster. Their focus was on the Westerner; his was on the native villager and peasant and the forces of nature—above all, the jungle—that controlled their lives. Even the dialogue, though necessarily in English, is said to demonstrate a sure grasp of Tamil and Sinhalese and the way simple people spoke it. Reviewing the book in *Blackwood's*, Sir Hugh Clifford, who spent his entire career in the tropics, commented on Leonard's remarkable understanding of the power of the jungle: "Mr Woolf is many years my junior in age and service, and has discovered in two years spent in the more arid jungles of Ceylon a fact which escaped me."

In Ceylon, Leonard accumulated a jumble of impressions that left him, as he acknowledged in his autobiography, in a state of political schizophrenia. On the one hand, he had worked hard to implement policies that were undeniably good for Ceylon and its people. Moreover, the British Empire at that time seemed as permanent as the sun that never set on it. To question its precepts and permanence, as he recorded in his short story "Pearls and Swine," was considered as outlandish as questioning the principles of the solar system. On the other hand, he was beginning to doubt not only the moral legitimacy of imperialism but also its effectiveness. In the end was it not the village headmen and the moneylenders in the cities, rather than the government agents, who had *real* power over the people?

Leonard Woolf's experiences in Ceylon are recorded in some 125 surviving letters—to Lytton Strachey, Saxon Sydney-Turner, R. C. Trevelyan, G. E. Moore, Desmond MacCarthy and John Maynard Keynes. By far the greatest number were written to Strachey, and they are the frankest and therefore the most interesting. Official correspondence by or about Woolf as an agent of the Ceylon government was destroyed in accordance with administrative practice, though his letter of resignation and related Colonial Office comments—which belong to a later period—are preserved in the Public Record Office. The loss of Leonard's letters to his family is unfortunate, since it is clear from the surviving replies that they dealt with a happier side of his life and with several political issues that did not arise with his Cambridge friends.

From Leonard's first letter on setting foot in Ceylon, it is obvious that correspondence was an emotional lifeline. Although at times pleasantly surprised by individuals once he came to know them, he despised his compatriots in the mass, describing them at one point as a "stupid degraded circle of degenerates and imbeciles." He was often in physical misery. Housing was at times squalid; the climate, the heat and the glare of the sun were brutal, and health problems were continual; he suffered from malaria, typhoid fever and all the common East-of-Suez intestinal disorders and skin problems. It always came back, though, to the pain of spiritual homesickness and fear of intellectual atrophy.

Eventually, in the spring of 1906, he wrote a drunken letter to Strachey declaring that he had made his will and planned to shoot himself.

Letters were vicarious conversations in this solitude of exile. "I feel I want to talk [to you] a little before I go to bed," is a remark found in one phrasing or another throughout the letters to Strachey. In his eagerness to get his thoughts on paper, his pen evidently ran away with him, and since he did not alter what he wrote, the letters are occasionally an awkwardly expressed stream of emotions. Such spontaneity has the advantage of offering the reader a sense of being carried back to the time and place. One careens through Jaffna in Jimmy Bowes's English gig and looks over Leonard's shoulder as he dashes off a letter in the moonlight after his lamp is blown out by the wind. However, as he himself found when rereading some of them nearly six decades later, while working on his autobiography, the letters overemphasize the bleakness, frustration and anger of the moment and understate his excitement and pleasures.

Entirely different was the correspondence with his family. Judging by their responses, Leonard's letters usually related entertaining anecdotes of his day-to-day life and passed over in silence most of the physical and metaphysical miseries that he shared with Strachey. Theirs were largely about family affairs, including the news—unwelcome to Leonard, who was still essentially apolitical and conservative—that his brothers had become enthusiastic supporters of a new socialist group in Parliament, the Labour Party, and that his sisters were very active in the woman suffrage movement. Above all, the correspondence makes plain that Leonard remained deeply devoted to his family. Having gone into the Colonial Service out of a sense of duty, to provide financial support, he showered them with gifts and money. During his years in Ceylon, his pay averaged around 480 rupees (£32) a month, and he regularly sent a portion of this home. On winning £690 in a sweepstake in 1908, he gave 250 of it to the family. For all his generosity—to his colleagues as well—he was careful with his money, and on leaving the island had managed to accumulate savings of £570 and investments of £517.

There also survive about 150 letters to Leonard from his Cambridge friends. The most important are from Strachey, and excerpts are occasionally included to provide some idea of the news about Cambridge to which Leonard was responding. These exchanges demonstrate the strength of the friendship between the two at a dark time in their lives and show how each often believed in the other more than in himself. Leonard's "blaze" letter of February 1905 and Strachey's reply in March of the following year to "the last despairing cry of the ghost of

a soul you once knew" are touching examples of a splendid com-
radeship that endured across thousands of miles.

In time—around the midpoint of his years in Ceylon—the challenge
of work and fascination with the country supplanted Leonard's curiosity about old friends. He wrote fewer letters and eventually brought
the correspondence with Strachey to an abrupt close; after years of
encouraging a visit, he scotched any idea of his coming to Ceylon.
Leonard had changed; as he wrote to Strachey in October 1908, "I
have no connection with yesterday: I do not recognize it nor myself
in it." He was growing; Strachey was stagnating. Increasingly they
had been talking past one another, and Strachey's gossip and tangled
love affairs must have become intolerably trivial to someone faced
with, among other things, an epidemic of cattle disease that threatened
the very livelihood of tens of thousands of wretched peasants. The
break in the correspondence marked a break in an emotional intimacy
that was never fully restored.

Their exchanges concluded on a bizarre note. Although Strachey's
letters had for years made references to Virginia and Vanessa Stephen,
only once had these aroused any comment: Leonard's admission that
he had fallen in love at first sight with Vanessa, on meeting her at
Cambridge in 1903. After her marriage, Strachey began speculating
on who might marry Virginia, and in a letter in 1908 that has been
lost, he alluded in some way to Leonard. Leonard's receptive response
surprised Strachey, who immediately took it on himself to promote an
alliance between the two persons he most admired, pressing Leonard
to return at once to marry. For more than six months, Leonard ignored
the appeals, and in his final letter reluctantly dismissed the idea. Adding a further curious touch, during this discourse between the two,
Bella Woolf broke in with her views on the sort of woman Leonard
should marry, an intervention that was either inspired by Strachey,
whom Bella had seen a few weeks earlier, or was uncanny in its timing.

For all their hardship and depression, the years in Ceylon and particularly the experience of governing Hambantota by himself marked
a high point in Leonard's life. By the time he left for a year's leave,
he had learned about the law, the courts, finance, bureaucracy and
human nature in the rough. He had discovered the pleasures of female
companionship and distaste for sex without love. And he had proved
he could deal equally well with peasants, British planters, village headmen, whores, colonial governors and retired empresses. Having arrived
in Ceylon, as he himself said, "an arrogant, conceited, and quick-
tempered young man," he left, as others said of him, a confident,
serious and reserved one. He departed from Hambantota on May 20,

1911; his horse, his pets and his books remained behind. He was due to be back on station in exactly a year.

*　　*　　*

To Lytton Strachey

Nov 26, 1904.   S.S. 'Syria'

I can only write incoherently, as incoherency seems very much the atmosphere of a P. & O. It has seemed very much of a whirl ever since I got on board. I don't read or think or feel, but just play chess & bridge, & talk, for the most part, pure dulness. There is a comic Irishman at whom I laugh a great deal, & an army captain, so tall & nice & demi-semi-Gothic that he very often reminds me of the real thing. There is an earl, & a tea planter & a most outrageous & disgusting Maltese. My 'fellow cadet' is, I am afraid, completely a dullard; he has already told me five times that the advantage of the Ceylon Civil Service over the Indian is that you don't pay for your pension. He is a little like [Walter] Lamb was before we took him in hand.[1] The females are extraordinarily dull. It is impossible to write in this smoking room, everyone is talking, & a wretch keeps on interrupting me & it is too cold to sit outside. I feel as if I had been born & lived my whole life in this ship. Cambridge seems very misty & far away; if I don't hear from you at Marseilles, I shall think it has all been a dream. The final week was really rather appalling, & I was quite wrecked by the dreariness of the first night on board.

I have been irretrievably interrupted, & it is too late now to write any more.

Yr
L.

1. The fellow cadet was Edward Millington, who in fact had an undistinguished career in the field in Ceylon. (Sir) Walter Lamb (1882–1961) was a contemporary at Trinity and Secretary of the Royal Academy of Arts 1913–51; LW and Strachey considered him an officious mediocrity.

Dec. 4, 1904   S.S. Syria

. . . We're very nearly in the Red Sea now, & the sun is shining, & it's noon, but there is no glare & no bright colours, a very pale blue sky, pale yellow sand, & soft reds & browns of the hills. I am in fact almost shivering with cold writing here on deck. . . . But it began at Port Said, with its filth & the coaling which I suppose you have seen, & swarming Arab crowd in the streets, who followed one of the hideous ladies & myself about the town imploring us aloud to buy French letters. I became enraged after bellowing at them to go in several languages, lashed at them wildly with my stick, & hit a solitary policeman very hard upon the shin. You have seen it all of course, & the canal with its weird colours under searchlight by night, & its melancholy sand, & its melancholy camels by day.

Dec. 6, 1904

God! There is no doubt about the heat now that it has come: I simply streamed with sweat, dressing at 8 this morning. I did nothing yesterday practically but play bridge, quoits, chess & dance. After everyone had told everyone else that it was the dullest ship they had ever been on, committees were formed 'to amuse the ladies': the consequence has been a wild round of tournamental gaieties. There is no one of course really to talk to; the Irishman & captain are the best, the latter went as far yesterday as to laugh at a very mild joke against God. I don't talk very much to the females; they are mostly either very old & pompous or very young & flighty. The cultured old maid Miss Birstingler sings Schumann for me after most of the other people have gone to bed; she adores repartee & witty conversation, she says, & her idea of it seems to be just to flatly contradict everything which anyone says. . . .

                                     Your
                                     L.

To Lytton Strachey

Dec. 12, 1904   S.S. Syria

. . . We go on in the same old way every day. I am somewhat hated
on board, I think, as I talk to very few people—they are for the most
part so intolerably boring. I have found, however, a rather wonderful
female. She is Irish & somewhat like B. G. Brown [a Trinity scholar]
in so far as she lends herself to brilliant conversations. We have got
as far as the immortality of the soul, & whether love is a physical
alteration, & one feels so monstrous on a P. & O. that I found myself
very nearly touching on sodomy. I actually did get to it—in conversation—with the captain, & I got a very interesting & practical description of its existence in the army. We could not land at Aden
because of plague there, & we got in so late that it was already dark.
There has been nothing to look at but the ugliness of my fellow passengers, flying fish, sunsets &, until to-day, a wonderful green sea.
When it's very hot, I sleep on deck & it's very charming with the stars
& the noise of the sea & the waking up at sunrise.

GRAND ORIENTAL HOTEL, COLOMBO

Dec 16, 1904

I've been here 5½ hours, in an immense hotel with miles of corridors
& thousands of rooms, a gallery in which I sit writing, a band playing,
& the motleyest of motley crowds. I'm partially drunk, I think, with
the complete unreality of it all & a very little whiskey. I feel as if I
were playing the buffoon in a vast comic opera. You *can't* exist, nor
grey old Cambridge, nor Bob Trevy nor the Yen. I can't believe I have
ever spoken to you, or rather I shouldn't if I did not want to so much
now. I have a servant of whom I know practically nothing but who
for the past hour has waited on me hand & foot. I have been in
rickshaws with the female to an hotel just outside the town which
seemed to come straight out of the Gaiety stage. I have dined with
two other females from the ship & have fled here now to sit bewildered
& aghast. There are odd buffaloes shambling about alone in the streets
outside, great red & white silent looking buildings & masses of trees—
it's no good telling you what there is for you know it quite well yourself,
I expect, & as I say it seems ridiculously a dream to me.
    The ship remained the same to the end. I got absurdly intimate with

the female, who eventually & suddenly poured out to me the 'story of her life' which was very amusing to hear & probably untrue, but would be too boring to retail. She was a neurotic & probably an erotic, & lent me Poems & Ballads first series with all the violent passages marked. She was extraordinarily a female, & consequently extraordinarily indecent.

Dec 17, 1904

I have never felt so lonely in my life as I do at the present moment. I have tried to talk to Millington for the last hours, but he is without sense, or feeling or intelligence or character, a dolt, a stone, a fool, an imbecile, a toad. I thought nothing could have been worse than the first days on the Syria, but that was nothing to the enormous & gloomy solitude of this. If only you were here, everything would be changed, for the place itself is wonderful & superb. I shall die, I hope, very soon; at any rate I feel as if I shall. It has rained all day & a thick moist heat is over everything.

I have called on the Colonial Secretary, where I saw what I suppose I must call my future colleagues. They seemed less crass than Millington, & immediately asked us to dinner. I am going to be sent away from Colombo up country, but probably not until the second week in January—& where is unknown as yet.

This is the last word I can send you by this mail—I hope it won't depress you too much.

Your
L.

To Lytton Strachey

The Grand Oriental Hotel
Colombo, Ceylon

Dec. 20, 1904

. . . My letters I am afraid are one long whine, but to you I can't help it; I can only say again, if you only knew how I want to see you! This place even is absolutely beautiful & absolutely degraded. The people—the English are hell, the Australians Sodom & Gomorrah. But outside—I just see that it's heaven; I went for a bicycle ride this evening, & it was absolutely superb—the sunshine, the streets, the myriads, even the smells which too I just saw my degradation in loathing. How they must despise us our boorish idiotic Millingtons. They wander, perpetually chattering, up & down the roads under their wonderful palm trees, & they look at Millington ride by without a smile or a blink—they are, I feel, either Gods or animals.

I am sitting in this same damned gallery after dinner & they've just played *Pinafore*, like a funeral march. Do you feel my isolation, the continual creeping of depression. Yesterday we—M[illington] & I—dined with the cadets who live with a police magistrate & a nondescript in one bungalow. They were all very nice & kind, nearly all from Cambridge & one John Scott of Kings whom Hom knows.[1] Even they, I think, have become rather old & melancholy here, counting the years they must spend before their twelve-months leave. In the daytime I sit in a Kachcheri or Govt Office & sign my name to documents all of which say: 'Sir, I am directed to inform you that the Governor having considered the petition of X, H.E. refuses to interfere. By order L S Woolf for the Col. Sec.' Thank God they are sending me to an out-station on Jan 4: almost certainly to Jaffna, a dry & sweltering spot in the extreme north of the island.

Your
L.

Colombo is *not* spelt Columbo.

Thank God, Ive known people who are not Millington or females!

To Lytton Strachey

Dec. 28, 1904

The Grand Oriental Hotel
Colombo, Ceylon

I am sitting in the hotel garden surrounded by strange trees & masses of wonderful creepers, with carrion crows dropping on my head & your hated Charles lying under my seat. I have been reading the *Times Literary Supplement*, & your letter which for some unknown reason I got only a few minutes ago. . . .

We are to be sent to outstations next week, & I had the choice between two places Jaffna & Matara. I chose Jaffna because I was told it was the better. I leave for it on Sunday, training all that day to a place called Anuradhapura & then having to travel two days in a bullock cart through the jungle. I am rather sorry now that I didn't

---

1. (Sir) John B. Scott (1878–1946) served in Ceylon 1901–21.

choose Matara, as I have spent most of the past days with the Assistant Government Agent or head person of that place. He is called Cookson & is rather wonderful for Ceylon. He is old of course & married at Oxford, but he was at school with McTaggart & stays with him at Trinity when on leave. Almost his first question was whether I knew McT. & his second was whether I knew Roger Fry so that I was almost disappointed that his third was not 'Do you belong to the Society?'[1] He is the sort of person who might, if he had been to C., have been an embryo, & it is something to meet even that here. He was absolutely bitter about the life here: the people & the interminable gossip & shop. He told me he never found anyone to talk to, & then after port & whiskey poured out his soul to me in the garden after dinner. It was a queer scene & conversation, I thought, between an A.G.A. & the newest of cadets. . . .

Midnight. I find that the mail leaves to-morrow so I can't write more. You're at Lancaster Gate at this moment I suppose & at dinner: I see you all. Goodnight.

Your
L.

TO LYTTON STRACHEY

Jan 5 1905   Jaffna

I am in, what I suppose I must call home, at last, collapsed utterly, mangled by mosquitoes. I have just endured 40 hours of hell. I started from Anuradhapura in the bullock coach at 9 o'clock on Tuesday night & until 9 this morning was in utter physical pain. The coach is just a springless old waggonette with a cover on it & the place between the seats filled by a board. On this surface hard as stone & scored with mounds & ridges you & your servant & any other black or white passengers lie. For 36 hours I underwent jolting indescribable, flung now against an iron railing, now on a mail bag or box, now on Charles or a passenger. I could neither sit up nor lie down & every muscle &

1. J.M.E. McTaggart (1866–1925), the distinguished Hegelian philosopher, and an Apostle. Roger Fry (1866–1934), painter and art critic. LW, who met him through the Apostles and became an intimate friend, described his curious contradictions in *Beginning Again.*

bone in my body was & is aching. We went on day & night only stopping to change bullocks, & you can imagine how I slept. In the day one can only stare vacantly at the interminable jungle with its monotony of dreary luxuriance, at night the blackness is only broken by the ceaseless shouting of the driver to the bullocks & the perpetual thud of his stick upon their flanks. As I lay in that rocking hell, with a brainsplitting headache, listening to the swish of the rain on the car & the 'Da! Ya! Hut' of the driver through the eternity of last night, I thought of our cursing the first day's labour on the canoe expedition, of our luxurious rest at Morhanger, & then again of the paradise of a winter's tea in the shell [chair].[1] And now I'm in a bungalow with Southorn—I shall live with him, they call it (my God) "chum" here, probably for the next year—& I am lacerated with mosquitoes, & my body is, like the cat's, old & battered.[2] Shall I ever be comfortable again, shall I ever sit opposite to you before a fire & fribble & laugh & talk? You're the past & a delightful dream to me, an unreality which every now & then shoots up into the only real thing in the world. . . .

Jan 8.

I am to live, as I say, in a bungalow with Southorn, nice but, I fear, brainless, though, thank God, heavens above Millington. The bungalow is on the ramparts of an ancient Dutch fort, which is really beautiful. I am living in the fort now, in what used to be the Dutch governor's house, a wonderful place with enormous lofty rooms & a vast verandah. I have begun work already & very dull it is—every day to the Customs & the Kachcheri (the govt offices of the district) where I check the accounts of the province, test weights & measures, & issue orders which I hardly understand. Next week I shall probably get dismissed as the Govt Agent who is head of the district & Southorn who is second in command are both going away & I shall be left in charge completely alone. After the first day I expect the province to be in a state of revolt.

The 'society' here is strange, about 15 white people who all quarrel together. There is the G.A. at the head, a fat huge silent man, in his

1. LW described this rained-out canoe trip on the Ouse in August 1904 in *Sowing*.
2. (Sir) Wilfrid Thomas Southorn (1879–1957) served in the Ceylon Civil Service 1903–25, was Colonial Secretary of Hong Kong 1926–36, and Governor and Commander-in-Chief of the Gambia 1936–42. In 1921 he married LW's sister Bella, after the death of her first husband.

ways a little like Duff; he looks like a very old boy & probably has a sense of humour.[1] His wife is big & fat & talkative: she is probably wicked, completely tactless & purposely makes the most purely outrageous remarks I have ever heard from a female 'in mixed society.' Then there is a sort of demigoverness & companion, an old & painted hag engaged to a very young cadet, the famous John Scott of Kings. . . .

I am getting to know some of the few inhabitants of this place, & the most astonishing part of them is their black melancholia. The fort is rather like a very small college as regards people dropping in at any hour in pumps. I went round to Freeman, the District Judge after dinner last night to ask him about one of the accursed telegrams about salt &c which plague me at all hours. He is a little like his namesake the muleteer, but his surliness is frightful. Like everyone else here, he has no interest in anything except the work, & he talks about things as if there were a weight upon his tongue & his mind &, if he had any, his feelings—& it's just the same with Dowbeggin, a strange & rather gruff Supt of Police, & with them all.[2] They come down to the tennis courts every evening & sit round after the game, grimly silent or making short melancholy remarks in a low voice with their eyes fixed on the ground.

It's a sort of dull unhappiness that comes from the isolation & blankness & monotony. It is quite different to the dullness & melancholia at home; I believe people have it sometimes in Kipling & it is, I think, in the air of the country. I went for a walk the other night by the side of the lagoon at sunset; the beauty of it was supreme with the bright green of the paddy fields, the masses of palms, the sky every shade of red & yellow, & the sea every shade of blue; but for all the brilliancy of colour there was a heavy melancholy over it all.

Thai Pongal Day 1905

I don't know whether you know that this is a Tamil feast, but to me it is really, being Jaffnese, important enough to head my letter, for on

1. The Government Agent was John Penry Lewis (1854–1923), Ceylon Civil Service 1877–1910. Lazy and more interested in archeology than governing, he let LW do nine-tenths of his work. "He was a large, slow, fat, shy man with one of those leathery or rubbery faces which even in middle age, and still more in old age, remains the face of a bewildered and slightly grumpy child, or even infant" (*Growing*). James Duff Duff was an amiable Trinity classics don and an Apostle.
2. Herbert Freeman (b. 1864) entered the Ceylon Civil Service in 1885. (Sir) Herbert Dowbeggin (1880–1966) served in the Ceylon police from 1901 until his retirement in 1937.

it I don't have to go to that damned office. And if you had ever worked as I did yesterday & the day before, you would realize the importance of a holiday on which you only have 5 hours work out of the 24. And the insanity of the work! Signing letters & issuing licenses, & counting & receiving rupees, inspecting carriages, trying & fining miserable wretches, answering petitions, checking accounts which I don't understand, deciding questions about salt & coolies & family quarrels, & irrigation & injustices. I began work yesterday at 7.30 A.M. & only finished at five. So you can see that if anything is calculated to make you phenomenal, I am in it.

There is a police magistrate who is never seen & has 2000 paper covered books, a police superintendent, a sour District Judge, an impossible doctor, & several male & female missionaries. I dined with the G.A. last night—they only talked scandal about people whom I of course did not know, & very dull scandal, & after dinner we played bridge. I foresee dry rot of everything, no one to talk to & no time even to read: I shall go awhoring, I think, in desperation as women are so cheap & it doesn't matter if you do get syphilis in Jaffna. Write to me about Hobhouse & everything, & elect him at once if you haven't. . . . I can't believe about Keynes even; he *is* crass & his feelings are those of a frog.[1]

. . . There was a mad dog killed or rather stoned to death outside my verandah this morning & there is a mangled cat dying in a drain about 15 yards from where I sit writing to you. If you go outside, you see people hacking the heads off chickens before hencoops of temples & the headless bodies flying & fluttering about. It is a land of blood & mange. . . .

No time to go on, as I have to catch mail.

Your
L.

---

1. Strachey had sent angry letters about his competition with Keynes—"very much like a Homeric battle over a wounded hero"—for the affection of Arthur Hobhouse, whom Strachey was sponsoring for election to the Society. (Sir) Arthur Hobhouse (1889–1965) was later a solicitor and an active Liberal.

To Lytton Strachey

Jan 23rd 1905   Jaffna

I did not write last mail: I was tired with work & heat, when I could have; & though I wanted to, I just lay in a chair & did nothing. I am at last in my own bungalow, a sordid whitewashed ramshackle half-barn high up on what, I believe, is called a bastion. It is shadowed by enormous banyan trees, on which at night thousands of crows sit, & make the whole place resound with their flutterings & cursings & melancholy din. As yet there has been living with me the police magistrate Dutton, who has had the bungalow until now, but he goes today when Southorn returns.[1] He is, in a strange contradictory way, a good example of the melancholy mania of the men here. I have no reason to believe that he is not a genius, but I'm convinced he is a worm. He has thousands of books which he buys at random, & therefore the majority degraded, & I should think only reads Shakespeare, Milton & the degraded ones. All his spare time he spends in writing poetry, & for three hours a day with infinite patience for 12 years he has been simply trying to acquire a style. I saw one line of it & it contained the word 'elves'. He has no taste: has never been in love except with 'an ideal woman of his imagination' whom he would never marry because he has a horror of copulation. I give you this as an example of the supreme heights to which a conversation can rise in Jaffna—well a thousand years ago I walked & talked with Gods! The 'society' of this place is absolutely inconceivable; it exists only upon the tennis-court & in the G.A.'s house; the women are all whores or hags or missionaries or all three; & the men are, as I told you, sunk. The G.A.'s wife has the vulgarity of a tenth rate pantomime actress; her idea of liveliness is to kick up her legs & to scream the dullest of dull schoolboy 'smut' across the tennis court or the dinner table.

---

1. Bernard Dutton (1876–1912) entered the Ceylon Civil Service in 1899 and served as a police magistrate in Jaffna and Matara. One of LW's colleagues described him as "a bloody unwashed Board School bugger, who doesn't know one end of a woman from the other." His sad life was recounted by LW in a paper read to the Memoir Club, which was incorporated in *Growing*.

Jan 26

Your letter came to-day, as it always does, among petitions & drafts & reports & the daily tangle of red tape.[1] The only time—it sounds exaggerated but it's true—that I feel I am living is when I see it lying on my green baize table. It is also the only thing here that ever makes me laugh: it was always one of our supremacies—our poor dead blighted supremacies—that we could laugh. I think too I can remember them all; how we laughed for hours in that dingy old attic of mine & in the Goth's green room & Turner's yellow barn, in your rooms & the cloisters & all over Richmond Park. I haven't laughed like that since Nov 19th though I was hysterical often on the Syria, & I suppose I shan't again for 6 years, when I expect I at any rate shall be dried up.

Jan 27.

The curse of this place is that there is no time for anything: I write to you in snatches every day 'after office hours' just before tea & exercise which is a necessity unless you want to get boils & itch & fever & scab. I followed you through all your doings, but I don't really think you are right in imagining that I do more. I sit in the Kachcheri most of the day & sign my name, I play tennis, dine, read Henry James (Jaffna has a library which contains him & [Dinah Craik's] *John Halifax, Gentleman*), & go to bed. When I *do* anything it is always phenomenal & usually strange, for instance I went the other day with the G.A. to do what are called exemptions. The natives are bound to do a certain amount of labour every year upon the roads or else pay a commutation of 2 rupees.[2] If they are too old or ill to work they are exempted from the commutation, & all who think they have either excuse come up to be examined on a special day. They are drawn up in ranks & files of stinking loathesomeness, while we walked down the lines accompanied by Headmen inspecting each case. You have no conception of what degree of foulness a naked body is capable until you have done that: mere skeletons covered in sores, deformities in

1. The letter described a visit to the house on Gordon Square where the Stephen children had moved following the death of Sir Leslie: "On Sunday I called at the Gothic Mansion, & had tea with Vanessa and Virginia. The latter is rather wonderful—quite witty, full of things to say, & absolutely out of rapport with reality. The poor Vanessa has to keep her three mad brothers & sister in control. She looks wan & sad."
2. After Ceylon became a British colony, compulsory labor was abolished except for the construction of roads and the collection of cinnamon.

every part of the body, & one horrible fat naked brute whose only mode of progression possible was upon his buttocks & one leg, the other black shining swollen & suppurating stuck straight out in front of him. And yet the people are, as a rule, the men at any rate, as far as their bodies go, extraordinarily beautiful, which accounts perhaps for the apparent rampantness of sodomy. This, my dear, is Morocco, where a white man is murdered by his black catamite out of jealousy at hearing that the white man is to be married. . . .[1]

Your
L.

I want to talk to you even about Russia.[2]

To G. E. MOORE

Jan 28, 1905

Jaffna
Ceylon

My dear Moore,

I have been feeling very much that I want to write to you, but in a way I find it difficult because I don't know whether you won't in the end hate it, & think you ought to answer when you don't want to. . . .

Feb 5th 1905

. . . I believe Ceylon & India are the only places to live in, or would be, if there were only respectable people in them. There is an enormous fascination about it all, chiefly because everything is wonderfully beautiful. As it is, it is very nearly unbearable, for there is no one—in Jaffna at any rate—whom you can like or take any interest in or talk to. They are not in the least what I expected them to be, very cheerful & sporting: they are almost all bored & melancholy; they only

1. "Morocco" was private language referring to homosexuality. To this Strachey responded: "The reign of Sodomy pleases me. How romantic! But then—black! . . . The Exemptions left me pale & vomiting. In your place I should be dead in a week—from every sort of death. (1) Mere physical exhaustion. (2) Boils, itch, scab, etc. (3) Rage. (4) Horror at material objects. (5) Desire to copulate with a bronze bottom without copulating with a brown face. (6) Desire to rip up the belly of the G.A.'s wife. (7) Despair at receiving the weekly Turnerian despatch."
2. The 1905 revolution in Russia had broken out following the fall of Port Arthur to the Japanese on New Year's Day.

take interest in their work & after dinner go to sleep in long chairs.

Are you going to have a reading party this year? I shall miss it almost more than anything else. I wish you could write your book quickly & then travel, taking Ceylon en route.

Yours
L. S. Woolf[1]

To Lytton Strachey

Feb 11, 1905   Kayts

I am in an island called Kayts, & India I suppose is a stone's throw across the way. It is quite late at night & I am writing in the verandah of a Rest House, a government inn where you can get a bed, a chair & no food. I sailed here, with Southorn—God damn him—in a native boat to inspect customs houses & audit accounts. O if only you had been in that boat, it would indeed have been the depart pour Cythère; it's the only place to live in, the East, if you could only have the right people in it with you.[2] Can you see it all? The sun & the blue water, the boats with their great square sails, the quai crowded with people in their wonderful clothes, the melancholy islands we glided by, with their low deserted sandy beaches & the palm trees coming almost down to the sea. We should have glided on as we did on the Ouse, but there would have been no work or pain or the bitterness of Huntingdon, but I think we should have sailed on for ever to India & greater wonders still. And, instead, I gnashed my teeth at Southorn's interminable drone, ten thousand brainless Lambi rolled into one.[3]

Feb 12.

. . . I get your moments sometimes when nothing seems to matter & I suppose that most of the time we, or I at any rate, are passively inert to happiness or unhappiness. I mean that we are so persistently

1. In terms typical of him, Moore replied: ". . . The reason why I haven't written, in spite of wanting to, is that I don't know what to say. I have begun three letters to you already before this one; but I wouldn't finish them, because they were so bad. I am afraid I have nothing to say, which is worth saying: or if I have I cannot express it. . . ."
2. An allusion, frequent in the full correspondence between LW and Strachey, to Watteau's celebrated painting of a voyage to Cythera, the Greek island where love was supreme.
3. "Lambi" was meant as plural (Latin) of Walter Lamb.

automatic that most of the day is a trance. When I do think or feel, it is usually with rage or despair. Don't you feel often or always that there is so little time to lose, & that we are losing it so fast. The Christians are right there, I feel, it wouldn't matter if there were another life, if there were some chance of making up for the time we are cruelly forced to lose here. But to be hurrying to annihilation, & only to have lived for an hour or two out of twenty five years! And you say, as they all would say, 'I feel it's an episode': you don't seem to see that in a few minutes we shall be old & in a few hours dead, that it's an episode between youth & life, &, sterility & annihilation.

Did I tell you that I wrote to the Yen & have regretted it ever since, that I had a mouldy affectionate letter from the taupe, & the paper which he read at the Society & which I thought simply 'balls'.[1] I have introduced Yenism into Ceylon, & public business with peculiar results. There was a petition from some poor people who had been employed by the arrackrenter, the man who buys the sole license to sell & make arrack, a spirit extracted from the coconut palm. He used to allow the people who petitioned to draw & sell him arrack on certain conditions, which for this year he had determined to alter. The G.A. was going away, & told me to interview the parties & try to effect a settlement. I applied purely Yenistic arguments for two hours with, theoretically, wonderful results. The Tamils are extraordinarily subtle & they nodded with approval as the argument got more & more intricate in my endeavours to make the renter give way. At last I drove him to admit— & the argument really was fair, I think—that it would pay him better to give 30 cents to the petitioners for arrack than 24. The practical result was less encouraging, for he suddenly burst out 'Your arguments are very reasonable; I'll give 25 instead of 24, but I won't give a cent more than 25'. 'Not though you admit that it's to your advantage to give 30?' To which I got an emphatic 'No, Sir'.

Your
L.

---

1. Text in *Selected Letters of E. M. Forster*, Volume One, *1879–1920*, Mary Lago and P. N. Furbank, eds.

To Lytton Strachey

Feb 19th 1905

Jaffna
Ceylon

. . . *You* can't know how I hate the physical labor of sitting up &
holding a pen. And you probably will not get even this scrap for years—
all the mails have gone wrong & there is apparently a regular one only
every fortnight. I only want to curse you for a bit, & probably in a
way which you will think very silly. It's your last letter which roused
me.[1] Why, *why* should you sink into the dotard of Mutton Hole Corner.
I don't mean 'why' in the obvious way, because you're in it at all, &
I'm out of it; but simply—damn grammar—the plain common-sense
reason, that you have powers & can blaze if you only will. Good God,
if I were you, I should be immense; I should trample everything un-
derfoot. I should write, as you can if you only will, supremely. I should
simply 'go for' fame & money in a rush; they are the only satisfactory
things after all. I am sick of the good & love & the only things really
worth having; & it's only because I am a mediocrity that I pretend to
try to get them. They are just examples of what we always were cursing,
the infinity of desire & the finite satisfaction. It's no good being in love
if you are separated by 10,000 miles as you always are & are only
saved by that from quarrelling & sordid torture. I should trample on
all that if I had 'powers'; I should be wicked & superb like Parnell.[2]
To be what they call great is the only satisfactory thing, & you must
just—as you can—go & do it. Leave the snivelling Gayes & Turners
& Keynes & Hobhouses & me with them in this suburban little island,
& blaze.

Your
L.

1. A despondent letter that concluded, "Please take all that a weary dotard has to offer—
the querulous love of—THE HERMIT OF MUTTON-HOLE CORNER."
2. Charles Stewart Parnell (1846–1891), controversial Irish nationalist, ruined by involvement in a divorce case.

To Desmond MacCarthy

Feb 26, 1905.   Jaffna

Dear MacCarthy,
   . . . I am settled now, for a time at least, in the very North of the
Island, in the hottest of hot places, swarming with Tamils & about
fifteen English people. On the whole I prefer the Tamils: if you searched
the Universe, you could not find 15 more unapostolic people than the
15 English, & the worst of it is that they have so few of the good
qualities which it is possible to have & yet be unapostolic. We never
see one another except on the tennis court—a daily & almost religious
function, & as we sit round after the game making our melancholy
remarks, I often think of what you said the last time I saw you: 'The
worst thing will be that you will probably be among people who will
never understand what you say'.
   If there were only people who could understand what one says, I
should not regret having come here at all. You know what it's like, &
I remember you telling me of its charm. And it does have an enormous
charm for me, the queer tortuous people, the wonderful glaring beauty
of the country, & the still oppressive heat which tones it all down to
a strange melancholy. I think that is the strangest part about it, that
there is always a dull melancholy feeling over everything, even over
the chattering crowds in the bazaar.
   The books you gave me were a godsend at once.[1] I had to travel for
two nights & a day in a bullock waggon through the jungle in order
to reach this place. For discomfort it was simply hell. I had to lie on
my back on the hard floor of the waggon & was battered & jolted
along for 36 hours but I took one of the small Shakespeare volumes
with me in my pocket, & it helped me to forget my aching bones.
   Don't forget that you promised to visit me here.

                                                    Yours
                                                    L. S. Woolf

1. ". . . the Oxford Press miniature edition of Shakespeare and Milton in four volumes which
have accompanied me everywhere ever since" (*Sowing*).

80

Feb 26, 1904 [1905]   Jaffna

I feel very ill tonight, & I don't think I shall be able to finish a letter. I sweated for thirty minutes on a bicycle this afternoon under a ferocious sun round this melancholy peninsula. I don't know whether I have sunk into the dotage of professional middle-age, but it was in fulfillment of the theory that 'you ought to know your province'. The consequence is that my inside is completely deranged, my limbs ache & if I don't go to bed, I shall probably eat.

Feb 27th

I couldn't write any more last night & so missed the mail. It is late again to-night, & I have a long day, being quite alone again for some days, but I feel I want to talk a little before I go to bed.

I believe I have made the remark before but I can't help repeating it, that the people in rotten novels are astonishingly life like. All the English out here are continually saying things of which, if you saw them in a novel, you would say 'people don't say those sort of things'. They are always sentimentally soliloquising with an astounding pomposity. There is a horsey [Assistant] Superintendent of Police here, very loud & vulgar & goodnatured.[1] He took me for a drive the other day in what he calls his 'English gig', & as we bowled along under the palm trees, he gave me the following address interspersed with curses at the drivers of bullock carts who got in the way. 'Ah, my dear Woolf, how I hate this bloody island. I shall have something to say to the Almighty when I meet him. I don't ask for much, a little house in an English shire, with plenty of hunting & six or seven horses, & enough money to run up to London for a week when the frost comes— Get out, you ugly stinking fucking son of a black buggered bitch; you black bugger, you—I don't ask for much, I'd be happy as a king— you greasy fat Jaffna harlot, get out of the light, you black swine—& I don't get it'. It went on like this for a full half hour, & if you left out the curses & the language, you would find the same sort of stilted stuff in any of the swarms of 1st class books in the Union library.

---

1. James Stewart Bowes, who is briefly described in *Growing*.

March 5

I am hot & perspiring, but, before I say anything & forget it, De Vigny
has come. I haven't read him all, but I'm rather disappointed: isn't
he rather metallic? I read a good deal in odd moments, & a curious
mixture, I think. A book I have always meant to do, I finished last
week & could hardly put down at all, *The Life of Parnell*—I believe
you once said it was supreme. Also *The Life of Russell* by the same
man [R. B. O'Brien] & [Disraeli's] *Coningsby* which is absolutely
preposterous, & [Voltaire's] *La Dictionnaire Philosophique*. The more
I read him, his method & humour, the more I see that you are Voltaire
on the hearthrug. I wonder if you *will* ever come here. I feel somehow
you might, but I think you would die at once. The heat is quite inconceivable; as I ride to the katchcheri in the morning, the sun on my
hands is just as if I put them close up to the bars of a hot fire. The
dry season has only just begun & there is no rain now until October.
The grass has already turned brown, & all the weeds & leaves, except
on the big trees, are drooping & dying down: there is a hot wind &
clouds of dust. The place will soon be a wilderness. The glare of the
white dusty roads is intolerable, & makes one's head swim & eyeballs
ache & click. . . .

Your
L.

To Lytton Strachey

March 14th 1905

Jaffna
Ceylon

I must, I feel, just before going to bed at any rate say something. Last
mail I simply could not write. I can do nothing, & a letter home reduced
me to greater incapability. Jaffna now is always red hot, for we are in
between two monsoons, with intolerable sun & not a breath of wind.
Poor Charles—I think even you would pity him now, as a symbol at
any rate of what was—is dying of it, & I sometimes think that I may
too.

It was very blank last week to get no letter, but I'm not sure that
to-day did not make it worth while, for the effect of eight sheets is

accumulative.[1] It came as usual to the katchcheri, & I read it in between godless papers until I had to stop out of pure shame of alternate tears & bursts of laughter before clerks & peons & punkah boys.[2] It is the one consolation, & O do remember that, if, in the fatigue & desperate staleness & weariness of this place, I don't write or you see me fading away when I do.

There is so much, when I read it, that I want to tell you about it, but—& I curse God for it—I want to talk & not write it. . . . At any rate I should not have given a thought to Keynes & his sickly feelings— you should sweep on & carry him away. Of course—& I can hear you say 'you're so damned pessim (a sudden gust of wind of strange hurricanes, which spring up in a moment here, has just blown my lamp out & I write by moonlight now) istic'—you must be disappointed, you *do* go too quickly to essentials & you always want so much. I can't see any more & I can't keep this damned lamp alight, so good night.

March 15th

I am writing this in the kachcheri as there is little to do—but it will be broken [soon] enough by odd papers to attend to. This is a sordid place with white walls & iron bars through which the foul & motley crowd, which hangs about on the verandah, peer & pry. The monotony of life here, when I have time to think about it, appals & enrages me. The weariness of having a pundit from 7.30–9 A.M., the loathsome breakfast at 10, the pure futility of the work here until 4.30, the inevitable tennis at 5.15, the foul & melancholy dinner at 8, the dreary grind at Tamil & half an hour's read before I go to bed—it stretches out into an interminable 6 years vista of hopelessly regulated hours. The work, I suppose is not duller, is not as dull as what it would have been in a degraded London office, but is not this unending monotony certain to dry one up & to shatter one? The people in the station are absolutely hopeless, & as a rule most of them are out on circuit. There is a foul minded old Captain, lecherous & ungentlemanly in every sense, who has now retired & settled down to end his days here. He has an immense & loathesome wife: they come down every night to the tennis court & play the Duke & Duchess of the place; conversation is directed to them to a great extent: it consists of perfectly futile 'smut' & gossip. Otherwise I listen to interminable stories by Southorn, punc-

1. Strachey's letter was mostly a bitter lamentation at Keynes's having "stolen" Hobhouse from him.
2. Peons were messengers; punkah boys operated punkahs, large ceiling fans.

tuated only by his own laughter, or discuss with the Superintendent of Police whether a Singalese whore is better than a Tamil or a German better than both. Then there are two lady missionaries who play tennis & ask me to read the lessons in church: one of them probably has the most hideous (& immense) body now in existence. The other Miss Beeching (you can see her by her name) is essentially silly & stupid. . . .

Your
L.[1]

To Lytton Strachey

Jaffna
Ceylon

March 25th 1905

. . . I can't write anything to-day. I spend my time bathing Charles with warm water when out of sheer weakness he pumps [urinates] over himself as he lies on the ground. He is blind now & paralyzed.

Among other things I have very nearly been dismissed. There was a muddle about a travelling allowance, & I did not answer some letter from the Treasury, so at last the Treasurer, who thereby could not make up the accounts of the Colony for 1904, lost his temper & wrote a long letter to Government abusing me, which letter the Colonial Secretary forwarded to the G.A. 'for an explanation'.

The most astonishing & sordid thing I have yet seen out here was last week in court, a rape case. An old hag of a woman charged a boy of about 18 with raping her. You should have seen her in the witness box with the grinning table of lawyers, it was absolutely the depths. She had to describe minutely the whole operation, the position of his & her legs & thighs & hands & mouth. It was quite plain that she had let him copulate with her & then got annoyed & charged him: but even *she* collapsed in the box when asked 'How do you know that the male organ entered the female organ, did you see it?' Eventually she

1. In his response, Strachey remarked: "By God, don't you sometimes get a feeling of eminent satisfaction to see yourself towering above your loathsome companions? The thought of Keynes often acts upon *me* like a tonic. I whirl into the empyrean, and you must too. . . . Your people's horror (I mean your Jaffna people's) seems to thicken every week. Do they bow down before you? I believe, if they don't, they will. My theory is, you know, that eminence is always recognized by the debased. . . . You burn with a mystic unquenchable flame—a dark triumph, which circumstance may shake, but never shatter. I whizz and sparkle, and am always on the brink of going out."

said she had felt it. 'Have you ever felt the same thing in your dreams?'
At last she gasped out, Yes.

March 26

Charles is dead.

Your
L.

To Lytton Strachey

April 9, 1905

Jaffna
Ceylon

You cannot very well realize my feelings at the present moment: it is
raining. An unexpected thunderstorm has just broken over the place
& the rain is coming down in sheets. You don't know what it is to see
& smell it after the monotony of three months glare & the smell of
parched earth & dried up grass & leaves. . . .

10.30 P.M.

I am dead tired having bicycled about 35 miles. I had to inspect the
stumps of some trees which had been cut down near a big temple. A
violent dispute had arisen between two priests & one accused the other
of cutting down trees on crown land. I had to decide whether it was
crown land or not in the midst of a yelling mob of some hundreds of
people. I must now go to bed, although I probably shall not sleep being
perpetually now kept awake by a big owl I possess. He is a wonderful
bird: he looks hundreds of years old with the wisdom & malignancy
of a fiend; the beauty & texture of his feathers is indescribable, the
most astonishing mixture of greys & browns. All night long he chases
a rat round the dog kennel in which I keep him, but as he never catches
him & I never feed the rat, they are both slowly dying of starvation.
It is questionable whether in the end either will have strength enough
to eat the other.

Almost the first thing I read in Tamil was this: 'I saw a teacher &

his disciple sitting under a tree; the age of the disciple was eighty &
the age of the teacher eighteen'.

God, god!

Yr

L.

To Lytton Strachey

Jaffna

Ceylon

April 23, 1905

... A curious man has arrived here. He is half dead with consumption
but Govt will not give him leave: so they sent him here to be police
magistrate, because Jaffna is dry & supposed to cure consumption.
The first day on the bench nearly killed him, but even now they have
not given him leave & Dutton, the 'poet', is still here. Leak—the new
man—would be I am sure a Turner protégé—he looks but is not
deformed. He is usually in bed & talks incessantly with enormous
excitement, lecturing about the way to pronounce Tamil & mend bi-
cycles & rule the natives. He has a half naked female child usually
dressed in pyjamas, & a grubby looking semiburgher wife dressed in
a white dressing gown very open at the neck.[1] There are always several
spitoons & pos [chamber pots] about the room & a loathesome smell
of consumption, which I expect I shall catch.

Last week I had another study in sordidity which may amuse you—
the Jaffna hospital. I happened to be with Dutton (who is really doing
the magistrate's work) when he was summoned to the hospital to take
the dying deposition of a man who had his skull cracked in a brawl.
I walked over with him. The hospital consists of two long rooms bare
& whitewashed, with rows of plank beds down each wall. Horrible
looking dishes lay scattered about & on the planks lay three or four
natives without any covering but the clothes in which they had arrived,
their heads & bodies bandaged, groaning grunting & spitting on the
floor. Outside & on the verandah & therefore to all intents & purposes
in the room, squatted a crowd of patients & their friends talking,
quarrelling, chewing betel & spitting it out upon the floor. Among
these sat the dying man eating curry & rice out of a big dish, &
quarrelling with the man who is accused of having broken his head.
We could discover no attendant & so went off to ask the doctor what

1. Burghers were descendants of Portuguese and Dutch settlers.

it all meant. All he could tell us was that he had given strict direction that the man should lie quite still, doing nothing, as he might fall down dead at any moment. The whole thing was exactly what I imagine the 18th century hospitals were like.

I always said MacCarthy was rather wonderful—well I suppose you allowed that—& I had last week a wonderful (& of course charming) letter from him. He described commem. & briefly the meeting on Sheppard's paper.[1] He has a curious way of almost reaching heights & then suddenly dropping into the most absurd depths, usually owing to some silly & rather degraded phrase.

I can't stand this any more: there is a plague of insects in this bungalow tonight. I have already taken two cockroaches crawling up my legs & a cricket getting down my back, a huge flying beetle hit me in the eye, & there is a minor plague of small flies & mosquitoes. I am going to bed under the mosquito curtains.

By the bye have you read one of the supremest books *Pilgrimage to Al-Medinah & Mecca* by [Sir Richard] Burton? There is no doubt we must go to Egypt & Arabia, & after all it is true that 'Voyaging is Victory'. Even here in this squalid little place, you have the curious absorbing people, & now & then there is a strangeness & beauty about a place that you never could have dreamt of in England.
Good night.

Your
L.

To G. E. Moore

Kankesanturai
Ceylon

April 30, 1905

Dear Moore,

I was very glad to get your letter, but really, if it is any worry at all for you to write, please do not do it. What I find is that I continually want to write to people, but hate it when I come to do it. It is so difficult to say what you mean, & one knows how different from what you meant it & from what it would be in conversation, it will all sound. And then I loathe the actual writing.

I am writing this on a wonderful glaring white beach, which is

---

1. "Commem," an annual college celebration, commemorating the college benefactors. The meeting of the Apostles discussed a proposal to broaden membership in the Society.

composed not of sand or stones, but solely of millions of minute shells. The sun is simply blazing down on me, & there is no shade for the only trees are palmyrah & coconuts which are practically useless: I crept under the ruins of a Portugese fort & breakwater, but the smell of [large ink blot] + decaying crab drove me out into the sun again. I came here last night with another man to inspect a grain shed. It is a small port on the North East coast. I had to bring my bed with me & put it up in a hut on the beach, the hut being little more than a roof on four posts. The Portugese began to build a fort here & now there is little more than masses of fallen masonry, the white beach, & immense crabs crawling over everything. Why should not you have a secondary reading party here? It could at any rate consist of you, MacCarthy, Bob Trevy & the Strache, for you are at least not tied to your work, & the amount you would do when you came back would probably be immense.

+ my fountain pen is
affected by the sun

Jaffna

I meant to add to this tonight when I got back, but it is too late now, & I think I had better send it by the mail tomorrow.
Love to Ainsworth.

Yr
L. S. Woolf

To Desmond MacCarthy

Jaffna
Ceylon

May 14, 1905

Dear MacCarthy,
I was so glad to get your letter which at any rate brought me back a little to things I like better than this.[1] However I daresay I was in somewhat a more pessimistic mood than usual, when I wrote to you before. Of the people here I do absolutely despair: there certainly is not anyone at all with whom I could imagine anyone being in love; but here as everywhere the greater part of one's time is spent, as regards

1. The letter is quoted in full in *Sowing*.

feelings, in passivity: it only seems that when one does feel, one is more often & more hopelessly melancholy than elsewhere.

The people really are inconceivable. There are only about ten of them & they spend most of their spare moments in engineering quarrels over absolutely ludicrous things. The quarrels are always conducted by letter so that the meetings on the tennis ground are invariably dully affable. The Assistant Superintendent of Police hits the dog of the Inspector of Police when they are playing golf together—nothing is said at the time but the Inspector writes several sheets of note paper complaining of the indignity he has suffered. The District Judge puts up for the Tennis Club a European who (besides being a scoundrel) has married a native: he is blackballed, the Judge resigns, & everyone spends the next few weeks in writing letters to everyone else.

The most amusing man is the Assistant Superintendent of Police, & you can judge the rest from him. He has really only two topics of conversation: whores & horses. He comes up to the bungalow after dinner, lies on a long chair, drinks whiskey & soda, & enters into a minute examination of the points of each, the difference in breeds & nationality, how to rear & treat them. Sometimes he varies this for a few minutes by telling me about his mother, 'dear old lady', & she is the only person I have not heard him refer to as a 'bloody fucker'. . . .

Yrs
L. S. Woolf

Tell me about the reading party if you write again.

To Lytton Strachey

Jaffna
Ceylon

May 21, 1905

This has been a week of events, & that is one reason why I could not write to you. I have been turned out of the bungalow on the wall—which legally belongs to the Office Assistant—by Southorn being moved from Jaffna & the consumptive married Leak being appointed O.A. I have therefore been immersed in the worries of moving. I now live with the magistrate Dutton (of whom I wrote long ago) in a hot stuffy bungalow surrounded by trees, full of mosquitos & where not a breath of wind ever gets in. Also there is much more work for me now, as Leak is too ill to work more than half a day at the Kachcheri.

I have to do the Customs work & they have now made me Additional Police Magistrate. The most probable result is that I shall catch consumption.

A cataclysm is hourly expected here. Yesterday a headman came to the Kachcheri & reported that a hole had suddenly appeared in the midst of a field about 5 miles from Jaffna, that it had gradually in a few hours increased from about 3 to 90 square feet & that it was still increasing. I bicycled out to the place in the afternoon. It is in the middle of a perfectly flat plain & was the most astonishing sight I have ever seen. It is like a big pond with the water about a foot from the top, there is a curious heaving in the water, every five or ten minutes a crack appears in the earth round the edge, the crack widens & the earth topples over into the water which heaves & swirls & eddies. Hundreds of natives stand round, looking on with their usual appearance of complete indifference, & every time another foot of the ground disappears, a long 'aiyo, aiyo' goes up. The water is obviously from the sea which is about a mile & a half from the place & I expect that it means that Jaffna Peninsula is going to return to the seabed from which it came. If the sea once again begins coming in, there is absolutely nothing to stop it simply pouring over this huge flat plain which is never above & sometimes below sea-level. If so, this is my last letter to you—& for dullness is probably only equalled by the first, which I remember went to France. But there is nothing to say to you, nothing to tell you of except 'events'. I neither read nor think nor—in the old way—feel. I can tell you that I rode 12 miles, after the usual work, to the northern coast to inspect a leaky ship, in which the Govt is sending salt to Colombo; how I was rowed out in the moonlight side by side with the vast fat Chetty contractor who was responsible for the leaky ship;[1] how I climbed about in the hot hold with the water pouring in, & examined the master & crew sitting on a camp stool in a little reeking cabin; how I was rowed back through a little fleet of catamarans, fifty or sixty logs of wood bobbing on the sea each with a kneeling figure on it which outlined against the white sea looked like a ghost praying. I can't write about anything else; here they are the only realities, & the curious feelings they excite, the only pleasant feelings I have. Perhaps they are not the only ones; when I read your letters first, you are for the moment real again. I can laugh too over Bob Trevy—whose letter God damn it, I shall never answer—& every now & then you raise things even to the pitch of excitement. But for the rest it's either the curious feelings & excitement from these curious

1. The Chetty were the Tamil trading caste.

rare incidents & sights, or else the boredom of the work & the nausea of conversation.

May 22.

A dinner at the GA's prevented anything being added.

L.

To Robert Trevelyan

Jaffna
Ceylon

May 28, 1905

My dear Trevy,

I have been much longer than I intended & wanted to be in answering your letter & thanking you for your book [*The Birth of Parsival*]. But I'm terribly bad at letter writing & even in this void there is very little time for anything but work. What you say about your book is quite untrue—I was delighted that you had sent it to me, & should have been (to read it) in a far less boring place than Jaffna. I remember last year on a walk from Woody Bay station you told me something of the story.

It would be difficult to imagine a more phenomenal existence than that of Jaffna. . . . The most interesting part of it all is the people themselves—not the English, good God. They are, I was surprised to find, just what the oriental is popularly supposed to be, but with many more queer little traits—subtle & quickwitted, shifty & habitual liars, abnormally fatalistic. It is in the Police Court that their natures really 'come out'; every case is an intricate tangle of lies, for even if a man has a true case, he always buys witnesses who have never seen the thing take place, & answers your questions as he thinks that you want them answered. Again & again too, you will see a complainant or accused standing or squatting absolutely unmoved & apparently listless, not even listening to what is going on, while some witness is giving damning evidence against him. You know that he is probably using their favorite expression "If it must be, it must be".[1]

---

1. These experiences are echoed in the courtroom scenes in *The Village in the Jungle*.

I do hope you will write sometime again & tell me about your and other brothers' doings.[1]

Yours fraternally,
L. S. Woolf

To Lytton Strachey

June 4, 1905

Jaffna
Ceylon

. . . They have made me Additional Police Magistrate now. I spend the evenings trying to learn something about the law; in the day the actual work is something of a horror & a relief. At first it is a mere whirl: sitting in sheer ignorance up there in the hum of the court, writing down the evidence, listening to the proctors & witnesses, thinking of questions to ask, trying to make up your mind—all at the same time. I felt that at any moment I might raise your old cry: 'I resign'. But it is a relief after the dreary drudgery of the Kachcheri. Its sordidity is almost superb: you see all the curious people & listen to their intimate lying tales. It is impossible to feel that it is real, when I sit up there in the stifling heat & look out over the glaring waste to the fort & the sea & listen to an interminable story of how one man smashed in the skull of another with a stone because the latter asked him to repay a debt of 25 cents. It is absolutely incredible how futile life can be; & if one doesn't become engrossed in its futility, I don't see that there is anything to stop one going mad.

I live now, I believe you know, with Dutton. He could only exist in the 19th century. He is a timid egoistic maniac who writes poetry all day long or reads in a vague voracious way. His mind—I don't know about his body—is castrated. He read Moore in his bleareyed way & said that it had all been said much better before. Last night he said something which made me lose my temper & I burst at him with 'God damn you, you've never been in love'. He then told me that he had been 10 years in love with a 'girl' to whom he had never spoken. He has however hundreds of books in horrible print & binding—I found some Diderot among them, which I had not read—wonderful but quite mad.

1. Besides G. M. Trevelyan, the other brother was (Sir) Charles Philips Trevelyan (1870–1958), a Liberal and later Labour MP, who was expelled from the Labour Party in 1939 for supporting a popular front with the Communists.

Since writing the above I have called on the G.A. They are back from the Pearl Fishery now & I have had the inevitable dinner.[1] Mrs G.A. is the same as ever: her greeting to her husband when he comes into a room full of people is 'O Pen dear, you really are *too* fat, with your great ugly paunch sticking out before you'.

Did I tell you I'm to be moved shortly from Jaffna to the worst station in the Island, Batticoloa. It is completely cut off from civilization & about the only European there is the Government Agent who is a religious maniac.

αἴλινον αἴλινον εἰπε[2]

L

To Lytton Strachey

Jaffna
Ceylon

June 11, 1905

I am dying of fatigue & it is too late now to write anything. I left tonight for it, but I am acting for the Superintendent of Police who is away & had to do all the police papers after dinner.

I do nothing but play the first bar of the 5th Symphony on Dutton's crazy piano. Have I told you about it? All the notes have fallen in pieces & are now tied up with string. It is more dead than that in Trevenna(?) House. He plays on it for hours: Gilbert & Sullivan, Mozart, the Gaiety & every other Girl, & impossibly sentimental German abominations.

Otherwise I have tea with the GA & his wild wife.

I wanted to speak about your letter but it's too late now. Good night.

L.

---

1. The rich oyster banks off the northwest coast of Ceylon were fished for two months every winter, under the supervision of colonial officials from the Jaffna District.
2. "Sing woe, woe," from Aeschylus's *Agamemnon*.

To Lytton Strachey

June 25th 1905

Jaffna
Ceylon

I did not write to you last week because all Saturday & Sunday I spent bicycling & searching for the corpse of a small boy. The boy disappeared on Thursday night & as I was Supt of Police I was supposed to find him. It was a typical story & typical of what one has to do here. He was last seen going in a bullock cart towards the sea with a young man who keeps a dancing girl & therefore is always in want of money. The child's relations set off on the main road in a body towards the sea stopping every bullock cart they met. At 2 o'clock in the morning they met a cart with the young man in it: they dragged him out, searched him & found the child's jewellery on him. They then took him to the chief headman's house, beat him with sticks & whips, pushed pins down his nails & tortured him generally until he confessed that he took the boy to Kangesanturai, carried him out into the sea, knelt on him in the water until he drowned, took his gold ornaments & threw the body out into the sea. Which do you think would reduce me first: Somerset House or toiling over burning blinding white sand with a retinue of maniagars [district chiefs] & adigars [provincial chiefs] & policemen watching twenty or thirty naked coolies wade along the shore searching for the body of a boy?[1]

I often think of Trevy & 'You must keep up the intellectual side of your character'. Good god! I find there's very little side left of any kind after some hours ploughing through sand with the sun beating down on you, the sea glaring into your eyes & the sand burning your feet. I suppose if I walked into your room at 11 P.M. & sank into the shell, I might be able to talk to you about George Lyttelton & embryos & the Society & even yourself.[2] I might not feel as if a million years had passed, I might realize that there are people who talk about other things than the Police Court & the Kachcheri, tennis & the iniquities of the wife of the G.A. But I can't from here. The wine is too strong on Sunday when the furthest I get during the week is—now that they are back from the Pearl Fishery—the daily tea &

1. The Inland Revenue offices, where Sydney-Turner was working, were in Somerset House.
2. Strachey's letters at this time were filled with gossip about his unrequited passion for George Lyttelton (1883–1962), a Trinity undergraduate who became Assistant Master of Eton, about possible new Apostles and about the Society, which, according to Strachey, was "in high disrepute."

94

conversation (it is at least wonderful) in Mrs Lewis' drawing-
room. . . .

Yr
L

To Lytton Strachey

July 15 1905

Jaffna
Ceylon

I believe I did not write to you last week at all. Sunday, the only day
on which it seems possible to do anything, I was enmeshed into bicycling to the other coast & back to breakfast & play bridge with Mrs
Lewis who was staying there with her astonishing entourage. Then a
ship came in from Colombo which it was rumoured had ice on board,
so a boat was hired & I put off for it in order to feel again something
not lukewarm pass down my throat. That is about the only thing that
stands out as far as doing or indeed thinking goes for two weeks. You
think I shall be in a position to forgive God one day?

 . . . I had the thinnest of thin letters from the 'taupe' (it is typical
of him that one always spells even his nickname with a small letter)
(though it is true that I had as usual a thinner on a letter card from
Turner) full of Elizabeth & her German garden & his own pale
humour.[1]

July 16th

I was interrupted yesterday by a reception here. O god, O god, it's
absolutely & entirely incredible to what depths & madness one passes
here. Your Jewish parties with Mrs Russell are nothing to my perpetual
existence here.[2] I live with a cross between a zany & an atrophied
poet, a mean minded, utterly provincial town clerk with, as the Yen
would say, the nicest of nice feelings. He is hopelessly non-conformist,
an egoist self-conscious & nervous to sheer ridiculousness. I have drawn
him, as they say, 'into society', to the tennis court & interminable

1. Forster had spent the summer tutoring the daughters of Elizabeth von Arnim, an Aus-
tralian married to a German count. In 1898 she had published *Elizabeth and Her German
Garden* about her life and garden on an estate in Pomerania.
2. Strachey had accompanied Bertrand Russell's wife, Alys, to a dinner given by a rich
London Jewish family; there he had met the playwright Alfred Sutro, whom he described
as "utterly vulgar with the sort of placid easy-flowing vulgarity of *your* race."

conversations with the missionary ladies. (He is unwashed & ill-bred & to look at utterly ridiculous.) It is possible that he is palely in love with one of these horrors—at any rate they say he is.

In a moment of sheer madness (in which I am degradedly always now) I told the whole crew to come on here after a Jaffna 'At Home'—to which, because thank God I have never called on the female, I alone was uninvited. It makes me feel sick to write it almost but it will at any rate show you the surrounding tone. Dutton became distraught: he would leave Jaffna for the day, he wrote curious—almost Yenlike—letters to me to the Kachcheri, & finally when he decided to brave it out spent the whole morning in trying vainly to make his room not the foulest & hugest filthpacket on God's earth by putting up a kind of lodging house curtains of muslin & terribly pink flowered stuff. I lay in a long chair & gasped & let him have his way except when, after putting on a black coat & a collar & a dicky, he piled a table with the 100 best pictures in order that, as he remarked, if he suddenly found himself absolutely unable to say a word, he could turn to some female & say 'Would you like to look at pictures?' Well they came; 5 females dressed in the height of Ceylon fashion & the G.A. lumbering in their wake, & were fed on chocolate & lemonade & biscuits while Dutton in the background & upon his piano mended with string played the 5th Symphony & the Country Girl. The only method of life I find when one is simply engulfed is to be absolutely unrestrained, to pile madness on madness & degradation on degradation until I positively feel that if in the full circle I took down my trousers & pumped into, if there were such a thing, the fireplace, Mrs Lewis or someone would make a joke about it & it would pass off as rather an amusing incident. You must come out & see it all, it's really worth it, just to feel the atmosphere, for 6 months at any rate, its only when one feels that it's for 240 that one feels inclined to resign.

Yr
L.

Jaffna
July 23rd 1905   Ceylon

I am in my usual state—rather like an anchor, I feel, though more of lead than of iron.[1] I can't write to you, for what is there to write? Only, of what I feel, the weekly stream of querulous rage. Or what have I done? The Kachcheri, tennis & a state dinner at the G.A.'s. At the latter a wizened female from the Straits suddenly launched out to me against the Christians, & for quarter of an hour at any rate I was able to let myself go. If it is known here, it very nearly means transportation. Everyone believes in Hell or, if they don't, pretend to because, if they don't, they will never become G.A.'s.

I have just finished *The Golden Bowl* & am astounded. Did he invent us or we him? He uses *all* our words in their most technical sense & we can't have got them all from him. . . .[2]

Yr
L.

July 30, 1905   Jaffna

Your letter was chiefly about [Clive] Bell.[3] It's rather sad, certainly more so than I thought it was, for I always said that he was in love with one of them—though strangely I thought it was the other. In a way I should like never to come back again now—just to be left in the warmth to be roused weekly from the level of gentle boredom—for that of course *is* the level—by the wonder of your letters. For it is

1. In his prior letter, Strachey had pleaded: "For heaven's sake write. It's essential. I must feel my cable; and my anchor is in Ceylon."
2. "As to Henry James," Strachey replied, "I entirely agree—it's too extraordinary about his use of our words. I suppose there must be some common cause—for it's certain that neither has taken from the other. I also wonder whether it's because he's so horribly like us that I, at any rate, can't read him."
3. See Biographical Appendix. For some time Strachey had been speculating to LW about Bell's attraction to Vanessa and Virginia Stephen. In the letter LW was answering, Strachey had written: "He's wildly in love—and with Vanessa. I couldn't doubt that he's fallen into a sort of distraction—it seems at times to be almost a mania. When he's alone I'm convinced that he's haunted, desperately haunted, by visions of Vanessa; his frightened pathetic face shows it; and his small lascivious body oozes with disappointed lust."

wonderful; so often as you see it must be & certainly in this case: society & unreality, curiously mixed. It's like reading a story about people one has known. And after all I miss the real boredom & discomfort of it all—the interminable & irritating discomfort, as I imagine it is sometimes, of a Gothic At Home.[1] Now Turner? Is he purely wicked or just crassly stupid? By the same post came a—for him—long letter from him, also all about Bell. I am still not quite certain that I know what he (Bell) was driving at, but I think that he is probably in love more or less with some female or perhaps females & also that he is vaguely discontented because he has nothing particular to do. Do you think he never really grasps anything? You think that Bell is really wildly in love with her? The curious part is that I was too after they came up that May term to Cambridge, & still more curious that there is a mirage of it still left. She is so superbly like the Goth. I often used to wonder whether he was in love with the Goth because he was in love with her & I was in love with her, because with the Goth. At any rate I give it to you as a palliation.[2]

At present it's much worse, because as you rightly guess I'm in love with the G.A.'s wife. I suppose work is one reason, but the best is that she is the only person—male or female—in Jaffna not positively repulsive to look at. She has superb hair & arms, hideous hands, & a fat 'good looking' face. After that perhaps you may 'relapse into cynicism.' When I'm not working or playing tennis, I seem to be always at 'the Park' as the G.A.'s bungalow is wonderfully called—talking on immense verandahs in long chairs (usually mildly amused) or playing interminable bridge. When one really gets to the heights of unreality, one can be, I think, very nearly supreme. I positively burst out laughing last night at a wild dinner, to which I stayed with the swearing Superintendent of Police, the painted governess, the wizened Miss Moorhouse & Mrs. Lewis (the GA is in Colombo) when something suddenly recalled to me a dinner one Sat. with you & MacCarthy in the Yen's rooms. O le sale monde, le sale monde.

Yr
L.

1. Some months earlier Thoby Stephen had initiated regular Thursday evening soirées for his Cambridge friends. Strachey complained to LW that there flowed on these occasions little conversation and even less drink.
2. An amazed Strachey replied: "As for your having been in love with Vanessa, it's really scandalous, I think—I mean to allow such things to come out only about 2 years after their occurrence. Also, how very, very wild. I feel that I shall never get used to the contortions of life."

To Lytton Strachey

August 13, 1905

Jaffna
Ceylon

I wrote you a degraded enough letter two weeks ago but this I expect will be more so, or more probably it will be nothing at all. The Governor, his mustachioed wife & his suite arrive next Saturday to stay two weeks here & it's already on my nerves.[1] I have to help to see that King's House is prepared for him, to reckon out how many fishknives & pillow cases & pos he wants, to arrange how Her Excellency's maid shall get to Her Excellency's bedroom without passing through His Excellency's dressing room, the only possible way being, as it happens, for her to crawl through the window.

I am going to leave Dutton & this bungalow tomorrow, the heat here being unbearable. I am to live in an immense bungalow on the side of the lagoon with a man called Templer, the Assistant Conservator of Forests. He is, I suppose, almost the dullest man in the world but as he is nearly always in the jungle he won't interfere very much with me. He used to live with the Gayes & knows Turner. As he possesses a tame leopard & I now keep a raging wild stag, I expect to be killed between the three. . . .[2]

Yr
L.

To Lytton Strachey

August 21st 1905

Jaffna
Ceylon

Je suis delabré. It's all I can write. I have been playing under housemaid for the last week & it will go on for several days to come. The Governor & suite arrived on Sat. & of course a good deal of the preparations fell on me. I have counted the linen and put up decorations & shown H.E. round salt pans & arranged the flowers & sweated in frock coats & helped Mrs Lewis to make Lady Blake's bed. I have been to bed at

1. Sir Henry Blake (1840–1918) was Governor of Ceylon 1903–07; Lady Blake was the daughter of an MP and a sister of the Duchess of St. Albans. In a letter in 1964 LW wrote: "The Civil Service, in my time, thought him a very stupid man and that Lady Blake did most of the ruling. She was certainly a formidable woman."
2. The two men shared a liking for animals and eventually acquired, in addition to the deer and leopard, five dogs, a monkey and a mongoose.

1 & up at 5, I have been to church & I have ridden (?) 17 miles in the
midday heat until the sun scorched the skin off my hands & blew up
my bicycle tyres in order that I might see whether a Rest House had
properly been got ready for H.E. I don't know whether the whole
world is like Jaffna now; if it be, it's all hopelessly insane. I feel as if
I should like to go to sleep for a thousand years & wake up to find
myself dead. It is almost incredible that we are not immortal. Probably
it's (August 22nd) really just the opposite & we shall wake up after a
thousand years only to find that we have got to go through the same
insanity all over again. If I dont post this now, you'll never get it.

Yr
L.

How awful about Theodore. I just had a line last week from Turner
telling me about it.[1]

To Lytton Strachey

Sept 3, 1905

Poonaryn
Ceylon

I am sailing from the above place to Jaffna & as the wind is very
strong, the boat rocking about & the water continually splashing in,
writing is rather difficult. There is a kind of famine in Poonaryn &
Govt has started a Relief Work. The people build a road & get paid
in rice & paddy. I sailed over there yesterday to superintend it & am
returning this evening. It's a most extraordinary desert of sand: miles
upon miles of paddy fields with thick jungle beginning 4 miles from
the sea, & in the middle an old Dutch Fort converted into a Rest
House, in wh. I stayed. I have got a damnable headache from walking
about in the sun & trying to calculate how much rice each cooly ought
to get per day.

   Euphrosne arrived.[2] It is a queer medley. There are only 3 things
in it wh. I ever want to read again, the Cat, Ningamus & the thing
about the song, I forget its name. But you're right; Turner doesn't
show up badly; only it's all about as pale as he is himself; it's like the

1. Theodore Llewelyn Davies (see Biographical Appendix) had drowned while swimming.
2. This was an anthology of poems by Clive Bell, Walter Lamb, Strachey, Sydney-Turner,
LW and others. Strachey's contribution, "The Cat," was inspired by a childhood visit to
the Sphinx.

ghost of a ghost. Are all the poems wh. I don't know by our Bell, or has Turner's abortion also contributed? They made me very nearly as sick as when I read my own.

I don't think I wrote to you last week. If I didn't it was from pure joy at doing absolutely nothing, once the Governor had gone. There was a wonderful Garden Party at the Park to which everyone came in astonishing toilettes. H.E. is, I think, the crassest man to whom I have ever spoken. Lady Blake is an old bearded hag & the private secretary an ill-mannered cur. But the ADC was a charming pink-faced guardsman & was the only redeeming feature.

The discomfort of writing here is becoming unbearable. So I'll leave off to scrawl 2 words to Turner.

Yr

L.

To Lytton Strachey

Jaffna

Ceylon

Sept 25th 1905

I don't quite know why I have begun to rush this in the middle of Kachcheri business except that it gives me some pleasure just to send a letter of some sort once a week. I was going to write as usual on Sunday but simply could not. I rode to a place called Pt. Pedro on Sat afternoon partly on business partly in order to escape Jaffna. It is about 21 miles away. I thought I should come back by a mad way & started out down the coast where there are no roads only sand & palmyra trees. No one ever goes there & the sand has heaped itself up into great curves & ridges. It seemed to be absolutely uninhabited except for one enormous temple standing quite solitary in this wilderness of sand. At last the track I had been following disappeared altogether & I had to haul my bicycle across a dried up lagoon in the direction I imagined my road to lie. Eventually I found myself at a Rest House 12 miles from Jaffna: there I inspected the tracing of a new proposed road & pushed my bicycle through 2 miles of paddy fields. I got back at 7 scorched aching & sore, only to be met by a constable with a letter asking me to take a dying deposition of a man who had been stabbed in a fight. Only a Magistrate can do this so off I dragged myself to the hospital. It's fairly grim, the man was a mass of wounds, he lay on a bare wooden bed in the long gloomy room surrounded by all the other loathsome patients. It took an hour & a half to get his story out of him & it had to be interrupted by the man having to have his urine drawn, a filthy operation. In the end he became unconscious or pretended to be. It must be pleasant to be in a dying condition & be shouted at until you are forced to tell who stabbed you. I shall write an article (strictly anonymous) on Modern Humanitarianism in the East for the *Independent*. I wonder if things are really managed in England as they are here.

I don't think you realize how wonderfully vulgar the GA's wife is.

Morhanger Park, good God. Were we in the canoe this time last year?

Your,

L.

To Lytton Strachey

Jaffna
Ceylon

Oct 1, 1905

I suppose you want to know everything—well, I am worn out or rather merely supine through a night of purely degraded debauch. The pleasure of it is of course grossly exaggerated certainly with a halfcaste whore. The ridiculousness of existence never reaches such heights— the elaborate absurdity made me almost impuissant from amusement. And yet the sheer desperation of life here I really think alone made me go so far. Are you appalled or enraged—I am merely wonderfully amused. Now I am lying in a filthy native sailing boat, absolutely becalmed on my way to Poonaryn once more. There is no wind, a blank heavy heat. I have been here 3 hours & God knows when we shall really begin to move. Time & everything else seems to have stopped still. I suppose you still talk about the Good & Yenism & what is really real & read books which aren't Ordinances & speak to people who aren't whores or insane or inane. It all seems very queer when the only things I can possibly imagine as real are smells & the sun. Now I feel so damnably old. There are only two things which would *really* amuse me at the present moment: one is to talk to you & the other to talk to Jesus Christ.

Your

L.

To Lytton Strachey

Near Kurunegala
Ceylon

I am in a train on my way to Colombo for the examination. The train goes the whole way now & it takes 14 or 15 hours. I left yesterday & stayed the night at Anuradhapura with Southorn, the man I used to live with.

I long to write you a letter but I can't, I must learn some damned law for tomorrow's examination. I have a tale to tell you. My dear it was supremely wonderful & worth coming to Ceylon to hear, at least told as it was to me on the immense verandah by the dull man [G. D. Templer] with whom I live.

I can't resist it now, I must go on. I saw his amazingly ugly face simply shine with sweat in the moonlight at the remembrance of it all. He is an Assistant Conservator of Forests. He was at Trincomalee about two or three years ago staying in the Rest House. There were two other men staying there, one an Irrigation Engineer & the other Sir Hector Macdonald, who had come for a week to inspect the garrison.[1] He was very friendly, rather vulgar, exactly like an immensely strong good humoured Tommy. Templer had heard nothing of his reputation. Two days before he left they were talking at about 11 at night, when Macdonald suddenly stopped in the middle of a sentence, looked hard at him & said: 'I'll see you again tonight' & walked out of the room to his own bedroom.

Templer knew in a moment what he meant: he was at his wits end, his own bedroom had no lock on the door, he heard Macd. undressing, he knew of no house to which he could fly. He rushed into the I.E.'s room (wh. had a lock on the door) & said 'For God's sake, get out of the room & let me sleep here. I can't tell you why, but you must do it'. The I.E. went & Templer locked the door, put out the light & lay down on the bed. In about ¼ of an hour Macdonald came to the door & called him. He tried the door, asked him to open it, tried the window, called & swore. From 12 until 2 in the morning he stood outside trying to break in while Templer lay sweating with terror on the bed. "I thought if he got in & I resisted I should either get killed or there would be a most awful row & the ADC would come & no one would

1. Major General Sir Hector Macdonald (1853–1903), who rose from the ranks to become an officer and a popular Victorian military hero. ADC to Queen Victoria and King Edward VII, he was appointed military commander in Ceylon in 1902.

take my word against that of a great gun like Macdonald. I lay there & knew I should be ruined & listened to him shuffling about outside. At last about 2 he went off. I never slept a wink the whole night. I didn't know what to do when I went into the room to breakfast the next day. Macdonald looked up as I came in & said 'Your puttees are put on wrong' & he insisted on showing me himself how they ought to be put on. Then he said 'What are you going to do today?' I said I was going to play in a cricket match. 'O' he said, 'you needn't do that, I am going for a long drive & you must come with me'. I said I must play but he answered that it was absurd & he would at any rate order the carriage".

Then Templer's nerves seem to have given way, he determined on flight as he knew that Macd. had a special gunboat which was to take him to Colombo the next day. He went to the Rest House Keeper & ordered a cart & bulls & told him to tell the General that he had gone to a Rest House some 10 miles off. Then he got into the bullock cart & flew as hard as the bulls could go into the jungle towards the Rest House. Six miles out he met a District Engineer in a madam (or hut). He was so shattered that he poured his tale out to the D.E. The D.E. said 'Don't go to that R.H. for Macd. is certain to follow for he is probably mad. Turn off here & go another 8 miles & you will get to another Rest House at——.' So Templer turned off & flew on to the other Rest House, where he stayed two days in terror. When he got back to Trinco he heard that Macd., as soon as the R.H. Keeper told him where he had gone, got a trap & drove off at full speed to the other Rest House. He stayed the night there & drove back to Trinco the next day thereby missing the gunboat & having to go back overland to Colombo.

There is a curious sequel but it will keep.[1]

Your
L.

---

1. The sequel was that early in 1903 rumors that Macdonald had been overfriendly with several schoolboys reached the Governor of Ceylon, who directed him to return to London and seek a new post. The War Office, however, ordered him to return to Ceylon to clear his name through a court-martial. In Paris, on his way back, he shot himself. A story, still circulating in the 1980s, maintained that Macdonald faked the suicide, defected to the Germans, took the identity of Field Marshal Mackensen, who had purportedly just died of cancer, and during the First World War led German troops on the Eastern Front.

Punakari Rest House
Poonaryn

Oct 29th [1905]

. . . The taupe sent his book to me last week.[1] It is really extraordinary that it is as amusing as it is. It is a queer kind of twilight humour don't you think. I can imagine the taupes in their half lit burrows making jokes to one another in it or old ladies in musty close smelling suburban rooms revelling in it if they ever had any humour at all. He is, I suppose, certain to 'make a name' for everyone will call it clever. What enraged me in the book was the tragedy. If it is supposed to *be* a tragedy it's absolutely hopeless; if it's supposed to be amusing, it simply fails.

I came back from Colombo last Monday. I spent a week there of exams & mild dysentery. I was completely shattered after the first day; after forthing about 24 times & eating nothing for the 1st 2 days I still wanted to & couldn't on the 3rd.[2] There has never been a lower depth of degradation than Colombo society. It is all 'sets' & exclusiveness. The level of the men rises, I think, from that of a haberdasher's assistant up to that of the lowest Cambridge pseudo-blood. The women— my God—they really give me, with their pale dried up faces & drawling voices, the creeps. No one ever talks about anything more interesting than 'the service' or whether Mr A. is really engaged to Miss B. If you are in 'the service' you say 'what snobs the merchants are & really they only retail tin-tacks'; if you are a merchant, you say 'what snobs civil servants are'. The first hag you are introduced to at the Colombo Garden Club can tell you what you had for dinner two weeks ago in Jaffna. And through the midst of them goes the unending stream of passengers. That is what, for all its abominations, if you stay as I did at the hotel, gives it a real fascination. The vulgar hideous Australians, the magnificent young men, wonderful women in wonderful dresses, hopeless middle class families wandering about in frock coats & 'billy cock' hats under the full tropical sun, fat Germans, bored & flurried Frenchmen—I like to see them ceaselessly passing Mr Denham of the Colonial Secretary's office who 'thinks he runs Ceylon'.

Your
L.

1. Forster's first novel, *Where Angels Fear to Tread*.
2. "Forthing" was a contemporary euphemism for using a lavatory.

Jaffna
Ceylon.

Nov 12th 1905

Do you know that I have not had a line from you for 3 weeks? I heard from Turner about the fellowship election.[1] They are getting even more degraded at Trinity high table than even I could have imagined. We are really wonderful as failures, don't you think? It is remarkable that we all three broke down as soon as we tried to earn our livings. Here, of course, I am considered anything but a failure; it is by comparison, I think, with themselves & therefore less complimentary to me than uncomplimentary to them.

I have just passed my first examination [in law] in record time & people go about saying that I run the Northern Province by myself already. All this I put down entirely to a persistent use of the method.[2] At Trinity of course we used it purely aesthetically & theoretically; but it is a wonderful instrument & weapon used practically. No one in Jaffna & probably only one man in Ceylon (I have only seen him once, he is the Lieut. Governor) has ever tried to think what another man is thinking or feeling. . . . As a rule the Office Assistant (much more the cadet who is under him), if he ever does anything of any responsiblility, enrages all the other officials who call him a 'prig who thinks he can run the province'. The Government Agent is furious with Government & is ill, & therefore allows me to do pretty well what I like. It is only through the method that the other officials think me 'nice' & are so 'good & kind' to me that they say it is a shame that I'm overworked & help me to do things which 'as a rule it is a perfect scandal that a cadet be allowed to manage'. Even the crusty Provincial Engineer sent the District Engineer to help me supervise the making of a road as relief work, though he was mortally offended that his department had not been asked to carry it out.

This is a phenomenal & degraded letter, & it had better end so. I am to leave this bungalow in a week & shall live by myself. The only thing is that I can't get a bungalow. At present I foresee having to move into a huge dilapidated house some way down on the beach. I have been in curious ménages since the wonderful one à deux in [Trinity] Gt Court, but what do you think of my new one alone with

---

1. To his lasting disappointment, Strachey failed to be elected a fellow of Trinity, at least in part because his examiners were unsympathetic to his revised dissertation on Warren Hastings.
2. "The method" was described by LW in *Sowing* as "a kind of third-degree psychological investigation applied to the souls of one's friends . . . a kind of compulsory psychoanalysis."

a burgher concubine in a long bare whitewashed bungalow overlooking the lagoon, where time is only divided between reading Voltaire on the immense verandah & copulating in the vast & empty rooms where there is a perpetual smell of bats & damp & the paint & plaster peel off the walls & gather onto the stone floors.[1]

Yr
L.

To John Maynard Keynes

Jaffna
Ceylon.

Nov 17, 1905

My dear Keynes,

I have become tired of reading 'No 1 of 1897, An Ordinance relating to Claims to Forest, Chena, Waste & Unoccupied Lands', I am sick of Salt & Relief Works, of the births of illegitimate children & the deaths of venereal old men, & I remember that I have still a letter from you long unanswered. I am fuming in my whitewashed office under a punkah which the punkah boy never will pull. I don't think I have anything else to tell you. I have heard of the dim ghosts of the things & people you mention, but little more. . . . I live a life of strenuous unreality relieved by flashes of degradation. There is nothing to be said for the former, but a little I think for the latter. I can understand how a dipsomaniac, who really recognized his degradation, might feel his supremacy in his drunkenness. If you had to live perpetually with A.C. Turner, you would rejoice in the conversation of whores.[2] They at any rate are sometimes amusing.

When you can, write again.

Yours,
L S W

---

1. LW had taken with him to Ceylon the complete works of Voltaire in a fine 1784 edition of seventy volumes. "Socially and psychologically they did me no good, and materially . . . caused considerable difficulty when I was moved from one station to another. . . ." (*Growing*).

2. A. C. Turner as co-founder of the Anglican Fellowship in Cambridge would have been antipathetic to both Keynes and LW.

To Lytton Strachey

Dec 24th 1905   Jaffna

I'm back as you see in Jaffna, shattered completely; but it is at any
rate something to be in one's own house again & able to eat fish.[1]
Lord, the horror of those 3 weeks of perpetual fever & enemas (do
they spell it like that) in the noisy bungalow & later in the still noisier
hospital. Now there is all the complication of going on leave up-country
& the journey & packing which I feel I shall never face.

I wonder if I'm doing a stupid thing: I'm sending you all the letters
you have ever written me. You must swear to keep them for me until
I come back. I determined, when I was ill & had to let people get
things out of the drawer where I had locked them up, that it was too
dangerous to keep them in bulk like this. Besides one's servants read
everything in some mysterious way. I hate doing it, for I like to read
them but it's not safe in this precarious existence in which one has to
fly off & leave all one's belongings at a moment's notice.

I have so much I want to say about Duncan &—good God—James,
but I'm still unable really to write.[2]

Yr
L.

To Lytton Strachey

Dec 30, 1905   Jaffna

I sent off your letters today, & trembled as I did so. They asked me
what the value of the parcel was &, as I did not like to say Morocco,
I said £5. I have spent a curious week; two full days of it lying in a
long chair & reading the letters straight through in chronological order.
You must do it, but God! It's appalling—& if it's that for me what
will it be for you? One simply goes right through the last 6 years of
one's life, one lives them in detail again. I really think that, as you
say in one of them, we are the true Aristotelian friends, for it made

1. A few days after writing to Keynes, LW had been stricken with a serious case of typhoid
fever and was taken to an American missionary hospital, where he was left to sleep it off.
2. Strachey had written that he was deeply in love with his cousin Duncan Grant and that
his brother James, now at Trinity, was having an affair with Walter Lamb. Duncan Grant
(1885–1978) became one of the leading British painters of his time.

no difference, as I read them, that you were writing or that it was about you—I shivered &, if I could, wept. It's all very curious. I can see you now so well in 1900 & myself through you. I think we were rather loathsome then. We are wild in 1901 but only in 1902 are we magnificent. The strange thing is, to me, that the boom lasts so short a time: it is only for a few months that we are on the heights & happy for we obviously are happy for a time. The blackness begins to settle already in 1903, an extraordinary gloom into which we have been sinking more & more. You must keep the letters & return them if I ever return.

I am in the midst of the horrors of packing. I go up country to-morrow: a month in hotels in the hills. If I were not bankrupt it might be pleasant, but being ill has ruined me & I don't know how, except by cheques that are dishonoured, I can pay hotel bills.

Your
L.

To Robert Trevelyan

Jan 9th 1906

Adam's Peak Hotel
Hatton

My dear Trevy, I was very glad to get your letter & the cutting of MacCarthy's dramatic criticism. A breath of Apostolicism always comes on me with renewed astonishment in this country. Forster sent me his book &, as far as I can see from what you say, I agree with you about it. It amused & at the same time annoyed me, the latter feeling especially in the tragedy.

This is not a settled habitation for me; I am for a month a wanderer among the Ceylon mountains. I got typhoid fever in the middle of November in Jaffna & had a very bad time of it for 5 weeks. It leaves one terribly weak & in the heat of the low country it is impossible to regain one's strength, so I have had to take a month's leave up country. I don't care very much for wandering about in second rate hotels. Nearly all the people I know in Ceylon are in the low country so that as far as society goes I am confined to casual conversations with tea planters or American tourists. The latter are absolutely astonishing, their sole standards of value seem to be money & a curious form of liberty, which consists in forcing every man to learn nothing but how to make money. I always end by losing my temper with their abominable patriotism & offending them. I have just succeeded in doing this to an old gentleman who began a conversation by telling me that 400 000 dollars was nothing to him & who being childless & apparently taking a great fancy to me I thought at one moment might be induced to adopt me & leave his 'immense wealth' to me. However I could not stand his explanation of how disgracefully we ran England & the colonies & how much better America could & did run hers. 'You don't even educate the people here', he said. 'America is a free country. You are educated free of charge there. The state just takes you & teaches you a trade so that you can earn your living. In the schools you get paper & pens free of charge, lunch with three courses free of charge & hot or cold as you like, & as many books as you can carry home free of charge. The school buildings are 4 stories high & made of brick & heated all through by hot water pipes. And that's what we'd have in our colonies too'. He was offended when I hoped that they would not insist upon hot water pipes in Ceylon.

I hope you won't forget to let me know when you publish your next book, & will write again whenever you have nothing better to do.

Yours fraternally
L. S. Woolf

To Lytton Strachey

Jan 13, 1906

Bandarawela
Ceylon.

. . . God, how I wish I could talk to you! At present mine is a curious 'enfer'. I was four days in Kandy & three in Hatton, an immense empty hotel surrounded by an interminable series of tea-covered hills, & now I have practically settled down for two weeks here. You can't under-stand my mood—& I don't think I can give its tone to you at all—without an idea of this country. It has enmeshed me together with my appalling isolation. It is superb; don't you think it always is when you can see vast distances? Well, here wherever you walk you can see over enormous tracts, but instead of, as usually happens in these cases, seeing plains, it is one immense sea of hills. You stand upon one & they rise & fall all round you in great waves, not rugged but desolate, covered with coarse grass, almost always bare of trees. It is only to the east that there is anything dark & rugged where they rise up 2500 feet even above this place in a long dark chain covered with jungle. The air is wonderfully soft & clear & the sky a curiously pale blue. I walk out on to these & wander about from 7-9 every morning & from

4-6 every evening, the rest of the day I read Voltaire's letters, Huysmans & Henry James.

The only people I talk to are a man who drives a traction engine & an interminable procession of tea-planters. The latter are typically 'good fellows'. They ask me to come & stay with them & I accept & then put it off in terror. Somehow or other, though I can talk to them, there is a horrible feeling of boredom & awkwardness. One must always say the same things in the same cheery way, &, as I do, of course the awkwardness is only felt by myself. I have definitely promised to stay next week with two of them on their estates about 10 miles away. I shall have to but I dread it. I fly from them to read in my bedroom or to walk on the hills. It is then that I am obsessed by a strangely pleasant melancholia. I have immense visions of what I know inanition & incapacity will never let me carry out. I want to write & when I get back I will find my brain too dull even to remember what I had thought of an hour before. Is it complete death or merely the sinking into the gentle sleep of Ferdyism?[1] I found one of my old papers for the Society &, compared to what I could do now, it seemed magnificent. I am a De Musset with no passé at all. Finally all my hair is coming out. . . .

An American whom I met in Hatton Hotel gave me the following recipe for happily spending one's days: 'Take a quiet walk, have your meals, clean your boots, take out your clothes & see that they are all right, read & answer your letters, talk to anyone you come across, go to bed,' & 'fuck your wife' I added & enraged him.

Your
L.

To Lytton Strachey

Jan 28, 1906   Bandarawela

. . . I stayed with the planters some days &, of course, it was much better than I expected. One was a wild maniac of the kind I am always surprised at being able to get on with. . . . The other was curious: he had been at Selwyn [College, Cambridge] destined to the church. He had never thought until he began to read theology & that reduced him immediately to agnosticism. Then he became a private tutor, & tried

1. See footnote on Ferdinand Schiller, page 45, n. 1.

to reform the method of teaching, his object being to teach people to think. He is rather charming & strenuous & deals largely in philosophy. We had, before an admiring audience on whom he has completely impressed himself, a violent argument about the existence of time & he is now about to begin a study of *Principia Ethica*. One would hardly expect an evening like I had in an isolated hill-bungalow on a Ceylon tea estate.

When I returned here, I found a telegram asking me whether I would go as Koddu Superintendent to the Pearl Fishery.[1] It is supposed to be very unhealthy & tremendously hard work, but as it is possibly less dull than a Kachcheri & I shall get rs 15 a day besides my ordinary pay, I wired back yes. I return to Jaffna tomorrow & go, I suppose, in about a fortnight to Marichchukkaddi where the fishery takes place.

Your
L.

FROM LYTTON STRACHEY

Feb. 2nd 1906.

My letters have come—in their wonderful tin box—and I have spent an entire day reading them. I read yours to me too, and I felt like a drowning man, who sees the whole of his past life flash before his inward eye. I quite agree with you about the different phases, and the gathering gloom—though it struck me, I don't know with what truth, that your letters were more depressed than mine, though the depression itself seemed to be mine and not yours so much. But perhaps this only applies to 1903–4. I wonder if future readers—if there are any—will think our gloom justifiable. It made me feel horribly low— the mere repetition of it. I wanted to weep and wring my hands as if I still felt those old agonies & agitations. . . .

Your
G L S

1. Divers, merchants, traders—and criminals—came from all over South Asia and the Middle East for the two-month winter fishing. Oysters were collected by Arab divers, who took them to an enclosure, or *koddu*, where two-thirds were claimed by the Ceylon government and then auctioned. Since the pearls were extracted by allowing the oysters to rot for several days, the smell and sanitary conditions of the camp were appalling.

To Robert Trevelyan

Feb 11, 1906

Jaffna
Ceylon

My dear Trevy,

Very many thanks for Fry's book [*The Discourses of Sir Joshua Reynolds*]. It seems, though I have only had time to dip into it, extremely interesting. Whether I shall have time just to read a word of anything for the next two months is more than doubtful. I came back here on Feb 1st quite recovered, & start on Wednesday for the Pearl Fishery. There is a huge camp formed at a place called Marichchukkaddi of about 40 000 people. It is a desert of sand surrounded by jungle & it takes 1 to 3 days to get to by native sailing boat from here. There are only 4 Europeans to supervise the whole thing including the fishing, counting & selling of the Government oysters & as I am going as one of them there will not be much time for anything but work.[1] It is supposed to be extraordinarily unhealthy & everyone says I'm a fool to go after being ill—but its fever I believe is exaggerated.

I am very busy here too as the place is full of Arab divers who have to be got off tomorrow to the Fishery—so excuse this letter which is of a phenomenality.

Yours fraternally,
L. S. Woolf

To Lytton Strachey

March 4th 1906

Marichchukkaddi
Ceylon

I meant not to write to you this week; I meant, in the little time I can snatch, to write to Turner or Campbell or MacCarthy—I never do write to them now—but when I sit with the paper before me you are the only one to whom I really wish to talk. Two letters ago you spoke of our pessimism & wondered whether future generations would think it justified. God knows I feel it; I am stunned by the madness & bitterness of life. If you live in tempests & crises, I live in a hell of lunatics. It is not because I don't think of it all that I don't write of

1. In the event, one of the four went down with malaria and another became ill, leaving LW and the GA to manage alone.

Duncan, or even perhaps because I have grown out of understanding it, but have we not in a way said all that could be said &, if there is anything left, I could say it across a fireplace not across 9000 miles of sea.[1] The most that I remember of him is his impulsive charm & the spring (I think) evening ages ago when we canoed with him on the backs. I suppose that the dead spirits of Turner & I are alone in the world who could understand your last letter; with the rest it would mean Morocco & what I heard an old & a young whoremonger say the other night a propos to some Arabs (now at the Fishery I think) who caught a missionary last year in the Persian Gulf & buggered him until he was all but dead. I wonder what the Post Master here thought of it—apparently he opens all letters before delivering them.

I am half dead from weariness & want of sleep. It is 9 at night & I am writing by the flickering light of lamps in the babel & hell of the Koddu. I don't know if you realize what it is like, a huge fenced in square with 9 open huts running from end to end. Each hut is divided into compartments & the boats as they arrive have to bring in their loads of oysters, & deposit them in a compartment in 3 heaps, one of which goes to the divers & two to Government. The bank now being fished is 21 miles away & the boats instead of taking 4 or 5 hours to get in, take 24 to 36. The work is consequently going on day & night & I have only been in bed about 3 or 4 hours out of the last 72. With 6 or 7 thousand Arab divers penned into this space, shouting & gesticulating in the light of a few oil lamps, it is like walking about hour after hour in a hell twice as mad as the coaling at Port Said. It is merely cooly work supervising this & the counting & issuing of about one or two million oysters a day, for the Arabs will do anything if you hit them hard enough with a walking stick, an occupation in which I have been engaged for the most part of the last 3 days & nights.

There was a curious scene here on Thursday morning. I was in the Koddu from 9 in the evening of Wednesday till 9 on Thursday morning without a break. Just before daybreak an Arab chief came & told me that one of his men had died on the boat out on the banks & his body was still on board. Smallpox had broken out in the camp, so I kept the Arabs on board & sent for the doctor. When he came, I went down to the shore with him & six Arabs waded ashore with the dead body on their shoulders. They laid the dead body naked on the sand & the dawn just broke with its curiously soft pink light over everything. The brother of the dead man sat down at his head, muffled himself in a

---

1. Strachey, after writing letter upon letter on his obsession with Grant, had complained about LW's silence on the subject.

long cloak, & wept & wailed while the old chief addressed apparently a long exhortation to him. At last when the doctor said that it was not small-pox, I allowed them to go & they filed off, the legs of the corpse sticking rigidly out over their shoulders, along the shore, muttering as they went 'Khallas, Khallas' 'it is finished, it is finished'.

The last 10 lines I have written on March 5th. It is 4.30 A.M. & I am sitting down for the first time in 2 hours. I went to bed at 10.30 & got up at 1.30, & I shall be here another 12 hours.

Your
L.

To Lytton Strachey

March 21st 1906

Marichchukkaddi
Ceylon

I sometimes wonder whether I shall commit suicide before the six years are up & I can see you again; at this moment I feel as near as I have ever been. Depression is becoming, I believe, a mania with me, it sweeps upon & over me every eight or ten days, deeper each time. If you hear that I have died of sunstroke, you may be the only person to know that I have chosen that method of annihilation. It is due, I suppose, partly to the monotony of perpetual work, the glaring & scorching heat of this place, the want of sleep, & the loathesome food which one has to eat here. You don't know what it is to be, as I am now, so tired at 10 P.M. that every muscle in your body seems to be felt & to know that you have to keep awake until 2.30 A.M., only to begin another day of the same sort at half past seven. And then there are the flies—they are bred in the millions of rotting oysters that lie about the camp. All day long they fly about in clouds, hundreds & hundreds swarming over everything: not a scrap of food can be left uncovered for a second without becoming black with them. They infect the food in some foul way, for all day long I feel horribly sick & many people are actually sick four or five times regularly a day. They are crawling over one's face & hands all day long & owing to the putrid filth on which they feed every little scratch or spot on one becomes sore.

Can I write to you about Duncan or the Society out of this? Or shall I go on to tell you that I have had diarrhoea for 4 days & that I am once more becoming covered with eczema? What I am going to do is to tell you of my mental degradation once more. I never wrote to you about the incident at the time because I really was ashamed of the degraded stupidity of it but I feel it may amuse you to hear of it. There was a female in Jaffna, unmarried, ugly but terribly & femininely violent. She was fairly interesting (for Jaffna) & I used to talk more or less openly to her. Then in a mild way she began, I believe, to fall in love—at any rate she tried to begin an idiotic little intrigue. I was absolutely degraded, I know, but as I felt that I could completely control the situation, I let it go on in its silly little incidents, taking a faint pleasure in guiding it through the appalling gossip of Jaffna. Then she went away & began writing 8 page letters every other day to which I now & again sent probably hideous replies. But I had mapped out my whole campaign: I suddenly broke it up by not writing for three months & then as suddenly, & as the answer showed successfully, opened it up again on a new footing.

If I did not feel that I am in the bottommost pit, beyond the pale (?) of being & outside the gates of Yenism, I should never tell you this, but then it would never I suppose have happened. You may take it as the last despairing cry of the ghost of a soul you once knew in the real world.

[Unsigned]

FROM LYTTON STRACHEY

Ap[ril] 13th 1906

My dear, I have just got your nightmare of a letter, with the description of the flies, & the Jaffna lady, & the general horror. I hope that by the time you get this, you will have moved away from the Oysters, and that the depression will be less. It's too fearful that things should be as they are. I curse god daily—but for the sake of everything in the world don't talk as you have lately of your own "degradation". You must see that it's twaddle—utter twaddle, which is not only prima facie absurd, but contrary to all our opinions. I'm afraid I can say nothing to cheer you up. If I could speak I could perhaps—I want to horribly. Will you believe that? I can only hope that we will get through this someday, that we will live to inhabit our castles in Spain. Don't you hope this too? Please, please try to; and, if you can give me some sympathy too, I've got filthily muddled up here—in mental horrors— while you've been in material foulness. . . .

Your
GLS

The Grand Oriental Hotel

April 15th 1906   Colombo, Ceylon

This place always makes me feel unwell with its food & clammy heat & passengers. But there is enormous pleasure in eating decent food again after seven weeks of pure filth with a liberal mixture of flies & sand. The fishery ended last week & I am taking a week's leave after it to stay with an Irishman (& nothing else) at a place called Kegalla. I came down on Saturday, an incredibly unpleasant journey; first on Saturday night to Pamban in India in a little steamer packed with about 1000 Arabs & Tamils. They swarmed everywhere over all the decks & overflowed into the 3 small cabins & box of a saloon. They were seasick over one another most of the time. You may say what you like, but the Semitic is worth, at any rate in the East, 30 Aryans or Dravidians or whatever they are called. You should have seen the wretched Tamils huddling together, squabbling & complaining. But the Arab is superb, he has the grand manner, absolutely saturnine, no fuss or excitement, but one could see when day broke that every Arab had room to spare to stretch full length in his blanket on the deck. At least I have set foot in India now & found it Jaffna, but a wilderness more desolate even than Jaffna.

. . . You cannot, I believe, imagine this existence, Jaffna & Marich-chukkaddi & then these little plunges into Colombo. The patronage of the great, the dinner last night with the young blood of Ceylon, who 'will make a name for himself', & the Galle Face Hotel, the Inspector General of Police & the Colonial Secretary who joined us afterwards. We talk as if Ceylon is the universe. God I play on them but I wish I had someone to laugh at them with me. Sometimes I ruin it all, & I believe I quite did for myself at the Fishery. One of the 'people with power', the Auditor General, came up, a pompous Irishman who is supposed to be a wit. I sat next to him at dinner & made some remark to him which was completely ignored. He is of course always thinking of the next witticism he is going to make but also can only talk to women & men over thirty. At any rate my temper went & for the remainder of the evening I pretended that he did not exist & succeeded at least, I think, in making him feel uncomfortable.

This is all beneath contempt & my train is going.

Yr

L.

To Lytton Strachey

Jaffna
April 21, 1906   Ceylon

I'm drunk, so drunk that I can scarcely see the paper I'm writing on,
so that all that I say you can put down to that. I remember you once
wrote a drunken letter to me. I wish I could get like that, but—& this
is my curse—the drunker I get the more sober I am. Damn damn damn
damn damn   I took out my gun the other night, made my will &
prepared to shoot myself. God knows why I didn't; merely I suppose
the imbecility of weakness & the futility of ridiculous hopes. Whores
& vulgar gramophones, fools & wrecked intellects. Why am I caged
& penned & herded with these. I laugh when I read that San Francisco
is wiped out & weep over the wreck & ruin of my existence.[1]

I have been dining with the new G.A. here & have drunk myself
drunk after it from disgust at life & the impossibility of getting a
loathesome whore. Price the new G.A. is superb.[2] I feel like a baby in
his hands, he is an administrator, absolutely cold pure intellect. And
because he is great, because he will not lickspittle & kow-tow, &
because he is in the most damned of all places, a Crown Colony, he
is discredited, a wretched monolith of all that he ought to be.

I am on the edge of death or of being sick so good night

Your
L.

To Lytton Strachey

Jaffna
June 21, 1906   Ceylon

Do you remember once, on a Sunday afternoon, in your room, when
we were all there on the heights of an after breakfast conversation,
Ainsworth coming in in a brown mackintosh & umbrella, wild &
breathless, & soon reduced us to incoherent rage in which he could
only repeat at intervals: 'You are all in a very bad state of mind;
the state of mind of the Society is appalling'. I believe I felt

1. The great San Francisco earthquake had occurred three days earlier.
2. Ferdinando Hamlyn Price (b. 1855) served his entire career in the Ceylon Civil Service.
Highly intelligent but incorrigibly indolent, he let LW govern the district. LW learned two
principles from him: never use two words when one will do, and always answer a letter on
the day it arrives. LW left a memorable portrait of him and his wife in *Growing*.

rather like him when I read your letter about James & Norton. . . .[1]

Of course it is really all you. You have corrupted Cambridge just as Socrates corrupted Athens. The authorities would do very rightly if they did with you what they did with, I believe Marie Lloyd, excluded you altogether from Cambridge. Anytus too was perfectly right.[2] It was Socrates who ruined Athens & I expect to hear every day that Cambridge has, through you, had to shut up altogether & disband. For it seems to have completely broken out into open sodomy, or rather into an interminable series of reciprocal flirtations. And you, you are a grim dim spectre, the spirit of it all & the only one to feel & be torn.

Yr

L.[3]

To Saxon Sydney-Turner

Jaffna
Ceylon

June 24, 1906

I had a letter from Strachey last week, but I don't seem to have heard from you for some time. His was principally about James & Norton & the Society. I gather that they are what we should have been if we had lived a generation later.

Here an enterprising female has started a Shakespeare Reading Society. We read *As You Like It* on Friday. It was not quite as bad as it might have been & I had expected the worst. There was considerable difficulty over the word copulation. 'I press in here, Sir, amongst the rest of the country copulatives' was allowed to pass, because no one was quite sure whether it referred to grammar or sexual intercourse. It was only the weight of my assurance that it referred to the former that induced Touchstone not to leave it out. I was Jaques.

Your

L.

1. James Strachey and Henry Norton had blackballed Keynes's current favorite, Robert Furness. Henry (Harry) T. J. Norton (1886–1937), later Fellow of Trinity and noted mathematician.
2. The letter to which L W was responding had commented: "I wonder if you'ld be shocked if you were here. The whole place you know, has broken out into open sodomy, and even Sanger (they say) has been infected. The conversation is certainly wilder than it ever was." Marie Lloyd was a popular music-hall comedian. Anytus was Socrates's chief accuser.
3. Strachey answered, "As for my being Socrates, it is, after all, rather an important difference that I haven't yet been condemned to death. And shall I ever be? Won't the whole world be converted first? . . ."

To Robert Trevelyan

Mannar
Ceylon

August 19, 1906

My dear Trevy,

I was delighted to get your letter describing the [Apostles' annual] dinner. You do not know how pleasant it is to hear about it all from here.

The Pearl Fishery did me no harm though it was pure hell while it lasted, with no sleep & indescribable smells. After that I went back to Jaffna & am now acting for a month as Assistant Government Agent here. It is a curious place over 50 miles from the railway, no roads & no white people but myself. It is a fairly large district composed almost entirely of sand & jungle. It is rather like solitary confinement, as there is of course no one to speak to at all. I have bought a horse & ride, & otherwise only work & read. Mannar itself, my headquarters, is on an island, but I also have a considerable portion on the mainland under me. It means very little to do as the people are sterile & dying out & would have died out long ago but for our beneficent rule. At the present moment many of them are supposed to be dying of starvation owing to drought; Government has opened Relief Works on roads, but many of the people are high caste & their ancestors never carried earth on their heads. They therefore sit down & say they prefer to die of starvation rather than carry earth on their heads. And they are quite right, I think, don't you?

Your
L. S. Woolf

To Saxon Sydney-Turner

Kaddukkarankudiyiruppu,
Ceylon

Aug 27, 1906

I am camping out in a tent in the wilderness. I told you I believe I was coming for a month as AGA Mannar. I am now on circuit which means that I ride about 10 miles a day through a desolation of sand to visit a few huts which are called villages. My tent & luggage is carried in buffalo carts at the rate of 1½ miles an hour. I have forgotten how to talk, after two years ago forgetting how to think. It is very pleasant, one glides into the vegetable state of the East. There is no work no worries nothing to think of but the discomfort which becomes a habit. The nearest white man is 30 miles away, the nearest railway about 80 & India is a stone's throw across the water. I ride through the sand from 6 A.M. to 9 & lie in my tent during the heat of the day & read Dickens whom of course I now consider the greatest of novelists. At any rate he is astonishingly amusing in Kaddukkarankudiyiruppu (which means the village of the man of the Jungle).

I have discovered that the only method by which one can under these circumstances retain one's identity as a human being is, despite the discomfort, always to wear a starched collar.

Yr
L.

TO LYTTON STRACHEY

Sunday Nov 4th 1906

Jaffna,
Ceylon.

I tore up your last letter. Pure fright, it is not safe to keep, once opened, for a week in this place. It was the description of the intrigues ending in Keynes. It made me feel a little sick, as I see it did you. Personally I feel with the British Public, certainly in the case of Keynes who, if he has the face of a pig, has the soul of a goat. Perhaps the strength of the repulsion comes from two years among people who are all 'healthily' vicious, if they are vicious. But at last I would fall back upon the certain condemnation of Moore. I shall dislike Norton & Hobber [Hobhouse] will irritate me beyond endurance, & you will be grimly amused. Keynes, thank God, will be buried on his stool.

I was reading La Bruyere today with the irritation against Keynes at the back of my mind. He is in full the 'sot' of La Bruyere for his chief characteristic—with all his damned intelligence—is that once you have seen him, he never surprises you: il est uniforme, il ne se dément point: qui l'a vu une fois, l'a vu dans tous les instances et dans toutes les périodes de sa vie, c'est tout au plus le boeuf qui meugle ou le merle qui siffle, il est fixé et déterminé par sa nature et j'ose dire par son espèce: ce qui paroit le moins en lui c'est son ame, elle n'agit point, elle ne s'exerce point, elle se repose. It is as true of him, though we elected him [to the Apostles], as of the Inspector General of Police who will bore me tonight at dinner & whom we should never have dreamt of electing.

By the same post, I had a letter from the Goth. He is the one person to fall back upon. 'Strache was going to live in a cottage with Keynes, his brother & young Trinity.[1] I apprehend scandal. The Congolese contagion seems to spread in Cambridge not but what these young fellows are all humbugs'. He stands, doesn't he?

Yr
L.

To Lytton Strachey

Dec 12, 1906.   Jaffna

I have just got your letter.[2] I knew nothing before. The last I had heard was from Turner that he had seen him & he was recovering. I am overwhelmed, crushed. If I only had a soul to whom I could speak a word. It was only a week or two ago that I wrote to you what we had so often written & said, that he was an anchor. He was above everyone in his nobility. God! what an accursed thing life is, great stretches of dull insensibility & then these unbearable bitternesses. If I could only see you & talk to you!

Yr
L.

To Saxon Sydney-Turner

Jaffna
Ceylon

Dec 17, 1906

I did not write to you last mail when I got the news from the Strache & your line from Denmark. What can we say? Life can become no blacker than it is now.

I should like nothing better than his Milton.[3] Will you thank them

1. The three and Harry Norton (young Trinity) spent ten days together in a cottage near Inverness.
2. Strachey's letter began: "I can only hope that you may know the dreadful thing that has happened, from other letters or papers, for I feel that to break it to you is almost beyond my force. You must be prepared for something terrible. You will never see the Goth again. He died yesterday."
3. VS had asked Sydney-Turner to choose one of Thoby's books for LW.

for me? I wrote to Adrian when I got the Strache's letter, I don't know what.

Yr
L.

To Lytton Strachey

Dec 17, 1906

Jaffna,
Ceylon.

Yes, I half expected this news, but there is nothing that one can say about it.[1]

After all now nothing can be said. I had a letter from Turner today, & I read what Lamb says in the *C[ambridge] R[eview]*. Even Turner hurt me a little. If I could only see you & speak to you. I am ill with fever & I don't quite know what. I work & play golf with these ghosts but I seem to see & hear the Goth all day. It is appalling to think that it is only death that makes it altogether clear what he was to us.

Do you feel that now we have grown irreparably old? In a few days we have left the last shred of our youth centuries behind. And Bell? & Vanessa? I am too weary to mind the mockery of it all.

Did I tell you that only the other day I heard that [Rokeby] Law had died of typhoid too?

Write to me, whatever else you do.

Yr
L.

To Clive Bell

Dec 30, 1906

Jaffna,
Ceylon.

My dear Bell,

I have just heard from the Strache & Turner of your engagement & I send you many congratulations, & through you to Miss Stephen.

The news of the Goth's death was terrible to me. I scarcely knew that he was ill, before it came to me. It is difficult & at the same time

1. Vanessa Stephen had agreed to marry Clive Bell.

terribly easy to realize at this distance; the blow I mean is if anything greater but one will only fully realize the loss when one returns.

Yours
L. S. Woolf

To Lytton Strachey

Feb 10, 1907

Jaffna
Ceylon.

It was curious that I came in on Thursday evening rather aching from having been about 5 hours at a stretch in the saddle mostly under a blazing sun—when I found your letter with the first words almost 'I suppose you ride horses. Isn't it heavenly?' But it is really heavenly: especially, as I now sometimes can, to get away from Jaffna & everyone & ride all day from place to place. One begins to like the jogging along the hard straight glaring roads: the heat, the interminable barren stupid plains make it impossible for one to think; it is simply stupor. And now & again one comes to a great level stretch of coarse grass or sand & one can (& I do though one oughtn't) let the horse go like a maniac for a mile. I have a curious horse: he is an Arab or what they call an Arab one here which means that there is a tiny streak of Arab in him. Still he looks like one & at the back of his head the blood of his great-great-great-great-great-grandfathers still works. For he hates roads or any enclosed space & is always lazy on or in them, but as soon as he gets into an open space & especially on sand, he becomes mad, sweats with excitement & if one allow him puts up his head & stretches out his tail & tears away as hard as he can go. It is then that it is heavenly; it is better I think as a pleasure than copulation.

Your
L.

To Lytton Strachey

March 3, 1907

Jaffna

The invariable thing is that I cannot write because of work, & when that is the case, even if I could, it would only be about work.

You rather astonished me about the suffragists.[1] I don't think it really matters a damn whether they have votes or not, but I rather hate banners & processions & things. More women are fools, I believe, than men but there are so many men that are fools that I cannot see any harm in giving women votes if they want them. Is it Ceylon, or is it the Liberal Government but I am beginning to disbelieve in democracy. I should have been a liberal in 1840, now I think I am a Brahman. We are all doomed, I imagine; here we certainly are & therefore—for it can only be this enlarged—in India. You cannot imagine the fatuity of it in Jaffna. Theoretically everyone is told that he is equal with everyone else, while practically we try to be paternal, despotic, to be what we were & refused to remain 50 years ago. Of course when you get out into the jungle & the villages it is different; you are still absolute, the villager still comes to you to settle his disputes & help him when his crop fails & your own word is law. But the people are all coming into the towns & in the towns, it is becoming to my mind hell. All the old customs & manners are going, everyone is educated with the worst possible form of education the world has ever produced. The boys are taught to hate us not because we treat them as inferiors, but because we treat them as inferiors & tell them that they are their own equals.

I shall continue this next week. I must go now. There is only one thing, I believe, to save us & here no one cares really a damn about it.

Your
L.

To Saxon Sydney-Turner

March 10, 1907   Jaffna

I enclose a leaf of Jaffna tobacco. It is to be smoked in a pipe & is supposed to be exceptionally strong. I doubt if it equals our red Virginia.

My only news is that I had to shoot my dog yesterday & that I had to be present at an execution on Friday. It was really more unpleasant

---

1. Strachey had described his sister Philippa's role in organizing what was to be the first mass demonstration for woman suffrage. Flora Woolf wrote at the same time to say she and her sisters planned to attend the rally.

shooting the dog than hanging the man. The worst part is the preliminaries in the gallows, the fixing of the noose, the priest, the apparently interminable wait of three minutes until the exact moment 8 o'clock comes. The man himself did not care at all. He walked up the scaffold smiling. I heard the priest say to him on the scaffold, when he was waiting with the handkerchief over his face & the noose round his neck, உனக்கு பயமா 'Are you frightened?' & the man answered in the most casual of tones இல்லை 'Not a bit'.

Yr
L.

To Lytton Strachey

March 24, 1907   Jaffna

. . . By a series of accidents the Assistant Agency at Mannar became vacant. Government wired to the GA telling him to send me & actually appointed me to act as Assistant Agent. It was where I acted before for a month but it is almost certain that this time I should have remained there. There are no white people there & it is nearly all jungle, but I should have liked it above everything. Besides it is practically unheard of for anyone to get a district after only 2¼ years out here. When the wire came, the GA was away. I could have gone at once, but knowing that he would not like me to go, I waited for his permission. I have described him to you: he has been very nice to me, but is a master of intrigue & has no heart at all. I foresaw the whole thing, but I seemed to be fascinated by wanting to see how he would contort & manage it. *He* wanted me above all things to stay here, because I do much more work for him than he could get most Office Assistants to do. But of course he could not 'stand in the way of my career'. His line was that I was too young & that I should learn so much more by serving another year as Office Assistant. I was determined—partly because he had really been nice to me, I have almost lived in his house for a year—not to go without his full consent, but of course I checkmated that argument. I put him in such a position that I was practically bound to go or he would have practically to go back on his word. I went to bed on Thursday wondering how he would manage it but certain that he would prevent me going. He took his own way, quite wonderfully for it showed that he had grasped my position absolutely. It would take too long to explain the minutiae of his method. But the end was that he wired to Govt asking to be allowed to send Leak (the man who is theoretically my senior & superior here) instead of me *for the present* as it would be more convenient. What showed me that he had so completely grasped my position was that when he gave me the telegram he said 'Of course if you prefer it I will tear this up now & you can go off tonight'. At any rate the wire went & Leak is to go to Mannar. . . .

So I suppose I shall have another year at least of this accursed place.

You see the state of my mind. I wonder if this letter will amuse you or only bore you. Sometimes I wonder if it is all only a contortion of my brain.

I believe but am not certain that I have won about £100 in a sweep-stake.[1] If it's true I shall try to get leave & come home for three months before the end of the year.

Your
L.

To Lytton Strachey

April 28, 1907

Jaffna
Ceylon.

. . . I don't know when I last wrote to you. I went to Colombo last week to be examined in Tamil & the heat & the 26 hours train journey in 3 days nearly killed me. The week before the Governor came here. I charmed Lady Blake (who is really the Governor) by telling her about temples & things so that I had to dine there on execrable food & be bored for hours by talking to her. She is clever, foolish, mad & almost the ugliest woman I have seen. He is absolutely crass.

I never continued my lecture letter & today my head is whirring with slight fever. Since I wrote that I have for the first time read *The Competition Wallah*.[2] It is extraordinary; it might be the Northern Province in 1907 instead of Bengal in the sixties. Of course I agree we must now go the whole hog, we have gone too far to give up liberalism & we must put everything on the gamble: but it is almost as to [?one]

1. LW was a petty gambler, and his Ceylon account books record winnings from bridge, wagers and sweepstakes. It turned out that on this occasion he won only £17; the following year he won £690 in the Calcutta Turf Club Melbourne Cup sweepstakes.
2. A book published in 1868, by Sir George Otto Trevelyan. The term competition wallah is an Anglo-Indian colloquialism referring to persons admitted to the Indian Civil Service by competitive examination rather than through family or political connections.

against us. It can only succeed if the natives believe in us, & they don't. There was a sensational murder trial in Colombo last week. A fairly high caste Sinhalese got two men to shoot his cousin. The police tracked it all out wonderfully & the evidence was very strong. The murderer took poison in prison & died during the trial. After 100 years of our rule, there is scarcely a native in Jaffna who does not believe that Kotalawala was poisoned in prison by the orders of the Governor in order to get him out of the way. They don't understand & they don't believe in our methods.

[Unsigned]

To Lytton Strachey

May 19, 1907   Jaffna

My last letter stopped in the middle & I believe I sent it off just as it was. This will end at the beginning, it is only to tell you I am alive. . . .

Among other things I have been in love lately.[1] I believe really I am mad. It was, I think, pretty degraded for you to be in love with S.[2] But that is nothing to this. The only thing is that I am mad enough to be able to go on as if I weren't, as if nothing happened or existed. In another week I shall, I think, be petrified completely. It is none the less unpleasant & filthy. I am beginning to think it is always degraded being in love: after all 99/100ths of it is always the desire to copulate, otherwise it is only the shadow of itself, & a particular desire to copulate seems to me no less degraded than a general. One day I shall fall in love with a prostitute, I shan't marry her as I believe you once said I would when we were to meet Turner as the billiard marker, but my career will then be complete. Turner I imagine is very far from the billiard marker stage now.

Your
L.

1. With "Gwen," see *Growing*. She indirectly reentered LW's life in 1943 (see p. 345).
2. Even Strachey was uncertain whether the reference was to J.T. Sheppard or Bernard Swithinbank (1884–1958), a Balliol undergraduate to whom Strachey was much attracted at this time.

To Lytton Strachey

June 3rd 1907   Jaffna

I have not heard from you for some weeks but I suppose it is all right.
I may however see you soon. I think H.E. the Governor may dismiss
me. I am expecting the blow to fall some day this week. Really if it
were to happen, I should pack my boxes very readily. The people of
Jaffna have sent a memorial to H.E. against me & I have had to report
on it. Or rather 'the Jaffna Association' sent it, which consists of demi-
Europeanized lawyers & schoolmasters who are trying to ape the associations & agitations in India. They don't like the 'strong measures'
of Price & myself, & so of course they take the paying line that we
are anti-native. In my case they have pitched on things which are of
course not anti-native but in the main true. They are absolutely silly
& ludicrous but just what Blake (the Governor) will not understand
& will be furious over (he is quite hopeless, poor man). E.g. I don't
allow people to spit in the Kachcheri & made a rule to that effect. One
day a clerk spat; I ordered him to clean the spot; he refused, but, when
he saw I meant it, did it. Of course I knew he was of a caste to hate
doing it, but he was also a person who wanted a lesson given to him.
There are other things like that. I expect a row.

                                                    Yr
                                                    L.

To Lytton Strachey

                                                    Jaffna,
June 30, 1907   Ceylon.

. . . I have to go out on circuit tomorrow for I really do not know how
long. Apparently cholera has broken out about 20 miles from here in
the North of the peninsula. The Provincial Surgeon is not absolutely
sure that it is cholera but he is treating it as the true Asiatic & there is a
camp & everything. I am going out there tomorrow to see that everything is all right. It means rather a rush of things to do the day before. I
shall have to spend the rest of the day in reading a pleasant book on the
treatment of Cholera in Indian Cantonments. It is a dog's life to be a
Government Servant; nothing is your own neither your house nor your
time nor your mind nor your body nor your soul. What with trains &
the accursed telegraph it is all servant now & no government.

                                                    Yr
                                                    L.

To Lytton Strachey

Jaffna
Ceylon

I have already written in two letters that iced champagne, iced beer,
& a native judge last night, & a more than ordinarily furious heat
today have reduced me to impotency.

There are only two things that interest me at the present moment:
women (not from the point of view of whores for I happened to pass
a man's house at 11 o'clock the other night & went in to see him as I
saw he was still up. He asked me what people do not consider a curious
question in this godforsaken country 'Would you like a woman?' At
the moment I really did not know & did not care; but I went into the
room he told me & there saw a half naked woman sitting on a bed.
But I was too utterly bored really to feel even the mild disgust which
was my only feeling (if there was any). I just sat down on a chair
dumb with dejection & finally, without doing or saying anything, gave
her all the money I had on me & fled.) & Forster. My brother sent me
The Longest Journey. Don't you think it is an astonishing & irritating
production? What a success he will be! For people will think it all so
clever. I thought on every other page that he was really going to bring
something off, but it all fades away into dim humour & the dimmer
ghosts of unrealities. It might have been so magnificent & is a mere
formless meandering. The fact is I don't think he knows what reality
is, & as for experience the poor man does not realize that practically
it does not exist. Still his mind interests me, its curious way of touching
on things in the rather precise & charming way in which his hands (I
remember) used to touch things vaguely.[1]

This too is a loathesome letter.

Yr.
L.

---

1. Strachey responded: "Your superb letter on Forster and Women came to me here the
other day, and cheered me up. You are the only person to talk to, and one talks to everyone
but you. When you said that Forster doesn't realize that there's practically no such thing
as experience, I leapt for joy—and then subsided—for what's the good when you're not
there to see it?"

To Lytton Strachey

August 25th 1907   Kandy

Address letters to me to Kandy in future. I have been moved here, at
a moment's notice as Office Assistant.[1] I arrived last Monday. This is
the stream of life compared to the stagnant pond of Jaffna. Governors
& Colonial Secretaries & innumerable planters; also an interminable
succession of dinners & dances. For five days I have walked a wondering ghost among it all. A seal of silence has fallen on my lips & I
am unable to talk a word to a soul. I went for a picnic today, I sat in
a carriage next to & walked with a female for two hours without
uttering a word.

There is a great deal of work here & I can write no more.

I wish I could talk to you for 5 minutes.

                                                    Yr
                                                    L.[2]

To Lytton Strachey

                                                    Urugala,
Sept 15, 1907   Ceylon

I rode up here yesterday from Kandy & unfortunately I have to go
back again this afternoon. One might I think be happy in a place like
this for awhile. It is beautiful, right up in the hills & at present untouched by the planter & civilization. It is extraordinary dealing with
the Sinhalese after the demiEuropeanized ill-mannered Jaffna Tamil.
I arrived here after dark in a slight thunderstorm after riding 24 miles,
but the headmen & villagers met me in procession ½ a mile from the
village & brought me in with tom-toms & dancers. Then I had to stand
in the rain outside for ten minutes while each member of the crowd
came & prostrated himself or herself & touched the ground with his
forehead. I believe it is the only way in the East for each nation to be

1. On returning from home leave John Lewis, the former Government Agent in Jaffna, was
placed in charge of the Central Province at Kandy and immediately arranged to have LW
promoted and transferred there as Office Assistant.
2. "It all seems very mysterious," Strachey answered, "as the last I heard from you was
that you would probably shortly become absolute Lord of ten million blacks in the middle
of a desert. Is it better to be an office assistant in Kandy than an absolute Lord in—
Baticaloa?"

kept as it was before Adam; the Tamil will only shake you by the hand & practically never salaams, & is about the most ill-mannered man you could meet; the real Kandyan grovels on the ground & touches your boots but has remained a gentleman.

I have just read [Francis Cornford's] *Thucydides Mythistoricus*. It seems to me rather good, except that as a book it has the almost universal fault of not ending.

When are you going to do something? I have hopes whenever I do not get a letter for several weeks that you have shut yourself up to write a masterpiece & have no time to write letters. I expect however that when I get back to Kandy this time & find, as I hope, your letter, I shall be disappointed again. The time is approaching, I believe, when you must write or forever hold your peace. Or at any rate even if you do break out in your old age, it is not the same. You may write a masterpiece when you are forty but I insist upon your writing one also before you are thirty. When I unpacked my books in Kandy I read your poems in *Euphrosyne*. They are crude enough in places & it is curious how one sees now the faults which one never saw 3 years ago, but they have youth in them which is the great thing. You can write a masterpiece now with the youth in it; after 30 it will have the crusted settled certainty of middle age.

Yr
L.

To Lytton Strachey

Sept 29, 1907   Kandy

. . . I read *Madame Bovary* again as I went up to Hatton in the train last week to look after cattle disease. As I read it again, it seemed to me the saddest & most beautiful book I had ever read. Surely it is the beginning & end of realism. Was it he who discovered what no one seems to have noticed before the 19th Century, the futility & sordidness of actual existence? They never really saw it before, even *Candide*, for they always believed in some absurd fetish of the nobility of man. One can't believe in anything except beauty after reading Flaubert. Read the paragraph beginning 'Dans l'après midi, quelquefois, une tête d'homme apparaissait derrière les vitres de la salle. . . .' (page 70 in my copy); but the astonishing thing is that one really ought to have read straight through from the beginning to get the full effect of it. I had in this case & as paragraph succeeded paragraph & the inevitable sentences rolled out, it was overwhelming. One day I shall sit down & read straight on to the end: I don't think one would ever reach the end, I think one might die with Emma at

Il souffla bien fort ce jour-là

Et le jupon court s'envola.

I saw a most appalling spectacle the other day. I had to go (as Fiscal) to see four men hanged one morning. They were hanged two by two. I have a strong stomach but at best it is a horrible performance. I go to the cells & read over the warrant of execution & ask them whether they have anything to say. They nearly always say no. Then they are led out clothed in white, with curious white hats on their heads which at the last moment are drawn down to hide their faces. They are led up on to the scaffold & the ropes are placed round their necks. I have (in Kandy) to stand on a sort of verandah where I can actually see the man hanged. The signal has to be given by me. The first two were hanged all right but they gave one of the second too big a drop or something went wrong. The man's head was practically torn from his body & there was a great jet of blood which went up about 3 or 4 feet high, covering the gallows & priest who stands praying on the steps. The curious thing was that this man as he went to the gallows seemed to feel the rope round his neck: he kept twitching his head over into the exact position they hang in after death. Usually they are quite unmoved. One man kept on repeating two words of a Sinhalese prayer (I think) over & over again all the way to the gallows & even as he stood with the rope round his neck waiting for the drop.

I don't know why I have written all this to you except that whenever I stand waiting for the moment to give the signal, you & Turner & the room at Trinity come to my mind & the discussion in which Turner enraged us so by saying that he would not turn his head if anyone said there was a heap of corpses in the corner by the gyproom [college servants' pantry]. I don't think I should any more.

Yr

L.[1]

1. "I now find it very difficult," Strachey replied, "to taste real life in fiction. . . . I want beauty—but absolute Beauty—reigning supreme in Cythera." Lamenting his loveless life, he added, "Wouldn't you love anyone who loved you? . . . But it all works round to a horrid circle—because who's to begin?"

To Lytton Strachey

Your last letter really rather amused me though it gave me the impression of rather abysmal depression. No, I'm all for reality, even in novels, even to hangings & whores. I don't believe in L'Ile de Cythère; I believe perhaps in Le Grand Gilles.[1] But after all of course we can never disagree about that; we settled it all a hundred years ago—that after all it's only the reality which matters, though I may like it for the moment rather violent upon the earth & you in the serenity of Olympus.

One thing you must understand & that is that I am done for as regards England. I shall live & die in these appalling countries now. If I come back for good now I should do nothing but loaf until I died of starvation. What else could I do? And as for happiness—I don't believe in being happy even in England.

What you said about the eternal contortion also amused me, because it so happens that I am really in love with someone who is in love with me. It is not however pleasant because it is pretty degrading, I suppose, to be in love with practically a schoolgirl.[2] Also the complications are appalling when one has, as they say, to 'behave like a gentleman', when one does not intend to marry & when one lives in a country where everyone knows everything which everyone else does, says or thinks. Sometimes I think really I am only in love with silly intrigue & controlling a situation, & sometimes merely with two big cow eyes which could never understand anything which one said & look as if they understood everything that has ever been, is or will be. God, the futility & mania of existence sickens me. I went down to Colombo last week for an official dance at Queen's House for the King's birthday. But I can't tell you the story it is too futile. Good night.

L.

1. A reference to another of Watteau's paintings, of "Gilles," a tender-hearted man who never attained satisfaction.
2. "Rachel Robinson" in *Growing*; her real surname was Jowitt.

8 Dec 1907   Kandy

So the Society may end in the police court, a fitting end, don't you
think? . . .[1] Personally I should resign & change my name & vanish
into Italy or Sicily. If only in real life one could. Do you think it
possible? To glide silently out of even one's own life second class on
a Japanese boat: I have it all mapped out. It is the only thing; it would
be like a re-incarnation, being born again into the world with all one's
knowledge, all one's experience & all one's memories. One could not,
I imagine, help being supreme; one could burst forth then unhampered
& uncontrolled.

I find I become hopelessly emmeshed in my surroundings, but what
else can one do? I work, play tennis, then bridge & billiards at the
club & the interminable gossip & filth. I haven't read a book for two
months. It all seems to me to matter nothing at all; so much so that
I shall never, as you suggest, take the boat to England. I suppose poor
old Morocco & your grandmother do not exist anymore; but there is
more chance of my taking it to Sicily.

I played golf this morning with a descendant (how he can be I do
not know) of Nelson: he is positively the most utter worm that has
ever been born. He was suffering from diarrhoea of mind body & soul.
Is everyone now either a degenerate or a cow?

                                        Yr
                                        L.

2 Feb. 1908   Kandy

My dear Turner, I don't know how many months it is since I have
written to you. I feel that the stagnation of absence is creeping over
me. I scarcely write to anyone & even the Strache's letters are becoming
rare. Circumstances appear to me in the long run to be overwhelm-

1. In a previous letter, Strachey had written: "He [Hobhouse] went to America in the
summer—to learn 'business methods', and came back the other day. On his return his
mother awaited him with an opened letter—'Explain this'! He looked, and it was from
Greenwood, rank with sodomy. . . . She stormed and raved, and . . . wound up by accusing
the Society, if you please, of being a hotbed of unnatural vice."

ing, eventually it is impossible to keep one's head above them.

My sister [Bella] arrived here last Monday & I brought her up from Colombo on Wednesday. She stays for 3 or 4 months.

Yesterday the Empress Eugénie came to Kandy & as I was the only official here I had to receive her at the station in pomp.[1] It was most unpleasant as I could not hear a word of what she said to me. One of the curses of this place is that distinguished visitors make one's life a burden to one.

Yr

L.

To Lytton Strachey

8.4.08   Kandy

It seems months since you wrote & really I don't know when I did, or whether I shall ever again. And after all why should we—except that from Turner came the sestina written for your birthday. Wonderful don't you think? It made me answer it but I have not the energy to copy it or even finish it.

And isn't this an answer? There is a new cadet here under me; he is called Perks & was sent here because the other man became engaged to an emaciated & pasty faced girl & the grandmaternal Government of this Colony always banishes a cadet from a station if he becomes engaged to any female in it. According to the Ceylon Govt you may copulate but you must not marry or become engaged. Well Perks (!) is a nice quiet young man who has just come out. He treats me in an absolutely filial manner & I feel 9999 & act the father & guide to him.[2]

Otherwise, I live a life of domesticity with my sister when she is

1. Marie-Eugénie-Ignace-Augustine de Montijo (1826–1920), wife of Napoleon III, had fled to Britain after the collapse of the Third Empire in 1870. She enjoyed traveling, and on this occasion was, at the direction of Edward VII, given all official courtesies. Of his being presented to her, LW commented in *Growing*: "I felt vaguely that I ought to bow and kiss her hand, but that was beyond me, and instead we shook hands." Two years later, when German Crown Prince Wilhelm visited Ceylon to hunt game, Marie Woolf wrote, "You are young to be very grand, Len; the German Crown Prince's company is no joke & ought to make you sit up straight. But you'd rather sit a little less straight, I know."
2. Either the place or the climate was too much for the unfortunate Perks, who wasted away and died the following year. LW contributed to the purchase of a memorial stone.

here & work & am ill. Practically I do little else but work; I am emmeshed & immersed in it so much so that sometimes I think I shall just bury myself in it & never come back again. If I did & this were not a miserable little Crown Colony & if there were not just the one little thing in me which I feel is wanting to make me decide to do it & if I didn't die or marry a prostitute, why I suppose then I should become Colonial Secretary of some wonderful phantasmagorical British Utopia with a KCMG.

Shall I?

Did I tell you of my tea with the Empress Eugénie & her curious thin little jokes?

I believe I should have ended this letter with four pages but I am called away & if I don't put it in an envelope I know I shan't post it.

Your
L.

To Lytton Strachey

2nd October 1908

Hambantota
Ceylon

. . . The scene has changed here too & one changes inside too.[1] After all I am today & to be impinged upon by innumerable todays, the change is inevitable. I have no connection with yesterday: I do not recognize it nor myself in it. I am of & in today moulded & marked by innumerable things which have never touched you &, when I come back & find you all the same, someone will say quite truly, as Moore once said of Sanger or Crompton or someone who had already reached the twilight, 'Really they seem to be interested in none of these things.'[2]

And I suppose I am happy too, happier I expect as far as quantity goes than you. I work, God, how I work. I have reduced it to a method & exalted it to a mania. In Kandy I worked about 10 hours a day & played in tennis tournaments & went to intolerably dull dinners &

1. The change at home, as reported by Strachey, was that Keynes was leaving the India Office and had fallen in love with Duncan Grant. In Ceylon, LW had so impressed Sir Hugh Clifford, Colonial Secretary and Acting Governor, that he was again promoted, and put in charge of the Hambantota District.
2. This prompted Strachey to reply, ". . . As for what you say about changes of course I don't believe it, and nor do you. If you came back tomorrow you would be simply what [you]'ve always been—a person of sense."

duller dances & played bridge & drank & became the bosom friend of planters. So as a reward a month ago they sent me here as Assistant Government Agent. A 'reward' because it is what they call 'a change'. I am on my own in my district which is about 1000 sq miles with 100 000 people in it & I am supposed to be very 'young' to have got it. So I live at the Residency Hambantota. There are no Europeans in Hambantota itself at all except a white woman who was I believe a lodginghouse keeper's daughter & has married a rather low caste Sinhalese engineer who went to the Isle of Man & met her there & she thought he was an Indian prince & so married him. I have not yet seen her. O there is also an ex Boer prisoner who refuses to take an oath of allegiance to the King's successors though he is willing to take it to the King, for as he very truly remarks 'I know what sort of a king he is but I don't know what sort of successors they will be'. So the British Government refuse to allow him to go back & he lives here on 3d a day as a Forest Ranger in a Game Sanctuary under me. I think he will die very soon of malaria & curry & rice. 26 miles away on one side are two Europeans, a judge & a Supt of Police & 20 miles away on the other is another, an Irrigation Engineer. There is also another Irrigation Engineer who suffers from chronic indigestion & fever 20 miles away in the jungle, I dont quite know where.

But the house, really it is worth coming to Ceylon to live in it. It must orginally have been built by the Dutch with walls of astonishing thickness & an enormously broad verandah & vast high rooms. It stands on a promontory right away from the town & right over the sea. Day & night you hear the sea thundering away almost at the gates of the compound, which is vast with nothing in it but sand & 3 stunted trees & is surrounded by a wall which the wind which blows here has increasingly blown into ruins.

I have to stop now: perhaps by next mail the spirit will descend upon me again.

From Turner I now & then got almost charming letters. He seems to me to be mellowing but I never write to him.

Your

L.

23 Oct 1908   Wiraketiya

It is curious that whenever I take a piece of paper to write to Turner it always ends—or nearly always—in my writing to you.

I am what is called on circuit—travelling round the district at a leisurely 10 miles a day hearing complaints & disputes & settling the hundreds of odd matters which we are supposed to settle. It is rather a charming mode of living. For ten days at any rate practically nothing can touch me. The runners who carry the post usually go wrong, they are frightened by elephants or the rivers rise in the night & for all I know England may be in the hands of the Germans & a German Governor 'administering' in Colombo. I have a beautiful black horse & ride from stage to stage with one bullock cart trailing on ahead & another trailing on behind with clothes & saucepans beds & tables & I sleep in old Buddhist temples or tents or dingy dirty irrigation bungalows. I am in a dirty irrigation bungalow now in a charming village by the side of a great tank [reservoir]. One could grow into a peaceful old man in a week here among the coconut palms & the enormous trees. Yesterday evening one of the runners did turn up by chance & he brought your letter & one from Turner—yours with the dim recollection of the Ouse from a railway carriage window, & Swithin[bank] & Moore.[1] I wonder if I could speak to Moore now; I could if I had him here, but nose to nose as you used to say in his stuffy room on a sofa I know I should collapse utterly.

I am going to stop now to write to Turner though I know I shall not. I don't know why because I could & want to, but I hate the physical effort in this heat. Really Turner is coming out; he said something in his last letter which positively made me laugh out, but I don't know what it was.

                                                          Yr
                                                          LSW

1. Strachey also wrote that Clive, Vanessa and Virginia had gone to Italy together and added: "Don't you think it's the wildest romance? That that little canary-coloured creature we knew in [Trinity] New Court should have achieved that?—The two most beautiful and wittiest women in England!"

I detest Keynes don't you?[1] Looking back on him from 4 years, I see he is fundamentally evil if ever anyone was. God! fancy electing him & not the Goth. We shall never be able to answer for not electing the Goth. It is the one thing which I think is unpardonable.

Perhaps you had better send Turner this letter as mine to him.

L.

To Saxon Sydney-Turner

28.10.08   Kirama

I feel desolate & the horror of desolation &, like almost every other feeling, it undoubtedly comes from my stomach. I am doing a 14 days circuit in my district & after 8 days have reached this open bungalow at the foot of the hills. Really I suppose it is a delightful place surrounded by forest, scarcely touched by civilization. It is quite cool as I watch the mist come rolling down the hills across the tree tops. Yesterday morning I should have enjoyed it but tonight I am broken physically & mentally. I started to ride here at 4 yesterday afternoon in pelting rain. Some of the foul food which one is obliged to eat travelling like this from day to day in wilderness & jungles must have poisoned me or the cold rain perhaps did it, but I was suddenly smitten. I had to wade through paddy fields & streams to inspect a channel, being violently sick every 100 yards & I rode the last four miles into Kirama in the darkness the rain streaming down my back & out of my boots, vomiting over my horse's head every 5 minutes. The roof leaked, the wind blew through the wall-less Gansabhawa bungalow & I was sick most of the night. I sent a messenger 10 miles to get castor oil which arrived at 5 in the morning & now am just recovering.

I wonder if the stool in Somerset House is preferable. I am 41 miles from Hambantota. Before me is a stream which may turn into a torrent at any moment & cut me off for days. The roads are just passable for a horse but it will take me 5 days to do the 41 miles. Some of the inhabitants of this place are scarcely human. Every male be-

1. The comment was intended to soothe Strachey, who was devastated by having lost Duncan Grant to Keynes.

tween the ages of 18 & 55 in Ceylon is liable to a road tax of rs 1.50; if he does not pay by March 31st he is liable to a fine of rs 10 or in default a month's imprisonment. At every place I stop, crowds of these defaulters are brought up to me by the headmen for trial & sentence. They bring down to me wild savages from the hills, spectacles incredible to anyone who has not seen them. Naked except for a foul rag round their loins, limbs which are mere bones, stomachs distended with enormously enlarged spleens, their features eaten away by & their skin covered with sores from one of the most loathesome of existing diseases called parangi, or else wild apelike creatures with masses of tangled hair falling over their shoulders their black bodies covered with white scales of parangi scab hobbling along on legs enormous from elephantitis.

A pleasant letter this! I meant to send you some verse I wrote some months ago but it is locked away in my writing table at Hambantota so you must take this instead.

I thought of writing something about the Goth as you suggest. It ought to be done but the difficulties are immense. Perhaps I'll really try one day. I was reading his letters the other day. They make one weep with bitterness. He is complete in them for anyone who knew him, but I wonder whether they would convey anything to anyone who did not: for after all everything was in his character. Do you want me to send them? I don't like really parting with them; they must be copied & returned.

Yr
L.

To Lytton Strachey

25 November 1908   Hambantota

It is my birthday today. I have been reading Forster's last book [*A Room with a View*] & as last year, at about the same time, it has just stirred the fringe of my brain. It is almost a repetition of last year for do you remember the hanging? This time it came also upon a similar piece of 'reality'.

As I suppose you know I am everything here: policeman, magistrate, judge, & publican. I was just going to begin breakfast when a message came that a murder had been committed at a place with the wonderful name Tissamaharama. It is a wonderful place which one gets to through 20 miles of uninhabited jungle, & after 20 miles of nothing but trees & tangle you suddenly shoot out of it into a great plain of paddy fields & coconuts & dagobas & irrigation channels & tanks & then as suddenly on the other side into the jungle again. The orders of Government are that when murder is reported you go straight to the spot & look at the body & catch the murderer & take down the interminable evidence. So I got into an absurd Irish car[1] which I possess & drove straight off there. A man had kicked the woman with whom he lived to death because she had not got his dinner ready. They took me into the room of the hut where she was lying dead, & they stripped her naked for me to examine the wounds. Most women naked when alive are extraordinarily ugly, but dead they are repulsive & the most repulsive thing is the way the toes seem to stick up so straight & stark & dominate the room. But the most abominable thing was the smell. One gets accustomed to the smell of corruption of dead things here where the cattle are always dying of thirst & starvation & lie on the roadsides decaying: but I had no idea before that the smell of a decomposing human being is so infinitely fouler than anything else. Is that reality according to Forster? I believe last year I thought that he thought it is. But this book which appears to me to really rather good & sometimes thoroughly amusing is absolutely muddled, isn't it?

Isn't it dominated by a spectral Moore? He still seems to think that death is real & sightseeing unreal; I think I shall have to write to him & explain once more that it doesn't exist, that after all the smell of cheese is as real as the smell of a corpse. There is a curious twilight & pseudo mystery over his books which irritate me into this: to be petty & to like bad things may be bad but he always seems to hint mysteriously that they are unreal.

Yr

L.

1. A low-slung, open horse-drawn cart.

18.12.08

My dearest Len,
   . . . Your generosity exceeds all bounds; you are a dear, & we don't know how to thank you.[1] *It seems brutal to take so much from you— that is the only thing. Your splendid present comes as a 'boon and blessing' just now, for I have many bills, & Xmas presents to buy, & also I covet Schumann's & Grieg's songs & see visions of possessing them now.*
   . . . Your suffrage sentiments are horrible: Bella tells me she dealt with them, so I'll let you off this week & only be polite. The vote will be won by the time you come home, otherwise you would be decoyed to a "meetin' ". We went to one at the Queen's Hall last night & took Mr. Hamer, late editor of Little Folks.[2] *He was very pleased with it. Herbert also went—it was a great triumph, as he is violently anti— and thought the speeches excellent. . . .*

Your loving
Flora

To G. E. Moore

Hambantota
Ceylon

4 Jan 1909

Dear Moore
   I don't think you realize how pleased I was to get your letter & paper. Please send me the one of 1906.[3] I have not written to you because I didn't know whether you would like it & because I too really hate writing almost any letter. I read your paper but to tell the actual

---

1. From his £690 sweepstakes winning, LW sent £150 to Marie and £100 to Herbert. Marie had already written: "It is a pity the pleasure was denied you of being eye witness to the sensation your letter . . . created in the family circle."
2. A children's magazine to which Bella had been a regular contributor.
3. In another characteristic letter, Moore had written: "I don't think you would find me at all altered from what I was. The only difference I notice is that I seem to find it more and more difficult to write anything about philosophy. . . . Sometimes I seem to see how I could do it; very often I feel as if I can't or won't try; and, when I do try, I almost always seem to lose the thread; and there are many other different states of mind, too. . . ." The enclosed paper was "Professor James' 'Pragmatism' "; the 1906 monograph was "The Nature and Reality of Objects of Perception."

truth I was disappointed, disappointed in the way in which most papers disappoint one. I want your opus magnum which will tell me what things are true much more than papers which tell me that Pragmatism, which I don't believe in, is false. Really you must write the opus: isn't it fearfully dangerous not to begin, in the way I mean that the longer you don't, the harder eventually it must be ever to do so.

You say you don't think you have changed at all. I think I must have a good deal. This life here must have an effect on one. I practically do nothing but work & ride & shoot. This sort of work becomes an obsession; I do about 12 hours a day. The district of which I am in charge is about 1000 square miles & one is responsible for nearly everything in it. I mean in keeping order, collecting the revenue & doing innumerable other things with roads & irrigation works & education, besides acting as Police Magistrate & judge in civil cases. One has of course to be continually travelling through the district & there is of course no railway & very often no roads. It is the pleasantest part of the work, the riding from village to village mostly through jungle & the camping. I think really what makes it pleasant is that one has no time to think at all about anything but work & food & facts; one is perpetually doing something. Of course if it weren't for that, one would probably go mad for one is almost perpetually uncomfortable: it is almost always too hot & one rarely feels absolutely well, food is disgusting & there is very little water & what there is is brackish. Also there is no one to talk to at all. The nearest white man to me lives 20 miles away.

Give my love to Ainsworth, I have never written a line to him but, except for one letter in 3 months to Strachey, I don't think I write to anyone now.

Yours affectionately
L. S. Woolf

To Lytton Strachey

[Postmarked 1 February 1909]

Palatupana
Ceylon

I have just received your last letter in a hut in the middle of the jungle.[1] I am on my way to the Game Sanctuary a vast area of forest which

1. The letter, which Strachey subsequently described as "a melodramatic letter on Christmas Day," has not survived, but it evidently raised the question of LW's marrying Virginia Stephen.

the government in its forethought for the villager & as much for the sportsman has 'reserved': no one may shoot in it or live in it & so the buffalo lies down with the elephant & the elephant with the leopard & the leopard with the deer. I trail along with my caravan of carts & mudaliyars [district chiefs] & tents; there are no villages & no people & if I don't go out & shoot something my dinner is sardines & eternal chicken.

You have the atmosphere into which you launch your thunderbolts. It is a fairly simple frame of mind to walk 10 miles with a rifle in your hand & the only thought in your head to shoot a deer. And then you suddenly come with all the violence & the intricacies of feelings which after all perhaps after 4 years I understand. But I don't agree with you. The most wonderful of all would have been to marry Virginia. She is I imagine supreme & then the final solution would have been there, not a rise perhaps above all horrors but certainly not a fall, not a shirking of facts. Of course I suppose it is really impossible for the reason (if for no other) that I cannot place you in it—& that for me makes it impossible or shows only perhaps that everything has gone beyond me—but it certainly would be the only thing. It is undoubtedly the only way to happiness, to anything settled, to anything not these appalling alternations from violent pleasures to the depths of depression. I am sure of it for myself &, as I perpetually now live on the principle that nothing matters, I don't know why the devil I don't. But something or other always saves me just at the last moment from these degradations—their lasciviousness or their ugliness probably— though I believe if I did I should probably be happy. Do you think Virginia would have me? Wire to me if she accepts. I'll take the next boat home; & then when I arrived I should probably come straight to talk with you. You don't know what it is not to have talked to anyone for four years. By the bye one of the saddest things in Moore's letter I thought was this. He said that Ainsworth seemed so happy at being engaged. 'I wished I could be engaged too'. God! I wish I could write like that!

A curious little thing with regard to your previous letter may amuse you. There was one thing in it about D[uncan Grant] which on reading it first actually struck me with a horror. And then I suddenly remembered that a woman had once done it to me & it hadn't struck me as a horror at all. Two things are quite clear from this & one is that what I always say is true, reality is nothing, it is only in writing & imagination that things are wonderful or horrible or supreme, in reality they are sometimes just beautiful, nearly always ugly & always vague & dire.

I wonder if after all Virginia marries Turner.

Your
L.

I never thanked you for the books. I do read on these circuits in the middle of the day & they are a godsend especially as I have just got to the end practically of the last batch I ordered out. I suddenly thought I must now read Maupassant again & when I reread the tale about the child who is pinched on the buttocks by the adulterating captain I thought I was right. I also read [the Earl of Cromer's] *Modern Egypt* & you can deduce my state of mind by the fact that I think it is the greatest book written in the last 25 years. I wish you wouldn't write introductions but when you do you must send them to me.[1] What do you think of this

> *When I am dead & you forget*
>   *My kisses: in the stirring air*
> *Will you not shudder when my touch,*
>   *Grown nothing now, just stirs your hair?*
> *Will you not shudder when you feel*
>   *My arms about you in the mist;*
> *You will not know the dead man's lips*
>   *You will not know that you have kissed*
> *A dead man. Only there may come*
>   *A memory of a foreign land*
> *Of wind & sun & how you lay*
>   *By the salt marshes in the sand*
> *With someone. Some forgotten name*
>   *May murmur in the wind: but I*
> *Amid the havoc of all things*
>   *Know that our bodies never die.*

---

1. Strachey had written an introduction to Elizabeth Inchbold's *A Simple Story* the previous year.

FROM LYTTON STRACHEY

Feb 19th 1909

Your letter has this minute come—with your proposal to Virginia, and I must write a word or two of answer, though the post is all wrong. You are perfectly wonderful, and I want to throw my arms around your neck. Everything you say is so tremendously to the point! Isn't it odd that I've never really been in love with you? And I suppose never shall. You make me smile and shudder—oh! and long for you to be here. It's curious—are you after all happier than I am? In spite of the silence of four years? This is all rubbish, but I'm rather ill and rather excited—by your letter.

The day before yesterday I proposed to Virginia. As I did it, I saw that it would be death if she accepted me, and I managed, of course, to get out of it before the end of the conversation. . . . I think there's no doubt whatever that you ought to marry her. You would be great enough and you'll have the immense advantage of physical desire. . . . If you came and proposed she'd accept. She really would.

Your poem disproves your theory. Imaginations are nothing; facts are all. A penis actually erected—on becoming erect—is cataclysmal. In imagination it's a mere shade. That, in my view, is the point of art, which converts imaginations into actualities. But I'm sleepy and ill, and I've got to write on Swift, Stella, & Vanessa for the Spectator.

> *Your*
> *Lytton*

Friday 20th

I've had an éclaircissement with Virginia. She declared she was not in love with me, and I observed finally that I would not marry her. So things have simply reverted. Perhaps you'd better not mention these matters to Turner, who certainly is not upon the tapis. I told Vanessa to hand on your proposal, so perhaps you are.

> *G L S*[1]

1. LW apparently did not respond. Three months later Strachey continued his effort at matchmaking: ". . . If you come [home], as I think I've mentioned, you could marry Virginia, which would settle nearly every difficulty in the best possible way. Do try it. She's an astounding woman, and I'm the only man in the universe who would have refused her; even I sometimes have my doubts. You might, of course, propose by telegram, and she'ld probably accept. . . ." LW, in an insubstantial note to Strachey in July, still made no comment.

July 27th 09

My dearest Len,

   Your last letter made me very sorry because it was full of loneliness & that's one of the worst complaints to which flesh is the heir to. I was sorrier than ever that I couldn't join you in Hambantota, for I often think how much I should have enjoyed that verandah overlooking the sea (& how much I should have disenjoyed it when you were away!) but for all that you would have had someone to turn to—& that's what you need.[2] You'd better marry as soon as you have got into a class where the Govt. doesn't faint at matrimonial intentions. But I can't think of any girl that would suit you in Ceylon. You need a very special sort of girl—& if you don't find her, you'd better steer clear of matrimony. If you had met Lady Strachey in her young days you ought to have married her—& if her counterpart in youthfulness walks the earth, she's your girl—strong-minded & clever & a sense of humour. If you marry a weak character you'll squash her [indecipherable words]. You must *marry someone who can hold her own with you & yet be good-tempered. Well, I've no more time to continue this highly improving discourse—I can see you smiling with that queer crooked smile of yours & thinking: "What rot—pish!"*

   . . . Women stand to lose so much by marriage nowadays, at least women with brains, that it takes a great deal for them to go in for it. . . . All the sentimental gush over the joys of motherhood & so forth are only true where folk fall in love with head & heart—in nine cases out of ten it's mere animalism—you must *love with your* head *as much as with your heart or you're lost. Am I right? . . .*

Much love from
Bella

21 August 1909

   . . . Your destiny is clearly marked out for you, but will you allow it to work? You must marry Virginia. She's sitting waiting for you, is

2. Bella had returned to London at the conclusion of LW's tour in Kandy.

there any objection? She's the only woman in the world with sufficient brains; it's a miracle that she should exist; but if you're not careful you'll lose the opportunity. At any moment she might go off with heaven knows who—Duncan? Quite possible. She's young, wild, inquisitive, discontented, and longing to be in love. If I were you I should telegraph. But at any rate come and see her before the end of 1910. . . .

Aug. 24th . . . Write to me again for the Lord's sake, and quickly. I want to talk to you far more than to anyone else. If it weren't for the hideous expense I'd start tomorrow for Hambantota. . . .

Your loving
Lytton

Saxon (as he's now called) is I believe at this moment in Bayreuth with Virginia and Adrian. But you're safe so far as he's concerned; only I don't know what charming German Barons may not be there. Telegraph.

To Lytton Strachey

14.9.09   Hambantota

You cannot imagine the effect of your letters in Hambantota. They make me laugh & cry out loud. To imagine that really Sanger & Bob Trevy & MacCarthy & Virginia exist! I suppose they do in some dim existence move vaguely through life. I suppose everything isnt jungle & work. But its damnably difficult to believe it; but then really, when one takes off one's puttees for half a minute in 365 days & takes the pen from behind one's ear & gets down off one's stool or even when one is perched so perpetually upon it, it is so damnably difficult to believe in the reality of anything. Am I absolutely sunk if I dont believe in the reality of George Mallory?[1] I believe in the reality of you & (the reality of the unreality) of Turner, because if I didn't I suppose I should cease to believe in my own—which shows that the Trinity which we havent mentioned for how many thousand years still exists—& lapse into suicide.[2]

Of course I know that the one thing to do would be to marry Virginia.

1. In his previous letter, Strachey had written that he was utterly smitten with Mallory, the famous mountaineer. "His body—vast, pink, unbelievable—is a thing to melt into and die."
2. At Cambridge, LW, Strachey and Sydney-Turner called themselves "the Trinity of Trinity."

149

I am only frightened that when I come back in Dec 1910 I may. For though when one had & everything was completed & consummated, life would probably at last be supreme; the horrible preliminary complications, the ghastly complications too of virginity & marriage altogether appall me. Really if it were n't for that & for the question of money I actually would telegraph. But I wont &, as you say, she will probably marry a German baron & I, when I'm forty, will marry either a widow (I hope she will be one then) or an exprostitute.

It is only when I get your letters that I even think now of anything. To think of existence at all fills me with horror & sickness: the utter foulness, the stupid blind vindictive foulness of everything & of myself. Undoubtedly if I am ever to be saved, I should telegraph.

You seem to be perpetually unwell. Cannot you go off somewhere for a year until I come back to some perfect climate, I mean like Madeira (is that the place) & sit in a hammock & write & become absolutely well? I am afraid you could never stand Hambantota; it would simply kill you off.

I probably shall not write again until I come back at the end of 1910. If I can only pass a law exam here.

Yr
L.

To Saxon Sydney-Turner

12 June 1910   Hambantota

I really think I have written to you since you make out but at any rate I am sufficiently dim about when.

I applied for leave from 19th Nov. but I have heard that I shall not get it then. 'Exigencies of the Public Service'! The census has to be taken at the beginning of next year & as I am doing the preliminary work they will not let me go until it is over, which is March 1911. However you too have the misfortune to be a 'government servant' so you know that sort of nonsense.

My sister met Lytton some while ago; otherwise I should scarcely know that he still exists.

I have nothing to tell you which would interest you. I have written nothing for years except Administration Reports & the following which will probably tell you more about my 'state of mind' than anything else. I know both are putrid:

To Ponamma+

O Golden Mother, in this embrace of thine
Thy fruit of motherhood is bought & sold:
The cancerous kiss, the ecstacy is mine,
For then thy womb bears gold, Mother of Gold.

+Tamil girl's name meaning 'golden mother.'[1]

To Lytton Strachey[2]

9 Feb 1911   Hambantota

In any case I shall not leave before May 16th. I have half a promise
of leave from May 12th & so I have booked my passage by a boat
leaving on May 16th. But I rather doubt whether I could stop at all
on my way, as my sister is coming with me.[3] What I think I must do
is to go straight back to Putney & after staying there some time I shall
begin to wander. Won't you be back by June? I propose to go to France
to learn to speak French so you had better come & teach me.

I am raging at the moment so you will know why this is as it is. But
I am beyond flux—I really am on a fixed course probably to damnation
or beyond it. I expect you when we meet to pass me by because of it.
George Trevelyan if he still exists is the only person who will understand me.

The *Times* gave me quite a shock the other day to see that A.S.
[Gaye] is going to marry. I suppose he is rolling in money & fat by now.

Yr
L.

1. A second poem and conclusion to this letter have been lost.
2. Writing from his sister Dorothy's house on the French Riviera, Strachey proposed that
LW visit him there "if (as it's rumoured) you're returning this spring." He concluded,
"Letters seem to have lapsed for some time lately. Flux! Flux!"
3. Bella, now settled in Colombo with her husband, Robert Lock, was returning to London
for a brief visit.

11 Jan 1912

My dear Virginia, I must write to you before
I go to bed & can, I think, probably think more calmly.

I have not got any very clear recollection of what I
really said to you this afternoon but I am sure you know
why I came — I dont mean merely that I was in love but
that that together with uncertainty drives one to do these
things. Perhaps I was wrong, for before this week I always
intended not to tell you unless I felt sure that you were
in love & would marry me. I thought then that you liked
me but that was all. I never realised how much I loved
you until we talked about my going back to Ceylon. After
that I could think about nothing else but you. I got into
a state of hopeless uncertainty, whether you loved me or
could ever love me or even like me. God, I hope I shall
never spend such a time again as I spent here until
I telegraphed. Your telegram sent saying, I would speak

TO VIRGINIA STEPHEN

PART THREE

———

LIFE WITH
VIRGINIA

Leonard Woolf landed at Folkestone in June 1911 for a year's leave; his memoirs described the following six months as the most serenely happy of his life. He went to Cambridge, where he dined at Trinity high table and attended a meeting of the Society. He traveled around the country visiting friends and sat on the lawn of a remote Dartmoor cottage watching Strachey write his *Landmarks in French Literature* and Moore his *Ethics*. He stayed with relatives in Denmark and Sweden and in London he reveled in the amazing cultural outburst in painting, music, ballet and theater that marked the last years of the old Europe.

His memoirs did not mention that these months were also a time of considerable torment. He found himself at the critical crossroad of his life. His professional record left no doubt that he would rise to the top of the Colonial Service and crown his career with a knighthood and governorship. Even if such honors meant little to him, he loved Ceylon and was genuinely attracted by the prospect of devoting the rest of his career to the welfare of that country. On the other hand, he realized there might be a possibility of satisfying a deeper longing— for love and marriage with someone he esteemed, Virginia Stephen.

Virginia, Vanessa and Thoby Stephen must have had an irresistible charm and physical attraction. To meet them was evidently to be captivated by them, individually and almost interchangeably. When

Leonard first saw the two sisters, in Thoby's rooms at Trinity in the spring of 1903, he found that "their beauty literally took one's breath away . . . as it does when in a picture gallery you suddenly come face to face with a great Rembrandt or Velasquez." Awesome and beyond reach, they were a vision he had cherished for nearly seven years in the jungles of Ceylon. Vanessa had been lost to Clive Bell, but Virginia, as alluring as ever, was no longer just a vision. Within several weeks of his return he confided to his brother Edgar that he was already thinking of marrying her. His prospects, he realized, could not be good. Not only had she turned down one suitor after another, but Leonard was someone she scarcely knew.

When they finally became acquainted that fall, Virginia took to him quickly. She invited him to share a house in Bloomsbury with Keynes, Grant, her brother Adrian and herself. She even showed him some of her manuscripts, and he had been impressed. "One can see that you might write something astonishingly good," he assured her. Leonard had intended to avoid declaring himself until he knew his feelings were reciprocated; but infatuation turned into irrepressible passion, and early in the new year he proposed. Like every lover in history, he poured out his heart in piteous, emotional letters deprecating himself and idealizing his beloved, while quite objectively cataloguing what he found most attractive: her mind and character, her beauty, her wit and candor, and the fact that she was not inferior or submissive. He also recognized that, like all Stephens, she could be cold and self-absorbed. But when he wrote that "above all it is realities which we understand & which are important for us," he was using pure Apostolic terminology to say that in spite of their differences, they were kindred spirits in every important way. And, as he said in another letter: "I shall never be content now with the second best."

Virginia remained unconvinced that she wanted to marry Leonard or that she wanted to marry at all. She worried about her mental stability and whether she would be suitable as a wife. She was troubled by Leonard's physical desire and by his seeming "so foreign"—a reference to his being Jewish. Vanessa at least had no doubts. She admired both his toughness and his sensitivity; she encouraged him—her letter is included—while urging Virginia to ignore his being a Jew. "Leonard is the only person I have ever seen," she wrote, "whom I can imagine as the right husband for you."

The course of the romance and its influence on Leonard's career decision can be followed in the correspondence. If Virginia rejected him, he would return to Ceylon; it was a comfort to know, he wrote to Strachey, that a train was always waiting at Victoria to carry him

away. However, with his leave running out and Virginia still undecided, he needed additional time. He applied to the Ceylon government
for an extension, but since he could not divulge the reason for his
request, he was eventually refused. By then Virginia had given him
just enough hope that he decided to take the risk and resign. Although
the Colonial Office was so anxious to keep him that the Under Secretary
offered, on his own authority, to grant the extension, Leonard let the
resignation stand. Virginia may have felt that an act of such devotion
deserved another. Three weeks later she accepted his proposal, and
what became one of the important marital alliances in literary history
was formally concluded in August 1912.

They were remarkably well matched. They shared the same values
and ideals, obsession with work, simplicity of living, disdain for religion, disregard for money, love of independence and contempt for
convention and bourgeois respectability. Even in their psychological
contrasts, they were a good fit—Virginia's insecurity and need for
sustenance were balanced by Leonard's strength and devotion, her
delicacy and femininity by his solidity and toughness. Underlying
everything was an unshakable mutual respect and confidence that
lasted throughout their lives together. "I have no circumference; only
my inviolable centre," Virginia wrote of Leonard in 1938 in her diary,
a sentiment he undoubtedly reciprocated.

Leonard had fallen so deeply in love with Virginia that for a time
she almost seemed to have cast a spell over him. He drew away from
his family, especially his mother, of whom Virginia took a baleful
view, and refused to have any of them, even Marie, at his wedding.
"I think you can hardly realize how *very* deeply hurt she is about it,"
Flora wrote a week before the ceremony. "You have been so much
kinder and more thoughtful in many ways that I cannot understand
your attitude." He became more conscious than ever of being Jewish.
And he felt himself completely alienated from the middle-class mores
of his past. At the same time he found himself caught up in a social
set that he found effete and phony. These confused emotions were
reflected in *The Wise Virgins*, a strange and angry novel that he wrote
on returning from his honeymoon.

The book, to some extent a *roman à clef*, centered on Leonard's
courtship of Virginia and the contrasts between her social background
and his. Most of the characters, symbolic types modeled to a greater
or lesser extent on his family, friends and neighbors, were portrayed
in a hostile light. The picture of his mother and his brother Herbert,
who was changed to the father in the final text, and their neighbors
in Putney, was so mortifying to Marie and Bella that they never forgave

him. The antihero was a self-hating and crassly materialistic Jew. Only Vanessa and Virginia escaped his scourge. The book was in fact Leonard's homage to Virginia, whom he presents as existing on a plane above other women. It was also his monument of gratitude to her for saving him from the sort of conventional marriage that was the denouement of the novel. Virginia was both a wife whom he could love with all his heart and an emotional and intellectual companion who would make it possible to lead the sort of existence he had dreamed of ever since his Cambridge days—an independent life of thought and creativity.

After a honeymoon in France, Spain and Italy, the couple settled down to a career of writing. They began as they meant to go on. To be undisturbed, they abandoned Bloomsbury for Clifford's Inn and a weekend house near Lewes in Sussex, initially Asheham House and then Monk's House. Every morning they worked in their rooms with the aim of writing at least 500 words: Virginia of *The Voyage Out*, and Leonard of *The Wise Virgins* and a short story, "The Three Jews." Leonard was the first to be established as an author. His novel *The Village in the Jungle* had been submitted to Edward Arnold prior to his marriage; by the time he was back from his honeymoon, it had been accepted, and on publication it was a great critical success. He had in the meantime also become a prolific contributor of reviews and essays. But after a short time their plans began going seriously awry. In 1913 and again in 1915 Virginia suffered horrifying mental breakdowns, which destroyed the couple's prospects for a fully normal life.

From an early age, Virginia had been vulnerable to mental illness. Following the death of her mother in 1895 and that of her father in 1904, she had nervous disorders that developed, in the latter case at least, into psychosis and attempted suicide. Both in 1910, for no discernible reason, and in early 1912, after Leonard had proposed, she suffered bouts of extreme nervous tension and had to withdraw briefly to a discreet mental home run by Jean Thomas, for what was known as a rest cure, the standard treatment at the time. In January 1913 her health again became delicate, and Leonard began keeping an encrypted record of the symptoms that plagued her to some extent all her life—insomnia, hatred of food, anxiety and "rat-gnawing headaches" in the back of her head. Several months later, following the completion of *The Voyage Out*, she became deeply depressed. By July she was briefly back in the nursing home; within a month of leaving, she became suicidal, and on September 9 took an overdose of Veronal and nearly died. Although the law normally required committing someone in her condition to a mental institution, Leonard persuaded the doctors to let him care for her himself, assisted by several nurses, first at Dalingridge Place, the Sussex country house of Virginia's half-brother George Duckworth, and then at Asheham.

Gradually Virginia recovered, only suddenly to descend one morning in February 1915 into delusional madness. In the months that followed, she was often violent, spoke gibberish for days at a time, was insomniac for long periods and refused to see Leonard for nearly eight weeks. By July it appeared that her mind and character had been permanently shattered. Then slowly she began to recuperate and by 1916 had largely recovered. For the next twenty-five years, even though her mental health remained very fragile and several times hovered on the edge of breakdown, she led a happy, active and astonishingly productive life.

The cycle of illnesses is recorded in the letters, though only a sampling can be included. Those to Virginia were written during their few and brief separations when she was not seriously ill. Even though Leonard had at times to write in language akin to baby talk, these letters are the most affecting he ever wrote. By contrast, those to others are ruthlessly controlled, with something of the quality of military dispatches from the front during a battle—the shock of the unexpected attack, the uncertainty about how to respond, the weary murmurs of relief when recovery comes. Although he never allowed it to show, his own suffering—not just from months of unceasing strain but from her violence and rejection—must have been nearly unbearable. Friends often worried that he might go under.

During her earliest illnesses, Virginia was seen by Sir George Savage, an eminent neurologist and old family friend, who diagnosed the condition as neurasthenia and prescribed large amounts of rest and food. When Leonard first confronted the problem, he was bewildered. Obviously he had known that Virginia's health was extremely delicate, but he now realized that Vanessa and Adrian had not warned him of the full seriousness of her condition. He also lost all confidence in Savage and turned to five other doctors, only to find that they made the same diagnosis and recommended the same treatment. Three of them were leading neurologists of their time, but they left Leonard with the impression—no doubt accurate—of knowing next to nothing about mental illness. The few surviving notes from the doctors are included; laconic as they are, they provide some inkling of why Leonard must have felt utterly frustrated at the medical profession's kindliness and hopefulness—and its helplessness: the illnesses would occur when they would occur and they would pass when they would pass.

Under the circumstances, Leonard had to attempt to deal with the problem himself. When he came to write his autobiography, he was inclined to see Virginia's illness as what he understood to be manic-depression. A little later on, when two psychiatrists, with his encouragement, took an interest in the case, he balked at simple diagnostic labels of either manic-depression or schizophrenia. At the time, he could judge only by what he saw, and that was someone precariously poised on a tightrope of mental health, who usually maintained normal balance but who could very easily lose equilibrium, with the risk of a disastrous fall. The reason for this delicate balance, he thought, was that Virginia's physical and mental natures were in conflict—the one demanding repose, the other flight. That, he said, "was the crux of her life, the tragedy of genius." It was the age-old notion of genius and madness being somehow allied—a view shared by Virginia.

Today conjecture would run along different lines. Since bipolar depression is now regarded as highly genetic in origin, the disorder may well have been essentially a biochemical one inherited from the Stephen family, which had a background of depression and mental illness. Virginia's 1915 breakdown and some subsequent minor depressions, for example, had no evident link to any outside cause and may therefore have been of endogenous origin. But Virginia was also profoundly insecure, an emotional problem that must have been rooted in environmental factors of her childhood. Consequently depressions of greater or lesser severity were at times triggered by her inordinate anxiety over the critical response to her latest book. No doubt the two types of disorder interacted; being constitutionally vulnerable, she could be incapacitated by something that would leave a healthy person untouched.

The practical problem for Leonard was learning how to prevent neurosis and depression from developing into psychosis. As the letters show, he gradually concluded that what knocked Virginia off balance was physical fatigue and emotional strain, which caused headaches, insomnia and racing thoughts. He found that if she then rested in bed, ate well and did no work, she would recover in a week or so. He did not mention that she also had a compulsive need for constant affection, reassurance and approval, which it was up to him to provide. Alix Strachey, who observed the situation firsthand over many years, expressed a view shared by everyone else who knew them, when she said, "I am sure that he was the only person who could have kept her going."

Virginia herself, as her diaries show, independently came to recognize the need for a careful regimen and increasingly took her own precautions. She also found that there was a relationship between her headaches and her writing and that periods of rest and isolation were vital, not only to keep well, but to refresh her creative powers. Although she knew all this, it was often up to Leonard to enforce it—his letter to Lady Robert Cecil in March 1916 provides an early example.

Question has sometimes arisen whether Virginia's condition might have been cured by psychiatric treatment or, as it has been phrased, "why Leonard did not have her psychoanalyzed." After all, her brother Adrian and his wife, Karin, as well as her friends James and Alix Strachey were psychoanalysts, and Leonard was among the first persons in Britain to be acquainted with Freud's writings and was his principal English-language publisher.

One answer is that no psychiatrist is likely to have taken her as a patient, given her age and medical history. Throughout her lifetime her condition was not considered susceptible to psychoanalytical therapy. Freud referred as late as 1933 to "the radical inaccessibility of the psychoses to analytic treatment," adding that the best hope of dealing with them was an understanding of the "operation of the hormones." Another response is that Virginia herself felt no need for treatment. As her diaries record, she considered psychiatry ridiculous; apparently it was only after she met Freud in 1939 that she read his works. Furthermore, her attitude toward the Stephens and the Stracheys was such as to put her off analysis rather than to entice her into it. And since the most serious domestic disagreement was over the relatively simple matter of her eating and resting sufficiently, it strains credulity to think that Leonard could have persuaded Virginia to undertake anything as drastic as psychiatric treatment against what was clearly her will.

And he may not have been inclined to try. Unlike his wife, Leonard was deeply impressed by Freud's ideas. No one outside the medical profession did as much as he to introduce Freud to the English-language public or to popularize his ideas. However much he admired Freud for his general insights into human nature, on Freudian analysis as therapy, he was silent. In any case, being convinced that Virginia's mental instability and her creative powers were inseparably connected, he may well have concluded that to tamper with the one risked damaging the other. Alix Strachey has stated that this danger was real and that it would have been reasonable for Leonard to recognize it.

From the first year of his marriage onward, then, Leonard's life was governed by Virginia's health. Whether to have children, where to live and the hours to keep, when to go out and when to have friends in, when to travel and when to stay home, all had to be decided with that in mind. How much his professional career was also affected is obviously impossible to know. Given his intellectual curiosity, it is reasonable to assume he would have accepted various invitations to travel abroad—such as to the Soviet Union in 1922 to prepare a report for the Fabian Society and later to India to do a study for the Independent Labour Party. It is known that he longed to return to Ceylon and wanted to get to know Asia and the United States. He might have been a member of British delegations to the League of Nations. But the key question concerns politics: whether he would have preferred to be in the mainstream, rather than on the sidelines. When the *Evening Standard* interviewed him on the occasion of his eighty-fourth birthday and asked if he had any regrets, he said that, although he never looked back over his shoulder, he would rather have liked to be an MP. So perhaps he would have accepted the invitations to stand for Parliament in the 1929 and 1934 elections.

Marriage involved another sacrifice. Leonard was decidedly virile and in his letters to Virginia he wrote of his physical desire for her. She was equally frank in stating that she felt no corresponding attraction, and marriage did nothing to change her feelings. After a short time, the two did not sleep together in any sense of the expression, although they remained physically affectionate in other ways.

There is no answer to the question that often arises of how "poor Leonard" managed in a sexless marriage, given his generally passionate nature. None of his own correspondence makes any allusion to the matter, and the only letter to come to light that quotes him on it is one that Gerald Brenan wrote to Rosemary Dinnage in 1967:

... When in March 1923 they came out to visit me in my Spanish mountain village I hardly knew them, but, as people sometimes do with comparative strangers, they talked very freely to me. Leonard told me that when on their honeymoon he had tried to make love to her she had got into such a violent state of excitement that he had to stop, knowing as he did that these states were a prelude to her attacks of madness. This madness was of course hereditary, but her early seduction by her half brother was no doubt a predisposing factor. So Leonard, though I should say a strongly sexed man, had to give up all idea of ever having any sort of sexual satisfaction. He told me that he was ready to do this "because she was a genius." All through his life with her he kept to this, and to avoid upsetting her never even flirted with other women. The only return he asked of her was that she should do the same with other men, and here he had especially in mind Clive Bell, a rather boisterous womanizer, who tried to make up to her and (on one occasion) Ralph Partridge who kissed her naked in the bathroom. Some years later, so I was told, he had an affair with the parlour maid, but I doubt if Virginia knew of it as it took place only when he was alone in London and she at Rodmell. There could have been no question of her ever having children though she may occasionally have day-dreamed of it. She knew that her bouts of madness put her in a different category from other women.

In addition to the talk about an affair with the Woolfs' cook-housekeeper, Nellie Boxall—for which there is neither evidence nor plausibility—one other story is said to have made the rounds. According to Frances Partridge, there was gossip in the twenties, possibly originated by Lytton Strachey, that Leonard was having an affair with Mary Agnes Hamilton. Molly Hamilton, ostensibly as much a friend of Virginia's as of Leonard's, was a formidable woman—a Cambridge graduate, a Labour politician, who sat in the 1929–31 Parliament, a British delegate to the League of Nations, an official of the British Embassy in Washington during the Second World War and an author of thirty-two books, including novels and biographies of Ramsay MacDonald and Arthur Henderson. She has been suspected of having had an affair with Ramsay MacDonald and possibly with Hugh Dalton. All her papers were destroyed at her request after her death and, although her name appears in Leonard's diary—along with hundreds of others—his files do not contain any correspondence with her. As far as is known, letters that Keynes, Strachey and other friends exchanged among themselves make no reference to any such romance; and the rumor could not have been widespread, since Clive Bell would have picked it up and taken great pleasure in repeating it, which was not the case.

Most of those who knew Leonard well believe that after marriage he simply repressed his sex drive—or redirected it. Late in life he told Trekkie Parsons that he never had an affair with another woman. He said that even had he been so inclined, he would not have taken the risk, since, had Virginia learned of it, "it would have sent her mad." It is not clear in any case that sex was so crucial to him that it would have driven him to an extramarital relationship. His letters to Lytton Strachey before marriage expressed distaste for sex outside an intimate emotional relationship. In his review of the first volume of Michael Holroyd's biography of Strachey, Leonard criticized the author for taking far too seriously Strachey's "love affairs," invoking Shakespeare: "Men have died from time to time, and worms have eaten them, but not for love." The words may have had personal significance. Perhaps the void was filled in other ways. Work, as Freud pointed out, is often an outlet for erotic impulses, and Leonard's ability to devote himself wholeheartedly to whatever he took up was legendary.

Conversely, there is the question of Leonard's reaction to Virginia's affair with Vita Sackville-West between 1925 and 1928. It seems clear from Virginia's diaries that this involvement did not alter her feelings for Leonard or their relationship. Even so, given his deep attachment, he must have been hurt by Virginia's sharing her affections with another person. He accepted the situation with the forbearance and grace of a saint, and his letters to Vita, both then and in later years, show that he had a continuing fondness for her. Nonetheless, his letter to Vita in December 1925, when the two women first spent a night together, and those to Virginia in September 1928, when they went together to France, make melancholy reading.

It is the very devotion of Leonard and Virginia to one another that impoverishes this chapter of letters. Since they could rarely bear to be separated, following their marriage, they seldom had occasion to correspond. The letters also suffer from occasional gaps; a few letters *to* Leonard partly compensate. Though Virginia's health is a leitmotif of the correspondence, its importance should not distort the fact that the couple led a socially rich, deeply contented and amazingly productive life once the breakdowns had been conquered. The letters chronicle Leonard's day-to-day activities through these years—the pleasure of friends, annual vacations abroad, gardening, pets and the quiet weeks in the Sussex countryside. These were the ephemera behind which he wrote his books and articles, pursued his advisory role in the Labour Party, directed an ever more successful publishing enterprise, edited several journals and attended countless meetings of numerous political committees.

The letters give no idea of Leonard's despair as much of Europe declined into dictatorship and as war approached. Indeed, his letter to G. E. Moore about the identity of a plant at the moment France was falling to the Germans is a magnificent finale to his Apostolic ideals. Yet as a prominent socialist and Jew he had no doubt what lay in store for him and his wife if Britain were occupied. Neither of them would have wished to survive; even before the fall of France, they had planned suicide in the event of invasion. In fact they had no way of knowing just how direct was the danger. Not only did the Germans intend in the first hours of an invasion to drop paratroops on the downs where they lived, but Heinrich Himmler's Central Security Office had a list of persons for immediate arrest; on it stood: "Woolf, Leonhard, Schriftsteller" and "Woolf, Virginia, Schriftstellerin."

Early in 1941 Virginia became prey to depressions, which she acknowledged to Leonard, and fears of madness, which she kept to herself. In mid-March, on finishing her latest novel, *Between the Acts*, she was more desperate than at any time since 1915. By the time Leonard had grasped the full seriousness of the situation, the best he could do was to persuade her to see Octavia Wilberforce, her new doctor and an old social friend. Leonard confronted the horror of knowing that anything he might say or not say, do or not do, could precipitate a breakdown. He faced a cruel dilemma: either to place her under the continuous surveillance of nurses—with the risk of driving her to suicide—or to leave her on her own—with the hope that she would recover but with an equal risk that she would take advantage of the freedom and kill herself. The letters record the ensuing disaster.

For a time Leonard was utterly inconsolable and withdrew into deep solitude. Intellectually he was convinced he had done what at the time seemed both prudent and consistent with Virginia's dignity. He also believed, Stephen Spender recalls his having said not long afterward, that Virginia had acted rationally. Emotionally, however, he no doubt felt an inevitable sense of remorse and self-reproach. A note found after his death, which he evidently jotted down at the time, conveys his anguish:

They said: "Come to tea and let us comfort you." But it's no good. One must be crucified on one's own private cross.

It is a strange fact that a terrible pain in the heart can be interrupted by a little pain in the fourth toe of the right foot.

I know that V. will not come across the garden from the lodge, & yet I look in that direction for her. I know that she is drowned & yet I listen for her to come in at the door. I know that it is the last page & yet I turn it over. There is no limit to one's stupidity & selfishness.

* * *

Turisthotellet, Rättvik.

den 2 August 1911   N. Söderström

Les Frères Karamazov is one of the greatest of novels.[1] I cannot refrain from giving you this information. But I dont think that people really do think & feel like they do. Have you read it? & the extraordinary speech of Ivan about Christ & Christianity & socialism which goes on without stopping for about 50 pages? I am halfway through. The Agamemnon is childish compared to it. I read it in trains & on steamers in inextricable fjords & on great lakes, very slowly, as befits it, in perpetual sunshine; I shall never finish it I think or perhaps it will never end. And Edgar [Woolf] is always sitting by me reading the *Ordeal of Richard Feverel*.[2] We have done nothing which we intended to do. We went up the coast from Gotenberg towards Norway & stayed in a village in Bohusland which is bare rock broken into innumerable islands & fjords by the sea. It was really rather wonderful with its blue sea in the blazing sunshine. Then we wandered up a fjord to a detestable town called Uddevala & north by Trollhättan to Imsjou on Lake Siljan. Then we took a toy steamboat & sailed over the lake which was absolutely white under the terrific sun to Leksamd & thence here. It was pleasant to sit on deck reading *Les Frères* at the rate of a page an hour, gliding past the shores from which the fair haired naked men & women perpetually waved their hands to us.

The Monday after I left you I went to the Russian dancers.[3] It was wildly unreal. First the audience for it contained everyone I knew in Europe. There was James [Strachey] with Rupert [Brooke], [Charles] Sanger & Norah (isnt that her name? repulsive beyond belief), the Corporal with Virginia, [Edward] Marsh with Forster, & [John] Pollock with no one & everyone. They all said that the second thing which contained the slaughter of negroes in a harem was better than the first which was the carnival. But it wasnt. The first was absolutely divine. Nijinsky is certainly not a eunuch. Poor Sanger who was bored said it was sentimental! Well I suppose it was, but it was divine.

You ought to have come here with me. I do nothing but overeat

---

1. LW read it in French, Constance Garnett's first English translation not being available until the following year.
2. In a letter to LW in 1964, Edgar wrote: "I have been looking at my diary of our time in Sweden & see it was at Trollhattan that . . . you told me about Virginia & your difficulty about proposing & the idea of the Ceylon Civil Service."
3. Diaghilev's Ballets Russes was having a triumphal London season; on this occasion it performed *Le Carnival* and *Le Spectre de la Rose*.

myself & then lie in the sun & drink iced beer & smoke innumerable pipes, while Edgar talks about the Insurance Bill & Education & Trades Unions. It is all very pleasant to look at, & the air is wonderfully soft & warm & there is a gentle breeze & the people are mostly good looking & are very often wearing no clothes. They are all very stupid, & perpetually talk about art & culture. They collect facts without ever understanding them in the least. They are exactly what novels, newspapers & foreigners think that we are but what we are not at all. We are the only intelligent people in Europe, I am convinced; we are the only race which really understands things. I thought at first it might only seem so because we are the only race which understands English but I see now it goes much deeper. Two American women spoke to me for two minutes yesterday, & they were the only people seen by me since I left England who have understood me & things. I have also met a Swede who has been chauffeur to an American millionaire for 5 years in Chicago & the only language which he has learnt there appears to be German.

Yr
L.

To Lytton Strachey

1 Nov. [1911]   Lexham

I saw Virginia yesterday. They have taken Brunswick Sq. I am going to see it tomorrow as they can give me rooms there. I shall decide then.

I see it will be the beginning of hopelessness. To be in love with her—isn't that a danger? Isn't it always a danger which is never really worth the risk? That at any rate you of all can tell me.

I expect after two weeks I shall again take the train not to Morocco but Ceylon. It is something to feel that it is always waiting there for one at Victoria.

Only yesterday Virginia told me that you had given up the heart for the affections or some other soporific, I forget exactly which. And now apparently it has broken out again. It isnt work the risk, it isnt worth the risk, though I suppose we shall never believe it.

L.

To Virginia Stephen

[Telegram]
10 January 1912   Mells[1]

I must see you for an hour tomorrow Thursday I shall arrive town
12.50 and leave again 5 if I can come to Brunswick Square 1.15 can I
see you then. Leonard

To Virginia Stephen

                                                        Great Elm Rectory
11 Jan 1912   Frome   Somerset

My dear Virginia, I must write to you before I go to bed & can, I
think, probably think more calmly

I have not got any very clear recollection of what I really said to
you this afternoon but I am sure you know why I came—I dont mean
merely that I was in love but that that together with uncertainty drives
one to do these things. Perhaps I was wrong, for before this week I
always intended not to tell you unless I felt sure that you were in love
& would marry me. I thought then that you liked me but that was all.
I never realized how much I loved you until we talked about my going
back to Ceylon. After that I could think about nothing else but you.
I got into a state of hopeless uncertainty, whether you loved me or
could ever love me or even like me. God, I hope I shall never spend
such a time again as I spent here until I telegraphed. I wrote to you
once saying I would speak to you next Monday but then I felt I should
be mad if I waited until then to see you. So I wired. I knew you would
tell me exactly what you felt. You were exactly what I knew you are
& if I hadnt been in love before, I would now. It isnt, really it isnt,
merely because you are so beautiful—though of course that is a large
reason & so it should be—that I love you: it is your mind & your
character—I have never known anyone like you in that—wont you
believe that?

And now, I will do absolutely whatever you want. I dont think you
want me to go away, but if you did, I would at once. If not, I dont
see why we cannot go on the same as before—I think I can—& then
if you do find that you could love me you would tell me.

1. LW was visiting Leopold C. H. Douglas Campbell, then Rector of Frome, a village in
Somerset.

I hardly know whether I am saying what I mean or feel: I am extraordinarily tired. A dense mist covered the whole of Somerset & the train was late & I had to crawl my way from the station for 3 miles to the house.

Dont you think that the entrance of Walter almost proves the existence of a deity?[1]

Yr
L.

To Virginia Stephen

Jan 12 [1912]   [Frome]

I find the post doesn't go out until evening, so I can try & write about what, with you sitting there, it was so difficult to discuss calmly & dispassionately. I dont think I'm selfish enough not to be able to see it from your side as well. From mine, I'm sure now that apart from being in love, I should be right to say—& I would—that if I were in love, it would be worth the risk of everything to marry you. That of course—from your side—was the question you were continually putting yesterday & which probably you ought to. Being outside the ring of fire, you should be able to decide it far better than I inside it. God, I see the risk in marrying anyone & certainly me. I am selfish, jealous, cruel, lustful, a liar & probably worse still. I had said over & over again to myself that I would never marry anyone because of this, mostly because, I think, I felt I could never control these things with a woman who was inferior & would gradually enfuriate me by her inferiority & submission. (I have had to be motored to Bath & back & it is now evening again.) It is because you aren't that that the risk is so infinitely less. You may be vain, an egoist, untruthful as you say, but they are nothing compared to your other qualities: magnificence, intelligence, wit, beauty, directness. After all too we like one another, we like the same kinds of things & people, we are both intelligent & above all it is realities which we understand & which are important for us. You wanted me to give you reasons for my state of mind: here they are &

1. Walter Lamb's arrival had made it possible to conclude their conversation gracefully without driving it to a resolution. VS's replies are published in *The Letters of Virginia Woolf*, edited by Nigel Nicolson and Joanne Trautmann.

damnably truthful at any rate. I feel like knocking nails—with Walter & Sydney—into my coffin.[1] I would even go so far—in the cause of truth—as to admit the possibility of my desire for you blinding me to the knowledge that no woman ought to marry me—but I dont believe it in your case—if you ever did love me.

As you dont, you ought to be able to know now exactly what the risk would be if you were & married me.

The people have come for the post so I must stop.

Yr
L.

FROM VANESSA BELL

Jan 13 [*1912*]

Dear Leonard,
 I am writing to tell you that Virginia has told me about her talk with you & also to say how glad I shall be if you can have what you want. You're the only person I know whom I can imagine as her husband, which may seem to you a rash remark considering how little I know you. However I have faith in my instincts, at any rate as far as they imply what I think of you. Besides that, which perhaps isn't very important, I shall be so glad if you dont go back to Ceylon. It seems absurd that we shouldnt get the benefit of your existence.

Your
VB

1. (Sir) Sydney Waterlow (1878–1944), like Walter Lamb, had proposed to VS and been turned down. A child prodigy at Eton and brilliant classicist at Trinity, Waterlow served at various times and places in the diplomatic service, leading a life that, according to LW, "was in some ways stranger than fiction."

23 Feb 1912   38 Brunswick Sq. WC

My dear Virginia, I wrote to you before, a long letter, when I was in Essex & before I heard that you weren't to have letters.[1] Now I hear you are in Asheham so I suppose you may have them. I shall try to make this as dull & unexciting as possible & it will be if it is as things are without you.

I have just come from a concert at the Bechstein Hall; all Brahms, & some of it rather splendid I believe but I listened in snatches. It has seemed a curiously long day: Lytton to lunch hovering between crises & really at last embarked on writing a play—a tragedy.[2] Then Desmond telephoned that he wanted lunch & Sophie provided cold meat & he came & talked with Lytton for hours about the Society while I sank into a trance of boredom. We left him here writing an article in order to earn £3 & walked across Regent's Park to Chalk Farm where Lytton set out for Henry [Lamb] & I to the Life Class at Philip's studio in Fitzroy St.[3] The classes are rather amusing; Adrian was there today & strange females rather like Dorothea [VS's cousin] with Pekinese spaniels.

God it does seem like a long time since I shut that damned blue door on your face, & its really only twelve days. I went down that day to Essex & stayed until the Tuesday evening at first with two brothers & then, when they left, by myself. It is a miserable muddy & melancholy county. We hunted on the Saturday & the galloping was pleasant & I very nearly managed to kill my brother [Herbert]'s new horse which fell jumping a ditch & somehow stuck in it upside down until we hauled it out by chains.

Asheham last week end was beautiful & we laid the carpets which I hope you note are, thanks to Vanessa, laid most professionally. Clive was in great spirits & so was Adrian.

I wonder if this letter is dull enough. There is some pleasure in writing even it to you.

I thought I should see you this Friday but of course I shant now. I

---

1. LW's marriage proposal had been too much for VS's nerves, and their correspondence had been discontinued.
2. *A Son of Heaven*, completed in the fall, was performed in London in 1925 and again in 1949.
3. Henry Lamb (1883–1960), noted painter and younger brother of Walter, did a portrait of LW some weeks later (see page 518). LW was studying painting and at the same time having his portrait done by his brother Philip.

expect it is better for you not to. I do hope you havent worried or thought about anything in the world or in your wonderful world either. I think I shall have to go to Cambridge as Moore has written a long & piteous letter: he wants me to arrange the Easter reading party. I shall come back on Monday; I do hope you will have returned to life again then.

It is very late so good night.

Yr
L.

To the Under Secretary of State for the Colonies

25th April 1912

38 Brunswick Square
WC

Dear Sir,

With reference to your letter number 12288/1912 of 23 April I have the honour to report that, as I am unable to assume duties on May 20th, I regret that I must resign my post under the Ceylon Government from that date.

I am Sir
Your obedient servant
L. S. Woolf

To Virginia Stephen

29 April 1912

[38 Brunswick Square]

Dearest Virginia, I cant sleep not from desire but from thinking about you. I've been to the opera but for all that I heard of it I might have been sitting in this room. I've read two of your MSS from one of which at any rate one can see that you might write something astonishingly good. I want to see you to talk with you & now, though I suppose I shouldn't, I'm going to write utterly miserable what I should want to say to you & probably couldnt.

Since yesterday something seemed to rise up in you against me. It may be imagination on my part; if it is, you must forgive me: I dont think even you realize what it would mean to me. God, the happiness

I've had by being with you & talking with you as I've sometimes felt it mind to mind together & soul to soul. I know clearly enough what I feel for you. It is not only physical love though it is that of course & I count it the least part of it, it isn't only that I'm only happy with you, that I want to live with you; it's that I want your love too. It's true that I'm cold & reserved to other people; I dont feel affection ever easily: but apart from love I'm fond of you as I've never been of anyone or thing in the world. We often laugh about your lovableness but you dont know how lovable you are. It's what really keeps me awake far more than any desire. It's what worries me now, tears me two ways sometimes—for I wouldn't have you marry me, much as I love you, if I thought that it would bring you any unhappiness. Really this is true though it hurt me more than the worst physical pain your mere words that you told Vanessa that probably you would never marry anyone.

There is nothing that you've done which hasn't seemed to me absolutely right which hasn't made me love you more. I've never for a single moment thought you were treating me badly & I never shall, whether you marry me or not. I love you more for not deciding—I know the reasons. You are far finer, nobler, better than I am. It isn't difficult to be in love with you & when one is in love with anyone like you one has to make no allowances, no reservations. But I've many beastly qualities—though I've shown them to you deliberately often because I'm too fond of you not to want you to know that they do exist. For me to know that they do exist & to be in love with someone like you, that's where the pain comes in.

I dont want you to decide until you've finished your novel [*The Voyage Out*], I think you're right not to. I can go on as we've been doing for six months even, if you want it, or if you ever for a moment feel it would be easier, I will go away for a week or a month or longer—though not seeing you for a day makes me miserable now. But I believe I know how you feel now & one should speak out what one thinks. I should like to say it to you, only when I'm with you all sorts of feelings make it so difficult to say exactly what I mean—so that it's a good thing perhaps that I am writing to you. I believe you might very easily be in love now & almost equally easily never be—with me at any rate. I dont think much of the physical part of it though it must come in— but it's so elusive. If one happens to be born as I am, it is almost certain to be very strong, but even then it becomes so merged with one's other feelings. It was the least strong of my feelings for you when I fell in love & when I first told you. It has grown far more violent as my other feelings have grown stronger.

I think we're reaching a point at which everything will tremble in the balance. Sometimes I suppose you don't know exactly what you feel & really unimportant things become magnified. I have faults, vices, beastlinesses but even with them I do believe you ought to marry me & be in love—& it isn't only because so often I feel that if you never are, the best thing in life will have gone. I shall never be like you, never anything like it, but you seem to purge my faults from me. And I have the fire in me at any rate & the knowledge. I want to live & get the best things in life & so do you. You are the best thing in life & to live it with you would make it ten thousand times more worth living. I shall never be content now with the second best. And you, I'm sure, you see that if it could be lived like that by two people who know how to live—God, the chance of it is worth any risk almost.

Virginia, I dont know where I've got to. I'm just writing as I think. It's nearly 3 in the morning. I shall go for a walk & post this & then go to bed again. I only hope there's nothing in it to worry you. At any rate you must know that I love you as much as it is possible for one human being to love another. I would rather do anything than harm you in the slightest possible way. You mustn't worry or hurry—there's no need for it. You must finish your novel first & while you are doing it you must not try to decide. If you dont try to decide & we go on as we have been, I shall get plenty of happiness in the next two months. After all I've had more happiness in the last two months than in all the rest of my life put together.

And writing like this to you is like talking to you, it makes all depression go. I shall go to bed happy & sleep peacefully. I hope you are.

L.

To Virginia Stephen

30 April 1912   38 Brunswick Sq

My dear Virginia, I've had what's called a semi official letter from the Col. Office today. They now obviously want to grant me the leave.[1] I am replying that I will call & see the man on Friday morning—he asks me to—or if I do not, will send them a definite answer by that day. I should like to see you before I do. If you are coming back on

1. The correspondence is quoted in *Growing*.

[words illegible], can't I? on that evening. But if you decide that Asheham is too nice to leave, if you sent me a telegram tomorrow I'd come down for an hour or two on Thursday & get back here in the evening.

I wrote you a letter which perhaps I shouldn't have written last night. If it worried you, wipe it out of your mind. If I whined, I didn't mean to & have no right or reason to. I slept after it & wrote my 500 words this morning. I hope you did too.

Your
L.

To the Under Secretary of State for the Colonies

2nd May 1912

38, Brunswick Square
W.C.

Dear Sir,

In continuation of my letter of the 30th April, I think upon consideration that I should prefer not to state more exactly the nature of my private affairs & that my resignation should be accepted.

I must thank you for the trouble which you have taken in the matter & regret any inconvenience which I may have caused.

Yours faithfully
L. S. Woolf[1]

To Virginia Stephen

24 May 1912

The Union Society
Cambridge

Dearest & most beloved of all creatures!

Have you ever had a letter beginning like that? At any rate you never have had one in which the words were so near the truth of the writer's feelings—or rather so far below them. Dearest Virginia, beloved! The words dont give anything of how much I love you. It's just

---

1. Bella Woolf wrote from Ceylon that news of the resignation had caused a minor sensation there. It was speculated that he was gravely ill, had inherited a fortune from someone drowned on the *Titanic*, had decided on a new career.

175

like when I'm with you. If I try to say what I feel, I become stupid & stammering: it's like a wall of words rising up in front of me & there on the other side you're sitting so clear & beautiful & your dear face that I'd give everything in the world to see now. O Lord I dont know what I'm writing, I took this paper out of the Union & I'm writing now in my brother [Cecil]'s room with people all round me talking to one another & to me & if youre to get this letter as I promised it's got to be posted by 11.45 which is close upon me. But they dont exist for me, nothing does except you. I went to Moore after dinner & have been with him all the evening talking but I was thinking of you the whole time. I believe if ever you got to have a grain or particle of love for me, I should be happy for the rest of my life. You dont know what a wave of happiness comes over me when I see you smile & the tone, I always hope for, of happiness comes into your voice—as it does when the sad & worried moods are chased out. Dearest Virginia, I wish, God how I wish, I never caused them & that they could be chased out for ever.

I must post this now. I hope the Mandril went to its box early & isn't worried by anything in the world.[1] The end is as the beginning was & it always will be, that it's for me the dearest & most beloved creature in the world.

L.

To Lytton Strachey

38 Brunswick Square

2 June 1912
W.C.

Do you remember the year in which I was going to justify myself & my method of dealing with life? 1935 was it? I feel somehow that I've done it in 1912 or at any rate life's justified itself to me. Virginia is going to marry me. I'm so happy that that's the only thing that I can say to you, simply that I am. Lord, it is difficult to put one's happiness into words & it was so damned easy to put the miseries of life into them from Ceylon. At any rate after 13 years & the silences in them, youre the person I turn to first in the world to try to tell you of either.

L.

1. It was now that nicknames were adopted: LW was "Mongoose," VS was "Mandril."

To G. E. Moore

38, Brunswick Square,
W.C.

7 June 1912

My dear Moore,

I feel I should like to tell you myself that I am going to marry Virginia Stephen & that I am extraordinarily happy. When you know her as I hope you will, I dont think you'll be surprised.

Yours
Leonard Woolf

To Violet Dickinson[1]

38, Brunswick Square,
W.C.

7 June 1912

Dear Miss Dickinson,

It was very nice of you to write to me as you did & I should so much like to come with Virginia to see you. She has not been very well the last few days & is going away for the week end. I want her & she means to be very careful not to tire herself in any way & so it might not possible to come on Tuesday unless she is quite well by then. But we both want to come so much that we should like if we may to leave it open.

I am looking forward to meeting Virginia's old friends because I'm sure they, knowing her, will know how happy she's made me—& it's very pleasant receiving their congratulations.

Yours very sincerely
Leonard Woolf

---

1. Several days after agreeing to marry, VS wrote of her engagement to several old friends whom she held in almost daughterly affection; one of these was Violet Dickinson (1865–1948).

7 August 1912

My dear Len,

Thanks for [your] letter. To be quite frank, yes, it has hurt me extremely that you did not make it a point of having me at your marriage. I know full well that neither Virginia nor you had the least desire to slight me, why should you, but it has been a slight all the same.

You are the first of my sons who marries, it is one of the if not the most important day of your life. It would have compensated me for the very great hardships I have endured in bringing you all up by myself, if you had expressed the desire that you wished me before anyone else, to be witness to your happiness.

. . . It has been the custom from time immemorial that one's nearest relatives are paid the compliment of being invited to the marriage ceremony; to ignore that custom & to carry it so far as to leave out one's Parent, must strike one as an unheard of slight. A wedding entertainment no one asked for, you're wise in discarding it. However I will not say more; you have missed a great opportunity of giving me some happy moments—I have not had many lately! . . .

> *With very much love*
> *Ever, my dear Len,*
> *Your devoted*
> *Mother*

To Saxon Sydney-Turner

1 Sept 1912

Tarragona
Spain

No one has ever given or lent me anything more useful than your little Spanish dictionary. It is always in my hand or pocket. I can now carry on quite a long conversation out of its leaves. We stayed in an inn in a village under Montserrat—sleeping over a urinal, a pigstye & a washing tub which stank more than either—in which only one youth was said to know any language other than Spanish & that was French which was less in quantity & quality than our Spanish. Crowds stood around us while I looked up words in your dictionary & there was nothing which did not eventually become intelligible. Virginia of course has inspirations about dictionaries as when she suddenly in an emergency to which not even your dictionary could rise pronounced the word 'gazeosos' which procured us what we wanted—soda water.

This is the noblest of countries vitiated by a universal smell of stale wine. One is always standing on some height looking over a vast plain towards enormous hills rising one over the other into mountains—& always the smell of stale wine is strong in one's nostrils.

We must go out now to walk by the sea & listen to a military band. I'll write to you again if you write to me to Br. Sq. which I hope you will.

Love from Virginia.

L.

To MOLLY MACCARTHY[1]

28th Sept. 1912

Casa Biondetti
Venice

My Dear Molly,

Virginia is very lazy, she's lying on a sofa eating chocolates & reading & looking at pictures, including her own portrait, in the *Strand Magazine*.[2] She ought to be writing to you, but as I'm sure she won't before tea, I'm doing it for her.

I'm very sorry you're giving up Hoxton in a way, though really I don't much believe in that work after what I saw of it. Miss Booth wrote & asked me to become Secretary but I had to refuse as I don't know yet what I shall be doing or whether I'd have any time for it.[3]

I have, I believe, a considerable knowledge of your character, & one of its characteristics is curiosity. Therefore if Virginia were writing this letter she'd probably try to satisfy it. As I'm writing for her, have I got to try to do the same? The first question you want to know about is how we get on together. I believe you'd rather have Virginia's version than mine, but there's no chance of your getting that today. I don't feel like a married man which I think is a good test of happiness. I believe it would be far easier to satisfy your curiosity, if the opposite

1. See Biographical Appendix.
2. The "portrait," which bore an uncanny resemblance to VW, was in fact a sketch of a fictional character in a story in the March issue.
3. Hoxton was a slum in the East End of London where LW had briefly worked for the Charity Organization Society. Imogen Booth, head of the Society, was the daughter of Charles Booth, a well-known promoter of social causes.

were true & we had quarrelled & bored one another. It would be so much more amusing—but after all, you don't want to hear that I'm sorry we've got to be back in London next Thursday & that it's as pleasant to be with Virginia in the furnace of Spain as in the rain & biting wind of the Grand Canal of Venice. I never of course really did expect to be able to satisfy your curiosity.

We haven't yet got anywhere to go except two rooms in Brunswick Sq. But we hope to get rooms in the Temple & live a nomadic life. I expect you'll think that rather silly—but I hope when I die like a good Jew at 70 I shall still have no home.

Well, I'm now going to give Virginia her tea. She's made the great discovery that one can drink both tea & chocolate & coffee at the same time as buttered toast, cakes & ices for tea! I also benefit by this discovery.

L. S. W.[1]

To Edward Arnold

[Second week of November 1912]   [38 Brunswick Square]

Dear Mr Arnold,
   I have to thank you for your letter of the 11th [accepting *The Village in the Jungle*]. With regard to the expressions & passages referred to by you, do you think that you could return me the MS, as you suggested, & that your reader could just mark those objected to?
   . . . I should also wish to retain my copyright in the book.
   Of course I should be only too pleased to give you the first refusal [on the next book].[2]

Yours sincerely
L. S. Woolf

1. A postscript by VW is in her published letters.
2. In a condescending reply, Arnold predicted poor sales and deprecated LW's wish to keep the copyright, dismissing the notion that foreign publishers would have any interest in the book. It was in fact translated into Tamil, Sinhalese and several other languages. When first-year sales required not only a reprint but also a second edition, Arnold wrote that he heard "nothing but enthusiastic praise from everyone who has read it" and asked when he might expect another book from his talented author.

To Robert Trevelyan

31 Dec 1912

13, Cliffords Inn,
Fleet Street, E.C.

My dear Trevy,

Many thanks for the letters.[1] I have been to see Bruce Richmond &
he is going to give me a trial in reviewing & also in articles on industrial
questions. It was very nice of you to take the trouble for me.

I hope you'll find Ceylon more beautiful than India, though I expect
a good deal of it is vastly ugly too, especially to travel through.[2] I
believe you really have to take it in little bits by living in it, to see it
properly. Only I like personally even the bareness & parchedness.

I've just got the first proofs of my novel: it's coming out in Feb. It's
about Ceylon.

Yours
Leonard Woolf

FROM VANESSA BELL[3]

Jan 20 [1913]

My dear Leonard,

*Thank you for writing. Craig's opinion seems to be much more
definite & quite different from other doctors. I didnt know you had
been coming to think the same thing. But I am glad you do as I had
for some time been thinking so more and more definitely myself. Not
that I think Virginia any worse, for I quite agree with you in thinking
her certainly better since you married. But, I suppose from my own
experience, I have been coming to think that on the whole one does*

1. LW had asked Trevelyan for letters of reference as a book reviewer. One was to Bruce
Richmond (1871–1964), the founding editor of the *Times Literary Supplement*.
2. Trevelyan was at the time traveling in India and South Asia with two close Cambridge
friends, E. M. Forster and G. L. Dickinson.
3. Faced with the question whether to have children, LW raised the matter with Vanessa
and others familiar with VW's medical history. His diary records that he first saw Dr.
Maurice Craig (1866–1935), a leading London neurologist, and Jean Thomas, proprietor of
the nursing home where Virginia had stayed during earlier breakdowns. Both considered it
too risky. He later consulted Dr. Maurice Wright, a neurologist he had seen in 1911 about
his trembling hands, and Sir George Savage (1842–1921), the Stephen family doctor and a
noted specialist in mental disorders. They were in favor. And finally he spoke to Dr. T. B.
Hyslop (1864–1933), another neurologist, who advised putting off a decision for eighteen
months.

plunge into a new & unknown state of affairs when one starts a baby
& once its started there's no going back. One generally does it quite
rashly & of course generally its all right. But if there's any reason to
think it may not be, I believe one ought to take a good deal of trouble
to find out all about it & take all the precautions one can beforehand.
I wish I knew more of what Craig said. I suppose he thinks the risk
she runs is that of another bad nervous breakdown & I doubt if even
a baby would be worth that. . . .

Your
VB

To Virginia Woolf

Lexham,
Colinette Road, Putney.

8 April 1913

My dearest dearest Mandy, I am miserable without you.[1] I have been
wanting you all day, & I shant be happy until I see you tomorrow. I
shall come back to Asheham tomorrow if everything goes on as it is
now—because there is really nothing which one can do here. It is of
course extraordinarily serious & at first they seem to have thought it
hopeless. But he is going on amazingly well considering that it is a
fracture in two places. His temperature has gone down to nearly normal
& he was actually conscious this morning.

I am now going over to the hospital where mother is.

I love you & adore you & worship you Mandy & I never want
anything else in the world than you. Goodbye my dearest.

Your
M.

To Lytton Strachey

Asheham
Rodmell   Lewes

25 April 1913

I hear from Saxon, who is a mere disseminator of malicious gossip,
that you say that you ought to have written to me. As you have writ-

---

1. LW was in Putney with his family because his brother Herbert had fractured his skull
in a riding accident.

ten to him I certainly think you ought. At any rate I shall expect an answer to this & with more in it because I've never been able to write a letter to you. The only one I ever succeeded in writing was on June 10th last year & it was so long & so appalling that on the advice—if not compulsion—of Virginia I tore it up. It contained a detailed analysis of friendship of which I believe you would have thoroughly approved.

We practically live here. In the morning we write 750 words each: in the afternoon we dig: between tea & dinner we write 500 words each. After dinner Virginia reads the *Life of Mrs Humphry Ward* & I the Poor Law Minority Report. Saxon stayed with us for a week & was thoroughly bored except every five minutes when he remembered the Finnish for some recondite Tamil word. Also Marjorie [Strachey] on her way on foot from London to Bath via Cranbrook. We saw Ottoline [Morrell]—not here but in town—the same scene happened, which happens every time I see Ottoline.[1]

"Have you seen [Walter] Lamb lately?" she says.

"No, not lately" I say.

"You used to see a lot of Lamb at one time?" with her
eyes fixed on me.

"A good deal" with my eyes fixed on her.

"He used to tell you confidences?"

"O well I dont know about that."

We continue to stare at one another awkwardly. This has now happened three times; always the same, word for word! What *does* it mean?

Yr
L.

---

1. Ottoline Morrell (1873–1938), half sister of the Duke of Portland and wife of Philip Morrell, a Liberal MP, maintained an intellectual salon at Garsington Manor, near Oxford. LW compared her to "one of her own peacocks, drifting about the house and terraces in strange brightly-coloured shawls and other floating garments . . ." (*Beginning Again*).

To Virginia Woolf[1]

13, Cliffords Inn,

25 July [1913]   Fleet Street, E.C.

My darling Mandy,   I must just say goodnight to you again. I was so
happy, dearest, to see you come to see that you were much too nervous
about yourself, & I am still happy, & I shall go to bed & sleep happily
knowing that & that tomorrow I shall see you again so soon. Only rest
quietly & dont worry about anything in the world, & it wont be any
time before we're again having the best life that any two people can
have. And that is what you've given me from the moment you took
me into your service.

   Good night, dearest of all creatures,

                                        Your happy & loving
                                        & beloved
                                        Mongoose.

To Virginia Woolf

13, Cliffords Inn,

26 July [1913]   Fleet Street, E.C.

   My darling, I got back so well & quickly. The happiness of being
with you, dearest dearest Mandy, makes up for everything. So be good
& dont think of anything else but how I love you & how you love me
& what a time we shall have again in a few days. Good night, beloved.

                                        Your darling
                                        M.

To Virginia Woolf

13, Cliffords Inn,

27 July [1913]   Fleet Street, E.C.

   My sweetest Mandy,   If it weren't so late I should sing you a Mongoose song of joy which begins

1. Increasingly unwell, VW followed Dr. Savage's recommendation and spent two weeks at
Jean Thomas's rest home in Twickenham. LW normally spent part of every day there and
wrote to her on returning home.

I do adore
I do adore
I feel so certain after seeing you today that it will be much shorter
time to our being together again. Never talk again, dearest, of causing
me anything but the most perfect happiness, because literally & honestly that is what I get merely from sitting quietly reading by you. I
shall think of you tomorrow as a brave beast lying quietly in its straw
& cleaning its dear self from time to time by remembering that.

Your adoring
M.

To Virginia Woolf

13, Cliffords Inn,

28 July [1913]   Fleet Street, E.C.

My darling Mandy,   I've just heard from Jean [Thomas] that you
have had a good day & that Savage was very pleased with you & I
did the mongoose dance of joy. O Mandy, I do so look forward to
seeing you tomorrow.

I have been a lazy mongoose today. I lunched with Adrian & went
with him to see the great tennis match & then to Gordon Sq where I
had a long talk with Vanessa who sends you her love. Then I met
Keynes who asked me to come in after dinner which I foolishly said
I would do & so have to write to you now instead of at goodnight time.
I dined at the Cock [Tavern] & there met James [Strachey] & Herbert
[Woolf]. I will tell you all details tomorrow.

Every minute I live, Mandy dearest, I see more clearly that no one
is anything in the world to me, except you.

Your loving
M.

I have gone *up* in weight: I am 9 stone 12 pounds! & I had an
expensive dinner: fillet of beef.

A letter from George [Duckworth] which I will bring with me.

13, Cliffords Inn,
Fleet Street, E.C.

31 July 1913

My darling Mandy, I met Herbert by chance in the train & he came back here for a few moments & will post this for me. O Mandy, Mandy dearest, I dont believe even you know how I can think of nothing but you, how you are everything in the world to me—Do, do trust me that its only a matter of days for everything to be perfect again & that there is nothing to fear. We said so so often & now darling is the time to prove it. After all, it is really only a question of resting for a few days. I love you, dearest Mandy, as I always have & more than I have.

Your
M.

To Virginia Woolf

13, Cliffords Inn,
Fleet Street, E.C.

1 Aug [1913]

Darling Mandy, I've just got your letter. I wont decide until I hear from you tomorrow whether I shall go away for the weekend. I should like, my sweetest dearest Mandy, really to see you; because when I'm away from you, you simply always are before my eyes & dance, dance in my thoughts—you can't imagine how you obsess me & how I long to see you—but in a way I believe it is better for you not to see me for a few days. If I do go, I should simply go to Asheham with Adrian. Saxon is here & Adrian has asked us to come to Brunswick so I'm just off now. I played tennis hard for two hours. I'm very well. If I go to Asheham I should come back on Tuesday & come out to you on Wednesday. O Mandy darling, whatever may happen, you cant doubt of my love of you—if you only knew what it is to be parted from you for one night & how stale the world seems without you. So do, my dearest one, just rest quietly & then whatever else may happen by the end of next week we shall be together again. To have you strong & happy again & with me, a few days are nothing. You know that, my dearest Mistress Mandril, & you do know what a happy year we've had together & what another happy year will begin for us next week. I believe, Great One, you do want to take on your mongoose in service for another year—& if you'll only let him grovel before you & kiss your toes, he'll be happy. Goodnight, beloved.

Your
M.

To Virginia Woolf

2 Aug [1913] Lewes

We are at tea in Stone's. O I do wish my Mandy were here. This is to tell you dearest that I wont believe you even if you tell me those dreadful things again & I am happy because I *know* you love me & that next Thursday we shall be together again. As for me, I always will be your adoring

Mongoose

To Virginia Woolf

2 August 1913 Asheham

Dearest,   I dont want to go to bed without saying goodnight to you. I'm very sleepy & so I'm going to bed at 10 oclock! O how I wish you were here: I think hardly a minute has passed since I saw you this afternoon that I haven't thought of you. I hardly can bear waiting until I hear from you. Mandy darling, you wont, will you? again think things such as you said today—surely you must know what you mean to me—to be really separated from you would be absolutely unbearable. Whatever else is true, I do know that in the year you have grown fonder & fonder of me. It's because of that & because really my belief in you is so absolutely sure—because I know what our love has been in this year & how it has grown & that our feelings for each other have been something fine, just as you are not only the most loveable but also the finest human being I shall ever know—it's only these things that make separation from you for the few days for which it will last bearable.

I am happy, dearest, simply because of my absolute faith in you & the knowledge that in a week we shall be looking back at these days as a nightmare that is over. It isn't that I don't know what it means to you to do this—I would do anything to save you from having to do what you dont want to do—but honestly you do know that it's worth it.

I am so sleepy, I must go to bed. Be good, darling, darling Mandy—& remember that never for a moment have I ever been anything but absolutely honest with you—& that there is no reason in the world why you should reproach yourself with anything or think that you have done anything to be laughed at.

I believe that at this moment I love you more than I've ever loved you before & want you more.

On Wednesday darling I shall see you & on Thursday we shall be together for good. Goodnight, sweetest.

Your
M.

Eat well, wont you? & rest quietly.

To Virginia Woolf

3 Aug 1913   Asheham

My darling mistress,

I am writing at the end of the morning because I shall be able to post this this afternoon & you may get it tomorrow morning. I was getting sad when your telegram came & made me happy again—& now I am longing for your letter. We have sat in the garden in divine weather. Adrian is very nice but it's dull for him I think alone with me here. I have to try & get this review done.[1]

Mrs. Funnell has been ill with [?dianhosy], pains in the kidneys, & all over the body but is much better again today.[2]

I feel life will begin again at the end of the week when you take me down here with you once more. But, dearest one, if I *have* done anything wrong to you & which has displeased you, you would tell me,

1. An unsigned review, "Guild and Trade Union," published in the *Nation* on August 16, 1913.
2. Mrs. Funnell, wife of the local shepherd, did housework for the Woolfs. LW left a sympathetic sketch of her in *Beginning Again*.

wouldn't you? I do adore you so, Mandy, that I would do anything to change any beastliness in myself, if I knew how it had shown itself.

Your
M.

To Virginia Woolf

Monday [August 4, 1913]   Asheham

Dearest,   We're just off for a walk & we'll go to Firle so that I can post this & you will get it tomorrow. I'm very well & it is pleasant here, but I'm not happy without you. I longed for a word this morning but no letter came—because of course the Twickenham Sunday post is too late; only I didn't think of that at the time.

I shall finish my review by tomorrow I hope but it's bad. Probably I shall come up tomorrow morning & type it in the afternoon. I shall see you Wednesday, darling one. I would give anything to see you today.

Your
M.

To Virginia Woolf

                                                    13, Cliffords Inn
5 Aug. [1913]   Fleet Street, E.C.

My sweetest Mandy,   We came up by a morning train & I got my review off all right. Then I had tea with Cecil [Woolf] & saw Vanessa for a little. Cecil dined with me at the Cock & there was James [Strachey].

Tomorrow I shall see you—it is the one thing I look forward to. Mandy, Mandy, dearest one, if you wont be careful of yourself for your own sake, you must be for mine—dont you know that I'm lost away from you?

I sent you a little picture this afternoon.

Goodnight, beloved
Your
M.

FROM SIR GEORGE SAVAGE

Aug 28 1913

Dear Mr Woolf

    Thank you for your note as to Virginia. She must *have breakfast in bed. Rest before & after meals. Only take short walks but lie out in open air as much as possible, taking Robson's Hypophosphate after meals. The calm & rest will do the rest, but she must accept this "invalid" for a time.*

Yours very truly
G. H. Savage

FROM SIR GEORGE SAVAGE

Sept 9 1913

Dear Mr Woolf

    I hardly know how or what to write for the uncertainty of the patient leaves me helpless. I certainly prefer this present resting in the country but if she is to see Head & this reduces my responsibility it must be done quickly.[1]

I am
Yours truly
G. H. Savage

1. VW, while on vacation with LW at Holford in Somerset, deteriorated to the point of nervous collapse; she agreed to return to London to see Dr. Henry Head (1861–1940), a neurologist recommended by Roger Fry, who had consulted him about about his own wife's mental illness. It was around 6:00 P.M. on this day that VW took an overdose of Veronal.

Sept 11 1913

Dear Mr Woolf
   I shall be pleased to see Dr. Belfrage with you here on Saturday or Monday.[1] *I can arrange an hour to suit Belfrage. I am very much distressed at this happening.*

> *I am*
> *Yours truly*
> *G. H. Savage*

TO LYTTON STRACHEY

38 Brunswick Sq

Sunday 14 Sept 1913   WC

Things could not have gone better than they have the last few days. V. regained full consciousness on Friday, & no sort of complication arose. In fact there is every reason to believe that by tomorrow or Tuesday no effect of having taken the veronal will remain. Mentally she seems to be exactly where she was for the last week at Holford, only rather more cheerful & calmer & more inclined to see that it is illness & nothing moral. She remembers everything about it, & talks quite calmly about it—her courage, as it has been all through, is amazing in facing it all. I'll let you know again how things go. There will be a consultation tomorrow at which we shall decide what is to be done.
   It did me good to be able to talk to you.

> Your
> L.

1. Sydney Henning Belfrage (1871–1950) was the Bell family's tried-and-true physician and the doctor whom LW consulted almost exclusively for the next six months and occasionally thereafter. Belfrage became a specialist in nutrition and wrote several books on the connection between nutrition and some nervous disorders.

Sept. 15. 1913.

Dear Mr Woolf,
    The fee for consultation is 2 guineas. I am so sorry to hear your news. It is terribly sad to see so fine a mind as Mrs. Woolf's lose balance, but I do hope time & rest will restore the stability again.
    I should like to thank you for your book The Village in the Jungle. I have enjoyed it more than anything I have read for many a day.

                                        I remain
                                        Yours sincerely
                                        Maurice B. Wright

FROM VANESSA BELL

Sep 26 [1913]

Dearest Leonard,
    Im afraid youre having a very bad time of it just now with this horrible food question. I am very glad I saw you for all you told me made it quite clear that this is just the same as before, perhaps not quite as bad as the worst part but on the whole very much the same. I am sure she will get quite right again but you'll need patience for months I expect. To tell you the truth I am rather worried about you, for you looked to me fearfully tired. But it's no use saying this for you havent much choice as to what you will do & I am sure you have sense and unselfishness enough to take all the care you can of yourself. . . .

                                        Your
                                        VB

To Janet Case[1]

Dalingridge Place
Tuesday 30 Sept [1913]   Tye's Cross, via East Grinstead

My dear Janet,

Margaret [Llewelyn Davies][2] told me that you would come down here & of course I knew you would. I only wish you could, but Margaret will have told you why it seems impossible.

There was a moment when V. said she very much wanted to see you. I thought I would tell you this, & also—what I know to be true—that it would have made no permanent difference if she had seen you. I believe when she was well she told you that, if she was ever like this again, she thought she would listen to you. She used often to say the same things to me about me—that if I told her that she was ill & could get well by doing things, she would believe me, & that if she had known me at that time she never would have had her first breakdown. But it is not true of me or of you. One can see it is so purely a physical thing: she *cannot* believe.[3]

I know so well that you want to help her & me, that I like to tell you this—& also that if the time comes when she begins to get a little better, I believe you will be able to help enormously. I shall tell you at once then.

Your affect.
Leonard Woolf

To Lytton Strachey

Dalingridge Place
Friday Oct 10, 1913   Tye's Cross, East Grinstead

I very nearly decided to come to you—it is what I should have liked best—but as its the first time I'm leaving her, & it's most important that the eating difficulty should not start again, I think I had better go where I'm in reach of the telephone. Next time if I may I shall come to you.

She has been amazingly better this last week—in fact most of the

1. Janet Case (1862–1937), who had tutored VW in Greek in 1902–03, was a close friend.
2. See Biographical Appendix.
3. Presumably LW meant *psychological* thing.

day now she is completely herself to talk to & quite cheerful. She also sleeps very well. I think one may hope now that there will be no relapse.

L.

To Violet Dickinson

Dalingridge Place
19 Oct 1913   Tye's Cross

Dear Miss Dickinson,

Virginia is not quite so well again—the food difficulty being very great. But these ups & downs are I suppose only to be expected. She was much better in the middle of the week, but went back on Friday.

Yours sincerely
Leonard Woolf

From Sir George Savage

Oct 25 1913

Dear Mr Woolf

I was glad to get your letter. I recognize your anxiety & that of Virginia's relations & I also fully understand why you and they thought it well to seek further and younger advice. I am not professionally jealous but that, while I was supposed to be looking after her, several others were also being consulted without reference to me caused me pain. This was made greater when another specialist was called down & I heard nothing from anyone. Fees certainly never entered into my mind but consideration did. My one desire is that Virginia should once more be her bright self and I do not mind by whose instrumentality it comes.

I am
Yours truly
G. H. Savage

November 19th [19]13.

My dearest Len,
   . . . I have been thinking a great deal about our conversation on the subject of your book, & the more I think about it the less I am convinced by your point of view. I understood that you do not want to hurt people's feelings & you asked me if I thought it would do if you went carefully through the book & eliminated what was likely to do so. I gathered from what you said the other day that you are only altering a few names.

   I suppose that other people's criticism has outweighed mine. Miss Cox, I understand, considered my criticism foolish—and Virginia thinks the book better than The Village in the Jungle.[2] *As to the latter that is a legitimate question of opinion—but as to the former, it appears to me that Miss Cox cannot judge my point of view. . . .*

> *Love to Virginia and*
> *yourself from*
> *your B.*

To VIRGINIA WOOLF

4 Dec 1913   Clifford's Inn

My sweetest Mandy,   I'm just going to lunch at the Cock. I have got through most of the packing & arranging by working yesterday afternoon & this morning & if things go on like this I might possibly catch the 3.20 tomorrow.[3] You dont know & now—because of that terrible

---

1. Three months earlier LW had finished a draft of *The Wise Virgins* and sent it to Bella for comment; she responded with a nine-page critique, harshly condemning much of it as an unpardonable attack on the Woolf family and their Putney neighbors, the Rosses. Meanwhile, his brother Philip wrote that he had enjoyed the book but found it depressing; he considered the portrait of Marie Woolf deadly accurate and doubted that criticism by the family should be taken seriously.
2. Katharine ("Ka") Cox (1887–1937), an old and reliable friend of VW's and one of a group of Cambridge graduates known as Neo-Pagans.
3. Since it was too much strain on VW to live in central London, LW was vacating their rooms in Clifford's Inn. Virginia was at Asheham in the care of two nurses, the last of whom left in February.

company of bees & nits & all manner of horrid winged things buzzing in your brain—you dont believe how I long to see you when I'm away. The books are the devil. I started on them at once after lunch yesterday. After tea I went to Jos. May in Howland St & told him to send a man to make an estimate for moving & storing this morning. Then I dashed in to Gordon Sq where I saw Nessa & Clive & Lytton with rings in his ears. Went to the *Wild Duck* with Ka [Cox] & two young people. Met Duncan [Grant] in the pit & Dominic Spring Rice later here.[1] May's man came this morning & I've settled with him & will tell you all about it when I see you. Margaret [Llewelyn Davies] comes here to tea.

Dearest, I do hope you've been good & sensible & fairly happy. I do love you, Mandy, more & more than ever.

Your
M.

My coming tomorrow depends (a) on Col. Banister from whom I have not heard & (b) on whether I have to go & dine with Mother. If I dont come by the 3.20 I shant come until Sat.

FROM MARIE WOOLF

11 Dec. 1913

My dear Leonard

I am now returning you the Manuscript [of The Wise Virgins] *by Registered Post, the reading of which has given me more pain than evidently you intended. . . . You thought fit to hold us all up, in connection with others at Rickstead [Putney], to ridicule, contempt and pity. . . . You have not convinced me one jot that the people at Rickstead are one bit less valuable to the common working of the Universe, than the people at Bloomsbury. I don't know what the Lawrences [Stephens] are developing into in your next chapters but as far as I have made their acquaintance I have discovered nothing especially attractive, useful, or great. That God had made the Ladies [Vanessa and Virginia] tall and beautiful, was not their fault. I dare say Ethel would have chosen to be like them had she had a voice in*

---

1. Dominic Spring-Rice (1889–1940), son of the British Ambassador to Washington during the First World War, was a London socialite.

the matter.[1] *No Leonard, this style of writing is unworthy of you, you can do better, if only you would give first preference to the finer part of your nature and intellect. If you publish the book as it stands, I feel there will be a serious break between us. . . .*

With love
Your Mother.

TO LYTTON STRACHEY

12 Dec 1913

Asheham House
Rodmell   Lewes

I enclose my novel [*The Wise Virgins*]. Will you read it & let me have it back at the very earliest possible? And will you *really* be absolutely candid? Your opinion cannot possibly be more damnatory than all I have had except one. This is the position. My family think it a rotten bad book & forbid me to publish it. Now if it is rotten or even poorly, it isn't worth while bringing all these people about my ears, obviously. But if it's otherwise worth publishing, I shouldn't mind, I think, telling the whole lot of them to go to Hell. I am so sick of the whole affair, that I shall be relieved if you dont condemn it, but probably just as relieved if you do. So dont spare me.

V. goes on much the same, improving always a little, I think.

I heard from Arnold today that he is going to reprint *The Village in the Jungle*, as he has sold out the first edition. But I shall never write another book after these damned Virgins.

Your
L.[2]

---

1. Ethel Davis was one of two fictional unmarried sisters who were roughly modeled on Connie and Sylvia Ross. Sylvia married Edgar Woolf the following summer; Connie then lived much of the time with them.
2. Strachey, who had detested *The Village in the Jungle*—too many "blacks" in it—generally praised the new manuscript but suggested that it be put aside for at least six months. LW next gave it to Vanessa Bell, who passed it on to Adrian Stephen. No record has survived of Adrian's reaction, but Vanessa commented that, although the story would be bound to offend some of those portrayed in it, "feelings, after all, *arent* very important." Forster, who had heard about it from VW, wrote the following March to recommend against publication to avoid hurting Marie Woolf.

TO LYTTON STRACHEY

Your letter was splendid & very encouraging. I want very much to
talk to you as it's impossible to go into the question by letter. I shall
stay here now until after Xmas. Could I come to you for a night or
two possibly later on or will you be in town?

Things go on the same here. Craig, you know, does not expect
complete recovery until the spring. He says you can hardly ever get a
complete recovery at this time of the year, but that it comes in early
spring.

                                               Yr
                                               L.

TO JANET CASE

Dear Janet,

I feel I must let you know how much good you did & pleasure you
gave to Virginia (& to me too). She has been extraordinarily well
today, better I think than she has ever been, & really able to take a
steady view of things. And she has said two or three times how much
she enjoyed having you here & asked me whether I thought you would
come again. She was very well too all yesterday up to the time she
went to bed when we had a bad hour of it—but there hasn't been a
shadow over today.

The flowers you sent are like spring coming into the year. V. is going
to write to you tomorrow.

                                               Yours
                                               Leonard Woolf

I think it was very *good* of you to take the trouble to criticize my
'creations' before me. You can now explain to Margaret [Llewelyn
Davies] when you see her why I wrote to her some time ago that I
thought she would probably dislike my novel!

Feb 4 [*1914*]

Dear Woolf
  Thank you for your note. I quite agree that the time has come to place reliance on your wife's self-control and I am very glad for her sake that it is so. She must rejoice in her recovery and her entry into happier conditions of living. I do hope that your wife recognizes fully the enormous importance of ordering her life in the most careful & thorough fashion—the all important regularity of habits—the hours of rest, immutability of meal times & of going to bed. She should take life very quietly in the early hours of the day and be in bed no less than 10 hours out of the 24.
  Will you let me see her occasionally so that she may feel that there is still some slight supervision of her life from a medical standpoint. Please remember me very kindly & convey my congratulations and good wishes.

Yours sincerely
S. Henning Belfrage

TO EDWARD ARNOLD[1]

[Mid-February 1914]   [Asheham House]

Dear Mr Arnold,
  I have now been through the MS. I find that you have marked 36 places. Of these 36 I am prepared to alter or omit 28, that is to say all in which, as far as I am aware, plain speaking can be miscalled coarseness. There are however 8 places where I regret to say I cannot agree to omission & I propose as shortly as possible to give my reasons.
  The passages . . . in which the question of children is discussed by Gwen & Harry, & I consider that if they are omitted the whole conception of the book & the psychology of the characters is altered. If they are cut out, Gwen's act at the crisis is one of mere lust, an act

---

1. In a letter transmitting *The Wise Virgins* to his publisher, Edward Arnold, LW expressed hesitation about publishing the manuscript. Arnold replied that the book "demonstrates further evidence of your powers as a writer," though he requested "a few concessions to the taste of the reading public."

completely incongruous with her character. Further the whole moral significance of the book vanishes, & the moral significance is this: Harry is living in a circle of somewhat unnatural cultured persons & like them he indulges in a habit of wild exaggerated talk which he believes that he believes. The effect of such talk upon Gwen who is half in love with him is that her *imagination* (not her mere desires) is fired & she really believes & proceeds to act upon her belief. When the reality is as near to Harry as that, he finds that *he* dare not act up to his talk, because it was more talk than belief.

These five passages I cannot under any circumstances agree to cut out, though I will go through them & alter anything which might be misunderstood as coarse language. . . .

If you will agree to include these 8 passages & will allow me to make certain alterations in the book in order to avoid (if possible) the risk of people identifying themselves with certain characters, I shall be very pleased if you will make me an offer for the book.[1]

Yours sincerely
[L. S. Woolf]

To Virginia Woolf[2]

8 March 1914

The Lacket
Lockeridge, Marlborough, Wilts

Dearest One,   I'm very glad I came here. It is really very pleasant, though pouring incessantly. I had quite a good night & my head certainly is a bit better this morning.

I'll keep all gossip till we meet principally because I'm engaged in an argument against Lytton & [Harry] Norton on the Ulster Question—which prevents my writing this.[3] Goodbye beloved

Your
M.

1. LW eventually agreed to alter most of the eight contested passages as well.
2. Although VW was much improved, the unremitting strain of caring for her nearly broke LW's own health. With Janet Case and Ka Cox standing in for him at Asheham, he spent ten days with Lytton Strachey, who had withdrawn to a country cottage in Wiltshire to begin writing *Eminent Victorians*.
3. The Irish Home Rule bill, pending in Parliament, was caught in a bitter controversy over the inclusion of Ulster.

To Virginia Woolf

The Lacket
9 March 1914   Lockeridge   Near Marlborough

Dearest Mandy,   It is snowing hard & all yesterday it rained hard—
so I'm having my usual weather here. Norton left this morning. He
goes on Sat to Sicily for 2 months to work at his dissertation. I like
him though he's too clever for your sodden headed old Mongoose. We
have had much talk about it & about.

I'm going to stay on here for a bit. I slept very well again last night
& eat hugely. Yesterday was a very good day on the whole & so is
today—though my head is still rather troublesome.

I wish I were with you at Asheham—it's the one thing I feel perpetually when I'm away from you always. But I suppose it's sensible
to stay away now & try to get rid of this silly headache. And then
we'll be perfectly happy together again.

Your adoring
M.

To Virginia Woolf

The Lacket
Tuesday   10 March 1914   Lockeridge, Marlborough

Dearest One,   It is a divine morning so we're going off, before the
rain comes on again, to walk. I had another very good night & my
head troubles me only a very little this morning. I think I shall stay
here now & possibly go on to Bella for a night. Vanessa, I forgot to
tell you, told me she could come on 17th & 18th & would like to. So
I arranged that, & I'll go on the 18th if I'm all right to Kettering for
Margaret [Llewelyn Davies].[1]

Your letter came last night & I've read it over & over so you see
what joy it gave me & how I adore you.

Your
M.

1. Bella and her husband, Robert Lock, were living in Streetly, Staffordshire. Kettering was
one of several manufacturing towns LW planned to visit in connection with Women's Co-
operative Guild business.

There is a new book made for you, I believe, *Ouida: A Memoir* by Elizabeth Lee. I'm rather homesick for you, Mandy, this morning.

To Virginia Woolf

The Lacket
Tuesday   10 March 1914   Lockeridge, Marlborough

Beloved,   I feel I must write to you again today because my other letter was so hurried & tomorrow's may not reach you—with those abominable posts—until Friday—& your dearest letter has made me long for you more if possible even than before. I want to be with you so much—the world is such a bitter stale place except the bit of it that's you. I never want to leave you again for a single moment. And then at the same time I'm undecided about when I'm to come back. I feel this new air is doing me good—the head still troubles at times but today has certainly been much better. I could stay here until Sat or even Monday which would save me the travelling to Asheham on Sat & back to London to go to Kettering on Tues. Or I might go to Bella from here on Sat & thence on Tues to Kettering. I feel that from mere health point of view either of these is wiser. But I have such a longing for you that I dont want to do either, but come back to you. I cant make up my mind not to see you, dearest, for another week. And then it's foolish not to do everything to get perfectly fit. Which shall I do, mistress?

   Now I must go & take a bath. I go to bed at 9.30. Good night, my dearest Mandy.

Your
M.

If the Cascara [laxative] does not act you must get Liquor Paraffin *at once*

To Virginia Woolf

The Lacket,
11 March 1914   Lockeridge, Marlborough.

Beloved,   The happiest moment of the day is when at ½ past 4 we come in from a walk & I see your letter lying on the table. Sometimes in the last few days I've thought it may be a bad thing to love anyone as much as I love you—but I dont really believe it can be—only it cuts one off in some odd way from the rest of the world. Listening to Lytton & Norton, I sometimes almost hugged myself to think what you are to me & I am to you—they seemed so wandering & incomplete & everything so thin to them & to me—everything with you in it— o rich. All this morning I walked by myself in the woods, & for hardly a moment could I think of anything but you, it was just as if I had dropped back two years to the time before you took me into your service & I was down there on Exmoor. I want so much from you, dearest one—& when I'm with you I get it all, I believe, & I believe that I do when I get your letters saying that you do want me.

I've been out almost all day today in the sun walking slowly. It's good country but not as good as Sussex. I really am, I think, getting better, practically no pain today, only noises & dullness but not as much as before. Bella wants me to come to her this weekend & I think perhaps I had better do this: I can go from here to her fairly easily on Saturday. I can stay with her until Tuesday. Kettering is not far from Birmingham so that I might go there Tuesday night. That will save me a lot of travelling. I can do the factories with Worley on Wed. morning & might get to Asheham Wed. evening.[1] In any case I shd. come Thurs. morning. How I shall exist without seeing you until then, I dont know—but I feel it's absurd to give way to my longing for you & so possibly bring on this headache again by rushing backwards & forwards. But beloved Mandy if you want me for one little minute, do call me back as I believe the joy of your calling me back would prevent my ever having a headache again.

Lytton is very nice, hard at work on a short life of Cardinal Manning! He is probably going to join James [Strachey] in Moscow. We have not discussed Clive's book very much—it is condemned. You know that Ottoline has had a reconciliation with Vanessa & Roger? Lytton is very bitter against her.[2]

Let me know whether the Cascara acts properly again. Dearest creature, I shall do what I suggest about Bella—unless you wire to me.

1. J. J. Worley (1876–1944), member of the Midland District Council of the Associated Union of Co-operative Employees, had joined the Co-operative movement at the age of fourteen and was active in it for the rest of his life.

2. Cardinal Manning was the first of the character sketches in *Eminent Victorians*; the others were Florence Nightingale, Thomas Arnold and Gordon of Khartoum. Clive Bell's book, *Art*, marked its author's debut as an art critic. The imbroglio involving Ottoline Morrell, Roger Fry and Vanessa Bell went back to the time when Roger fell out of love with the former and in love with the latter.

And you'll post & write to me on Friday, Sat, Sun. & Mon. [+] morning to Tregonna, Streetly, Staffs. Would you also write me a line to say how you are on Mon. morning to Kettering, Poste Restante so that I shall in any case hear from you.

Your

M.

[+] After Monday morning it wd be no good posting to me but if you wanted me, you would wire to Streetly up to Tues after[noon] & after that to Kettering Post Restante.

To Virginia Woolf

The Lacket,

Lockeridge, Marlborough.

12 March 1914

Dearest One,   I am sitting here alone, Lytton in the next room writing of Cardinal Manning. I have just read the *Times* & the *Lit. Sup.* And that is about all I've done today. I hardly read & dont work, walking very slowly morning & afternoon, eating hugely, & going to bed at ½ past 9. I do feel considerably fitter but I do wish this dullness &c in the back of my head would go altogether.

You must get from Day's that book about Goldwin Smith which we saw reviewed in the *Nation*. It is by A. Haultain, & really is unmatchable.[1] "I knew both the Stephens" is one comment "They were both *hard* men, Leslie less hard, more genial than FitzJames.[2] They were both critics. Neither of them set out to construct anything, to prove anything, to establish anything. They were always criticizing what other people did."

Lytton is very nice: he isn't really ever very pernicketty with me, I think, because I go my own way a good deal. We laugh as much as usual. He has a very high opinion of my mistress.

But there's only one person I want. Will you really take me in your

1. Goldwin Smith (1823–1910), a British scholar and academic who spent the second half of his life in Canada and the United States, left a manuscript of reminiscences, which his private secretary, Arnold Haultain, published in 1913.
2. Sir James Fitzjames Stephen (1829–1894), a noted lawyer and judge, was Sir Leslie Stephen's brother.

arms & kiss me, when I'm allowed to run back to you next week? Mandy darling, I love you, I love you.

Your
M.

Bella & Cecil have had influenza & now Mother has it!

To Virginia Woolf

The Lacket

13 March 1914
Lockeridge

Sweetest Mandy, Do you know that I almost cried when I got your letter just now? Merely from longing for you. Is that foolish, dearest? I've been depressed & wanting you so much today.

It's a wretched day & my head has been worrying me again, not very bad, but it's disappointing that it does not go. However I suppose one must expect ups & downs.

I think I shall go to Bella. I dont think it does to stay too long here. Lytton is very nice but he's exacting. I very nearly enraged him this morning because I said I saw no reason to believe that the Greeks didn't love women! Also this isn't really a very comfortable house: there's only one comfortable chair & no sofa, so that it's rather miserable if one is not feeling well.

There is no doubt of one thing, beloved, & that is that we do suit each other in some amazing way. I've never been alone with anyone else for a few days without irritating & being irritated. And yet you can day after day & all day give me perfect happiness.

Lytton read me last night what he had written about Manning. It's very good & amusing. We argue & talk about books & Vanessa & Clive & Roger & Adrian. He thinks Nessa by nature a virgin & Adrian a cretin. He has a tremendous opinion of Mistress Mandril. He said this morning that your handwriting was the most "eminent" he had ever seen. I think sometimes he is rather jealous of your old Mongoose.

Dont think, dear one, that I'm ill. I'm not. Really I'm even today much better than I was when I came here. But I'm lonely without you. You cant realize how utterly you would end my life for me if you had taken that sleeping mixture successfully or if you ever dismissed me.

Some of the country round here is very good. Very open & rolling downs, & then there are very mystic mounds & tombs of prehistoric kings. But it doesn't 'dispose itself' in that amazing way of Sussex. It hasn't the character or the atmosphere.

I think you might like to read Purcell's life of Manning & W. Ward's life of Newman & another amusing book I looked at here is Hurrell Froude's *Remains*. I have read partly Newman's *Apologia*; he seems to me a self-sentimentalist. But Haultain's Goldwin Smith is the gem.

I feel the usual post-Stracheyan conviction of dust in my mouth & that it is useless for me ever to try to write again.

It is worth going away from you I always say in order to come back, but it's hard being away from you.

Your M.

Love to Ka. Will you thank her for her letter?
Has Cascara acted?

To Virginia Woolf

14 March 1914

Tregonna,
Streetly, Staffs.

Beloved,   I got here not long ago after quite an easy journey through Cheltenham & Birmingham. I am very much better today, scarcely any headache & feeling much more secure in the pate than I've done for many a long day. This is a comfortable villa house like Little Talland rather, with fine open country, speckled with similar villas around it.[1]

I fear very much that I shall not hear from you, dearest creature, today because I think I told you to write to Lockeridge too late. I am writing this early in the afternoon so that it may be certain to come to you Monday.

I kiss you, dearest one, in imagination & worship you, Mandril Sarcophagus Rarissima.

Your
M.

1. As a refuge after her 1910 mental breakdown VW had rented a house at Firle, in Sussex, and called it "Little Talland" after Talland House, the Stephen family vacation house in Cornwall.

To Virginia Woolf

15 March 1914

Tregonna,
Streetly, Staffs.

Dearest, I did get your letter last night after all which sent me to
bed as happy as I can be not having the great Brute in person. Yesterday
really was the best day I've had for weeks—my head practically well.
I didn't have a very good night last night & so I am feeling slightly
less spry today—but there is no doubt at all but that I shall return to
you completely recovered.

It is quite pleasant here: Bella very friendly & Lock also. I am sitting
in a comfortable chair! We are going to motor to Lichfield now which
is why I'm writing early to you.

I hope, Mandy dearest, you didn't mind my sending you an informal
paguino from here.

I had a letter from Margaret [Llewelyn Davies] last night—I had
written to her against the *Herald*—& she now agrees with me.[1]

I cut the enclosed out of a Birmingham evening paper.

I cant write because I'm continually interrupted. I love you, Mandy
dearest.

Your
M.

To Virginia Woolf

16 March 1914

Tregonna,
Streetly, Staffs.

Beloved Mandy, After all we didnt go to Lichfield yesterday because
the car went wrong & the rain rained—so we decided to go this afternoon. Today there is a hurricane of wind & rain varied with snow &
so I dont suppose we shall go after all.

I'm much better again today after a very good night. I've told you
the complete truth, Mistress, about myself the whole time, because I
knew well that you would dismiss me from your service if ever I told
you a lie.

1. The *Herald* was a left-wing, vaguely syndicalist daily newspaper founded in 1911; it was
taken over by the Labour Party and the trades unions in 1922 and published as the *Daily
Herald*.

There is a small black companion dog here, but I haven't much to say to him. I'm afraid you must have had a very bad time with those two at Asheham—beat them well, great one. You ought to have let me take Max with me.[1]

It is just possible that you may get this tomorrow morning—that is why I am writing it before lunch.

Tomorrow I go to Kettering & then joy, joy, joy! I shall see you, dearest one, again.

We have talked about my book & things seem more subdued.

Your
M.

To Virginia Woolf

Tregonna,

17 March 1914   Streetly, Staffs.

Dearest One,   You may see your old Mongoose trotting, galloping rather, back to you before you get this. I have n't heard from Worley at all & I've been telegraphing all over the kingdom to find out whether he is going to meet me tomorrow at Kettering. If I dont hear by 4 oclock, I shall return to London tonight & to Asheham tomorrow.

Yesterday we motored to Lichfield & then on round the country. I saw Johnson's birthplace & the chair he sat in & many other interesting things which I thought you would approve of my seeing. The wind & cold were too much for me & I got the headache again in the evening. However I'm really a good deal better today.

Lord, Lord! how I long to see you again, darling creature. I hope I dont hear from Worley.

Your
M.

1. The Woolfs had two dogs, Shot and Max.

To Janet Case

21 May 1914   Asheham

Dear Janet,

Things have been a little up & down but on the whole good lately. The weight dropped & I had to get V. to begin taking milk again which was rather awful.

. . . It's quite clear from what Craig wrote & said that V cannot be left completely alone yet, & on the other hand it naturally depresses her to feel that I get people to come here when I want to go off. . . .[1]

Yours
L S W

To Janet Case

30 June 1914   Asheham

My dear Janet,

I think you're the most remembering person I know. Your card again was the only thing which stood between us & no *Times* on Monday morning. Every Monday morning now a little Poem of praise of you goes up around Virginia's bed & breakfast from us both.

I should have liked to have looked in on you last week but it was quite impossible. London did V. no harm & after the first few hours the effect of the dentistry passed off. With some difficulty I got her to see Craig on Sat morning. He thought her distinctly better, but he is rather concerned about the fixity of the ideas about food, & he said "she would go to pieces very rapidly if she were left to have her own way."

She has been a good deal better again since we got back. We had George Moore & Desmond MacCarthy for the week end & she was quite happy.

1. LW was making plans to attend the annual conference of the Women's Co-operative Guild in Birmingham; Janet Case was once more to stand in for him at Asheham. It was on this occasion that LW drafted and VW signed a "contract" committing her to rest, eat and sleep properly and to be wise and happy.

I hope you'll *choose* a time & come yourself in July.

We both thought your letter in the *Nation* very good & not at all dead.[1]

LSW

To Lytton Strachey

17, The Green,
Richmond.

4 Jan 1914 [1915]

I've sent His Eminence to Henry [Lamb]. I think its very nearly perfect—far & away the best thing you've ever written. You must go on to Florence, Victoria, & General Gordon.[2] It's a great invention, this kind of biography & the material just fits your method. But it's almost inconceivable that you'll ever find any group quite so grotesque & grim as the Cardinals.

L.

To Lytton Strachey

17, The Green,
Richmond.

10 Feb 1915

When I wrote you I did so with two definite purposes both of which as soon as I began I forgot.

The first is that we have at last got a rather nice house here—a "Georgian residence" as the agents call it. We shall go in in March. And we think of setting up a printing press in the cellarage. Now Ray tells us you know all about printing presses. Is this true & can you tell us how & where one gets them & what they cost?[3]

1. The letter was a rousing feminist statement on behalf of women's rights and a stinging denunciation of efforts by Catholic groups to prevent the WCG from endorsing a divorce-law reform to extend women's prerogatives and protections.
2. Strachey's sketch of Cardinal Manning, after nine months of writing and revision, was finally done. Queen Victoria, to have been the subject of another essay, was saved for full biographical treatment.
3. The Georgian residence was Hogarth House in Richmond, chosen because it was far enough from central London to insure calm for VW but close enough for easy visits. Ray was Rachel Strachey.

The second is that Marjorie dined with us the other night & told us her amazing history. I thought she seemed verging on nervous breakdown. But V. wants very much to know what *you* think about the affair.[1]

L.

[In VW's hand:]
Have you read Pope?
Have you read Sir Leslie on Pope? Well—
what do you think of it?[2]

To John Hills[3]

17, The Green,
Richmond.

7 March 1915

Dear Jack,

I'm sorry to say Virginia is again seriously ill. She had been very much better up to about a fortnight ago & she liked Richmond so much that we had just taken a house here. The doctor thought it a very good place for her. Then about two weeks ago she suddenly got one of her old headaches. We went at once to Craig who is now her doctor & she has been practically in bed ever since. The doctors think there is very serious danger that another complete breakdown is coming. We are living in rooms here until we get into our new house which we were going to do on March 25th. It is very difficult to know exactly what to do & the doctors are not yet decided. There is to be another consultation here Tuesday, at which I think it will be finally decided what is to be done. I now have two nurses here.

What I want to ask you is whether you would give directions that the £100 which you allow Virginia & which is paid to her at the end of March should be paid into her account at once. It would be very

1. Marjorie Strachey had fallen in love with Josiah Wedgwood, scion of the pottery family and a Liberal MP, who was married and had seven children.
2. VW had been reading Pope's poetry and her father's biography *Alexander Pope* (1880), all of it with pleasure and the latter with evident pride.
3. John Hills (1867–1938), a solicitor and MP, had married VW's half sister, Stella Duckworth, who died three months after the wedding in 1897. Following her death, Hills made over the income from their marriage settlement to VW and Vanessa.

good of you if you would. The expenses with nurses &c are so heavy
& much of it one has to pay at once. The last year has left us with
very little balance, but if the £100 can be paid earlier I can get along
for a month or two which will give me time to make arrangements.

Yours sincerely
Leonard Woolf

If you give directions, will you say that the money should be paid
into her account at the London County & Westminster Bank, Richmond Branch? We had to change our bank when we came here.

To Violet Dickinson

Hogarth House,
28 April 1915   Richmond.

Dear Violet,
I had meant to let you know how things went. I am afraid they are
very bad. She is worse than I have ever seen her before. She hasn't
had a minute's sleep in the last 60 hours. I have seen Craig again this
afternoon. He is very pessimistic. And yet a fortnight ago she seemed
to be doing so splendidly. She ate so well & put on weight, & even
now she is a stone heavier than she was ever in her life before. I would
let you know if there were anything you could do but I'm afraid there
is nothing that anyone can do.

Yours
Leonard Woolf

To Violet Dickinson

Hogarth House,
1 May 1915   Richmond.

Dear Violet,
It was very nice to see you & to be able to talk to you. Virginia had
no sleep last night but is rather more clear this morning.
I hope *I* didn't give you the impression that Vanessa washed her
hands of it. She really cares enormously & has always done everything

she could. She has always come whenever any big change had to be considered.

Yours sincerely
Leonard Woolf

Hogarth House,
Richmond.

10 May 1915

Dear Violet,

I went to [Ian] Mackenzie Saturday a week ago & he saw her the same day when she was too bad to realize him at all.[1] I saw him several times afterwards, took Vanessa to see him & then Vanessa & I went to Craig who had had a consultation with him. He was very anxious to undertake the case. But finally we decided not to make any change at present. This was partly because I did not feel fully confident in him & partly because V. took a turn for the better last week & one does not want to risk an upset. She is much less excited & has stopped the incoherent talking to a great extent. She is also sleeping splendidly without drugs.

Yours
Leonard Woolf

Hogarth House,
Richmond.

12 July 1915

V. has been really a good deal better lately, I think. All the excitement has gone & she has been quite contented to rest & eat. The only thing is that she suddenly turned very violently against me about 4 weeks ago, & although it is a little better lately, she is still very opposed. It makes it all rather more difficult of course. Craig says its very common & will pass away.

Yours
L S W.

1. Mackenzie cannot be identified.

20 September 1915   Asheham

We are here once more in superb sunshine. V. is a good deal better.
I hear you've written a very good Russian play about Clive. We both
want to read it. Will you send it here? And I should like to read about
Miss Nightingale.[1]

                                                    L.

To Lady Robert Cecil

                                                    Hogarth House
8 March 1916   Paradise Road   Richmond

Dear Lady Robert Cecil,
Virginia is most frightfully sorry not to be able to come after all
today. She has been rather rushed with things these last days, & today
she has a headache. She is absolutely forbidden by the doctors to do
anything at all when these headaches return—& (though she would
have flaunted their orders today in order to see you) I have stept in
& insisted on her keeping in & doing nothing. But she hopes you will
let her come instead some day later.

                                                    Yours sincerely,
                                                    Leonard Woolf

To Margaret Llewelyn Davies

[Early May 1916]   [Hogarth House, Richmond]

Dear Margaret,
I am in great trouble about conscription.[2] I shall of course apply
for exemption on grounds of health (shaking hands) & domestic hardship. Craig ought to give me a pretty strong letter about V—but I am
not hopeful of the results. I feel I am a conscientious objector—for I

1. The Russian play was *Old Lyttoff*; the sketch of Florence Nightingale was completed in
late June.
2. In January 1916, Parliament enacted a conscription bill for unmarried men; in late April,
the exemption of married men was lifted.

loathe the thought of taking any part in this war—& yet I feel very much the difficulty, from the point of view of reason, of the position. I go to see Craig on Wednesday to hear what he says about V.[1]

The *Labour Leader*[2] has given me the sack because I'm not descriptive—which I regret very much. I will let you have the Taxation lecture this evening or tomorrow.

Leonard

To Lytton Strachey

27 Oct., 1916   Hogarth.

I return the MS. which I thought amazingly good.[3] It made me laugh until I cried twice, once at "where he remained for the next thirty-six hours" and once at the painful mystery of the animal world. It is almost incredible that such a person should have existed. Do hurry up with the General.

Have you heard that Moore is engaged to a Miss Ely who "is very young compared to me"? They marry about the New Year, he says.[4]

L.

To Virginia Woolf[5]
[Postcard]
[October 29, 1917]   In train to Bolton

I've had a very easy & quite comfortable journey. Tea at Manchester & I shall get dinner at Bolton. I got to M. about 5 nearly ½ hour before time. *Do* look after yourself. Love.

L.

1. Craig thought that VW would probably have a breakdown. Both he and Maurice Wright wrote letters declaring LW unfit to serve on the grounds both of VW's medical condition and of his trembling hands. LW was formally exempted on June 30 and again the following year.
2. The weekly journal of the Independent Labour Party.
3. The chapter on Dr. Arnold; only General Gordon remained to be written.
4. Dorothy Ely (1892–1977) was a classics student at Newnham College, Cambridge, when she met Moore, whose lectures she attended.
5. Now deeply engaged in work on international government, LW spent several days lecturing on the subject to Women's Co-operative Societies in industrial cities. At each stop he was the guest of a local member of the Society.

To Virginia Woolf
[Postcard]
Tuesday [October 30, 1917]   Broome House

I've had quite a comfortable day here & am just starting for Oldham.
They are very "kindly" people. Love.

L

To Virginia Woolf

30 Nov [October] 1917   Manchester Station

My dearest dearest Mistress,   I am on my way to the Eckhards & this
½ hour will be well employed writing to you.[1] O I do miss you so my
sweetest Mistress, & being away from you shows how much more &
more each year I love you. It would have been so different to have had
you jumping about all over Lancashire by my side.

It has, however, been comfortable. You needn't fear my being
starved if they're all like Mrs Booth. A party of 3 accompanied me
back to the house from the lecture, & a spread of boiled haddock,
apple tart, tea, toast, butter, marmalade, & cake in front of a huge
fire awaited us. We ate large quantities at 11 P.M. & at 11.30 I was fast
asleep. A fire in my bedroom & a hot bath in the morning. Mrs Booth
is Scotch of the upper working class, very kind but rather sticky in
conversation. Another woman was there of the ultra-pacifist type &
full of good conversation culled from Morel, Bertie [Russell], & Goldie
[Dickinson] & watered by a dim understanding.[2]

The lecture was fairly successful: it was infinitely too long & rather
difficult to cut. A horrid (literally) & dirty person in the chair, very
proud of having been a century ago at Oxford & said to have been
Herbert Fisher's tutor—a statement I doubt.[3] An audience of 50—
three quarters pacifist & ¼ militarist. They asked many questions but
it was a little too difficult for them. I think I shall have to cut it down
& deliver it from notes only.

1. The Eckhards were a prosperous middle-class family whom LW knew through their son-in-law Sydney Waterlow. LW regarded Mrs. Eckhard as typical of "those immensely energetic, dominating Jewish matriarchs," for whom he had mixed feelings.
2. E. D. Morel (1873–1924), author and journalist, was a leading proponent of greater democratic control of foreign policy.
3. H. A. L. Fisher (1865–1940), the historian and statesman, was VW's cousin.

I must post this now. Beloved, you are being sensible? You dont know how many times a day I think of you & always with a longing to see you, talk to you, & kiss you.

Your adoring
M.

To Virginia Woolf

Werneth Park,
Oldham.

31 October 1917

Dearest One,   I'm really in the same place on the same seat as when I wrote to you yesterday waiting for the same train to Didsbury. But I took this paper to try & give you some flavour of the incredible place in which Goose M was strawed last night. O Lord, I wish you could have seen its hideous pomposity & Miss Lees![1] A pinched little spinster rotted & rotting with wealth & snobbery. And Lord & Lady Emmott— no relation unfortunately of the great & noble insect tribe—who were staying in the house.[2]

But first about yesterday. Your letter came in the morning, & blew away from me a slight despondency which was accumulating from a longing for you. I hadn't expected to see your handwriting or an envelope quite as soon—& it was such a joy.

I had a quiet morning by myself & then Mrs E[ckhard] & a queer daughter, appropriately called Beetle, appeared. Mrs E is really rather nice, very impulsive & downright & at first sight objectionable. In the afternoon she suddenly determined to pull up or cut down all the trees in her garden. So we set to & you can imagine that I thoroughly enjoyed myself with saw & pick axe.

I want to post this before my train leaves, so if it breaks off suddenly, you will understand.

Then to Manchester where I dined well & caught the train to Wemeth. Miss Lees met me in a car & drove me to the lecture. The lecture [was] much more successful. I wrote out a few notes & delivered it straight from them which I find much better than reading it. The audience about 50 & very nice & more intelligent than at Bolton.

1. Marjorie Lees was the daughter of Sarah Lees (1842–1935), widow of a rich industrialist who spent most of her time and fortune on improving Oldham, a center of the cotton trade and by general repute the ugliest town in Britain.
2. Alfred Emmott, 1st Baron Emmott of Oldham (1858–1926), was at this time Director of the War Trade Department. "Emmet" is Old English for "ant."

Beloved, I adore you & every feather on your magnificent form. I wonder if you've really missed me one millionth of my longing for you.

If I've time, I'll continue this at Didsbury, but if I wait, [you] wont get it at Charleston.[1]

> Good bye, sweetest mistress,
> Your servant
> M.

The largest canine, a St Bernard, I've ever seen, has just been up to & making friends with me.

To Virginia Woolf

Nov 1 1917

Broome House
Didsbury   Manchester

My darling Mistress, Your letter—No 2—only arrived this morning, so it takes a long time from Asheham & I shall send this to Hogarth where it will meet you I hope tomorrow. It was sad not hearing from you yesterday but I thought it was probable that I should n't & it made up for it to find the letter on today's breakfast table.

It is pleasant having a morning without a train journey for I dont go on to Maclesfield until the afternoon. I'm going to see Scott of the *M G* on my way there.[2] There is a sameness about my days here. Most of yesterday I spent talking to Mrs Eckhard who is a real character. She dates most things in her life from the day on which she had her appendix removed. She has a curiously restless & eager mind & though old, fights against age in the right way. We spent the afternoon trying to uproot a large tree, Mrs E. using an axe with great vigour & inefficiency. Then Margaret Ashton—the woman who was chairman of the Suffrage Meeting we went to—came to dinner. She took the chair at my lecture & we went in to Manchester together. She is one of those "public work" elderly women of enormous & too unrestrained energy. Very nice but hardly ever stopping to think. There were about 70 or 80 at the lecture which went off fairly well. I dont think I'm a good

1. Charleston, a farmhouse in Sussex, was the home of Vanessa Bell and Duncan Grant.
2. C. P. Scott (1846–1932) edited the *Manchester Guardian* from 1872 to 1929 and made it one of the world's most respected newspapers. LW wanted to discuss with him the Ceylon government's handling of an outbreak of civil violence two years before.

propagandist lecturer. What I say is too calculated to make people think & they wont & dont. There was a soldier & an officer in the audience. The soldier made a violent revolutionary speech. He said he had begun the war as a jingo, he was now a complete pacifist. Mr Eckhard & one of the innumerable Miss Eckhards were at the lecture. He is the queerest gray little German you can imagine, with a little wrinkled twitching face: very [indistinct word] & speaking perpetually at a tremendous pace with a "you know" & a "you see" between each sentence. I had no idea there were so many Miss Eckhards: I thought there was one & there are four.

I had a hot-water bottle last night & slept like a marmot & was given early tea in bed at 8.

I do hope Asheham had been properly aired & warmed—it really was scandalous of Mrs A.[1] I shall never leave you again, I think, partly because you want a Stewart Goose to look after you & partly because life is so intolerable without you. I keep on thinking this morning that it's only today & to-morrow now before I see you again. We'll go & fetch poor old Tinker from the vet in the afternoon & walk by the river & then we'll come back to tea & sit over the fire & talk.

Good bye, my dearest One

Your servant
M.

I am very well & not a bit tired.

To Violet Dickinson

15 Dec. 1917

Hogarth House,
Paradise Road, Richmond, Surrey.

Dear Violet,

It was very nice of you to write to me. My brother was not in the same regiment of Hussars as Edward Horner—he was in the 20th—but he had been through all the fighting as cavalry safely.[2] Then in the muddle in Bourlon Wood they were sent dismounted to support

1. Mrs. Attfield, a neighbor and housekeeper at Asheham, had failed to have the house ready for VW's arrival.
2. Cecil and Philip Woolf were officers in the XXth Hussars. Both were wounded on November 27; Philip recovered, but Cecil died three days later. Horner, also killed in the war, was the son of Lady Horner, a well-known cultural figure.

the Guards, and there he was killed and another of my brothers, who was in the same regiment, wounded by the same shell. The wounded one is in hospital in London and is going on very well. But it is rather appalling for him as the two had been absolutely inseparable since they were children.

Virginia sends her love.

Yours
Leonard Woolf

FROM MAURICE CRAIG

April 8th, 1918.

Dear Mr. Woolf,
I am sorry to hear that your wife is still losing weight. It will be important for her to rest more and more in bed until the weight improves and for her to take as much milk as possible. It is very doubtful if you will get extra meat, but I have put it in.

Yours very truly,
Maurice Craig

TO LYTTON STRACHEY

1 Sept. 1918.   Asheham

. . . I dont like these pregnant women. Karin and Adrian (who is by no means pregnant) have just left us.[1] Karin has the appetite of ten horse-leeches. For seven days I tried to fill her up and make her refuse something. I increased the helpings until I thought no human being could possibly stand it. She blew and puffed and heaved and swelled, but it all went down; so I told V. to order a very heavy suet pudding for lunch and when it appeared, I heaped Karin's plate like Pelion on Ossa. Half way through she stopped and gazed out the window, sighed heavily, and a curious twitching appeared to take place about the

1. Karin Stephen was pregnant with her second daughter, Judith.

stomach and abdomen. We sat expecting either an explosion or a premature birth, but after another deep sigh, she finished her plate of suet. Next day she went to Brighton and bought a bottle of liquid cascara which broke in Adrian's pocket.

L.

To Margaret Llewelyn Davies

8 Sept. 1918   Asheham.

My dear Margaret,

It was very nice to get a letter from you again. I have often been on the point of writing and then been overcome by the inertia of the country. I am sorry you haven't been well again, but very often it is true that the good effects of a change and rest come when they're over, I think. At any rate, though I agree with your Hebrew blessing, I cant imagine anyone who is further than you from tragic failure.[1]

First, I propose to answer categorically your categorical questions:

(1) V. has been very well and I too.

(2) The garden has produced 1 cwt. potatoes, some broad beans, French beans, Japanese anemones, nasturtia, phlox and dahlias and a forest of weeds. I spend nearly every afternoon in it.

(3) Weekends: Bonwick (of the *Nation*), Carrington, Pernel Strachey, and for a whole fortnight we had Adrian & Karin who failed to get lodgings anywhere. Next week-end is the culminating glory of Asheham and the Woolfs, for the Webbs are coming. . . .[2] [*sic*]

(4) Output of my mind 500 words per diem, output of V.'s ditto 300 words per diem.

(5) Input of my mind: Church Missionary Society's Reports from 1888 to the present day, all the war-books published since June, and all the weekly, monthly and daily papers. Input of V.'s ditto: Sophocles,

---

1. The Hebrew blessing, as she quoted it, was: "Blessed be thou who hast not made me a heathen; blessed be thou who hast not made me a bondman; blessed be thou who hast not made me a woman," to which she added, "dear Leonard, do write to one of the tragic failures of humanity."

2. Alfred Bonwick (1883–1949), business manager of the Rowntree Trust, was involved in the negotiations for a political journal, which LW hoped to establish but which Ramsay MacDonald scuttled. Dora Carrington (1893–1932), the painter. For the Webbs, see Biographical Appendix.

Milton, and an Italian whom I forget, Flaubert's Letters, and all the poetry and criticism published since June.

(6) I have had proofs of the Co-op, book [*Co-operation and the Future of Industry*] and returned them corrected. It will be a nasty looking vol.

(7) The *International Review* will begin in Jan. but I'm afraid it will not have my Labour Committee. The MacDonald story is too long and complicated to write: I'll tell it you when we meet.

I rather expected you to send me the material for the Co-op memo but perhaps things are not far enough forward. We shall not return [to Hogarth House] before October. Sept. is so magnificent here and the servants have to go on their holidays.

I had a letter from my brother [Philip] last week. He has been back in France for a good time and was in the first part of this fighting, but I gather that he is now second in command of a squadron which means that he is at headquarters. I saw him just before he went out, and he seemed more cheerful than he had been before.

This Russian intervention is far the most beastly thing which has happened in the war. For us to start killing Russians merely because they wont fight is really the limit.[1]

V. sends her love.

Leonard

To Molly MacCarthy

Monk's House

17/6/21
Rodmell, near Lewes, Sussex

Dear Molly,

I enclose the script of Desmond's Table-Talk.[2] I'm afraid it's not very well done. Let us know what you think of it.

We have had to fly here for 10 days. Virginia is rather better but will have to take a rest for at least 10 days.

I hope you have now realized that NOTHING MATTERS & have also

---

1. Several months after Russia withdrew from the war in March 1918, an Allied force under British command occupied areas in the northern part of the country.

2. Desmond MacCarthy was renowned as a brilliant conversationalist; to record a sample of his wit and charm for posterity, LW arranged for a stenographer, discreetly hidden, to take down his conversation at the dinner table. To everyone's disappointment, the transcription conveyed no wit, charm or interest.

experienced the exhilarating effects of that belief. I should have liked to continue my diagnosis & therapeusis. *Nothing* matters.

Yours
Leonard Woolf

V. wants me to add that she would very much have liked to see you but was allowed to see no one.

To Lytton Strachey

Hogarth House,
17/7/21   Paradise Road, Richmond, Surrey.

Virginia is being allowed gradually to return to life and see visitors, the two terms being apparently synonymous. She would very much like during the next week to see any day at 4.30 the particle of life going about under the name of G. L. Strachey. But she says that it must not on any account put itself out if it has other engagements or it would be the slightest bore to come all the way out here. But, if not, could it suggest a day, as she returns to life only about three times a week at 4.30 and has to map out the programme of resurrections.

L.

To Margaret Llewelyn Davies

16 Aug 1922   Monk's House

Dear Margaret,
    Every post brings a letter or a present from you, & it is so nice that I am debating whether the best way to get this to go on would be by answering or not answering. I hope I have chosen the right line.
    We have been here 2 weeks, & only 2 days & the last [were] fine. But the garden is very pleasant. I do think you should come & see it, if not us, this year—but I despair of ever seeing you.
    Virginia has had a bad time of it with doctors. The pathologist diagnosed tuberculosis. Our doctor [D. J. Fergusson] disagreed. So we

had to go up for the day last week to a specialist. I am glad to say he agrees with our doctor. The temperature continues—probably due to pneumonia microbes in the throat, which they are now treating by painting the throat. Doctors are very nice but their knowledge is limited, as I told our doctor, to being able occasionally to say with certainty that there is no hope.

I am afraid from what you say that you too are not really fit yet. What a plague the body is. If it is not tuberculosis, it's mumps which is now devastating Vanessa's household.

Here ends medicine, for I myself remain well. I am going to give up the *Contemporary* [*Review*], as Massingham has asked me to take Brailsford's place on the *Nation* when he goes.[1] I am also to give an address to the Southern Section Conference in Jan. So I feel I'm getting on in the Coop. world.

I do hope Lilian is better.[2]

When shall we see you?

Leonard[3]

To Margaret Llewelyn Davies

Hogarth House

22 February, 1923   Paradise Road   Richmond, Surrey

My dear Margaret,

Every night before I go to sleep I say to myself: "Another day gone by and I have not written, as I intended, to Margaret." But I will not tonight. We have been through a perpetual whirl of changes and impending disasters which still continue and which yet seem so insignificant as to be non-existent. Mr T. S. Eliot, the poet, continually consults us as to his future. Leo Myers the novelist is going to do the same. Philip Morrell came to dinner on Sunday and appeared again on Monday unannounced just as we thought we were settling in for a rare quiet evening. On April 7 we are faced by bankruptcy owing

---

1. H. W. Massingham (1860–1924), famous editor of the *Nation* 1907–23. "He was a small, neatly dressed, quiet-spoken man whose face had the look of one of those small, brindled, reserved mongrels who eye one with motionless suspicion . . ." (*Downhill All the Way*). H. N. Brailsford (1873–1958), the distinguished journalist.
2. Lilian Harris (1866–1949) was Davies's companion and Assistant Secretary of the Women's Co-operative Guild.
3. VW's postscript is published in her letters.

to the end of the *Nation* and propose to leave for Granada in Spain. . . .[1]

We went to see Katherine Stephen last week and she asked us whom we could suggest to be made the Principal of Newnham. I said at once "Margaret Davies", so that if the post is offered to you—she thought it an excellent suggestion—you must really take it.[2]

I was rather disappointed that Lilian would not write the League's obituary. I believe she would do it very well.

I do hope you are better and that the day will soon come when we see you again.

Leonard

To Margaret Llewelyn Davies

c.o. Gerald Brenan
5 April 1923   Yegen, Ugijar, Granada, Spain

Dear Margaret,

You see that bankruptcy has driven us to a peak of the Sierra Nevada. All yesterday we sat on the backs of two mules, on the top of all our luggage, from 9 in the morning to 9 in the evening, & crawled up the bed of a torrent among orange trees & olives & almonds & pomegranates to reach this little village where Brenan, aged 28, lives alone with 3000 books on £60 a year, the son of a retired army officer who has disinherited him because he refused to go into the guards.[3] In Granada we stayed two days with a man called Temple who was Governor of Nigeria & who seemed to know Crompton [Llewelyn Davies] very well.[4]

It is a superb country. We are about 4 to 5 thousand feet up, above on the tops of the mountains is perpetural snow & one can see the

1. Leopold Myers (1881–1944), a Trinity contemporary of LW's had just published a novel, *The Orissers*. Philip Morrell (1870–1943), husband of Lady Ottoline Morrell, was a Liberal MP 1906–18. The *Nation* had been transformed by H. W. Massingham from a Liberal into a Labour journal, provoking its owners to sell it.
2. Katherine Stephen (1856–1924), VW's cousin and Principal of Newnham College, Cambridge 1911–20, was succeeded by Pernel Strachey.
3. Gerald Brenan (1894–1987), after serving in the army in the First World War, went to live on a mountain in Spain. In time he became an expert on the country and an object of national veneration. He recorded the Woolfs' visit in two books of reminiscences, *South from Granada* and *Personal Record 1920–1972*.
4. Charles Temple (1871–1929), Lieutenant Governor of Nigeria 1914–17.

Mediterranean. We stay here for a week or 10 days & then drift slowly back along the coast & through Toulouse to Paris, expecting to be back about the 27th. Virginia has been well & stood yesterday, which was really very strenuous, remarkably well.

I have been asked to become Literary Editor of the *Nation*. The offer was made 2 days before we started. I should rather not, but the question of money has made me say that I will on certain conditions— but I dont know whether the conditions will be accepted.

V. sends her love. We wish we could hear from you, but our movements are too uncertain to make it possible to give you an address to write to.

I do hope you are better.

Leonard

To Gerald Brenan

Hotel de Londres

23/4/23
Paris

My dear Gerald,

Here we are arrived without mishap & quite well. The journey was easy & pleasant & V. has slept well the whole time, the hotels being quiet, smellless, & bugless. The train journey to Valencia was really remarkable—through miles & miles of orange trees & the Valencia plain under the setting sun seemed too fertile to be real outside the pages of Moses.

Hotel Cuatro Naciones, Valencia, is to be recommended. Next day to Perpignan, a long & rather tiring journey which ended in a small but comfortable hotel where the paté de fois gras was divine. We went for a longish walk in the morning in rather charming country. In the afternoon we set out again & stayed the night not at Toulouse but at Montauban. Our hotel must have been built in the 17th or 18th century—a vast building with all the rooms built round a central hall or well. It was a very simple cheap hotel & the town itself would be worth staying a few days in. Yesterday we came on here & I leave tomorrow.[1]

Our holiday has been an immense success due entirely to you. It would be silly to try to thank you properly. But I do hope we were

1. VW remained briefly in Paris after LW returned to conclude arrangements with the *Nation*.

not too exacting & trying—so that some day you will ask us again. And I hope too your journey home was not very tedious.

Yours
Leonard Woolf

To Virginia Woolf

24 April [1923]   [London]

I am on the train from Victoria to Richmond after a very easy journey. Train from Paris packed & if I had not started at 9.15, I should not have got a corner seat. Sea quite calm & a very sunny, but rather cold day, here. On the station at Paris I suddenly heard: "Mr Woolf, I dont suppose you remember me", looked round, & saw Mrs Dominic Spring-Rice, ex Mrs Garrett Jones, ex Miss Garrett. I had a long talk with her on the boat. At Newhaven I bought *The Times*, opened it, & the first thing that caught my eye was that her father had died yesterday.[1] She certainly did not know. Ought I to have broken the news? At any rate, I didnt.

My cough is already better. Do come back Friday, for your mongoose misses you.

L.

To T. S. Eliot[2]

30 April, 1925   52 Tavistock Square
                                                London, W.C.1

Dear Tom,

I am very very glad if I can be of any use to you with advice, and you must not hesitate to ask it (or anything else) without apology.[3]

As to the writing, the difficulty is that it all depends on what is the actual cause of the nervous disturbance. I am convinced myself that,

1. Samuel Garrett, a highly regarded London solicitor, had died unexpectedly.
2. See Biographical Appendix.
3. Eliot had turned to LW for help in trying to deal with the deepening mental problems of his wife, Vivien. They exchanged more than thirty letters and lunched together weekly around this time. Peter Ackroyd's biography of Eliot misinterprets these contacts as relating to a breakdown of Eliot himself.

if the real cause is nerve exhaustion, anything which excites or tires the brain is bad and that therefore writing is bad. In these cases you must begin with food and rest which alone begin to produce stability. When the stability begins, then a little work like writing is good, but only at first in minute quantities. When Virginia was recovering from acute nerve exhaustion, she began by limiting her writing strictly to half an hour a day, and only increased it when, after months, she was convinced that she would stand the strain of more.

Of course, if the cause is not exhaustion, but something entirely different, this would not apply, and, if the writing did not cause fatigue or even excitement, it might, I imagine, do good.

On thinking the matter over, I should be disposed to go to Wright rather than Head. Head can be rather brusk in manner.

Yours
Leonard Woolf

Virginia would like to give Vivien a copy of *The Common Reader*, but does not like to do so unless you think that it would be right to do so.

To Vita Sackville-West[1]

16/12/25

52 Tavistock Square
London, W.C.1.

Dear Vita,

I enclose Virginia & hope she will behave. The only thing I ask is that you will be adamant in sending her off to bed not 1 minute later than 11 P.M. She ought not to talk for too long a stretch at a time. It is good of you to have her. I hope to be able to come for a night.[2]

Yours
Leonard Woolf

---

1. See Biographical Appendix.
2. A physical relationship between the two women apparently began during this visit by VW to Long Barn, Vita Sackville-West's house in Kent. LW joined them several days later and spent the night there.

To Vita Sackville-West

[July 26, 1926]

Monk's House
Rodmell, Lewes, Sussex

Dear Vita,

The puppy, whom we have christened Fanny (after trying innumerable names from Boadicea to Vita), is absolutely charming.[1] She is beautiful, full of spirits, has a will of her own and is intelligent. She refuses to sleep anywhere except in my room and usually insists upon a game in the middle of the night. Grizel unfortunately is extremely jealous. I dont know how to thank you enough for her, but I wish you would let me pay what you would get for her in the market. Will you?

Your book is as difficult to name as Fanny. I dont like Persian Apparatus. What about Persian Pictures or Persian Letters? You have thought of two titles of genius, so you must think of a third. . . .[2]

Yours
Leonard Woolf

[In VW's hand:]
Spectacles
Horn: left on table by fire in Sitting Room
Should be immensely grateful for return
Sibyl to-morrow

To Virginia Woolf

28/7/27

52 Tavistock Square,
London, W.C.1.

Dearest, it was melancholy to see you fade away in the train, and Pinka cannot understand what has happened.[3] She insisted upon going in at once to your room this morning to see whether you were or were not in bed. Nothing has happened. Of course, Fred did not turn up

1. Fanny (1926–1935), later renamed Pinker, also known as Pinka, has taken her place in literature as the model for Flush, Elizabeth Barrett Browning's spaniel, in VW's eponymous novel.
2. *Passenger to Teheran*, the eventual title, was about Vita Sackville-West's two-month visit to Persia earlier that year.
3. VW had gone to stay with Ethel Sands and Nan Hudson at their house in Normandy, where she met and was sketched by Jacques-Emile Blanche.

last night, and I do not expect to see him again.[1] I am looking forward to Saturday and the return of all animals.

I saw Dadie [Rylands] this morning. He denies that he said anything of the sort to Topsy, and is furious with her. He is going up to Cambridge today and will face Peter at once. It is curious, but I gather that Topsy is very touchy about us.[2]

Several letters have arrived for you, but I am keeping them; they are from Saxon, Leys, and I think Pipsy.[3]

Love from the two solitary animals

M[ongoose]
P[inka]

To Vanessa Bell[4]

7 February, 1928

52 Tavistock Square,
London, W.C.1.

My dear Vanessa,

. . . I hope you will continue to write letters [from France] as your adventures are very interesting at this distance. It is strange to hear of there being a sun or that it is possible to sit out of doors any where. We have not succeeded in using our car until last Sunday and then we started in a black drizzle and often drove over roads flooded a foot or two by the Thames, which now covers half of Southern England.

Hardy and Meredith between them very nearly did for V.[5] At any rate they succeeded in giving her a headache. However she was sensible, and it seems to have gone now.

I expect V. has told you all the news about Tom Eliot becoming an Anglican in a desperate effort to show that even in religion he is not

---

1. The Woolfs had just bought their first car, a used Singer; Fred Pape was giving them driving lessons, successfully in LW's case.
2. The brouhaha between George ("Dadie") Rylands, apprentice manager of Hogarth Press, and Mr. and Mrs. F. L. Lucas—"Peter" and "Topsy"—concerned a manuscript Peter had submitted to the Hogarth Press.
3. Norman Leys (1875–1944) was an expert on Kenya, whose book on the subject Hogarth Press had recently published. Pipsy was Philip Morrell, then in love with VW.
4. Beginning in 1927, Vanessa Bell spent part of most years at Cassis, on the Riviera, where she had bought a small house.
5. VW had just completed for the *Times Literary Supplement* two major articles: one on Hardy, who had died a short time before, and the other on Meredith.

American, of Desmond starting a new monthly literary review, of Bob Trevelyan having become Bob Philips and having inherited £10,000 a year and Welcome—so I wont repeat it all.[1]

Yours
Leonard

To VANESSA BELL

13 February, 1928

The Hogarth Press
52 Tavistock Square
London, W.C.1.

My dear Vanessa,

Many thanks for the [book jacket] design for America—which seemed to me one of your best and too good for Americans. I have sent it on to Doubleday Page.[2]

Clive has returned in the highest spirits. We dined with him last night and lunch with him and Bobo Tuesday. Roger [Fry] has returned also in the highest spirits and is now extremely intimate with Lady Astor, Lady Colefax, and the Duke of York, to whom he is going to lecture on Cezanne in the house of Sir Philip Sassoon.[3] He *and Helen* were at Clive's. He began a long story in which Helen I and Helen II both appeared and got inextricably confused, with Helen II sitting beside him rather uncomfortable.[4] We also lunched with Jack and Mary [Hutchinson] domestically. She seems to have recovered health and spirits, but there was nothing of interest, I think, to record.[5]

The weather here is completely out of hand. It rarely stops raining and hurricane succeeds hurricane, blowing our windows bodily away and removing part of the ceiling even inside my bedroom. According to Roger it could easily be cured by melting a small ice cap in Greenland

1. Desmond MacCarthy's review was *Life and Letters*, an intellectual and cultural monthly which ran from 1928 until 1950, though MacCarthy edited it for only the first five years. Trevelyan's mother, whose maiden name was Philips, had recently died, leaving Robert a legacy of £10,000 annually and Welcombe, a house at Stratford-upon-Avon.
2. The book cannot be identified.
3. Bobo was Beatrice Mayor, a playwright and Clive Bell's latest companion. Nancy Viscountess Astor (1879–1964) and Sibyl Lady Colefax (d. 1950) were prominent hostesses in the interwar period; the Woolfs occasionally went to the latter's parties. The Duke of York became King George VI in 1936. Sir Philip Sassoon (1888–1939) was at this time Under Secretary of State for Air.
4. Helen I was Fry's wife; Helen II was Helen Anrep, legal wife of the Russian mosaicist Boris von Anrep and de facto wife of Fry after 1926.
5. The Hutchinsons were social friends; Clive Bell had broken off an affair with Mary a year before.

which would not really be difficult. It was melted in 700 A.D. for a short time when Europe had perfect weather.

You will see from the above that London and your friends have not altered much since you left.

Yours
Leonard Woolf

To Vanessa Bell

11 April, 1928   Aurillac [France]

Dear Vanessa,

We got here tonight though with considerable difficulty. We had a hard time of it after leaving you. The road was very stony & we punctured 3 times in 40 miles. Also it rained hard & the road twisted & turned in the mountains. Our last puncture was at 6 p.m. in the rain & we had to change wheels in semidarkness & drive down to Florac in the dark. However, it was all right & we found an admirable inn. We were 25 miles short of our time table & started to do 130 miles to this place. We began well with sunshine & superb country. At 12.30 it began to snow heavily & we had lunch. After lunch we started with snow falling slightly through forests. The snow covered everything & one might have thought one was in midwinter. It then cleared & a nail ran into & punctured a front tyre. We then climbed another mountain & ran into a terrific snowstorm. It was impossible to see through the windscreen & we had to drive with it open. It was so cold that icicles hung from the windscreen. We crawled along for some time & then came to a tunnel in the mountain which ran for about ¼ of a mile or more & was lit by electric light very dimly so that one had to drive with lights on. On the other side it was not snowing & we got on all right arriving here about 6.45.

I hope you got back all right & that the rain did not reach your part of the country.

We hope to reach Guéret tomorrow.

Yours
Leonard

To Virginia Woolf[1]

Monk's House,
Rodmell, near Lewes, Sussex.

25/9/28

I am sending you this letter for Vita which came this morning from Harold.[2] There was a letter for you asking you to "be careful about her, and see she doesnt get sore throats, or drink drain water, or sprain her ankle. And cheer her up, Virginia, about life and the importance of writing books and how it matters little being nimbleminded. I do hope you enjoy yourselves and that you return ready to face the birth of Orlando".[3]

There is also a letter from Janet Vaughan enclosing a card from Mrs Ernest Franklin inviting you to Porchester Terrace on Oct 4 at 8.30 to meet Dora Gordine, a Swedish sculptor.[4]

I was terribly sad to see you go and moped with the Pinka family for a long time[5]—it was the summer dying out of the year, and the chill of autumn in fact immediately descended and today I woke up to a regular grey, damp Rodmell autumn with the clouds right at the foot of the downs and the smell of dead leaves burning. It began to rain already yesterday afternoon and I spent it tinkering at the car. Quentin came and painted the gramophone and after tea I took him for a walk on the watermeadows and discussed his change of character and view of life. Then I read Dorothy Osborne until bedtime.[6]

I think I must catch the post with this to make sure of your getting it—it is immediately after breakfast now. One Mongoose, Pinka, four puppies, all sad, send their love.

L.

1. VW left the day before for a week's trip to France with Vita Sackville-West.
2. Harold Nicolson (1886–1968), who married Vita Sackville-West in 1913, was in the Foreign Service from 1909 until 1929, when he took up writing and journalism. He sat in Parliament 1935–45. LW did not have a high regard for him.
3. *Orlando*, VW's novel about Vita Sackville-West, was soon to be published.
4. (Dame) Janet Vaughan (b. 1899), daughter of VW's cousin William Vaughn, was at this time a medical researcher.
5. Pinka had given birth several weeks earlier.
6. For Quentin Bell, see Biographical Appendix. *The Letters of Dorothy Osborne to William Temple* had just been reviewed by VW for the *Times Literary Supplement* and the *New Republic*.

26 Sept 1928

Monk's House,
Rodmell, near Lewes, Sussex.

My dearest M, It was a joy to see your letter this morning for I had scarcely expected one. It is very dreary here without you & the minor animals—I could not live without them despite their curious ways.

Quentin came after lunch yesterday & finished his work. We took another walk & at 7 I drove him (& Nellie & Gladys for whom I had an invitation) to Charleston.[1] Lytton was, I thought, slightly piano, but I quite enjoyed the evening. We talked war memories & then gave Raymond[2] a complete genealogy & family tree of the Stephen & Strachey families with character sketches of every member to the third & fourth generation reaching as far as Emmie Fisher & Aunt Sally whose surname Vanessa could not remember.

Today the weather has got back to perfection, bright sun & windless—I hope Saulieu has it. I have gathered apples & now shall take Pinka for a walk. She & the Pups send love—they grow & eat & eat & grow.

There were no letters for you this morning & nothing of much interest for me other than the letter from Paris. Write to me again just to say you are well each day if nothing else.

Love to Vita. It will be a great relief her taking Pinka & family.

I dont think I really like Dorothy Osborne very much.

I hope you wont make a habit of deserting me.

Your
M.

27/9/28

Monk's House

My dearest M. I'm not sure you'll get this but I'll send you a line on the chance that it gets to you on Sat. Not that I've anything to tell you except that I look forward to Tuesday & am dull & wretched without you.

A perfect day again here—work morning & no letters of interest—

---

1. Nellie Boxall was the Woolfs' maid-cook; Gladys may have been her niece.
2. Raymond Mortimer (1895–1980), the noted literary critic.

apple picking afternoon. I drove in to Lewes before tea, taking Nellie & Gladys, to sell my apples. I met Vanessa there. Clinker has been brought to bed last night of 4 puppies. Three are coal black & one black & white. She made some fuss about it & Vanessa had to be called in by Julian at 4 a.m.[1] However all are doing well.

Your letter from Saulieu came this morning. I was glad of it. Write, write again.

I had the records sent by train & fetched them this afternoon. There are an immense number—I shall have to do nothing but play them the next 24 hours as I have to write about them this weekend.[2]

Every animal here sends its love including

Your M.

To Vanessa Bell

28/1/29   52 Tavistock Square, W.C.1

My dear Vanessa,

We have had an extraordinary time since we left you.[3] We got to the Hook all right and on board and V. took a dose of Somnifene. It was pretty rough. When I woke her in the morning she was in a very curious state, so giddy that it was with the greatest difficulty I got her off the boat and into the train, as she could hardly walk and was in a kind of drugged state. She says she had only taken 20 drops. She has been in bed ever since. The giddiness lasted off and on for about another 24 hours and she has now one of the oldfashioned headaches and a rather bad one. . . .[4]

Your
Leonard Woolf

---

1. For Julian Bell, see Biographical Appendix.
2. As literary editor of the *Nation*, LW also wrote reviews of musical recordings.
3. The Woolfs, joined by Vanessa and Quentin Bell and Duncan Grant, had spent a week in mid-January in Berlin, where Harold Nicolson was second-ranking official in the British Embassy.
4. They had returned home by way of the Hook of Holland, where VW took an overdose of the drug to ward off seasickness. She was ill for three weeks and unable to work for another three.

Dear Vita,

I am sending you three novels which, I think, deserve inclusion. If, as is certain, you now have too many, will you eject some of the first lot I sent you?[1]

Virginia has been a good deal better the last two days though she is still not right & is more or less in bed. The slightest thing is apt to bring symptoms back. But this has always been the case when she has been so near breaking point, & I think, if she keeps quite quiet, for another week, it will pass away. She has not really had such a severe attack as this for the last 3 or 4 years. It was not, of course, due to anything like influenza or sea-sickness cures, but simply to her over-doing it & particularly not going to bed at 11 for all those nights running. It has been proved over & over again in the last 10 years that even 2 late nights running are definitely dangerous for her & this time it was 7 or 8. It was mad.

I should not write much to her about the causes of it, if I were you, or let her know that I have given you this account of causes—which I do, because she told me that you said you'ld like to hear of her state from me. Until she is once more completely stabilized, one does not know that she may not suddenly become worried. She is not in the least at the moment.

Yours
L S W

I must add that it would be absurd for you to blame yourself in the least for what happened—& I have an uneasy feeling—& unexplained—that you may. Whatever you & Harold did, made things less tiring, in fact. The blame is entirely upon us—& as a matter of fact I do not blame even myself. I knew the danger but decided before we came that, as we were coming, the danger had to be risked & that to interfere, as I always do in London, would do no good & only spoil things with the continual nagging which that kind of shepherding always involves. But if you had not been there, things would have been worse.

1. Sackville-West was regularly commissioned by LW to review books for the *Nation*.

To Virginia Woolf

4/10/29   52, Tavistock Square, W.C.1.

Dearest M, I got on quite all right. I started well with a cheerful
memento mori. You know that place at Chailey where we turn off the
main road across the heath to Hayward's Heath, where the car some
weeks ago ran into the sign post & carried it away into a field & ever
afterwards the sign post has been on the ground. Well, there in exactly
the same place were two policemen, 4 or 5 cars & vans drawn up &
the remains of a car burning in the same field. Apparently it was
Captain Bolton of Lewes being burnt to death, but I did not stop to
see. He ran over the bank & through the hedge into the field & the
car burst into flames.

I have already been rung up by Mary.

Nellie wants me to remind you to bring her cake tins.

Limited edition *R of O. O.* oversubscribed—862 ordered ordinary
edition.[1]

I hope you've been well & sensible & that I shall see you tomorrow.
Love to Pinka & the 2 carp.

                                              M.

To T. S. Eliot
                                              Castle Hotel
5/5/30   Taunton

Dear Tom,

Somehow or other I feel that it is really suitable to write to you from
Taunton to thank you for *Ash Wednesday*. We are touring the West
Country partly for pure pleasure & partly—an excuse—for travelling
our books. Bath—Bristol—Wells—Glastonbury—Taunton. Do you
know these astonishing places? You begin in the purest 18th century
& travel back to, I suppose, B.C. Alfred tumbles over Arthur & Arthur
stumbles over Monmouth or Sedgemoor. If I did not always feel that
I dated from Sumeria & Assyria & that winged bulls were my family

---

1. VW's *A Room of One's Own* was published in October in a limited edition of 492 numbered
and signed copies. The regular edition had an initial printing of 3,000 copies; within six
months 22,000 copies had been sold in Britain and the United States.

portraits, I should be impressed. At any rate, one seems to get older & older from place to place & even the hotels are built out of ruins. The elderly females who are their only inhabitants are the oldest ruins of all. Which brings me back via the *Waste Land* to *Ash Wednesday*. You are the only living poet I can read twice; only in your case, I cannot stop at twice & go on rereading until something from outside intervenes to stop me. The usual thing happened to me the other evening with *Ash Wednesday*. It is amazingly beautiful. I dislike the doctrine, as you probably know, but the poetry remains & shows how unimportant belief or unbelief may be.

Virginia sends her love & joins me in thanks.

Yours
Leonard Woolf

T o W i l l i a m P l o m e r [1]

8 July, 1930

52 Tavistock Square
London W.C.I.

My dear William,

I was so glad to hear from you again, as I had a fear that you might, as people do, have blazed for a moment and then faded out of our lives like a comet. I hope you wont. "How wise William is", we said when we read your letter—not to immure yourself, I mean, in Bayswater with the hum of literary gnats perpetually in your ears, but only to dip now and then, as I trust you will, into this iron-laced society. Greece sounds perfect and we are always talking of going there but always prevented by the iron tentacles that have hold of us and in a minute or two we shall be too old. . . .

Write again whenever you have the time and mind.

Yours
Leonard Woolf

---

1. William Plomer (1903–1973), novelist, poet and librettist.

238

To T. S. ELIOT

Monk's House
25 September, 1930   Rodmell, near Lewes   Sussex.

My dear Tom,
    It is always pleasant to get a letter from you. We shall be here until
the first or second week in October and we must then meet again.
Your name is often mentioned in these walls, for none of the Cambridge
younger generation can keep for very long off the subject of "Eliot's
poetry". We have otherwise vegetated the summer here, usually cold,
wet, but happy.
    I shall be interested to see the Gongora.[1]

                              Yours
                              Leonard Woolf

To LYTTON STRACHEY

Picture postcard]
[April 23, 1931]   Bergerac [France]

We visited Montaigne's tower this morning. It is the tower to which I
have drawn an arrow overleaf. Apparently untouched with the 3 win-
dowed library & the bedroom below. And the prospect from his windows, as he said, divine. An old saddle & an old chair, said to be his.[2]

                              L W

To DONALD BRACE[3]   The Hogarth Press
                                         52, Tavistock Square
9 February, 1932   London, W.C.1.

Dear Mr Brace,
    We had mentioned your idea of a book about Mrs Woolf to Harold
Nicolson but I do not think he could do it. I feel that Rebecca West

1. Luis de Góngora (1561–1627), eminent Spanish poet. LW did not publish whatever of his
Eliot sent.
2. It was in the tower adjacent to the family castle that Montaigne wrote the essays that
LW and Strachey esteemed. This was LW's last note to Strachey, who died of cancer eight
months later.
3. Donald Brace (1881–1955), the Woolfs' American publisher, had proposed commissioning
a book about VW, initially approaching E. M. Forster.

would be the best person probably.[1] We do not know her very well, so that I think it would be as well for you to write to her direct if you decide to go on with it.

Lytton Strachey's death has been a great blow to us. It was a terrible time as it went on for so long at one moment seeming hopeless and then again there would be a rally which made up hope that he might recover. . . .

With kind regards

Yours sincerely
Leonard Woolf

To William Plomer

29 April 1932   Athens

My dear William

We have had a very good time. Your books & information have been extraordinarily useful & we have enjoyed ourselves immensely. We returned yesterday from a tour in the Peloponnesus to Sparta & Mistra. It is one of the most lovely countries I've seen, particularly the Argolid plain. We went by car & were on the whole extremely comfortable. The weather is fairly good, varying from real heat to icy cold in two minutes.

The Greeks seem to me the kindest & most charming people in ordinary intercourse of life in Europe.

We must meet when we return. We hope to go to Delphi tomorrow for two or three days.

The Melathron was full up so we came to the Majestic which is comfortable & moderate.

Yours
L W

1. Rebecca West (1892–1983), author and literary critic.

To Margaret Llewelyn Davies

June 10, 1933   52, Tavistock Square, W.C.1.

Dear Margaret,
   I was so glad to get your letter and had put it by for the week end to
answer. We have been away for some time and when one gets back and
finds the accumulation of some weeks, one begins to doubt the wisdom
of ever going away. However we did enjoy it very much. We took the car
across to Dieppe and drove through France by the Riviera to Italy. We
got as far as Siena where we stayed for some days and then came back
by Lucca, Parma, Piacenza, Avignon, Orléans, and Chartres. Do you
know the country between Pisa and Siena, round about Volterra? It is
about the loveliest country I have seen in Italy and we very nearly decided to stay there for the remainder of our lives. . . .

                                   Leonard

To Francis Hackett[1]   The Political Quarterly
                                        52 Tavistock Square,
12 May, 1934   London, W.C.1

My dear Hackett,
   . . . We drove from Kerry to Galway emerging on the west coast from
Kilfenora opposite the Aran islands on a day half grey and rain and half
sun. The cliffs were covered with gentians and I dont think outside
Greece I have ever seen anything more beautiful. Why is the country in
Ireland so beautiful and the towns and even the villages so horrible?
The first day after we landed when we found ourselves in a land un-
ruined by bungalows and motor-cars, we felt it was the only place left in
the world to live in. But now I dont think I could possibly *live* there; the
poverty of the people and a kind of fly-blownness on the towns, villages
and society were so depressing. Or is that my own imagination?
   I hope you'll let us know in time next time you come here.

                                   Yours
                                   Leonard Woolf

1. Francis Hackett (1883–1962), born in Ireland, lived in the United States after 1901 and
was co-editor of the *New Republic* 1914–22. He returned to Ireland, but abandoned it for
Denmark. LW consulted him occasionally on Irish questions.

To Virginia Woolf[1]

14/7/36   52, Tavistock Square, W.C.1.

My dearest M,

I had a very easy drive, arrived 10.10, & a good lunch. [Hogarth]
Press all the morning. I am dining with Willy [Robson] as he has
[Hugh] Dalton coming & he will have to be back at the House [of
Commons] so I hope to get away early. I have arranged to see Elly
[Rendel] tomorrow 10.30.[2]

I hope you are all right & somnolent, & entertained by the marmots
to whom I send my profound respect.

The Times Book Club rang up to say that they have not got the
book you ordered so will you send a card for another as I did not like
to take one out on spec.

Yr
L.

To Margaret Llewelyn Davies

                                                        Monk's House,
30 December, 1936   Rodmell, near Lewes   Sussex.

My dear Margaret,

It was very pleasant to see your handwriting again and to hear
from you. We have been here from just before Christmas. I had
intended writing in the late summer and suggesting that we should
come over to see you again. But Virginia was not really well for
the first three quarters of the year and we did as little as possible. The last three months she has been ever so much better and
has now finished her book. I heard of you from Desmond. If later
on you feel that you would care to see us for an hour or so, let me
know.

I haven't seen Richard for ages, though I sometimes hear of him

---

1. Now in the final stage of work on *The Years*, a novel that gave her considerable difficulty,
VW was on the verge of a breakdown and remained for much of the year in Rodmell.
2. William Robson (1895–1980) was an expert on administrative law and local government;
he and LW co-edited the *Political Quarterly* for many years. Hugh Dalton (1887–1962) was
a Labour Party leader. Frances Elinor Rendel (1885–1942), daughter of Lytton Strachey's
sister Elinor, was VW's doctor after 1924.

from Ann, who is a very remarkable girl.[1] So is Judith, the other daughter of Adrian. In October we went over and fetched her from Bedales [School], of which she is head girl, gave her lunch in Petersfield and then took her out to Bertie Russell. We are publishing an immense work in two vols for him, the letters and diaries of his mother and father, one of the most fascinating books I've read for a long time. We had to go and discuss business with him in his extraordinary tower, Telegraph House.[2] He teaches Judith philosophy.

I still go on doing the Labour Party Committee and am slowly proceeding with the second vol. of my book [After the Deluge]. But there seem to be incessant interruptions, for instance the other day I was rung up to say that the whole staff of the [New] Statesman was ill and most of them unconscious and would I write the Diary until they recovered?

We had so many apples here this year that I expect we shall have none at all next season, but I spend my afternoons in the pleasantest of all occupations, pruning the fruit trees. But I suppose that unfortunately we shall have to go back to London next week. The country seems to be the only place where one gets any work done at all, certainly any writing. [Victor] Gollancz asked me to do him a book in his new cheap series on Cooperation; I felt I ought to for the good of the cause, but simply could not face it. . . .[3]

Virginia had a letter from Janet [Case] a week or so ago. It is sad that she is so unwell.

Virginia sends her love and all good wishes to you both from

Yours
Leonard

---

1. Richard Llewelyn Davies (1912–1981), nephew of Margaret, married Ann Stephen, VW's niece, in 1938; later divorced, Ann married Richard Synge, winner of the Nobel Prize for chemistry in 1952.
2. *The Amberley Papers: The Diaries and Letters of Lord and Lady Amberley*, edited by Russell and Patricia Spence, his third wife. Telegraph House, in the South Downs of Sussex, was one of a series of eighteenth-century semaphore stations between London and the naval base at Portsmouth.
3. (Sir) Victor Gollancz (1893–1967), the noted publisher and promoter of left-wing causes.

Jany. 31st 1939.

Dear Mr Woolf,

Handicapped in the use of your language I think I could not give full expression to my satisfaction of having met you and your lady.

The condemnation delivered by the Norwegian judge I take to be a misrepresentation or a bad joke by a malicious journalist.[1]

Yours sincerely
Sigm. Freud

TO MARGARET LLEWELYN DAVIES

21 October, 1939

Monk's House
Rodmell near Lewes   Sussex

My dear Margaret,

We were so pleased to get your letter. We have been up in town for a week and I left it to answer until I got back to some quiet. We are making Rodmell our more or less permanent residence, but go up to London for a week at a time. London is really a nightmare because of the perpetual talk of persons with inside and invariably false information. That is much worse than the difficulties of getting about—which are, however, none the less a nuisance.

We landed ourselves in considerable difficulties by our move. We decided in June to take a house in Mecklenburgh Square and move there from Tavistock Square which in any case we should have had to give up at the end of next year. The Mecklenburgh Square house is absolutely perfect—quite quiet and with a beautiful outlook over the square. Unfortunately the war broke out actually on the day of moving. Next day all the men disappeared, leaving us with the furniture &c piled up in heaps—no carpenters, no electric light, no means of washing or cooking. However eventually we have got it fairly straight and at any rate just livable in. The nuisance is that we still have the

1. The Woolfs had taken tea with Freud on January 28. During the conversation, LW mentioned the trial a short time before of a man who had stolen several books, among them one by Freud; in fining the thief, the judge commented that he had considered sentencing him to the harsher punishment of having to read all Freud's works. Freud seemed quite amused, according to LW, though he somehow misunderstood the magistrate to be Norwegian.

Tavistock Square house for a year on our hands and now of course no one will take it.

It is so pleasant here that one can almost forget war and horrors. We arranged to move part of our staff from the Hogarth Press here if London becomes uninhabitable and we have them down for short spells from time to time. Otherwise we live as we always do alone. Rodmell was to have 95 evacuated children from London and we made all preparations in the village to receive them; but they got lost somewhere on the way from London and never turned up. Then when we had all settled down again, suddenly at 5 on a Sunday evening omnibuses arrived without warning containing 28 expectant mothers and about 40 or 50 of their children. They came from Bermondsey and Battersea. All arrangements had to be made over again and by 8 oclock we had settled them in. But they hated the country and got on pretty badly with their hosts. After a week about 25% had returned to their homes and there are now practically none left.

Vanessa and her family are at Charleston. Quentin volunteered before the war began—indeed last year—for anti-aircraft work, but was rejected owing to the fact that he had had trouble with his lungs There was therefore no question, I think, of his being called up, but he has got a job on a farm near Charleston. It is very hard work, but it means that at least he is living at home.

When we were in town, we had a message from Mrs Webb to say that she would very much like to see us, so we went last Monday and lunched with her at Mrs Drake's.[1] I had not seen her for years. She really is amazing in mind—I could see no difference at all, but I am afraid that physically she is extremely weak. Sidney has practically recovered.[2]

My mother died earlier in the year. She was 88, but in mind and body invincible. The only thing was that she was liable to fall. If she had ever allowed any one to do anything for her she would have been all right, but this she would not do. The consequence was that she had one fall after another. She fell against a table in her room and broke a rib and the shock was too much for her.

I am afraid this is a dismal letter. I wish we could see you and Lilian, but we send you both our love.

Yours,
Leonard

1. Barbara Drake (1876–1963), Beatrice Webb's niece and a devoted Fabian.
2. He had suffered a stroke in January 1938.

To G. E. Moore

Monk's House
7 February, 1940   Rodmell near Lewes   Sussex

Dear Moore,
   It was very pleasant to see your handwriting once more. . . . I should
like to see you, but not at Commem. I hate ceremonies and dinners
more and more and I should much rather see you in slippers over your
or my fire. Why should you not come and spend a week end with us
here? You did once years and years ago at Asheham which is now an
immense cement works which you can see from our garden. Almost
any week end or week day when we are not in town would suit us if
you would suggest it. If you cant, I shall come up one day in the spring
and see you at Cambridge.

Yours
Leonard Woolf

To G. E. Moore

Monk's House
27 May, 1940   Rodmell

Dear Moore,
   I dont know why I told you that the plant I gave you is Anthemis.
It is not. Its name is Dimorphotheca Ecklonis. It wont stand a winter
out of doors. I take it in in October, cut it right down and pot it.
   We enjoyed seeing you immensely. I hope you will come again.[1]

Yours
Leonard Woolf

1. Moore, accompanied by Desmond MacCarthy, had spent the preceding weekend at Monk's
House. In *The Journey Not the Arrival Matters*, LW records the meeting with the warmest
nostalgia: "I could shut my eyes and *feel* myself back in 1903, in Moore's room in the
Cloisters of Trinity." This was the last time LW and Moore saw one another.

Monk's House

14 November, 1940   Rodmell   near Lewes   Sussex

My dear Margaret,

It was delightful to get a long letter from you again and to know that you are in the north [Cumbria]. We are both well and safe. We have been living mainly here with visits of a few days at a time to London for business. But we have now been completely bombed out of London and have to live here the whole time and only go up when necessary for the day. First the house in Mecklenburgh Square was rather wrecked by bombs falling in the Square, that is to say the windows were blown out and many of the ceilings down. We had just had it patched up when another large bomb fell in the street at the back of the Square and fairly well wrecked us again. All the windows were blown in, the bookcases blown off the walls, and the ceilings came down. The place is uninhabitable and we are now trying to remove the books and furniture. Another bomb fell on 52 Tavistock Square, which we still have on lease, and completely destroyed it. Vanessa and all her family are well, but they are in the same plight as we. Vanessa's studio in Fitzroy Street was completely destroyed with everything which she possesses there by an incendiary bomb. So she and the whole family now live permanently at Charleston which is 7 miles from here.

This all sounds rather gloomy and one might imagine from it that the greater part of London is destroyed. As a matter of fact, when one goes there, one is astonished at how little damage has really been done. Bloomsbury happens to have suffered more, I think, than any other district except the East End—which is bad luck for us. But there is a great deal to be said for living in the country any way. . . .

Much love from us both and we hope you will write to us again some time.

Leonard

To Robert Trevelyan

8 January, 1941

Monk's House
Rodmell   near Lewes   Sussex

Dear Bob,

I want to say how much we enjoyed your *Epistle*.[1] In these days of confused bitterness its form and content were both refreshing. Your translations and the two conversations were equally or even more refreshing. By a curious coincidence I had been reading Horace's satires after an interval of I dont know how many years. I never read the classics except in bed before I get up in the morning and I nearly always read Greek. But the other day I thought I would try Horace again and began the Satires. I liked it better than I had expected for I had recollections of being bored by Horace's hexameters. Your translations are extraordinarily satisfactory and satisfying.

I hope we may see you soon.

Yours
Leonard Woolf

To Margaret Llewelyn Davies

4 March, 1941

Monk's House
Rodmell near Lewes   Sussex

My dear Margaret,

I was so glad to hear from you again. We are both very well, living entirely here. I did write you a letter a little while back and I am not sure how much I told you of our experiences or whether you ever got it. Our house in Tavistock Square has been completely destroyed. The house we took in Mecklenburgh Square has been rendered completely uninhabitable. We have had to hire rooms in the village here and remove all our books and furniture. The books are a nightmare as the bookcases were blown off the walls and the ceilings came down on the top of the piles of books. They are now stacked in huge piles in a large room which used to be the village shop.

All this means that we have nowhere to stay a night in London and so have to go up for the day when we have business there. But we dont do it more than we have to as travelling is often a wearisome

---

1. *Epistle* was a privately printed poem, based on a translation of bits of Horace and composed in the form of questions and answers.

affair. We have had to evacuate the Hogarth Press from London and have put it in Letchworth as our printers [Garden City Press] offered to let us rooms in their works. I had to go and do some work there the week before last. I did three hours work in the office and it took me 17 hours travelling. We stayed the night in Cambridge which we had not seen for a long time.

Here we have been very peaceful lately. The Nazis drop an occasional bomb in the neighbourhood, but it is months since we had anything near us. I like country life, even with bombs, much better than London without. The garden is just beginning to break into life with crocuses and iris reticulata under the apple trees.[1] We too had a pretty stiff winter here, very cold and snow, but I dont suppose it is anything to yours up north.

We have had some interesting letters from France from the Bussys who live in Nice. She is Lytton Strachey's elder sister [Dorothy] and is married to a French painter [Simon Bussy]. They are quite well and cheerful now though the food shortage is very bad there too. They had rather a bad time during the debacle, and for a short time after it many people were anti-British, but they say the feeling has now completely changed. At first some of the people she knew looked askance at her because she was English, but her popularity is now greater than it was before the war.

I am afraid this is a dull letter. I wish we could meet and talk once more. Virginia was interested to hear you are reading her book and sends her love, as do I.

Yours
Leonard Woolf

1. In *Downhill All the Way* LW wrote: "One afternoon [in the late summer of 1939] I was planting in the orchard under an apple-tree iris reticulata, those lovely violet flowers which, like the daffodils, 'come before the swallow dares and take the winds of March with beauty'. Suddenly I heard Virginia's voice calling to me from the sitting-room window: 'Hitler is making a speech'. I shouted back: 'I shan't come. I'm planting iris and they will be flowering long after he is dead.' Last March, 21 years after Hitler committed suicide in the bunker, a few of those violet flowers still flowered under the apple-tree in the orchard."

To John Lehmann[1]

28/3/41 [morning]   [Monk's House][2]

Dear John,

I enclose a letter from Virginia. The fact is that she is on the verge of a complete nervous break down and is seriously ill. The war, food &c have been telling on her and I have seen it coming on for some time. It is out of the question for her to touch the book [*Between the Acts*] now and so we must put it off indefinitely. Send it back to me and *dont answer this letter*. I will come up to town and discuss the whole thing with you when I can. I am sorry for your and the Press sake; there seems some fate against you in the publishing world. The whole thing is a nightmare. Would you mind writing a note to V saying that you're very sorry that we shant be able to publish in the spring, but that we will hope for the autumn?

                                        Yours
                                        Leonard Woolf

To Vita Sackville-West

28/3/41 [evening]   Monk's House

My dear Vita

I do not want you to see in the paper or hear possibly on the wireless the terrible thing that has happened to Virginia. She has been really very ill these last weeks & was terrified that she was going mad again. It was, I suppose, the strain of the war & finishing her book & she could not rest or eat. Today she went for a walk leaving behind a letter saying that she was committing suicide. I think she has drowned herself as I found her stick floating in the river, but we have not found the body. I know what you will feel & what you felt for her. She was very fond of you. She has been through hell these last days

                                        Yours
                                        Leonard

1. See Biographical Appendix.
2. The letter was written on Hogarth Press stationery.

To John Lehmann

Monk's House

Dear John,

The most terrible thing has happened. I wrote to you yesterday explaining how ill V was getting. I had [to] take her against her will to see a doctor the day before. All the old symptoms were returning and she thought she was going mad. Yesterday morning she committed suicide. She had said she was going for a short walk and I found a note from her saying that she knew she was going mad and had decided to kill herself. I found her walking stick floating in the river. They have not found the body yet. I thought I would let you know as I know you will feel it as a shock, but it is probably better that you should not tell other people before the body is found

Leonard

From Octavia Wilberforce[1]

March 29/41

Dear Leonard,

I want to thank you for telling me all that most revealing history yesterday. I'd had one intuitive flash which left an uneasy feeling in my mind the day she talked about Ld. David Cecil's letter. "I was raving mad for 4 years during the last war." You'll know the approximate date of his letter but roughly I should say it was perhaps 6–8 weeks ago?[2]

I went home that evening asking myself Is she afraid, association-

---

1. Octavia Wilberforce (1888–1963), descendant of the antislavery Wilberforces, had been a social friend of the Woolfs since 1928, and in the preceding months had become VW's physician. LW described her, in *The Journey Not the Arrival Matters*, as "large, strong, solid, slow growing, completely reliable, like an English oak."

2. Lord David Cecil (1902–1986), the biographer and Goldsmiths' Professor of English Literature at Oxford 1948–69. The letter was presumably one, undated, in which Lord David expressed admiration for VW's biography of Roger Fry, published in July 1940. He commented that he was preparing for his lectures at Oxford—he was then a tutor at Wadham College—and added in what was evidently the critical passage for VW, ". . . It involves deliberately liberating one's mind from the war: but I do not know why we should contemplate events we cannot alleviate."

repetition-& so on, the many memories haunt one—that perhaps this *war is going to repeat history?*

 The more I think of our talks together the more I feel that she did throw herself into them—now & again asked if I had black moods etc, was I *never depressed. Anything I could think of I tried to do, to distract.*

 After our talk yesterday I feel convinced in my mind: 1. That with the war on with its associations & all its horrors, we had no chance. 2. I dont believe any *other man could have helped & sustained her & steered her thru' the unhappy times so wonderfully. 3. If by any accident she had been the one to survive, it would have been the most heartbreaking catastrophe imaginable.*

 I have no words to begin to express my deep sympathy for you but I do beg of you always to remember that on Thursday [March 27] (I hadn't asked anything about it) she suddenly said "I've been so very *happy with Leonard" with much feeling & warmth in her face. I have only known her so short a while but I felt I'd known her quite well! It was such an unforgetable joy to be with her & feel the brilliance of her mind. And if I feel quite stricken, what must it be for you after all these many years. You have all my deepest sympathy.*

 And I would like to say how proud I am that you did both come to me, as I told her at the time "there is nobody in England I want more to help". I also told her that I'd stake my all on getting her better. This reassurance she would have forgotten when the voices took possession. Again I am so sorry.

Yours very sincerely
Octavia Wilberforce

The milk etc will continue as usual please. I know she'd expect that of me and it would help me if you can make use of it. Later the cows may dry off—but not just yet.[1]

---

1. An attached document written by Wilberforce, apparently a record of her conversation with VW on March 27, is not transcribed.

March 31, 1941

My dear Leonard,

I have no words of grief. Your letter stunned me, and at present I can only think of you, with feelings I will not attempt to express. The loveliest mind and spirit I ever knew, immortal both to the world and us who loved her. It was so utterly unexpected as I did not know she had been ill lately & had had a letter from her only about a fortnight ago.

I do not like to send you a telegram as you may be trying to keep it private for the moment, but you will know that that was my only reason.

This is not really a hard letter to write as you will know something of what I feel and words are unnecessary. For you I feel a really overwhelming sorrow, and for myself a loss which can never diminish.

Vita.

I am more touched than I can say by your having written to me.

To Geoffrey Dawson[1]

Monk's House
1 April, 1941   Rodmell near Lewes   Sussex

Dear Mr Dawson,

I feel that I had better let you know the following facts, so that you may use them in *The Times* in any way you may think best. There is reason to think that my wife was drowned in the river here last Friday, but the body has not been recovered. She had not been well for some weeks and has all her life suffered from neurasthenia. On Thursday she had been with me to see a doctor and had returned very depressed. On Friday morning she went out for a walk and I found a letter from her to me saying that she was going mad and would not this time recover. Her walking stick was found floating in the river and she was seen by two or three people near the spot where it was found. She was

---

1. Geoffrey Dawson (1874–1944), editor of *The Times*.

not seen again anywhere, and, though the body has not been recovered, I feel now that there is no hope that she is alive.[1]

Yours truly
Leonard Woolf

TO MARGARET LLEWELYN DAVIES

Monk's House
Rodmell near Lewes   Sussex

1 April, 1941

My dear Margaret,

I do not know how to write this letter to you and break the news, for I know how you will feel it. Virginia has not been well for some weeks. The strain of the war and of finishing a book produced the old effects of nerve exhaustion. Then the food difficulty began badly again and was very hard to deal with. She lost weight terribly. But it was only the last few weeks that I really became alarmed. She found it difficult to concentrate and was herself afraid that she would never get right again. It has been torture for her these weeks. Last Thursday after vainly trying to persuade her to go to bed and try a real rest cure for at least a week, I rang up a doctor and fixed an appointment for the afternoon and persuaded her to go with me. But it was no good. I was not certain whether the old suicidal impulses were there, and wrongly came to the conclusion that they were not. On Friday morning she went out for a walk leaving a letter for me saying that she knew she was going mad and that this time she would never recover, and could not face it.

It is over now. You know what it was like before and I can never forget what you were at that time. She said in her letter that she had been completely happy until this terrible disease came on her and I think it was true, I know it was true. She would have got better again this time too, if one could have prevented this. Of course, I could have prevented it by immediately getting nurses and I suppose I ought to say I was wrong not to have done so. I have been proved wrong and yet I know myself that I would do the same again. One had to make up one's mind which would do the greater harm—to insist, in which

1. On its main news page on April 3 *The Times* reported "with regret that it must now be presumed that Mrs Leonard Woolf (Virginia Woolf, the novelist and essayist) who has been missing since last Friday, has been drowned in the Sussex Ouse at Rodmell, near Lewes." An obituary was carried on another page. The BBC announced her death on its evening news broadcast that day.

case I knew it would be a complete break down at once and attempt at suicide, or to run the risk and try to prevent the last symptoms coming on. I say this to you because I know you will understand.

Yours
Leonard

To John Lehmann

Monk's House
Rodmell

3/4/41

Dear John,

Many thanks for your letter. I knew how you would feel. I should like to have a talk with you. I could come up and meet you in town any day next week except Thursday and meet you any time after 11.15.

The body has not been found. If it is and there is an inquest, I should have to be here for it, but in that case I would let you know. You will have seen that the papers now have it. I gave the facts to Geoffrey Dawson as it seemed to me that that was the best thing to do. But the result is of course that all last night and this morning the Press Association and other papers are ringing me up.

I presume that you did not send the MS of V's book as I have not received it. She was pleased when she got your letter about it. I still think it a very remarkable book. I had expected from what she had said and feared to find a loss of vigour. I may be wrong, but it seemed to me the opposite, to be more vigorous and pulled to gether than most of her other books, to have more depth and to be very moving. I also thought that the strange symbolism gave it an almost terifying profundity and beauty.

LW

To Donald Brace

Monk's House
Rodmell near Lewes   Sussex

6 April, 1941

Dear Mr Brace,

I must thank you for your telegram and your sympathy. . . . My wife always appreciated your kindness and courtesy to her and looked upon you as a friend as well as a publisher.

The book, which was fiction, was finished. She had given it to me

255

to read the week before this happened and I thought it extraordinarily good; in fact, in some ways it is better, I think, than anything she has written. For the moment this encouraged her, but her doubts soon returned and she was convinced that it was hopelessly bad. As I saw that it would be disastrous for her to worry about it, I suggested that we should give up all idea of publishing it this season (as we had intended), that she should put the whole thing on one side, and that in a month or two, when she felt better, we would consider the whole thing again. She agreed to this and I was going to write to you about it. I may of course be wrong in my view of it, for some of it must have been written under the strain or threat of this illness. I shall get the book read here by someone else, and if the opinion confirms mine, I shall publish it.[1] In that case I will send you proofs as I expect you will want to see it.

Once more I must thank you for your kindness and sympathy.[2]

Yours sincerely
Leonard Woolf

To Vita Sackville-West

Monk's House
Rodmell

6/4/41

My dear Vita,

I just want to say that your poem which I have read this moment moved me profoundly & to thank you for it. It expresses perfectly what was Virginia & what one felt in & to her.[3]

If you go to Vanessa, as I believe you may, & could come on here for a few minutes, remember that I should always like to see you. But if you feel that you cant, I shall understand.

They have been dragging the river the last week, but are now, I think, abandoning the search.[4]

Will you thank Harold from me for his letter?

Yours
Leonard

1. The other person was Vanessa Bell, who recommended publication.
2. LW received more than 200 condolence letters and sent handwritten replies to each.
3. The poem, "In Memoriam: Virginia Woolf," was published in the *Observer* of April 6.
4. VW's body was found on April 18 and identified by LW on that day; an inquest was held the next day. He went alone to the cremation and was deeply offended when music was played from Gluck's *Orfeo*, which promised a future reunion; he felt the music made a mockery of his pain at Virginia's extinction.

To H. G. Wells[1]

Monk's House
11 April 1941   Rodmell near Lewes   Sussex

My dear Wells,

Your letter touched me & I want to thank you for it. I have always had an impersonal admiration for you since I was a boy & a personal affection since we met over the League in the other world war. What you say therefore means something to me.

Yours ever
Leonard Woolf

To Mary Hutchinson

28 April, 1941   Monk's House, Rodmell

My dear Mary,

I want to thank you for your letter & for what I know you & Barbara feel.[2] I want you to know too that the reports in the papers are completely inaccurate—even the words in her last letter are given quite wrong.[3] Virginia had been fairly well until the end of last year, though she had got terribly thin. Indeed it was barely three weeks before the end that I became alarmed; some of the old symptoms began to return & she feared that she would go mad again & became convinced that if she did she would not this time recover. If she could have been induced to go to bed & rest, it would have cleared away, as it had more than once in the last 25 years. But she felt it would be no good & that she would not recover. She never felt or wrote that she could not go on any longer "in these terrible times"—as the reports make her out to have said. What she actually wrote in her letter to me was:

1. H. G. Wells (1866–1946), author and old friend, had written: "I've been wanting to write to you these days about this distressful break in your life & finding it difficult to say what I had to say. You see I knew you & your work very well. . . . I think you are as strong & clear on the human outlook as anybody else in the world & I am concerned before anything else that you should carry on. . . ."
2. Barbara Rothschild (b. 1911), daughter of Mary and St John ("Jack") Hutchinson, and wife of Victor Rothschild (3rd Baron Rothschild).
3. At the inquest, the coroner quoted VW as having written in her last letter that she could not "go on any longer in these terrible times" and he added that she was "of an extremely sensitive nature."

"I feel certain that I am going mad again. I feel we cant go through another of those terrible times. And I shant recover this time."

Will you tell Barbara & Jack how much I appreciated their writing to me?

Yours ever
Leonard

To the Editor of the Sunday Times

[Published May 4, 1941]   Rodmell, Sussex.

Sir,—In view of Mrs. Hicks's letter in your last issue, I feel that I should not silently allow it to remain on record that Virginia Woolf committed suicide because she could not face the "terrible times" through which all of us are going.[1] For this is not true. The idea that this was so is due to a misreporting which has appeared in almost every newspaper of the words which she wrote in her last letter to me. The newspapers give the words as:

I feel I cannot go on any longer in these terrible times.
This is not what she wrote; the words which she wrote are:

I feel certain that I am going mad again. I feel we can't go through another of those terrible times. And I shan't recover this time.
She had had a mental breakdown about twenty-five years ago; the old symptoms began to return about three weeks before she took her life, and she thought that this time she would not recover. Like everyone else, she felt the general strain of the war, and the return of her illness was no doubt partly due to that strain. But the words of her letter and everything which she ever said prove that she took her life, not because she could not "carry on," but because she thought she was going mad again and would not this time recover.

Leonard Woolf

---

1. Commenting on the coroner's report, Kathleen Hicks, wife of the Bishop of Lincoln, had written that there were many persons, possibly more sensitive than Virginia Woolf, who had lost everything in the war but who continued to "take their part nobly in this fight for God against the devil."

To Vita Sackville-West

8/5/41   Monk's House

My dear Vita,
  I was glad to hear from you again. Later on I might feel I want a
day or two away & then I should like to see you & Sissinghurst. At
present I feel I am better here.
  The Bishop's wife is a strange woman. She wrote me today an
incredible letter & forgot even to sign it.[1] I don't know whether it is
a strange thing, but I keep on thinking how amused Virginia would
have been by the extraordinary things people write to me about her.

                                             Yours ever
                                             Leonard

To Vita Sackville-West

                                                    Monk's House
24 May, 1941   Rodmell

My dear Vita,
  Virginia has left you one of her MSS with instructions to me to
choose it and now the probate people have asked me to inform them
which it is to be. I thought of choosing *Flush*, which would also include
some of the *Common Reader*, as they are in the same MS book. The
only thing against it is that Chaper I is not there. I expect it is in
another book and will eventually turn up, but at present I have not
come across it. Would you like to have this or would you prefer to
have *The Years*?[2]
  I liked your reminiscences in *Horizon*; they were so characteristic
of Virginia.[3]

                                             Yours
                                             LW

1. Mrs. Hicks said the point of her letter to the *Sunday Times* "was to save anyone who
was on the verge from thinking . . . one was justified in taking one's life."
2. Sackville-West replied that she would prefer *The Waves* but would accept *The Common
Reader* or *Mrs. Dalloway*. She added that the manuscript of *Orlando*, which VW had given
her years before, contained many unpublished passages.
3. The May *Horizon* was a memorial number on VW; Sackville-West's piece included the
lapidary comment: "Tenuousness and purity were in her baptismal name, and a hint of the
fang in the other."

Monk's House
29 May, 1941   Rodmell

My dear Vita,

I am glad you are outspoken, as always, and I will be. *The Waves* is the only one in particular which I should much like to keep, partly for sentimental reasons, and partly because I think I may some time write something about Virginia's actual method of writing. I should like to compare her first draft with the final draft and also with what she says in her diaries at the moment about writing them. It happens that the last part of *The Waves* is extraordinarily interesting from this point of view as she gives a description in her diary of the actual writing of it.

I had thought of *Mrs Dalloway*, but I could only find half of it and oddly enough the second half in two versions. I have now made another search and have found the first volume. *The Common Reader* is very scattered and not nearly complete. So I think I had better say it will be *Mrs Dalloway*. If however you would really much rather have *The Waves*, I trust you to say so and I will make it that and should not feel it in the least, not nearly as much as that you should not be getting what you like. So I trust you to be absolutely frank on this point.[1]

I should very much like to see the unpublished passages in *Orlando* which I have quite forgotten. If they are as good as the rest, I think they ought some time to be published. Would it be possible to have them typed (at my expense)?[2]

I am very glad *Grand Canyon* will be finished by July, for that makes it possible to publish in the autumn.

Yours ever
Leonard Woolf

1. She eventually accepted *Mrs. Dalloway*.
2. On seeing them, LW found the passages too inchoate to be published; however, Sackville-West read one on the BBC and it was published in the *Listener* in January 1955.

To Vita Sackville-West

Monk's House
23 June, 1941   Rodmell   near Lewes   Sussex

Dear Vita,

Here is the book.[1] I am also sending the MS of *Mrs Dalloway*. I presume that it is legal for me to do so before the estate is settled. The first vol. is called *The Hours* which is what V. intended the title to be originally.

The garden here has been rather knocked about by the weather. I think I have less fruit than any year since we came here.

Yours
Leonard Woolf

1. An advance copy of *Between the Acts*.

HOGARTH HOUSE,
PARADISE ROAD,
RICHMOND,
S. W.

TELEPHONE:
RICHMOND, 496.

19 Oct. 1918.

Dear Mr Eliot,

My wife and I have started a small
private Printing Press, and we print and publish
privately short works which would not otherwise
find a publisher easily. We have been told by
Roger Fry that you have some poems which you wish
to find a publisher for. We both very much liked
your book, Prufrock; and I wonder whether you would
care to let us look at the poems with a view to printing them.

Yours very truly

Leonard Woolf

I should add that we are amateurs at printing
but we could, if you liked, let you see our
last production.

TO T. S. ELIOT

PART FOUR

PUBLISHER
AND EDITOR

The lives of Leonard and Virginia Woolf revolved around books—reading, reviewing, printing, publishing and, above all, writing them. The Woolfs even thought of having their own bookshop and literary review. Of his wife, Leonard commented that she spent virtually every waking moment thinking about her writing. Although no single vocation could contain him, throughout his life writing was Leonard's central interest and his greatest satisfaction, if also at times his deepest disappointment. He began as a boy, contributing verses and stories to the *Jewish Chronicle*, and went on almost to the moment of his death, nearly eighty years later. In the intervening years he published two novels, four short stories, a play, more than thirty works of nonfiction, a five-volume autobiography, well over a thousand reviews and essays, dozens of pamphlets on international political questions and countless memoranda for the Labour Party and the Fabian Society. As manager of a publishing house, he read mountains of manuscripts and published more than a thousand of them, thirty-four printed by hand. And at one time or another he was an editor or director of *War and Peace*, the *International Review*, the *Contemporary Review*, the *Nation*, the *New Statesman* and the *Political Quarterly*.

If being a writer was Leonard's great objective in life, the type of writing was determined by circumstance. His original intention was to write novels and short stories and, on the side, essays and reviews. He was off to an excellent start with *The Village in the Jungle*. However, it was not to be. Virginia's breakdowns forced him to find an immediate source of income to finance her medical expenses. Moreover, whether because it was only a modest critical success or because of his family's hostile reaction, *The Wise Virgins* caused him to give up his career as a novelist. Perhaps he thought the fictional muse had abandoned him; in any case, he realized she would not provide an adequate income—the royalties from both novels averaged £6 a year in their time. Meanwhile, the outbreak of the First World War had transformed him from a nonpolitical animal, in his idiom, into an active figure on the political left and a recognized expert on international organization. As a consequence, within a few years of marriage he found himself writing works on an entirely new range of topics and deeply immersed in journalism.

But even a relatively placid life of writing, if now nonfiction, was not Leonard's destiny. Intrigued by the idea of dabbling in printing, he and Virginia in 1917 bought a tabletop press and taught themselves how to use it. The small hand machine was intended as an exciting hobby and as therapy for Virginia, to take her mind off writing. Although the purpose was printing rather than publishing, they called their enterprise the Hogarth Press, after Hogarth House, their eighteenth-century residence in Richmond.

The venture was launched in July 1917 with a laboriously produced edition in 150 copies of *Two Stories*, Leonard's "Three Jews" and Virginia's "The Mark on the Wall." Now intrigued, they went on to print Katherine Mansfield's *Prelude*, T. S. Eliot's *Poems* and Virginia's *Kew Gardens*. *Kew Gardens* was such an unexpected success that Leonard had to turn to a commercial firm to rush a second edition into print. With that simple step, the Woolfs crossed the threshold from an afternoon pastime of printing to one of publishing—as Leonard later remarked, "something which we had never intended or originally envisaged." Then, with a flight of inspiration that was to typify their publishing, they brought out T. S. Eliot's *The Waste Land* and also the first English-language translations of works by Gorki, Dostoevsky, Bunin, Tolstoi and Freud. By 1924, the Hogarth Press was not only an established firm but also a house with an exciting reputation. The manuscripts flowed in, not just from authors in Britain, but also from William Plomer in Zululand, Robert Graves in Cairo, Edmund Blunden in Tokyo, Italo Svevo in Trieste, Conrad Aiken in Boston, Gertrude Stein in Paris and Edwin Muir in Vienna.

At this point Leonard made a decision that was central to the character and success of the Press: it would remain a small, personal, part-time business, poised between amateurism and professionalism. At first all the work was done on the dining-room table at Hogarth House—the pages printed, stitched and bound; the books wrapped, addressed and invoiced and the business correspondence typed. When the Woolfs moved to Tavistock Square in 1924, the Press went into the ground floor—the old kitchen, pantries and billiard room—and a small staff was engaged. Even then, Leonard and Virginia continued to do almost everything themselves. They read the manuscripts, drew up contracts with a commercial printing firm, commissioned jacket illustrations, wrapped and posted the books, designed the advertising and, when there was time, traveled to bookshops around the country to find new outlets. Leonard kept the financial accounts and for many years maintained a meticulous record of each book sold, with the date and the name of the buyer. And every afternoon from two to four Virginia set type while Leonard printed books they occasionally still produced themselves. Even in its heyday the Hogarth Press was a makeshift, even quirky operation, run on a shoestring with a clerk, a secretary and a passing parade of assistants. But Leonard managed it with an efficiency equal to that of the best houses in London. From the acceptance of a manuscript to its publication was a matter of about three months; never did the Press fail to get a book out on time, never did it fail to fill an order promptly.

What transformed this amateur endeavor—almost inadvertently—into a firm that became a legend in twentieth-century publishing was a combination of literary talent, publishing ideals and financial shrewdness.

The key was the Woolfs' exceptional intellectual skills. Virginia was one of the outstanding critics of her time; Leonard was in his own right a highly respected literary journalist. Literature had been his consuming interest at Cambridge; he was exceptionally well read and had been developing his critical abilities since his days at St. Paul's. Moreover, with his expertise in political affairs, he was able to add a dimension that most of the prestigious older houses lacked. Inevitably he and Virginia failed to recognize a few promising authors and overrated some of their own. But they built up a list of authors that was second to none in British publishing at the time. It included many of the leading names of twentieth-century English fiction and poetry, the major contemporary Russian writers, such European avant-garde poets as Rilke, Lorca and Cavafy, Freud and most of the leading psychiatrists, and a grand miscellany of outstanding writers on literary, social and political topics.

Virginia's role in the Press was modest. As she gained fame, with the publication of *To the Lighthouse* in 1927 and *Orlando* the following year, her name became a great asset. For a novelist to be accepted by Hogarth was taken to mean that he was accepted by Virginia Woolf—just as for a poet to be taken by Faber meant that he had been approved by T. S. Eliot. But apart from sharing in some of the menial labor, she read only manuscripts of novels and literary works. All the rest—poetry, politics, psychiatry, history and so on—was Leonard's province. Even so, titles were published only if they both agreed; in the rare case they did not, they turned to a friend, such as Raymond Mortimer, for an independent opinion. Eventually they used Cecil Day-Lewis as a regular outside reader and established an advisory committee—which included Rosamond Lehmann, Stephen Spender, Wysten Auden, Christopher Isherwood and Vita Sackville-West—to suggest new authors and occasionally to assess a manuscript.

The second ingredient in the Press's success was the distinctive purpose Leonard gave it. This might be summed up in a phrase very typical of him, which he once used in another connection: to throw a few stones in the stagnant pool of human thought in the hope of causing a ripple or two. At first he envisaged the Press simply as a service—to provide an outlet for unknown and unorthodox authors whose works were unacceptable to other houses. But very soon he recognized that he could use it creatively—to sponsor the experimental in fiction and poetry, to educate the public on politics and history, to introduce foreign authors to the English-language world and to provide an outlet for psychoanalytical writings. Since his days at Cambridge, he had been impressed by the implacable resistance of society to whatever was new, unconventional and innovative. He had observed the ridicule directed at such contemporaries as Freud, Ibsen, Stravinsky and Cézanne. If his professional life had any single intellectual theme, it was the desire to propagate new ideas, to stimulate thinking and to disseminate alternative views—even when they were unpopular and, indeed, antithetical to his own. When asked in 1966 why he had brought out *The Waste Land*, his response could have been the motto of the Hogarth Press: No one else would have published it.

Leonard published what he considered to have genuine intellectual or literary merit and only that. He was pleased when a book sold well, but never published one simply because it might. On the contrary; the Hogarth Press files hold many a letter to an author saying in so many words: My wife and I think highly of your book and are pleased to publish it; it will not be a popular success but you should not be discouraged, because it is a work of genuine value. Even when a writer was a proven nonseller, they were not deterred from accepting another of his works. Leonard took repeated financial risks in bringing out book after book that he knew might lose money and whose losses were compensated by those that were profitable. Poetry was a particular problem. Since it never sold well, it was not a commercial proposition. But he saw it as part of his publishing duty to give poets their chance. To save printing costs, he and Virginia printed much of it themselves. Eventually Lady Gerald Wellesley agreed to subsidize losses on poetry to the extent of £200 a year in exchange for being co-editor with Leonard of the poetry published by the Press.

Because many Hogarth authors are now among the most widely known in our culture—five became Nobel Prize winners—it takes an effort to realize that most were unheard of when the Hogarth Press first published them, and that the Press was in many cases the vehicle that carried them to fame. Even Sigmund Freud was only just becoming a household name when Leonard agreed to publish his *Collected Papers*, and for years Leonard had difficulty finding an American house interested in buying publication rights. His courage in accepting manuscripts that had been turned down by other London houses was the turning point—or starting point—in many a writer's career.

It was a corollary of his publishing philosophy that he did not wait for manuscripts to turn up, but commissioned works on topics he considered important. To this end he also inaugurated various series on a broad range of cultural, social and political topics. Imaginative in concept, these works were commercially risky, since they were usually published as pamphlets, which booksellers shunned because of their low mark-up value. On the literary side were "The Hogarth Essays," "The Hogarth Essays on Literature," "Hogarth Living Poets," "Hogarth Stories," "New Writings," "Daylight," "Poets of Tomorrow" and "The New Hogarth Library." Social and political issues were addressed in the "Merttens Lectures on War and Peace"— done for the Quakers—"Hogarth Sixpenny Pamphlets" and "Day to Day Pamphlets." One of this last series was Mussolini's *The Political and Social Doctrine of Fascism*, which circulated widely as a primary source book on the subject. To balance it, Leonard asked R. Palme Dutt, a founder of the British Communist Party, to write a companion piece. There were also "Biographies through the Eyes of Contemporaries" and "World Makers and World Shakers," short biographies for older children. One of the most inventive but commercially least successful was "The Hogarth Letters." Some of these were entertaining, such as E. M. Forster's to Madan Blanchard; others were deeply serious, such as Louis Golding's to Adolf Hitler, which Leonard commissioned a full year before the Nazis came to power. Together the various series represented a corpus of excellent minor works by major figures in their field, all of which would otherwise never have been written. Though a few are classics, by and large Leonard overestimated the public's intellectual curiosity, and the series failed to gain the readership they merited.

Leonard's greatest gamble was in committing himself to publish works on psychiatry, in particular those of Freud. Stanley Unwin, the noted publisher, who had brought out two of Freud's works early in the century, had refused to publish any further psychoanalytical writings and warned Leonard against doing so. The project appeared commercially unpromising and involved a substantial capital outlay. Leonard decided to do it because no other publisher could be found and he felt a sense of duty to disseminate Freud's ideas. As can be seen in a sampling of the correspondence, the adventure was an editorial odyssey that began in 1924, progressed through the publication of Freud's individual books and culminated in 1966 in the twenty-four-volume *Standard Edition* of his complete works. Freud's position as the great seminal influence of the century was achieved through his conquest of the English-speaking world, a triumph in which Leonard, however indirectly, had a part.

Such was the enterprise that began with a £38 tabletop printing press, a box of type and a self-instruction manual, which two rank amateurs operated as a casual diversion. But for all the Woolfs' literary skill and Leonard's ideals and imagination, the Hogarth Press would have foundered on launching had it not been for one further element: Leonard's managerial and financial savvy. The supreme paradox of the Hogarth Press is that its reputation and success resulted precisely from Leonard's indifference to the conventional measure of reputation and success: moneymaking.

By keeping the Press a small, spare operation and by refusing to outbid other publishers by offering large advances, he did not need to worry about profits. This enabled him to take risks on unknown authors that other firms could not. Eventually some Hogarth authors were bought away by other publishers. Leonard accepted their move gracefully, as can be seen in letters to Cecil Day-Lewis and William Plomer, who remained friends. But he was angered when an author whose early work had been published at financial risk—or loss—bolted without a word of explanation as soon he had become established through Hogarth. And he was deeply offended when Ernst Freud, who handled his father's publishing interests, and Ernest Jones, who controlled the Institute of Psycho-Analysis, treated him treacherously as soon as Sigmund Freud was dead.

For all his economies, Leonard was as generous as possible with Hogarth authors, even though he and Virginia claimed no compensation for their labors and took from the profits only what was not put back in the firm. At first they paid their authors a quarter of any profits; in later years, royalties were at the standard rate and in some circumstances were paid—for example, to Freud—when there was no obligation to do so. Leonard returned subsidiary rights even when, as in the case of Eliot, it meant forgoing significant future royalties. Usually he was willing to abrogate a contractual right of first refusal for an author's next work. His loyalty to authors was not often matched by theirs to him. Two notable exceptions, as the letters bear witness, were Sigmund Freud and Vita Sackville-West.

It has sometimes been maintained that Leonard's penny-pinching attitude toward advances and book promotion was self-defeating, the reason he lost some of his outstanding discoveries. What is overlooked is that this policy was an essential part of his ethic as a publisher. His aim was to discover writers, not produce celebrities; if celebrities left him, that was their concern. Linked to this was his firm conviction that good books sell themselves. And in fact his biggest moneymakers, in addition to books by Virginia, were by those authors who stuck with the Press. Perhaps there is some poetic justice in the fact that many of those who did abandon the Press had done their best work when they were Hogarth authors.

A striking feature of the letters in the Hogarth Press files is the picture that emerges of a friendly, almost familial business. From one or two letters included here, it can be seen that Leonard and Virginia looked on their authors as friends rather than producers of commercial products. To be a Hogarth author, however insignificant, usually meant not simply having one's books published by the Woolfs, but also invitations for a weekend at Rodmell or an evening at Tavistock Square. It included the privilege of writing whatever one wished. Once in a while Leonard suggested ways to improve a text, but he loathed asking for changes and never insisted.

The more successful the Press became, the more deeply were the Woolfs plunged into a quandary from which they could never extricate themselves. As writers—and in Leonard's case a writer active in politics and in editing one journal or another—they found their growing enterprise an increasing intrusion on their time. Although any publisher would gladly have taken their list, and a good many offered to do so, they could never quite bring themselves to give it up. For Leonard, it offered an outlet for his energies and ideals. For Virginia, what had began as physical therapy continued to be psychologically vital in allowing her to feel completely free to engage in literary experimentation without having to worry about a publisher's reaction.

None of the efforts over the years to find effective managerial assistance worked out. Alix Strachey, not yet launched on her psychoanalytical career, was the first to try; she quit the first day, out of boredom. Barbara Hiles followed; she worked for a share of the profits, which at the end of her tenure amounted to the noble sum of a half-crown. Then several bright young literati arrived from Oxford and Cambridge: Ralph Partridge in 1920, followed by George Rylands, who stayed for five months in 1924 and then returned to a fellowship at King's, succeeded by the amiable but singularly ineffective Angus Davidson until 1929, and finally by John Lehmann, who put in a year before suddenly decamping for Central Europe. At one time or another Marjorie Thomson, Bernadette Murphy, Mrs. Cartwright and Peggy Belsher also had a try. In 1928, as a favor to a friend, Leonard took on sixteen-year-old Richard Kennedy as an apprentice. Although the lad struggled for two years before admitting defeat, he made his mark forty years later with *A Boy at the Hogarth Press*, an inimitable memoir of the firm aetate 1928–30. In his autobiography Leonard frankly acknowledged that he had not always been an easy employer and that it had been unfair to expect anyone of real intelligence to work for a low wage in a dreary basement and do what at times was menial labor, even for the thrill of association with Virginia Woolf and the Hogarth Press.

Finally, in 1938, the problem was solved. John Lehmann returned to London and bought Virginia's half-share of the Press and became general manager. Leonard continued to oversee operations, to read all the manuscripts, and he retained control over Freud's works. But for the next eight years the day-to-day administration was largely in Lehmann's capable hands. The times were far from easy. When the Woolfs' house was damaged in the blitz, Lehmann evacuated the press to Letchworth, in Hertfordshire, with Leonard keeping in touch from Rodmell. In view of the acute paper shortage and the policy of giving preference to works by Freud, reprints of Virginia's writings and poems by Lehmann's protégés, few new titles could be issued. But with the bombing of book warehouses and the wartime thirst for books, the firm quickly sold out its stocks and fairly prospered during these years.

Virginia had foreseen problems in partnership from the start. "I think I suspect our first breach with John. It'll be over his fashion complex," she noted in her diary in 1938. And it was this issue—which manuscripts to publish—that proved explosive. On the first occasion when Leonard took issue with Lehmann, in 1943 over the publication of a small book of poems by Terence Tiller, he was subjected to verbal abuse that continued until he finally gave in. In subsequent autobiographical writings, Lehmann said that the dispute over "author-policy" was the heart of the discord and the reason he despaired for his ideals and the future of the Press. Yet the Press had operated from its earliest days on the strict principle of publishing only when both partners agreed. Moreover, during Lehmann's eight years as a partner, the Press published about a hundred books; on no more than two or three occasions did Leonard demur at Lehmann's decisions. Contrary to Lehmann's later assertions, Leonard favored publication of Saul Bellow's *Dangling Man* and there was no disagreement over works by several other authors that Leonard purportedly opposed. To be sure, Leonard did not think the Press should use its limited paper supply for a selection of Tennyson by Auden and for Sartre's *Les Mouches*; this was as close as he ever came to exercising a "veto." Lehmann gave himself away when he argued for taking these two works, which he admitted were not very good, solely to get their names on the Press's list, an argument that was antithetical to Leonard's publishing principles. In reality, this controversy masked Lehmann's deeper discontent—Leonard's continued presence in the firm. In 1946 Lehmann decided to try to oust Leonard by dissolving the partnership in the hope of forcing him to sell his share. Instead, he was himself bought out and went off to establish his own publishing firm, which failed some years later.

By selling Lehmann's equity to Chatto & Windus, in an association that left Hogarth Press autonomous, Leonard found what he had always wanted—a staff to administer the firm, leaving him free to manage the editorial side. In contrast to the relationship with Lehmann, Leonard and Ian Parsons, a director of Chatto, collaborated in perfect harmony for the next twenty years. Leonard ran the press along the old lines—if with less gusto—and into his eighties was still guiding the publication of Freud's works. The year after the publication of *The Standard Edition of the Complete Psychological Works of Sigmund Freud*, Leonard brought his publishing career to an end. He had been with the Press fifty years.

Leonard Woolf's work as an editor, reviewer and essayist was dedicated to the same objectives as his work as a publisher. Although he enjoyed writing, he took up journalism primarily because he needed money, and he never let it be more than a sideline to his other activities.

Nonetheless, he threw himself into it with his usual verve. His output was amazing. In the three years 1913 to 1916, when he was nursing his wife through her worst bouts of insanity, starting a political career and writing several books, he turned out more than 150 review articles and essays. No less impressive was his repertoire. For the *Times Literary Supplement*, he reviewed literary works; for the *New Statesman*, he produced reviews and essays on international affairs; for the *Co-operative News*, he wrote on economic and feminist issues. He wrote, for a while, a regular report on parliamentary debates for the *Labour Leader*. And for the *Independent Review*, the *Athenaeum*, the *Nation* and the *Economic Journal*, he wrote pieces that ranged from art to zoology. Some of the articles were quite original. For example, his critique in the *New Weekly* in June 1914 of Freud's *Psychopathology of Everyday Life* was the first article in a nonmedical journal on Freud's theories.

Leonard's career as a critic and essayist continued almost to the time of his death. His last article, an obituary appreciation of Kingsley Martin written in the spring of 1969 for the *Political Quarterly*, was fully as rigorous in style and substance as anything he had written nearly sixty years earlier. The articles in the intervening years, though undervalued and largely forgotten today, are probably his best writing.

His work as an editor began in 1916 with *War and Peace*, a monthly founded by Norman Angell. At the end of the war he wanted to turn the journal into an international socialist review on foreign affairs and induced the Rowntree Trust to finance it. Ramsay MacDonald undercut the project, but the Rowntrees were intrigued and induced Leonard to edit a similar publication without socialist links; this became the *International Review*. The publication was filled with documentation and had brilliant contributors; but it was too dryly intellectual and failed financially at the end of 1919. The Rowntrees then persuaded him to edit a new international section of the *Contemporary Review*, which he did for two years. When Keynes took over the *Nation* in 1923, he invited Leonard to be editor of either the political or—T. S. Eliot having declined it—the literary side. Leonard, too far to the left to have much patience with Keynes's liberalism, chose the latter.

As with the Hogarth Press, Leonard used his journals as vehicles for discovering new talent, circulating new ideas and alternative viewpoints and educating readers about national and international issues. Beginning with his old Cambridge friends—including Strachey, whom he cajoled into writing iconoclastic reviews in the style that was soon to make him famous in *Eminent Victorians*—he built over the years a formidably impressive retinue of reviewers on literary, political and social questions. "I doubt," he wrote, without exaggeration, "whether any weekly paper has ever had such a constellation of stars shining in it as I got for the *Nation*." The stars included just about every notable British writer and thinker of the time. His own weekly column in the *Nation*, "The World of Books," was of high critical quality. As a result, the literary side was fully up to the standard of the political and economic pages and helped to make the *Nation* the most influential and highly regarded of the three main weeklies during the 1920s.

Leonard never liked journalistic life, with its deadlines, scramble for adequate space and what he described as its practitioners' "hallucinatory overestimation" of their own importance. Moreover, when he began to introduce his intellectual principles into the *Nation*, he immediately clashed head on with Hubert Henderson, the editor-in-chief. Leonard's instinct was to give his reviewers freedom to write as they wished. As Richard Aldington was moved to comment: "I write for you with more ease and zest than for any other editor I ever worked for. . . . You give all the liberty one could reasonably ask, and yet at the same time I always feel perfectly confident you wouldn't allow me to print anything really foolish or unwise." Leonard also opened his pages to unknown young writers and in so doing launched the careers of some of the most outstanding critics of the time. But the Liberal Henderson could stomach neither Leonard's liberal editing principles nor what he regarded as Leonard's literary incestuousness—making the journal a mouthpiece for Bloomsbury friends, an assertion, by almost any definition of Bloomsbury, that was demonstrably false. The two repeatedly disagreed as well over the space allowed for the literary side of the journal. In exasperation Leonard resigned several times, only to be persuaded by Keynes to stay on. But as his need for outside income declined, once the Hogarth Press began to turn a profit, he reduced the time spent on journalism and finally left the *Nation* in 1930. He continued, however, to have a strong interest in political journalism, co-editing the *Political Quarterly* and serving as a director of the *New Statesman* until his eighty-fifth year.

By rough estimate there survive about 3,000 letters that Leonard wrote in connection with his career as a publisher and editor, a small portion of the total number he wrote. Collectively they provide an excellent glimpse into the publishing and editing world during a half-century. The correspondence necessarily has serious gaps. Some are the result of wartime destruction; some, because most books were accepted upon submission and left no paper trail. Letters were selected not for the fame of the person addressed, but to give a sense of the evolution of the Hogarth Press and Leonard's editing career and to illustrate his techniques and philosophy in both professions. In view of the importance of Freud's works, enough correspondence has been included to make it possible to follow two publications from conception to completion—*Moses and Monotheism* and the *Standard Edition*. The titanic struggle between Leonard and John Lehmann after 1943 is recorded in correspondence that would fill a volume of its own; a few representative letters are included.

The correspondence in this chapter illustrates other aspects of Leonard's career as a publisher. One tragicomic series of problems was that caused by the stringent libel laws and philistine social standards, which brought him into difficulties with the government of India, a major book distributor, and his printing firm. Through the years Leonard was at the forefront of those who sought to prevent the suppression of works and the arrest of persons for "obscenity"—of Radclyffe Hall in 1928 for her novel *Well of Loneliness* and "Count" Potock in 1932 for his poems.

Time has obscured Leonard Woolf's contribution to British literary and intellectual life. Had he done nothing more than publish the works of his wife and Sigmund Freud, he would have made a major and lasting contribution to the cultural life of the century. The works published by the Hogarth Press are Leonard Woolf's greatest tangible legacy.

*   *   *

TO ROBERT TREVELYAN[1]

Hogarth House,
[Early August 1917]   Paradise Road, Richmond, Surrey

Dear Bob,

Many thanks for your letter. I am glad you liked the *Stories*. I thought Virginia's extraordinarily good. As for the printing, I quite agree with your criticisms. We still have a lot to learn: but I think we are definitely improving, and with our new type it is distinctly easier. We are also going to get a better machine. I am very sorry you had a faulty copy, and now enclose it rectified.

1. The text of this letter was printed on the Woolfs' hand press.

We took your *Pterodamozels* to Asheham and read them there.[1] I like it very much. It carries one along, and the choruses seemed to me most successful.

Yours
Leonard Woolf

[In handwriting]
The above is our new type.

TO LYTTON STRACHEY

Hogarth House
Richmond.

19 Jan 1918.

I thought your review of Morley just what I had hoped for. I have called it "A Statesman", but was unable to do Dilke.[2] Would you do us another for next month. There is a book just out on Li-Hung-Chang by J.O.P. Bland which might be quite amusing. I thought you might deal with Li as a Diplomatist and in connection with Diplomacy which would bring him within our orbit and might give you great scope. Will you? By Feb 14?

A curious scene at Belsize Park: V. and I at tea with her Ladyship. V. very innocently: "Well, Lady Strachey, and what do you think of Tidmarsh?"[3] An awkward pause and some very indistinct remarks from her Ladyship. A pause. Then across the table to me: "What do you think of it all?" (She was referring to the general European situation, but I naturally thought that she referred to Tidmarsh.) I prepare to give a very full and definite opinion on the moral and social problem involved in Lytton and Carrington cohabiting at Tidmarsh. Tableau.

L S W

1. *Pterodamozels: An Operatic Fable*, a two-act play.
2. The review of the memoirs of Viscount Morley, author and prominent Liberal Party figure, was one of five articles LW commissioned from Strachey for *War and Peace*. They were published in 1933 as *Characters and Commentaries*.
3. Strachey was sharing a house with Dora Carrington in the Berkshire village of Tidmarsh, an unconventional ménage that troubled his socially conventional mother, who resided in Belsize Park Gardens.

1917 Club
[May 6, 1918]   4, Gerrard Street, W.1.

Would you do a short & amusing article on "Peace Traps & Peace Offensives" by May 17th? I think you could, you know.

Rowntree has been greatly bitten by my scheme for a *Review* & will certainly finance it unless the expense proves too terrific.[1] He has asked me to edit it if he does start it & is now having estimates made. It would start at once. A new vista has now opened which might, if one only had the energy to push it, be made to end in something really worth doing. But I've just had gas & an enormous tooth removed & everything is fading into insignificance except James & Alix & Adrian talking on the other side of this table.

L

To Lytton Strachey

22 Sept. 1918   Asheham

It has definitely been decided that the *Review* is to come into being. The question is now whether it is to appear first in January or before, and I shall go up some time this week to discuss it. I dont think it will be able to come out until January, so that it does not matter about "Bismarck" for the moment. But I hope you'll do it as soon as you're recovered.[2]

What a devilish thing the body and particularly the guts are (or is?). (V. induced me to buy *The King's English*, a book which teaches you exactly how not to write. The difficulty is that that is precisely what it does do, and now I cannot write a sentence, because as soon as I get one down, I see that it is exactly like some horror of Miss Corelli's quoted as a warning in that damned book.[3] Also it has made me unable to read a book, because the whole time I observe mistakes of punctuation in it.)

1. Arnold Rowntree, of the chocolate manufacturing and philanthropic family, was a promoter of international and liberal causes.
2. LW had asked Strachey to review a new biography of Bismarck for the first issue of the *International Review*.
3. The famous book by H. W. and F. G. Fowler cited passages from the writings of Marie Corelli as examples of grammatical and stylistic solecisms.

Last week we had the Webbs here and George Young, a most curious entertainment. Young insisted upon travelling from Portsmouth in order to see the Webbs for two hours. He walked from Lewes in a waterspout, and then stayed of course for 24 hours. He is just what Hilton was at Cambridge plus 50 years.[1] The Webbs were rather nice. Webb said that the use of marriage was that it was a waste paper basket for the emotions: you just swept up all your emotions and deposited them in it, and then got on with your work. Mrs Webb agreed.

Now Gertler is here talking about Gertler.[2]

L.

To T. S. ELIOT

Hogarth House

19 Oct. 1918.   Paradise Road   Richmond, S.W.

Dear Mr Eliot,

My wife and I have started a small private Printing Press, and we print and publish privately short works which would not otherwise find a publisher easily. We have been told by Roger Fry that you have some poems which you wish to find a publisher for. We both very much liked your book, *Prufrock*; and I wonder whether you would care to let us look at the poems with a view to printing them.

Yours very truly
Leonard Woolf

I should add that we are amateurs at printing but we could, if you liked, let you see our last production.[3]

---

1. (Sir) George Young (1872–1952), civil servant and Labour candidate for Parliament, was considered by LW "a nice, absurd, cantankerous man." His younger brother, Edward Hilton Young (1879–1960), LW's contemporary at Trinity, was known as a sphinx without a riddle.
2. Mark Gertler (1891–1939), the painter. Of this occasion, VW recorded in her diary that they had talked "about Gertler to Gertler for some 30 hours."
3. The last production was Katherine Mansfield's *Prelude*. Eliot accepted LW's offer, and *Poems*, the fourth Hogarth Press book, was printed by the Woolfs the following spring in 190 copies. It sold out in a year, with total receipts of £18-10-4 and a net profit of £12-8-6, of which Eliot's share was £3-2-6.

To H. G. WELLS   The International Review
                                                10, Adelphi Terrace,
8 Feb 1919   London, W.C.2

My dear Wells,

I am sending the first three chapters to the printer today, though I think the first two will form the instalment for the March number.[1]

I feel, after reading the *Undying Fire*, that I have all the more to thank you for letting me have it. I like it immensely, more than anything else I've read of yours, & I've read, I suppose, all. It's not only that it's beautiful, but you've got a kind of large truth in it & over it which is rarely felt & seized & still more rarely communicated. When I read *God the Invisible King*, I didn't agree with you in the least— but I'm sure you're right in this.

                                                Yours ever
                                                Leonard Woolf

To EDWARD MARSH
                                                Hogarth House,
11 May, 1919   Paradise Road, Richmond, Surrey.

My dear Marsh,

I had not thought of publishing L. Strachey's parerga, partly because, I must confess, I think them extraordinarily poor. There were great points in his *Eminent Victorians* which was a thoroughly amusing book. But his article ["Lady Hester Stanhope"] in the *Athenaeum* seemed to me weak and mechanical, as if his method had already become a trick and his style a formula. But in any case the regular flies of the publishing world are already buzzing round the ointment.

                                                Yours
                                                Leonard Woolf

1. LW launched his *International Review* with a stellar group of contributors, even inducing Wells to serialize his latest novel.

9/6/21 Hogarth House

Dear Ralph and Partridge,

We were very glad to get your letters and, if I were not the worst letter writer in Europe, I should have answered before.

I dont know that there is much news to tell you. We have just been for our annual treat at the Richmond Horse Show. Various people with nervous break-down, in various stages of incipient lunacy, [Harry] Norton and Molly MacCarthy for instance, have been to dine and ask our advice. We have acquired two goslings from your friend Mrs Barker. I am on the point of quarrelling with my old friend Sydney Waterlow because I do not like Middleton Murry.[2]

The Press progresses. The sales now are Tchekhov 487, *Monday or Tuesday* 434, *Stories of the East* 261. We have practically finished binding up Prewett and he wants me to distribute them.[3] He is the vaguest man I've ever struck, but I suppose I shall have to do it. We continue to exchange letters. We have received quite a good poem from a woman and have offered to print it ourselves, and are to see her next Sunday. We are going to start printing Clive's poems and have also agreed to print Fredigonde's so we ought to have a flight of poets in the autumn.[4] I hope you approve.

Give my love to Lytton if he is with you. I hope he will see my reference to him in the *Daily Herald*.[5]

Yours
L S W

1. Ralph Partridge (1894–1960), at this time an assistant at the Hogarth Press, and Dora Carrington had married several weeks earlier and were on a honeymoon in Venice with Lytton Strachey.
2. John Middleton Murry (1889–1957), literary critic and husband of Katherine Mansfield. "I once reviewed in the *Nation* a book of his simply by mixing up indiscriminately quotations from the book and quotations from Pecksniff. I defied anyone to disentangle them, and I do not think anyone ever did—but the Murry-Pecksniff paragraphs made perfect sense" (*Beginning Again*).
3. *The Note-Books of Anton Tchekhov*, edited by Maxim Gorky. *Monday or Tuesday* was by VW, and *Stories of the East* by LW. Frank Prewett's *Poems* were published in August; Prewett was a Canadian farmer and a friend of the poet Siegfried Sassoon, through whom he may have met the Woolfs.
4. The woman was Ruth Manning-Sanders, her poem was *Karn*; Clive Bell's *Poems* appeared in December of that year, and Fredegond Shove's *Daybreak* in May 1922.
5. In a review (June 8) of two books on British economic history, LW had written: "Neither

The Hogarth Press
                                                 Hogarth House
2 January, 1922   Paradise Road   Richmond   Surrey

Dear Mr Unwin,

   . . . I considered carefully the question and, while of course there
would be very great advantages from our point of view in distributing
through you, for the present at any rate we must, I think, go on as
we are. The Press by its own momentum some time ago grew into a
concern which was much more than a mere hobby for our spare time,
and, as we were not willing ourselves to manage it as a business, we
took in some one who would.[2] Your letter arrived at a moment when
we were in doubts whether to continue in this way, but we have
eventually decided that for the present at any rate we must go on in
our semi-amateurish way.

                                                 Yours sincerely
                                                 Leonard Woolf

To T. S. Eliot

                                                 Hogarth House
25 May, 1922   Paradise Road   Richmond, Surrey

Dear Eliot,
   I enclose the rest of the Dostoevskii as far as we have got it, so that
you can see yourself what it looks like.[3] There is still a little more, but

---

of these books can be classified under the heading 'light and easy reading,' and their authors
would probably argue that if you want entertainment and amusement, you must go to Miss
Dell or Mr. Lytton Strachey and not to a Regius Professor of Ecclesiastical History or an
Assistant Professor of Economics. No doubt there is something in the argument, though we
have never seen why the professors should not make the path of the student of economics
and industrial history a little easier and a little gayer without any loss of efficiency or
dignity."
1. (Sir) Stanley Unwin (1884–1968), one of the leading publishers of his time, probably met
LW through the Fabian Society. By 1918 he had published three of his early works. He was
one of the publishers who wanted to absorb the Hogarth Press.
2. Marjorie Thomson, who replaced Ralph Partridge.
3. Eliot was about to launch and edit a literary review, the *Criterion*. To give the publication
a pan-European accent, he turned to LW for extracts from Russian books that the Hogarth
Press planned to publish. The Dostoevsky work, which Eliot used in the first issue, was the
sketch of a novel, planned but never written, entitled "The Life of a Great Sinner." This
and other Russian texts came to LW through a Russian émigré, Samuel Solomonovitch
Koteliansky (1881–1955), who translated them with the Woolfs' assistance.

Leonard and Herbert, c. 1885

Leonard (l.) and Bella (r.), c. 1894

Woolf family in 1886: Herbert, Harold, Marie, nurse with Flora, Clara, Edgar, Bella, Sidney, Leonard

Leonard and colleagues in Jaffna, c. 1905

Leonard in Hambantota, December 1908

Leonard and the Hamers, c. 1910

Leonard and Bella at Hatton,
March 1908

Leonard and the headman of the Central Province in front of the Kandy
kachcheri, 1908

Leonard and Virginia at Dalingridge Place, July 1912

Walk morn. Sat in glen.
Walk w V even. V. calm &
happy at first in morn. Then
v. worried & great difficulty
over food. Ate v. little.
Worry nearly all day but not
as acute as yesterday. Calm
& happy after dinner but
slight return just before
sleep. V. good night.
(Delusions persisted I think
all day) Great difficulty over
food all day

Encrypted diary entry with transliteration

"Contract" between Leonard and Virginia

Lytton Strachey and Saxon Sydney-
Turner, c. 1914

Leonard and E. M. Forster at Asheham
House, June 1913

Leonard and G. E. Moore at Asheham
House, June 1914

Leonard and Margaret Llewelyn
Davies in Cornwall, September 1916

Roger Fry, Clive Bell, Duncan Grant, Lytton Strachey, Saxon Sydney-Turner and Vanessa Bell at Asheham House, September 1913

Leonard, Quentin and Julian Bell, J. M. Keynes, Clive Bell, and (front) Mary Hutchinson and Duncan Grant at Charleston, 1921

Monk's House, 1919

Monk's House dining room (photographed after Leonard's death)

Leonard and Vita Sackville-West at Monk's House, 1933

Leonard and Virginia at Studland, September 1923

Leonard and Virginia in Hyde Park, June 1925

Leonard, Virginia, Margery and Roger Fry in front of the Olympieum in Athens, April 1932

Leonard and Pinka in Monk's House garden, 1931

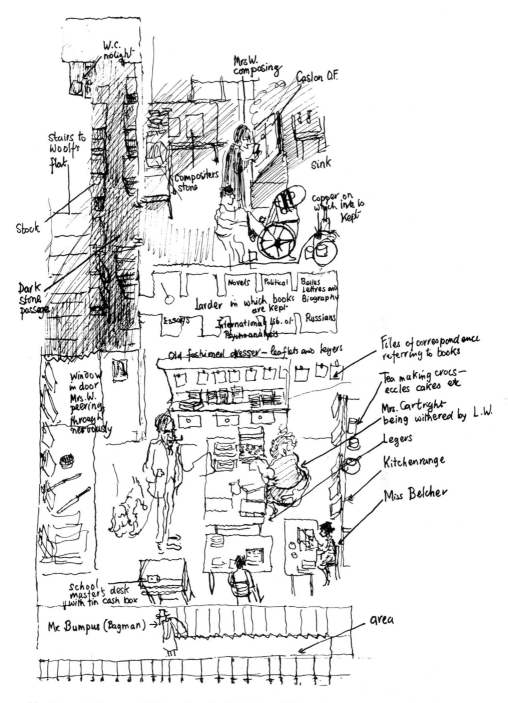

The Hogarth Press, c. 1928, as sketched by Richard Kennedy

Page from Hogarth Press account book, recording sales of T. S. Eliot's *Poems*

Leonard and John Lehmann in Lehmann's flat, 1944

Oil portrait of Leonard Woolf by Henry Lamb, 1912

Oil by Duncan Grant, c. 1912

Pencil sketch by Vanessa Bell, c. 1938

Oil by Trekkie Parsons, 1945

Leonard reading Virginia's diary at Monk's House, 1967

Leonard and his Border collies at Monk's House, c. 1968

Leonard in his greenhouse at Monk's House, c. 1966

Bust of Leonard by Charlotte
Hewer, 1968

Leonard and Trekkie Parsons at Charleston, June 1969

we have not yet obtained the Russian of this. The difficulty, I see for you, is length. We should have to publish the whole in book form before Christmas, probably in November, so that it would be no use to you except in the October issue.

Let me know what you think. If it is no good, Koteliansky has two other suggestions: (1) There is a book just published consisting of 12 letters exchanged between the best living Russian poet and the best living Russian critic who were in a Bolshevik kind of Convalescent Home. The letters discuss the influence of culture in the modern world and according to Koteliansky are very good. He says that one or two of them could be published alone if there were difficulty regarding length. (2) Kot. again says that there is a most interesting writer, Rosanov, who died a little time ago, who wrote volumes of "pensées". He says they are very good and have never been translated.[1]

Yours
Leonard Woolf

To Lytton Strachey   The Nation and The Athenaeum
10, Adelphi Terrace
4th May, 1923   London   W.C.2

I expect you have heard that, having failed as (a) a civil servant, (b) a novelist, (c) an editor, (d) a publicist, I have now sunk to the last rung on which stand Jack Squire, Desmond MacCarthy, Edward Shanks, and Penguin—literary journalism. I am now Literary Editor of *The Nation and Athenaeum*, and I would not even have sunk to that, if I had not been told that you had agreed to write for it, for with your help I may be able to keep my head above the waters impregnated by the Eagles, Penguins, and Hawks.[2]

This means that I hope and pray that you will write something for June. Do you want me to suggest subjects or is that an impertinence? For instance, I see that the new Nonesuch Press is publishing "the first complete edition" of Congreve from the original quartos. It is an

1. The poet was V. I. Ivanov (1866–1949) and the critic M. O. Gershenzohn (1869–1925). V. V. Razonov (1856–1919) was an eccentric, reactionary avant-garde writer and journalist; his *pensées* were later translated and published by Koteliansky in two volumes, *Solitaria* and *Fallen Leaves*.
2. "Solomon Eagle" was the pseudonym of J. C. Squire (1884–1958) as literary editor of the *New Statesman*; Desmond MacCarthy, who succeeded Squire, was "Affable Hawk"; Edward Shanks was a poet and critic.

expensive "limited" edition and therefore it is just possible that they will not send us a review copy, even if we ask for it. But if I got it and sent it to you, would you write an article on Congreve? If not Congreve, Tunis?

L S W[1]

To Hubert Henderson[2]   The Nation and The Athenaeum
10, Adelphi Terrace
26/9/23   London, W.C.2

Dear Hubert,

Coming back in the train last night it struck me that probably in the heat of argument I had not made one point clear to you.[3] I do not think that there is nothing in what you say about these young men. There is, and I dare say that I have not treated them with as firm a hand as is desirable. I am perfectly willing to read them a lecture and I will be more careful with the kind of book which is sent them though I think it would be a great mistake only to give them second class books and writers to cut their teeth on. I also agree with you that one does not want too much youth (though I think that the world and newspapers, on the whole, suffer from too much age). I will bear all these things in mind. I know too that you have to bear the brunt of the criticism on the Board of my delinquencies and I am sorry for it. But, if you dont mind my saying so, your life will be impossible if you pay too much attention to every criticism of every review and article which is in *The Nation*. Every one of the articles and reviews will always be disliked by someone, and every week everyone who reads the *Nation* will dislike some article or review in it. I have heard at least 20 diametrically opposite opinions of the literary side. The answer

1. To this, Strachey responded: "It all sounds very deplorable. . . . But I've no doubt that you'll tirer yourself d'affaire with the utmost competence. However, I entirely deny that I agreed to write for your dreadful paper, though I shouldn't object to reviewing Congreve if you can get the edition. . . ." In fact, Strachey became one of LW's regular reviewers, contributing seventeen articles, simultaneously published in the *New Republic*, which were brought out in 1931 as *Portraits in Miniature*.
2. (Sir) Hubert Henderson (1890–1952), an economist and pupil of Keynes, was appointed editor of the *Nation* when Keynes assumed control. "Hubert's articles . . . seemed to me extremely able, but conscientiously to hit the bull's-eye on the wrong target" (*Downhill All the Way*).
3. The Woolfs, with Henderson, had been visiting Keynes at Studland, where a vehement argument had broken out over George Rylands and Raymond Mortimer, two young critics whom LW had just taken into his stable of *Nation* reviewers.

to the question so often put to one: "why on earth do you put in A?", is in nine cases out of ten: "I put in A, because, though you do not like him, there are dozens of people who do, just as I put in B because you like him, though there are dozens of people who dont."

As I say, I think there is more in what you said than I perhaps showed in the vehemence of controversy. My main point was that I really could not agree to the return of the reviews because I am convinced it would have been most unfair.[1] It would have been to send a first offender to jail for a month on the ground that he was drunk and disorderly when in fact he had only got a little merry on ginger ale.

I feel too that I ought to say in writing what I said to you verbally. I do think that we differ rather fundamentally in our tastes. (I naturally think that I am right and you wrong, but not, I assure you, in the supercilious sense that is thought to be characteristic of "Bloomsbury". It is simply that if I think a piece of writing good, I think that I am right—and there is an end of it; I admit that I may be completely wrong.) But I think this makes the position much more difficult for you than for me, because I choose the things and you have to take the rather drastic step of vetoing them after selection. . . .

. . . It was understood on both sides that I was only to take the job on trial until the end of the year so that it would be perfectly natural for me to disappear at the end of December. If you feel this, you need only tell me unofficially and I will simply tell the Board that I find that I cannot go on after December 31.

Yours
Leonard Woolf[2]

1. The reviews were Mortimer's critique of three plays by A. A. Milne ("they could not be more conventional and less true to life") and Rylands's review of plays by Lady Gregory and Florence Darwin.
2. Henderson replied that while he did "not mind" Rylands "if properly controlled," he disliked Mortimer, adding that the book reviews were not "sufficiently appreciative of the better type of non-Bloomsbury writing." But he acknowledged that the real issue was who would control the literary side of the paper.

To Harold Nicolson

6th July 1924

[The Hogarth Press
52 Tavistock Square]

Dear Nicolson,

We are starting a venture in the press of critical essays which we propose to publish in pamphlet form. By all the laws of publishing, they are foredoomed to failure because every publisher knows that the pamphlet is unsalable. However we are going to attempt it and we are beginning with pamphlets by Roger Fry, my wife, and a Miss Bosanquet on Henry James (she was his secretary). I wonder whether you would allow us to consider your lecture on Byron as a possible addition to our series? We cannot resist asking you, as my wife thinks that you have not decided upon publishing it elsewhere.[1]

Yours sincerely
Leonard Woolf

To Norman Leys

July 18, 1924

[The Hogarth Press
52 Tavistock Square]

Dear Leys,

I do not wish to be guilty of "unprofessional conduct". But on the other hand I do not want you to sign a bad agreement.[2] We are very curious publishers ourselves. It began purely as a hobby of printing and has grown of its own motion until now my wife and I cannot deal with it ourselves. Consequently we have a young woman manager and we have just taken in a young man as a partner [George Rylands]. Whether we can ensure the publicity that an old established firm gets I cannot say—probably we do not get the same results as they do with travelling bookshops particularly in the provinces. On the other hand I have no respect at all for their cut and dried methods. . . .

We have published ourselves novels and poetry and one "serious" work—Stephen Reynolds' *Letters* which was published at 16/-. We are also branching out and becoming the publishers to The Psycho-

1. Nicolson did not offer his lecture, in commemoration of the centenary of Byron's death, but in 1927 contributed his *Development of English Biography*, which became a classic.
2. Leys, who knew LW from their collaborative work in the Labour Party, had asked if Unwin's terms for his book *Kenya* were fair.

Analytical Press. Frankly if Unwin will give you a fair and reasonable agreement, I think you ought to stick to him as it has gone so far and is already rather late if you are to get it out in the autumn. But if he wont then you ought to try some other publisher, and, in my opinion, at any rate let us see exactly what we can produce for you.[1]

Yours
Leonard Woolf

TO STANLEY UNWIN

Monk's House

7 August, 1924   Rodmell   Lewes   Sussex

Dear Unwin,

Mr Rylands sent me your letter on here. Very many thanks for taking the trouble to give us the information.

I do not wonder at your being amused at our becoming your successor over the psycho-analysis undertaking. There has been plenty of amusement on my side already over the way that some of the people do business. I dont expect much profit, although the only thing which I have undertaken to publish (besides taking over the old stock) is the *Collected Papers* [of Freud]. The ideas of some people in the International Psycho-Analytical Press with regard to some of the other books contemplated seemed to me purely fantastic. My contract is with Dr Jones and Dr Rickman representing the Press.[2] If I end up without loss, profit, or lawsuit, I shall congratulate myself. But I shall have had a good deal of amusement.

Yours sincerely
Leonard Woolf[3]

1. Leys preferred the Hogarth Press. *Kenya* has been described as "one of the most influential pieces of writing on African colonialism during the interwar years." It had further editions in 1925 and 1926 and was reprinted in 1973.
2. Ernest Jones (1879–1958), one of Freud's closest collaborators and a pioneer of psychoanalysis in Britain and Canada. John Rickman (1891–1951), president of the British Psycho-Analytical Society 1947–50 and editor of the *International Journal of Psycho-Analysis* 1948–49.
3. Unwin responded, "My thankfulness that I am at the end of my troubles with this agency, and not in your shoes, is intense."

To Edmund Blunden[1]

Monk's House
14 August, 1924   Rodmell, Lewes, Sussex

My dear Blunden,

It was a very pleasant sight this morning when the postman stumped into my garden with a letter addressed from the other side of the world in your old English handwriting. It was pleasanter too to read what was inside, and to see that you still remember Yalding Bridge, the *Nation*, and me. I know the feeling of the expatriated—that one has sunk into a curious dream world composed mostly of lethargy and visions, very fleeting, of English streams, roast beef and Yorkshire pudding, or the view from Hungerford Bridge.

Looking out upon Hungerford Bridge the other day from that narrow slip of a room where Mrs Jones sits roaring with laughter down the telephone and Harold Wright interviews people with the best bedside manner which ever brought a man to Harley Street and wealth[2]— looking out, I say, upon Hungerford Bridge while lightning flashed and the thunder roared loud enough to drown Mrs Jones's laughter at the telephone, I was talking to H. W. Massingham sheltering from the rain which was as heavy as any that you have seen between the Indian Ocean and Tokyo, I was talking about you, and what had been heard of you—and Mrs Jones between a peal of thunder and a peal of laughter said that I ought to write to you. And I said that I should like to, but that it is a year's effort to get myself to write a letter, but that if they would tell me an address I would. And several times I have taken my typewriter in my hand, metaphorically, and thought of you, but—

Then came the postman on this very English summer day, just the right kind of soft delicious heat and the thrushes and blackbirds eating my apples lazily on the path—for I gathered three bushels of July pippins yesterday from an ancient apple tree and the thrushes and blackbirds are gorging themselves on the debris—and I felt that, if I didnt write to you to-day, I never should this side of meeting you years hence in the *Nation* office. So this is the first letter that I've written— a real letter, I mean, to a friend—these six months at least.

I envy you being in Japan, although I daresay often you cannot yourself see the reason, though you will when you are once more back again among us. You will find everything here just where you left it,

1. Edmund Blunden (1896–1974), poet, biographer and literary scholar, was Professor of English at Tokyo Imperial University.
2. Alice Jones was Henderson's secretary. Harold Wright (1883–1934), another of Keynes's economics students, was assistant editor of the *Nation* 1923–30, and editor 1930–31.

for, you know, those who are left behind go on doing the same thing day by day ad infinitum. Which is one reason why they have nothing to say in their letters.

I admired your book on Clare very much.[1] It passed through my hands en route for a reviewer last week, and it looked so good that I coveted it for my own. But then Conrad had died suddenly over the week end and necessitated a hurried "World of Books", leaving me with one already written on my hands. Otherwise I should have kept that copy and done a "W. of B." on it.

Your wife sent me two poems of yours which I like immensely and shall use, though I am as usual snowed under with other poems which I ought never to have accepted.[2] As you say, my poets are not very good, but one can hardly resist accepting anything which is not very bad after reading the mass that is sent in.

Dont forget your promise to write a book for the Hogarth Press. Seriously we want one from you very much—and soon.

Write again whenever the spirit moves you. Is there any book or thing that I could ever send you?

Yours
Leonard Woolf

To Vita Sackville-West

[The Hogarth Press
28 November, 1924   52 Tavistock Square]

Dear Vita,
. . . Your mother is magnificent, but I can see quite uncontrollable.[3] But she is perfectly right, and, as a publisher, I welcome both her ideas and enthusiasm. I only hope that we are doing our part of the publishing with half her fertility of ideas. The book is not booming, but is selling slowly, and I hope it will quicken up in the next few weeks. Its sales are, in fact, behaving very much as I personally expected. I

1. *Madrigals & Chronicles: Being newly found Poems written by John Clare*, which Blunden edited.
2. The poems were "Elegy," published on September 27 and "Unteachable," published on October 11, 1924.
3. Sackville-West's *Seducers in Ecuador*, described by LW as "a curious little story which no ordinary publisher would have looked at," had just been published; it was her first book with the Hogarth Press. Her mother, Lady Sackville, whose eccentricity increased with age, had suggested ways of promoting sales in France.

went last week and consulted an Advertising Service Agents (i.e. advertising experts) called "Ogeden & Spencer" about it. They drafted me an advertising scheme for the book during the next three weeks, i.e. the amount which we ought to spend, the form of advertisement, and the papers in which to go. I have accepted their scheme which I must say I thought rather good, but if you see a rather vulgarly worded advertisement you will know how it has originated.

I know the author of the review in the [New] Statesman. He did not like the book, I am afraid.[1] It is a very odd thing about books, reviewers, readers, and publishers; the three latter simply hate any author to write any book which is not practically identical with his or her last book. *Seducers* is different from your previous books, and you can see—dont you think?—that many of the reviewers are puzzled or irritated or both by this fact. But there was a good review in yesterday's *Times Literary Supplement*, and my man, [Edwin] Muir, was intelligent.

Yours
Leonard Woolf

To John Maynard Keynes The Nation and The Athenaeum

10, Adelphi Terrace

13/12/24 London, W. C. 2

Dear Maynard,

I wish you would look at the enclosed figures of the average space apportioned to the several branches in the *Nation* and [New] *Statesman* during the last four normal issues. . . .

You are making the paper more and more political precisely at the moment when—owing to the position of the Liberal Party—you are bound temporarily at any rate to lose a little on the political side. You are materially deteriorating the literary side precisely at the moment when Sharp—very cleverly, I think—is all out, not only to do you on the political side, but at the same time to strike you as hard as he can on the literary.[2] Hence he gives his literary side an average of 5 pages

1. John Franklin had poked gentle fun at it, along with seven other novels he reviewed.
2. Clifford Sharp (1883–1935), editor of the *New Statesman* from its foundation in 1913 until its amalgamation with the *Nation* in 1931. "I got to feel something towards him which might perhaps be called affection. It was the affection which one sometimes acquires for an old, mangy, surly, slightly dangerous dog. One is rather proud of being one of the few people whom he will—with a growl—allow to pat him gingerly on the head" (*Beginning Again*).

more than his political while you give yours 1½ pages less. I am sure the latter policy is wrong.[1]

Yours
Leonard Woolf

To WILLIAM PLOMER

The Hogarth Press
52 Tavistock Square

28 April, 1925

London, W.C.I.

Dear Mr Plomer,

My wife has now read *Turbott Wolfe* and agrees with me about it.[2] I must apologise once more for the delay in our coming to a decision. We should like to publish the book this autumn, and will put it in hand at once if you agree to our terms. . . .

There is however one other thing. I am still rather worried by the question of identity of characters with real people. If there is any character which can be even remotely identified with a real person in S. Africa, both you and we will be liable to a libel action, and heavy damages might be given against us. According to the contract usual in publishing, you are bound to make good to us any loss which we may sustain from such an action, but we should be personally responsible to the plaintiff in such an action and should have to recover again from you—which, I understand, would not be possible. You will excuse my plain speaking, but we are not wealthy people, and heavy damages might be a most serious thing for us. I do therefore most earnestly ask you to consider this very carefully, and, if you think that there is a remote possibility of identification in any case, that you will make alterations in the MS. The delay in returning the MS would be unfortunate, but I assure you that a libel action of this kind might be disastrous, and that it is essential to make it impossible. Remember that the mere fact that you have changed the names of real places and persons is not an answer in a libel action. Any incident in the life of a character which is identical with that in the life of a real person is

---

1. Although this and subsequent appeals were unavailing, LW generally got forty percent of the space for his side of the paper.
2. Plomer, born in South Africa of British parents, was then living in Zululand. In his memoirs he commented that since the manuscript had been written "with a hard pencil on thin paper, [the Woolfs] must have had a strong curiosity to read it at all." It was a groundbreaking work on racialism in South Africa.

sufficient to identify the character with the person—also any personal characteristic.

Again it will presumably be published under your own name, so that any incidents which actually happened in the vicinity where you live and which were transferred to any character in your book would be held to identify characters with real persons living in your vicinity.

Yours sincerely
Leonard Woolf

To Thomas Hardy   The Nation and The Athenaeum
                                              10, Adelphi Terrace
2 June, 1925   London, W.C.2.

Dear Mr Hardy,
   I do not know how to thank you sufficiently for sending me the poem. It has always been my ambition to have something of yours in *The Nation*. It is extremely good of you.[1]

Yours sincerely
Leonard Woolf

To Herbert Palmer[2]   The Hogarth Press
                                              52 Tavistock Square,
14 July, 1925   London, W.C.1.

Dear Mr Palmer,
   The reason why we cannot send you second proofs is simply this: my wife and I are printing your poems [*Songs of Salvation Sin & Satire*] ourselves, i.e. literally with our own hands as I told you. We do it in our spare time. We are amateur printers, and naturally our stock of type is small. We have not enough type to keep it standing and we distribute it sheet by sheet. I have already machined the first sheets which you returned corrected and I propose to machine the last this week end if possible. You will therefore understand that it is

---

1. Although Hardy was best known as a novelist, LW admired him as a poet. The poem, "Coming Up Oxford Street: Evening," appeared on June 13, 1925.
2. Herbert Palmer (1880–1961), an impoverished poet and critic whom LW encouraged by publishing three volumes of his work.

impossible to make corrections in the first sheets. I could send you a revise of the last sheet but that means that you will hold the thing up indefinitely as I cannot be sure of being able to finish it off before I go away for the summer.

I am very sorry that this is the case, but it is the case with everything which we have ever printed ourselves and must of necessity be so. You know our work—it is amateur printing, but it the only way of producing poetry with a reasonable chance of no loss.

Yours sincerely
Leonard Woolf

To Hugh Walpole[1]

Monk's House
Rodmell, near Lewes   Sussex

19 August, 1925

Dear Mr Walpole,

I am sorry that you thought Aldington's article grossly unfair, but far from resenting your writing to me about it, I am glad you did.[2] I admit that I did not very much like the tone of some of it, but I dont think I thought it was as offensive as you did. I am however very strict with myself in forcing myself not to interfere in any way with the liberty of expression of an author whose name is to be signed, provided that he keeps within certain bounds of decency and courtesy.

But I wish very much that you yourself would write me an article on American literature apropos of that review or without any reference to it, whichever you may prefer. The ignorance of contemporary American literature here is very great, and it would be really interesting if you would write about it. Will you do so, and in that case, could you give me any idea when I might have the article.

Yours sincerely
Leonard Woolf

---

1. (Sir) Hugh Walpole (1884–1941), popular novelist and literary figure.
2. Richard Aldington (1892–1962), poet, novelist, critic and biographer, had written a stridently anti-American review of *Definitions* by H. S. Canby, a Yale University English professor. So low was Canby, according to Aldington, he might even take seriously a novel by Hugh Walpole.

[The Nation and The Athenaeum
38, Great James Street]

13/8/26

Dear Hubert,

I do not think that this is an example of truculence on my part. The complete rejection of a review seems to me an extremely truculent action, and when it is proposed out of hand to reject as harmless a review as this of Aldington's—who, as I said, is a well known and practised writer—it is, to put it plainly, to my mind, childish. Personally I wont have anything to do with it, it seems to me so silly. But if I am directed by the Board to inform Mr Aldington that they consider his review impossible to print in the *Nation*, I will do so, and at the same time I can say that I did my utmost to prevent such a thing happening on the *Nation*.

The reason why I propose to refer it to the Board—apart from the fact that I dont want the *Nation* to make a fool of itself—is that you assumed that I would write and tell Aldington that it was rejected. That seems to imply that I am as responsible as before. On the other hand, if I am not responsible, I will certainly not write to Aldington rejecting the review.

The fact that Aldington is a regular reviewer for *The Times Literary Supplement* is extremely relevant. It is an extremely respectable and sober paper and they would not tolerate him for a moment if he wrote the kind of stuff you would have hypnotized yourself into believing that he writes. No one writes quite the same in any two papers, but it is ludicrous to pretend that he could write week after week for Bruce Richmond and then write unprintable reviews for me. That one or two sentences are too violent in a review or not quite the tone one likes is one thing—and a case for cutting or altering, as indeed, I had already done in one sentence at least in this review—but simply to reject a mild and harmless and rather, if anything, pompous review like that—really it is ludicrous. . . .[1]

Yours sincerely
Leonard Woolf

1. LW apparently lost this argument, Aldington's only review in the following weeks being an innocuous one on German literature. Aldington refused to write further reviews for the *Nation* after LW had accepted an article by a critic who had run off with Aldington's wife.

To Jonathan Cape[1]

[The Nation and Athenaeum
16 December, 1926   38, Great James Street]

Dear Mr Cape,
   I am very sorry that the reviews in the *Nation* have irritated you,
but I think you probably underestimate the difficulties of the literary
editor and reviewers in a weekly paper. Every week for at least fourteen
weeks in the autumn I take in my hand, open, examine and hesitate
over on an average fifty books which, in my opinion, might well be
given a column review (on the average) in the paper. If the space
actually available for reviews, including my own page, is 11 columns
a week, I am lucky. That is to say that in the autumn season books
for which their authors and publishers might legitimately expect 700
columns as a minimum have to be dealt with somehow or other in
150. In fact, the disproportion is very much greater, for various reasons—the desire of readers for at least one "long" review, the desire
of readers to see books reviewed which I would certainly not include
in the 50 per week worthy of review, etc. Under such circumstances,
a choice of books for review and allocation of space result which I
never pretend to defend; it is, I know, illogical and unreasonable, but—
and it causes me more thought and worry than any other occupation
of the week—I cannot see how it can be anything else.
   As to the particular cases you mention, the course of events as seen
from my side may interest you. Adequate space for reviews of novels
in the autumn season in the weekly press is, as you know, completely
impossible. They have to be done in batches, in shorter notices, or
ignored. To include a novel in a batch for a "review" is, I have always
imagined, the best of these three courses. I deliberately included your
two American novels in a batch, because I do not think sufficient notice
is given normally in the press to American writers. . . .[2]
   As to the relative merits of papers in the present and the past, I
always think of Burnand's answer to some one who complained that
Punch is not as good as it was: "my dear fellow, it never was."[3]

Yours sincerely
Leonard Woolf

1. Jonathan Cape (1879–1960), the highly regarded head of one of the leading London
publishing houses; he badly wanted to absorb the Hogarth Press.
2. The novels, Ruth Suckow's *The Odyssey of a Nice Girl* and Louis Bromfield's *Early
Autumn*, were reviewed with eight other books, including works by D. H. Lawrence and
Lion Feuchtwanger. Of them, the reviewer commented, "The faster American life becomes,
the slower American fiction is getting."
3. Sir Francis Burnand (1836–1917) was editor of *Punch* 1880–1906.

To Edmund Blunden

26 July, 1927

52 Tavistock Square
London W. C. 1.

Dear Blunden,

I dont know how long it is since I had a letter from you which I enjoyed and never answered, but I remember it was about Plomer and Murry-Pecksniff and Aldous [Huxley]. The time, I hope, is now approaching when we shall see you in propria persona, a little Japanned, I daresay, but I am sure still Blunden. I am glad you like Plomer: I have never met him, but I have great hopes of him on paper and the ferocity of his youth; also he writes very nice letters. We are publishing a book of his [*I Speak of Africa*] this autumn and he has just sent us some poems which, I think, you have read.

I still write a page ["World of Books"] in the *Nation* but do little else there. I have been to Sicily and Rome lately and Rome seems to me the best city that I have seen yet on earth.

Well, come back to London soon.

Yours
Leonard Woolf

To Herbert Read[1]

4 March, 1928

[The Hogarth Press
52 Tavistock Square]

Dear Read,

I should like to stick to the arrangement of your lecture series volume [*Phases of English Poetry*] for the autumn, so that, in that case, we should want to have it by the end of July.

I think that [Harold] Nicolson's *Development of Biography* is the nearest in form to what I originally conceived the series as being. Neither of the other two is quite as "expository" as I had intended.[2] On the other hand, I do not think that a series need be too uniform and that a considerable amount of latitude to the writer is a good thing. As regards audience, I had in mind mainly the intelligent, par-

1. (Sir) Herbert Read (1893–1968), art critic, editor, poet and literary critic, was one of LW's regular *Nation* reviewers.
2. F. L. Lucas's *Tragedy in Relation to Aristotle's* POETICS and Allardyce Nicoll's *Studies in Shakespeare*.

ticularly the intelligent student and therefore also the intelligent teacher. The series is for the advanced, not the elementary, intelligent student, and therefore I should include the good Mechanics Institute in the provinces as well as the man or woman who is reading English literature at one of the Universities for degree purposes. What in fact gave me the idea of the series was reading some English literature examination papers for the Cambridge Tripos. The questions asked were really very good questions, and it struck me that I knew of very few books which would help a student to think about and discuss such questions in an intelligent manner. I enclose our prospectus.

Yours sincerely
Leonard Woolf

To T. S. Eliot

13 March, 1928

The Hogarth Press
52 Tavistock Square
London, W.C.1

Dear Tom,

We have considered MacLeish, but I am afraid the decision is unfavourable.[1] He is intelligent, but he is too much under the influence of Mr T. S. Eliot. I like Mr Eliot from the pure and undefiled source of his own inspiration, and not bottled at second hand with the analyst's certificate on the label. I am sorry, but the young must really begin to find some legs of their own to stand on. Am I to return the MS to you?

Yours
Leonard Woolf

---

1. Archibald MacLeish (1892–1982), American poet and playwright. The work was probably *The Hamlet of A. MacLeish*, published that year in America.

To Rubinstein, Nash & Co.

10 October, 1928   [52 Tavistock Square]

Dear Sirs,
    With reference to your letter addressed to me at *The Nation*, I shall
be glad to give any support in my power in the matter and should be
prepared to give evidence [in] regard to the decency of the book.[1]

                                              Yours faithfully
                                              Leonard Woolf

To T. S. Eliot

                                              52 Tavistock Square
25/10/28   London, W.C.1.

Dear Tom,
    I could lunch with you tomorrow Friday week and should like to.
    I am glad you think well of Jeffers: he is, I feel, an interesting poet
at the least. . . .[2]
    I think one ought to give evidence in the [Radclyffe Hall] case if
possible, though I dont like the people. But the book is perfectly decent
and it is monstrous to suppress it.

                                              Yours
                                              Leonard Woolf

1. In the summer of 1928 Jonathan Cape published Radclyffe Hall's *The Well of Loneliness*,
a novel with a lesbian theme. The Home Secretary, Sir William Joynson-Hicks, threatened
legal action unless the book was withdrawn. The matter reached the courts, and Harold
Rubinstein, a solicitor and a prolific playwright, led the defense. G. B. Shaw and John
Galsworthy, President of PEN, among other prominent authors, refused to testify for the
book; LW, who had reviewed it sympathetically in the *Nation*, was among those who offered
to do so. The judge refused to call any defense witness and found against the book, which
he declared obscene and ordered to be destroyed. On learning of VW's death, Hall wrote
to LW, "I remember her always as she looked that day, twelve years ago, when you and
she befriended the author of *The Well of Loneliness* at Bow Street. . . ."
2. Robinson Jeffers (1887–1962), noted American poet. LW was about to bring out *Roan
Stallion, Tamar, and Other Poems*, the work that established him. In his letter, Eliot had
congratulated LW for publishing the book, which he said was the best verse out of America
for many years.

298

To William Plomer   The Hogarth Press
                                      52 Tavistock Square
3 February, 1929   London, W. C. 1.

Dear Plomer,
   Many thanks for your very nice letter. I am so glad that you are
coming here and that we shall at last meet. There is no need to apologise
for your letters to me. I have always been pleased at getting them; as
for the things that you mention in them, I was conscious that much
was due to extreme youth and circumstances and to your merits too.
Every one who has anything in them is bound, I think, to be intolerant
and savage and hubristic at least up to a certain age, and it is perhaps
a defect of the elderly that we lose our bite with our teeth.
   We hope to publish *Paper Houses* in March, so that I suppose we
had better keep your copies here for you.[1] I am looking forward to
reading your new things. I feel sure you are going the right way to
prepare yourself for writing a first-rate novel.

                                      Yours
                                      Leonard Woolf

To Cecil Day-Lewis[2]
                                      [The Hogarth Press
24 March, 1929   52 Tavistock Square]

Dear Mr Lewis,
   I like your poem very much and we should be glad to publish it
next autumn. It is a remarkable piece of work, though I do not think
it will have what publishers call "a wide appeal". I enclose an agreement for your approval and signature if you approve the terms. We
would publish in our Living Poets Series.

                                      Yours sincerely
                                      Leonard Woolf

1. A collection of stories about Plomer's life in Japan, where he had taught English for two
years.
2. Cecil Day-Lewis (1904–1972), who wrote as C. Day Lewis, had submitted his first book
of poetry, *Transition Poem*, which had been rejected by other publishers. A schoolmaster
at this time, he was Professor of Poetry at Oxford 1951–56 and Poet Laureate 1968–72.

To Humbert Wolfe[1]

[The Hogarth Press
25 March, 1929   52 Tavistock Square]

Dear Humbert Wolfe,

Many thanks for your letter about Lowenfels. As a matter of fact
Tom Eliot sent me his poem for us to consider. I thought it had promise,
as you say, but also that it was, as you say, unformed. To be quite
honest too, it rather bored me. Lady Gerald Wellesley, who edits our
series, did not like it at all.[2] In the end we turned it down. The difficulty
of deciding what to publish, out of the mass of "poetry" one is sent,
is very great, and I feel more and more that if Shakespeare presented
himself in the basement to the Hogarth Press, it is even betting that
he would be informed that his work "interested us but we regret being
unable to offer to publish it", while Tupper was appearing in the Living
Poets. . . .[3]

Yours sincerely
Leonard Woolf

To Kingsley Martin

52, Tavistock Square
26 July, 1929   W.C.I.

My dear Martin,

There is no need for you to feel bad.[4] I always tell the truth unless there is a very good reason for telling a lie, and in this case there
was no need for me to do so. The *Quarterly* interests me and I like
having a finger in interesting pies, but as I said (truthfully) I have

1. Humbert Wolfe (1886–1940), though an outstanding civil servant, is best known as a
poet. He wrote to recommend Walter Lowenfels (1897–1976), an American poet then living
in Paris.
2. Lady Gerald Wellesley (1889–1956) was a poet admired by Yeats, if by few others. She
used some of her wealth to sponsor young and unknown poets through publication by the
Hogarth Press.
3. M. F. Tupper (1810–1889), a popular and prolific writer of trite verse.
4. Kingsley Martin (see Biographical Appendix) and William Robson, then professor at the
London School of Economics, were about to establish the *Political Quarterly*. After sounding
out LW to be editor, Martin decided to take the position himself. A year later he resigned,
and LW and Robson became joint editors. LW was sole editor from 1940 until 1946, co-
editor again with Robson until 1959 and literary editor until 1962.

not really the time for it and was glad to get out of it for that reason. . . .

> Yours
> Leonard Woolf

To John Maynard Keynes

14 December, 1929

52 Tavistock Square
London, W.C.1.

Dear Maynard,

I understand from Henderson that the Board [of the *Nation*] has officially approved of Blunden if Wright succeeds to the editorship. I think therefore that I ought now officially to inform you in writing that I should like to resign my post of Literary Editor from the end of the year. I have told Wright, however, that I am prepared to go on doing the work until the middle of February, if it is found that Blunden cannot arrange to take it on before then.[1]

> Yours
> Leonard Woolf

To Robinson Jeffers

3 January, 1930

52 Tavistock Square
London, W.C.1.

Dear Robinson Jeffers,

It was very pleasant to get your letter, but unpleasant to find that it meant that we should not see you again.[2] We enjoyed your visit and had looked forward to the possibility of another. Perhaps if some day we come to America and California, you may allow us to visit you.

I have only just been sent your book *Dear Judas*. I hope we may be able to publish an edition here.[3]

---

1. LW stayed until February; Henderson left for a position in Whitehall and was succeeded by Wright. With LW and Henderson gone, Keynes decided in 1931 to merge the *Nation* with the *New Statesman*, with Kingsley Martin as editor.
2. Jeffers returned to the United States to live in isolation on the California coast at Carmel.
3. *Dear Judas and Other Poems* was published by the Hogarth Press in November.

My wife joins me in remembrances both to you and to your wife.

Yours sincerely
Leonard Woolf

To Vita Sackville-West

[The Hogarth Press
9 March, 1930   52 Tavistock Square]

Dear Vita,

We found your MS [of *The Edwardians*] awaiting us and, of course, Virginia pounced on it and I have had no chance. She approves so violently that I shall send it off to the printer and read it in proof to save time. Will you let me have the second MS you promised so that I may take it at once to the Book Society?

Do you think you could possibly give the chapters names? . . .[1]

Yours
Leonard Woolf

To George Kennedy[2]

[The Hogarth Press
15 May, 1930   52 Tavistock Square]

Dear Kennedy,

I have not written to you before about Richard, partly because I understood that he was keeping you informed of developments here, and partly because I had hoped to meet you at the Cranium and have a talk. I am sure he is right to leave us in September and take a course at University College. As you know, I was always doubtful of his prospects here, and lately it has become obvious that his good qualities are not really suitable to the kind of work which necessarily falls to

1. In the first six months 30,000 copies were sold, making the novel the press's first runaway best seller and adding greatly to its profits.
2. A noted architect, whose nephew Richard had been taken on in 1928 as a trainee at the Hogarth Press.

his share in a small publishing business. In many ways we shall be sorry to lose him, but I am sure he is right to make the decision to go now.[1]

Yours sincerely
Leonard Woolf

To John Lehmann   The Hogarth Press
                                                        52, Tavistock Square
19 December, 1930   London, W.C.1.

Dear Mr Lehmann,

We like your book of poems very much and would be glad to publish them. I propose to send them now to Lady Gerald [Wellesley] who edits our Hogarth Living Poets Series and see whether she agrees with us to do them in the Autumn season. I am afraid that we are full up for this spring and that our spring list is already printing. I hope you will not think it too long to wait for the autumn.

Dadie [Rylands], whom I saw yesterday, talked to me about your possibly wishing to come to the Press and become a publisher. We are ourselves in some doubt as to the future, for the Press is taking up much more of our time than we care to give it. I should like to have a talk with you on the subject. Would there be any chance of your being able to come and see us when we return after Christmas about January 6?[2]

Yours sincerely
Leonard Woolf

To E. M. Forster

                                                        [The Hogarth Press
13 March, 1931   52 Tavistock Square]

Dear Morgan,

We are thinking of starting a new series of pamphlets in the autumn and we very much hope that you will be one of the first contributors.

1. Richard Kennedy (1912–1989) became a prolific illustrator of books and book jackets.
2. At their meeting LW offered to sell Lehmann three-quarters of the Hogarth Press capital and with it responsibility for running the firm. Lehmann could not raise the money and was instead taken on as apprentice manager with a salary and a percentage of profits.

The only conditions are that it should be in letter form and anything between 4000 and 10,000 words. . . . We ought to have the MS by the end of June.

I hope you will do this. You may write the letter to any one, dead or alive, real or imaginary, on any subject.

Yours
Leonard Woolf

TO SIGMUND FREUD

[The Hogarth Press

14th April, 1931   52 Tavistock Square]

Dear Dr. Freud,

We are sending you a cheque for £23.3.3d., royalties on account of the books published by us together with a statement. You will probably notice that we are paying a royalty on your two books *Beyond the Pleasure Principle* and *Group Psychology* on which we have not previously paid a royalty and I think I ought to explain how this comes about. When we took over the publication of the Institute of Psycho-Analysis, the Institute had already published six volumes. We purchased the stock and rights in these six volumes for a sum down and there was no obligation for the payment of royalties to authors. We have now repaid the original cost to us of the stock of these volumes and, although we are not under legal obligation to do so, we do not think it would be fair, now that we are making a profit, not to pay a royalty to the authors. We are therefore paying a royalty of 10% on the copies sold by us during the year and we shall continue to do so in the future.[1]

Yours sincerely
Leonard Woolf

---

1. LW followed a similar practice with the other writers—J. J. Putnam, Sandor Ferenczi, J. C. Flugel and Ernest Jones—whom the Press inherited when it contracted to be the publisher for the Institute.

To Ernest Jones

[The Hogarth Press
52 Tavistock Square]

April 15th, 1931.

Dear Dr. Jones,

An American publisher has suggested to me that he and I might get Freud to write his autobiography, and he suggests that I should make a certain proposition on the subject to Freud. It seems to me that such a book would not be suitable for the Psycho-Analytical Library, but I do not of course wish to do anything in a matter like this without consulting you first. If you agree with me that it would not be suitable, I will go on with it on my own, but if you think that such a book ought to appear in the Library perhaps we might discuss the matter on my return to England in about a fortnight's time.[1]

Yours
Leonard Woolf

To E. M. Forster

[The Hogarth Press
52 Tavistock Square]

12 June, 1931

Dear Morgan,

I think the *Letter* [*to Madan Blanchard*] perfect. Many thanks. Its only fault is its shortness, but I feel it might spoil it to lengthen it. Could you let me see the portrait of Lee Boo? It would be nice to include him if we could. I am afraid that, being a series, it ought to have a uniform cover.

Yours
L W[2]

---

1. Freud agreed to the proposal, and *An Autobiographical Study* was published by the Hogarth Press in 1935 as part of the International Psycho-Analytical Library.
2. Forster replied: "Thank you for your letter, and I am so glad that you like mine. I enjoyed writing it, but one never knows whether this means success. . . . The final foot note could have told much that was amusing—Madan took off all his clothes after the sloop left, was universally disrespected by the natives, given only one wife and perished obscurely. But this, too, proved intractable."

To William Plomer   The Hogarth Press
                                          52 Tavistock Square
11 Feb, 1932   London W.C.1

Dear William,
   I am lunching with Forster tomorrow and at 3 I am interviewing
here the friend of the poet who has just been sent to jail for 6 months
for taking an indecent poem to a printer. I intend to try to get Forster
to come back with me and take part in the interview. (I am contem-
plating a letter of protest to the papers and also an appeal against the
sentence.)[1] I suggest that you can come as well and join the interview
and that after they go, if possible, we discuss your book.

                                                  Yours
                                                  L W

From H. G. Wells

March 7th, 1932.

My dear Leonard Woolf,
   *A friend tells me you have quoted one of the more brilliant of the
younger critics as saying I am "a thinker who cannot think". Who
was it? He says you don't name the m[ore] b[rilliant] of the y[ounger]
c[ritic]s. I can't quite see why. But do tell me.*[2]

                                                  Yours ever,
                                                  H. G. Wells

1. A few days earlier Geoffrey Potocki de Montalk, a New Zealander, claimant to the Polish
throne and notorious anti-Semite, had been sentenced under obscenity laws. In fact he had
merely asked a printer to print for private circulation a salacious poem. At the request of
the poet's friend Douglas Glass, LW contributed and collected enough money to finance an
appeal, and Harold Rubinstein took the case. The Appeal Court upheld the conviction.
2. Wells, notoriously touchy, was referring to a review in the *New Statesman* of his *The
World, Wealth and Happiness of Mankind*. LW had praised the book, citing the offending
words only to rebut them.

52 Tavistock Square
W.C.I.

11 March, 1932

My dear Wells,

The writer to whom I referred is A. L. Rowse, the young Oxford economist who is now at the London School of Economics.[1] What I actually wrote was "The other day one of the younger generation, an extremely clever and serious writer on politics and economics, summarily dismissed Mr Wells as a thinker who could not think." I now feel that perhaps I ought not to have said this. When I wrote it, I thought he had said it in his book *Politics and the Younger Generation*. I have just looked at this book again and find that it is not there. I now remember that it was in an article which he submitted to me for the *Political Quarterly* and which I could not accept. However, I believe it is coming out in *The Criterion* so that he *will* say it.

Yours
Leonard Woolf

From H. G. Wells

March 13th, 1932

Dear Leonard Woolf,

It seems to me you ought to do something in the way of a public repudiation of that pseudo-quotation. On the face of it, it looks as though you wanted the thing said and hadn't the guts to say it on your own. Do you want to leave it at that?

Yours etc.,
H. G. Wells

1. A. L. Rowse (b. 1903), historian, essayist and poet.

To H. G. Wells

19 March, 1932

52 Tavistock Square
W.C.1.

Dear Wells,

I am not quite sure whether your card is serious or not. If you have seen my review, I cannot believe that it is. I read your book with the greatest admiration and said so quite clearly in my review. That the result should be your falling foul of me is only one more curious instance of the danger of praising an author's work. Why if I wanted to say that you are a thinker who cannot think, I should "not have the guts" to do so, I cannot imagine. I am not conscious of being in the least afraid of expressing such opinions as I have in print.

I suggested to the editor that I should write a letter to the *New Statesman* explaining what I had done and your objection, though it seems to me that the result would only be to make you look slightly ridiculous, which personally I have not the least desire to do. The editor himself did not seem to be at all anxious to have the letter. However if you want me to do so, I will. Perhaps you will let me know?

Yours
Leonard Woolf

FROM H. G. WELLS

March 23rd, 1932.

Dear Woolf,

I don't think it will mend matters if you write a letter to the New Statesman *in order to make me "look slightly ridiculous". I quite understand that the editor would not want you to do so. The letter you ought to write is plainly this;—*

'In a review of the Work, Wealth and Happiness of Mankind *in the N.S. of (date) I said (quote the passage under discussion). I made this statement in order to enhance the credit of Mr Wells with your readers and as a delicately indirect way of conveying my own admiration for his work. There was no word of truth in that statement, objection has been made to it, and I tender now my sincere apologies both to Mr Wells and to the rising young*

economist to whom, in the first excitement of being challenged, I
ascribed it.'

That I think would be a simple, honest way out for you. What else,
in the name of decency, can you do?

> *Yours very sincerely,*
> *H. G. Wells.*

To H. G. Wells

52 Tavistock Square

25 March, 1932
W.C.1.

Dear Wells,

I have written to the *New Statesman* explaining the facts and expressing regret for my inaccurate statement. It will not satisfy you
because you obviously made up your mind from the first that I had
invented the statement—which is not true—and I am not going to
apologize for doing something which I did not do. The statement exists;
it was written by a young writer on politics; I had read it in the last
six weeks. I was apparently wrong in thinking it was by Rowse and I
am prepared to express my regret for the error. I do not imagine that
you will believe what I say but that does not alter the fact that it is
true.

> Yours sincerely
> Leonard Woolf

From H. G. Wells

[c. March 27, 1932]

Dear Woolf,

I find it a little difficult to accept this new "young writer on politics"
who now appears in the place of Rowse. Who is he? I gather you have
still to find him. Can you blame me now if I doubt his existence? I
have sent a telegram to Kingsley Martin asking him to publish nothing
in this affair until I have seen him about it. It seems to me that you
ought either to produce your sample of the younger generation and
his dated statement or do a handsome climb-down.

Shall we publish this correspondence? Then people can draw their own conclusions?

> *Yours etc.,*
> *H. G. Wells.*

To H. G. Wells

4 April 1932   52 Tavistock Square, W.C.1.

Dear Wells,

I have today received a letter from Rowse (in answer to one of mine apologizing for having dragged him into the controversy) in which he says:

"Please do not apologise: there was really no need to. I thought it odd that Wells should take notice of a stray remark like that, and I told him when he wrote me that you were remembering something like that which I *had* said in conversation. And I think—and told him so —that by means of quoting the remark you had established a very interesting point . . ."[sic]

It seems strange to me that you never told me that after all Rowse himself admitted that he had made that remark. When you publish the correspondence you will of course include this letter from me.

> Yours sincerely
> Leonard Woolf

From H. G. Wells

April 2nd, 1932.[1]

Dear Woolf,

Having worried you as much as I can, I think the incident may terminate without publication. I was acutely hurt and exasperated by what I thought was a stroke of ungenerous and disingenuous detraction from you, because you have always been of importance in my mind. It seems you didn't mean it. I begin to think you didn't and

1. With Wells in the South of France, letters sometimes crossed.

anyhow we are too much in the same camp to knock the paint off
each other in the sight of our enemies.

Yours very sincerely,
H. G. Wells.

To Rosamond Lehmann[1]

[Monk's House
Rodmell, Lewes, Sussex]

7 September, 1932

Dear Rosamond,

I suppose you know that John has left us. I had seen him on the Friday and he had said nothing. On the next Wednesday evening he walked out of the Press without saying a word about his intentions to Miss Johnston (except that he would be in at 2.30 the next day) and wrote a letter to me simply saying that he had decided not to accept the new arrangement (which was to begin the next day and which he had already accepted). His behaviour seemed to me to be so either outrageous or childish that I decided to have nothing more to do with him and simply did not reply, for under the circumstances there is nothing to say but that. However when I went up yesterday they told me that either you or your sister had been ringing up to find out where he was. I thought therefore that I had better let you know all that I know about his movements since Wednesday of last week. It all seems to me very strange, but I hope he is all right.

Yours sincerely
Leonard Woolf

From Ernest Jones

4th Oct. 1932.

Dear Mr. Woolf,

I have been in correspondence with Freud about his new book [New Introductory Lectures on Psycho-Analysis]. *He is rather difficult in the matter, owing to a bee in his bonnet about publishing a translation*

---

1. Rosamond Lehmann (b. 1901), John's sister and wife of the painter Wogan Philipps, wrote several novels that shocked the "moral majority" of the time.

simultaneously in England and America. The motives for this are (1) Pressure from the Americans, who feel that his works are not sufficiently accessible in America, (2) A desire to get as much money as possible; he devotes this to the Verlag in Vienna which at present is in a parlous financial condition,[1] *(3) a feeling, I fear partly justified, that he has behaved over-generously in the past and that we have taken undue advantage of it. . . .*

Yours sincerely,
Ernest Jones

TO ERNEST JONES   The Hogarth Press
                                                 52 Tavistock Square
7th October 1932   London, W.C.1.

Dear Dr. Jones,

Many thanks for your letter of October 4th. The position is, I think, a little difficult. In the main Freud has really no grounds for complaint against us, I feel. Up to the publication of *Civilization and its Discontents* no American publisher would look at any of his books that we publish, and over and over again American publishers who are continuously coming to see us when they are over here, when shown his books or any books that we were publishing in the [International Psycho-Analytical] Library, remarked that there was no sale for psychoanalytical books in America.

Just before the publication of *Civilization and its Discontents* there was a sudden flare up of interest in Freud and in psychoanalysis generally once more in the United States. We received telegrams about *Civilization and its Discontents* from I do not know how many publishers. We sold the rights in that book, as you know, to an American publisher, Harrison Smith and Jonathan Cape, and we paid Freud his share according to our agreement.

In view of the interest at present displayed in Freud's books I think perhaps it is reasonable for Freud to feel that that agreement was not very generous to him, and that he ought to have had a larger share of the royalties. But one must remember that before that book was taken, as I pointed out above, we had to work very hard to try and get Freud taken in the United States, with no result at all.

1. The Internationaler Psychoanalytischer Verlag, founded in Vienna in 1919, was Freud's publishing house; it was always in financial difficulty.

312

I have paid Freud royalties on *The Pleasure Principle* and *Group Psychology* for last year as I promised to do, though of course we were under no obligation in the matter. I may also mention that originally, when we took over the publications of the Institute and were on the point of taking the risk of publishing the *Collected Papers*, one of the big publishers here [Stanley Unwin], who is a friend of mine, got to hear, not from me, that I was going to do this, and, as a friend, came to me and strongly advised me not to do so as I would almost certainly lose a large sum of money over the transaction. The fact that the transaction has, as a matter of fact, turned out very well does not alter the fact that at that time we were obviously taking a considerable risk in publishing Freud, and, as you know, no American publisher would look at the publication of those volumes.

I cannot therefore allow that so far as we are concerned we have taken any undue advantage of Freud's generosity. On the other hand I do not wish it to be said, even incorrectly, that we are doing so, and therefore with regard to his next book, so far as we are concerned, I would suggest that as regards the American rights, if Freud wishes to deal with them by himself, he should do so. If he is prepared to give us the American rights, which simplifies the question of translation for the two countries, we should take any percentage of the royalties paid by America which he considers fair. . . .

Yours sincerely
Leonard Woolf[1]

To Cecil Day-Lewis

23 December, 1932

The Hogarth Press
52, Tavistock Square
London, W.C.1.

Dear Mr Day Lewis,

I have just read your MS [of *The Magnetic Mountain*] and wish to thank you for it, not only as a publisher but as a reader—an unfortunately rare desire for a publisher. It is certainly, I think, the best

---

1. Jones sent a copy of this letter to Martin Freud (1889–1967), Freud's eldest son and business manager, with the comment, "I have discussed the matter with Mr. Woolf (i.e. Hogarth Press) who does our publishing and who is a very honest man." To LW, Jones replied: "There is not the slightest question in anybody's mind about the way in which the Hogarth Press has treated Freud. When I used the word 'we' I should have explained that this referred only to the analysts in England, the Institute. It is in itself a moot question, but in any case does not involve the Hogarth Press. . . ."

thing you've done, but also the best long poem that I have read for many a long day. It has the extraordinary merit, too, for me, that it is not only poetry but about interesting things, and so alive, whereas nearly all "poetry" today seems to me, even when you have to admit that it is poetry, to be about things and themes which no longer have the faintest interest for or connection with me. There is no doubt that we shall wish to publish it this spring. But I must send it to Lady Gerald Wellesley first and I will write you again as soon as possible. . . .

Yours sincerely
Leonard Woolf

To Rebecca West

19th January 1933

[The Hogarth Press
52 Tavistock Square]

Dear Mrs Andrews,[1]

Very many thanks for sending us the MS [of *A Letter to a Grandfather*] and also the page which had been left out. I like the *Letter* enormously and dont know when I have read anything which interested me so much. I am not quite certain that I understand your meaning, because I think it is really extraordinarily difficult and subtle. But I shall read it again.

There is one small point which it may be impertinent on my part to raise, but as I read I was pulled up by your reference to Rousseau. He seems to me to be essentially so different from the other two as regards belief. But I may be quite wrong about this.[2]

Many thanks again for letting us have the Letter.

Yours sincerely
Leonard Woolf

1. Rebecca West had married Henry Andrews, a merchant banker, in 1930.
2. The others were Hume and Voltaire, who, according to West, "dreamed of an orgasm of the universe when achieved justice, pity, candour, honesty and sense, should fuse into a substitute for God."

[The Hogarth Press

21st February 1933   52 Tavistock Square]

Dear Blunden,

I have a proposition to make to you which I hope you will consider, and which I really think might interest you. I do not know whether you know a series of biographies in French which consist entirely of contemporary records about the biographee.[1] For instance there is Stendhal "raconté par ceux qui l'ont vu", and Voltaire "raconté par ceux qui l'ont vu". Each consists of contemporary accounts and documents of the biographee, together with any important documents such as birth certificates, reports by secret police and the military authorities. The French ones that I have read seem to me to be fascinating, and I do not know of any similar biographies in England about English people, and I have been meaning for some time to try some here.

Would you consider doing Lamb in this way? I think he would be a very good person to begin with, and I imagine that you practically have the material already. . . .[2]

Yours sincerely
Leonard Woolf

To WILLIAM PLOMER   The Hogarth Press
                                           52 Tavistock Square
April 2nd 1933.   London W.C.1.

My dear William,

I cannot pretend that I was not sorry to get your letter; I do not like to think of the publishing tie between us being broken, but it will not, I hope, make any difference to our other ties.[3] It has been a pleasure

1 The idea had occurred to LW while visiting a bookshop in France two years earlier.
2. Blunden's *Charles Lamb: His Life Recorded by His Contemporaries* was published in 1934. The series never caught on, and there was only one other in it, E. M. Delafield's *The Brontës*.
3. Plomer was one of several Hogarth authors financially lured to Jonathan Cape by Rupert Hart-Davis, Cape's reader.

to publish your books, because from the first they had a considerable appeal to us.

> Yours
> Leonard Woolf

To J. B. LEISHMAN[1]

[The Hogarth Press
52 Tavistock Square]

27 August, 1933

Dear Mr Leishman,

As the moment approaches at which I shall have to sign an Agreement with the Insel-Verlag, I feel a great repugnance to do so, and I am going to throw myself upon your mercy.[2] The more I think about the present situation in Germany, the more barbarous does the behaviour of the Government seem to me, and I feel that I do not want to have any personal or business relations with those who support or tolerate it. I know that I ought to have thought about this before I embarked upon the negotiations with you and the Insel-Verlag, and if you think my attitude unreasonable, I will carry out my undertaking. But if you see your way to releasing me from it, I should be greatly obliged. In that case I shall write to Insel-Verlag and say that I cannot sign an agreement with them as long as the present conditions exist in Germany.

> Yours sincerely
> Leonard Woolf

To VITA SACKVILLE-WEST

[The Hogarth Press
52 Tavistock Square]

4 September, 1933

My dear Vita,

It does not surprise me that a publisher [Heinemann] should try to buy you away from the Press or, knowing you, that your instinct is to

1. James Blair Leishman (1902–1963), Lecturer in English Literature at University College, Southampton 1926–46, Senior Lecturer in English Literature at Oxford 1947–63, became the standard translator of Rilke in Britain.
2. The contract was for poems of Rilke, who was one of LW's favorite poets. The Hogarth Press introduced translations of his works to Britain.

refuse.[1] But it rather worries *me*—I mean that I do not think that any feeling of friendship really ought to influence you if your material interests are to be in any way unfavourably affected. My own opinion, for what it is worth, is as follows—I think it is as nearly impartial as possible in the circumstances, and we have of course had to consider the matter to some extent in an impartial way in Virginia's case. Long before we as publishers were as established and flourishing as we now are, the question arose whether she should accept much more tempting offers from other publishers (in one case a royalty of 35% for her next novel). We decided that if it meant a serious loss financially to her it would be absurd for her to go on with the Press, but that taking everything into consideration we did not believe that in the long run it would. We still believe that.

Now this is what I think. I dont believe that any publisher—I am assuming a certain amount of honesty, intelligence, and business capacity—can really do much to sell a book published at a given price. There would not be 500 copies difference in the sale of a book if you took it to Chatto and Faber, and it was a novel by you published at 7/6. The same applies to Constable and possibly to Heinemann and Cape, though I am doubtful about Heinemann's competence. It applies, I believe, also to the Hogarth Press, Secker, and perhaps one other small publisher. The reason is that provided that a publisher is recognized by the press as publishing good books (so that the book is assured of reviews) and by booksellers and libraries as publishing books which are really demanded by the public, and provided that he understands his business enough to have copies printed and bound to meet the demand (not every publisher is competent enough to do this!), the book really sells itself. Therefore in the case of you and Virginia, if you go to the Hogarth Press or to any of seven or eight other publishers, whose methods are more or less the same, I do not believe that your actual sales will be materially affected in the long run. . . .

There remains however the sum down which some publishers are prepared to pay in order to get authors away from their existing publishers. There is no doubt that a successful author can make a considerable sum from time to time by changing publishers in this way. The reason is this: Every publisher to some extent finances his losses on his unsuccessful books by the amount which he makes out of his successful books. In other words the really successful author gets less than he should get, probably, out of his publisher. It therefore pays a

---

1. When Sackville-West received an enticing offer of a substantial advance four years earlier, LW had written similarly.

publisher every now and then to put a large sum down and buy an author away from another publisher.

I will give you an interesting example. We have published five books of a particular author at 7/6 each. On the first we made a profit of £29-3-4, on the second a loss of £23-8-6, on the third a loss of £65-13-1½, on the fourth a loss of £32-8-7, on the fifth a profit of £796-0-7½.[1] (These figures are gross profits and losses; i.e. they include only actual expenditures on production of the book and advertising, nothing allowed for salaries, rent, overhead &c.) Another publisher has now bought this author from us; it should pay him quite well to put down £500, even if he only makes say £300 to £500 out of the next book (which is in fact all he will make at the highest).

The conclusion of the whole matter is

1. That I dont think that you ought to stay with us if you feel that your material interests will be seriously affected

2. I am not prepared to adopt the system of putting large sums down as advances which means gambling on books

3. I do think there is something to be said against publishers in that they underpay the very successful author in royalties. I think, for instance, that our scale of royalties for novels, if really fair, should be somthing like 15% on the first 3,000, 20% 3000 to 10,000, 25% 10,000 to 25,000, and 30% over 25,000. If you publish another novel with us, I should be willing to pay on that scale.

Yours
Leonard Woolf[2]

To J. B. Leishman

The Hogarth Press
52, Tavistock Square   W.C.1

11 September, 1933

Dear Mr Leishman,

I have to thank you for your letter and the generous way in which you received my proposal to break my agreement.[3] I see the force of

---

1. The author was William Plomer and the books were, respectively, *Turbott Wolfe*, *I Speak of Africa*, *Paper Houses*, *Sado* and *The Case is Altered*.
2. She replied: "I am sorry now that I ever mentioned the £1000 bribe, as I really only did it as a joke and had no intention of giving you the impression that it was only a feeling of friendship that kept me with Hogarth Press. I would never for a moment consider accepting that kind of offer or of going to the firm that could make it. I am as happy as I can be with the Hogarth Press and would not change my publisher for the world."
3. Leishman, then in Germany, replied that he shared LW's repugnance for the Nazi regime but considered it important to maintain links with "good Germans."

some of your arguments, but on the whole I am not really convinced. It seems to me the only way of showing people in Germany what the view of non-Germans is with regard to the barbarism—which you yourself say is desirable—is by individual action such as the kind I suggested.

Despite this I have decided to sign the agreement with the Insel-Verlag and I have now done so. I have discussed the matter with various people here and I find that few share my view. I am afraid that I still maintain it, but I do not think that in a case like this I should act upon it, particularly where I have already gone so far both with you and the Insel-Verlag. The chance of doing any good and the good that one might do are so small; the possibility of forming a sound or unprejudiced opinion is so doubtful that I do not think that I should be justified in going back on what amounts to an undertaking.

I am sorry to have put you to a considerable amount of trouble in this way.

Yours sincerely
Leonard Woolf

To Ivan Bunin[1]

[The Hogarth Press
November 21st, 1933   52 Tavistock Square]

Dear M. Bunin,
I should like to congratulate you on having won the Nobel Prize. As you know, it is many years since my wife and I began to admire your work, when, in fact, we saw the translation of *The Gentleman from San Francisco*. We are both therefore particularly pleased that it should have been recognized in this way.

Yours sincerely,
Leonard Woolf

---

1. Ivan Bunin (1870–1953), novelist and poet who fled to France after the October Revolution, was the first Russian to be awarded the Nobel Prize for Literature. *The Gentleman from San Francisco* is thought to have been an important consideration in his selection. The work had been published by the Hogarth Press in 1922, in a translation by LW, S. S. Koteliansky and D. H. Lawrence.

To John L. Graham

[The Hogarth Press
10 January, 1934   52 Tavistock Square]

Dear Mr Graham,

Many thanks for your letter. I am afraid that "very great interest" is a sort of stock publishers' phrase, but it meant in this case that both my wife and I thought that there were very great merits in your novel [*Good Merchant*]. You see things and people for yourself and are able to convey the vision to the reader; the book has a flavour of its own; and you can make words perform their duty economically and according to your wishes and not theirs. We thought (and hoped) that there were signs of immaturity and that you were young. That was why I wrote to you—it naturally makes a difference, when it comes to the problem of whether one is or is not to offer to publish a book, if the book if a first attempt or if it is the work of an old gentleman. We should much like to publish the novel and would do so next autumn. . . .

We have a cottage at Rodmell and are often down there. We shall be there until next Sunday and if you happened to be in the neighbourhood and wished to discuss anything, dont hesitate to look in. If not, perhaps some other time it might be possible to meet or if you are in town and would like to discuss any point at any time, let me know.[1]

Yours truly
Leonard Woolf

1. Graham proved to be a disappointment; he submitted other novels, which the Woolfs rejected. Every rejection, however, was accompanied by an invitation to Monk's House to play bowls.

To W. H. Smith & Son, Ltd.[1]

[The Hogarth Press
52 Tavistock Square]

February 6th, 1934

van der Post. *In a Province*[2]

Dear Sirs,

We understand from our traveller that your original order for copies of this book, to be published on February 15th, had been cancelled, and that you are "banning" the book. We should be greatly obliged if you would let us know whether this is correct, and if so, on what grounds the book is objected to?

Yours faithfully
Leonard Woolf

To W. H. Smith & Son, Ltd.

[The Hogarth Press
52 Tavistock Square]

February 8th 1934

Dear Sirs,

With reference to your letter L/GCB/HH of February 7th, I have to thank you for your courtesy in letting me know the reason for banning the book. On the other hand, I cannot help saying that it seems to me extraordinarily strong measures to ban a novel which, I imagine, is one of the least "sexual", indecent, or improper that could possibly be written, because of a single expression to which, as you say, many people might take objection.[3]

Yours faithfully
Leonard Woolf

1. In 1848 William Henry Smith founded a chain of bookshops that became the largest in Britain. Smith, a devout Methodist, who later became First Lord of the Admiralty both in real life and in *HMS Pinafore*, refused to sell books considered offensive—Hardy's *Jude the Obscure* was one casualty—and his firm continued the practice.
2. (Sir) Laurens van der Post (b. 1906), South African-born novelist and travel writer.
3. The offending passage reads: " '. . . You know when I sit next to you, I sort of get excited, sexually, you know.' 'That's nothing,' said the girl, determined to show that she was more emancipated than he. 'All the young men who sit next to me get much more than that.' "

To Laurens van der Post

[The Hogarth Press
February 8th, 1934   52 Tavistock Square]

Dear Mr van der Post,
  I am sorry to say that W. H. Smith & Son have banned your book
and cancelled the orders both for libraries and shops which they had
given to us because of "a certain expression which appears towards
the end of page 202". They gave me the reason, when asked, and
added that they considered that objection might be taken to this
expression by many people reading the book. I am afraid it may
damage the sale because one cannot very well advertize the fact.

                                              Yours very truly,
                                              Leonard Woolf

To Vita Sackville-West

[The Hogarth Press
July 17th, 1934   52 Tavistock Square]

Dear Vita,
  I have read your MS [of *The Dark Island*] with considerable excitement, which was maintained to the end. I do not know whether
you will like my saying it, but I like it ever so much better than *Family
History*.
  I am sending it to the printer at once, and hope that we shall be
able to send you proofs very soon. There is only one point which I
think you ought to consider. Where Lady Lester says: "I always
thought he had a prostrate gland", I take it to be a very indecent joke,
though the virgin minds of my wife and staff were unable to see it. I
expect the minds of the readers at Smith's Library are as prurient as
mine, and that they will say it is an indecent joke.
  We had a very unfortunate incident with a book which we published
last season, in which there was an isolated expression rather like this,
and Smith's banned the book altogether. Personally I do not think it
is worth facing the risk if it is just a casual expression which is not
material to the book, and I think it worth your while considering the
advisability of altering it in the proof. I take the word "prostrate" to
be deliberate, and the point of the joke? It is not irrelevant that the

only two people besides myself who have read it have not seen the joke because they thought that "prostrate" was the right word.

> Yours
> Leonard Woolf

TO CECIL DAY-LEWIS

Jan. 18th, 1935.

[The Hogarth Press
52 Tavistock Square]

Dear Mr. Lewis,

I will modify Clause 12 and except detective novels as I do not believe there is any good in a publisher insisting upon this kind of condition if the author does not want to publish with him.[1] But I hope you will not misunderstand me when I say that I do not think it reasonable, or possible, for authors—and still more agents—to send all the books which they think cannot have a sale to one publisher, and all the books which they think might have a sale to another.

> Yours sincerely
> Leonard Woolf

TO HERBERT READ

3/2/35

52, Tavistock Square,
W.C.1.

My dear Read,

Your article in the [London] Mercury interests me very much. I agree with practically everything you say. The publishers and booksellers between them are destroying the sale of books other than "best-sellers" and publishing is already little more than a gamble in which the only thing aimed at is the creation by hook or crook of a "best-seller"....[2]

Your scheme is very interesting and, if it could be worked, would

---

1. Needing £100 for repairs to the roof of his house, Day-Lewis decided to earn the sum by pseudonymously writing mystery novels for Collins. Clause 12 gave Hogarth Press the right of first refusal on any of his manuscripts.
2. Read's article, "The Sweated Author," argued that members of no trade or profession, including fishermen and coal miners, received such a low proportion of the product of their labor as authors. Morever, since the goal of most publishers was quick profits, works that did not promise to be best sellers were rejected, which meant that all works of literary merit were eliminated. His proposed remedy was the formation of an authors' guild, which would arrange to print and distribute books more economically and leave a greater share of the sale price to the author.

do an immense amount of good. My only doubt is whether you could possibly get an adequate sale. The curse of the capitalist system is that it debauches the consumer. The publishers, [commercial lending] libraries, and booksellers between them have created a state of affairs in which the habit of buying serious books is confined to a handful of people. . . .

Yours
Leonard Woolf

To Herbert Read

52, Tavistock Square,
London W. C. 1.

5 February, 1935

My dear Read,

I am trying to finish a short book [*Quack, Quack!*], but when it is off my hands I will have another shot at an article on publishing. . . .

I agree that there may be an average 3000 potential buyers for a serious work, though I should have put the figure at much higher than 500, but rather lower than 3000. But under existing conditions the chances are 1000 to 1 against your being able to make 50% of your potential buyers actual buyers for any particular book; they are 500 to 1 against your making 25% of them actual. You have therefore to get a revolution in the book trade or the habits of the reading public to touch the fringe of the subject. If I had not been a socialist before, publishing would have made me one.

From the serious author's point of view, the trade is corrupted from top to bottom. Why, even the travelling is heavily weighted against him and his interest, for in a great deal of the travelling the only way in which the traveller can earn a living wage is to do utterly useless work, i.e. collect orders for best sellers or for permanent sellers which the publisher would get in any case, and he would starve if he did the work necessary for selling the serious books. If you want to see the hopeless inefficiency and futility of the capitalist system from the inside, become a publisher. To talk to 95% of the booksellers about books is like a nightmare in which you found yourself discussing meat with a butcher who held Shaw's views on meat, meat-eating and meat selling.

We should like to come and see you some evening.

Yours
Leonard Woolf

To Insel Verlag

June 27th, 1935

[The Hogarth Press
52 Tavistock Square]

Dear Sirs,

I have just published a book here called *Quack Quack!* which deals to some extent with Germany.[1] I had thought myself that the book might interest Germans, but that there was no chance of it being allowed in a translation under the present regime. I did not, therefore, send you a copy. However, one of the best-known publishers here has written to me especially to suggest that you would like to see a copy and consider it for the German translation rights. If you would care to see one, I should be happy to send it to you.[2]

Yours faithfully,
Leonard Woolf

To Garden City Press[3]

16 August, 1935

[The Hogarth Press
52 Tavistock Square]

Dear Sirs,

I have only just received the copy of your letter of August 2, which never reached the office. I should be obliged if you would be good enough to inform me whether any of the passages marked by you are such that you definitely refuse to print them, and if so, which. I have considered them carefully and I cannot see that any of them could possibly be construed as libellous. The majority of them are purely matters of opinion, e.g. do you seriously maintain that we have reached

1. The book was about irrationality in Western society, in particular its virulent form in German and Italian fascism; it included photographs of Hitler and Mussolini, each juxtaposed with photographs of primitive war-god effigies with similar facial expressions.
2. The publisher was Stanley Unwin, who had a long connection with the German publishing world. The inquiry must have been either a hoax or an attempt to test literary freedom in Germany. On submission the book was indignantly rejected.
3. A printing firm often used by the Hogarth Press; its lawyers had reviewed the text of Raymond Postgate's *What to do with the B.B.C.* Postgate (1896–1971) was a noted left-wing writer and gastronome.

a point at which we may not say that it is scandalous that a public corporation should not publish accounts (p. 13)?[1]

Yours faithfully
Leonard Woolf

To the Secretary of State for India

[The Hogarth Press
6 September, 1935   52 Tavistock Square]

Sir,
    We have the honour to invite your consideration of the following facts. At the end of last year we received an order from, so far as we know, a perfectly respectable Indian bookseller, The Oriental Book Society of Benares, for two copies each of the following books: *The Dark Island* by V. Sackville-West and *How to Make a Revolution* by Raymond Postgate. These books were despatched by post. In April of this year we heard from the purchasers that they had not been delivered. We immediately wrote to the General Post Office here and asked them to make enquiries. On August 31, four months later, we received the following reply from the Assistant Controller of the London Postal Service:

> "With reference to your application of the 26th April concerning a book packet addressed to the Oriental Book Society, Benares, I have to inform you that I have now received a reply to my enquiry abroad. The packet was detained by the Indian Police owing to the nature of the books."

We have the honour to point out to you that these books have been seized by the Indian Police and Government, and no intimation of any sort has been sent either to us or to the importing firm. We are members of the Publishers Association of Great Britain and are, we venture to say, well known as reputable and respectable publishers of books of the highest class. As to the books seized in this way, V. Sackville-West (the Hon. Mrs. Harold Nicolson) is a distinguished poet and novelist

---

1. Among the passages objected to was one asserting that the BBC employed "whisky-sodden comedians." According to the Garden City Press solicitor, the passage would be ground for action not only by the BBC, but by "any comedian who may like to identify himself with this paragraph." The passage was dropped from the published text.

and if we had not the evidence of the Assistant Controller's letter, we should not have believed that this novel of hers would have been forbidden entry into India and that the Indian Police would seize copies consigned by us to Indian booksellers. As to the other book, we presume that it was seized solely because of the title; no one who had read it would, we venture to assert, find in it anything warranting its suppression. It is an objective, historical analysis of revolutions and attempts at revolutions during the 19th and 20th centuries; in so far as it has a moral, it is that under modern conditions fundamental political and social changes cannot be attained by violent methods; it contains a devastating criticism of communist tactics and methods; the author is a well known publicist and journalist. We are prepared if you so desire it, to submit to you copies of these books and of reviews of them in *The Times Literary Supplement* and other first-class papers confirming our statements.

The matter, we submit, is a serious one for a publisher, like ourselves, who does not publish, and has no wish to publish, books for pornographic or seditious purposes, the only two purposes for which presumably the Government of India seizes books. Yet if these two books can be seized, without notice or intimation, by the Indian police, we see no reason why any book on our list will not at any moment suffer the same fate, and the uncertainty and risk will make trade in books with India impossible.

In view of these facts we have the honour to request that some information may be given to us why these books were seized and whether in future we must expect that any books of the same kind sent by us to India may be suppressed without notice or intimation either to us or to the importers.

We remain, Sir,
Your obedient servants
Leonard Woolf
THE HOGARTH PRESS[1]

1. The reply, five months later, stated that the India Office had determined that Postgate's book "could not from the nature of its contents, be permitted to circulate in India . . . and importation of this book has been prohibited. . . . The aim of the authorities in India is to prevent the circulation in that country of literature calculated to encourage the growth of revolutionary movements and . . . capable of creating harm." *Dark Island*, the response went on, had been erroneously detained because it was in the same package. Postgate's was not the only Hogarth Press book banned by the Indian government. Before sending to India any book touching on politics, LW normally first submitted it to the India Office, which checked with the government of India, for an opinion.

To Cecil Day-Lewis

[The Hogarth Press
December 3rd, 1935   52 Tavistock Square]

Dear Day Lewis,
   Many thanks for your letter and for the MS, which I shall read with
great interest, and I am sure will want to publish.[1]
   I am very sorry, of course, that you are going to leave the Hogarth
Press, but it was not unexpected. I think you are quite right to do so
from your point of view.

                                        Yours sincerely
                                        Leonard Woolf

To John Rickman

[The Hogarth Press
23 December, 1936   52 Tavistock Square]

Dear Rickman,
   You will, I know, think me obstinate, churlish, and money-grubbing,
and I dare say I am, but I cannot agree with you.[2] I am a little tired
of large publishers taking no risk with authors in the early stages,
leaving it to the publishers like ourselves to take those risks, waiting
until one out of fifty authors on whom the risk has been taken by the
small publisher becomes famous, and then devising some method of
raking all the profit off the author and the small publisher. In 1924
the Institute had, I believe, made a considerable loss on their psycho-
analytic publications. I know that at least one large publisher refused
to risk money on Freud's *Collected Papers* and when he heard that
we were going to do so, he wrote to warn me "in a friendly way"
against it, saying that we should have to tie up over £1000 in it (which
was correct) and that in his opinion we should never see our money
back. He was wrong, but that is no reason why, now that Freud is
not a risk, I should hand over the publication of his works to the large

1. In submitting a new poem, *Noah and the Waters*, Day-Lewis said it would be the last
offered to the Hogarth Press, adding: "I could not be surprised if, under these circumstances,
you did not feel inclined to publish this book, though I very much hope you will." Day-
Lewis was another of Hart-Davis's acquisitions for Jonathan Cape.
2. Rickman wanted to publish an anthology of excerpts from Freud's works in Dent's
Everyman's Library series. LW considered "potted Freud" bad Freud and bad business,
offering to publish instead a general summary of Freud's writings.

328

publishers. That is what the proposition amounts to. I think it will damage the sale of our books; in that I may be wrong, but I am not going to risk it. . . . I am prepared to publish the kind of book which I suggested to you or I would, if you are keen on it, publish an anthology myself, but I cannot agree to handing over the publication of Freud's works to Messrs Dent.[1]

Yours sincerely
Leonard Woolf

To J. R. ACKERLEY[2]

52, Tavistock Square
W.C.1.

3 November, 1937

Dear Joe,

I feel I must say that the under-housemaid snobbery of the B.B.C. makes me queasy. I note that one is not allowed to say that a politician cannot compete with the popularity of little princesses, though one may say that he cannot compete with that of film stars. Are reviewers expected to remember to write with the standards of the under-housemaid in mind; if so, it would be better to add it to the instructions on the slip enclosed with review books.

Yours
Leonard Woolf[3]

To J. R. ACKERLEY

Monk's House,
Rodmell, near Lewes, Sussex.

6/11/37

My dear Joe,

I am glad that you did not mind my writing as I did and that you even found it timely. It must be torture to be inside the machine. That

---

1. In the end LW agreed to publish *A General Selection from the Works of Sigmund Freud*, edited by Rickman, the first in a Hogarth Press series known as Psycho-Analytical Epitomes.
2. Joseph Randolph Ackerley (1896–1967), writer and literary editor of *The Listener* 1935–59. At his request LW reviewed Frederick Maurice's *Haldane: 1856–1915* and Herbert Asquith's *Moments of Memory*. A reference to the princesses Elizabeth and Margaret Rose had been cut from the review on the ground of lèse majesté.
3. Ackerley replied that his superiors had insisted on the deletion over his objection.

the B.B.C. should be reactionary and politically and intellectually dishonest is what one would expect and forgive, knowing the kind of people who always get in control of those kind of machines, but what makes them so contemptible is that, even according to their own servants' hall standards, they habitually choose the tenth rate in everything, from their musichall programmes and social lickspitlers and royal bumsuckers right down their scale to the singers of Schubert songs, the conductors of their classical concerts and the writers of their reviews.

We should like to see you. The next week or so we are rather overcrowded, but I shall suggest a day for you to dine with us if you will after that.

Yours

Leonard Woolf

To John Lehmann[1]

52, Tavistock Square

W.C.1.

9/12/37

Dear John,

I look forward to seeing you when you get back. Rodker rang me up and told me that he had people prepared to buy the Press from me at my price provided that the figures were satisfactory when disclosed to them.[2] I replied that I had morally given an option on the Press to other people since my first interview with him and that I therefore could not open negotiations with him. He asked me when I would be able to tell him whether the option was exercised. I said that I could probably tell him before the end of the year something more definite. We have done very well with [Vita Sackville-West's] *Pepita*. If it sells much more, our profits this year will be so large that I shall be tempted to put the price up on you![3]

Yours

Leonard Woolf

1. The Woolfs, VW in particular, were now seriously thinking of selling the Press. Lehmann wanted to get back into publishing, in part to find an outlet for avant-garde poetry, and had proposed buying it.
2. John Rodker (1894–1955), translator and poet who lived much of his life in Paris. Another prospective buyer was Martin Secker, who had just severed his connection with Secker & Warburg Ltd.
3. Unable to raise funds to buy the Press himself, Lehmann tried, vainly, to interest Christopher Isherwood, Wystan Auden and Stephen Spender in purchasing it with him. He eventually bought VW's half-interest for £3,000 and became general manager in April 1938.

To J. B. Leishman[1]

[The Hogarth Press
December 15th, 1937   52 Tavistock Square]

Dear Mr. Leishman,

As far as I am concerned, you misunderstand the position entirely, and in no circumstances am I prepared now to publish a translation by you alone. It was not I but you who suggested Stephen Spender and the collaboration. It was owing to your suggestion, therefore, that I spent a great deal of time and trouble interviewing the American publisher and got from him quite a good agreement. It was Spender's name which induced Norton to make the agreement, and I know that he will not publish the translation unless Spender is included.[2] Without the American edition, the whole thing breaks down. . . . Therefore, if there is any question of publishing a translation by only one translator, it is more probable that I should choose Spender than you.

Yours sincerely
Leonard Woolf

To W. W. Norton   The Hogarth Press
52, Tavistock Square,
January 12th, 1938   London, W.C.1.

Dear Mr. Norton,

I am extremely sorry about what has happened. As I thought, it might inconvenience you, but I am afraid that I am in no way to blame.

I told you exactly how things stood when you were here, and you saw Spender yourself. I was led to believe that they would get to work at once, and that the translation would be completed quite soon, as Leishman had already done a considerable amount of work upon it. The truth is that first of all Spender got ill and so could not meet Leishman, and then when he recovered, great friction arose between them. In fact, at one moment, Leishman flatly refused to have anything more to do with Spender. It was only when I told Leishman that I would certainly not publish the translation by him alone, and that I

1. At LW's invitation, Leishman had agreed to do a new translation of Rilke's *Duino Elegies* and had decided to do it with (Sir) Stephen Spender (b. 1909), the poet and critic.
2. William Norton (1891–1945), President of W. W. Norton Publishers 1924–45.

was pretty certain that you would follow the same course, that there was a meeting between the two at which amicable relations were established. But now that I see how badly they run in this double harness, I am not at all sure that the thing will be completed, and in any case, I see endless trouble and delay. That is why I wrote my previous letter as soon as I was certain about this. All I can say now is that if they remain amicable, there is a possibility, I suppose, of their finishing it in time for the Autumn season, but considering the trouble that I have had already, I am, as I said, very doubtful even about this.[1]

Yours sincerely
Leonard Woolf

To Bertrand Russell

February 15th, 1938

[The Hogarth Press
52 Tavistock Square]

Dear Russell,

As a member of the Bookstall Committee of the Jewish National Fund Exhibition and Fair, I have been asked whether I would get some of the authors of books published by the Hogarth Press to sign copies which can be sold on the stall. The published price of each volume will be paid. Would you be prepared to sign copies of the *Amberley Papers*? It would be very good of you if you would.

Yours sincerely
Leonard Woolf

1. The collaboration continued but was so difficult that the work was not finished until April 1939, when there was a squabble over the introduction, which Leishman wrote and which gave most of the credit for the translation to himself.

[The Hogarth Press
February 18th 1938   52 Tavistock Square]

Dear Lady Russell,

I really don't think that I deserve to be quite so magisterially lectured. I suppose that technically I ought to have said 'you and your
wife'. But I was not giving, or going to, a party. I was doing what I
had been asked to do, namely to take advantage of the snobbery of
people who would pay for the signature of the author of *Principia
Mathematica* in order to get money to rescue certain miserable Jews.
I had been explicitly asked to get Bertie, if I could, by the secretary
of the committee, and that was why I wrote to him without thinking
anything more about it. I naturally thought, if I thought at all about
it, that 'you' meant the two authors. But I really don't think any the
better of Bertie because I know that at a bazaar some snob will probably
pay more than the published price for his book if it is signed by him,
nor do I think the worse of you if I doubt whether in your case the
snob would. And I may add that I do not think any the better of my
own wife or the worse of myself because as a matter of fact she was
one of the people whose books I was asked to get signed, and I—an
extraordinary fact—was not.

Yours sincerely
Leonard Woolf

To Ernest Jones

[The Hogarth Press
7 July, 1938   52 Tavistock Square]

Dear Dr Jones,

I saw Dr Martin Freud today and discussed with him the question
of his father's new book.[2] He has been offered an advance of £500 by

---

1. Incensed that LW had asked only her husband to autograph *The Amberley Papers*,
although she was co-editor, Lady Russell had written to ask: "Would you at a party confine
your polite attentions to those who were old friends, rich, famous, popular, and already
overwhelmed with attentions, ignoring altogether poor, shabby, young, shy and generally
insignificant newcomers?"
2. Sigmund Freud had arrived in Britain a month before with an unfinished manuscript
about Moses, based on the notion that Moses was an Egyptian and the Biblical account of
his life was fictional. As Ernest Jones had told LW: "He saw no prospect of publishing it
while he lived in Catholic Austria. . . ."

Cassell. An advance of such a sum is an impossibility for a book published in the [Psycho-Analytical] Library. It would be possible to bring out one of Freud's books in a popular form and go out for a popular public and thus pay an advance of £500. But the Library is well known as a scientific series producing books of a serious nature for specialists and students. You would never get a popular public therefore to believe that a book published in it was for them. I do not think that we should attempt to compete with this offer. I explained my view to Dr. Martin Freud and he understood it. He said that he was anxious not to break with the Institute or the Hogarth Press, but that in the present circumstances it was imperative for them to make as much as possible out of the book. He hoped that if his father later on produced any technical work, it would be published in the Library.

I hope that you will agree with me and approve of what I have done.

It would, of course, be possible for us to compete with this offer and offer to bring the book out in popular form outside the Library, but I do not think that, as publishers with the Institute of the Library, we ought to do this.

Yours sincerely
Leonard Woolf[1]

To Ernest Jones

12 July, 1938

[The Hogarth Press
52 Tavistock Square]

Dear Dr. Jones,

. . . I would be prepared to go up to £500 as advance, if you thought it advisable, on these terms, and we would spend about £200 to £250 on advertising. But I do not want to offer less than Cassell if you think that there would be little chance of Freud accepting less. Also do you think it would be possible to ask Freud to let us see what has been written of the book before we actually make the offer. Unless the book is really the kind to appeal to the general

---

1. Jones replied: "I want to tell you that Professor Freud would very much prefer that you publish the Moses book, provided that the financial difference to him from Cassell's offer would not be too great."

public, I do not think it would be wise to embark upon this kind of gamble.

Yours sincerely
Leonard Woolf[1]

FROM ERNEST JONES

October 20th 1938.

Dear Mr. Woolf,

. . . I want to say about the Moses *that there is no prospect of finishing it in the next couple of weeks for your January publishing. It will surely take us into the New Year and probably into the Spring. Perhaps you will let me know your next date for publishing.*

I am sorry to say there is some basis for Mrs. Knopf's criticism.[2] There is no doubt that the book is rather badly strung together, not having been written as a whole. It is hard to explain the reason for this in a sentence and I also feel that I am not myself the best judge, since I read the various sections at different times as they came along. It would be valuable to have the opinion of someone who would read through the whole book consecutively and, if you like, I could send it to you for this purpose. . . .

The book certainly sparkles with valuable ideas and is very interestingly and characteristically written, but it has, owing to certain circumstances, been badly planned. Freud himself has two introductions written before and after the Anschluss, which explain all this and also contain some pointed comments on the Nazi régime.

Yours sincerely,
Ernest Jones

1. Jones responded that, much as he needed money, Freud wanted to keep the Hogarth Press as his publisher. LW and Martin Freud reached an agreement and sold the American rights to Alfred A. Knopf.
2. Blanche Knopf, director of Alfred A. Knopf, had written to LW of her reaction on seeing Freud's manuscript: ". . . I am extremely disturbed. The work is really rather incomplete and surely unsatisfactory as it stands. We both paid big advances for this book and surely we did this on the assumption that we could reach correspondingly big audiences with it. Not only that, but for Professor Freud's sake, to get the widest possible hearing for his ideas. . . ."

To Ernest Jones

22 October, 1938.

[The Hogarth Press
52 Tavistock Square]

Dear Dr Jones,

Your letter is very disturbing. As you know, I was from the first extremely doubtful whether it would be possible to make a book of this sort into a popular selling book and was therefore against competing with Cassell. I was persuaded to do so by your account of the book which certainly (to quote Mrs Knopf) gave me the assumption that we might reach audiences commensurate with the advances we were asked to make on the book. It now looks both from her and your account that there is little chance of this with the book as it stands. I should like to see the book, but my German is not good enough to make it possible for me to form a judgment if over half the book is not translated and I think I must wait until the translation is complete. In any case I presume that nothing can be done in the way of revision until it is complete. . . .

Yours sincerely
Leonard Woolf

From Ernest Jones

November 9th 1938.

Dear Mr. Woolf,

You will be pleased to hear that Professor Freud has been working again at the troublesome third part and has made some improvements as well as omitting some repetitions.

Mr. Strachey was good enough to read through the whole book and I enclose a very Stracheyian report of his on it, which I am sure will interest you.[1]

*Yours sincerely,
Ernest Jones*

---

1. James Strachey reported as his first impressions: "The form of the book is a little eccentric: it has three prefaces—two of them about half way through and the third about three-quarters of the way through. The plan also involves a certain amount of repetition, though not as much as one expects—for each repetition brings out fresh aspects of the material. . . . The work, in fact, seems to me in every way characteristic of its author. People who dislike his earlier books are not likely to be pleased by this one. On the other hand Freud's admirers will find that *Moses* comes up to their expectations. In particular, it must not for a moment be thought that this is a mere re-hash of former material. The main thesis is itself a new one and the thought is throughout as original and acute as ever."

[The Hogarth Press
15th March, 1939.   52 Tavistock Square]

Dear Dr. Freud,

I hope you will forgive me for bothering you about the title for your book. I understand from Dr. Jones that you do not like the idea of having the title *Moses* and want it to remain *Moses and Monotheism*. From the publishing point of view it is, I am sure, a great mistake to have the long title, for in England many people will be frightened by the word monotheism. Would you, therefore, agree to its appearing under the shorter title?[1]

With kind regards from myself and my wife,

Yours sincerely
Leonard Woolf

May 20th 1939

Dear Mr Woolf,

Accept my hearty thanks for the advance copy of Moses and Monotheism *you were so kind to send me. The outfit of the book is very satisfactory and the reproduction of the grandiose face of Michelangelo's statue on the jacket is the most impressive you could have chosen.*

By the way, it is rather a bit of irony that this face should be so full a contradiction to the content of the book. The Moses of my construction living under the XVIIIth dynasty could only be clean shaven. I know no such representation is to be found in [the] arts.

With high regards
Yours sincerely
Sigm. Freud

1. Freud would not agree.

12th December, 1939

Dear Woolf,

In reply to your letter of the 7th, we are ourselves in negotiation with Dr. Ernest Jones concerning the possibility of publishing the complete works of Freud. As his first publishers, [+] and also as the publishers of two of his most important works, we seem to be the appropriate people for the job. Do you not agree?

Yours sincerely,
Stanley Unwin

[+] *It took some courage in those days*

To Stanley Unwin

[The Hogarth Press

14 December, 1939   37 Mecklenburgh Square, W.C.1.]

Dear Unwin,

Many thanks for your letter. I am afraid that I do not agree with you. For the last 15 years all Freud's works have been published here by us for the Institute of Psycho-Analysis and in the International Psycho-Analytical Library. In those 15 years thirteen volumes have been published in this way. A priori I should have said that the appropriate way to publish the complete edition would have been in the Library in the same way.

I agree that it required courage to publish Freud in the early days. But it was only after you turned down the *Collected Papers* that the Institute came to me and asked me to take over the Library and publish the papers. I always remember that you behaved in a very kind and generous way to me then, when I was an extremely inexperienced publisher. You wrote to me saying that you had heard that I was considering the publication of the four volumes of collected papers and that as a friend you warned me that it was a most hazardous

1. After Freud's death, in September 1939, LW proposed to Ernest Jones publishing Freud's complete works. Early in December he learned that Jones had asked Stanley Unwin to be the publisher. The news prompted an immediate letter, which does not survive, from LW to Unwin.

undertaking, involving very heavy capital outlay and the possibility of considerable loss. The fact that I did not take your advice and that, as it happened, the venture turned out all right does not prevent me from realizing now that your advice was probably sound.

I must say that your statement that Dr Jones is negotiating with you concerning the possibility of publishing the complete works astonishes me in view of the correspondence which I have been having with him on the same subject. I shall be interested to hear how it is proposed to deal with the copyrights in the 13 volumes published by us.

Yours sincerely
Leonard Woolf

To Ernest Jones

24 December, 1939

[The Hogarth Press
37 Mecklenburgh Square]

Dear Dr Jones,

Your letter, as you no doubt intended, does not clear up the situation, so far as we are concerned. It is disquietening to find, after publishing for 15 years for the Institute, that we are treated with, to say the least, a curious lack of candour.

About a month ago we suggested to you that we would seriously consider publishing a complete edition of Freud. You agreed and informed us that the Institute was also considering the question. Immediately afterwards I was told quite casually by a friend who has nothing to do with psycho-analysis or publishing that he had heard that negotiations were going on between Allen & Unwin and members of the Freud family for the publication of a complete edition. We informed you of this and you replied that it was "unfortunately very far indeed from any question of negotiations with publishers", that you had "happened to meet Stanley Unwin" and "naturally mentioned" the matter to him. Meanwhile I had taken the precaution to write tentatively to Stanley Unwin myself about the question of copyrights. He replied: "We are ourselves in negotiations with Dr Ernest Jones concerning the possibility of publishing the complete works of Freud." In your last letter you again say that "we are far from the stage of considering publishing negotiations". One or other of these

339

statements is clearly not true, and the situation therefore remains obscure and, for us, extremely unsatisfactory.

Yours faithfully
Leonard Woolf

To Ernest Jones

9 January, 1940

[The Hogarth Press
37 Mecklenburgh Square]

Dear Dr Jones,

I have to thank you for the explanation and apology contained in your letter. I of course accept them and agree that the matter is now cleared up in a way in which for us it had hitherto not been. I am particularly glad of this because we had always looked upon our psychoanalytical publications (and our relations with the Institute) with pleasure and a certain measure of pride.

Yours sincerely
Leonard Woolf[1]

To J. R. Ackerley

25 September, 1941

Monk's House
Rodmell, near Lewes, Sussex

Dear Joe,

I notice in the review which I wrote of Priestley's book that I was not allowed to say that he was Prometheus Unbound or that he had just a tinge of Pecksniff in his attitude and diction.[2] I quite understand why the organ of the B.B.C. was averse to saying that he was unbound when not broadcasting. But as regards the second excision, while of course I know that, the review being unsigned, I have no locus standi

1. After further exchanges, it was agreed that the Hogarth Press and Allen & Unwin would jointly produce the work but that publication should be postponed until after the war. By then Unwin had lost interest.
2. J. B. Priestley (1894–1984), journalist, critic, novelist, playwright, short-story writer, literary editor of the *New Statesman* and scriptwriter for films and radio. His *Out of the People* was one of a number of books LW reviewed in an unsigned article in the *Listener* on September 18, 1941.

for a protest, purely as a matter of interest and future guidance, I should much like to know why you cut out such a very mild and, I think, true remark. Priestley is so popular and so British that it would be rather odd if he did not have a tinge of Mr Pecksniff and, in your official position, I should have thought that it might even have endeared him to you.

Yours
Leonard Woolf

To John Lehmann   The Hogarth Press
                                                37 Mecklenburgh Square
3/4/42   London, W.C.1

J. L.

I enclose the MS of *Grand Canyon*.[1] It is not a good book, I'm afraid and I doubt whether, were it not by Vita, one would consider it. It would, I suppose, be difficult to refuse it and I should personally be against refusing it unless you are very certain it is not good enough. I find it extremely difficult to judge this kind of book. It is obviously in many ways absurd, but I dont know how absurd it may seem to other people and how many people like that kind of absurdity. My mind reels before Vita and the universe. The consequence is that, though I usually feel pretty certain as to what sales one should count on with a book (though of course one knows one may always very likely be wrong), here I have no idea of what one should guess at. The guess I do make is about 4000.

Do you expect me to write to Vita?[2]

I dont think I shall be in town next week at all, but I shall be up the week after.

L W

1. This was Vita Sackville-West's latest novel, a weird tale about Hitler's conquest of the world.
2. When Lehmann objected to the book as "profoundly defeatist," LW agreed to reject it. Although his letter to Sackville-West has been lost, it is quoted by her biographer, Victoria Glendinning, as opening: "This is one of the most unpleasant letters I have ever had to write, primarily because as an author you have always treated us so extraordinarily well that it seems almost unthinkable that the Hogarth Press should reject a book of yours." She was devastated and never again published with the Press. The novel, rejected also by Heinemann, was brought out, after alterations, by Michael Joseph.

To John Lehmann

30/1/43   [Monk's House]

J. L.
I think I had better see it [*The Three Rings* by Barbara Baker]. At least I dont feel quite happy, from what you say, that we must be so authoritarian with the author. I think . . . she has as good a right to her opinion as we have. . . . I should therefore be disinclined to insist upon our view in this case. The opening chapter is much more important. But here again it does not seem to me to be a question of the "amount" which she has done but the result. A priori simply to cut out the first chapter and begin with the second chapter appeals strongly to me and may completely have done the trick. Shaw once told me that the secret of good writing is always to cut out the first paragraph of an article or the first chapter of a book—and there is a lot in it.

[L W]

To John Lehmann

                                                     Monks House
17/5/43   Rodmell   near Lewes, Sussex

J. L.
I return Tiller.[1] I have read it with the greatest care and I have reread his first book. I am afraid that I am definitely against publishing this. All the faults in the previous poems are now exaggerated and there are hardly any of their merits, except perhaps in the last poem. I do not think I am really a very stupid person, but except in the last poem the greater part of what he says is to me, except in the vaguest and most useless sense, unintelligible. What I do understand is rather feeble and very dreary stuff. The preface is silly and shows fundamentally why the poems are so often silly. He does not understand what a synthesis is. It is no good just stating vaguely that there is the emergence of a reconciliation and synthesis. You have to state what the reconciliation of the contradiction is. There is no emergence, no reconciliation, no synthesis anywhere in these poems; even the thesis and negation are blurred. Consider carefully the figures in the margin of

1. Terence Tiller, whose *Poems* had been published by the Press the year before, had submitted a new collection, "The Inward Animal."

342

the first poem and the meaning of each section and you will see at once that the dialectic is empty and fraudulent. That is why the poems are nearly always just a collection of words. I am against using our paper on this kind of thing.

L W

To John Lehmann

22/5/43 [Monk's House]

Dear John,   It would be absurd for us to quarrel over Tiller. Surely it is essential that differences of opinion between us about the merits of works submitted for publication should be treated absolutely objectively and not as reflecting upon ourselves personally and we must be at liberty to express our own opinions in our own way without minding our p's and q's. Of course I am biased, but so are you and so is everyone in matters of taste. The mere fact that, as you admit yourself, I have given you wide discretion with regard to poetry shows, I think, that I have treated these matters with an open mind. But I am not prepared to waive my right to see, judge, and if so advised reject every book before publication. I do not say my judgment is right, but I cannot admit that I have yet reached the stage of not being able to form an intelligent judgment of Tiller; if it has been reached, it is obviously time that I retired from publishing. My judgment is that the book is not good enough to be published by the Hogarth Press. That is no reflection upon you or Tiller, and it is not, I suggest, fantastic either that I should make that judgment or, making it, reject the book. You have the same right with regard to any book, and it is essential that each should be absolutely free and equal in this respect, and that, as I said before, a difference of opinion and the exercise of the right of veto should not be treated as a personal matter.

L W

To John Lehmann

8/6/43   [Monk's House]

Dear John,
    . . . I think that the Press should not publish third-rate work either
because it is a work of an established writer like Vita or because it is
that of the young and "promising" like Tiller. I agreed at once to
reject Vita's novel which was an extremely difficult and painful thing
to do, particularly as it was the first thing submitted by her after
Virginia's death. I think that one must treat the young and promising
in exactly the same way if they produce bad stuff and that one must
not allow personal reasons to interfere. . . .

    I will be perfectly frank with you. I set great store by the Press not
publishing anything, so long as I am still connected with it, which is
third-rate, however well-known or unknown or young or promising
or paying the author may be, and irrespective of modes and fashions.
I have considerable misgivings therefore about your statements with
regard to your having "supported" an author and that being any
argument in favour of publishing an inferior book by him. I think that
the name and standard of the Press, such as they are, have been
established by an exactly opposite method, i.e. independent judgment
by two people as to whether in their opinion any publication is or is
not up to their standard. . . .

                                                    L W

To John Lehmann

                                                    Monk's House
10/7/43   Rodmell, near Lewes   Sussex

J. L.
I have reread Tiller. As to its merits, I remain of the same opinion
still. I should be very sorry to see the Hogarth Press publish much
poetry of the standard of this book whatever the previous reputation
or promise of the writer. I must also repeat that I think it lamentable
that an author of Tiller's age and gifts should be encouraged to proceed
on a path which must inevitably destroy such talent as he has; to do
so is neither kindness to the author nor good publishing.
    In view however of the particular facts in this case, namely that it

is extremely difficult with him out of England to deal with him and that you are so anxious to publish the book, I am prepared to agree to its publication. I do so with the greatest hesitation and misgiving. . . .

L W

To John Lehmann

Monk's House
18/9/43 Rodmell

J. L.

. . . *Citrus Culture.* The position is this. Stephenson is a boring Ceylon planter. I do not know him at all. But when I was 25 and his wife was 17, we had an absurd, amusing, and romantic affair in the first station I was sent to in Ceylon.[1] I thank God that I have never seen her again as I believe she now weighs 22 stone. On the strength of this, he wrote me some imbecile letters asking me to publish this book in the Hogarth Press. . . . It is monstrous that the sins of one's youth should be visited upon one in shape of a citrus manual 40 years later.

L W

From John Lehmann

15 October 1943

. . . I scarcely trust myself to put into words what I feel about the way you have handled our relationship in the press during the present year. I feel you are badly out of touch and your interventions either (and increasingly) irrelevant or petulant. As you clearly have ceased to trust me, and never ask my advice—as I have been the one in charge during the last three years of rapid changes and complex difficulties there are things I am in a much better position to judge than you— but only issue orders, or make categorical demands, I frankly despair for the future.

J L

1. She was disguised as "Gwen" in *Growing*.

345

Monk's House
Rodmell

23/10/43

Dear John,

Your attitude and language to me during the last 12 months or so are absolutely inexplicable to me. I have treated you with the greatest restraint only to be met at every point with the grossest rudeness. In no other of my many business relations am I consistently told that I am senile, out of touch, irrelevant, and petulant, and I do not believe that it is true of my ability to deal with publishing matters. It is not a question of my ceasing to trust you or not asking your advice. (You rarely give me any information about anything until the matter is settled and therefore how can I ask your advice. I dont quite see also where the asking of advice comes in in our relationship.) But the moment I express any opinion of any sort or kind about anything, you say I am not "trusting" you or that I am "giving orders" or "making categorical demands". No partner has ever given another partner a freer hand than I did to you or treated him with more consideration. Instead of showing some appreciation of the fact, you have in the past 12 months shown more and more resentment of my having any say connected with the Press, twisting every remark of mine into "interference" or "orders" and treating me with a rudeness such as I have never experienced from anyone with whom I have had relations before. . . .

The last thing in the world that I want is to quarrel with you or to have another perfectly unnecessary breakup in the Press. If on the other hand you do want to break up the partnership, say so in a reasonable way. You keep on speaking about your "position and rights", but your position and rights are precisely the same as mine. We are partners and I claim no position or rights which I do not completely accord to you, but you on your side have no position and no rights superior to mine. That is the meaning, legal and moral, of a partnership and of a partnership agreement. . . .

L W

To Anna Freud[1]

11 March, 1944

Monk's House,
Rodmell, near Lewes, Sussex

Dear Dr Anna Freud,

I have more than once lately been asked by people whether there is a reliable biographical work on your father. I was talking to Karin Stephen on the subject the other day and we both felt that the time had come when a book should be published on his contribution to the sum of human knowledge and containing a really adequate biography. I suggested that perhaps she herself might write such a book and she was prepared to consider the suggestion. But we both also felt that the biographical part could not be written from the material at present available and without your encouragement or cooperation. It seemed to me essential therefore to put the matter before you and see what you yourself felt about it and whether, if you view it favourably, you would be good enough to have a talk with Karin Stephen about it.[2]

Yours sincerely
Leonard Woolf

To John Lehmann

18/4/45

[Monk's House]

J L

I return Sartre['s *Les Mouches*]. I have grave doubts whether we should bind ourselves to publish the translations you suggest under present circumstances. Surely there will be any amount of things old and new for which we shall require paper for a long time much more worth our while than translations from the French of extremely exotic stuff

1. Anna Freud (1895–1982), Sigmund Freud's favorite child, was in practice her father's literary executor.
2. Anna Freud responded: "The question of a reliable biography on my father has been approached several times lately. Personally, I think, that it will have to wait still. The only reliable material to be utilized are his own letters which are scattered all over the world. . . . So far as I know Ernest Jones is very interested in that question and has compiled some material. There are two other people of my knowledge who could undertake such a task and would be fitted for it through close co-operation and detailed personal knowledge. One is the novelist Arnold Zweig, now in Palestine; the other is Princess Marie Bonaparte, now in Capetown. I myself would, for evident reasons, not approach the task. But, I think, whoever it is would have to wait for the end of the war."

347

which neither of us is enthusiastic about. Of course this is quite clever enough, but I am getting so tired of these retellings of the Atreidae story.

L W

To John Maynard Keynes

19/5/45

Monk's House
Lewes, Sussex

Dear Maynard,

I entirely agree about the article, although the responsibility is of course mine.[1] It is appalling. . . . The pages with material which I had not read were promised for 2.30. The front page however was only ready for me to read at 5. When I read it, I felt as you do about it and told Vallance so. It was considerably worse than it is now. The difficulty was that the article ought to have been rewritten entirely, but in the state the printers were in that meant beginning all over again on Friday for them and quite probably not getting the paper out until Monday. I also had an engagement which made it necessary for me to catch the 6.45 latest to Lewes. In the end I told Vallance that he must put in certain alterations and additions which I thought would make the article tolerable. But I agree that they did not and that it would probably have been better to have rewritten the article and have held up the printing.

As regards what action it is your duty to take, I think it would be wrong to confuse this case with any thing against Kingsley. It should be raised at the Board meeting, but the responsibility is mine and it shouldn't be counted against Kingsley.

On the general question, after my experience of the last four weeks I think it is a mistake to have MacKenzie on the paper.[2] I like him and he is extremely intelligent, but it is hopeless to have communists in "key positions". However I understand that he is not going on. I dont understand Vallance. Up to this incident I had always thought

1. LW, who edited the *New Statesman* during May in Kingsley Martin's absence, had received an outraged letter from Keynes about the lead article in the previous week's issue. The article, by assistant editor Aylmer Vallance, was, as LW wrote in *The Journey Not the Arrival Matters*, "full of the slants, snides, sneers, and smears which Communists and Fellow Travellers habitually employ as means for building a perfect society." Vallance had deliberately submitted the article late.
2. Norman MacKenzie (b. 1921), assistant editor of the *New Statesman* 1943–62.

him to be a first rate journalist and second rate in everything else, but also some one whom one could trust to be reasonable up to a point.

Yours
Leonard Woolf

24.1.46.

Dear Leonard,
. . . It must have been clear to you, even as far back as the Autumn of 1943 . . . that a gulf had opened between us that only a miracle could close—given the temperaments and aims that each of us knows the other to have. . . .

I am not complaining of interference in my defined rights as Manager; I have no complaints at all there; it is a flaw more fundamental in our relationship which each successive row or disagreement has seemed to me to reveal more clearly. And if there is no more confidence between us, how can we make a success of publishing in the future? I would therefore like you to take this letter as notice in the sense of Clause 15 of our Articles of Partnership, and inform me what course you propose to follow. . . .

Yours
J. L.

To John Lehmann

Monk's House
Rodmell, Lewes   Sussex

26/1/46

Dear John,
I received this morning your letter of 24 January giving me notice under Article 15 of our Deed of Partnership calling upon me to dissolve the Partnership. I shall exercize my option to buy you out on the terms provided for in that article and this is the formal notice which I am required to give you within three weeks. . . .

Yours
Leonard Woolf

To John Mavrogordato[1]

17/3/46   [Monk's House]

Dear Professor Mavrogordato,

I daresay you have heard that John Lehmann is leaving the Hogarth Press and that I am taking over things again by myself. I have been going into the question and correspondence regarding your translation of Cavafy.[2] I tried to get a translation published 20 years ago, so that it seems familiar, especially as the same exasperating muddle occurred then because at the last moment Cavafy always fought shy of any firm agreement. The same thing, I find, has happened in the last two years. I do not think it possible to publish without getting an agreement signed by Singopoulo. . . .[3] On the other hand, if you agreed, and I could get Singopoulo to agree, I would gladly publish a selection of your translations without the Greek text. I should be greatly obliged to you if you would let me know what you feel about it. . . .

Yours sincerely
Leonard Woolf

To Donald Brace

                                                    [The Hogarth Press
23/5/46   40-42 William IV Street]

Dear Mr Brace,

I have more than once in past years discussed the possibility of an edition of [Freud's] collected works with Freud's representatives, but there have always been difficulties which prevented it being undertaken. I have recently had a talk with his son and daughter and they are anxious now that an attempt should be made to bring out an English edition.[4] The German edition in 18 volumes, now being published here, is almost complete and the English edition should follow

1. John Mavrogordato (1882–1970), Fellow of Exeter College, Oxford, and Bywater and Sotheby Professor of Byzantine and Modern Greek Language and Literature.
2. Constantine Cavafy (1863–1933), the Greek poet, who was born and lived in Alexandria. He was a friend of E. M. Forster.
3. Alexander Singopoulos was Cavafy's literary executor.
4. Ernst Freud (1892–1970), Sigmund Freud's youngest son, an architect. He had emigrated from Berlin to London in 1933. When Martin arrived in Britain with his father in 1938, Ernst eased him aside and took over management of his father's publications.

it. If we do it, it would clearly be advisable if possible that we should do it in collaboration with an American publisher. The Freuds are in favour of the complete translation being made here under an editor chosen by themselves and the Institute of Psycho-Analysis. The preliminary costs would be considerable, but the demand here and, as I know, on your side is very large, and if the preliminary costs could be shared between the English and American publishers, I have myself no doubt about the financial success of the publication. Would you be interested in the proposal? If you were, I would go into the whole question in greater detail. There are, for instance, considerable difficulties regarding copyright which have to be considered.

With kind regards

Yours sincerely
Leonard Woolf[1]

To E. M. Forster

20/11/46

[The Hogarth Press
40-42 William IV Street]

Dear Morgan,

I have just had one of the great triumphs of my life. I have received from Singopoulo a signed agreement giving me the right to publish Cavafy in Mavro's translation. I shall do it complete. The triumph would be complete if you would write an introduction to it. Would you?

Yours
Leonard Woolf

To Ernst Freud

1/10/47

[The Hogarth Press
40-42 William IV Street]

Dear Mr Freud,

I have seen James Strachey twice since I wrote to you, but what I learn from him does not encourage me to go on with these negotiations. I do not feel that we have the confidence from you without which the

1. Brace offered terms that were rejected by Ernst Freud.

relations of publisher and author are extremely difficult. I learnt, quite accidentally, from him that you have given an unpublished work of your father's to be published by Imago and that you now propose to give another important book, translated by James himself, to the same publishers.[1] This is the first I have heard about this. According to James, who naturally thought that we should have been given the first option on these books, he was told by you that they had been offered to us and refused on the ground that we had no paper. As you are aware, this is not the case. No one had the courtesy even ever to say a word about the matter to me and the first I heard of it was from James himself. You are also aware that in the last two years we have reprinted seven or eight of your father's books, including the *Collected Papers*, as well as your sister's book [*The Ego and the Mechanisms of Defence*], so that the idea that we could not find paper for two short new books of your father's is ludicrous. When I protested against the [Freud-Fliess] letters having been given to another publisher without a word to us, you told me that you yourself disliked it, but that it had been done by the Princess.[2] I have known many cases in which authors have treated publishers or publishers authors with discourtesy or worse, but I do not remember any in which the treatment is stranger than this. I understand that you have given one book definitely to be published by Imago but that the transaction with regard to the *Three Contributions* has not been completed. Would you be good enough to let me know whether we shall be given an option to publish it.[3]

Yours sincerely,
Leonard Woolf

1. The works, unpublished in Britain, were *The Question of Lay Analysis* and *Three Contributions on Sexual Theory*. Both had been given to John Rodker, who in 1938 had founded the Imago Publishing Company with the evident intention, and now with Ernst Freud's cooperation, of supplanting the Hogarth Press as the publisher of psychoanalytical works.
2. The letters, exchanged by Sigmund Freud and Wilhelm Fliess in 1887–1902, had been purchased by Princess Marie Bonaparte (1882–1962) from a Berlin dealer in 1937. She was a close friend of both Sigmund Freud and Rodker.
3. Unrepentent as ever, Freud did not relent.

To Roger Machell[1]

[The Hogarth Press
40-42 William IV Street]

9th February, 1949

Dear Mr. Machell,
   With reference to your letter of the 2nd of February, I communicated with Mr. Ernst Freud again about the Brill translations and I enclose a copy of his reply.[2]
   As regards the proposed edition, the last proposal was for an edition of 24 volumes of which the last would be indices. We reckon that the total number of words would be something over two million and the average length of each volume would be round about 212 pages. James Strachey would translate, or retranslate, and edit the whole series and it was proposed to pay him a fee of £1000 a year for doing this. He reckons that it will take him six years to complete the job. Our proposal to an American publisher was that they should go halves with us in the cost of translating and editing and would take from us a minium of 2000 sets. . . .
   The whole project would be supervised by the Institute of Psycho-Analysis and the Freud family, with both of whom James Strachey has worked for years. . . .[3]

Yours sincerely
Leonard Woolf

To John Mavrogordato

The Hogarth Press Ltd
40-42 William IV Street
London WC2

17th May, 1949

Dear Mr. Mavrogordato,
   Your letter of May 13th distresses me, though I understand that you may justly feel that we have not treated you well. I was put into an extremely awkward position because, as you know, I had asked E. M.

1. London representative of Harper & Brothers, who was trying to negotiate terms for the publication of the *Standard Edition* acceptable to Ernst Freud.
2. It was financially critical that the *Standard Edition* should be salable in both Britain and the United States. The American copyrights, which Sigmund Freud had dispersed with abandon, had therefore to be traced and acquired. Most difficult was persuading the estate of Abraham Brill to permit Brill's poor translations to be redone.
3. LW eventually abandoned efforts to find an American co-publisher, deciding to risk publication by the Hogarth Press alone.

Forster to write an introduction and he had agreed to do so. I thought that obviously it was well worth waiting for him as it would have given the book a much better chance if it had an introduction by him. The MS was sent to him and has been in his hands up to a short time ago. I have seen him from time to time in the interval and, each time, as there seemed to be some real chance of his writing the introduction, I reluctantly left things as they were. However, a few weeks ago, he told me that he felt that he could not do it. The MS was returned and I tried to get T. S. Eliot to take Forster's place and it seemed for a moment as if I should succeed, but, in the end, he had too much on hand already to be able to undertake it. This, of course, added to the delay.[1] We were then on the point of taking steps to publish the book, when the opportunity occurred of getting an introduction from Mr. Rex Warner.[2] He is now writing the introduction and as soon as we get it, the book will be put into production. I can only apologise to you for the delay, though I hope you will agree that there was some reason to wait in the hope of an introduction by Forster.

Yours sincerely
Leonard Woolf

To Sir Francis Meynell[3]

16.3.51   [Monk's House]

Dear Sir Francis Meynell,

Yes, it was certainly unreasonable. The facts are these. Just before the war, Stephen Spender rang me up one day and asked me whether I could take some cases of type which he had had from you. I had no desire to take them but I had a good deal of type of my own and room to store them so that I agreed and fetched them round in my car to my house in Mecklenburgh Square. I was never quite certain whether, in fact, you had given them to him or lent them to him or even what

1. LW also approached Sir Maurice Bowra (1898–1971), Warden of Wadham College, Oxford, 1938–71, and Professor of Poetry at Oxford, 1946–51, who replied that since some poems were pornographic he could not risk the "letters from clergymen and lawyers, rows and trouble" that would inevitably descend upon him.
2. Rex Warner (1905–1986), classicist and Director of the British Institute at Athens 1945–47.
3. Sir Francis Meynell (1891–1975), founder of the Nonesuch Press and typographic adviser to H.M. Stationery Office, had written to ask if it was unreasonable of him to be surprised that LW had ruined some cases of type that belonged to him.

my exact position was in regard to them. At any rate, I never used the type and quite soon afterwards the house in Mecklenburgh Square was completely shattered by bombs and uninhabitable. The room in which the type was, was wrecked and it was some time before I could get either my furniture or the type and printing machine removed. I then had to hire a room in this village and have everything sent down in removal vans and they were all stacked in the room until the end of the war. When I took the house in Victoria Square, they were again loaded into removal vans and sent there but I have never had the time or inclination to examine them and I sold my own printing machine and all my type. I explained this to Stephen Spender and considering what the stuff went through I was astonished that any of it existed at all. As you never lent me the type and I had had no communication with you, and did not you know whether you were even still the owner, not unnaturally, I think, I did not say anything to you about it. I am, however, extremely sorry that it should be in the state in which it is.

Yours sincerely
Leonard Woolf[1]

To Sir Francis Meynell

28 April 1951   [Monk's House]

Dear Sir Francis Meynell,

I see from your letter that you are determined to believe that I borrowed your type from you, by my fault ruined it, and then refused to say that I was sorry, and that that entitles you to be offensive to me. I do not grudge you that kind of satisfaction if it is the kind of thing which gives you pleasure. I have already told you that I am extremely sorry that your type was reduced to the state in which it is, but that I never wished to borrow it, never used it, and could not possibly have prevented bombs from wrecking the room in which I stored it. You disbelieve what I say, and the only possible excuse for your rudeness is a single inaccurate sentence in a letter from Stephen Spender to you 12 years ago. Why should my wife and I "want to do

1. Meynell replied: "I had no intention of stirring in you so deep a sense of guilt. I meant merely to give you a second opportunity for a little ordinary courtesy. Now I must resort to the soothing tactics of the modern (circ.1930) mother. 'Hush, my dear, hush. Of course you can break the toys you borrowed, and of course you needn't say you're sorry.' "

some printing of our own during the blackout" and want to borrow 6 cases of your Janson type when we habitually did printing of our own and had done so continually for 20 years and had over 50 cases of Caslon O.F. type in the room into which we put your 6 cases? However, obviously, our views of what is reasonable and mannerly are so different that there is no real point in my writing this.

Yours sincerely
Leonard Woolf[1]

To the *Observer*

[The Hogarth Press
London W.C.2.]

14 October 1951

Sir,— In your Profile of Professor Day Lewis there was an amusing account of the Hogarth Press and its early ventures in the publication of poetry. Mr. Day Lewis's "first volume of poetry," you say, "was published by the Hogarth Press in 1929, and plunged into an almost instantaneous oblivion. . . . At that time it was the habit of its publishers, Leonard and Virginia Woolf, to recline on the formidable piles of their unsold poetry. . . ."

I feel that in defence of the poets whom we published I should say that the implication that their works did not sell is incorrect. The first book of poetry which we published was *Poems* by T. S. Eliot, in 1919, and in 1923 we published *The Waste Land*. By 1929 we had published works by V. Sackville-West, Frances Cornford, Robert Graves, William Plomer, R. C. Trevelyan, Herbert Read, Conrad Aiken, Edwin Muir and J. Middleton Murry.

The sale of poetry in England is normally very small and these poets were not well-known writers when we first published their work. But not very much of their poetry remained unsold—certainly not enough to sit, let alone to recline, on.

Yours etc.
Leonard Woolf

1. Meynell, who had been convinced LW had borrowed the type, now responded: "I have respected you too long and too much to feel happy about leaving this quarrel where it is. Therefore I write to tell you that I accept your view. . . ."

To J. B. LEISHMAN

[The Hogarth Press Ltd
11th June, 1952   40-42 William IV Street]

Dear Leishman,

We have been much concerned about this translation and, after discussing it several times with Mr. Parsons, we have decided that I should write to you about it.[1] We do not think that the translation as it stands is really publishable. What distresses us is that it is often unintelligible and there seem to be far too many un-English words. The kind of thing I mean is best shown perhaps by example and here are two:

".... like joy thats already
been too long feigningly held, makes blissfully more
the hopedest alarm of the find.

Doesn't so much visibility tempt you? Think:
from the jubilant grab of the other
To, in sudden excess, overflow!...."

Neither Mr. Parsons nor I can see that the English, without a knowledge of German, is intelligible in either of these passages. Is there anything in German of the first passage which requires the use of a word like 'hopedest' which is not English at all? We feel that it would be a great disservice both to Rilke and to the Hogarth Press to publish the translation as it is, but we do not want to do anything without consulting you. Do you think it is possible that you could go through the translation and rectify these things?

Yours sincerely
Leonard Woolf

1. For Ian Parsons, see Biographical Appendix. The work was Rilke's *Correspondence in Verse with Erika Mitterer* and raised in acute form the extraordinary difficulty of translating Rilke. Alterations in the text were made.

To J. R. Ackerley

[The Hogarth Press
3/12/54   40-42 William IV Street]

Dear Joe,
  I think Ian [Parsons] has told you that I would be writing to you
about your MS which he and I have both read.[1] We agree in thinking
it extremely good as a "thing in itself"—a work of art. I enjoyed it
and your skill immensely—it is a work of great fascination. But when
it comes to publishing, in contemplation I doubt the possibility. There
are two or rather three questions, the first and second would be both
yours and ours, the third yours. The first is decency. I think with a
few alterations this could be got over even with the present furor
puritannicus. The second is libel. We feel here that it is almost certain
that you could not avoid the most serious libel actions and that no
alterations are possible which would not destroy the book. The third
is simply whether you could really from your point of view publish.
No one except you can really be the final judge of this, but for what
it is worth my opinion would be—no.
  I hope I shall see you some time again.

                                                   Yours
                                                   Leonard Woolf[2]

To J. R. Ackerley

[The Hogarth Press
7/12/54   40-42 William IV Street]

Dear Joe,
  There is no doubt that the book is very amusing and that you have
done what you meant to do. But it would be taken by many people
much more seriously than it is meant and more autobiographical—a
Liber Amoris Homosexualis in which the object is not a lodging-house
keeper's daughter, but turns out to be an Alsatian dog, and a bitch
at that. That is to say in answer to your question, yes, I do mean both.
Why I would hesitate from your point of view is precisely that they

1. The manuscript was *We Think the World of You*, an autobiographical novel about how
a man's love for another man was replaced by his love for a dog.
2. In a friendly reply Ackerley asked whether the advice against publication was because
he would be frowned on for admitting his homosexuality or laughed at for his relationship
to his dog. He added that the book was intended to be comic, not serious.

would have you both ways, askance for the homosexuality and contempt for your amorous naivety. I am very glad that Hazlitt published the *Liber Amoris*, but I dont know what I should have advised him to do so if he had come and asked my advice. Or least I should have said to him what I am now saying to you. "Well, you know, *they* will be rather . . ."[*sic*]

Yours
Leonard Woolf[1]

To Lyn Irvine Newman[2]

1/8/57   [Monk's House]

Dear Lyn,

You misunderstand my position a good deal. I admire and sympathize with much of the Christianity of Christ, though some of it is impractical and some nonsense. If he had brought me the Sermon on the Mount in 1920 I should have published it with the greatest pleasure (and would probably been the only publisher in London who would have done so) and I am sure that he would have been quite willing to be published by someone with my views. What I dont like is the Christianity of the Churches, of the Archbishop of Canterbury, Queen Elizabeth II, the Pope, and the Moderator of the Church of Scotland which worships respectability and a synthetic deity composed of 90% Mamon and 10% God.

Also I dont agree with your thanking God that you are not as other men are—which again is contrary to the Christianity of Christ and at the root of your not wanting to be published by the Hogarth Press. What you say about Freud shows this. I think Freud made remarkable contributions to knowledge and wrote first class books, but there is much of his which I dont agree with and some of it I think is nonsense. He went on giving us his books to publish from 1924 until his death, almost certainly knowing this or at any rate not thinking about it,

1. Ackerley next submitted the manuscript to Fredric Warburg, who declined to publish it on the ground that Ackerley would face immediate arrest as a practicing homosexual. After repeated rejections and revisions, the book was finally published in 1960 and was a popular and critical success.
2. Lyn Irvine Newman (1901–1973), an old social friend of the Woolfs, had written to criticize LW for a variety of shortcomings, including his attitude toward religion, his failings as a publisher and his choice of authors.

because he knew that we took him and his books seriously (which very few did in 1924) and were competent publishers.

You are quite wrong about Laurens van der Post. He is not bogus; he is one of the sincerest of men. Some of what he writes is very good and some of it, in my opinion, unmitigated nonsense. But he believes it just as Christ and Freud did theirs. He knows what I think, but gives us his books because he knows we take things seriously, because we were the only publisher who 30 years ago would publish his first book, and because he knows that we sell anything between 25,000 and 300,000 of what he writes today. As for Mrs [Anne Morrow] Lindbergh, she is not, I should say, in the very least degree bogus—sentimental, yes, but not bogus.

. . . It gives one an unworthy pleasure to find one's expectations about human nature, even of one's friends, confirmed. On the other hand it is this which makes our disagreement comparatively unimportant. For the fact that I disagree with your brand of Christianity and think that it has led you to act (I think) wrongly in the present instance does not alter my affection for you.[1]

Yours
Leonard Woolf

To E. M. Forster

2.10.63 [Monk's House]

Dear Morgan,

Show [magazine] wrote to me out of the blue and asked me whether they could consider publishing extracts from my Volume III [*Beginning Again*]. I sent them the first chapter and they chose about 5,000 words out of it for which they offered me $500 which I accepted. They are a most curious glossy paper to publish anything of mine or even yours. Aldous [Huxley] once on a boat coming from America got very friendly with the proprietor of one of those kind of American magazines, who, after three days out, asked him to write an article for which he offered him a fabulous sum and Aldous accepted. The last day before they reached England, when they became still more friendly, Aldous asked him why he had asked him for an article. The proprietor then said that they had reached the point, which is not unusual with a large

1. She refused to entrust her memoirs to the Hogarth Press.

scale illustrated paper, when they wanted to reduce their circulation and he thought it was a very respectable way to do it. I rather thought that *Show* must have reached the same point. I have a copy of it if you would like to see it. . . .

Yours
Leonard Woolf

To Esther Salaman[1]

3/6/64   [Monk's House]

Dear Esther,

It was a very pleasant surprise to get your letter. I was really sorry when you took against me (quite wrongly, as I then thought and still think), for I liked you very much and also Myer and your children, when I saw your family sitting round that night at dinner.[2] Sorry, but not hurt or angry or shocked, as I would have been 30 years ago, because one of the consolations of age, I find, is that one is no longer surprised or shocked by anything that anyone does and so one is practically never hurt personally.

But according to my standards, you did behave badly. . . . I took a very great deal of trouble over your book, partly because I was your publisher, but also partly because we had become friends. I told you exactly what I thought about the book. What else could I do? You had consulted me as a professional, as a publisher, as an "expert" in the particular field of novels and their writing and publication. What would you think of Myer if he concealed or altered scientific facts as he saw them in order to please or displease or placate or not hurt someone to whom he had to give a professional opinion? Yet you took against me merely because I gave you an honest opinion which was not what you wanted. I dont of course know what your unconscious told you about my behaviour. It may have revealed to you a truth of which I am unaware, but I certainly do not agree that the unconscious mind reveals deeper truths about someone else than plain common or garden common sense does. And—as far as the unconscious is con-

1. She had written to praise the third volume of LW's autobiography; one of her books had been published by Hogarth Press and one rejected.
2. Myer Salaman was Director of the Department of Cancer Research, London Hospital Medical College.

cerned—isn't it possible that one reason why you were so angry with me was that in the depths of your mind you knew that what I said was unbiased and probably true.

However, all that is long ago and now I send my love to you all and hope everything is well with you.

Yours
Leonard Woolf

To William Plomer

21.10.64

Monk's House
Rodmell, Lewes, Sussex

Dear William,

. . . I was rather amused by Laurens [van der Post]'s preface to the book.[1] It is very good in its way, as Laurens practically always is, but it is of inordinate length. It made me sardonically suggest that possibly the book ought to be called Preface by Laurens van der Post of a novel by William Plomer.

I hope I will see you in the near future.

Yours
Leonard

To John Campbell[2]

18/6/65

[Monk's House]

Dear Jock,

In thinking over this question of Paul [Johnson], as discussed yesterday, I still face the greatest reluctance to appointing a Roman Catholic, a communist, or any other denominationalist who subjects his will and actions in principle absolutely to an organization or party.[3]

1. *Turbott Wolfe* had been reissued with a preface of forty-seven pages to what was a short novel.
2. John M. Campbell (b. 1912), industrialist and chairman of the *New Statesman* board of directors 1964–81; he was made a life peer in 1966.
3. Paul Johnson (b. 1928), Catholic journalist and author, was the proposed candidate to replace John Freeman as editor of the *New Statesman*. LW had for years disagreed with his views on a variety of topics.

But if and when the time comes to appoint Paul, as all the rest of the Board are in favour of appointing him, I would not oppose it, since I think it would be a great pity that his appointment would not be unanimously agreed by the Board. I do feel however that we have an obligation to John [Freeman] to give him more time before altering our decision to give him leave of absence.[1]

Yours sincerely
Leonard Woolf

To John Campbell

19/6/65   [Monk's House]

Dear Jock,
   Many thanks for your letter. I have resigned twice in the last ten years on the ground of senility, and withdrew the resignations at the request of the chairman. I will therefore this time take the opportunity of not standing for reelection. It was been a pleasure to be a member under your chairmanship; please convey my farewell good wishes to the board.

Yours sincerely
Leonard Woolf

To Ian Parsons

10/10/65   [Monk's House]

Dear Ian,
   I have come to the conclusion that the time has come when I should cease to draw a salary from the Hogarth Press and come to the office once a week. The reasons are (1) I do not think that I do much, if any, useful work. The fact is that H.P. is more and more amalgamated with Chatto and there is not therefore sufficient independent work for me to do. For instance, very few MSS now come to the H.P. (2) I want to give as much time as possible to my book.[2]

1. John Freeman (b. 1915), Labour MP 1945–55; editor of the *New Statesman* 1961–65, High Commissioner in India, 1965–68, and Ambassador to the United States 1969–71.
2. The final volumes of his autobiography.

I should rather like to remain on the board without salary unless there is any objection. If I live until 1967, I shall have been in the Press for 50 years and that would be an appropriate moment for complete retirement.

Yours
Leonard

To Ian Parsons

23/3/66   [Monk's House]

Dear Ian,

I read the article about Tom.[1] The sales facts are as follows. We published *Poems* in May 1919. We printed 200 copies. The first copy sold to a bookseller was one copy to James Bain on May 29. We sold 4 copies to the Poetry Bookshop on June 12 and 7 to Hatchards on June 18. The first order from Simpkin [a book wholesaler] was for 15 on July 25, and their last was for 7 on October 15. After 12 months we had sold 168 copies. By September 17, 1920 we had sold 183 copies and the book was out of print.

We published *The Waste Land* on 12 Sept., 1923. By the end of 1923 we had sold 306 copies; in the first six months of 1924 we sold 79 copies, and in the next six months 49. The book went out of print on February 11 1925, when we had sold 443 copies.

When we published *Poems* Tom was practically unknown and so he was in 1923 when we published *Waste Land*. A few people, like ourselves, thought him a very good poet, but the general view was that he was unintelligible and ridiculous. The Literary Establishment continued to think *Waste Land* absurd, but it had an immediate success with the young. After 1925 MSS poured into the H[ogarth] P[ress] of poems imitating *Waste Land* in vocabulary, rhythm, subject, and obscurity.

The sales of *Homage to John Dryden* show the kind of general reputation which Tom had seven or eight years after we published

1. In the *Critical Quarterly*, George Watson, a Cambridge don and literary critic, had contested the view that "Eliot had to fight hard and long to establish himself as the first living poet of the English speaking world" and argued that "acclaim for his early poems was, for all practical purposes, instantaneous." Parsons rebutted his argument with data from this letter.

Poems.[1] We published *Homage* at the end of 1924. By the beginning of 1926 we had sold 565 copies; in the next six months we sold 162 copies, and in the following six months 196. So by the end of 1926, it had taken us two years to sell 923 copies.

Yours
Leonard

To Alix Strachey

10.5.67 [Monk's House]

Dear Alix,

I was very glad you liked my note.[2] James's death was a shock as I had no idea that he was ill. The Authors' Society wrote to me the other day and asked me whether I would receive the prize on behalf of James as they did not like approaching you. I told them that they really ought to approach you and if you couldn't do it, it would be better to get Anna Freud or some officer of the Psycho-Analytical Institute.[3]

Yours
Leonard Woolf

To A. L. Barker

22.11.67 [Monk's House]

Dear Miss Barker,

I have been reading your book again and I want to say how pleased I am that we are publishing it.[4] I think it is extremely good. I am

---

1. *Homage to John Dryden: Three Essays on Poetry of the Seventeenth Century* was the fourth in the series of Hogarth Essays.
2. An obituary appreciation of James Strachey in *The Times*, which had ignored his death.
3. For his translation of Freud's works into English, culminating in the production of the *Standard Edition*, James Strachey had been awarded the Schlegel-Tieck Prize by the Society of Authors but died prior to the award ceremony. The prize was accepted by Donald Winnicott, president of the British Psycho-Analytical Society; LW attended the ceremony but, inexplicably, Anna Freud and Alix Strachey did not.
4. A. L. Barker (b. 1918), author and literary critic; the book was *The Middling: Chapters in the Life of Ellie Toms.*

afraid the sales of your books must have disappointed you and this one so far has not sold nearly as well as it deserves. But you are one of the writers who for years may not sell anything like the number which they ought to sell. This is no comfort to you but it is not a publisher's excuse. Your books are so good and original that in any case they are the kind which it takes a long time for the people who appreciate them to get hold of; and I am sure you must be aware that there is something in them which is part of their being so good but, at the same time, a large number of intelligent readers would not appreciate. All this may not be much of a consolation to you though it is very much of a consolation to me as your publisher. I hope you will go on writing out of yourself no matter what happens.

Yours sincerely
Leonard Woolf

To Barbara Middleton

29/1/68   [Monk's House]

Dear Mrs Middleton,
    Mrs Smallwood has shown me your letter and, as I read all three novels submitted by you and am largely responsible for the acceptance and rejections, and as I am always very sorry not to be able to continue with an author whom we have published, I should like to make more clear what I felt about *The Golden Key* and *The Black Swan*.
    The fact that a book pays, and that *Tidal Water* paid its way, is an important fact and makes one want to publish the next book submitted, but I have always been against publishing any book which one thinks falls below a certain standard, merely because it will probably pay.
    The judgment of standard is ultimately a personal matter. Personally I am slightly suspicious of the idea that good books are "compulsively readable". I should have said that on the whole the opposite is true. A novel first of all should have a central idea, and, if it is a great novel, every sentence must be determined and controlled by the central idea. I do not expect novels submitted to the Hogarth Press to be great novels, but I expect them to be to some extent determined by the same standards—or rather I do not publish them unless they do.
    Your first novel seemed to me to have "promise" though it was what I can only call "thin on the ground". The content of a novel must bear a certain relation to its size and will be or ought to be different from

the content of a short story—just as the content of a Keats sonnet will be different from that of *Endymion*.

If Keats had tried to write *Endymion* out of the content suitable for a sonnet, his poetry would have been thin on the ground. That is what I was thinking of when I said that the content of your novel was only strong enough to bear the weight of a short story—inadequate for a full length novel. This has nothing to do with its being "written with my heart's blood". Of course the heart's blood is important, but it is the emotion which controls or should control the tension of the book. But when you come to write the first sentence and every damned sentence after it, you dont write it with your heart's blood but with your brain and your typewriter—or you should do. Are you going to write: "He sat down in the comfortable armchair and lit a cigarette", and dozens of other sentences like that? There will be no heart's blood about that. But if you get your content/size wrong, you will write dozens of sentences like that and your novel will be thin on the ground—ultimately because each sentence wanders on its own account instead of being determined and controlled by the idea, the central idea of the book—and note it is the idea, not the heart's blood, which in this way should determine and control each individual sentence.

Yours sincerely
Leonard Woolf

17, The Green,
Richmond.

21 Dec 1914

Dear Mrs Webb,

Very many thanks for
your letter. I should much like, if the executive
of the Fabian Society approve, to do the work on
Internationalism which you suggest & in the way
you suggest — namely that I should act as
Secretary to a small Committee of the Research
Department & that the report would be published
with my name attached as the Author. The only stipulation
which I would make is that the committee would
not require anything to appear over my name

TO BEATRICE WEBB

PART FIVE

———

"Socialist
of a Rather
Peculiar Sort"

Political affairs were Leonard Woolf's central professional interest. Yet, like much else in his life, involvement in politics came about more by chance than by design. He had left Cambridge and gone to Ceylon in a state of political innocence. After single-handedly governing 100,000 people, he returned home mildly curious about how his own country was ruled. Mild curiosity was transformed into active engagement by several women. Margaret Vaughan, one of Virginia's cousins, enticed him into charitable work in the East End of London; the shock at the sight of the human wreckage of the capitalist system converted him literally overnight into a socialist. Margaret Llewelyn Davies, a woman so formidable that Virginia said she "could compel a steam roller to waltz," introduced him to the Women's Co-operative Guild, which gave him a glimpse of what life was like for working-class wives. Through his wife and her friends he became active in the woman suffrage movement. And Beatrice Webb recruited him into the Fabian Society and the Labour Party. By mid-1913 Leonard had been through a personal political revolution and emerged simultaneously a feminist and a socialist, albeit, as he himself said, "a socialist of a rather peculiar sort."

The qualification is crucial. Capitalism may have made Leonard a convinced socialist, but Cambridge had left him with a moral independence that took priority over everything. No doctrine, group or institution could ever command his unqualified commitment. He would work unremittingly for socialism, the Women's Co-operative Guild, the Fabian Society and the Labour Party, but none would be more than a means to a higher goal. E. M. Forster's statement, which came straight out of Cambridge Apostolicism, that if he had to choose between betraying his country and betraying his friends, he hoped he would have the guts to betray his country is not one Leonard would have made. Both friends and country were subordinate to his ethical and social ideals.

These ideals, reduced to their basic elements, were simple, even if they appeared at the time to be either dangerously revolutionary or naïvely utopian. At home he wanted a socialist welfare state as a way of achieving social equality and social justice. Abroad he envisaged replacing "a psychology of a conflict of interests" with "a psychology of common interests"; more concretely, exchanging nationalistic real-politik and rival alliance systems for collective-security arrangements and arms control. In imperial affairs, he called for an acceptance of racial and ethnic equality and a recognition of the right of every nation to govern itself.

Historians usually place Leonard Woolf in the intellectual tradition of British Radicalism. And in fact he was closely linked through friend-ship and his Cambridge connections with many of the prominent twentieth-century incarnations of this spirit—J. A. Hobson, Norman Angell, E. D. Morel, G. L. Dickinson, G. P. Gooch, the Trevelyans and Buxtons, Bertrand Russell and Helene Maria Swanwick. He was also associated through membership in both the Independent Labour Party, the left wing of the Labour Party, and the Union of Democratic Control, the Liberal-Labour group founded in September 1914 to agitate for parliamentary oversight of foreign policy. To a greater or lesser extent he shared the Radicals' preconceptions—that the more socialism and democracy, the less chance of social discord and war; that capitalists and conservatives were responsible for most national and international ills; that as the First World War had resulted from alliances and armaments competition, so collective security and disarmament would insure peace. Ultimately, however, Leonard's politics were based not on ideology but on independent pragmatic analysis, and this eventually led him to part company with all of his early ideological companions.

Leonard had two traits that further qualified his relationship with institutional politics. The motive behind his engagement was a sense of duty; the aim was service, not power. This quality was the pure essence of Cambridge and can in fact be traced to a paper he read to the Apostles in May 1903, which argued that philosophers had a responsibility to commend to princes those policies that "will produce the best possible results." The other quality, developed in Ceylon, was a remarkable capacity for empathy. His unusual ability to understand the feelings of Sinhalese villagers was transformed into a similar capacity to comprehend working-class disenfranchised women, the London proletariat, the blacks in Africa and the desire of colonials to be independent.

But in practical politics it is between principle and expediency, between ideals and policies that the shadow falls. Duty and empathy never won a parliamentary debate, an argument with a government minister or an election. The naked desire for power and the willingness to sacrifice principles for it were notions Leonard had great difficulty grasping. The point is illustrated by a letter in 1929 to Sidney Webb, Colonial Secretary in the Labour government of the time, about the treatment of the blacks in Kenya. Leonard had already been to see Webb personally to protest the fact that white settlers in Kenya were taxed proportionately far less than blacks but received a vastly higher portion of the colony's budget for the education of their children and for the construction of roads to their estates. After getting a brush-off, he went back to Webb in writing, and the text and tone of the letter are instructive. He simply could not believe that Webb—and the Labour Party leadership—had no intention of implementing the party's colonial program; he could not credit that a socialist would fail to sympathize with the impoverished natives. Some years later, as he recounts in *Downhill All the Way*, he had a somewhat similar experience with Clement Attlee over India.

His frustration steadily mounted as the party and the trade unions compromised or abandoned one socialist position after another. As he wrote to Julian Bell in 1935, "Nine tenths of the Trade Unionists even are not socialists and are indeed as much scared of socialism as the old ladies of Balham & Tooting." He remained loyal, though, and worked for the party with the utmost devotion. He saw no alternative. Labour was at least headed in the right direction at home and was less inclined to follow nationalistic and militaristic policies abroad. And so, as he wrote in another letter, "in 999 cases out of 1000 I should prefer to vote for a bad Labour candidate rather than a good Tory candidate."

Leonard's commitment to ideals rather than institutions can be seen in other ways, large and small. All the paraphernalia of class privilege and social ritual were instinctively repugnant to him. Titles and official honors he found ridiculous, and it pained him when a person he respected accepted one. He refused a Companion of Honour when Prime Minister Harold Wilson offered it and would not accept an invitation to a Buckingham Palace garden party. Respectability and respectable institutions, social organizations and London clubs left him queasy. Typically he declined to join PEN and, soon after helping to establish them, resigned from the Royal Institute of International Affairs and the Executive Council of the League of Nations Union. And though he held conservatives and capitalists to be the twin pillars of social privilege and the class system, it was people who subordinated themselves to a millennial ideology who earned his particular mistrust. For him, as for George Orwell, Communism and Roman Catholicism were the great anathemas, propounding the notion of absolute, knowable truths and universal laws—supernatural or dialectical—which govern human life.

What troubled Leonard about messianic beliefs, secular or religious, was their social effect. In practice they were the enemy of toleration, and toleration was the keystone of civilized society. Two men he ardently admired were Erasmus and Montaigne, men whose principles and example might have saved Europe from the wars of religion. Therein lay another of his deepest beliefs: Intolerance eventually breeds violence, and violence always destroys civilization. In one of the most despairing comments in his autobiography, he asked rhetorically, "What is the point, one feels, of any political, social, scientific, or intellectual activity if civilized people in the twentieth century not only accept as divine truth the myths dreamed by Palestinian Jews two or three thousand years ago or by German Jews a hundred years ago, but also condemn to Hell, death, or Siberia those who disagree with them?"

This is the ideological background of the correspondence in this chapter. The letters record seventy-five years of Leonard's political activity. Unfortunately they cannot give a fully rounded impression of his career. Party work was carried out in committees and private meetings; most of his important contributions were recorded in minutes and lengthy memoranda for the party executive. His views on issues of the day were elaborated in books, articles and pamphlets. Moreover, this is an area of his professional work where the losses of correspondence are particularly severe. Judging by his diaries, he devoted more of his time in 1916 and 1917 to the woman suffrage movement than any other interest, but not a single letter on his work survives. Similarly his activities with regard to the various interwar issues—the Bolshevik revolution, the Black and Tans, Russian famine relief, the General Strike, the Irish problem, reform of the foreign-policy machinery and the diplomatic service and the Nazis' seizure of power, to mention a few—have left no epistolary record. His voluminous correspondence with E. W. Perera, a Colombo lawyer, concerning his efforts to arrange an official inquiry into the 1915 riots in Ceylon could not be retrieved from the National Archives of Sri Lanka, and there are no letters from him on the subject in the Public Record Office. Nothing could be found on his contacts with European socialists between the wars or his meetings with Chaim Weizmann, Sir Lewis Namier and others on Zionism. Despite the losses, the letters and several memoranda in this chapter lay out his views on the broad questions of foreign and imperial policy and offer a more personal and intimate dimension than do his published works. Though the specific topics are now passé, the underlying issues he addressed live on today and his views are as relevant and cogent as ever.

The earliest letters record Leonard's plunge into the gray world of the Women's Co-operative Guild. He was deeply impressed by these working-class women, and his first project was a study of wages and working conditions of women in industry. The inequity of women's wages was a subject he was still writing about at the end of his life. He became a regular contributor to *Co-operative News* and in the following several years produced seven books on the cooperative movement. He had great expectations for Cooperation, which he wanted to transform into an instrument of political education for women and ultimately a feminist force within the political left, able to stand up equally to capitalist entrepreneurs and to male-dominated trade unions. The goal was a chimera, the only one he chased in his political life.

Leonard's work in the Guild quickly caught the attention of Beatrice Webb, who brought him into the Fabian Society. At this point, fate, now in the shape of the First World War, intervened further to change the course of his career. Although not a pacifist, like most of his Cambridge friends, he opposed British entry into the war and favored a negotiated settlement. In his view the conflict had resulted from a criminally reckless "war party" in each of the major powers; Britain had allowed itself to be drawn in as a result of secret agreements and Parliament's lack of control over foreign policy. He was obsessed with the conviction that the war had resulted from wild miscalculation and was the greatest offense against reason and civilization in modern history. So when the Webbs and G. B. Shaw asked him to write a study for the Fabians on the causes of war and how to reduce them, he immediately accepted. His letter to Beatrice Webb about this was the beginning of his political career.

Leonard's report was published in 1916 under the title *International Government*. Though its concepts are commonplace today, it was highly original at the time and no doubt the most influential book he ever produced. His starting point was that it was "impossible to make war impossible, but possible to make it less probable." To this end he proposed the establishment of an international authority to provide the machinery and moral impetus to settle disputes. His study was a key document in the work leading to the founding of the League of Nations. The proposals and the principles behind them were largely incorporated in the Covenant of the League and were retained in the United Nations Charter. The premise that had animated Leonard and guided all his political work thereafter was the conviction that national interests are not necessarily opposed and that military force should be used only for defensive purposes.

His work took a new turn in the last year of the war. By then the Labour Party was on its way to replacing the Liberals as the second force in British politics. Its leaders, mostly trade unionists, had no knowledge of foreign affairs and established a committee to advise them. Leonard agreed to be Secretary and for the next quarter-century or so he and the committee sent the party executive hundreds of policy analyses and recommendations. He wrote an initial series of memoranda during the last months of the war that are remarkable in their farsightedness and their courage in countering the anti-German mood at the time. These documents opposed the proposal to set up the League of Nations as an anti-German military alliance; they attacked the war-guilt clause, the imposition of huge reparations and the exclusion of Germany and Austria from the League. What is of most interest is the heart of his argument—that a stable international order had to be based on cooperation among states rather than on military competition, an obvious point, no doubt, but one that was certainly not accepted at the time and that took another world war before it was grasped by the states concerned.

Leonard hoped that out of the wreckage of the war would emerge, if not a new world, at least a radically different approach to international relations. The peace settlement of 1919 consequently came as a profound shock; both its terms and the way they were reached seemed to him politically and morally compromised. The treatment of Germany was bound in his view to encumber the very political and economic recovery vital to Europe. Of the Versailles Treaty he commented: "It is not a peace but a truce." He thought something might be salvaged if relations between states could gradually be placed on a new basis and if his own country followed different foreign-policy principles. His hopes were pinned on two institutions. The League of Nations might render the old balance-of-power politics obsolete and develop into an effective instrument for the peaceful settlement of international disputes. And the Labour Party might wean Britain away from a foreign policy based on narrow nationalism and reliance on military force.

Imperial issues were Leonard's other great interest. When the Advisory Committee on Imperial Questions was established in 1924, he agreed to be Secretary. There were two key colonial issues between the wars. One centered on the question of self-government. In Leonard's view, every nation should have the right to govern, or misgovern, itself. As early as 1918, he had advocated immediate independence for India as well as for Ceylon, Burma, Egypt, Iraq and Ireland, a view iterated in a 1926 memorandum included here. It was this position that earned him Beatrice Webb's malediction "an anti-imperialist fanatic." But what motivated him was neither fanaticism nor woolly-minded idealism. "The perpetual tragedy of history," he insisted over and over, "is that things are perpetually being done ten or twenty years too late." In his opinion the growth of nationalism made the transfer of power inevitable; the only question was whether it would be timely, willing and peaceful or late, grudging and violent. No one else conducted so persistent a campaign on behalf of a rapid, voluntary and peaceful transition. Meanwhile, Ceylon continued to engage his personal attention and his memorandum in 1938 on a solution to the Tamil-Sinhalese problem is striking in its foresight, being very close to the settlement reached fully fifty years later, after a decade of brutal civil violence.

The other imperial issue that engaged his attention was the special problem of Africa. In *Empire and Commerce in Africa*, which he wrote in 1918, Leonard had condemned the expansion of the British Empire into the subcontinent. He accepted that self-government for the African colonies was not yet possible and would only open the way to rule by white settlers. But he insisted that independence and majority rule must be the goal and, to lead directly to it, that policies should be implemented for the education and training of the native population. The most pressing problem lay in East Africa, with its large white population. Leonard wanted to forestall the establishment of white-controlled indigenous legislatures, to counteract racial discrimination—the color bar—and to insure that the Colonial Office and local

377

governments administered the colonies in the interest of the native population rather than the white minority.

All the policy proposals of the two advisory committees were approved by the party executive. But Leonard feared that unless the party formally committed itself to implementing them, once in power, the recommendations would be no more than platitudes. Hence his tactical objective was to get such a commitment. In this he failed. When in November 1928 he sent Ramsay MacDonald a memorandum entitled "First Measures in Foreign Affairs Which Might Be Taken by a Labour Government," MacDonald typically replied: "Something a little more advisory and less mandatory would be an improvement." The trouble was that Leonard and the other committee members were on the left of the party. The leaders were extreme moderates, who had no intention of altering the direction of colonial rule and thereby antagonizing the middle class, on whom electoral success depended.

So in the end Leonard's recommendations were ignored. In East Africa, successive British governments followed policies favorable to the whites. In Asia, they "sought honourably to dishonour" the promise of self-government, counterbalancing every dollop of concession by a dollop of regression. Leonard was particularly bitter that his party failed to do even the little it might have done during its brief stints in power in 1924 and 1929–31. Several committee members resigned in frustration. Leonard stayed to fight another day, in accord with a political beatitude of his own invention: "Blessed is he who expects nothing, for unexpectedly he may somewhere, some time achieve something."

Leonard's disillusionment with imperial policy was negligible compared to his bottomless despair over foreign policy in these years. His views were well summed up in his parliamentary campaign platform for the 1922 election: The keystone of peace in Europe was collaboration among Britain, France and Germany; world peace required close cooperation between Europe and the United States; disarmament must be a central objective. Above all came the League of Nations. Either there would be a strong League or there would be a return to the old military competition, leaving Europe poised for another war. These views were generally shared by the Labour and Liberal parties and a few independent Conservatives, such as Lord Robert Cecil. But it was the Tory Party that governed for seventeen of the twenty years between wars, and Leonard never doubted that its rhetorical support for the League was as insincere as its rhetorical promise of self-government for India.

The nightmare years began with Hitler's rise to power. Few in Britain

378

recognized the nature of the Nazi regime as early as Leonard. "According to standards of what has been thought to be civilization for the last two thousand years, it is one of the most savage and senseless dictatorships that has been tolerated by a civilized European population for at least two centuries" is the way he described it in the *Political Quarterly* a few months after the Nazi takeover. He was also quicker than most in recognizing the collective threat that Germany, Japan and Italy posed to the world order. Gradually it became clear to him that there were three possible responses: appeasement, a military alliance accompanied by rearmament or common action on behalf of the League. It was the third course he favored, even while recognizing that the collective-security principles of the League might entail going to war. This brought him into conflict with the powerful pacifist element in the Labour Party, as his letters to Kingsley Martin and H. M. Swanwick testify.

The refusal of Britain and France to enforce the Covenant when Italy invaded Abyssinia left in ruins everything Leonard had hoped for since 1918. It meant, as he wrote to Julian Bell, "The League is dead; collective security is dead and rotten." A black nihilism steals into his letters at this point. A year later, when Britain and France permitted the Germans to occupy the Rhineland, he realized that Hitler was free to change the European order through force. With the German annexation of Austria in 1938, Leonard concluded that the sole chance of avoiding either war or further surrenders was rapid rearmament and a broad antifascist alliance. This was the position he advocated in several advisory-committee memoranda; it split the committee and the party down the middle.

On one point—alliance with the Soviet Union—Leonard wavered. Having considered the tsarist regime the most loathsome in Europe, he had welcomed the Russian Revolution and helped to organize the 1917 Club to celebrate the Tsar's downfall. The first decision he and the Labour Party advisory committee made in 1918 was to oppose Western military intervention in the Russian civil war. Soon afterward he personally called for a normalization of diplomatic and economic relations. But, although he always had a soft spot in his heart for the Soviet Union, he was by 1920 disillusioned with Lenin and developed a particular loathing of the Soviet government, in a way more intense than that he had of Nazi Germany, since he saw it as a corruption of a noble ideal. By 1938 he regarded Germany as so immediate a threat to European peace, however, that he saw no alternative to an Anglo-Soviet military pact. Since this was not the policy of the Conservative government, he looked to Churchill as the only possible leader and lent his support to those trying to arrange a coalition government under him.

During the war Leonard went on with his work for the party, giving his attention to such issues as economic recovery, postwar colonial policy and a successor organization to the League. With Labour's victory in 1945, he resigned his advisory positions, but he continued to work for the Fabian Society and to write books and articles on foreign affairs. There was much in the postwar world that gave him great satisfaction. In his own country a broad welfare system was established and poverty largely done away with. As the class structure became more indistinct, there was greater equality of opportunity. The colonies were given independence. Political and military rivalry in Western Europe were replaced by cooperation. But there was also much that caused him to despair—the cold war, the failure of the United Nations, and the spread of Communism.

His views on many of these issues emerge from letters to Kingsley Martin, to whom he wrote both as a friend and as editor of the *New Statesman*, of which he himself was now a director. In the thirties Leonard had gradually weaned Martin from the leftist-pacifist notion of all war as capitalistic and had convinced him that Italy and Germany were a menace that might have to be resisted by force. What prompted the postwar correspondence, of which only a portion is included, was not just Martin's apologetic line toward the Soviets and the Chinese and his carping attitude toward the United States, but the underlying intellectual muddle that he felt obfuscated critical moral and political issues. This, Leonard considered unforgivable, even writing in an obituary of Martin in the *Political Quarterly* that under his editorship the journal had been a supply line for "a weekly dose of political, social and cultural irritation."

From this postwar correspondence, two themes emerge above all others. It was Leonard's deepest and longest-held belief—discussed with much feeling at the very outset and again at the very end of his autobiography—that there is no higher value than the individual. This he regarded as the moral keystone of the Renaissance. Treating human beings as anonymous, impersonal objects for some higher goal was what had opened the floodgates to all the greater and lesser horrors of the century. He therefore argued that the end cannot justify the means when the means involve killing people—whether Israeli schoolchildren by Arabs or Arabs by Israelis or Communist political leaders by other Communist political leaders or two and a half million Nationalist Chinese by Communist Chinese or Vietnamese by Americans. In his youth the massacre of several thousand Armenians had unleashed a public furor. Now murder on an infinitely worse scale was met with widespread indifference and apologetics by humane editors of enlightened publications. It was this loss after 1914 of a sense of human mercy and justice that convinced him civilization had been killed by the shot in Sarajevo.

The other theme of these letters is the issue he had wrestled with ever since that momentous occasion: how to control human aggression. Whether mankind would succeed was the supreme question. He would have agreed with Freud that the founder of civilization was the first person who had hurled an epithet at his enemy rather than a spear. His political life had been dedicated to encouraging the use of epithets.

* * *

To Margaret Llewelyn Davies

[Postmarked June 13, 1913]

13, Cliffords Inn,
Fleet Street, E.C.

Dear Margaret,

I feel we must thank you for the Congress. I dont know when I've enjoyed anything so much & Virginia feels the same. It was simply absorbing from beginning to end, & everything about it was splendid. I only hope you'll allow us to come again another year. Virginia is so enthusiastic that she will not rest until she is sent some day as a delegate.

Yours

[In VW's hand]   L S W

This is quite true about both of us. Being
ignorant doesnt mean that one cant at least
appreciate. (however, being ignorant only
applies to me) V.W.

To Margaret Llewelyn Davies

27 July 1914   Asheham

Dear Margaret,
Many thanks for your letter. I have had a proof of the article from the *Coop[erative] News*.[1]
I spent a night at Barrow House going up there Monday and coming down Tuesday evening. I opened the discussion on Cooperation & tried to show that there were no limits to the movement in the control of industry. The Webbs, Shaw, Cole & a whole host of young Oxford "rebels" were there.[2] I dont understand Cole; he was very nice to talk to & seemed quite "sympathetic" to the movement, but then made a speech quite hostile to both the theory & practice of Cooperation. He & the rebels are all mad on Guild Socialism. Mrs Webb seems to come more & more over to Cooperation, but perhaps that is because, as I gathered, the Webbs are considered rather out-of-date there! The whole conference seems to me a vague & rather dreary affair & how Shaw & the Webbs, who must know it all by heart, can stand it year after year amazes me. I met two very nice people—an old man from Middlesborough, a W[orkers'] E[ducational] A[ssociation] & housing man. I dont know his name but he was enthusiastic about your Guild women in Middlesborough, especially a Mrs Ramsay. Then a very intelligent American editor called Lippman.[3]
We go to Wooler in Northumberland on Aug 7th.

                                                    Leonard

1. "Co-operative Tradition and Freedom of Discussion," arguing that the Women's Co-operative Guild should not hold itself aloof from political and social issues, appeared on August 1, 1914.
2. Barrow House, near Keswick, was the meeting place of the Fabian Society summer schools 1912–15. G. B. Shaw was one of the earliest and most active Fabians. G. D. H. Cole (1889–1959), Oxford don and prolific writer, joined the Fabian Society in 1908 and was later its chairman; his ambiguities were famous: "Mr. G. D. H. Cole is a bit of a puzzle/ With a Bolshevik soul and a Fabian muzzle."
3. Walter Lippmann (1889–1974), the distinguished American political journalist, spent much of this summer in Britain meeting prominent political intellectuals. LW wrote of their encounter on this occasion in *Beginning Again*.

To Margaret Llewelyn Davies

The Cottage Hotel

13 Aug 1914   Wooler   Northumberland

Dear Margaret,
    . . . I think I must have been rather unjust to the people here. I dont think they're callous but they come from Newcastle & are absolutely imperturbable. They are amazing people on nearer acquaintance with a surprising knowledge of trade, art & literature.
    I still really dont believe that Germany wanted war. I think that as soon as Russia mobilized, things fell absolutely into the hands of the small mad war party. And you know what any Govt is with experts. If the expert says: "With Russia mobilizing you must declare war at once or you'll be overwhelmed, & strategy makes it imperative to invade France through Belgium or you'll be overwhelmed", hardly any Govt would stand up against them. I wish I could believe that it really meant the end of kings & militarism.

L S Woolf

To Margaret Llewelyn Davies

Cottage Hotel

20 Aug 1914   Wooler   Northumberland

Dear Margaret,
    We both enjoyed your letter immensely—especially about the Queen.[1] Really these great ladies are too ridiculous!
    B. H. in the [New] Statesman is, I believe, Dudley Ward, a friend of Ka Cox & married to a German—but I'm not absolutely certain. I thought Bertie Russell in the Nation was very good, didn't you?[2] It does seem to me clear that we were practically pledged to help France & Russia, & that the really fatal thing was that while this egged on Russia, Grey didn't dare clearly tell Germany under what circum-

---

1. Queen Mary was organizing a mass knitting campaign in support of the war effort. The ultimate effect was to damage the woolen knitted-goods industry.
2. Dudley Ward (1885–1957) was Berlin correspondent of the Economist. The New Statesman article described the popular mood in Germany at the outbreak of the war. Russell's long letter in the Nation was epitomized in one sentence: "And all this madness, all this rage, all this flaming death of our civilization and our hopes, has been brought about because a set of official gentlemen, living luxurious lives, mostly stupid, and all without imagination or heart, have chosen that it should occur rather than that anyone of them should suffer some infinitesimal rebuff to his country's pride."

stances we would interfere.[1] We were simply playing into the hands of the war party in both countries, & when Grey did try to extricate himself & take a strong line, it was too late because the war party had got the upper hand. . . .

Leonard

To Beatrice Webb

17, The Green
Richmond.

21 Dec 1914

Dear Mrs Webb,
Very many thanks for your letter.[2] I should much like, if the executive of the Fabian Society approve, to do the work on Internationalism which you suggest & in the way you suggest—namely that I should act as Secretary to a small committee of the Research Deparment & that the report would be published with my name attached as the Author. The only stipulation which I would make is that the committee would not require anything to appear over my name of which I was not the author or with which I did not agree. I presume that this could be arranged provided that the other members of the committee in case of disagreement had the right of appending to the report their dissent or suggestions over their own names.

Leonard Sidney Woolf

To Lytton Strachey

17, The Green,
Richmond.

8 Feb 1915

I am writing this from Rye—Ye Old Flushing Inn. We came here for the week end to find every house & inn filled with soldiers. We thought we should have to return to Richmond, but at the last moment

1. Sir Edward Grey (1862–1933), British Foreign Secretary. Most British Cabinet officials "were so anxious for peace and uncertain of the public attitude that they had failed to give a clear warning which might have strengthened [German Chancellor] Bethmann Hollweg in his feeble efforts to withstand his own war party" (B. H. Liddell Hart, *History of the First World War*).
2. Her letter, which inaugurated LW's political career, asked him to do a study of "international control over Foreign Policy, Armaments and methods of war-fare."

we desperately came here & found absolute comfort. No one in the house except ourselves & very good food. It appears to be some sort of cross between a club & a hotel.

I have been absolutely submerged in Internationalism. The result will I imagine be the lowest pit of dullness. It would make it easier if I knew something about history. I met my "Committee" last week— 14 wretched creatures led by the Webbs, Eagle, & Shaw.[1] The only thing they did was to pass a resolution that they would not even ask me what I was going to do. . . .

L.

To the *Nation*

November 29th, 1916

Hogarth House
Richmond

Sir,— There is one point in connection with the German Chancellor's speech which has, I believe, not been pointed out, but which is of importance for anyone taking a broad view of international relations.[2] The passage in that speech proclaiming Germany's readiness to join a "union of peoples," and accepting "an arbitration court and the peaceful liquidation of conflicting antagonisms" as a method of developing international relations, is essentially a reversal of the official German attitude towards such methods and relations throughout the twenty years preceding 1914. It was one of the most disquieting symptoms of German foreign policy before the war that her statesmen consistently opposed any extension of organized international cooperation which would make the appeal to force in any way more difficult. . . .

Yet if we are to judge from the tone of the comment of the majority of our newspapers on this speech, we are to pay no attention to any sign in our enemies of a willingness to accept the principles for which we are fighting, or rather we should do everything to weaken that willingness in Germany. However long the war goes on, it can only end satisfactorily for us by the responsible statesmen of Germany expressing a willingness to agree to accept our conditions. That is the way in which all other wars have ended, and the only way in which

1. Eagle was the literary pseudonym of J. C. Squire, an active Fabian.
2. Theobald Bethmann Hollweg (1856–1921), chancellor 1909–17, a proponent of a negotiated peace settlement, had spoken before the Reichstag.

385

a war can end, unless the belligerents are exterminated. Yet at the moment we seem to have adopted the policy of not stating what our conditions are and of refusing to pay any attention to any sign of willingness on our opponents' part to accept them.

Yours &.,
Leonard S. Woolf

To Margaret Llewelyn Davies

4 August, 1917

Asheham House
Rodmell, Lewes

Dear Margaret

. . . Dont you think this affair with Henderson and the Government is excellent?[1] I am going to try to get up to London on Friday for the Labour Party Conference, as it seems to me much the most important thing that has happened to Labour during the War. I only hope that Henderson does not wobble. If he stands firm against the jingoes, with Thomas and the railway men and Smillie and the miners, to back him, it might be the making of the Labour Party.[2] I only hope that the I[ndependent] L[abour] P[arty] will have the sense to see that it would be a time to let all by-gones be by-gones and simply back Henderson. I suppose it's too much to expect of the Labour Party that they would have the sense to come out of the Government. But it's amazing that they dont see after last week that their friends will take the very first opportunity of rounding upon them, as soon as they got all they can out of them.

Leonard

1. Arthur Henderson (1863–1935), a Labour Party leader and member of the war cabinet, wanted to attend a proposed meeting of the Socialist International in Stockholm, where it was hoped an agreement on war aims might be reached that would lead to a negotiated peace.
2. Henderson did not wobble, and the party supported his proposal to attend the Stockholm conference. J. H. Thomas (1874–1949) was a railway union leader; Robert Smillie (1857–1940) was leader of the Scottish Miners' Federation, of whom LW wrote affectionately in *Beginning Again*.

To Margaret Llewelyn Davies

Asheham House
Rodmell, Lewes

25 August, 1917

Dear Margaret,

. . . It has been superb here and the days have raced by. We had rather a long spell of visitors and are now rejoicing in the feeling of being absolutely alone. I went up again for the second Conference which was disappointing after the first. The policy of Snowden and the I.L.P. was hopeless as I felt from the first it probably would be.[1] Instead of making that embittered speech, Snowden ought to have said that what the I.L.P wanted was the Conference and were quite willing to waive all right to special representation. If he had done that the majority for Stockholm would have remained huge and the minority would almost certainly have secured representation. Instead of that they have now lost everything. But Snowden and the I.L.P.ers are so bitter and truculent that they can see nothing except a tiny segment of the horizon. In their way they are almost as bad as the bellicose Thornes and Roberts's.[2] Snowden apparently defended his policy by saying that he had the Labour Party on the run, and he did not see why therefore the I.L.P. should give up the reins. Anything more childish one can hardly imagine. What a bore it all is: extremists hopeless because they are as blind as mad bulls, and moderates hopeless because they are moderate![3]

Leonard

1. Philip Snowden (1864–1937), Chairman of the Independent Labour Party 1903–06, a pacifist during the First World War, Chancellor of the Exchequer 1924 and 1929–31. In LW's view, Snowden was less concerned about whether the Stockholm meeting would take place than about separate ILP representation if it did.
2. W. J. Thorne (1857–1946) was an active trade unionist. G. H. Roberts (1869–1928) quit the ILP in 1914 and eventually went over to the Tories.
3. In the end neither the British nor the French government would grant exit visas, and the Stockholm conference did not materialize. Henderson resigned from the government and devoted himself to revamping the party's organization and program.

To Margaret Llewelyn Davies

23 Sept [1918]   Asheham

Dear Margaret
    . . . The Webbs were really rather nice & human—in a strange
inhuman way—as guests. I got no more entangled. George Young also
came. Do you know him? A brother of Hilton & Geoffrey. Mrs Webb
is surprisingly old & worn, I think, & talking of retirement & the end.
"No," Webb said to her, "we shant retire or end like that. I know
exactly what our end will be. It will come when one of us has a stroke.
About the age of 65."

                                                    Leonard.

Memorandum to the Parliamentary Labour Party

November 8th 1918

          Advisory Committee on International Questions
            Note on Self-Government for Ceylon

    I wish to bring the following question before the Committee. The
[Executive] Committee has already dealt with the question of reform
in India.[1] Now the Crown Colony of Ceylon is from the point of view
of self-government in almost precisely the same position as India. There
is first the same demand for responsible Government, and the same
system of autocratic bureaucracy. The peoples of Ceylon are certainly
on the average the equals of the peoples of India in education and
political capacity. The only real difference is that in Ceylon there has
been no violent political unrest or terrorism.
    If a large measure of responsible Government be granted to India
and not to Ceylon, the position will be grotesque and impossible. Why
within the British Empire should the Tamils of Southern India be
allowed to manage their own affairs while the Tamils of northern
Ceylon are denied all rights of self-government? Yet that apparently
is the position which the Colonial Office desires to bring into existence.
To all questions in the House of Commons with regard to the necessity

1. In 1917 the British government promised the people of India "responsible government
. . . as an integral part of the British Empire."

388

for bringing Ceylon reform into line with the proposed Indian reforms, the Secretary of State [for the Colonies] presents the blank wall answer that the time is not opportune for discussing the question. But again why is the time opportune not only for discussion but for giving responsible Government to the Tamils of Southern India, if it is not opportune for considering the demand for responsible government from the Tamils of Northern Ceylon?

The truth of course is that if a measure of responsible government is not granted to Ceylon in the period of reconstruction after the war, it will be delayed for years—and it looks as though the Colonial Office desires this. It is essential therefore that the Government should undertake to give the same measure of responsible government to Ceylon as it gives to India. This is a matter in which, I suggest, the Labour Party could rightly take action by asking for a pledge from the Government that at least an equal measure of reform will be introduced into the Ceylon as into the Indian Constitution.

LEONARD WOOLF

To Margaret Llewelyn Davies

Monk's House

5 April 1920

Rodmell

Dear Margaret,

. . . I hope you dont think I'm anti-Bolshevik. I'm not. I think they're the only people who've made an honest and serious attempt to practice what I believe in. But I cant help seeing their faults & mistakes which, if persisted in, will undo the good they've done. Perhaps however it's only the original sin of Governments.

I am afraid you must be very worried over the Guild. Advice & other people's opinions are always useless, but I'm quite sure if you resign & take a holiday, you'll find things overwhelm you again as soon as you come back.[1] One thing you ought to do is to organize a women's wing of the Labour Party.

Yours
Leonard

1. She retired the following year, after more than thirty years of voluntary work for the Women's Co-operative Guild.

To Sidney Webb

31st May 1920
[Hogarth House
Richmond, Surrey]

Dear Webb,
I have been asked by the Seven Universities' Democratic Association whether I will stand at the next election as their candidate.[1] Of course, as a member of the Labour Party I could not stand against a Labour candidate, but I understand that last time, when [J. A.] Hobson stood for them, the Labour Party treated him as their candidate. Do you think there would be any possibility of their doing the same with me, and that I could be given an assurance at this time that if I accept I shall not find myself opposed by a Labour candidate?[2]

Yours sincerely
Leonard Woolf

To Lord Robert Cecil[3]

11th April 1921
[Hogarth House]

Dear Lord Robert Cecil,
I have to thank you very much for your letter, and also for taking the trouble to write me about my book.[4]
. . . In our society the interests of the workers *are* in conflict with the interests of the capitalists—not all their interests, but all their main economic interests—because the whole of society is organized on the assumption and basis of such a conflict. The capitalist is forced to

1. Until 1948 English universities were represented in Parliament, with two seats each for Cambridge, London and Oxford and two for the remaining seven. It was the combined-universities constituency for which LW was asked to be a candidate.
2. Webb replied: "You may certainly proceed with confidence," and when the general election was held in 1922, LW was in fact treated as the Labour candidate. Reckoning his chances of election to be nil, he spoke at only four of the universities. He came third in the polling.
3. Edgar Algernon Robert Gascoyne-Cecil (1864–1958), independent Conservative in the House of Commons 1906–23 and a founder of the League of Nations. He was awarded the Nobel Peace Prize in 1937 and was created Viscount Cecil of Chelwood in 1923.
4. He had praised *International Government* while questioning LW's contention that national interests could be more easily reconciled than class interests. "I know," he had written, "you have the authority of the Prime Minister in support but that does not recommend it to me. . . . Is not class war and class consciousness and all the rest of it really only another form of the same vice as underlies extreme nationalism?"

struggle to increase his profits, or economically he will be lost, the worker is forced to struggle to increase or maintain his wages, or he will be lost: but to maintain or increase profits necessitates a struggle by the capitalist against the worker to decrease or prevent an increase of wages, and vice versa.

This is a completely different situation from that which exists in the world of nations. There is nothing in the organization of the society of nations which assumes and makes inevitable such a conflict of interests, although of course, as I said, some of the interests of some nations are in conflict with some of the interests of other nations.

. . . Personally I think that the class war and the conflict of class interests are the greatest curses, and that the first thing that one should aim at is to abolish this conflict and class war. I think you want exactly the same kind of cooperation between individuals and classes in a nation as you want between nations, but that you cannot possibly get it so long as society is organized as it is today. I have just written a book [*Socialism and Co-operation*] which ought to be published in a week or so, dealing very largely with this point, and if you will allow me I will send you a copy of it as soon as it comes out.

Yours sincerely,
Leonard Woolf

To Margery Waterlow[1]

14 January, 1925   [52 Tavistock Square]

Dear Margery,

There is nothing impertinent about your letter. But you do not, I think, touch upon the point which, in my opinion, is absolutely indefensible with regard to this Chinese Committee business. The point is not whether there are not just as good or better people who might be put upon the Committee instead of Bertie and Goldie. I daresay there may be, and if they had been appointed to it originally, I should have said nothing against it. I should have said nothing, too, if worse people had originally been appointed. The point is that one Prime

---

1. Margery Waterlow née Eckhard (1883–1973), second wife of Sydney Waterlow, had taken issue with LW for criticizing the Baldwin government's removal of Bertrand Russell and G. L. Dickinson from the Boxer Indemnity Committee. Of Russell she wrote: "I met him at dinner recently and came to the conclusion that he looks evil and grows worse as he grows older."

Minister having appointed two people of considerable distinction but whose views are not acceptable to the official world, within ten days of a Conservative Government coming into power the new government as its first official act kicks these two persons off the Committee. Such a thing has never been done before and is contrary to every tradition of decency and courtesy. What would the papers—and the Foreign Office too—have said if MacDonald had used the first fortnight of his coming into power to kick well-known capitalists off committees who had been appointed by Baldwin? If I have any say in the Labour Party when it next comes into office, I shall recommend them to kick all conservatives off such committees wholesale.

As to the personal question about Goldie and Bertie. I do not agree in everything with either. But how you or Sydney can maintain that either in intelligence or in decency they are not infinitely superior to 99 per cent of respectable conservatives appointed to Government Committees, I really cannot imagine. If everyone who was old, "looked wicked", or was even half imbecile had to be ignominiously kicked off Government committees, committees would all lose three quarters of their most respectable and distinguished members.

I hope we shall soon meet again and continue the discussion verbally.

Yours
Leonard Woolf

To Ramsay MacDonald[1]

52 Tavistock Square
19 June, 1925   London, W.C.1.

Dear MacDonald,

A good many people think that it might do some good for Salvemini[2]—at any rate as regards his treatment in prison—if a question of a non-provocative kind, but showing that responsible people here were concerned, were asked in Parliament, e.g. possibly in the form "whether the Professor Salvemini just arrested by the Italian Government is the same Professor Salvemini who gave the series of historical lectures in London last year". I do not know whether you

1. James Ramsay MacDonald (1866–1937), chairman of the Independent Labour Party 1906–09, leader of the Labour Party 1911–14 and 1922–31, Prime Minister 1924, 1929–31 and 1931–35. He was one of the few persons LW deeply disliked.
2. Gaetano Salvemini (1873–1957), the eminent Italian historian and antifascist.

think this advisable or, whether if you do you would consider asking such a question yourself. Could you possibly let me have a word saying what you think about it on Monday?[1]

Yours sincerely
Leonard Woolf

MEMORANDUM TO THE TRADES UNION
CONGRESS AND THE LABOUR PARTY

Questionnaire on Subject Peoples

by Mr. L. S. Woolf [2]

Should these peoples be granted self-government immediately?

It is necessary to consider different classes of peoples separately.

(1) *Mandated territory in Asia.* This consists of (a) Irak, which should be given self-government immediately; (b) Palestine, which should be given self-government in accordance with the terms of the Mandate and Balfour Declaration.

(2) *Crown Colonies etc.*, excluding those in Africa. The measure of self-government demanded by the inhabitants of these territories, e.g. Ceylon, should be granted immediately.

(3) *African territories.* Here the African inhabitants are not in a position to govern themselves. In many places, e.g. Kenya, the grant of self-government would merely mean that the inhabitants would fall into the power of the white settlers, who would usurp all political power. The immediate grant of self-government would be disastrous.

. . . The only thing which can be done immediately is to do everything possible to prepare the peoples for self-government. This can only be done by: (a) Preventing political power falling into the hands of [white] minorities who will use it for their own political and economic interests. It follows that the central legislative and executive power must remain completely in the hands of the Imperial Government—i.e., the Colonial Office which is responsible to the two Houses of Parliament. No measure of "responsible government" can at present be granted and it should never be granted unless and until it is certain that the Gov-

1. MacDonald, an admirer of Mussolini, responded that it would not be possible.
2. This memorandum, submitted on behalf of the Advisory Committee on Imperial Questions in January 1926, may have been in anticipation of the Imperial Conference of this year, which dealt with intra-Empire relations.

ernment will be responsible to and controlled by the African inhabitants; (b) Education of the native inhabitants. This must be undertaken in two ways:– (1) General education: this must aim at making the inhabitants capable of understanding and dealing with the political, economic, and social conditions of the modern world which are the result of the penetration of Africa by European civilization. . . . (2) Political education: this can only be achieved by training the inhabitants in local self-government wherever this is possible. Whereever there are self-governing local organs, these should be encouraged and developed by the central government; where such do not exist they should be created. The aim should be gradually to extend the area and powers of these local self-governing organs.

To Sidney Webb[1]

24 October, 1929   [52 Tavistock Square]

My dear Webb,

I hope you wont think it an impertinence on my part, after the patience with which you heard us and the time you gave us, if I now trouble you in writing.[2] I only do so because there are just two points which I could not mention at the time and one which seems to me so crucial that I should like, if possible, to make clear my position. I will begin with the two points not mentioned at our interview.

1. I submit that it is most important that the Labour Government should show by acts pretty promptly that it is not going to be contented with a mere iteration of general principles regarding trusteeship. Now there is prima facie evidence for believing that the incidence of taxation in Kenya is grossly unfair to the native and that the apportionment of a fair or adequate proportion of the revenue to native interests and areas has not been insisted on. I suggest that this is a case in which the Secretary of State [for the Colonies] might take immediate action. . . .

2. Ever since the Labour Government came in and even before, I have felt that it is extraordinarily important that it should find someone

1. Webb was appointed Secretary of State for the Colonies and raised to the peerage, as Baron Passfield, during MacDonald's second Labour government.
2. Webb's meeting with LW and C. R. Buxton, Chairman of the Advisory Committee on Imperial Questions, is recounted in *Downhill All the Way*, though mistakenly dated 1930.

who, as Governor in Kenya, would not be afraid to stand up to the planters if necessary. The only man in the service of whom I have ever heard anything which would make me think that he might do so is Clementi who is now Governor in Hong Kong.[1] I do not know him personally, but my brother-in-law [Southorn] is Colonial Secretary there and I have heard a good deal about Clementi from my sister [Bella]. I must admit that I do not set very great store by her judgment; on the other hand, I have got the impression that it is just possible that, properly instructed by a Secretary of State, he would be less pliable to the wrong kind of settler than previous Governors. I hope it is not impertinent of me to write this, but I thought you might like to know even a vague impression of this kind.

3. The third point is . . . that the Government of Kenya has displayed deplorable weakness in many respects where the settlers have pressed their interests against those of the natives. The last demand of the settlers has been (1) the abolition of the official majority and (2) an increase of the elected European members. Now is it wise for a Labour Government, by one of its first acts, still further to weaken the [Kenyan] Government's position by giving in to either or both of these demands? Is it likely that the local administration will be encouraged to stand up to the settlers or that the settlers will be encouraged to moderate their previous attitude towards the government, if the first act of the Secretary of State [for the Colonies] is to concede what has hitherto been refused on the ground that it would weaken the government? An increase of the elected Europeans would, I submit, be especially disastrous from this point of view. . . .

I hope you will forgive me for putting the case as I see it so strongly and at such length.

Yours sincerely
Leonard Woolf

---

1. Sir Cecil Clementi (1875–1947) was an outstanding member of the Colonial Civil Service; he served with distinction in Hong Kong, British Guiana, Ceylon, and the Malay States.

To Frank Hardie[1]

52 Tavistock Square
11 October, 1933   W.C.1.

Dear Mr Hardie,

Many thanks for your letter and for the copy of your article which I had already read with great interest.[2] I think we probably agree to the extent of about 95%. Even on the subject of isolation I have always been strongly drawn to the policy under certain conditions. But the conditions do not at present exist and I feel the gravest doubts as to their ever existing. It is not merely the millionaire press of which I am afraid, but the whole psychology of nationalism and patriotism which has been generated since 1900. In deciding on a long term policy it would be fatal to ignore that psychology. You cannot ignore the fate of the isolationalist policy of the United States where it had an infinitely better chance of succeeding than it would ever have here in the next ten years. And nothing seems to me quite so bad as an isolationist policy which misfires.

Yours sincerely
Leonard Woolf

To Philip Noel-Baker[3]

Monk's House
11 March, 1934   Rodmell, near Lewes   Sussex.

My dear Phil,

. . . You know that I entirely agree with you about collective security and that nothing but it can stand between the world and war. The disorientation in the forces on the Left with regard to the League is appalling. The sanctions madmen I have never been able to understand; they are people who believe in political absolute truths and like all absolutists end in the clouds or the mire. But I see the difficulties

1. Frank Hardie (b. 1911), best known as the President of the Oxford Union who organized the "King and Country" debate in February 1933, was a lecturer at the London School of Economics.
2. "Youth, Socialism and Peace" had appeared in the *Week-end Review*, September 30, 1933. It advocated general European disarmament or, failing that, British unilateral disarmament and a policy of isolationism.
3. Philip Noel-Baker (1889–1982), member of the League of Nations Secretariat 1920–22, Labour MP 1929–31, 1936–70, Air Minister 1946–47, Commonwealth Minister 1947–50, was one of LW's closest political friends. He received the Nobel Peace Prize in 1959.

of the Cripps, Attlees, Laskis, and even Brailsfords at the moment, and I am sure that some restatement of the Party's League policy is required. . . .[1]

Yours
Leonard Woolf

TO THE *NEW STATESMAN*[2]

16 February 1935   [Monk's House]

Sir,— You have started a very live hare—or rather two hares—in the discussion on war and capitalism, and I am sure that we shall see them go hopping off most lively in opposite directions. Brailsford has already gone off on the back of one, and next week I suppose we shall see the nimble Angell rip away on the other. But since they both wish to get to the same destination, would it not be wiser to pause for a second and consider whether they won't have a better chance of getting there by putting the two hares into double harness?

. . . "Where are the causes of war?" is the right question. Angell says: "In people's heads"; Brailsford says: "In the economic structure of society." Both are right, but both are wrong when they implicitly deny or ignore the causes which the other is insisting on.

Brailsford in his letter has shown Angell to be wrong, by insisting—I think, rightly—on the enormous effect of the economic structure of present-day society upon the policy of imperialist and protectionist states. It creates a situation in which states drift or are forced into war and it puts into the heads of individuals and classes ideas regarding their economic interests which almost inevitably result in war, if those individuals and classes have—and they do have—a major say in determining policy. Angell's thesis does not apply, I agree, to this actual world of armed, protectionist, capitalist, imperialist states; it applies only to an ideal world of reasonable, free trade, mild-mannered capitalists. The Socialist analysis is indeed irrefutable if it is put in its

1. The left of the party condemned the League as a cartel of sated capitalist states; the right supported it but were frightened of sanctions.
2. In the February 2 issue, Kingsley Martin had attacked Norman Angell's *Preface to Peace*, just published, for its faulty analysis of the causes of war. The following week Noel Brailsford, in a letter to the editor, criticized Angell for ignoring economic factors. LW's letter here and subsequent replies by Angell and others were published in a small book, *Does Capitalism Cause War?*

397

right form, i.e., that the existing protectionist, imperialist structure of capitalist society must almost inevitably sooner or later produce war, whatever may be in the heads of the masses of the population.

But that, of course, is not exactly what Brailsford says. Just as Angell ignores the truth in Brailsford's thesis, so Brailsford ignores the truth in Angell's thesis. The causes of war are much too complex and multifarious to be covered exclusively either by economics or by psychology. I claim to be a Socialist, but I have never understood how the extreme Marxist or even the non-extreme Marxist who claims to be orthodox can believe that the world is as simple as he tells us it is. The millions who fought in the last war on Brailsford's theory (and mine and Marx's) were fighting for everything which was contrary to their own economic interests. They fought—and will fight again—because they had in their heads the delusions which Angell has given up his life to exposing. It seems to me fantastic to say that those delusions—which have nothing to do with economics and which aim at things contrary to the economic interests of the masses who cherish them—are part of "the economic structure of capitalist society." Many of them are, in fact, compatible with a Socialist structure of society. If they did not exist, the governing classes in a capitalist society would certainly find it much more difficult to obtain the support of the masses for war or for the policies which end in war. For a Socialist to refuse to admit and to combat these non-economic causes seems to me blind and absolutely disastrous both to peace and Socialism.

Leonard Woolf

To Ursula Roberts[1]

52 Tavistock Square
22 March 1935   W.C.1.

Dear Mrs Roberts,

I have the greatest sympathy with PAX in principle, but I am not at all happy about it in the exact form in which you have it now. . . .

One of the main reasons why I am a member of the Labour Party is that, on the whole its record is in foreign affairs more pacific than that of the others and that I feel that it is more likely in the future to stand for peace and disarmament. It follows that in 999 cases out of

1. The pen name of Susan Miles, a poet and pacifist, active in peace movements.

a 1000 I should prefer to vote for a bad Labour candidate rather than a good Tory candidate, no matter what they swore themselves to be in favour of during an election campaign. . . .

I also feel that, apart from anything else, you should confine yourself strictly to Peace and cut out Righteousness and Goodwill. The two latter terms are not without ambiguity. The last war was felt by the vast majority of the populations of all the countries engaged in it to be a righteous war. The sooner ordinary people become convinced that an unrighteous peace is infinitely preferable to these righteous wars, the better it will be for the world. But then one must tell them quite frankly to forget about the righteousness and only think about the peace.

Yours sincerely
Leonard Woolf

To the New Statesman

29 June 1935   52 Tavistock Square, W.C.1

Sir,— I agree with every word in Prof. Tawney's letter.[1] But isn't there a corollary to it—with regard to the House of Lords? As long as that House exists, he says, the Labour Party must have members in it. I believe that constitutionally a Labour Government must have a certain number of Secretaries or Under-Secretaries of State there. But I have never understood why the Party and Labour Peers should play the Tories' game by treating the House of Lords seriously and taking part in its farcical debates. For over 100 years it has been purely a partisan and party House, a part of the Tory political machine. When a Tory or "National" Government is in office, it goes out of business, except as a rubber stamp; when the Tories are in opposition, it vetoes or destroys all the Government's major measures.

A Labour Government should refuse to take part in this political farce. Its Bills should be introduced with a first reading speech which should always be the same, namely, that as their Tory Lordships have already made up their party minds, it would be a waste of time to intrude in their debates. No Labour Peer should ever say anything else there. As long as the House of Lords exists as a part of the Tory

1. R. H. Tawney (1880–1962), the eminent socialist scholar, had protested against Labour Party members' acceptance of political honors.

machine, the Labour Government should continue the Tory Lord Chancellor (without, of course, a seat in the Cabinet) in office; if he refused, they should appoint a hack Tory lawyer to sit on the Woolsack during the sittings of the Upper House.

Leonard Woolf

To Kingsley Martin[1]

Monk's House,
Rodmell, near Lewes, Sussex

29/9/35

Dear Kingsley,

You say that I wear blinkers. Of course, we all wear the blinkers of our opinions. But let me put on record what they are so that they and I may be judged by events.

Those who have supported the League system with knowledge and a sense of responsibility have done so for certain explicit reasons. They have included the Labour Party, yourself, and myself. We have maintained that the pre-war system of independent sovereign states, judges in their own disputes, each using its power as the instrument of its policy, must inevitably lead to war and, sooner or later, to a world war. We have maintained that a League system which binds all states to abide by a pacific system of settlement and to place the force of its individual members behind a victim of aggression and against an aggressor was the only possible means of preventing another world war in the near future. We have maintained over and over again that the pooled use of force in such an eventuality was not war in the old sense of the word. We have maintained again and again, right up to the day before yesterday, that capitalist governments and the National Government in particular ought to apply the League system and carry out their obligations under clauses 11, 12, 15 and 16 of the Covenant. We or at least I have done this with my eyes open to the following facts:

1. The great international issue in the fall of 1935 was whether the League should impose sanctions on Italy for invading Abyssinia. Martin was now moving away from his long-held pacifism, but he was criticized by LW for flinching at giving his—and the *New Statesman's*—full support to Baldwin's "National government," which had committed itself to sanctions. Martin, unsympathetic to LW's single-minded insistence on opposing Mussolini, had written: "You seem to me to wear blinkers just as I seem to you to flutter."

A. that the use of this system may lead to sanctions and sanctions may lead to war and that in a world of capitalist, imperialist, nationalist states and governments the use of force by the League to resist a clear case of aggression may degenerate into something difficult to distinguish from any other capitalist, imperialist, nationalist war;

B. that an international system which makes the elimination of war practically a certainty is in the next two or three hundred years practically out of the question; that the more or less firm establishment of the League system would make war more improbable; that capitalism is one of the chief causes (long-term causes) of war; that the League without socialism will not prevent war permanently (and that socialism without the League—or a League—will not prevent war).

I see nothing in the present situation which makes me think that we were wrong in these views. But if that is the case, how can we turn round now and say either

A. that we will never support a capitalist government which proposes to apply sanctions against an obvious aggressor

or B. that the League's use of sanctions is nothing but a capitalist war of the old type

or C. that anyone or any organization which "supports the League" against Italy is "merely patriotic"? . . .

The danger of the whole thing sliding into a patriotic war is of course there and is probably great. But Mussolini had provided us with so clear a case of aggression under a League system that if we and the Labour Party keep our heads and remain firm to those reasons and principles which made us support a League system, we can, I believe, make the Labour movement and the country see what is involved and force the Government to apply the Covenant in the way and for the ends which for the last ten years we have been demanding. . . .

I add the following as the determining factors in my political beliefs and particular opinions:

A. The idea that people are politically all-white or all-black is false; the mind is mongrel

B. The idea that you can choose between a course of action which is good and leads to all good and a course of action which is bad and leads to all bad is an almost universal delusion and leads to political and social disaster. In 999,999 cases out of a million, the choice is between two evils and two courses both of which will lead to evil; the wise man is he who by reason or instinct chooses the less evil course leading to the lesser evil. (E.g. Course I. Destruction of League system, destruction of Abyssinia by Italy, inevitable European war. Course II. Use of sanctions, war with Italy, possibility of degeneration into common or garden war.)

C. Things happen very slowly.

L W

To Julian Bell

52 Tavistock Square
24/11/35   W.C.1.

Dear Julian,

Your letters are very interesting and make me long once more for Asia. It all sounds extraordinarily familiar. I dont know whether you have already got to the inevitable stage at which our doings here sound incredibly far away and parochial. If not there are probably two things you would like to hear about from me—Abyssinia & the election.

Abyssinia, I think, is one of those political miracles which happen occasionally and always when you least expect them.[1] The explanation is not nearly as simple as most people and of course the good Marxian seem to think. The psychological elements to be noted are these. The Peace Ballot which gave a nasty jar to the National Government.[2] They thought that it showed that there were really thousands of electors who wanted peace and not the kind of peace which Sir John Simon was laying up for them.[3] It made them think seriously of the League and what they knew was called collective security as questions which might influence votes in an election. They felt that the Simon attitude on the Manchurian business had really possibly become a stick to beat them with and that it might not be safe too openly to do the same thing again.[4] I think that therefore in a vague way the notion of really using the League as a method of collectively preventing a war had ceased for the moment to be in their view pure eyewash and moonshine. In a vague way too the idea of the League as the only

1. Following the Italian invasion of Abyssinia a month before, the League invoked economic sanctions against Italy.
2. In the fall of 1934 the League of Nations Union had conducted a house-to-house poll of roughly 12 million people; the result showed overwhelming support for the collective-security principles of the League, with a majority for war if necessary to oppose aggression.
3. Sir John Simon (1873–1954), Foreign Secretary at this time and soon to be Home Secretary. LW saw him as a proto-appeaser.
4. Following the Japanese invasion of Manchuria, Simon had extricated Britain from the conflict by accepting Japan's *fait accompli* without condoning its use of force.

402

method of possibly stopping the inevitable world war had really permeated quite a large number of heads. When Musso played the dictator and rather overplayed it at Geneva, he at once got Eden and those in the Cabinet who felt the League had to be taken more seriously up against him.[1] There was a struggle in the Cabinet between the Leaguites and the Simon-MacDonald anti-Leaguers. The Cabinet as usual wobbled, while Musso played the strong man to perfection and made every diplomatic mistake that he could possibly make, even putting his friends the French in an impossible position.

Then he went just one inch too far. He threatened, not only the League but the British Empire. That finally cooked his goose, for only the super-geese like Garvin did not see what the U S S R saw months ago—that the League is the only last possible faint hope of preventing a world war and is the bulwark against war on all the pacific socialist, democratic and imperialist satiated states against the Fascist and dissatisfied powers.[2] The whole Cabinet simply had to go over to a real League position. . . .

The position is therefore extremely confused and complicated. You have behind the League now a mixture of real pacifism and common sense and also of the toughest imperialism masquerading as the dove of peace and in addition the pleasing spectacle of the Communist lion lying down with the capitalist dove. What will happen, god knows. It is obvious that behind the scenes there is still a pretty strong drive to do a dirty deal with Musso and call it peace. Musso himself seems to be such a complete imbecile and muddler that it will be diffcult even for Garvin, the Bank of England, and M. Laval [French Premier] to get him out of his mess. Most people now agree with what Maynard [Keynes] would have told him in June that his whole plan of campaign in Abyssinia is wrong; he has sent ten times too many men there. He is not the first dictator who has found megalomania fatal to him.

The election was of course a wretched disappointment.[3] I went down to Patcham and drove voters to the poll in a drizzling rain until I was dizzy. We got 50 or 60 seats less than I had expected. We were dished by

(a) The split among the leaders on the League question and sanctions.

1. Anthony Eden (1897–1977), then Minister without Portfolio for League of Nations Affairs; Foreign Secretary, 1935–38, 1940–45, 1951–55; and Prime Minister, 1955–57.
2. J. L. Garvin, editor of the *Observer* 1908–42. In the *Political Quarterly* of January 1936, LW wrote: "Week after week Mr Garvin pours out a flood of vituperative misrepresentation over everyone who says a word on behalf of the League system or of trying to prevent Italy attacking and conquering Abyssinia."
3. In the general election of this year, the Conservatives won 425 seats; Labour recovered from its 1931 electoral disaster but won only 154 seats.

Thousands of people, I think, felt quite rightly that for a party to attack the Government violently for not using sanctions against Japan and then be in two minds as to whether sanctions were not altogether taboo when they were going to be used [against Italy] was not a safe party to have in control of the country when people like Hitler and Musso are about the place.

(b) The corollary of this, the complete absence of any responsible leader in the Party, any one man whom the man in the street can think of when he thinks of Baldwin, Churchill, Lloyd George.

(c) The fact that the party calls itself socialist and has done literally nothing to convert even a small minority of the country to socialism. Nine tenths of the Trade Unionists even are not socialists and are indeed as much scared of socialism as the old ladies of Balham & Tooting.

(d) The fact that in nearly every constituency the fight is one between a wealthy and a poor party. It is extraordinary what a difference this makes even in the one matter of cars.

I must stop, but I will write again. Your proofs have arrived.[1]

Yours
L W

To Julian Bell

52 Tavistock Square,
W.C.1.

16/1/36

My dear Julian,

Many thanks for your letter. If I have an opportunity, I will suggest your reporting any crisis.[2]

As for what happened here over the Hoare-Laval business, I cannot pretend to know exactly what happened, but I reconstruct it somewhat as follows and I doubt its being very far from the truth.[3] The majority, probably the overwhelming majority, of the Cabinet have always been

1. Against their better judgment, the Woolfs had published Bell's *Work for Winter and other poems.*
2. LW tried, without success, to find a newspaper willing to publish reports by Bell on events in China.
3. Within two weeks of LW's prior letter, the British government, as he had predicted, sought to reach a Manchurian-style compromise with Italy. Laval and British Foreign Secretary Sir Samuel Hoare worked out a deal that would give Italy almost all of Abyssinia. The plan was leaked, British opinion was outraged and Hoare had to resign.

in favour of doing a deal with Musso and calling it peace. They neither understand nor in fact do they like the notion of collective security or the League system. By peace they understand giving the greater part of Abyssinia to Italy in accordance with the 1906 treaty, the terms of which recur in one form or other in every settlement proposed by this and the French Government. The Foreign Office expert [Maurice Peterson] had been for weeks in Paris elaborating a "peace plan" with the Quai d'Orsay. The peace plan was once more the 1906 partition dished up in a slightly new sauce. Hoare goes to Paris with Vansittart, who many people say is the real villain of the piece.[1] The Quai d'Orsay, Laval, Vansittart, and the F[oreign] O[ffice] expert then all pressed the plan on the wretched Hoare. He swallowed it whole and remitted it to the Cabinet. Eden and one or two others probably thought it was going rather far to hand over the unconquered Abyssinia to the bungling Musso, but the rest of the Cabinet were all in favour, now that the election was over, of shelving the League and getting back to what are called realities.

Several considerations help to turn the thoughts of these imbeciles in that direction. (1) They dont like the idea of Musso coming down with a big bump (2) Most people think that the Italian army is in a hopeless mess (3) The imposition of an oil embargo might make the Italian position impossible and (a) they dont really want to make it impossible and (b) they think that if it is, Musso may go quite mad and bomb the British fleet. Result: the whole Cabinet swallowed the whole Hoare-Laval plan.

Next day they found themselves, to their amazement and I must say to mine, in the middle of an absolute blizzard. One talks of "public opinion" and usually it simply means nothing at all, but really for the first time one made its acquaintance. It simply swept through everything, including even the newspapers. I did not meet one solitary person who did not think the thing outrageous. Even retired colonels turned against the Government. I think the indecency of the exposure so soon after all the League of Nations blather from Government speakers at the election and after Hoare's speech in the Assembly was too much for the country to stomach, and also what weighed heavily with ordinary people was the cool treachery of handing the wretched Abyssinians over to Italy when they had made "such a gallant fight" and the Italians seemed to be completely stalemated.

Well, the only way out was to chuck Hoare and chucked he was.

1. Robert Vansittart (1881–1957), Permanent Under-Secretary in the Foreign Office, was notoriously anti-German and favored placating Mussolini to forestall his turning to Hitler.

The odd thing is that it is Baldwin and not Hoare who has suffered most in reputation. Perhaps it isn't really odd. We are a country of sportsmen and it is felt that Baldwin did not play the game, while Hoare, though he was wrong, did and took his punishment "like a man". I doubt whether "Trust Baldwin" will ever be a good slogan again.

I think it possible that people here rather exaggerate the mess that Musso is in. Certainly all one hears personally from Italy goes to show that he has practically the whole country behind him, though that may change at any moment.

You may like to see what the *Week* says on the subject. I dont vouch for its accuracy.[1]

L.

To Julian Bell

29/3/36

52 Tavistock Square
W.C.1.

My dear Julian,

It was a terrible nuisance about your proofs which, as you now know, never arrived, but I hope you find we spotted any actual mistakes.

We go here politically from crisis to crisis. The latest, Hitler's coup in the Rhineland, was pretty exciting while it lasted. It is now going to be simply a race between the economic breakdown of the Fascist governments and a European war, and obviously Hitler will prefer war to collapse. The lengths we have gone are shown by the complete disintegration of opinion here. The Govt has to all intents and purposes destroyed the League and the collective security system, but now says precisely what the Labour Party urged them to say two years ago, when there was still time, "The League and the security system are the pivot of our policy". Their policy is now pivoting on a vacuum. It is really the policy of 1911 all over again, i.e. getting entangled in commitments the exact meaning of which no one, including the Government, understands. The result is that hundreds and thousands of ordinary people are in favour of complete isolation or, deceived com-

1. The *Week*, a newsletter put out from 1933 to 1946 by Claude Cockburn, a maverick Communist journalist, maintained that there was serious agrarian trouble in southern Italy and that the Italian army was hopelessly bogged down in Abyssinia.

pletely by Nazi propaganda, are becoming pro-German & anti-French.

Excuse more and also the haziness of this, but I am suffering from a violent cold in the head.[1]

I am afraid your poems have not done very well. Politics have been so terrifying that one has not been able to sell poetry at all this season.

L.

To Julian Bell

5 July, 1936

52 Tavistock Square
W.C.1.

My dear Julian,

. . . The political chaos here in all parties and practically all heads, except my own, is very distressing. The Labour Party drives me mad. The official policy of the Parliamentary Party is muddle-headed and silly beyond belief. What is the point of calling upon Mr Eden and Baldwin and Neville Chamberlain to keep on sanctions?[2] You might as well call upon Mussolini to apply sanctions to himself. It will now simply be manoeuvering for alliances and armaments, and whatever comes out of it will be labelled "the League of Nations".

Yours
L W

To Charles Singer[3]

25 September, 1936

[The Hogarth Press
52 Tavistock Square]

Dear Dr Singer,

Very many thanks for your letter. It is extremely good of you to take so much trouble and interest over and in this book, and I feel

1. "Excuse more" was a Woolf family term of apology for not writing more.
2. Neville Chamberlain (1869–1940), Chancellor of the Exchequer and soon to become Prime Minister, had just denounced sanctions as "the very midsummer of madness."
3. Charles Singer (1876–1960), a noted physician and Professor of the History of Medicine at the University of London. Son of a rabbi, he was active in helping scholars who were victims of Nazism.

rather churlish at not being able to agree to all your suggestions.[1] My real difficulty is that if I bring out a second edition so soon after the first and omit things like references to our own attitude towards our own monarchy or the appendix on anti-semitism, it looks as if I no longer hold those views—which is not the case. Also my experience is that it is fatal to cut out arguments which people will not like. If you cut out what the Conservative will not like at one end and the extreme Left will not like at the other, you get the sort of twilight—intellectual twilight—which is characteristic of B.B.C. talks. After all my real point is that the attitude of the Balliol undergraduate who objects to my writing as I do about our own monarchy is symptomatic of Quack, Quack. If I talk of the German's attitude towards the Kaiser or Hitler, he is quite happy, but he gets angry if any one says that his attitude towards the King is not very different. If I write about the German quackery and cut out all reference to the English, I only bolster up and cover up the very thing which it was my purpose to uncover.

I hope you will not think that I am merely obstinate and obstructive over this.[2]

Yours sincerely,
Leonard Woolf

To Charles Singer

5th October, 1936

[The Hogarth Press
52 Tavistock Square]

Dear Dr. Singer,

I am afraid I still, to be honest, do not agree with you; but I am convinced that the more one disagrees with criticism of one's own writing, the more likely one is to be wrong and, at any rate, it is extremely salutary to give way to them. I am therefore prepared to cut out the appendix, and I have already agreed to making the alterations about the King, so that I think this really meets your important points. . . .[3]

Yours sincerely,
Leonard Woolf

1. Singer had written to praise *Quack, Quack!* and to urge LW to publish a cheap edition, to give it wider currency. Maintaining that it was important for the book to convert conservatives to its line of argument, he suggested softening critical references to the royal family and removing the appendix on anti-Semitism.
2. Singer persisted, sending LW a long list of suggested changes.
3. The revised, cheap edition sold well and had to be reprinted the following year.

52 Tavistock Squre
W.C.1.

15/11/36

Dear Julian,

I have been very remiss. I have often meant to write, but really the kind of things you want me to write about are so abominable that I shrink from it. If only you wanted to hear about Sally (you dont even know that she is Pinka's successor) or Mitz the marmoset or any other defence against reality, I would gladly send you pages. But what I suppose you want to hear about are the realities—Hitler, Mussolini, Franco.

The difficulty is that by the time you get this some new horror will have started up in Poland or Czechoslovakia or Iceland or even Paris or London, and the ruins and corpses of Madrid will no longer be even of "interest". At the moment for the first time for two years it looks as if there is a faint, faint chance of a Fascist being beaten. Franco has been held up for 9 days outside Madrid, and whereas 7 days ago it looked 100 to 1 on his taking it, people are now saying that he may after all be beaten.

The Labour Party has cut a poor figure once more. It is split hopelessly into two and even the two halves are themselves fluid. It began in favour of non-intervention and swung over in the space of three days at the Edinburgh Conference to be against the non-intervention pact. The fact is that 9 out of 10 people cannot make up their mind to face realities and base their policy on them. The League is dead; collective security is dead and rotten. The alternatives are isolation (with or without rearmament) or an alliance of the non-Fascist powers against the Fascists. Spain was the first test case of the new dispensation of a world without the League. The corollary of isolation was non-intervention; the corollary of alliance was to support the Spanish Government, to get France and the U S S R to do the same, and to risk war or trouble with Germany and/or Italy. Our Government was of course in favour of non-intervention, for it is really in its shilly-shallying way isolationist, and in any case is not sufficiently anti-fascist as to be pro-socialist.

The Labour Party is composed partly of people who are pacifist and therefore not prepared really for an alliance against fascism, partly of a small number of people who would be prepared for an alliance, and partly of those who want to oppose fascism up to but not over the edge of war. You can see the muddle. The first and third classes together make the Party vote for non-intervention; then the third class is carried away by its emotions and "working class solidarity" to want to support the Spanish government and reverses its previous vote without really considering whether it is prepared to fight Germany and Italy if our support of the Spanish Government led to war, or threat of war.

The same muddle-headedness and confusion are splitting the party over rearmament. I have come myself to be in favour of isolation at any rate as a temporary policy for this country. It is too late to stop a European war by an alliance; in fact it would probably precipitate a war. Also for an alliance policy you must have governments in Britain and France, at least, which know their minds, keep cool, and are prepared to stand firmly together. Such governments dont exist. And what applies to the government applies mutatis mutandis to the Labour Party as an opposition party. It does not know its own mind, and that is not the state of mind in which it can put forward a policy of alliance. The best that one can hope is that we may stumble and stagger together into an ignoble policy of isolation, that the guns will not go off or the bombs begin to fall for a year or two, and that something meanwhile "may turn up." Meanwhile the Spaniards are shouting: "Long live Death."

Yours
Leonard

To Julian Bell

13/12/36

52 Tavistock Square
W.C.1.

My dear Julian,

I have just got your letter about coming home. I think it is rather a good idea to try and get an unpaid secretaryship to one of the Labour leaders. . . .

I suppose as a matter of fact this may never reach you, so I wont waste my words on the air. This king business has been the most curious event of an absolutely insane epoch.[1] I imagine that we cannot now go further in romantic idiocy.

It is very pleasant to think we shall be talking to you about all this in a very little while.

LW

1. Edward VIII had abdicated two days earlier.

19 February, 1937   52 Tavistock Square, W.C.1.

Dear Julian,
    . . . I had an opportunity of talking to the Spanish Ambassador here the other day in a confidential manner. He is a nice depressed little man and I ventured to consult him about your wish to go and fight for them. He said that of course they were doing absolutely nothing to enlist any one, but that as a matter of fact they did not want untrained men. Any one with technical knowledge was of immense value to them, but not otherwise. I asked him whether there were any other jobs than the army in which one could be of service. He said again that really only skilled technical jobs. He said people came to them and said they were prepared to do anything, even drive a lorry, but that it was no good having lorry drivers who could not speak Spanish. If a man who cant speak Spanish tries to drive a lorry from Madrid to Valencia today he finds it extremely difficult, whereas they have lorry drivers who are Spaniards. I asked him whether if at any time he heard of any job which might be of use to them and suitable for you, he would let me know, and he said he would.

                                    Yours
                                    Leonard

To John Lehmann
                                    52, Tavistock Square
21 July, 1937   W.C.1.

Dear John,
    . . . I dont know whether you have heard that Julian has been killed in Spain. The news came last night. There is nothing to be said except about the sheer waste and futility of it all. It is the War all over again, when one was rung up to be told that Rupert [Brooke] was dead or one's brother killed, and one knew that it was only in order to produce the kind of world we are now living in. Horrible.

                                    L W

To H. M. Swanwick[1]

1 October, 1937

Monk's House,
Rodmell, near Lewes, Sussex.

Dear Mrs Swanwick,

I was very glad to get your letter and to see that we had not really quarrelled.[2] After all, we have, I believe, always been after the same things, and that seems to me what is most important.

But in the present condition of the world I do also think that the question of means to those ends in the international sphere is of vital importance. It is not merely a question of reason, but of political (and historical) judgment, which is a mixture of reason and instinct. It is there that you and I differ, and it is because we both feel the appalling results of a mistake in judgment on this question at the present moment that we have probably both been led into verbal overemphasis of our case, you in your book and I in my review of it.

I should like to make one more attempt to make my position clear, because I think you misunderstand it. To make stable peace probable or war improbable, two things are necessary.

The first may be defined as a minimum of international justice. That is what you insist upon in your book and I too, I think, have always insisted upon, particularly in the first ten years after the war. . . . I still believe that if the governments of Britain and France had set themselves to right wrongs, conditions would have been established in which the League would have worked and peace in Europe might not have been broken for 25 or 50 years.

But under no conceivable circumstances could any system of absolute justice be established internationally in the 20th century; there would always be wrongs or conditions which some peoples or nations considered wrongs. Also you have to start with things as they are, and things as they are include armies, navies, and air forces, and a tradition of centuries encouraging the use of force as an instrument of national policy and as a legitimate method of righting what are thought to be wrongs.

Here comes in the appalling problem of fear which it seems to me

---

1. Helena Maria Swanwick (1864–1939), noted writer and lecturer on international politics, was active in League of Nations affairs. LW had known her since 1914, when both were members of the Union of Democratic Control, of which she was a founder.
2. The two had exchanged letters the previous week about LW's critical review in the *New Statesman* of Swanwick's book *Collective Insecurity*. Swanwick was a pacifist and an outspoken opponent of sanctions, which in her view had destroyed the League. In her subsequent book, *The Roots of Peace*, she answered LW's review and denounced him as a "sanctionist."

that pacifists habitually burke. For these conditions breed fear which dominates international relations, for given armies and navies and no international control of force, the only apparent possibility of ensuring your safety is the imbecile method of trying to make yourself stronger than your neighbour. Hence, however just you might make the international system, in order to make it pacific and in order to relax this fear and so make a reversal of the wheels possible, you must somehow or other deal with this problem of force and existing forces.

Just as between 1918 and 1928, I believe, the other part of the problem was most important, so since 1928 it is this problem of force and fear which dominates the situation. To tell people to disarm when they are terrified of their neighbours' arms seems to me hopeless and to preach the international justice programme in the present state of Europe without dealing with this dominating problem of force does seem to me to be saying in effect "Be good, sweet maid".

The only conceivable way of dealing with the force problem seems to me to be some sort of system of "collective security", a system of collective resistance to any state resorting to war. Of course, I know that such a system may be misused, that it involves terrible dangers, but I can see no other way in which it would be possible to create a sense of security and so make disarmament possible. The League was potentially such a system. I do not think that the breakdown of sanctions itself involves the destruction of the League. But the fact that the potential collective security system of the League was never used has convinced 99 persons out of every 100 that the League as an instrument of preventing war is dead and that there is no safety in collective systems and that therefore the only safety is to be found in increasing national armaments to a maximum.

So you come round once more to the problem of dealing with existing force and the fear of force, and you come round to it again and again from whatever point you start from because in existing circumstances—unlike the years 1918 to 1928—it is the dominating question.

Yours sincerely
Leonard Woolf

17 November, 1937   [52 Tavistock Square]

Dear Mr Graham,

I was interested in your letter, but it contains a large number of misunderstandings, misstatements and errors:

1. My article was not an attack upon the Soviet Union nor was it an endeavour to reduce the faith (whatever that may be) of *D[aily] H[erald]* readers.[2] So far as my politics are concerned, the thing which I should desire more than any other is that the Soviet Union should succeed as a socialist state, and it is because of that that I consider it to be a right and duty to point out anything which jeopardises that success. I am no less anxious than you to prevent the spread of fascism and I agree with you that the Soviet Union might be the greatest bulwark against its spread. There are certain parts of the internal policy of the Soviet Government which are obviously weakening it both internally and externally as a bulwark against fascism, and it is a duty of those who are friends of that government and wish it success to say so openly. It is you, not I, who in this respect are blind and cannot see this and think that everyone who says a word in criticism of soviet policy is either a liberal or a fascist or both.

2. I am not a liberal and never have been one. Ever since I began to take part in politics—which is over 25 years ago—I have been a socialist. Where you go wrong is in thinking that freedom of thought is somehow or other a crime in a socialist and that socialism consists in a continuous mumbling and remumbling of phrases from Marx, Lenin, and Stalin and abuse of people who differ from you on any point at all.

3. You are quite wrong in supposing that I have not studied the history of the Russian Communist Party, the record of Stalin, and the works of Lenin.

4. If you will reread what I wrote, you will discover that you were so convinced that I was attacking the Soviet Union that you did not even take the trouble to read what I wrote. I gave infinitely higher praise to the Webbs' book than to Gide's; I did not of course compare them and what you say about it being "unseemly" to talk of them at the

---

1. A Communist writer; his *War and Peace in the Soviet Union* was published in 1934.
2. The article, "You want freedom—yes, but what sort?" published in the *Daily Herald* of November 5, 1937, contrasted the "positive freedom" of dictatorship with the "negative freedom" of the Western liberal tradition.

same time is simply silly and schoolboyish.[1] What I said was that Gide is as honest a socialist as the Webbs and that the fact that they came to such different conclusions as to the present policy of the Soviet Government is a fact worth investigating. So it is.

5. What you say about freedom amounts to this: that because the *Daily Herald* and the British Trade Unions refuse freedom to some people on some points, any refusal of freedom to anyone on any point is justified by the Soviet Government. That is only adding to the "great deal of rubbish written", as you say, "on the subject of freedom."

6. When you say that in the Soviet Union "there is freedom to express your opinion about anything", you must know that it is untrue.

Yours sincerely
Leonard Woolf

To Victor Gollancz[2]

27 October, 1938   [52 Tavistock Square]

Dear Gollancz,

I have thought over the question of the book which you asked me to write for the Left Book Club. I have made a very rough outline of the kind of book I think I might be able to do, though I would not bind myself to follow it slavishly, but it contains the kind of topics I would deal with. I have no doubt that I could make a book of 50,000 words as a minimum out of it. If it is the kind of book you had in mind, I should be prepared to sign an agreement, provided that you did not tie me down to produce it by a given date. I would do it as quickly as possible.

1. LW had praised the Webbs' notorious book *The Soviet Union: A New Civilization* as a splendid compilation of data about Russia but noted that it failed to explain why "the present ruler of the republic has had to shoot, imprison, or dismiss from office practically all the statesmen, administrators, and generals who were responsible for the establishment of Soviet communism." He also referred to André Gide's *Afterthoughts*, which recorded the author's disillusionment with Communism following a visit to the Soviet Union.
2. Gollancz had written that his view of the Soviet Union had changed and that he now felt freedom to be at risk not only from the fascists but also from the Soviets. He said he wished to commission a book about "the defence of western civilization" by a democratic socialist and could think of no one better than LW. The book was to be for the Left Book Club, which Gollancz had founded in 1936 to combat fascism and promote far-left, generally pro-Communist, causes. Since a Club book could usually count on a quarter-million readers, the Club was a formidable influence and the most successful Communist-front organization of the interwar period.

I hope you will not mind my just mentioning one other point. Some of the topics with which I would deal raise acute controversy among different sections of the Left and I daresay some of my opinions would be much disliked by a good many members of the Left Book Club. I assume that I should have complete freedom in the expression of opinion within the law of libel and obscene libel.[1]

Yours sincerely
Leonard Woolf

MEMORANDUM TO THE LABOUR PARTY

November, 1938

ADVISORY COMMITTEE ON IMPERIAL QUESTIONS

Memorandum on the Demands for Reform of the Ceylon Constitution By L. S. Woolf.

The Ceylon Constitution, which resulted from the report of the Donoughmore Commission, has now been in operation for nearly ten years and demands are being put forward by the Sinhalese for revision in order that the people may be given an increased measure of responsible government. . . .[2]

The Committee is of the opinion that the time has come for a further measure of self-government and of an appreciable measure of responsible government and that the Party should adopt this as its policy. . . .

In order to achieve this the Party should support . . . alterations in the Constitution. . . .

Provision should be made for the protection of minorities. This applies in particular to the Tamils who oppose revision of the Constitution and the grant of further measures of self-government on the ground that the Sinhalese have used and will use their majority against the interests of the Tamils. Consideration should also be given to the

---

1. Although he had never before so committed himself, Gollancz agreed. The book was to be entitled *Barbarians at the Gate*.

2. A constitution, based on the recommendations of a commission headed by Lord Donoughmore, was promulgated in 1931. In introducing universal suffrage, it inflamed rivalry between Sinhalese and Tamils, the latter opposing any advance toward self-government unless their position was protected.

possibility of ensuring a large measure of devolution or even of introducing a federal system on the Swiss model. . . .

The Swiss federal canton system has proved extraordinarily successful under circumstances very similar to those in Ceylon, i.e., the co-existence in a single democratic state of communities of very different size, sharply distinguished from one another by race, language and religion. Thus the German speaking Swiss with a population of 2,750,000 occupy the numerical position of the Sinhalese, the French speaking Swiss with 824,000, that of the Tamils and the Italian speaking Swiss with 284,000 that of the Moormen. The democratic canton and federal system in Switzerland has safeguarded the legitimate interests of the minorities.[1]

To Norman Leys

22/2/39   52, Tavistock Square, W.C.I.

Dear Leys,

Many thanks for your two letters.[2] In principle I agree entirely with you. The real difficulty, as we found, with Passfield, you know, was how to get the Labour Government when it is sitting there in power to implement its promises. Now your memo really asks them now to make a promise to make a promise when they get in. As you say yourself "the problem is how to ensure that these two steps will in fact be taken within a month of the next L[abour] G[overnment]'s taking office", but you dont suggest *how* to solve that problem. My own belief is that possibly the only way is (a) to get the Party to pledge itself in advance to take certain general and specific steps (b) to work out the specific steps of supreme importance now and get the Party to endorse them. The steps under (b) should be five or six of key importance, e.g., to remove discrimination in the Kenya Highlands. But if we recommended such steps we should have to advise the Party of the kind of opposition which it would have

1. LW was the first person to propose a federal solution to the Tamil-Sinhalese conflict. It was this sort of arrangement that was adopted by the government of Sri Lanka in 1987.
2. Leys announced his intention of rejoining the Advisory Committee on Imperial Questions, from which he had resigned in 1931 because of the Labour government's conservative colonial policy in Africa.

to face and of the measures which it would have to take to meet them.

I will speak to Buxton today and if he agrees, I will circulate your memo for discussion.[1]

Yours
Leonard Woolf

To VICTOR GOLLANCZ

23 June, 1939.   [52 Tavistock Square]

Dear Gollancz,

I must say that your letter rather astonishes me—not least that you now propose in any case to postpone publication of the book for over seven months, i.e. nine months after you receive the MS and 10 months after you knew the date at which you were to receive it. . . .[2] The book was written—at your suggestion—to meet an immediate situation; in 1940 or 1941 all my examples &c may be out of date and the whole thing will sound silly or possibly we shall be at war—which will solve the difficulty.

. . . I am not hostile to the Soviet Government, but I know that any criticism of that Government or its policy is interpreted by many people as hostility, and it was for that very reason that I put the matter quite plainly to you before we signed the agreement. Now what I foresaw has happened, and because I deal in a book of which the subject is tolerance both in the U.S.S.R. and in fascist countries, I am accused of "hostility" to the Soviet Government. But that is precisely the subject which in your letter to me and in our conversation you asked me to deal with. I claim to be as good a socialist as any member of the selection committee of the Left Book Club and to be equally desirous

1. Charles Roden Buxton (1875–1942), a Labour MP, was Chairman of the Advisory Committee on Imperial Questions. Leys's draft memo began: "The Labour government of 1929–31 left scarcely a mark on Africa" and went on to criticize Sidney Webb for acting "as if [racial] discrimation was a danger when it had long since become an accomplished fact."
2. Appalled by the criticism of the Soviet Union in the manuscript LW had submitted, Gollancz had written on the previous day to say that publication of the text could be used by "reactionaries and fascists" against the Soviets, would provoke the resignation of 10,000 Left Book Club members, could jeopardize Anglo-Soviet negotiations then under way and would for technical reasons be impossible until the following year.

with them of the success of the Soviet Union.[1] For the Soviet Union as a socialist state I have like you an affection (though not for the Governments and governing cliques—which is a very different pair of shoes). It is just because of this that I think it essential to point out errors in policy which, as I explain in the book itself, seem to me fatal to the ultimate aim of socialism or communism. That is the main object of the book and of course it will be treated as lèse-majesté by people whose attitude towards socialism or communism is the same as that of the Tory to the British Empire.

I am prepared to consider any suggestions from you, Strachey, and Harold, and will welcome them. I would alter anything which you convinced me might read as hostile to the Soviet Union, because, as I say, I am not hostile and would be very sorry to give that impression to an unbiased person. But I am not prepared to alter or "tone down" the main argument of the book on the ground that now is not the time to tell the truth because of the delicate international situation or because what one says may be used for propaganda by one's enemy. Everyone has been saying that on one side or another since August, 1914.

I propose to cable Harcourt, Brace that they can bring the book out in the U.S.A. at once as publication here is indefinitely postponed. But I must say that I think it extraordinarily unfair, in view of what has happened, to postpone publication in this way.

Yours sincerely
Leonard Woolf

To Victor Gollancz

27 June, 1939   [52 Tavistock Square]

Dear Gollancz,

I think you have rather misunderstood my letter. That there should be criticism or suggestions from any of you is not what I object to; in fact, as I said, I welcome them and I shall be only too glad to discuss them with you at the earliest possible moment. When will you be ready for such a discussion?

1. Committee members were, in addition to Gollancz, Harold Laski (1893–1950), and John Strachey (1901–63), a Communist, though not a member of the party.

... A publisher's guarantee that an author can express freely opinions which he knows will be unpopular is not really of much value to the author if, when he delivers the MS, publication is indefinitely postponed because of the unpopularity of his views. If you treated all Left Book Club books as you are treating mine, you could never pubish a book on controversial subjects which was not out of date, for they would all be published over a year after they had been written—which is obviously not the case. When do you expect to be able to begin to consider when it will be possible to publish this book in the Left Book Club and when will the final decision be made as to its date?

Yours sincerely
Leonard Woolf[1]

To Victor Gollancz

29 June, 1939   [52 Tavistock Square]

Dear Gollancz,

"To put it bluntly", as you say, I do not believe in the necessity for an indefinite postponement of my book—nor does anyone with any publishing experience to whom I have told the circumstances—nor in fact did you yourself until Strachey had read the MS, otherwise you would not have put it in your spring list.

As an author I am not interested in speculations regarding the imaginary influence which my book will have on international negotiations or the membership of the Left Book Club;[2] I am interested in two things only: (1) that the book shall be published within a reasonable time and that it shall not therefore be indefinitely postponed until it is just out of date and all the edge taken off it, (2) that I am paid for my labours within a reasonable time.

You politely draw my attention by implication to the fact that unlike Rhys Williams I have no legal stipulation from you regarding when the book shall be published.[3] I am fully aware of the fact, but if it is to be a question of law, as you know, that does not mean that the

---

1. In reply, Gollancz said it was clear that LW, "to put it bluntly," did not believe his reasons for postponement. Gollancz's biographer, Ruth Dudley Edwards, has written: "Victor was indeed lying. . . ."
2. Anglo-Soviet talks over some form of alliance were then taking place in Moscow.
3. The Left Book Club had published Williams's *The Soviets*, a book that Gollancz himself described as "a hundred percent friendly to the Soviet Union."

publisher can indefinitely postpone the publication of a book and I am not without legal remedy.

After all this correspondence and after you have had the MS in your hands for two months, although I agreed to meet your wishes in every way so far as considering objections and criticism and discussing them, I am still in precisely the same position as at first with regard to the only points which interest me. All that I know now is that publication is "indefinitely postponed". Does this mean

(1) that you will not publish the book in the autumn season despite the fact that you announced it for the spring season?

(2) that you refuse to give me a definite date for the publication of this book?

I shall be greatly obliged if you will give me an answer to these two questions as early as possible.

Yours sincerely
Leonard Woolf[1]

To Victor Gollancz

2 July, 1939   [52 Tavistock Square]

Dear Gollancz,

. . . I think throughout this correspondence you have misunderstood my position because you obviously do not believe that I intend my words to mean exactly what they do mean and that so far as I know they are true. If anything that I wrote had or might have any real effect upon the Anglo-Soviet negotiations or any large effect upon the membership of the Left Book Club, I should be enormously interested. I do not suffer from any false or excessive modesty, but I am not really quite so silly or so vain as to believe that this book will have the slightest influence upon the first or that it could possibly affect the membership of the Left Book Club to the extent of more than a baker's dozen. (After years on the *Nation* I know all about the people who write in and say "I have been a subscriber to your paper for 20 years, but after reading your article by Mr Gollancz in the last issue, I shall

1. Gollancz responded that the book would be published sometime during the first three months of 1940. He added in a postscript: "I cannot really believe that you mean 'As an author, I am not interested in speculations regarding the imaginary influence which my book will have on international negotiations.' "

never read it again," and what effect this kind of thing has on circulation.) As I said, therefore, I simply am not interested in speculations regarding the imaginary influence of my book, flattering though they may be.

Your sincerely
Leonard Woolf

To Victor Gollancz

22 August, 1939 [52 Tavistock Square]

Dear Gollancz,

I now return the MS of *Barbarians at the Gate* finally revised for the press. I think I have accepted practically every one of the verbal suggestions made by you, Strachey, and Laski.[1] I have made certain alterations in view of Strachey's larger criticisms and have added a disquisition on the dictatorship of the proletariat, which he was anxious for me to do. There remain, of course, as between him and me fundamental differences of opinion as to the interpretation of history (and of Marx) which cannot be resolved except by a Hegelian dialectic of which I am unfortunately incapable.[2]

Yours sincerely
Leonard Woolf

1. At a meeting of the four, postponed until July 25, Strachey reproved LW for failing to see that Stalin was a reluctant dictator and his mode of rule motivated solely by the need to defend Soviet Communism from internal and external subversives.
2. The next day, the Nazi-Soviet nonagression pact was signed; suddenly, all the technical obstacles to the publication of LW's book vanished. Even so, when published in November, it was paired with *The Socialist Sixth of the World*, an avidly pro-Soviet book by Hewlett Johnson, the "Red Dean of Canterbury," and it received a review in the Club's *Left News* by Strachey, who described it as "almost wholly mistaken."

To Aneurin Bevan[1]

28 September, 1939 [Monk's House]

Dear Bevan,

It is very good of you and the Board [of the *Tribune*] to write as you do. I took the review of course simply as an expression of personal opinion.[2] I have long since arrived at the stage at which reviewers can give one little pleasure and no pain. Sloan's review gave me no pain, but a little pleasure because it amused me. The somewhat violent language I put down to mere exuberance of youth.

Yours sincerely
Leonard Woolf

FROM THE MARQUESS OF CREWE[3]

July 29th 1940.

Dear Mr Woolf,

I read your article on the Politician and the Intellectual, in the New Statesman of July 20th, and I hope that you will excuse a much older man who has enjoyed the company of many of both sorts for troubling you with a few observations on it.[4]

. . . I suppose that in sheer power of mind Gladstone was ahead of any man of letters or of science in his own or the succeeding generation. . . . But is the divorce as complete as you make it? You do not mention Bulwer Lytton, Cornewall Lewis (some of whose essays are worth

1. Aneurin Bevan (1897–1960), noted Labour MP for the Welsh mining constituency of Ebbw Vale 1929–60, was a founder of the left-wing weekly *Tribune*, which he edited from 1942 to 1945.
2. *Barbarians at the Gate* received a vituperative review in the *Tribune* by Pat Sloan, who remarked, "If Mr. Woolf would read Lenin and Stalin he would see he has lied as glibly as the *Daily Express* about their attitude to democracy." LW's was the first Left Book Club work to criticize the Soviet Union, and it scandalized Club members and others on the far left.
3. Robert Offley Ashburton Crewe-Milnes (1858–1945), Viceroy of Ireland 1892–95, leader of Liberals in the House of Lords 1908–25, 1936–44, Colonial Secretary 1908–10, Secretary of State for India 1910–15, President of the Board of Education 1915–16, Ambassador at Paris 1922–28, Secretary of State for War 1931.
4. The article discussed the anti-intellectual temper in Britain, arguing that "the divorce of the British intelligentsia from practical affairs has had profound and disastrous results upon our politics, our politicians, and our intellectuals."

reading still), George [Otto] Trevelyan, and curiously enough, James Bryce, among "intellectuals" who held Cabinet office. (By the way, I like the old term "scholar" better than "intellectual.")

From the opposite point of view, should we not suffer if all the best minds were given to affairs? Carlyle might have upset any coach; & I cannot conceive Faraday or Darwin in Parliament. Thackeray tried to get there, but would have been no good. And one has to think of the loss involved. Surely Shaw & H. G. Wells are better as they are? And if I may say so, Mrs. Woolf would take a higher place in the House of Commons than any of the excellent ladies who are there; but if she wrote less in consequence it would be a misfortune. And would not the like have been true of your father-in-law, for whom I had great admiration?

. . . But I must stop. May I say how much I enjoyed the irony of the whole article?

Yours sincerely
CREWE

TO THE MARQUESS OF CREWE

30 July, 1940

[37 Mecklenburgh Square,
London W.C.1.]

Dear Lord Crewe,

I have to thank you for your extremely interesting letter. I agree with almost all you say. I certainly should have mentioned James Bryce. I do not myself like the word "intellectual", but I do not think it is altogether synonymous with the old word "scholar". It answers more to the still less pleasant word "intelligentsia", but which indicates a real class and one much wider than the scholar. I think that it is not unfair to say that it covers a class of person who by training or trade or both is accustomed largely to rely upon the intellect as an instrument. And I think that it is also true that we traditionally . . . mistrust the use of that instrument in practical and particularly political affairs and that owing to changes in society this mistrust is nationally more dangerous than it was in the 19th century. Actually in many branches of affairs the logic of events is compelling ordinary people to make the change, even though the mistrust continues to exist higher up. For instance a young Oxford man whom I know entered the Navy at the beginning of the war as a rating. He tells me that the Petty Officer in

424

the Navy is an intellectual; he is compelled to be, because he is continually having to deal with complicated scientific instruments and with complicated problems which can only be solved by the use of the intellect. And what applies to the Petty Officer applies in a modified degree even to the ordinary rating.

I completely agree with what you say in the latter part of your letter. I did not mean to imply that I thought that all the intellectuals should take an active part in politics. I should be very sorry to see writers and scientists flocking into the House of Commons; they should in 99 cases out of 100 stick to their job. But it is not good either for their job or for politics that the one should be completely divorced from the other.

Yours sincerely
Leonard Woolf

To Clement Attlee[1]

24 August, 1940   [Monk's House]

Dear Attlee,

I hesitate to trouble you at the present moment, but the following case is so extraordinary that I cannot resist putting it before you. I have known most of the Freud family ever since Freud himself came here from Vienna. His daughter Dr Anna Freud now writes to me and says that his son Dr Martin Freud has been interned since July and that Martin Freud's son, a boy of 19, has now been sent off to Australia.[2] Freud and his family, when they came here, were welcomed as distinguished guests and victims of the Nazis. I have never heard a word from any of them which did not seem to show they were anything but absolutely opposed to everything connected with the Nazis and Hitler. That any of them should now be interned as dangerous and that a

---

1. Clement Attlee (1883–1967), at this time Lord Privy Seal in Churchill's war cabinet. LW, who knew him in the Labour Party and the Fabian Society, found him "mouselike" but "when you least expected it, would suddenly show himself to be a masterful or even savage mouse."

2. In a security panic after the fall of France, all German and Austrian refugees, except Jewish women, were interned for longer or shorter periods. Martin Freud and his son Walter as well as the family's maid Paula Fichtl were among them. Martin was sent to the Isle of Man, Walter to Australia.

grandson of Freud should have to be sent off to Australia by the Government seems to me amazing.

There may, of course, be some reason of which I am not aware, but I do suggest that it is a case which deserves to be seriously considered.

Yours sincerely
Leonard Woolf[1]

To A. L. Rowse

24 May, 1941

Monk's House
Rodmell near Lewes Sussex

My dear Rowse,

Very many thanks for your letter and words of sympathy which I greatly appreciate.

Your article is a terrific indictment of Baldwin, but I am sure that you overdo it verbally and defeat your object.[2] This is particularly the case on the first page; which I am returning to you and I hope you will reconsider it. As it stands, it is too definitely libellous and it is quite possible to tell the truth about B[aldwin] and say what you want to say without being libellous. It is also, I am sure, false psychologically. People like Baldwin do not deliberately deceive the people—they are not deliberate confidence tricksters—they keep their own minds in compartments and can therefore believe that they trust the people and yet conceal some vital thing from the people in order to make sure of winning an election. That is what makes them so dangerous in this country. I have made some alterations for your consideration in order to retain your meaning and avoid libel. But I have also cut out the last few sentences and hope you will substitute something different for the following reasons.

First, there is no real interest in imagining what Baldwin thinks in the watches of the night—he probably thinks that he did everything for the best and that he had bad luck and that his critics are very unfair to him. It seems to me slightly cheap and silly to imagine old

1. Attlee responded that he would immediately take up the matter with the Home Secretary. The two men were among the first internees to be released and soon afterward were commissioned in the British army.
2. The article, submitted to LW for the *Political Quarterly*, was one of the harshest attacks at the time on former Prime Minister Stanley Baldwin; it concluded: "But what can the man think in the still watches of the night, when he contemplates the ordeal his country is going through as a result of the years, the locust years, in which he held power."

Baldwin's bulbous nose over the white sheets of a sleepless repentance.

Second, you say more than once that his career raises "the crucial question of leadership" in a democracy, but you say nothing about this "crucial question" itself. I suggest that you end with a few words about it. And I also suggest that the danger of the question and of the political confidence trick is most clearly not confined to democracies and that you should point this out. The power of both Hitler and Mussolini internally has been very largely built up on the confidence trick. Mutatis mutandis there is very little difference between the confidence trick of Mussolini and that of Baldwin and the Italians are paying for it very much in the same way as we are. If we win this war, as I believe we shall, the Germans and Italians will pay much dearer for their confidence trickster rulers than we shall. In fact despite its defects, democracy has more defence against the confidence trick than the authoriarian system. Look at Italy, Poland, Yugoslavia. The future of democracy—the future of Europe, indeed—depends to some extent on this very question—whether the people will learn to trust only the leaders who tell them the truth, however unpleasant that may be, and will drum out at the earliest possible moment the medicine men and the confidence tricksters who are just shuffling the cards for their own or their class or their "party" interests.

I do hope you will reconsider this ending and end not on the miserable Baldwin but your "searching light upon the crucial question for the future." I am sure you will enormously improve the effect of the article.[1]

Yours
Leonard Woolf

TO ERNEST BARKER[2]

Monk's House
Rodmell, near Lewes   Sussex

17 August, 1941

Dear Mr Barker,

I am afraid that we are either not talking about the same things or are differing fundamentally about facts. . . .

1. Rowse made few changes, leaving Baldwin in the still watches of the night. The article, published in the July-September issue, was republished in 1947 in his *End of an Epoch*.
2. (Sir) Ernest Barker (1874–1960), Principal of King's College, London, 1920–28, Professor of Political Science at Cambridge 1928–39. LW wrote a commendatory review of his *Ideas and Ideals of the British Empire* in the *Political Quarterly*; Barker expressed his appreciation but challenged certain of LW's arguments.

As regards the colour bar, I am afraid that I disagree completely with your statement of fact. I do not think that the British Government has fought steadily aganst the colour bar in Southern Rhodesia, in Northern Rhodesia, or in Kenya. In Southern Rhodesia we have completely abandoned the Africans to a handful of white men to institute the worst kind of colour bar system—economic, educational, and social—retaining a paper control which we do not attempt to exercize in fact. We are on the road to the same thing in Northern Rhodesia; we have complete power to stop the thing there, but we do not attempt to do so. The colour bar has been introduced into Kenya in its most degraded, degrading, and dishonest forms (have you ever examined the facts with regard to European and native education in Kenya?), and for years the British Government have provided the settlers with the legislative and administrative power and measures demanded by them in order that they may enforce it.

I do not wish to be misunderstood on this point. I have never denied that the ideas and ideals of the empire as explained by you exist and have been and are frequently applied in practice. But that is all the more reason surely for stating clearly in a book such as yours the facts in those cases in which there is a flagrant and dangerous violation of the ideas and ideals. Particularly at the present moment when, as you of course know, there is great danger that these unBritish ideas and ideals will spread from South Africa and Southern Rhodesia all over British Africa after the war.

Yours sincerely
Leonard Woolf

MEMORANDUM TO THE LABOUR PARTY

[1941]

Advisory Committee on Imperial Questions
Draft Report on Palestine
by
Leonard S. Woolf

The position in Palestine is governed by the Mandate to Great Britain, administered under the League of Nations. . . .

The fact is that it is not possible to reconcile the promises made originally to the two communities, as they are now understood and interpreted by the Arabs and Jews. But at the end of the war so many changes will have been made in the political pattern of the world and of the Middle East that it should be possible to tackle the problem de novo and to find a solution in which the differences of the two communities may be reconciled and forgotten. If this is to be successful, the policy to be formulated must be based upon the following principles:

1) The aim should be to do the least possible violence to the promises made and the least possible injustice to both Arabs and Jews;

2) The aim should be to establish a regime which will give time and opportunity for healing the breach and composing the difference between the two communities and which, when that has been accomplished, will make it possible for Jews and Arabs to co-operate peacefully in a self-governing Palestine.

It follows that the first principle of the settlement must be preservation of the integrity of Palestine and a rejection of all proposals to partition it between Arabs and Jews. Partition is a policy of despair and, under existing circumstances, is so desperate as to be almost inevitably disastrous.

. . . There are two crucial questions of internal policy upon which a clear decision must be taken and, when taken, honestly and fearlessly carried out: Jewish immigration and the sale and purchase of land. Here in particular the settlement should be one which does the minimum injustice to the two communities. The Arab demand for prohibition or drastic restriction upon Jewish immigration and of sale of land to Jews springs from their fear that they will be reduced to the position of a minority in the country. The solution appears to be to allow the continuation of Jewish immigration and of the sale of land by Arabs to Jews, but subject to reasonable restriction. Restriction upon immigration may be defined as reasonable provided its sole purpose is to prevent the Arabs from being reduced to a minority and provided that the country can absorb the immigrants economically. It would, therefore, not be reasonable at the present moment to allow unrestricted immigration. But it is clear, on the other hand, that a considerable immigration could be allowed without in any way endangering the present position of the Arab population, and if the Arabs could be convinced that the Administration was determined to safeguard them legitimately, much of the opposition might die down. Within those limits Jews should be allowed and encouraged to enter and develop the country. It would be well for the Administration in this matter to proceed cautiously but firmly, and to make it its first object to convince both parties of its impartial care for their rights and interests. Much the same applies to the land question. But it is easier here to define what is a reasonable restriction. Restrictions are only reasonable if they are in fact necessary to safeguard the Arab cultivator and small owner; they are not reasonable if their object is really to prevent Jews from acquiring land.

TO BEATRICE WEBB

Monk's House
17 January, 1942.   Rodmell, near Lewes   Sussex

Dear Mrs Webb,

When the days get a bit longer I should very much like to come down and see you and Mr Webb one afternoon. I will, if I may, later on write and see whether it is convenient to you.

I have often lately been reminded of my work with Mr Webb during the last war on the international post-war policy. I am secretary of a [Labour Party] sub-committee of Shinwell's Reconstruction Committee which is dealing with international affairs and all the same problems are arising again—most of them in a more acute form. It is uphill going. There is, I think, a kind of disorientation about Labour people—perhaps not unnaturally.

I agree with what you say about the punishment of the guilty.[1] I cannot see that mass trials after the war will do any good when there is no law upon which to base them. I understand that the Russians have become extraordinarily embittered in the last few weeks by the proofs of German brutality and barbarity which they find in the reoccupied territory. There is no doubt that German "ruthlessness" breeds a state of mind which destroys sobriety and saneness of judgment both in themselves and their opponents.

Yours sincerely
Leonard Woolf

1. She had referred to a press report about war-crimes trials after the war, commenting that there was no legal basis for them.

Monk's House
3/4/42
Rodmell

Dear Willie,

I have read the documents about the German socialists.[2] I shall not be up in London next week. I will either send them to you or bring them up with me the following week.

I hope you wont mind my saying that I think the whole thing most unpleasant and inadvisable. Every really informed person has known the truth about the matter for years. It lies half way between you and Phil Baker. The difficulty is that at the present moment it is quite impossible to convey that truth to uninformed persons or even to informed persons who are not unbiased. It was just the same in the last war, when one had people like Morel at one end—honest people who were so biased in favour of Germany that you could not argue with them—and at the other end bitter-enders so biased against Germans that you could not argue with them, and in between a mass of ignorant people whose emotions made them incapable of judging between the two. So today the truth in your case—and it is only half the truth—is misused by Vansittart and his fellow bitter-enders for their own no doubt honest but fatal purposes.

The truth, as I see it, is this. Once war has broken out—and, what is more important, when the international system is dominated by the fear or threat of war—99 per cent of the population is nationalist. Defeat in a modern war is or seems to be the ultimate disaster, and everything else is swept away by the fear of it. This applies to all Europeans, not exclusively to Germans, and to all sections of the population including international socialists, unless and until there is a complete breakdown in the national morale. Intelligent and honest socialists saw and said this before 1914; they never pretended that international socialism would, as it then existed, be strong enough to prevent a war or that when a nation was imminently threatened by or involved in war, socialists would not support their governments.

So far the German socialists did exactly what all other socialists did,

1. William Gillies (1885–1958), a Glasgow Fabian who began work in Labour Party headquarters in 1915; in 1920 he was appointed Overseas (later International) Secretary of the party executive. Although it is unclear whether he had any real influence, his extreme anti-German and anti-Communist views caused him to be dismissed in 1944.
2. Gillies had drafted material denouncing German Social Democrats for their conduct during the First World War and in the last days of the Weimar Republic. He wished to publish the documents in order to discredit Social Democrats in exile in Britain and to counter Philip Noel-Baker, whom he thought "a romanticist as regards Germany."

and it is easy enough to condemn them out of their own mouth. All these quotations are no proof of the Vansittart case, though of course they are and will be misused to support it. The Germans themselves in your documents use them to a considerable extent to pay off purely personal scores—which is what makes the documents smell so unpleasantly.

The truth in your case, however, which Phil and the others do not admit, is important, but it is not easy to explain and quite impossible to get over to most people during a war. In this attitude towards the national safety and to the Government when national safety is once threatened, Germans and German socialists are just like everyone else and there is really nothing strange or particularly significant in the fact that Scheidemann supported an annexationist Government or that Loebe is almost the only German socialist today pure enough in heart and intellect to long for the defeat of the Germans.[1] But what is true and significant is that, *in degree*, the Germans have always been worse socialists and more crude nationalists than most other Europeans. The difficulty is to explain honestly and clearly exactly what this means and how it has come about. Your documents dont do it, and that is why I object to them. I could do it, but it would take a book and not a letter—so I wont attempt it.

Yours sincerely
Leonard Woolf

To H. N. Brailsford

Monk's House
Rodmell, near Lewes   Sussex

17/10/43

Dear Noel,

I have read your MS and think it extremely interesting.[2] In the main I agree with most of your larger conclusions. There is one general important point and a few minor ones on which I have criticism and I will take the general question first, because in dealing with that I shall also get rid of some of the others.

1. Philip Scheidemann (1865–1939), first Chancellor of the Weimar Republic; Paul Löbe (1875–1967), President of the Reichstag 1920–32.
2. As Chairman of the Fabian Society's International Bureau, LW had encouraged Brailsford to set down his views on postwar Europe in a pamphlet for the Society. Brailsford expanded the pamphlet into a book, *Our Settlement with Germany*, which he submitted in draft to LW for comment. The text reflected Brailsford's immutably philo-German views.

I disagree entirely with the Vansittartites, both in their historical interpretation of Germans and in their proposals for dealing with Germany. But I do think that the communal psychology—and therefore history—of the German people has presented a problem since 1848 which is different from that of the other European peoples. The elements of that psychology can of course be seen in the other peoples and therefore it is true that, as you say, the aggressive nationalism of Prussia and Germany differs from ours and the French and Italians in degree. But differences in degree, when they are large enough and when combined with other factors, often amount in the end to differences in kind, and I think that this has become the case with German aggressive nationalism. The historical record of German governments, internal and external, alone supports this view and no other European nation since 1870 can approach the Germans for the crazy exaggeration of nationalistic psychology. This is not due to any original sin in Germans or a different constitution of the German mind; it is due to a combination of historical causes, geographical facts, and a German communal psychology which is itself the effect of historical causes and geographical facts. . . .

My own feeling is that one ought to admit to the full that the German communal psychology as it exists today, presents an appalling problem in a way in which the communal psychology of Frenchmen, Englishmen, and Dutchmen does not. Your conclusions, which are the important thing, are not invalidated but strengthened by the admission. If that psychology continues, there can be no peace in Europe. There is no reason to believe that it need continue, after a German defeat, if the German people are treated equitably and given a chance of cooperating in a new European order of peace and prosperity. The task of creating such an order is of course now of incredible difficulty. The one way of making it absolutely impossible and to ensure the continuance of militarist-nationalist German psychology would be a Punic peace.

I hope you wont mind my putting down my thoughts in this categoric way, but it is difficult to put them down succinctly. . . .

Yours
Leonard Woolf

Monk's House

16 October 1949 Rodmell, near Lewes, Sussex

Sir,

After 30 years instruction from nazis and communists, surely it must be possible to think up a better defence of judicial murders than that contained in Mr Kingsley Martin's article.[1] His argument runs: Because Popes massacred heretics for an issue which "was once held to justify them", because "Christians" (does he mean all Christians?) "are *as ready as*" (my italics) "Communists to act as if the end justifies the means", because some people "applauded the indiscriminate bombing of open cities", therefore it is misguided, trivial, and superficial to condemn the trial, verdict, and execution of good Communists by good Communists on framed and false charges. I seem to remember to have heard that it was said by them of old time that two wrongs dont make a right, but Mr Martin's doctrine is that one wrong anywhere at any time makes everything right for ever after. The difficulty is that, if this is true, it knocks the bottom not only out of Christianity, law, justice, truth and civilization (which would, of course, be all to the good), but also out of communism (which would be a tragedy) and nazism (which has, of course, been destroyed by Stalin). . . . It also knocks the bottom out of an article by Mr Martin which I read in another paper a few days ago in which he argued that it was wrong to retain the death penalty for murder in Britain. And as for the last sentence in Mr Martin's present article, if all murder of innocent persons is right, it is a little sentimental to worry about the fact that the person whom we murder happens to be our "comrade".

I feel that if I gave my thought to it, I could find a better argument than this for judicial murders on the grand scale. But it is not my business, for I am one of those Rip van Winkles who has always condemned the murders of Socrates, Christ, and Giordano Bruno as well as that of Mr Rajk.

Leonard Woolf[2]

1. In 1949 there began in Eastern Europe a series of "show trials" of Communist leaders. The first was of Lazlo Rajk, Hungarian Interior Minister, who confessed to and was executed for a variety of fabricated crimes. Martin's article was a bit of tortured logic that neither condemned nor justified Rajk's trial.
2. Martin wrote back that he and other members of the staff assumed that the letter was "some kind of joke" and that on maturer reflection LW would not want it published. After

Monk's House
24.10.49   Rodmell, Lewes, Sussex

Dear Kingsley,

I was very glad to get your letter because I think it means that you are no longer angry. The point, I admit, is an extremely difficult one, and I suppose it is true that sometimes the end justifies the means. But I doubt whether one should ever act on it and the argument that the end justifies the means is used so much with such frightful results that I think a paper like the *New Statesman* should be very, very chary of using it. I do not really agree with the argument as put even in your letter about "trivial and superficial", and, as put in your article, it shocked me and still shocks me. It implies a justification of any judicial murder by a Government because it always allows the Government to say it is trivial and superficial to condemn the execution of "x" because we are executing "x" as a deliberate act of policy involving a great issue. If our whole sense of justice had not been perverted in the last 30 years, I do not believe that you or anyone else would use that argument about a gang of low-class Hungarian politicians deliberately murdering by judicial process members of another gang, not with regard to a great issue but with regard to an internal struggle for power.

Yours,
L W

Shall we bury the hatchet at lunch tomorrow?

To Kingsley Martin

15.11.51   [Monk's House]

Dear Kingsley,

I was amused to get your letter as I expected it and could almost have written it for you. About once a year I write a letter to the *New*

---

a further exchange of correspondence, the letter was published with an editor's note stating that "nothing in Mr. Woolf's letter stands since the article had attacked both popes and communists."

Statesman and the editor refuses to print it on the grounds that it is both unintelligible and unintelligent. He has shown it to Dick [Crossman], Aylmer [Vallance], Norman [MacKenzie], J. B. S. Haldane, the office cat, a high Cabinet minister and they all agree.[1] When I read letters from Haldane and others which are printed in the *Statesman* I feel I must agree too, though I suppose it is just conceivable that it is the other way round. . . .

Yours,
L W

To Kingsley Martin

24/11/51   [Monk's House]

Dear Kingsley,

When A accuses B of "insincerity", it nearly always means that A does not like to admit to himself that he knows exactly what B is quite clearly saying and quite clearly means. It is true that I did not write with all the paraphernalia of unreality and pomposity that seems to be required in newspaper controversies and that I made the mistake of being mildly sarcastic, but you know perfectly well what I meant and that I said it. I think, mean, and say that

(1) The facts regarding the international situation are no longer honestly presented in the *NS*;

(2) The policy of the *NS* is ill-advised and calculated to produce the opposite effect of what I assume the editor to desire;

(3) The emphasis is such that the American policy and case are presented with gross unfairness;

(4) The emphasis is such that the Russian case and policy are treated in exactly the opposite way;

(5) In general the communist or pro-communist and the anti-American are allowed any amount of space, but any criticism of the Soviet Govt or system is toned down or goes into the wastepaper basket or editor's drawer;

(6) In particular the editor always finds some reason—in my opinion

1. Richard Crossman (1907–1974), Labour MP 1945–74, Cabinet Minister in Harold Wilson's governments, and Editor of the *New Statesman* 1970–72; J. B. S. Haldane (1892–1964), noted geneticist and biochemist, was a Communist, a fact that prompted LW repeatedly to call for his dismissal from the journal's board.

a bad reason—why L. Woolf should not express any or all of the above 5 sincere beliefs in the correspondence column of the *NS*.

Perhaps I should add that I believe (1) that there is a great deal to say impartially and usefully against American policy; (2) that there is a great deal to say impartially and usefully against German rearmament; (3) that I dislike emotional journalism.

Yours

L W

To the Editor of the *New Statesman*

	Monk's House
September 6, 1952	Rodmell, Lewes, Sussex

Sir,– Critic, in last week's Diary, says that he hopes that the 32 Englishmen who have gone on a visit to Peking will tell us on their return whether "the executions" of 1½ million Chinese by their Government in the last few years "were really necessary." It would be useful and interesting if Critic would give some indication to them and to us under what circumstances the execution of 1½ million persons by a Government is "really necessary."

Leonard Woolf[1]

To Kingsley Martin[2]

	Monk's House
23/8/53	Rodmell, Lewes, Sussex

Dear Kingsley

I daresay (though of course I do not believe) that I am as prejudiced on the other side of the fence as you are on yours, and that that is why so much in the *NS* distresses me. If the kind of thing which Balogh wrote appeared once a month I would pass it as easily as what I do

---

1. "Critic," alias Kingsley Martin, replied in the same issue that "you cannot carry out a revolution with rose water" and that the victims were Kuomintang soldiers whom the Communists had classified as bandits. The matter did not end there, however; see p. 450.
2. Martin had written to express himself puzzled by LW's criticism of an article in the *New Statesman* on Soviet economic growth.

every morning after breakfast.[1] It is, however, a question of emphasis, cumulative action, and the slant of an implication. The smell of the Baloghs, the emphasis, the accumulated innuendos, the slants of innumerable sentences give the impression to me—but also to many other people—that the *NS* in now habitually pro-Soviet and anti-American. Take August 15: it begins with an article in which all the vim is against the Americans. . . .

The first leader is still more anti-American.[2] I am completely against the American policy toward Rhee and I agree that there should have been an article pointing out its dangers and the right policy for the British Govt.[3] But your article is anti-American because all through it assumes the worst of everything connected with America, Americans, and American policy. This is not counterbalanced by the one sentence in which you surreptitiously admit that nine-tenths of what you have been saying is exaggerated anti-American propaganda.

There are two notes in the Diary which show how absolutely fair the *NS* is in criticizing the Russians as much as the Americans, but you will observe that in every case there is an insertion . . . to insinuate that the Americans are just as bad as, if not worse than, the Russians.

There follows an anti-American Sagittarius and the anti-American letter, the only point of which seems to be that only an American woman would give her dog a 450 franc steak.[4]

So back to Balogh. I have a profound mistrust of Tommy based on long experience in the L[abour] P[arty], the Fabian Society, and elsewhere. His judgment—political, economic, and social—seems to me as good as that of a mentally deficient boy of 16. I mistrust everything he says unless supported by incontrovertible evidence. Nine-tenths of what he says in the article is unsupported by any evidence except his hypothetical deductions from some rather doubtful figures. Like every-

1. Thomas Balogh (1905–1982), an Oxford economist and economic adviser to the Labour Party and several foreign governments, was a power in Harold Wilson's governments. In the article at issue, he maintained that it was difficult for "Western politicians and propagandists" to acknowledge the "tremendous dynamism" of the Soviet economy, which in ten years would give the Soviet Union "an absolute preponderance economically over Western Europe."
2. It lambasted Britain's agreement with the United States to resist another attack by North Korea against South Korea.
3. Syngman Rhee (1875–1965), the authoritarian ruler of South Korea after 1945, enjoyed what publicly appeared to be the full support of the U.S. government.
4. "Sagittarius," alias Olga Miller, had written satirical verse for the *New Statesman* since 1934; after 1945 her doggerel had an anti-American tone, as in the case to which LW referred, which concluded: "America replies to her outraged Allies/ That everything is just as it should be—/ U.N. is not disgraced/ But on the States is based/ While the States are firmly based on Syngman Rhee."

thing which he writes, you cannot be quite certain of what he really means you to think that he means. The smell and slant and implication here are that the Soviet economic system is so good that the standard of life in Russia will soon be higher than that of Britain or the USA. . . .

L W[1]

TO MARGERY PERHAM[2]

24.8.55   [Monk's House]

Dear Miss Perham,

It was extremely pleasant to get your letter. I wrote *Empire and Commerce in Africa* so long ago and I hardly think that I have read it since I wrote it so that there is not much in it that I remember.[3] But I am sure that my views with regard to economic imperialism have altered since then. I don't think that I ever said that it did no good but I daresay it did a good deal more good than I thought it did when I wrote the book. I daresay too that I was unfair to Lugard though not entirely, for I remember how distasteful a good deal of what he said seemed to me at the time and I don't think I can have been altogether wrong about him.

Did you ever come across [Charles] Temple, who was in the Nigerian Civil Service, second in command to Lugard and often acting for him. He wrote rather a good book about Africa. He read *Empire and Commerce* after his retirement and when he lived in Granada; hearing that Virginia and I were going to stay in the mountains above, he asked us to come and spend the night at his house. I had a long talk with him and he was very bitter against Lugard, claiming that a great deal

1. Martin answered: "Your letter distressed me and I am keeping myself from replying until I've time and the mood to do it properly. I think that so far from being pro-Soviet and anti-American, we are now so anxious not to give this impression that we suppress a great deal of news and comment that we ought to include!"
2. (Dame) Margery Perham (1895–1982), Fellow of Nuffield College, Oxford, 1939–63, and doyenne of Africanists at Oxford, had begun a biography of Lord Lugard, the famous imperialist, whom LW had savaged in his *Empire and Commerce in Africa*.
3. She had written: "I should like to say how deeply impressed I was with the imagination and intellectual courage shown in this book. . . . I wondered, as I read it, whether, looking back, you would be inclined to modify any of your views. You must surely see that Economic Imperialism in the hands of a man like Lugard . . . has been used for the benefit of the people. . . ."

of the credit for indirect rule etc., which Lugard claimed himself, ought to have gone to him, Temple. I took this with a grain of salt as he was a vain man but felt that there may have been a little in it.

I remember your coming here years ago with Hilda Matheson, wasn't it?[1] I hope if ever you are nearby again that you will look in.

Yours sincerely,
Leonard Woolf

To Kingsley Martin

3/8/56   Monk's House

Dear Kingsley,

I am sorry that I got angry yesterday, which never does any good to anyone but I dont think you realize how contemptuously (or should I say just rudely) you treat me the moment I disagree with anything you say in the *NS*—and though I always intend to follow Christ's teaching, Jehovah always breaks through. . . .

The internationalization problem is not just academic, because if you dont get some real international control of the Canal, you will undoubtedly have a war there, not perhaps today, but in a very near tomorrow. . . .[2]

The Soviet Government by its support of Nasser is playing the same kind of stupid dangerous game [as the British government]. My main disagreement with you and the people who mistakenly think they are the only true Left is that you are doing on the other side just what the Government is doing. You encourage and find excuses for the sort of nationalist threatening of a Nasser which you would howl against if it was made by a miserable French or British Government or by the imperialist USA. You never say what is true—that if Krushchev and Nasser go on acting as they do—i.e. like nationalist, imperialist warmongers—sooner or later some bloody fool like Eden, Mollet, Dulles or Krushchev will take some step which will precipitate a war. You never say what is true, that the imperialism and nationalism of a

1. Hilda Matheson (1888–1940), an official of the BBC.
2. On July 26 President Gamal Abdel Nasser nationalized the Suez Canal and closed it to Israeli shipping; at the time of this letter the British and French governments were trying to force him into a compromise settlement.

communist Russian Government or a dago Egyptian Government is no better than and is today more dangerous than that of any British or American Government. I think this refusal of "the Left" to have the courage of what were its convictions whenever someone with a Russian or a black, brown, or yellow face is concerned encourages the most dangerous thuggery by downtrodden Russians, Chinese, Egyptians just as the *Times* and the conservative backbencher encourage the most dangerous bellicosity in a weak-kneed conservative Government.

I think you and Krushchev and the *Times* and Eden have produced a very nasty international situation, and having now helped to produce it you ask me what policy I advocate. I am against war even if it is made by Russia or Egypt. I am therefore naturally against it being made by Eden. I am therefore against France and Britain taking military action against Egypt if Nasser refuses internationalization. In that event Britain should take the matter to the United Nations. . . .[1]

Yours
L W

FROM KINGSLEY MARTIN

[*c. 9 November 1956*]

Dear Leonard,

When I called on you this afternoon I hoped to exchange a memory or two about Greece and the islands and perhaps to pick your brain about the meaning of equality which I have to lecture about, with Crossland, to the Fabians.[2] *I have always enjoyed coming to see you anyway. Now I wish I'd stayed at home. Such a meaningless wrangle, as it seemed to me deliberately and unnecessarily provoked, has been more tiring to me and involved as much waste of spirit as a usual week's work.*

. . . I only wonder whether it never occurs to you that I've been giving my life to trying to make a decent paper and just when I am wondering whether you, as a friend, director and colleague will not

1. Israel, supported by Britain and France, attacked Egypt on October 29.
2. Anthony Crossland (1918–1977), Labour Party leader and theoretician of democratic socialism.

be finding something to be pleased about in the paper or to talk about interestingly . . . you simply start off on what appears to me an obsessive hare. Thats how it looks to me and I have to fight with myself at much expense of spirit not to rankle.

K M

To Kingsley Martin

11/11/56

Monk's House
Rodmell, near Lewes   Sussex

Dear Kingsley,

I am sorry that you were distressed and thought it a meaningless wrangle and deliberately provoked. I dont think it meaningless because it seems to me we are disagreeing about one of the most fundamental of political and social problems of the day. . . .

How deeply you misundertand what I say is shown by your use of the words "Soviet iniquities". I have never wanted the *NS* to dilate on Soviet "iniquities" nor do I think that "my friend" did. My and (I think) his point is that it is not Stalinism or Stalin or any particular communist or any "moral" delinquency or iniquity which produces the reactionary barbarism in Russia and its satellites, but the anti-democratic, anti-libertarian, autocratic, police-state organization which is, since Lenin, an integral part of the theory and practice of communism.

On the other hand since 1789 some form of democratic government in which the government is responsible to and ejectable by the people with freedom of speech and [assembly] is an integral part of what we call European civilization. It is therefore against the political autocracy and dictatorship of *communism* that we should protest fearlessly and do everything in our power to support democratic governments and democratic elements in communist countries. It is this which I think you and the *NS* have not done and do not do.

. . . What they [Russian leaders] rightly fear in Hungary is the demand of the revolting workers for free elections, free parties, and free speech, because they know perfectly well that if the Hungarian workers won this, it would be extremely unlikely that the workers of the other satellite countries and even of Russia would long tolerate the dictatorship of communist parties. And the reason is—what I tried to

say, but you would not listen to—that since 1789 the political psychology of Europeans, workers and bourgeoisie alike, puts upon certain
forms of political and social liberties a very high value.

Yours
L W

To Hugh Gaitskell[1]

28.5.58   [Monk's House]

Dear Hugh,
   Ever since I passed you in the Rome airport and we greeted one
another, I have contemplated writing to you on a subject which I feel
very strongly about. Last Sunday I met an ancient Winchester schoolmaster of yours, Murray Hicks, and we talked about this subject and
he feels as strongly about it as I do and urged me to write to you. The
thing is that I think the Labour party ought to pledge itself, if it returns
to power, to return the Elgin Marbles to Greece.[2] When we passed one
another in Rome I was on my way to Athens which I had not seen for
20 years and they have enormously improved the Parthenon. It seems
to me absurd that the Marbles should moulder in the British Museum
and not go up where they belong, side by side with some which are
still up there. I think it would greatly increase our prestige abroad if
we did it, though some old fogies here would start whimpering in *The
Times*. But they are not people who would vote Labour in any case
so that we could eat our cake and have it. Do think this over. It would
be a good slogan for the Labour party to nationalise here and also to
nationalise in Greece. You might make a condition with the Greeks
that they gave us casts of the Marbles in return for our generosity.

Yours,
Leonard Woolf[3]

1. Hugh Gaitskell (1906–1963), leader of the Labour Party 1955–63.
2. In 1801 Lord Elgin, British Ambassador to the Ottoman Empire and art collector, received
permission to remove "some stones" from the Acropolis. The stones were the frieze of the
Parthenon, a caryatid and a column; in 1816 they were purchased by an act of Parliament
and placed in the British Museum.
3. Gaitskell was noncommittal in his reply. When LW learned some years later that the
marbles would not be reaffixed to the Parthenon, he decided they should remain in London,
where they would be accessible to a larger number of viewers than in Athens.

To Margaret Cleeve[1]

6.8.58

Monk's House
Rodmell, Lewes, Sussex

Dear Miss Cleeve,

I don't know that I can really give you the kind of information you want as I had very little to do with the Royal Institute of International Affairs. After the War I used to meet a small group of people which inluded H. G. Wells, Lionel Curtis, Gilbert Murray, William Archer, to discuss with them Wells's idea of combining to write a History of the World.[2] Wells's own [*Outline of*] *History* was the result but I know that we used also to discuss the Institute. At that time there was a great interest in secret diplomacy, owing to the publication by the Bolsheviks of the secret treaties and also interest in the possibility of democratic control of foreign policy. I certainly and some of the others hoped that the Institute would do something to educate people about foreign affairs and, at the same time, introduce some democratic control of foreign policy.

I went to one of the earliest meetings of the Institute at which Lord Grey gave a speech about foreign policy and made the astonishing statement that except for the treaties made during the War and published by the Soviet Government, there had never been any secret treaties in the Foreign Office. Nobody challenged this statement, including myself, though to my mind, it was obviously untrue.[3] Walking home after the meeting I came to the conclusion that if no one in a large audience challenged this statement and I had not had the courage to do so myself, I ought to resign. When I got back home I wrote a letter resigning from the Royal Institute of International Affairs and never joined it again.

Yours sincerely,
Leonard Woolf

1. A long-time member of the staff of the Royal Institute of International Affairs, she was collecting material for a history of the organization; she wrote to LW because he was a founding member. No study has ever been written.
2. Lionel Curtis (1872–1955), who straddled the worlds of academia and public affairs, was an expert on South African, colonial and commonwealth affairs. Gilbert Murray (1866–1957), the leading Greek scholar of his time, was a committed internationalist. William Archer (1856–1924), a drama critic, was active in the League of Nations Union and similar bodies.
3. LW had in mind at least the secret articles of the Anglo-French Entente of 1904, which Grey consistently deprecated—dishonestly in the judgment of LW and diplomatic historians—as "of no importance." In 1914 and afterward LW accused Grey of being committed *in petto* to support France and therefore of failing to do what he could to forestall the war.

To Isaiah Berlin[1]

6/7/59   [Monk's House]

Dear Isaiah Berlin,
    . . . I have been rereading with admiration the last few days your
Two Concepts of Liberty. I find it both fascinating and illuminating.
There is one point which puzzles me a little. You say that "there seems
to be scarcely any consciousness of individual liberty as a political
ideal in the ancient world" and you agree with Condorcet's statement
that the nation of individual rights is absent from the legal conceptions
of the Romans and Greeks. But does not the Thucydidean Pericles
state the ideal of individual liberty as clearly as it has ever been
envisaged. I should also have thought that the consciousness of it was
in fact implicit in many places in Herodotus, even in the *Antigone*,
and sometimes in Euripides. Condorcet's use of the idea of "legal
conception" in this connection is misleading. In our sense there must
have been hardly any "law" or "legal conception" in Athens; the
framework of life was often regulated by custom where we regulate it
by law or legal conception. And the ideal of individual liberty has
according to Pericles been built into the framework of Athenian life
consciously and deliberately. What he says may be denied, but I dont
think one can deny that he had the consciousness of individual liberty
as a political ideal.

                                          Yours
                                          Leonard Woolf[2]

1. (Sir) Isaiah Berlin (b. 1909), eminent Oxford scholar and author. His inaugural lecture
as Chichele Professor of Social and Political Theory had recently been published.
2. In a long reply Berlin defended his argument about the absence of a notion of *individual*
rights in ancient society, but concluded: "However, I may be hoplessly mistaken about this.
The Professor of Greek History in this University—Andrewes—quoting another Professor
of Greek History—Gomme—agrees with you. I am shaken, but still obdurate."

To Isaiah Berlin

9/7/59   [Monk's House]

Dear Isaiah Berlin,
    . . . I agree with nine-tenths of what you say—in fact, like you I'm
"shaken but obdurate". What orginally puzzled me was your statement
that "there seems to be scarcely any consciousness of individual liberty
as a political *ideal* in the ancient world." But it is precisely as a
"political ideal" that Pericles and even Herodotus talk about individual
liberty. In your letter you write about the Greeks' consciousness of
individual liberty as a political *right*. That surely is quite different and
I think it is true, as you say, that there is scarcely any Greek consciousness of a right to individual liberty in the modern sense. This is
partly, I think, because there was such a very small area of law at any
rate in Athens. Even so, in the conversations between Antigone and
Kreon and between Haimon and Kreon in the *Antigone* the dispute
comes very near to a dispute over a *right*, something, as you say, the
violation of which is a violation of some ultimate principle.

                                                    Yours
                                                    Leonard Woolf

To Hugh Dakin[1]

10.12.59   [Monk's House]

Dear Mr. Dakin,
    I found your letter extremely interesting, though we are so far apart
in our views that I doubt whether it is much good continuing the
controversy. It is, of course, really the old question of the egg before
the hen or the hen before the egg. My position is that you and people
like you go on saying that people who are not white and English are
not yet able to govern themselves but, of course, you are going to give
them the right to govern themselves when they are fit to govern themselves, until they break out into savage violence. Sooner or later this
has happened all over the British Empire with disastrous results. Of
course I do not say that the black man's civilization or barbarism is

1. A Rhodesian student who had criticized LW's article "The Colour of Our Mammies" in
the July issue of *Encounter*.

446

the same as ours and I know that he will make a mess of governing himself. But would you really say that the Europeans, at any rate in Germany, Poland, Hungary, Spain and Russia have made a great success of it? I did not say in my article that the blacks were more civilized than the whites but I do think that, looking back over history, the obstinate stupidity of people like Lord Robins and Sir Roy Welensky is staggering.[1] That does not mean that I am claiming any superiority; otherwise you have to say that anyone who disagrees with anyone else about anything is claiming superiority. I do not agree with you that *any* belief that one does not oneself hold must seem ridiculous.

That is my position. Your position is that if I say the hen precedes the egg, you say the egg precedes the hen, i.e., you say that it is people like me who cause the Africans to want to be self-governing and make them use violence against the good white people and so you put anyone, who is black and wants to begin to govern himself, into jail or a concentration camp.

Yours faithfully,
Leonard Woolf

To Margaret Cole[2]

5/7/62   [Monk's House]

Dear Margaret,

I am very sorry to have hurt you. I ought not to have reviewed your book. I wanted to read it, but being a publisher and ex-literary editor, I never buy books and am apt to review a book if I want to read it. Having embarked on a review, I felt an obligation to say what I thought about it as I would if I had not known the author. What you say now shows, I think, that I was correct in saying that your depreciation of the Webbs is unconscious. There is hardly a single word of praise of them or of Shaw in your book. No one who did not already know a great deal about the [Fabian] Society and what the Webbs really did in it and in the Labour party and movement could possibly get any

1. Thomas Robins, 1st Baron Robins (1884–1962), a prominent Rhodesian business leader. Sir Roy Welensky (b. 1907), a leader of white trades unions in Rhodesia and Prime Minister of the Federation of Rhodesia and Nyasaland 1956–63. Both men were white supremacists.
2. (Dame) Margaret Cole (1893–1980), wife of economist G. D. H. Cole, was active in the Labour Party and the Fabian Society. LW's review in the *Political Quarterly* of her book *The Story of Fabian Socialism* had provoked her protest.

idea of what it was from your book. This shocks me. On the other hand you seem to relish never giving them the benefit of any doubt as to their dishonesty, pettiness, snobbery, or absurdity. Indeed, you again and again slip in a word or sentence which denigrates or depreciates them, as you will see if you carefully reread the passages to which I referred you. . . .

Of course Sidney and Beatrice were in many ways ridiculous and unscrupulous. It is eminently right to say so. That they were often exasperating is also obvious and should be recorded. But, for good or bad, they had an immense influence upon the Fabian Society and the Labour movement; I dont think your book gives any recognition to this, whereas the sneering and sniping leave the uninformed reader with the impression that they were merely silly or negligible.

They were certainly not that, and there was also another quality in them (the existence of which no one could guess from your description of them): a curious simplicity and sincerity, benignity and unvindictiveness, which made them, beneath their surface ridiculousness and enfuriatingness, exceedingly nice persons. That is why, though they often annoyed me, I had a considerable affection for them—and still have.

Yours sincerely
Leonard Woolf

To the *New Statesman*

Monk's House
Rodmell   Sussex

30 November 1962

Sir,– Hitler and the Nazis, in Germany and the countries which they occupied, arrested millions of men, women and children and herded them into concentration camps where they deliberately starved and tortured them; they deliberately murdered in gas chambers millions of these inoffensive persons, stripping them naked and driving them mercilessly to their death. Mr A. J. P. Taylor,[1] in reviewing a book about the Irish famine of last century, takes the opportunity to argue by inference and insinuation that the British government of 1846, in particular Lord John Russell and Sir Charles Trevelyan, were no better than the Nazis, for under their administration 'all Ireland was a Belsen'

---

1. A. J. P. Taylor (b. 1906), Fellow of Magdalen College, Oxford, 1938–76 and controversial historian of modern Europe, had just reviewed Cecil Woodham-Smith's *The Great Hunger*.

and owing to them 'nearly two million Irish people died of starvation and fever within five years'. He does not mention the fact that, whereas the Nazis deliberately created Belsen and deliberately gassed the millions of men, women and children, Russell and Trevelyan had no responsibility of any kind for creating the famine. They came into office on 6 July 1846 when the crop had already failed. It is difficult to understand the reason for Mr Taylor's passion for whitewashing Hitler and the Nazis. That a serious historian who has lived through the years 1933 to 1945 should seriously write such stuff in a serious journal is horrifying and terrifying.

Leonard Woolf

To Samuel Lessere[1]

16/12/62   [Monk's House]

Dear Mr Lessere,
  I do not think I am "motivated" in this by the fact that I'm Jewish. That over 6 million persons should have been deliberately in cold blood slaughtered with the greatest cruelty and suffering seems to me appalling whether they are Poles, Americans, Jews, Germans, communists or even cats and dogs. That you should really think it necessary to "redress the balance" (what balance?) and that it really makes a difference whether they were Jews or not Jews, and that what the "Mosley gang" did is really comparable with the deliberate torture and slaughter in a space of four years of over 6 million Poles, Jews, Russians, socialists, communists, old and sick people, shows to what a state of muddled barbarism an American citizen has been reduced in the year 1962.
  I have never said that there is anything "diabolic" about Taylor, only that he is disastrously mistaken. I have never said or thought that there is any inherent evil in the Germans or that there is no evil in other peoples. I am not concerned with wickedness, but with the effects of what people do and it seems to me appalling that Taylor (or an American citizen) should airily say: "After all what is all this fuss about Hitler and the Germans torturing 6 million people and driving them naked into gas chambers and flogging and starving them in Belsen; after all they were only Jews or Germans or sick people or

1. An American resident in France.

449

Poles or Americans; and after all we are all wicked, and after all Mosley or Lord John Russell or Moses or Jesus Christ were in their own way just as bad and after all no one can say that he is holier than another—so let them get on with the good work of persecuting those they dont happen to like, for after all. . . .[*sic*]"

Yours sincerely
Leonard Woolf

To Kingsley Martin

7.5.63   [Monk's House]

Dear Kingsley,

I got back here yesterday and am much better. . . .[1] I used my enforced inanition to jot down what seemed to me the heads of the difference between you and me with regard to the question raised by Hyams in his book and by you in the memorandum which you sent me. I have put it down crudely because I think it is only in that way that my position will be clear to you. I append it on a separate sheet.

Yours
Leonard

[Appended sheet]

It is never the case that—as Roman Catholics, communists, and you assert—you know something so certainly to be so good in itself, that it justifies you to do anything, however vast the evil, as a means to it.

It is never right for an individual or a government to do any vast evil as a means to some hypothetical good. That is why the question: "Is the execution of 1½ million subjects by the [Chinese] government really necessary?" is both shocking and ludicrous. . . .

In real life individuals and governments are continually confronted by situations in which, owing to their own or other people's actions,

1. LW had returned from two weeks in a hospital following an operation; during his confinement he had received a memorandum from Martin about Edward Hyams's book, *The New Statesman: 1913–1963*, which referred to LW's letter to the *New Statesman* on the execution of several million Chinese. Hyams had commented: "That the reproach should have come from Leonard Woolf was of particular interest to insiders: it was long assumed, rightly or wrongly, that Leonard Woolf was one of the few people whose influence with Kingsley Martin was strong."

whatever they do the result will almost certainly be evil. Here they have to consider solely the probable results of their actions and choose that which seems likely to produce the least immediately evil results. This can never justify the immediate doing positively of great evil. . . . Thus (1) it could never justify the execution of even 10,000 subjects as "really necessary;" (2) it might—though I rather doubt it—have justified a warning to Germany in July 1914 that if she declared war on France, we would come to the aid of France—i.e. in order, by risking an evil, our becoming involved in war, to try to prevent the evil of war breaking out; (3) I think it would have justified a warning to Hitler after the invasion of Austria that any further act of aggression would be resisted by force; (4) the League Covenant to resist aggression against a member and all the sanctions clauses are justified accordingly; (5) all nuclear war is ruled out because no evil, alternative to a nuclear war, could be more evil than a nuclear war.

. . . I believe I know what is good and that some of the things which I believe are true, but I dont think my knowledge is so certain that it justifies me in injuring, torturing, or killing other people. So although up to a point I am a Marxist, I do not think that that justifies me in harming in any way even a non-Marxist flea.

. . . Another [difference]: you are a Fellow Traveller who likes to find a justification for anything which the communist does because he seems to have the same end as you and vice versa to condemn the American. I am prejudiced against the communist just because he seems to have the same end as I and turns out so obviously not to have it.

Another: you rate economics and metaphysics above freedom; I rate freedom above economics and hate and distrust all metaphysics. . . .[1]

To William Humphrey[2]

26/11/64   [Monk's House]

My dear Bill,
. . . I saw yesterday in the *Times* that the Italian elections had gone rather as you feared with more communist gains—but they did not

1. In reply Martin repeated the syllogism of his memo to LW: If Britain was justified in declaring war in 1939, even though millions were killed as a result, it was inconsistent to condemn Mao for executing millions in the belief he was forestalling a third world war.
2. An American writer who met LW through Ian Parsons, the British publisher of his first novel.

seem to be very great and they were only municipal elections. The Labour Government here, as you have probably seen, is in rather stormy waters. Harold Wilson, whom I dont like, has done better than I expected, but I mistrust his economic advisers, particularly Balogh.[1] They mistake violence for strength, and though I think their economic measures were generally right, they seem to have messed things up by the crude way they put them into operation.

Love to you both.

Leonard

To Harold Wilson

11/5/66   [Monk's House]

Dear Harold,

I got back from the USA this morning and that is why I have not answered your letter before—for which I must apologize. It is extremely good of you to think of submitting my name to the Queen for an honour and to ask me whether this would be agreeable to me.[2] I have always been (heretically) against the giving and accepting of honours and have often in the past said so. Much as I appreciate your kindness, I cannot therefore accept it, but I hope that you will not think the worse of me. Years ago Ramsay MacDonald offered the same honour to Virginia, and, sharing my views, she asked to be forgiven for not accepting it and I drafted her reply in much the same words as I am now using for my own.

It is ages ago that we were both on the Fabian Executive, and, remembering that, I have more than once been on the point of writing to you and saying how much I admire what you have done for the party and the brilliant result of it in the last election, but I thought you might regard it as an impertinence. Now I venture to say it.

Yours sincerely,
Leonard Woolf

1. In the general election a few weeks earlier, Labour came to power with Harold Wilson as Prime Minister but held an overall parliamentary majority of only four seats.
2. Wilson had offered LW membership in the Order of the Companions of Honour.

To the Editor of *The Times*[1]

25/3/68

Monk's House
Rodmell, Lewes, Sussex

Sir,

Lady Fisher of Lambeth says that the Arabs attacking Israelis from Jordan are not terrorists or saboteurs, but heroes and brave men. The act of sabotage for which the Israelis staged the reprisal (which personally I do not defend) was to blow up a bus containing children. I wonder whether the late Archbishop of Canterbury or Jesus Christ would agree with Lady Fisher of Lambeth.

Yours &c
Leonard Woolf

To Lord Fisher of Lambeth[2]

1/4/68

[Monk's House]

Dear Lord Fisher,

Many thanks for your letter. I am sorry that we should again find ourselves on opposite sides of the fence—and the fence itself this time seeming to be almost the opposite of the previous one.[2] The answer to your question is the difference between the nature and intentions of the acts in the case of the Arabs and, say, of the acts of the French Maquis. The French acted violently against a German army of occupation; they did not go into German territory and lay mines to blow up a busload of German children. (Nor by the way, did the Germans proclaim that they would not negotiate with the French and were determined to exterminate them.) Under these circumstances it seemed to me unfortunate to castigate us for not recognizing the heroism and bravery of the men who had just blown up a busload of Israeli children

1. Following a report of a reprisal raid by Israeli forces against Arab guerrillas, Rosamond Fisher, wife of the retired Archbishop of Canterbury, had written a letter to the paper comparing the Arabs to the heroic French underground during the Second World War.
2. Geoffrey Fisher (1887–1972), headmaster of Repton School 1914–32, Bishop of Chester 1932–39, Bishop of London 1939–45, Archbishop of Canterbury 1945–61, was made a life peer in 1961.
3. LW and Lord Fisher had exchanged letters about immortality the previous year; see pp. 552–54.

and to make no reference whatsoever to the nature of this brave and heroic act. I may be wrong, of course, and you and Lady Fisher may be right—I am always sceptical about my own (and other people's) beliefs; the only thing which I feel some certainty about, if you will pardon me saying so, is that this time Jesus Christ would agree with me and not with you and Lady Fisher.

I should like to add that, though I am an (atheistical) Jew, I have no prejudice against Arabs; I used to deal with the Arabs of the Persian Gulf. I liked them very much and we got on well together.

Yours sincerely,
Leonard Woolf

To Lord Fisher of Lambeth

4/4/68

Monk's House
Rodmell, Lewes, Sussex

Dear Lord Fisher,

You write: "Lady Fisher was drawing attention to the simple fact that the French people and the Arab people hold the title of Resisters against the invaders and masters of their own homeland. Are you disagreeing with that?" This is like saying to a man: "Have you stopped beating your wife? Answer the simple question by yes or no." But it is not a simple question in either case, and I cannot give a simple answer.

I must first state my own attitude to the terrible situation in the Middle East. From the first moment of the Balfour Declaration I was against Zionism on the ground that to introduce Jews into an Arab occupied territory with the ultimate prospect of establishing an independent Jewish state would lead to racial trouble. Verbally and in writing I said this. Sir Lewis Namier was an old friend of mine and I have spent hours listening to his arguments to convince me of the necessity for Zionism. He once induced me to go and see Weizmann in order to be converted by him.[1] I had a two hour talk with Weizmann and remained unconverted. This was in the twenties.

After 1930 and the advent of Hitler and still more after the massacre of the millions of Jews in Europe, the withdrawal of us from Palestine,

1. Sir Lewis Namier (1888–1960), eminent historian; Chaim Weizmann (1874–1952), Zionist leader and the first President of Israel.

the enormous increase in the Israeli population, and the unsuccessful attack of the Arabs on the Israelis, the situation was entirely altered. In history and politics you have got to deal with situations as they are, not as they were twenty, thirty, forty, or fifty years ago. There is now an established Israeli state with a large and immensely energetic population. It could only be destroyed now by a massacre of the inhabitants. This is what Nasser and the Arab states have again and again announced as their policy. They have once tried unsuccessfully to execute it. By closing the Suez Canal and the Gulf to the Israelis and insisting upon the withdrawal of the United Nations contingents, Nasser proclaimed his intention of trying again. The Israelis attacked the Arabs and Nasser was once more beaten.

I deplore this situation which is a terrible one. But to say that it is a simple one and like that of the German invasion and occupation of France seems to me to ignore both reality and morality. The crux is that unless the Arabs can be induced to negotiate with Israel, there can only be an unending horror of violence and bloodshed. Do you really think that it is feasible for the Arabs now to destroy the state of Israel? Or that, if they can, that means anything less than the slaughter of most of the population of Israel? And do you really think it right to approve and incite the Arabs attempting to do this by acts of violence, terror and sabotage, which include the blowing up of busloads of Israeli children?

It seems to me that the situation in and around Israel is so appalling and so delicate that no one ought to say anything to exacerbate it or to incite either side to further violence. What shocked me in Lady Fisher's letter was that that seemed to be what she was doing, inciting the Arabs to further acts of terror and bloodshed against the Israelis, soldiers and civilians, and ignoring the dreadful results, e.g. the killing and maiming of Israeli children as in the act of sabotage which had just taken place.

You say: "We need not go to Jesus Christ for a ruling on this." But with all respect to you and Lady Fisher, this was the relevant point of my letter. If nine out of ten people had written her letter, I should have deplored it, but I should not have been so horrified as to write a letter to the *Times*. I am, as you well know, not a Christian, but there are many things in the doctrines and sayings of Christ, as reported in the New Testament, which have a strong appeal to me. Among these in particular was his uncompromising attitude towards violence and cruelty, the notion, for instance, that anything can be justified by anything—e.g. the massacre of children by the heroism and bravery of patriotism. After all as Head of the Church of England you had stood officially for his doctrine, and I still think that as your wife there is, as it were, some moral obligation on Lady Fisher not even to seem to flout that doctrine.

Yours sincerely
Leonard Woolf

To Lord Fisher of Lambeth

Monk's House
Rodmell, Lewes, Sussex

6/4/68

Dear Lord Fisher,

We differ so profoundly on ethics, politics, and metaphysics that it is only natural that the longer we correspond the further apart we drift. But there are some points in your letter where you misstate or misunderstand what I believe and said which I should like to make clear. I do not believe and never said that "Israel should be left to keep her war gains in self-defence." My position was: (1) So long as the Arabs refuse to recognize or negotiate with the Israeli Government and publicly proclaim their intention of destroying the state and people of Israel, it is improbable that the Israelis will give up their war gains and return to the dangerous position which they occupied before Nasser made the United Nations contingent withdraw; (2) So long as the Arabs adopt the above attitude to Israel, there is no moral obligation on the Israelis to withdraw; (3) Acts of terrorism, violence, and sabotage by the Arabs, particularly the shooting of policemen and civilians, the throwing of bombs among civilians, and the killing and maiming of children will not cause the Israelis to withdraw and can only lead to further useless violence, bloodshed, and cruelty; (4) Such useless acts of violence, bloodshed, and cruelty by the Arabs are morally wrong, and would be morally wrong whatever the nationality of the "heroes and brave men" who performed them; (5) People who incite or condone this useless violence, terrorism, and sabotage by the Arabs are morally wrong and politically foolish; (6) If Arabs would state that they are prepared to make peace and negotiate with Israel, I think that the Israelis would probably agree to a reasonable settlement of frontiers; but it is only by negotiating that it can be discovered whether this is so.

As you will see from the above, I disagree profoundly with the argument in your letter that you can separate morality from politics.

That principle is untrue and has caused more disasters and been used as an excuse for more cruelty and evil than almost any other human delusion. The question whether Arabs (or Israelis or Frenchmen) should shoot policemen in the back or kill and maim children is both moral and political, i.e. is it morally wrong and is it politically effective? I condemn it on both grounds, while you and Lady Fisher approve it on both. That is where we differ.

As regards Christ and the New Testament and violence, I have read Luke's Gospel many times and have heard the arguments to prove that he would approve war, violence, and all the rest of it many times, and have heard many times about the difference between the Kingdom of God and the Kingdom of Caesar, but when I read the sermon on the mount, I am convinced that he would have thought the shooting of policemen in the back and the killing of children in the name of nationalism and patriotism, no matter who did it, morally wrong. Here again we differ.

I accept, of course, your statement that Lady Fisher did not *intend* to incite and condone Arab violence. But I am not alone in misunderstanding her. . . .

Yours sincerely
Leonard Woolf

To Lord Fisher of Lambeth

12/4/68 [Monk's House]

Dear Lord Fisher,

You say that the answer to the question

"Are not all so-called terrorists or saboteurs, whatever kind of violence they use and whatever the political motives, brave men when they are acting for their own country and homeland when it is under the heel of a conqueror?"

is Yes, and you add that it is a question of moral judgment. I agree that it is a question purely of moral judgment. But my answer is the most emphatic NO, no matter who these terrorists may be—Jews, Arabs, French, or British. To say yes is to make a moral judgment that the end justifies the means, a principle which, I think, is horribly immoral and has for thousands of years been used to justify every kind of evil and crime. I think that for anyone anywhere at any time to shoot a policeman in the back or kill a child because he is acting for his own country and homeland when it is under the heel of a conqueror is unjustifiable and morally wrong. The end does not justify the means. You hold the opposite and that is really the nub of our disagreement and of this correspondence.

Yours sincerely
Leonard Woolf

Monks House
2/7/51

Dearest, It is rather late to begin a letter, but this is only to say goodnight. Rodmell, Sussex, London, England, Great Britain, the Commonwealth, & English Speaking Union are very dreary without you. (I have, as you will see, been listening to speeches by Eisenhower, Salisbury, Attlee, & Winston at an English Speaking Union banquet. Eisenhower was rather impressive.)

I went to London today, lunched with Willie & a Russian. I got into a carriage at East Croydon & after the train had started found that it was labelled LADIES ONLY. I apologised for my intrusion to 8 ladies & 6 of them assured me that it did not matter at all. Two in the seats at the further end looked resentful & started a conversation at the top of their voices absolutely incredible. One looked & dressed exactly like Mabel. The other gave an account — obviously to impress us — of the dinner she wished to order but could not get at her club. "No champagne

PART SIX

LATER YEARS

With the twin calamities of the death of Europe in 1939 and the death of Virginia in 1941, Leonard Woolf's political and personal worlds lay in ruins. A profound loneliness fell over him. That he was not spiritually broken, Leonard ascribed to his Jewish heritage—the sense consciously or unconsciously imbibed that fate might be defied through iron self-control and unremitting hard work. In fact, the twenty-eight remaining years of his life, far from being a period of anticlimax and decline, were a time of undiminished activity and great happiness. As politics and publishing demanded less of his time, other activities filled their place. He continued to take a lively interest in the *New Statesman* and the *Political Quarterly*, wrote regular book reviews, and broadcast for the BBC on literary topics and his reminiscences. He devoted more time to working on his own books, and in the last twenty years of his life published no fewer than a dozen of them. He joined the Royal Horticultural Society, the Glyndebourne Festival Society, the Ancient Monuments Society, the National Cactus and Succulent Society, the National Trust, the British Pteridological Society, the Zoological Society of London, the Sussex Beekeepers' Association and the Sussex County Cricket Club; he became a member of the India Club and the Athenaeum; he was elected Fellow of the Royal Society of Arts and the Royal Society of Literature; he was appointed to the Council of the Fawcett Library Trust and the Society of Authors. He was for many years President of the Monday Literary Club of Lewes, Clerk of the Parish Council of Rodmell and President of the Rodmell Horticulture Society.

One of the most demanding activities of these later years, as it developed, was dealing with Virginia's literary estate. Her papers were in great disorder, partly because of her untidiness and partly as a result of the confused removal of the Woolfs' effects from London after the bomb damage to their house on Mecklenburgh Square. After sifting and organizing a great mass of papers, he was able to bring out three volumes of her essays and some previously unpublished fictional writings. He also extracted passages from her thirty-notebook diary that dealt with the art of writing and published them in 1953 as *A Writer's Diary*. Up to then surprisingly little was known about Virginia as a person or even as a writer. This well-edited volume aroused serious critical interest, initially with a literary elite and gradually with an ever-wider readership.

By the mid-fifties there began arriving at Monk's House what eventually swelled into a seemingly endless stream of scholars with questions about every facet of Virginia's life and work. Leonard gave each an interview, lunch or tea and a tour of his garden. He read their manuscripts, offered comments and helped some with their careers. With his encouragement several of them found and published further essays by Virginia that had been written anonymously or lost sight of. There also arrived scores of letters inquiring about Virginia and her writing: what she thought of psychoanalysis; whether she was clairvoyant, thought of her books as music, had read Plotinus, Freud, Jung, R. A. M. Stevenson's *Velasquez*, Frazer's *Golden Bough*, Bergson or Karin Stephen on Bergson, Jane Harrison, Tagore or Baudelaire; whether she had attended a lecture by Wittgenstein; whether she was influenced by Roger Fry, Charles Mauron, Berkeley, Proust, Joyce, the Fabian socialists or the Impressionist painters; whether so-and-so in real life was the model for this or that character in one of her novels. To each, Leonard wrote a brief reply, trying—sometimes without success—to set the record straight.

Eventually the question arose of the disposition of Virginia's original manuscripts. In the 1940s Leonard had given away two of them and, while usually fending off requests from dealers, had agreed to sell for a modest sum the original text of two essays. Then in 1956 he was approached by two American dealers who wished to purchase the bulk of Virginia's *Nachlass*. Evidently he saw the sale as an opportunity to promote interest in his wife's work and a way of insuring that her

464

papers would have a single repository. He agreed to the sale on the condition that the collection would be kept intact, preferably in an American university library, and made readily accessible to scholars. When his brother Philip objected to the manuscripts leaving the country, Leonard explained why he thought they should be in the United States. He neglected to mention that no library in Britain showed interest in having them.

A more vexing question was whether to publish some of Virginia's letters. Instinctively Leonard did not like the idea. To publish the intimate ones, as he wrote to Vita Sackville-West in 1948, would not be possible; yet to bring out only the impersonal ones would leave a distorted impression. There the matter stood until January 1955, when he suddenly received the page proofs of a biography of Virginia, *The Moth and the Star*, which contained quotations from her letters to Vita Sackville-West. No steps had been taken by the American author, Aileen Pippett, or by the publisher, Little, Brown, to secure Leonard's permission to use the letters. He was less angered by the deception— and gave permission for the book to be published in the United States and Canada—than by the fact that the book, by publicizing bits of letters out of context, did precisely what he wanted to avoid. The incident forced his hand, and he decided to prepare a volume of general correspondence.

Before then, however, he and James Strachey brought out a slim volume of bowdlerized correspondence between Virginia and Lytton. The book received few favorable reviews. Leonard's uneasiness was increased by the critical reaction to memoirs that had been published around the same time by Clive Bell and David Garnett, which he felt indirectly reflected on Virginia. At length, after consulting his fellow directors at the Hogarth Press in the fall of 1957, he decided against publishing any letters. He was convinced that in the hostile critical climate they would be turned against Virginia, damaging her reputation and inflaming antagonism toward her social circle—Bloomsbury. On both points he was exceedingly sensitive.

Nothing in his later life concerned Leonard more than Virginia's literary status, which for many years after her death rested on her novels alone. Her position in English letters at that time not only was generally held to be relatively minor, but in some quarters was under harsh critical assault. Rare indeed was it when anyone in a British university had a good word to say for her work. During her lifetime Leonard had chided her for caring so much about critical opinion and for hoping to gain immortality through her novels. Yet, deep down, he evidently thought of her writings almost as though they were her children. Anyone who attacked the novels in writing or in a radio broadcast or who had the temerity to maintain that they were no longer being read was fairly certain to receive a polite—or stiff—note of rebuttal. His argument was simple. One could like or dislike Virginia's novels, but one had to take them seriously and recognize that they deal with some of the most important issues with which an artist can deal. Whether she failed or succeeded in what she was trying to do could be debated; he made no exaggerated claims. *The Waves*, in his judgment, was one of the great works of English literature. He also admired *To the Lighthouse* and, though he wavered here, *Between the Acts*. That is as far as he went. But, as he once remarked of a review by F. R. Leavis, "to ignore *what they are about* and simply say that they are 'vacant' and 'pointless' and have no 'concern for any appearance of grasp or point' (whatever exactly the Professor of English Literature may mean by that) seems to me just silly."

His reaction to attacks on Bloomsbury was similar. The critics did not take seriously what deserved to be taken seriously. In reality Bloomsbury was nothing more than a group of a dozen or so friends, most of whom had met at Cambridge and later lived in the same London borough, who had matured together and who shared a general intellectual outlook. They had started out as intellectual rebels seeking liberation from the past and new paths into the future. In their various ways they had then excelled and, though their emotional ties never broke, had steadily grown apart and saw one another less and less until little remained of Bloomsbury but memories. Yet almost from the start Bloomsbury had been misrepresented as an exclusive and monolithic cartel of self-admiring aesthetes who propounded a doctrine about everything from the arts to politics and who aspired to control the cultural media and fasten a dictatorship over the country's intellectual life.

So there were always two Bloomsburys—the real one and the mythical one. Leonard could therefore at one moment write explicitly about Bloomsbury and discuss those who were part of it while at another deny that there was such an entity or refer to "what came to be called Bloomsbury." Eventually his exasperation at the attacks on "Bloomsbury" gave way to an equal irritation with the ostensibly friendly products of the Bloomsbury industry, which went into business in the mid-sixties. These writings distorted Bloomsbury almost as grotesquely by, again, concentrating on individuals rather than ideas and on titillating details about personal lives rather than on professional contributions to cultural and intellectual life. It was the magnification of incidentals—sexual tittle-tattle, stray scribblings—that created the fog he saw settling around the lives of those he knew. And not just those he knew, as can be seen in a letter to Baroness Asquith about the publication of Lady Cynthia Asquith's diaries.

This "washing of dirty linen in public," as he once phrased it, was what he was determined to prevent in the case of Virginia. As he wrote to Nigel Nicolson, "Personally I have no feelings against the publication of anything, agreeable or disagreeable about myself or my relations, friends, and acquaintances. . . . All that one should do is to do nothing to add to the distortion." This is why he would not publish selections from Virginia's letters, why he extracted from her diaries those parts related to her writing while excluding gossip and comments on people, why he expurgated her correspondence with Strachey and vetoed the separate publication of her letters to Vita Sackville-West. And it was the motivation behind his choice of a biographer. Even when conscientiously done—as was Roy Harrod's of Keynes—Leonard found the biographies of those he knew to have failed in their understanding of the subject's character. He therefore wanted not only a sound scholar but also someone who had known Virginia personally. His choice eventually fell on her nephew Quentin Bell, who had been around her all his life and who had demonstrated his scholarship in his biography of John Ruskin. The last thing Leonard desired was hagiography or, as he said in his preface to *A Writer's Diary*, the equivalent of a Royal Academy picture which smooths out "the wrinkles, warts, frowns, and asperities." What he wanted was a full, rounded portrait, showing the whole person.

Since his intent was not always understood, Leonard was, not surprisingly, criticized on occasion for going too far the other way. Was it not inexplicably prudish, even hypocritical, for a truth-worshiping disciple of Moore to ignore in an otherwise candid autobiography the sexual activities of his friends, a very high proportion of whom were homosexuals and lesbians? He addressed the point directly, if cursorily, in a letter to Melvin Lasky of *Encounter* and indirectly in one to Lucy Norton. In neither did he fully explain himself. Although he no doubt disapproved of philandering, he was indifferent to the nature of a person's sex life. But he loathed gossip, especially about sex; whether the relationship was heterosexual or homosexual was a matter of indifference to him and was met with equal silence. He was in any case obsessively discreet—in large part because of his experience as a publisher—about anything that could cause pain to living persons or that could be construed as libelous. And he was convinced, perhaps because of his own situation, that sexual affairs were not very important in the context of one's life and work. A person's monument was to be found in his accomplishments.

Several letters record the criticism Leonard also received from a quite different quarter. For Bella and, unexpectedly, Edgar Woolf the wound created by *The Wise Virgins* never healed. They remained touchy almost to the point of paranoia about the attitude of Virginia and Leonard toward the Woolf family and took strong offense at passages in *A Writer's Diary* and *Principia Politica*. Edgar's malediction, included here, was terrible. Bella nursed a deep grudge because of Leonard's published references to their mother's social conventionality and a presumed unfavorable reference to herself in Virginia's diary. Although Edgar later recanted and visited Monk's House several times, the exchange of letters between Leonard and Bella, shortly before her death, is a sad close to their relationship.

The great preoccupation of the final decade of Leonard's life was, appropriately enough, writing his memoirs. For this, paradoxically, several academics deserve thanks. One of Leonard's very few self-deceptions was that he was indifferent to adverse criticism, perhaps because he had never had to contend with much. But when his political study *Principia Politica* received hostile reviews from a number of Oxford dons, he was devastated. Following the failure of *The Wise Virgins*, he had turned away from novel writing; now he gave up any thought of further political analysis and, after recommending autobiography to E. M. Forster, took his own advice. The result was not only an overall critical success but also one of the great autobiographies of the century.

From 1940 onward, the physical and psychological center of Leonard's life was Monk's House and especially its garden. There, daily life followed a regular pace and pattern—writing and answering mail in the mornings, gardening in the afternoons and reading in the evenings. Music remained of profound importance; Beethoven, closely followed by Mozart and Bach, meant most to him, but his taste extended to Berg and Schönberg as well. He continued to take a keen interest in classics, often reading Greek or Latin before breakfast. Friends, old and new, were more welcome than ever for a meal or a night; for both, a game of bowls was *de rigueur*. As always there were pets, a dog and a cat or two at any time. The death of Virginia meant release from unceasing strain and worry. Gradually, friends noticed, the tense, on-guard man of the past became more relaxed and easygoing.

On his weekly visits to London in the summer following Virginia's death, Leonard made a point of seeing Alice Ritchie, a Hogarth Press author, who was gravely ill. Alice was living in Victoria Square with her sister Trekkie and Trekkie's husband, Ian Parsons; after Alice's death, Leonard continued to see Trekkie and soon fell in love. Happily married, Trekkie was for a time taken aback by Leonard's attentions— "I have been really surprised that you should enjoy my company and I have thought it must be 'the novelty,' " she wrote to him—but gradually she recognized the central place she filled in his life. Neighbors in Victoria Square after 1943 and in Sussex after the war, they saw one another almost daily, and it was with her that he traveled to Greece, Israel, Ceylon, the United States, Canada and often to France. Their close companionship lasted until his death and was the basis of the emotional contentment of his later years. Although Leonard mentioned this friendship in his autobiography, his letters convey far better the strength of his feelings. The correspondence, some of which is included, trailed off after the war because the only occasion to write was when Trekkie and her husband were abroad.

Letters in this chapter also touch, if sometimes only briefly, on a number of important issues in Leonard's life that did not emerge in earlier correspondence. One of these is the question of his Judaism. Leonard's parents were Reformed Jews, and though the children attended synagogue and learned a little Hebrew, the family atmosphere was not religious. Leonard disclaimed ever having had any positive belief in God, sin or immortality; his announcement at fourteen that he would no longer go to synagogue produced maternal tears but no family crisis. Indeed, from his generation on, the entire Woolf family lived outside the Jewish community; none of Leonard's brothers or sisters was a practicing Jew, none married a Jew and none brought up their children as Jews. Leonard eventually came to find Judaism, as he did most other religions, quite repugnant, once describing it as the primitive beliefs of desert savages. Even the anti-Semitic pogroms of the Nazis did not cause him, as it did many another non-believing Jew, to assert his ethnic identity or to reenter the Jewish community. And when in later years he wrote of the victims of the Nazis, he never singled out Jews above other groups and always made clear he considered Stalin as much a monster as Hitler.

Leonard had not the slightest reluctance in acknowledging his ethnic identity as a Jew. In his autobiography he pronounced his hierarchy of loyalties to be "my family; 'race' (Jews); my country, England in particular and the British Empire generally; places with which I have been connected. . . ." If anything, he seems to have felt a mild pride in being Jewish, and this no doubt prompted him in 1957 to visit Israel, which on the whole impressed him deeply. Otherwise his background meant little to him and played no role in his social or professional life, which was carried out exclusively among Gentiles. Of his few Jewish friends, William Robson was the closest.

Leonard was reticent about anti-Semitism in his life, as some reviewers of his autobiography observed. When one of them challenged him, he insisted, as can be seen in the reply here, that it had not touched him personally. And it seems true that he never suffered any disability, either at Cambridge—where he was the first Jew to be elected to the Apostles—or in his later professional career. Yet his being a Jew had certainly arisen during his courtship of Virginia and was cause for comment by Virginia and his friends in later years. In May 1913 Vanessa Bell wrote, "I owe you a letter & I'm afraid of getting in trouble if I dont pay what I owe the Jews." In writing to Vanessa in 1917 and 1918, Keynes referred to "Virginia and the Jew" and his pleasure at visiting Asheham and finding Virginia "but no Jew." Harold Nicolson recorded in his diary a conversation he had in 1930 with Leonard and Hugh Dalton about easing the social qualifications for entry into the British Foreign Service: "The awkward question of the Jews arises. I admit that is the snag. Jews are far more interested in international life than are Englishmen, and if we opened the service it might be flooded by clever Jews. It was a little difficult to argue this point frankly with Leonard there." And Quentin Bell recalls a visit by the Woolfs to the Bells at Charleston, when in the general chatter a question was asked. "Let the Jew answer," Virginia exclaimed. To which Leonard replied, "I won't answer until you ask me properly."

It is impossible to know to what extent he encountered comments of this sort and what he made of them. Trekkie Parsons and Quentin Bell believe that such jibes annoyed but never really troubled him. Anti-Semitism was in his view simply one more social neurosis. "The thing is so irrational," he wrote in one letter, "that a long course of psychoanalysis alone would uncover its origin in any particular case." Hence, he could at one time be deeply incensed by it—as when he blasted Bertrand Russell's "aristocratic anti-semitism" in a review in the *Political Quarterly* of Russell's memoirs. Yet at another he could be remarkably casual—as when he replied to a correspondent that he considered T. S. Eliot's mild traces of anti-Semitism to be so trivial a matter that he could not even recall his conversations with Eliot about it.

A more vivid issue in the late letters is religious belief. Unlike Virginia and all his friends, for whom God was dead and religion a matter of total indifference, Leonard never ceased to be intrigued by the subject. *Principia Politica* was almost as much about religion as about

470

politics and was a book that could not conceivably have been written by anyone else in Bloomsbury. He regarded any form of worship as an irrational desire for consoling fantasies and considered prayer to be "one of the oddest freaks of human psychology." Both had become all the more bizarre since, as he commented in a striking simile, the status of God in the twentieth century had undergone a change parallel to that of the British monarch: although each continued to receive great reverence, both had lost their power to their ministers.

The subject embroiled him in controversy as a result of a two-part BBC television interview in March 1967. The program concluded with Leonard affirming a "strong disbelief" in immortality, a remark more than any other that touched an extremely sensitive nerve in viewers, some sixty of whom were moved to protest to him in writing. No one liked a good argument more than Leonard, and no one could have given him more pleasure to argue with than a retired Archbishop of Canterbury, who was the first to communicate. Most of the correspondents were friendly, if patronizing; many volunteered to pray for him and sent devotional writings. Some, including the interviewer, Malcolm Muggeridge, were astonished that Leonard did not expect to meet Virginia in heaven. A few were outraged that he should voice his heretical views precisely at Eastertime, and a few others were downright offensive and earned an angry response.

The "debate" over religion is also an incidental sign of Leonard's undiminished intellectual vigor as he approached his eighty-eighth year. He was well aware of the horrors that could accompany aging. In a particularly bitter comment in his autobiography, he remarked on "the stupid wastefulness of a system which requires that human beings with great labour and pain should spend years in acquiring knowledge, experience, and skill, and then just when at last they might use all this in the service of mankind and for their own happiness, they lose their teeth and their hair and their wits, and are hurriedly bundled, together with all that they have learnt, into the grave and nothingness."

His own last years were rich and happy ones. He lost neither his hair, his wits, his health nor his memory. He does not appear to have been afflicted by recollections of happy days now vanished. Nor did he need the conventional buttresses of the aged, the solace of religion and the love of a doting family. Unlike many intellectually ambitious and dedicated men—such as his own father-in-law—his last years were not tortured by a sense of having failed to fulfill himself. Of course, like any Englishman who grew up at the turn of the century, he never fully recovered from seeing the dream of a civilized world destroyed between 1914 and 1945. And the sense of personal failure at not having been able to do anything to prevent it was profound. But after a lifetime of trying to cultivate reason in a small corner of the British political, intellectual and literary worlds, he was content to put the past behind him and cultivate his garden in a corner of Sussex. No doubt part of him deeply felt that his life was symbolized by Swinburne's weary river winding its course to the sea. But even more was he ultimately convinced, with Montaigne, that what mattered was not the arrival but the journey.

The end of Leonard's life came gently. In mid-April 1969 he was suddenly incapacitated, whether by stroke or brain tumor is unclear, and his memory and speech were briefly impaired. When Trekkie Parsons asked him the names of his brothers and sisters, his wife or herself, he smiled and murmured Swinburne's lines:

> *And the best and the worst of this is*
> *That neither is most to blame,*
> *If you have forgotten my kisses*
> *And I have forgotten your name.*

Under Trekkie's care he soon recovered, and for a time followed his normal routine, mornings at his desk—correcting the page proofs of the last volume of his autobiography and typing responses to letters—and afternoons in his garden. But he was slowly declining. He wrote what was probably his last letter—about his book *A Calendar of Consolation*—on July 7. During the following weeks his greatest pleasure came when Quentin Bell visited and read passages from the draft manuscript of his biography of Virginia. Indignant—outraged—at the prospect of dying, he clung defiantly to life, but shortly after four in the morning of August 14 it deserted him.

In *The Journey Not the Arrival Matters* he wrote of his wife's death: "I buried Virginia's ashes at the foot of the great elm tree on the bank of the great lawn in the garden, called the Croft, which looks out over the field and the water-meadows. There were two great elms there with boughs interlaced which we always called Leonard and Virginia. In the first week of January 1943, in a great gale one of the elms was blown down."

Leonard's ashes were buried under the surviving elm.

*   *   *

Monk's House

16 June, 1941   Rodmell near Lewes   Sussex

My dear Margaret,

. . . I am going on here by myself. I do a fair amount of work one way and another, though I have not really been writing anything lately. I muddle about with the Press, the Labour Party, and the Fabians and go up to town every now and then to meetings. In the afternoons I garden and I usually see Vanessa once a week. I always sleep—in fact, I am almost ashamed to say that I have never had a bad night in my life and I hardly ever dream. Materially life is quite easy here and, though it is difficult to get some things, one can always get something to eat and enough of it. . . .

My love to Lilian and to yourself.

Yours ever
Leonard Woolf

To Violet Dickinson

Monk's House

6 July, 1941   Rodmell near Lewes   Sussex

My dear Violet,

I am very well; I practically always am. I spent four weeks in bed with typhoid in 1906 and during the next 30 years had only about three or four days ill in bed, and that malaria. I dont really find much difficulty with food. For years we have had a very nice woman here whom we give a cottage to live in and she comes in and cooks breakfast and lunch and we have always cooked dinner for ourselves.[1] I continue in the same way. I live a good deal on fish and macaroni, keep seven fowls which provide eggs, and get as much milk as I want, and the garden has always produced all the vegetables which we could eat. We have also always made our own jam from our own fruit and I keep four hives of bees which supply honey. So I dont do too badly.

1. The cook-housekeeper was Louie Everest, née West (1912–1977), who had worked at Monk's House since 1934.

We have had no rain here for 23 days, but it is rather surprising how things have stood up to it.

Yours
Leonard Woolf

To Margaret Llewelyn Davies

23/2/42

Monk's House
Rodmell

My dear Margaret, I was so glad to get a letter from you again. I am still here in the main, but I have taken a flat in Cliffords Inn and usually stay there for two or three nights a week. I could have got Mecklenburgh Square patched up, but the difficulties of service &c if one is not regularly in London seemed too great. I hate flats, but this is a service flat where one can get food, so that one can go there and leave it again at a moment's notice. I have a good many committees and things in London and I found the journey up and down two or three days a week with a four mile bicycle ride in the winter darkness too unpleasant. We were in Cliffords Inn in the last war, but the old buildings where we had rooms have been all pulled down and an immense block of modern flats built in their place.

I quite often see Judith [Stephen]; she dined with me in town the week before last. Whether she will marry Leslie [Humphrey] I dont know; I advised her not to—which was a rash thing to do—but I dont think he is the right person for her.[1] I have not seen Ann [Stephen] since she came back to England as she is working hard up in Leeds. Judith is doing very well in the Ministry of Works.

. . . I imagine that the cold up where you are [in Cumbria] must be pretty bad; even here it is most unpleasant and London under snow with no one to clear the streets some weeks ago was appalling.

Please give my love to Lilian.

Yours ever
Leonard Woolf

1. She eventually married Nigel Henderson, a professional photographer.

TO GEOFFREY KEYNES[1]

16 August, 1942

Monk's House
Rodmell, Lewes, Sussex

Dear Geoffrey,

The difficulty about a portrait is that I simply do not know of a single one in existence. Virginia hated to be painted or photographed.[2] It is just possible that Vanessa has one and I will talk to her when I see her, but I rather doubt it.

Virginia always wrote her first draft of anything in handwriting and I have a good many of these MSS. She then typed them out, altering the whole time, usually several times. I think you justly deserve one if you want one. I enclose the first draft of a short book we published in 1930, printing it ourselves, *On Being Ill*, which in some ways it is appropriate you should have, but if you would rather have something else let me know and I will see whether it is in existence.

I am not sure whether the Fitzwilliam has one of her MS. I know that either the Bodleian or Fitzwilliam did ask her for one and I rather think she sent them something.[3] I suppose there would be no harm in my asking them.

Yours
Leonard Woolf

TO TREKKIE PARSONS[4]

29/3/43

Monk's House

Dearest tiger,

. . . The time passing is a terrible feeling. It comes, I think, some time or other to everyone. But you are too young for it; you still have what I think is probably the best part of the day before you. It is when

1. (Sir) Geoffrey Keynes (1887–1982), brother of John Maynard, was a surgeon and bibliophile. He had saved VW's life in 1913 when she took an overdose of Veronal. He had inquired about a portrait of her or manuscript by her.
2. LW had forgotten Vanessa Bell's painting done in 1934 and the watercolor sketch of it. Although that was the only full-scale oil portrait of the mature VW, there were other paintings and sketches, by Vanessa Bell, Roger Fry, Duncan Grant and Jacques-Emile Blanche.
3. In 1942 LW gave the Fitzwilliam Museum in Cambridge "Women in Fiction," the first draft of what became *A Room of One's Own*. *On Being Ill* was bequeathed by Keynes to the University Library, Cambridge.
4. See Biographical Appendix.

evening really comes and one realizes that there are only a very few hours before bedtime that the moment comes when one must stand up and defy fate. And that, I believe, is really the only way to meet it and to deal with God, death, and life. If only one can recognize fate as fate, the inevitable as inevitable, even one's own fate becomes impersonal. Then you can stand up and defy the universe, which is the only right attitude for a human being; "I dont like you," you can say, "I dont like what you do and are going to do to me; I despise you and your ways; but the responsibility is yours, not mine; so go ahead, go your way, and, while there is still time, I propose to go mine."

This is more a sermon than a letter, I'm afraid. It is written to the accompaniment of a continual wailing of sirens, alerts and all clears following one another at intervals of five minutes all the morning—which seems to be appropriate.

Would you come to Kew with me if I could snatch an afternoon next week? I had thought to come up tomorrow, but all my engagements have got into a tangle and I think I shall make that an excuse for cutting them all, staying here, and doing some work in quiet. But I shall be up Tuesday, Wednesday next week. Do you hate dining in restaurants? If you dont, would you dine with me at the Akropolis Restaurant in Percy Street on Wednesday, the 7th; it is a Greek restaurant which means that the food is Turkish and, I think, rather good.

Ever yours
L.

To Trekkie Parsons

3/4/43   Monk's House

Dearest Tiger, How terrifying are the words you dont, as you say, mince! Terrifying, because they not only apply to lithography but life. I am sure that I am sullenly scummed up and snaked off. And then you have resensitized me, but dont, please, gum me up and leave me finally snaked off and scummed up. Your use of words unminced shows that you ought to be a writer as well as a painter.

Defiance is exhausting. But the attitude should not be pure defiance, but a mixture of defiance and resignation. It was the Greek attitude to fate. The defiance which leads to acceptance of and contempt for one's own fate. That is what makes their heroes like Prometheus and poor old Oedipus so admirable; they shriek with agony or rage, and yet deep down they quite calmly defy and accept the inevitable. . . .

How I wish you were here today. The garden has suddenly changed from yellow to blue and violet, hyacinth, scillas, grape hyacinth, and aubretia; there is a pear tree in full flower, and one or two fritillaries in the grass. I do hope your painting has been going well.

Ever your
L.

To Sidney Webb

Monk's House
Rodmell

2 May, 1943

My dear Webb,

I have been thinking of you and Mrs Webb so much during the last 24 hours that I feel I must say something to you personally, however vain and inadequate.[1] It would be impossible to give a real idea of what you both did and meant for people of my generation, and the debt we owe you is immense. But quite apart from that, it was impossible to know Mrs Webb, as I did, without acquiring for her great affection, besides admiration and gratitude—and, if I may say so, for yourself. I have been thinking with pleasure and regret of the days which you spent with us years ago near here at Asheham House and of my meeting Mrs Webb only a short time ago at Mrs Drake's and noticing how the years had left completely untouched the vigour and brightness of her mind.

Yours sincerely
Leonard Woolf

1. Beatrice Webb had died on April 30, 1943. Following Sidney's death, in October 1947, the Webbs' ashes were interred in Westminster Abbey, the first couple so honored.

Monk's House
Rodmell

27/5/43

Dearest, I hung the picture over the mantelpiece this morning. It *is* good of you to lend it to me. I like it immensely. It is not dull or tedious. But it is austere, which seems to me right, for the austerity of beauty is in your painting—what I mean by the integrity of your living.

I had my talk with John [Lehmann]. He began about everything but the matter which we both were thinking of—which is the eastern method of manoeuvre & bad tactics, in my opinion. Tension until I suggested that we should settle our difference. Considerable tension but I did *not* lose my temper. We parted amicably but with toes still dug in.

When I got back here tonight, I did wish you were with me to see the pond covered with the bloodred & the cream waterlilies & bright blue sky, reflected in it.

The devil is I so often want to be with you. I shant see you now really for 3 weeks, I suppose, which seems a terribly long time. I told you it was a week of bad things hammering on me. You know, it's really rather awful to be as fond of anyone as I have become of you the last six months, dearest tiger. I suppose it's all right if you're 3 or 6 or 36 (though I doubt it) but it's disgraceful at 63. The happiest people must be those whose affections are nil or tepid . . . they dont get the supreme pleasure of the oasis but then they also miss the pains & emptiness of the desert. The desert is unfortunately so much larger as a rule than the oasis. You would never guess, I believe, that every time you say, as you do, "Well, good-bye, Leonard" & look at me with the sternness—& at the same time kindness which I like so much—before disappearing into the Russell Square tube, as I turn away I think of Thucydides, the greatest & most astringent of all historians. The reason is that no one for the last 2500 years has succeeded in giving a more perfect description of that desert feeling which comes over me in Bernard Street than Thucydides. (He himself says it was Pericles who said it & he may be right. I daresay Pericles learnt it from Aspasia.) "It is as though the spring had died out of the year."

I hope you'll forgive me for writing another volume like this. It's really your fault. I begin to write you a short letter to thank you for the picture & you make me think aloud on paper. At any rate I'm glad to think you'll see the border. My recollection is that Edinburgh is a nice place. But if you can snatch even one day for the Cheviots you should. You'll see a new thing in light & sky. And I know the hills are made for you. They are cousins to our downs, but quite different & yet you cant mistake the relationship. Have you ever been to Abbotsford? If you haven't, you ought not to miss that, just to see what the human mind is capable of in the way of houses if it really sets its mind to it.

Goodnight my dearest tiger, & forgive me my trespasses.

Yours
L.

To Trekkie Parsons

26/8/43   Monk's House

Dearest Tiger,   I do hope the mental gooseflesh didn't last long. I hate to see you worried in that way. I wish I could analyze it out of you. It is, I'm sure, a very complicated and subtle thing & my mind at the moment is not up to the task though I've been thinking of it & you off and on ever since I saw you yesterday.

I've been thinking of you in other connections too. You've become so intertwined in my thoughts & feelings particularly here & in the garden that when you aren't here I have continually a strange sense of your presence & absence at the same moment. There has just been a violent storm of rain with a clear sky in the west & a great rainbow over the church, & we were looking at it together as we did only a few weeks ago & yet you weren't here. And last night when I got back in the evening it was incredibly beautiful with a sky like the sky we had at Whipsnade, but quite different here, & the sun & long shadows chasing one another very slowly & softly across the water meadows & up [Mount] Caburn. I walked on the terrace, & it was just as though you were by my side telling me all about the clouds & yet hopelessly different because you weren't. The garden, too, at the moment is, I think, rather wonderful, having burst into a new florescence with clouds of Japanese anemones, & they also were strangely coloured by this feeling of presence & absence, because you haven't seen this particular moment & yet seemed so near.

I sent you four figs in a tin. I chose them not quite ripe as I thought they might travel better & be ripe when they arrive. But this may be a mistake. If so, let me know & I'll send really ripe ones another time.

I forgot to tell you that I examined the Tiger, tiger poem with great

479

care again the other evening, & came to the conclusion that we were wrong & that "What dread hand? And what dread feet?" must refer to God.[1] All the other whats refer to God or the materials or instruments which he uses to make you. Secondly you are always referred to in the second person—thine eyes, thy heart. Thirdly I dont believe that you have hands in the poem.

I began this letter after tea but am finishing it long after dinner & in the interval have developed a violent cold in the head which perhaps accounts for why I felt so muzzy in the brain.

Still more Belladonna lilies have begun to poke out their pink snakelike heads.

Good night, dearest. Write to me from Dartmoor if it's not a nuisance to you & write a short story.

Ever your
L.

I liked the picture you did of the orchard. The caption of the lithograph should be "*We* dont believe a word of it."[2]

To Trekkie Parsons

3/9/43   Monk's House

My dearest,   I meant to write to you yesterday, but couldn't because I had the Labour Party meeting here & Quentin [Bell] stayed the night & came early in order to play bowls. I have been thinking & thinking about you & your work this last slowly passing week, with not a sight of you, & I have so much I want to say. I want to say it, but not that I should seem overinsistent & nagging, worrying & disturbing to what is inmost in you. I think you do know that it is because you & your work—which means too your happiness—are to me now infinitely the most important things in life. And not, I really believe, merely that you & everything connected with you are so personally dear to me. I can judge you objectively, as the philosophers love to say, & I know that "objectively" too you are really important because of what you

1. The poem was one of William Blake's *Songs of Experience*.
2. As a jest at his innate skepticism, Trekkie Parsons had done a lithograph that pictured LW saying to the Archangel Gabriel, "I don't believe a word of it."

have it in you to produce. From that point of view far the most important of anyone I know, & after all, as you always say, I do know quite a lot.

I think you have got to a vital stage in your painting life & that you can & must burst out into a new & superb florescence like the Japanese anemones in the garden. And it depends almost entirely—& that's why I feel I must write so insistently—upon your having, your regaining self confidence which in a subtle way you have lost. I think that you've got to face the fact that you've lost it, & deliberately conquer it & that as soon as you do, it will have an astonishingly releasing effect upon you & your work. If you were not you, there are very good reasons why you should no longer be confident—& that too one must face & not belittle. I am sure it began . . . at the very moment when sympathy & encouragement were essential. And then, as you said in your letter once, it is impossible not to be affected by the continual shutting of doors in one's face. This is one of the main things one must face. I set no store of any sort or kind by failure & success. I mean that there is no relation between success & real value or importance. You might be a complete failure to the end with public, agents, shows &c. & it wouldn't make a shiver or quiver for one second in my belief in your value & importance as a painter. But it would be silly to pretend that success or failure does not have important effects upon even the greatest artists, even those who deep down set no real store upon them. I think success has a releasing effect upon them even when they really know that it means essentially nothing. It is pleasant in itself & it relieves them of the worry of having to consider what their impact upon the outside world will be.

Failure has just the opposite effect. It forces one in upon oneself. This may produce the privacy & secrecy which we talked about. If one is by nature a tough, one damns the outside world, sets one's teeth, & produces masterpieces which no one pays any attention to until one is senile or dead—even so I think the effect is not good. But if one is not a tough—& I dont think you are—even if deep down you remain certain of your solid core, superficially your self-confidence will be affected. The devil of it is that it may affect you as an artist & then two things happen. First, the outside world is always enormously impressed by self-confidence & vice versa, & as it has an uncanny instinct for spotting them, a vicious circle is set up. Second, the artist who has superficially lost confidence, often unconsciously, continuously underestimates his powers & therefore does not fully use them—he becomes too unambitious, in a sense, in his works—he is always, as it were, writing sketches & short stories when he should be writing full scale novels—& as he is always producing below his real power, he is perpetually conscious of something lacking in what he produces.

I believe that something like this has happened to you, & the problem is to reverse the process. You have something in you—I feel it, see it so often, dearest, that I cant be mistaken—so strong & so beautiful, something of the utmost importance that you must break through this spider's web which prevents you often from giving full expression to it. How to break through? Of course, the main thing is simply to be confident, to see things exactly as they are—it sounds a lame conclusion, & would be with anyone but you, for one of the things which I adore in you is the way you do see things exactly as they are with your great eyes wide open (& that is why those "blue pools" are the most beautiful eyes I have ever seen). But I believe there's another thing to do, though here my ignorance of the art of painting makes it difficult for me to know how it would apply there. But if you were a writer, I should say: "In your next book, instead of chosing a theme & form which you think within your powers, choose ones which you think a good deal above your powers. And having done so, force yourself all through not to think of it again until the whole book is complete. Except that you may occasionally say to yourself: 'There's nothing I cant do.' "

I must catch the post. What a letter! I wont apologize because you know what causes it. . . .

Your devoted
L.

To Molly MacCarthy

Monk's House
Rodmell

25/9/43

Dearest Molly,

I can but obey you, and you do with immense skill make it sound very nice to have to.[1] Whether when I come to sit down with my nose to the typewriter I shall find the writing of my memoir quite so glam-

---

1. This was a summons to read recollections to the Memoir Club. LW read five papers—about his youth, Cambridge and Ceylon—all but one of which he later incorporated bodily into *Sowing* or *Growing*.

orous as it is in your description, I have already some slight doubt. But I will do my best.

I wish we met some times not at the Memoir Club. I suppose you wouldn't come and see the apples here some day?

Yours
Leonard

30/10/43   Monk's House

Dearest (I suppose I mustn't say & most beautiful) of creatures,
    . . . I dont think I'm really romantic, though if I am about you, I have a good excuse. It is not romantic, though it may be dangerous, to love anyone like you as much as I love you. It's romantic to love someone passionately who isn't worth a passion—it's dangerous to love passionately someone worth a passion—& the more worth, the more dangerous. If ever anyone was worth a passion, dearest, it's you. Sometimes when I leave you, a—I daresay unreasonable—terror comes over me, that I shall weary, bore, annoy you & that next time I see you I shall find that you cant tolerate me. I dont really know why you should, particularly the appalling resistance & persistence which I know I possess & cannot control, which is due to some horrible fire in my entrails & must be a weariness of flesh & mind to other people. I had hoped that age would put it out but I dont really think it does. It makes things obsess me. But only once before in my life has it made a person obsess me. And it's because you are in every way so worth an obsession & passion that my terrors are not unreasonable.

I should like to write you another four pages on the subject of female beauty, but I feel I had better not, if I dont want to weary you. But I may say this, mayn't I?, that your self-portraits show that even a painter has no idea of what she herself really looks like. I could give good reasons for this which are not invalidated by her hairdresser's mirror.

Your other pictures give me extraordinary pleasure.

If I love you, dearest of tigers, it is because you are so lovable, so that if I weary you, you must forgive me, since the Prime Cause is you.

Your devoted
L.

483

I am beginning to enjoy *Don Quixote.* I like "damsels there were in times past that at the end of fourscore years old, all which time they never slept one day under a roof, went as entire & pure maidens to their graves as the very mother that bore them."

To Vanessa Bell

Monk's House
Rodmell

26/2/44

Dearest Vanessa,

Harcourt, Brace have enquired about a jacket by you for *A Haunted House*. I think you usually send them the drawing. Or would you like us to send a copy of the jacket?[1]

I have been up in town all the week. The raids are not at all pleasant. My sister [Flora] who took a flat on Wednesday of last week was bombed out of it on Friday and very nearly killed. She and her daughter are now homeless and it looks as if I shall have to give them temporary lodging at Victoria Square.[2] I went to get a book out of the London Library on Thursday morning and found it so damaged by Wednesday night's raid that one could not get books out.

Would you let me know about the jacket at Victoria Square as I shall be there next week from Monday to Thursday.

Your
L.

To Trekkie Parsons

11/5/44   Monk's House

Darling, . . . I get more happiness from an hour with you than from a year away from you & it really outweighs all the longing for you & missing you when you aren't there. I cant pretend that I dont miss

1. *A Haunted House* was a collection of VW's short stories, some never before published, which LW brought out in 1944.
2. Unable to endure the new Clifford's Inn, LW moved back into several makeshift rooms at Mecklenburgh Square in April 1942; when that proved too uncomfortable after a year, he rented a house at 24 Victoria Square.

you & long for you—here more than anywhere. But you have turned a passive, neutral existence into life of passionate happiness. To know you & love you has been the best thing in life. . . .

I am afraid you'll never be as fond of me as Kingsley. He rang me up this morning & asked me to come & lunch with him. I refused. As soon as I got back here, the telephone rang—Kingsley. Would I lunch Monday? No. Would I write an article on the I.L.O.? (You dont know what that is.) Would I review a book by Elspeth Huxley? If you say two Nos, you feel you must say a Yes instead of a third No & so I said Yes out of sheer weakness. I dont want to write about the I.L.O. or review Elspeth—& now I shall have to read about the I.L.O. all Friday & Saturday & write about it all Sunday morning.[1]

Darling tiger, I must begin on the I.L.O. at once & say good night to you. (Peat as I wrote this put out a paw & gently smudged the word "say" to show, I suppose, that he said it too.[2] He was in the sunniest patch of the flower bed by the front door when I arrived.) And say that I love you, adore you, & kiss your toe—I mean, my toe.

Your
L.

To Margaret Thwaites[3]

29/5/44

Monk's House
Rodmell, Lewes, Sussex

Dear Miss Thwaites,

I return your MS which I have read with great interest. It seems to me a very solid piece of work and though there are of course details over which we would disagree, in the main I find myself in close agreement with your conclusions. Your analysis and criticism of *The Waves* are particularly good. I have a rather less high opinion of *The Years* than you have, perhaps, but you may be right.

The only point on which I do not agree with you is the influence of Bergson. I doubt whether Mrs Woolf had read any Bergson and the statement in Delattre that she attended lectures in Manchester is, I

---

1. LW's unsigned article on the International Labour Organization, "Choppy Seas for the I.L.O.," appeared on May 20, 1944; his review of *Race and Politics in Kenya: A Correspondence between Elspeth Huxley and Margery Perham* on June 3, 1944.
2. Peat was a recently acquired cat.
3. Of the University of Leeds.

think, entirely without foundation.[1] I feel sure that I should have known if she had before 1911 and I know as a fact that she did not do so after 1911.

Her sister-in-law who wrote *The Misuse of the Mind* was Mrs Adrian Stephen (not Bell); she married Adrian Stephen, my wife's brother, and her maiden name was Karin Costelloe.[2] I happen to know that Mrs Woolf had not read that book; indeed the one type of book she hardly ever read was the philosophical & metaphysical.

Yours sincerely
Leonard Woolf

To Trekkie Parsons

> *In demarcating the affecto-symbolic substrate underlying the be-*
> *havior of man, we have attempted to contrast the incitements that*
> *pertain to this conditioned reaction-segment, and thus segregate the*
> *organism's epigenic behavior-reactions from the motivations of*
> *man's organism as an orthogenic whole.*

7/7/44   Monk's House

Tiger dearest, We thought the chimpanzee book jargon; what do you think of the above from a pamphlet sent me this morning.

Here is an interesting fact from my book on geology. Burton ale has a very fine & peculiar quality due to the salts in the water used in making it. The salts were deposited in a kind of Dead Sea which covered that part of England when it was more or less desert about 100 million years ago. God works in a mysterious way & obviously has an ingenious mind. It is rather like Saxon [Sydney-Turner]'s. It would be like him to take the trouble to create a Dead Sea & then cover it up with rocks for millions of years in order—10 million years later—to give a peculiar flavour to beer.

Do you remember in Proust that Swann always thought the same as the Princess in unimportant things? I think the marvel is that we always think the same about the important things. It sounds conceited

1. Floris Delattre reported this in his *Le Roman Psychologique de Virginia Woolf* (1932). LW was no more successful than VW in convincing scholars that she had never read Bergson.
2. Karin Stephen was a devotee of Bergson; her book was subtitled *A Study of Bergson's Attack on Intellectualism* and was published with an introduction by the philosopher himself.

for me to say that—but I felt it at once as a miracle & the miracle has persisted. And you said the other day that from the first you felt you could say anything—& everything—to me. Aren't the two things connected? Isn't it therefore probable, dearest, that this accounts for my passion for you—in part & a large part—& that there is something in you which causes it? Not just a phantom in my mind. Not a fortuitous fixation, as the jargonists would say.

I am getting to not being able to go to bed without writing to you. How I wish, dearest, I could give you a bulls-eye, a hot water bottle, & say it to you. Perhaps, perhaps. . . . [*sic*]

> I love you
> L!

I think persicifolium can only mean Persian leaved but what that can mean I dont know

To T. S. Eliot

25/8/46

Monk's House,
Rodmell, Lewes, Sussex

Dear Tom,

It was nice to hear from you again. We published two books of Muir's poems—the first, *First Poems* and the second, *Chorus of the Newly Dead*. I have one copy of the first and must have one of the second, but cannot find it. We printed them ourselves and I dont want to lose the only copy I have. Can I be certain of Tate returning it if I send it?[1]

I should very much like to see you again. I live most of the time here, but come up to town for a night or so most weeks. I left Mecklenburgh Square and took a house in Victoria Square—No 24. I could give you a mutton pie and coffee if you would come and lunch there one day when I am up.

> Yours
> L W

1. Allen Tate (1899–1979), the American poet and critic, wished to introduce the poetry of Edwin Muir (1887–1959) to the United States and had written to Eliot for copies of his works published by the Hogarth Press.

Monk's House
13.10.48   Rodmell, Lewes, Sussex

Dear Vita,

Many people have been urging me to publish some of Virginia's letters and I have been getting a certain number from people from time to time to look them through and see whether it is possible. That is why I told Harold that I should like to see some of yours if you had no objection. I very much doubt whether the thing is really feasible or desirable. The difficulty is that the really personal letters are unpublishable and it seems to me that if one publishes only the impersonal ones, one gives a totally false impression of the character. This was certainly the case with the first volume of Rupert Brooke's letters which were published. I don't know what you feel about this.

I should very much like to come over and see you for a day but the difficulty is that I have not enough petrol to manage it. I will try to save enough, if I can, to do so as I should [like] to see Sissinghurst again and you.

Yours,
Leonard

To R. G. Howarth[1]

Monk's House,
17.2.50   Rodmell, Lewes, Sussex.

Dear Mr. Howarth,

The quotation in *To the Lighthouse* was from an unpublished poem by a very curious man called Charles Elton.[2] He was a landed gentleman and a relation of the Strachey family. He occasionally wrote poetry at night and read what he had produced to his family at breakfast. He wrote "Luriana," which I think is a poem of the very highest class, and also another, which is not quite so good. There is nothing of his, I believe, outside these two poems, which is very good. The text of "Luriana" was given to me by Lytton Strachey. It remained unpublished for years but I rather think that Harold Nicolson and V. Sack-

1. Howarth taught in the Department of English of the University of Sydney.
2. The poem was taken down, according to another of LW's letters, by Philippa Strachey.

ville-West obtained a manuscript copy and published it in an anthology.[1]

Your sincerely,
Leonard Woolf

To Trekkie Parsons

13/3/50   Monk's House

O dearest, dearest, I wish you were sitting over there & we were listening, as we used to at this hour, to a Beethoven quartet or a Mozart concerto. Shall we ever again, when you return from your crucifixion on the cross of boredom, which has claims to be the worst of the many unpleasant crosses?

My brain is a puddle tonight. I have sat down to myself for the first time today when it is almost time to go to bed. First the Hort. Sy. meeting which dithered on interminably in its usual way. Then I had to go to Frank Dean & Freeth to try to make arrangements for getting the sideshow materials. More dithering conversation & no means of getting them. So I drove to Lewes to to get hold of Collins.[2] No Collins. Back to Rodmell. Dinner. Drove once more to Lewes & at last Collins. "Well-er-yes-er-Mr Woolf-er-we must see what we can do-yes-er--well-yes-it-is-er-rather awkward-well-er-yes-well, Mr Woolf, we must see what we can do-of course, there's Burchett-yes, & then of course there's Moon-well, er, we must see what we can do-yes." So we are seeing what we can do.

Louie [Everest] returned today in time to do my breakfast. She enjoyed herself enormously in the Black Forest & gave a most entertaining account of her adventures. She obviously was a great success with the Germans & behaved with the greatest common sense. It astonishes me how she manages to combine 80 per cent of real intelligence with 20 per cent sheer imbecility. She cant stop telling you her experiences. Her conversations with cemetery keepers, police men, Americans, restaurant keepers are fascinating. I dont think she liked Annalise's people much. She stayed with them for three days.[3]

1. The anthology was *Another World Than This* . . .
2. Dean, the village blacksmith, Freeth, a farmhand, and Collins, the village police constable, were to help in arranging the amusements for the Rodmell horticulture show.
3. Annalise West, the German-born wife of Louie's brother, was the Parsons' housekeeper.

The wood warbler came & settled on my ladder today within a few feet of me.

Dearest, you see how puddled is my brain.

But puddle or not I love you.

Your
L.

TO FLORA WOOLF

23.5.51   [Monk's House]

Dear Flora,

I had heard that you had once more set sail for Africa but was very glad to get your letter and hear news from you yourself. I always thought that Kenya must be a superb country, the only blot being the inhabitants. I should like to come out and see not the inhabitants but yourself and the giraffes, but I don't suppose that I will. I don't think there is any news worth telling you from here but I should like to hear how things go with you again.[1]

Yours,
Leonard

TO G. E. MOORE

                                                    Monk's House
18 June, 1951   Rodmell near Lewes   Sussex

My dear Moore,

It is late to write to you, but I want to say how glad I am that they have decided that you should confer merit on the order. It is remarkable that the Order of Merit should be so philosophical. I wish I sometimes saw you, but I am never in Cambridge and you never in Rodmell except when the Germans are overrunning Europe.[2]

Yours
Leonard Woolf

1. Flora lived from 1949 until 1953 in South Africa, Rhodesia and Kenya. In speaking of the "inhabitants" in Kenya, LW had in mind the white settlers.
2. In the King's birthday honors, Moore had been granted the Order of Merit. The order was "philosophical" because it was already held by Russell and Whitehead. Moore had last visited LW in late May 1940.

2/7/51   Monks House

Dearest,   It is rather late to begin a letter, but this is only to say goodnight. Rodmell, Sussex, London, England, Great Britain, the Commonwealth, & English Speaking Union are very dreary without you. (I have, as you well see, been listening to speeches by Eisenhower, Salisbury, Attlee, & Winston at an English Speaking Union banquet. Eisenhower was rather impressive.)

I went to Londay today, lunched with Willie [Robson] & a Russian. I got into a carriage at East Croydon & after the train had started found that it was labelled LADIES ONLY. I apologized for my intrusion to 8 ladies & 6 of them assured me that it did not matter at all. Two in the seats at the further end looked resentful & started a conversation at the top of their voices, absolutely incredible. One looked & dressed exactly like Mabel [Trekkie's mother-in-law]. The other gave an account—obviously to impress us—of the dinner she wished to order but could not get at her club. "No champagne cocktails, my dear. How can one give a dinner without champagne cocktails?" The rest of the carriage dissolved in laughter.

It has been heavenly weather. Laurens's strange plant opened a flower as I came into the greenhouse tonight.[1] It is green of a slightly yellowish hue & later developed a darkish streak. I suppose it may change to red later. I went into the garden for a moment at 11 & the scent of the honeysuckle—which is a sheet of bloom—was amazing. The little hypeastrum which I got from South Africa is most beautiful, bright red with a white centre. One of the crinums has shot up its flower. Two flowers opened on the prickly pear.

All my news, you see, is of flowers. But they are of no value if you are not with me—for, though you dont approve of the word, I love you.

L.

The only other news is that Dr Rickman is dead. This is news for Ian.[2]

---

1. Laurens van der Post and LW occasionally sent one another unusual plants.
2. John Rickman was in charge of publications for the Institute of Psycho-Analysis.

To FREDERICK ADAMS[1]

14.1.52   [Monk's House]

Dear Mr. Adams,

I am sure you will be interested to know that I have at last been able to trace the origin of the pamphlet which you enquired about.[2] I did it by eventually discovering who lived in the house from which it originated in 1930. It turned out to be the literary agent, [Spencer] Curtis Brown. He did not answer a letter of enquiry at first, but has now sent the following information—

"The Broadsheet Press was published for a few months only on a small hand press and I and my friend H. Stewart, were publishers, printers and distributors. The pamphlet you mention was, I think, the last produced. It is simply a parody of Virginia Woolf's essay style and describes a wholly imaginary event and it was written, as I remember, by Yvonne Kapp".

It is not entirely true that the event described was wholly imaginary. I enquired about this from a friend of mine who is a psycho-analyst [James Strachey] and as a matter of fact, there was a meeting and presentation of the kind described.[3] Yvonne Kapp was the wife of a fairly well known caricaturist, who did caricatures of people like Bernard Shaw and others in the *New Statesman*.

Yours sincerely,
Leonard Woolf

To MOLLY MACCARTHY

                                                    Monk's House
10/6/52   Rodmell, near Lewes   Sussex

My dear Molly,

I felt as if I had lost a whole piece of my life at a blow when I saw the news of Desmond's death in the paper. And that is what it really means. It is true of only a very few persons that they are part of one's life in this way and you were both that to Virginia and me. The feeling

1. Adams was Director of the Pierpont Morgan Library in New York.
2. A pamphlet entitled *Mrs Woolf Attends the Proceedings of the British Psycho-analytical Society* and *The Snobbery of Modernism* (Paper No. 5 of the Broadsheet Press, June 1930).
3. A cigar cutter went to Ernest Jones.

is always the same even though, as one grows old, one tends, as I do, not to move much from one's own house. I hardly ever saw Desmond in recent years except at the Memoir Club, but the feeling was and is the same. And for you too. I should like to see you some time and would come out for an hour some day if you would care for me to do so.

Your
Leonard

FROM EDGAR WOOLF

27-II-53

Dear Leonard,

I have just finished reading Virginia's Diaries [A Writer's Diary] *and* Principia Politica. *It is not for me to question the decency of a man selling his wife's tragedy for gold. But in your preface you state some entries are suppressed so as not to cause pain to people. In your own book you go out of your way to disparage & hold up to ridicule our family, not because it has anything to do with the argument of your book, but because you think it adds somehow to your stature. For some reason all Labour people think it adds to their stature, if they can say they are gutter-snipers.*

As a boy you were mean & a bully—not that I ever allowed you to bully me, but Herbert and Harold did.

I saw little of you until I went to Sweden with you in 1911, when I realized how mean you were in your outlook. After that I have seen little of you.

You showed what a cad you were when you published the Wise Virgins—*after solemnly promising not to! Desmond MacCarthy's idea of a masterpiece!*

Unfortunately people know I am your brother & I have the greatest objection to other people being given a lying and utterly caddish picture of our parents & our home. And I believe on good evidence you have done the same thing before.

Having always been the lickspittle of greater intellects, you suffer from the deformity of the little man, who thinks it makes him greater to cry out "See how I have risen above my degraded beginnings."

Unfortunately with your mean nature you'll go on the same way &

493

*delight in causing pain to all of us. But Virginia's Diary shows you
up for what you are better than any words of mine.*

Edgar[1]

To Mary Lyon

13.1.55   Monk's House

Dear Miss Lyon,
   With reference to your letter of December 30th, most of the revisions
of the essays were destroyed at the time.[2] The only reason why I was
able to find one of them and send it to the author of a review was that
it had been written just before my wife's death and the various revisions
were lying about her room. I doubt very much whether I could find
anything of this kind which would be of any use to you. However, if
you come to London, I would be willing to let you examine the first
draft of one of the books. These are in handwriting and were always
very much revised before publication.

                                                    Yours truly,
                                                    Leonard Woolf

To Vita Sackville-West

                                                    Monk's House,
13th January, 1955   Rodmell, Nr. Lewes,   Sussex.

Dear Vita,
   I yesterday received from Little, Brown, the American publishers,
a copy of the proofs of Mrs. Pippett's book about Virginia [*The Moth
and the Star*]. She told me last May that she was sending me a draft

1. In *Sowing*, LW, without identifying Edgar as the author, characterized this as "the
bitterest letter which I have ever received" and expressed shock that he "should have known
someone intimately for over half a century and have liked him, and never in all those years
been aware of his hatred and contempt. . . ." Such was his astonishment that he replied
only in 1959 and then to ask permission to quote the letter in his autobiography.
2. Lyon, at work on a thesis for Radcliffe College entitled "Virginia Woolf as a Critic," had
asked to see drafts of VW's reviews. She cited, as an example, VW's review, the last she
wrote, of a biography of Hester Lynch Thrale by James Clifford, which VW had rewritten
eight or nine times.

of her book in order that I could see what she was using from the letters which you had lent her. This she never did. Early in December, she wrote to me saying that the publishers were sending me by air mail a copy of the completed typescript. This they never did. I was horrified to find in the proofs that she had quoted an immense amount from Virginia's letters to you and that she had stated in the preface that I had given her permission to do this. I never gave any permission at all and I have written to the publishers today to say that I have not and do not give permission, the copyright being mine. I don't know what you feel about the matter but I have the greatest objection to a large number of snippets from what are obviously first-class letters being published in this kind of book. It destroys to a great extent the desirability and possibility of publishing the letters themselves. I have, of course, not seen the letters and do not know their bulk and what proportion is publishable. But if they are to be published, I think they ought to be published by the Hogarth Press as a volume of letters by Virginia Woolf. What do you feel about it?[1]

Yours,
Leonard Woolf

To T. S. Eliot

2/4/55

Monk's House
Rodmell near Lewes   Sussex

Dear Tom,
Though I dont really like the kind of thing which Mlle Nathan is doing, being in France, it seemed so remote that I have given her a good deal of material in the shape of photographs—which is what she mainly wants. I have not given her letters and I would rather that you did not.[2]
The whole subject of Virginia's letters has become very difficult. I should very much like to examine the ones which you have with a view to a volume of letters. But I should like still more first to have a talk with you not only about this. Could you lunch some day? I am

1. Sackville-West replied that she had incorrectly assumed LW had given Pippett permission to quote letters. She was strongly in favor of their full publication.
2. In 1956 Monique Nathan published *Virginia Woolf par elle-même*, a romantically illustrated book that evoked strong interest in the subject in France.

going to France for a bit at the end of April, but would you perhaps lunch with me at the Athenaeum on Wednesday, April 13, at 1?

Yours
L W

FROM CLIVE BELL

6 August 1955

Dear Leonard,
I think I have collected the bulk of Virginia's letters to me: probably I shall come across two or three odd ones later. Very roughly they fall into two categories—early and late. You won't be surprised to hear that all are brilliant and the later are scurrilous to a degree. These of course are the ones that amuse me most. They are full of pastime and prodigality and fascinating gossip (possibly untrue) about my friends. I fear they are at present unpublishable. To be sure they contain a few pretty compliments to myself which could offend no one; but these might look oddly standing by themselves. The case of the earlier ones is different. The better part of these is concerned with writing and with ideas—more often than not with Virginia's writing and ideas—and with books in general. Though to one as old and frivolous as I gossip is the thing, to the young and thoughtful I believe the early letters might be of profound importance. They are certainly interesting. But God! how touchy we were in our young days. . . .

Clive[1]

TO GERALD BRENAN

11/8/55

Monk's House
Rodmell, Lewes, Sussex

Dear Gerald,
I have read these [draft pages of *South from Granada*] with great interest and pleasure and I have only one criticism. You repeat the

1. Vanessa Bell had written six months earlier to say of the letters she had seen, "I dont think they could be published now as they are and it would spoil them to leave out that sort of thing [gossip about friends] as the way of saying it is always very characteristic."

commonly made statement that "Bloomsbury" "regarded all but a few chosen people as being beyond the pale." This is really quite untrue. It is true that Lytton had a facade of arrogance and that he did more or less condemn a large number of people to outer darkness. I personally over and over again abused him for doing so. The general statement is quite untrue of Virginia, Roger, Desmond, Clive, Duncan, Morgan or myself, who after all were all "Bloomsbury" (Desmond and Morgan were certainly regarded by all of us as "Bloomsbury" by the way). It is also not true that Bloomsbury despised people who fought in the [First World] war. Personally I was not a C.O. and was twice rejected on medical grounds.[1]

Many thanks for the letters which I will read and return to you later. . . .

Yours
L W

To Jill Day-Lewis[2]

2/10/55

Monk's House, Rodmell
Lewes, Sussex

My dear Degenerate,

I have just been listening to your voice. You read it perfectly and the more difficult it became, the better you did it, I think. And it is very difficult—and also better than I expected, I mean as a book, because I dont think it is anything like as good as *The Waves* or the *Lighthouse*.

I rather feel that the BBC—while justified in cutting out complete sentences—should not cut pieces out of a sentence and should not alter words, e.g. Hatchards.[3]

I hope I shall see you soon again.

Your affectionate
co-degenerate
L.

1. Although he would not accept the fact that MacCarthy and Forster were part of Bloomsbury, Brenan otherwise altered his text.
2. Jill Balcon, the actress, was Cecil Day-Lewis's second wife. She had read extracts from *Mrs. Dalloway* on the BBC.
3. On the ground that it does not "advertise" commercial firms, references to Hatchards bookshop and Rumpelmayer's had to be omitted.

From E. M. Forster

Dec 7th 1955

Dear Leonard,

I hope you got the two or three letters of Virginia's which I sent you some weeks ago. But this is also to ask you whether you can advise me what to do with my life—that is to say from the literary point of view. You have advised me well in the past.[1]

I have finished the Marianne Thornton biography, and miss it. . . . But what next? I used to like reviewing, but find it so snippety and unrewarding, and as long as royalties come trickling in, there is no urgent need to make money. I want another long piece of work, which I might hope to live to print. . . .

Don't hurry to answer this letter, indeed you may never answer it, but since you have known me and my possibilities so long, some suggestion might occur to you.

Yours ever
Morgan

To E. M. Forster

Monk's House
Rodmell, Lewes, Sussex

14/12/55

Dear Morgan,

I received the letters and am having them typed. I will send them back to you in a week or two. I have already collected a mass of Virginia's letters from various people and am making a selection. James and I are also going to bring out a (small) volume of letters between Lytton and her.

I wish I could "advise" you, but I find it a very difficult problem. It ought to be autobiography. I am sure you could do a perfect one ab ovo if you could get into the mood and rhythm. You would have to take a deep breath and really start ovo with your last words always getting further and further in the future and sitting down every morn-

---

1. In 1922, crippled by depression and unable to go on with *A Passage to India*, Forster wrote: "I want to talk over my situation with you. There is no one whom I would so willingly consult, and I know you will help me if you can." LW persuaded him to give up reviewing and finish his novel.

ing to it and ruminating on old letters and memories. If you really cant do that, then, I think, you should do a biography. I always feel that it would be possible to write a good biography of almost any one and with infinite pleasure if one had the time and the library at hand as you have. I dont think it matters much who it is to be, provided it is a time which interests you and pleases you. And there should be a good deal but not much reading to do.

If you would like to lunch one day in London and talk about it, after the end of the year I could manage almost any day, but particularly Tuesdays when I am up at the office.

Yours
Leonard Woolf

To Frances Hamill[1]

27/8/56   [Monk's House]

Dear Miss Hamill,
I have been through the Virginia Woolf MSS and I enclose a list of them.[2] I should be willing to sell the 11 items provided that they were bought en bloc either by Harvard or Yale with an undertaking that they would be kept together and made available for serious students. I would consider an offer made by either. . . .[3]

Yours sincerely
Leonard Woolf

1. In the 1950s two Chicago rare-book and manuscript dealers, Frances Hamill and Margery Barker, began purchasing the papers of modern British literary figures and became an important conduit between owners and American collectors.
2. *Jacob's Room*; *To the Lighthouse*; *The Waves*; *Flush* and part of *The Common Reader*; *The Years*; *Between the Acts*; *Roger Fry* and notes on *Roger Fry*; *Three Guineas*; *Mrs Dalloway*; "Gas at Abbotsford"; essays and short stories; and notes on books read.
3. The manuscripts, with VW's diaries, were eventually purchased by the Berg Collection of the New York Public Library, though LW retained possession of the diaries during his lifetime.

To Philip Woolf

17/9/56

Monk's House
Rodmell, Lewes, Sussex

Dear Phil,

I daresay you are right and I am wrong about the MSS; these things are difficult. I had no idea of selling or getting rid of them, but was approached by the Americans with the possibility of Yale or Harvard acquiring all the MSS of the books and all the notebooks, keeping them together and making them available for students. It so happened that I had been much impressed both by the way in which these American universities do this kind of thing and the interest and intelligence of their students. For instance, there was a student [Mary Lyon] from Harvard over here this year who was writing a thesis on Virginia's novels. She was extremely intelligent and took immense trouble to get the information she wanted. She found a number of Virginia's essays and articles published in journals but not signed of which I was ignorant and I paid her a fee to search them out and collect them. She did the whole thing extraordinarily well and I shall be able to publish another book of essays by Virginia.[1] I have never come across anything like this here and I feel that if the MSS went to Cambridge or Oxford, they would be stuffed away somewhere and no one would ever look at them again except that one would be shown from time to time to the public under a glass case.

I wish you had written to Virginia about her books; nothing would have given her greater pleasure. I wish you would come and spend a few days here some time.

Yours,
Leonard

To John McCallum[2]

8 January 1957

The Hogarth Press Ltd.
40-42 William IV Street
London, W.C.2.

Dear Mr. McCallum,

Many thanks for sending me the reviews of the Woolf/Strachey Letters. They are very interesting, but the variation of pro and con has also been noticeable here.

1. *Granite and Rainbow: Essays*, published in 1958.
2. Head of the Trade Department of Harcourt, Brace and Company.

I look forward very much to seeing you in the Spring.

Many thanks, too, for *Ulysses in Paris*. It recalls the moment when Miss Harriet Weaver brought us the MS of *Ulysses* and we tried without success to get an English printer to print it.[1]

Yours sincerely,
Leonard Woolf

To SIMON NOWELL-SMITH[2]

17/1/57   [Monk's House]

Dear Mr Nowell-Smith,

I should be glad to be of any assistance, but I doubt whether there are unpublished references to the Library. I will have a look. My wife of course used it much and was once found to have about 50 books unreturned. The Library tradition that the Stephen girls were a bit wild was, I believe, due to Mr Cox who is said to have told a very respectable friend of the Stephen family—possibly Mrs Whitehead—that it was a great pity that they had done so badly for themselves, one marrying a man called Bell and the other a man called Woolf.[3] Later when my wife rehabilitated herself by becoming a well-known writer, Mr Cox relented even to me and we became very good friends. I dont suppose this is suitable for the history, but I should be delighted for you to put it in as it is characteristic of the amusing atmosphere of the Library and Mr Cox when I first knew them. . . .

Yours sincerely
Leonard Woolf

1. *Ulysses in Paris* was by Sylvia Beach (1887–1962), who knew Joyce and was the first to publish *Ulysses*, in France. Harriet Weaver (1876–1961), a rich social worker with keen literary interests, is best remembered as Joyce's promoter. In 1918 she asked the Woolfs to publish *Ulysses*; since the text was too long to be printed on their hand press, and no other printer would touch it out of fear of prosecution for obscenity, it had to be returned.
2. Librarian of the London Library 1950–56, Nowell-Smith had in mind writing a history of the institution and asked LW about any unpublished references to it in VW's writings.
3. Frederick Cox (1865–1955) served in the Library from 1882 to 1951. VW records in her diary another of Cox's comments: "Ah, strange to see what's become of those two girls. Brought up in such a nice home too. But then, they were never *baptised*." Evelyn Whitehead, wife of the philosopher A. N. Whitehead, was a woman of strong opinions, particularly about social appearances.

To Sylvia Townsend Warner[1]

18/2/57

Monk's House
Rodmell, Lewes, Sussex

Dear Sylvia,

It was extremely pleasant to get your letter. I enjoyed your visit so much and I only regret that you never came when Virginia was alive. I hope you will come soon again and Valentine too. I was so sorry to hear from Norah [Smallwood] about her being ill.

Yours
Leonard Woolf

To John McCallum

20 February 1957

The Hogarth Press Ltd.,
40-42, William IV St.,
London, W.C.2.

Dear Mr. McCallum,

. . . I do not think that there is any prospect of further portions of Virginia Woolf's Diary being published over here or in America in the near future. It would raise too many difficult questions, both of personal feeling and of copyright.

On the other hand, I was led into considerable difficulty with regard to the letters which were quoted in Mrs. Pippett's book, as certain commitments were made without my knowing it and it was almost impossible for me to forbid publication, though I did not at all like the way in which the letters were presented. I do not really like books of selected letters from all over the place, but after this incident I decided that it would be advisable to publish a volume of letters of all sorts of different people. I have a considerable number and I am in the process of making a selection, which would fill one if not two good-sized volumes. At the same time owing to the researches of a young American, I have discovered quite a number of essays by Virginia Woolf which were published in the *Times Literary Supplement* and other papers, and are quite as good as any which have appeared in *The Common Reader* and other volumes. I am at present engaged on getting together a volume of these essays and I should, of course,

1. Sylvia Townsend Warner (1893–1978), poet, novelist and short-story writer, had visited Monk's House for the first time a few days earlier. She lived with Valentine Ackland, who at the time had pneumonia. Smallwood was a director of Chatto & Windus.

be very glad if Harcourt Brace would publish it. I ought to have it ready in a month or two. The volume of letters will take rather longer to get into publishable form.

I am sorry that we shan't see you this Spring, but look forward to the Autumn.

Yours sincerely,
Leonard Woolf

To Constance Edwards[1]

31/7/57   [Monk's House]

Dear Mrs Edwards,

The £102 overpaid income tax returned to me was as unexpected a windfall, as if I had won £102 on a premium bond. I think you ought to go on a holiday and should use £20 of this windfall. When—and only when—you win £1000 on a premium bond you can pay it back to me.

Yours
Leonard Woolf

To Vita Sackville-West   The Hogarth Press Ltd
                                          40–42 William IV Street
24 September 1957   London WC2

Dear Vita,

We have now considered and discussed here at great length the question of publishing the letters. As you know, I originally decided that in order to avoid the continual requests of people to be allowed some of Virginia's letters, it would be advisable for me to publish a volume of selected letters. Then came your suggestion that all the letters to you should be published in a separate volume. In the interval Bunny Garnett and Clive's books have been published, and I think that they have both done a considerable harm to the reputation of

1. Edwards was LW's secretary at Monk's House. During those periods of his life when he had any money—in Ceylon and after 1930— LW was a generous lender and donor.

Bloomsbury and therefore in particular to Virginia's.[1] I have decided, therefore, not to proceed with my original intention of producing a volume of letters to various people because I am sure it is not the moment to do so, as the kind of thing which was said about the two books, not without reason, would almost certainly again be said by reviewers about the letters whatever they might be. I think this applies *a fortiori* to the volume of letters to you. It simply isn't the moment to publish them. I am sorry about this because I know you feel that it would be a good thing to publish them.

I will return the letters to you, but would you have any objection to my having copies made of them before I do so? I should like to be able to have them by me so that I could again study them from time to time and see whether my present opinion changed. The moment it did so I should, of course, let you know.

Yours,
Leonard

To Vita Sackville-West

Monk's House
Rodmell, Lewes, Sussex

27/9/57

Dear Vita,

Very many thanks for your letter. I am sorry we disagree and I would have liked, I hope you believe, to do what you want. But I feel very strongly—as do others more impartial than myself—that there has been too much washing of intimate Bloomsbury linen lately. This has encouraged naturally the inevitable turn of the tide against what is called Bloomsbury. To publish this great mass of very intimate letters would still further encourage it and the professional writers who dislike Bloomsbury. They would not get a fair press at the present time. I will return them to you after getting them typed and I will give instructions to the typist to be careful of the order.

Yours
Leonard

1. David ("Bunny") Garnett (1892–1981), novelist and critic, in 1942 married Angelica Bell (see Biographical Appendix). His *The Flowers of the Forest* (1955) and Clive Bell's *Old Friends* (1956) were autobiographical reminiscences.

To *The Times*[1]

4 October 1957

Monk's House
Rodmell, Lewes, Sussex

Sir – May I support Mrs. Lee . . . and urge that the suggestion be carried to its logical conclusion? To be fond of fat old dogs is undoubtedly reprehensible sentimentality, and the wholesale destruction of such dogs eminently desirable. But I, like many other people, am disturbed by the sight of many fat old persons, some "without teeth or good eyesight, living their joyless and unhealthy lives" and kept alive by sentimental persons who are fond of them, "when true affection," to quote Mrs. Lee, "would lead to a quick and painless extermination at skilled hands." Surely these fat old persons should be destroyed with the fat old dogs? I may add that I am myself old (though, in the circumstances glad to say, thin).

Yours &c.,
Leonard Woolf

To William Plomer

14/3/58

Monk's House
Rodmell, Lewes, Sussex

Dear William,

I was so glad to get your book and have waited to write until I had read it. I liked it immensely. It was very nice to read what you say about Virginia and me.[2] But apart from that it is to me a book of great character and distinction giving both the personal and the cosmic flavour of time past with the intangible aloofness and intimacy which are so rarely mixed into autobiographies in the right proportions.

1. A report that a man had been sentenced to six months in jail for kicking a dog in a park had provoked a protesting letter from the Warden of All Souls, John Sparrow, and a supporting one from Margaret Lee, who proposed that "fat old dogs, some without teeth or good eyesight, whose unhealthy and joyless lives are prolonged to satisfy the self-centered whim of their owners" should be exterminated.
2. In *At Home: Memoirs*, Plomer wrote that he had valued the Woolfs' friendship as much as anything in his life. He also commented that LW had predicted the outbreak of the Second World War almost to the day, though before the event he had been considered a crank.

I hope you will come over to lunch one day after the middle of April when I shall return from a holiday in France.

Yours
Leonard Woolf

To Evangeline L.[1]

22/8/58   [Monk's House]

Dear Evangeline,
I hope you will not mind my saying that I am sure that I should not write to you or you to me. I am sure that it is not good for you. I think you should quite seriously write a novel, taking it seriously yourself and not writing to me until you have finished it.

Yours
Leonard Woolf

To Evangeline L.

25/8/58   [Monk's House]

Dear Mrs L——,
I do not know whether your two cables are serious, but I replied on Saturday that you must not come here. I was already concerned about your letters and had written to you last week saying that I was sure that it was bad for you to go on in this way and that you must not write any more. Of course you must on no account come here as it would be impossible for me to see you. And really you must not send me any more cables or letters. Your cable to my office was opened by my secretary as usual. When you first wrote to me, I thought you were

1. In his later years LW received enormous quantities of fan mail, some individual correspondents deluging him with as many as 400 or more letters. Evangeline L. of Los Angeles sent him more than 500 letters, as well as books, advice and pots of jam. She was also determined that he should have a plant from her garden, flew with it on her lap from California to London, took a taxi to Rodmell, deposited the gift on the doorstep of Monk's House and immediately returned home without having seen LW, who was working in his garden.

amusing yourself with a joke and I answered, wrongly I see now, in the same vein. But for the last few weeks you have let yourself go too far and you must really stop the whole thing.

Yours sincerely
Leonard Woolf

To David Garnett

Monk's House
Rodmell, Lewes, Sussex

8/2/59

Dear Bunny,

It is an interesting suggestion [to do a Bloomsbury picture book]. But on reflection I am definitely against it and would not be the publisher. Two reasons in the main. It would be met by the usual chorus of anti-bloomsburiansis which is more virulent among reviewers than elsewhere and must therefore be considered if you are considering publishing a book. But apart from that it would have a slight taste of the kind of "publicity" I dont much like. Perhaps this is old-fashioned in the worst sense—but I cant get over it or rationalize it.

Yours
Leonard

To Sylvia Townsend Warner

Monk's House
Rodmell, Lewes, Sussex

15/2/59

Dear Sylvia,

It is extraordinarily nice of you to write like that.[1] Though I dont normally like public and particularly respectable functions, I very much liked being asked by you to take the chair. And I thought your lecture perfect in every way and really enjoyed it. I was told that I ought to have said more from the chair and I hope you did not feel that I had treated you niggardly in that way. It was not in any way

---

1. LW had presided at a meeting of the Royal Society of Authors at which Warner spoke on "Women as Writers." After the event she wrote: "I wanted to say at the beginning of the lecture that all women writers owe you a debt of gratitude for what you did for one particular woman writer. But I don't think these things should be said in public; so let me say it now. I have long wanted to."

from lack of appreciation, admiration, and affection, but simply from a feeling that the chairman—certainly if it is I—should really be heard as little as possible.

Yours
Leonard Woolf

To Paul F. Mattheisen[1]

11.3.59 [Monk's House]

Dear Mr. Mattheisen,

I can never make out where Leslie Stephen's letters are or whether they are still in existence. It would be just worth your while to write to Mrs. Bell, Charleston, Firle, Nr. Lewes, Sussex.[2]

My wife, of course, knew Gosse who had known her as a child. I think he, like some of their old friends, disapproved of the way in which the children took a house and lived entirely on their own after the death of Sir Leslie. I only know of a single time when there was actual correspondence between my wife and Gosse. As you know, he was a terribly respectable, irritable, peevish and snobbish man. When we published *Early Impressions* by Leslie Stephen, Gosse reviewed it in *The Sunday Times*. We were told that he was very offended because my wife never wrote and thanked him for the review. I think she did then write to him and that he wrote to her but I do not know where the letters are.

I hope if you are writing about Gosse you will put in the story about him and Walter Raleigh, which shows up Gosse's waspish nature very well.[3]

Yours sincerely,
Leonard Woolf

1. Mattheisen was writing a biography of Sir Edmund Gosse (1849–1928), the distinguished man of letters. Gosse's literary reputation had suffered from charges of poor scholarship, leveled by the critic John Churton Collins.
2. The letters mysteriously turned up, with other valuable correspondence, in 1971 and were sold by Bertram Rota Ltd. to the New York Public Library.
3. Sir Walter Raleigh (1861–1922) was Professor of English Literature at Liverpool, Glasgow and Oxford.

To Paul F. Mattheisen

18.3.59   [Monk's House]

Dear Mr. Mattheisen,
   The story about Gosse I heard direct from Raleigh himself or he told it to Lytton Strachey who told it to me. I am not quite sure at this distance of time which it was. Raleigh was sitting in the Athenaeum when Gosse suddenly came across the room to him with a magazine in his hand and said to him in some excitement, tapping the magazine: "Look he's written a book; now's your chance." Raleigh looked and saw that it was a review of a book by Churton Collins, I think. He couldn't understand what Gosse meant and said so. Gosse then excitedly said to him: "Don't you remember that bad review he gave your book? Why don't you review this and pay him back?" According to Raleigh, Gosse seemed to be perfectly serious.[1]

                                                     Yours sincerely,
                                                     Leonard Woolf

To Edgar Woolf[2]
                                                     Monk's House
31/7/59   Rodmell, Lewes, Sussex

Dear Edgar,   I have never understood how you could convince yourself that what I wrote showed that I thought the family contemptible and published books in order to make money out of Virginia—except that of course one knows that people will go to almost any length to convince themselves of what is false in order to be able to cause pain to other people. Fortunately or unfortunately I have reached the age at which what people say or think of one no longer causes pain. But

1. Gosse's irritation had also been vented against LW for an article unfavorable to R. L. Stevenson in the *Nation* in 1924; he wrote to a friend, "I don't think he is an 'idiot' rather a perverse, partially-educated alien German, who has thrown in his lot violently with Bolshevism and Mr Joyce's 'Ulysses' and 'the great sexual emancipation' and all the rest of the nasty fads of the hour."
2. In response to LW's request for permission to quote Edgar's letter of November 27, 1953 in *Sowing*, Edgar claimed he had no recollection of the letter, adding that LW apparently no longer considered his family so contemptible.

if one is writing a truthful autobiography, one ought, I think, to show if one can, what one's family thinks of one—& what it is like. That is why I think your letter should go in. . . .

[No close or signature on copy]

To Dame Peggy Ashcroft[1]

14.10.59

Monk's House
Rodmell, Lewes, Sussex

Dear Peggy,

The record arrived and Trekkie and I listened to one side of it last night. We enjoyed it so enormously that we exercised great restraint in order to hear the other side tonight and prolong the pleasure. We both thought it absolutely marvellous. Everything was remarkable but the Tennyson and the Swift were superb. I have never heard anyone give poetry in the way that you do because you not only give every word and the rhythm perfectly but you never for a single second overdo the emotion and that, I think, is the supreme test.

I cannot thank you enough for giving me this record and I only wish, as I said before, that you had done the record of Virginia.

Yours,
Leonard

To Dame Peggy Ashcroft

8/11/59

Monk's House
Rodmell, Lewes, Sussex

My dear Peggy,

I feel that before I do anything else this morning I must thank you.[2] It was wonderful; you seemed to me perfect down to the minutest point (or perhaps one ought to say, up to). You are far and away the best English actor I have seen—I mean actor both the finger and the ear. I saw Sarah Bernhardt several times, Duse twice (once in *The*

1. Peggy Ashcroft (b. 1907), the noted actress, was appointed Dame Commander Order of the British Empire in 1956.
2. Dame Peggy was playing Rebecca in Ibsen's *Rosmersholm*.

Doll's House), and Coquelin.[1] There was something great about each of them, with Coquelin at the top in Molière. You stand with them. I cant tell you how moving it was, but there was something more to it than just "moving" as I am sure there always is when there is perfect interpretation of a character in a play by a great dramatist. I feel it is rather impertinent and pompous to say these things to you, but I cant get Rebecca and you out of my head this morning.

Yours ever
Leonard

FROM BELLA WOOLF[2]

13.11.59.

My dear Leonard,
   Forgive all defects of typing etc. My hand shakes so much and I see so badly.
   . . . Now regarding your request for the photographs of our Parents. As I told you before most of the family photographs went up in the blitz with Lady's [Marie Woolf's] possessions. I have however a photograph of Papa taken in wig and gown when he took silk and one of Lady (a very good one taken by Mendelssohn) when she was presented to Queen Victoria. Both photographs are of the same date and Papa's is what people call a 'speaking likeness'. . . .[3] Now I am going to be quite frank with you. I know that you know how pained I was by your description of your relationship with our Mother in your book Principia Politica—*I hope I have got the name right—there was not one word of appreciation. Moreover in your broadcast about the Grandparents, you mentioned Papa but not one word of our Mother. . . .[4]*
   Tom and I found, like many others, no clue to the meaning of this strange life into which we are thrust and came to the conclusion that the best things to do were to do your job as well as possible and be

1. Eleonora Duse (1858–1924), famous Italian actress and one of the great tragediennes of the theater; Constant-Benoît Coquelin (1841–1909), noted for his performances of Molière.
2. LW had asked Bella for photographs of their parents for his autobiography.
3. These are the photographs in *Sowing*.
4. "My Parents and Grandparents," broadcast on the BBC Third Programme in June 1959, was an excerpt from what became the first chapter of *Sowing*. The text contained several, albeit not many, words about Marie Woolf.

as kind as possible. Probably you don't agree with me for otherwise
you would not have revealed the contempt Virginia had for us in that
passage about Mrs. Collett in A Writer's Diary. . . .[1]

Love from
Bella

To Bella Woolf

Monk's House,
Rodmell, Nr. Lewes   Sussex.

18.11.59

Dear Bella,

Many thanks for your letter. . . .

It is very difficult to write about the . . . question which you raise because we probably take different views about it. At any rate, I don't think myself that I ever said anything derogatory of mother or of the family and that the family has read things into passages which are not there at all. For instance, you have always completely misread the passage in Virginia's diary about Mrs. Collett. The sentence "from that we did not expect anything much" does not refer to you at all; it simply means that she had not expected a Lord Mayor's daughter-in-law to be the kind of person to ridicule the Jubilee and the Lord Mayor. I knew that I had probably got the facts wrong [in the draft of *Sowing*] with regard to dates etc., and I should be much obliged if you would let me know any corrections, the earlier the better.

Yours,
Leonard

---

1. The pertinent passage, in the entry for April 27, 1935, states: ". . . the only cure she said was to go to Hong Kong & stay with Bella. From that we did not expect anything much, to tell the truth; whereas she [Mrs. Collett] ridiculed the Jubilee, the Lord Mayor & told us all about life in the Mansion House."

Monk's House
                                        Rodmell near Lewes
28/8/60   Sussex

Dear Lady Huntingdon,
   The reason why I have been so long is that I have found the decision
so difficult and now I am terribly sorry to disappoint you. I feel in my
bones, as you probably guess, that it isn't the moment to "open the
archives", as it were. I felt also that you were so sympathetic that, if
they were opened at all, they might be opened to you. But the very
generosity of your proposal and your sympathy would make it the
more difficult, and the more unfair to you, when the feeling in my
bones began to work. There is also another consideration which weighs
with and on me. I am writing my autobiography and the first volume,
which brings me down to the end of Cambridge, will be published
next week. I have begun the second and am at present writing about
my seven years in Ceylon. After that comes my return to London and
marriage and Virginia. I had not thought of this before I talked to
you, but now I think I should find it confusing and disturbing to write
myself about this and her and at the same time to be closely concerned
with the writing of her biography by someone else. I feel that at least
until I have got to that part of my book and see the shape of it, it
would be wrong from both points of view to get involved with a
biography. I wish this were not the case and I am really sorry to say
no and to have given you unnecessary worry.

                                        Yours sincerely
                                        Leonard Woolf

From Sir Roy Harrod[2]

31.viii.60

Dear Leonard,
   This is to thank you for the most enjoyable hours that Sowing *has
given me. . . . I was very cross with you for your review of my Maynard,*

1. The author Margaret Lane, Countess of Huntingdon, had proposed writing a biography
of VW.
2. Sir Roy Harrod (1900–1978), Student of Christ Church, Oxford, 1924–67, had recently
completed *The Life of John Maynard Keynes*, which LW had described as a failure in an
unsigned review in the *Listener*.

which I thought spiteful. . . . I have no doubt that there were correct points in your criticisms. But it seemed that you failed to give praise where that was due. Happily for me, I subsequently got the highest tributes from writers of great distinction. . . . I am sure that no living person could have written anything remotely to match it. Lytton, had he been still alive, could doubtless have done a better portrait, but he could not have appraised Maynard's economics & active career . . . with such authority. . . . I have returned to mention this old grievance, because you were so very kind to me at the Cranium the other day.

Yrs
Roy Harrod

P.S. Why did you say of me "who was not himself an Apostle." I nowhere hinted this & it would be impossible as an Oxford man. . . . I was slightly intrigued the other day that it was I, rather than any Apostle, who wrote to that Apostle, Guy Burgess, with whom I have a desultory correspondence, to suggest that he might respond to the Appeal of the Cambridge Arts Theatre.[1] He sent me a cheque for £25 to carry on the work of Apostle Maynard.

To Sir Roy Harrod

2/9/60   [Monk's House]

Dear Roy,

Your letter interested me very much and I'm very glad you liked my book. I wish you could have reviewed it, for I should have liked to have your full dress opinion of it. But if we had changed places, I'm sure I should have said no. Reviewing is almost always a stupid occupation. Space, time, editors contrive to make it impossible for one to say what one wants to say.

Which brings me to your book. I ought never to have reviewed it and I am quite prepared to believe that I did not do it justice. But I was not spiteful. I have never felt the slightest spite against you or it and I dont think that spite is one of my many vices. Irritation and an irritable pen or typewriter are, and there were certain things in your

1. Guy Burgess (1911–1963), who defected to the Soviet Union in 1951, had been an Apostle while at Cambridge. Keynes had financed the construction and operation of the Cambridge Arts Theatre.

book which irritated me, as indeed the review showed. I dont think these faults in the book were unimportant, but it was wrong of me not to insist upon its very great merits. That I did not was partly due to the little space I had allowed me. But you had grounds for being angry with me.

I had no arrière pensée in saying that you were not an Apostle. It was simply that 999 of 1000 readers would not have the faintest idea whether you were or were not and it seemed to me slightly important that it should be clear to them that you were not. I did not mean it in the slightest degree "spitefully". I had great doubts about how to write about the Society, but so much has in fact been written about it in recent years and it was so important to my thesis that I came to the conclusion that it would be silly not to go the whole hog.

How very interesting about Guy Burgess.

I hope we may meet again soon at the Cranium. I enjoyed our talk very much.

Yours
Leonard Woolf

To Minna Green[1]

26.10.60   [Monk's House]

Dear Miss Green,

I was very glad to hear from you again after so many years. As regards the first question, I personally think that Freud is a very great man and that he discovered things about the human mind which are quite new and very important. Of course he was wrong about a lot of things as all great men and pioneers must be and some of his followers talk complete nonsense. But there is a tremendous lot of truth in what he says. As regards your second question, of course I should like to believe things which would make the world more reasonable but I believe that the mere fact that a very large number of people believe a thing that would make the world a better place if it were true, is no reason for believing that it is true.

Yours sincerely,
Leonard Woolf

1. Minna Green was LW's secretary at the *International Review* and the *Contemporary Review* 1919–22.

To WILLIAM PLOMER

23/11/60

Monk's House
Rodmell, Lewes, Sussex

Dear William,

I can think of no better [birthday] present than Chateau d'Yquem 1949—absolutely none, and only you could have had the brilliant idea of sending it to me. There are a few things which have a quality which makes them stand out by themselves from their own class, quite different things like Richebourg (Domaine de la Romanée Conti), Doyenne du Comice pears, Beethoven's slow movements, and Ch. D'Yquem certainly is one of them. I wish you would come and drink it with me. Will you give the enclosed to Charles?[1]

Yours
Leonard

To SYLVIA TOWNSEND WARNER[2]

5/12/60

Monk's House
Rodmell, Lewes, Sussex

Dear Sylvia,

Your letters are always the nicest in my post, and you are one of the rare people who thank when it is they who should be thanked. Certainly it is I [who ought] to thank you in every way, simply for coming here and the pleasure it was to see you here and then for your talk which was in every way superb and delighted everyone.

Yours
Leonard

1. Charles Erdman, a refugee from the Nazis, lived with Plomer until the latter's death.
2. She had spoken to the Monday Literary Club, a distinguished Lewes literary insititution, of which LW was President from 1954 until 1969.

To C. H. Johns[1]

26/1/61   [Monk's House]

Dear Sir,

    With reference to your CHJ/OH of 24 January, I acknowledge receipt of my cheque. I would however point out that I do not "wish to resign membership of the Society", of which I have been a member for many years. It is you who have summarily turned me out of the Society by deciding that 55 miles is less than 50 miles.

Yours faithfully
Leonard Woolf

To Sir Solly Zuckerman[2]

24/2/61   [Monk's House]

Dear Sir Solly Zuckerman,

    I have to thank you for your extremely nice letter and I gladly enclose a cheque for £5 in payment of my subscription. I should, as a matter of fact, have been quite willing to pay the additional £3 but was slightly annoyed by the categorical tone of Mr Johns' letters. . . . As regards judging by the crow flying distance, I feel that a Zoological Society should be very careful not to confuse birds with mammals. I am sure the Rodmell crow would have no objection to be considered as a resident within 50 miles whereas a mammal like myself might well object to being included in the category of crows.

Yours sincerely
Leonard Woolf

---

1. Johns was Establishments Officer of the Zoological Society of London, who had returned LW's annual dues for underpayment. Dues were now higher for residents within fifty miles of Charing Cross, measured "as the crow flies" even if road and rail distance was greater.
2. Sir Solly Zuckerman (b. 1904), professor, noted scientist and secretary of the Zoological Society had seen LW's name on a list of resignations and wrote: "I should hate anyone of your distinction ceasing to be a Fellow."

To Nancy Carline

27/11/61

Monk's House
Rodmell near Lewes   Sussex

Dear Mrs Carline,

We very much enjoyed seeing you and your husband, and also the pictures and house and garden. I have looked up my old diaries and find that I saw a great deal of Henry Lamb in January, February, and March 1912 and that he must have painted a portrait of me in March. There are entries, for instance, on March 24 and 25 that I lunched with and sat for him.[1]

Many thanks for the card.

Yours sincerely
Leonard Woolf

To William Plomer

30/11/61

Monk's House
Rodmell, Lewes, Sussex

Dear William,

It was very nice of you and Charles to cheer me on the 25th for just clearing the 81st fence in the great steeplechase. This will be the style in which I write—if I do write—the 3rd vol. of my autobiography. You wrote a charming review of vol 2 in the *Listener*. I am afraid the 3rd volume will be very difficult—beset by inhibitions.

Yours
Leonard

1. Richard and Nancy Carline owned Lamb's portrait of LW, one of eight known oil portraits of him: two by Duncan Grant (1911–13), one by Philip Woolf (1912), one by Vanessa Bell (1939–40) and three by Trekkie Parsons (1945–60). He also appears with others in two oils by Vanessa Bell and one by Duncan Grant. Quentin Bell did a study of him that he later used as a model for the head of Christ in his painting of the Supper at Emmaeus in the Berwick church in Sussex. In addition, there are drawings, sketches and lithographs by Vanessa Bell, Dora Carrington, Richard Kennedy and Trekkie Parsons and a caricature by David Levine.

To Alice Cameron

17.1.62 [Monk's House]

Dear Mrs. Cameron,

I was very much interested by your letter.[1] I suppose that there is really no certain answer to the question you raise about the conflict. In a sense I don't feel it as a conflict because I have the greatest contempt for so many of the things which I really want. Personally, there are a large number of things which give me considerable pleasure but I, at the same time, know that they are completely worthless except for the pleasure they give me. Success is only one of the things and I think the reason why I despise success, though I want to have it, is that most of the successful people one knows are very despicable.

Yours sincerely,
Leonard Woolf

To Angus Wilson[2]

8/3/62 [Monk's House]

Dear Mr Wilson,

I hope that you will forgive me bothering you with this letter though you do not know me. My excuse is that a few days ago I read an article on the novel by you. Like everything else of yours which I have read, it interested me very greatly and nearly everything in it seemed to me convincing. One point, however, occurred to me and at the back of my mind has worried me ever since I read your article. It is in order to get it out of the back of mind that I am impertinently putting it before you.

As I understand your article, you roughly divide novels into A, those which deal with the personal relations of human beings as individuals; and B, those which deal with the relations of human beings to society or to one another as members of a particular society in a particular place and time. My wife's books you classify as A and as a writer you

1. She had asked LW about his statement in *Growing* (p. 178) that "deep down" he sought success while at the same time despising it.
2. (Sir) Angus Wilson (b. 1913), novelist and critic. His article "Against New Orthodoxies" had just appeared in *Books and Bookmen*.

reacted against A books, but you now think your reaction went too far or has produced a reaction in favour of B books which has gone too far. The point which I would put to you it this: that there is a third class of novel, C, which deals with the relations of human beings to one another and also to the universe. Perhaps I can explain what I mean by taking novels which seem to me indubitably masterpieces or at least of the highest class and classifying them as A, B, or C. *Pride and Prejudice* seems to me pure A; *Madame Bovary* is almost entirely A. Turgenev's *Fathers and Children* and many of Dickens' novels are B. *War and Peace*, *The Brothers Karamazov*, and some of Hardy's novels are C. And if you go outside the novel I should say that *As You Like It* and *Romeo and Juliet* are A, *Lear* and the *Tempest* C.

Leaving for the moment entirely on one side the question of their merits or success, I think that my wife, at any rate in her later books, was writing C books. She was obsessed (as her criticism and *A Writer's Diary* show and also her conversation) with what she called "reality" and "life" in relation to human beings and therefore to the novelist's problem of dealing with the relations of human beings to one another and to "reality", to the universe. *Night and Day* and *The Years* which seem to me her worst books are A books. *The Voyage Out*, *Jacob's Room* and *Mrs Dalloway* are mainly A books, but at the end of *The Voyage Out*, occasionally in *Jacob's Room*, and more profoundly in *Mrs Dalloway* the C themes creep in. Those themes are more persistent and clearer in *To the Lighthouse*. *The Waves* is pure C; it is not about the relations of human beings to one another simply as individuals; it is about those relations but also about the relations to "reality", to the universe—the relation of friendship, love, life, death to "reality." I am not discussing whether the book is a good book or a bad book, but merely what it is actually about. Surely it is not about simply the human relations of a small number of people as revealed by feminine sensitivity any more than it is about their relations as members of a particular class in a particular society at a particular time; it is about their relations to one another under the shadow of love, life, and death in the context, not of society, but the universe.

When it comes to a question of values, I feel I should put my cards on the table since I am almost certainly personally prejudiced where my wife's books are concerned. I think that the only one of her books which is probably really successful and great is *The Waves*. I think it is great because she did what she meant to do—i.e. write, not an A book nor a B book, but a C book. I also think that you can have, and that there are, masterpieces by all kinds of different writers, which are

A books, and B books, and C books. People who write first class novels like you or my wife naturally react against novels of a particular class. She reacted against the B class and you reacted against the A class. Fundamentally she went much too far in her reaction against B, just as you went too far against A—but pragmatically as serious writers at a particular moment of time you were both right. People like myself who dont write novels can perhaps see more objectively that *Pride and Prejudice*, *Crotchet Castle*, *The Brothers Karamazov*, *Anglo-Saxon Attitudes*, *Jane Eyre*, *Wuthering Heights*, *Domby and Son*, *The Waves*, *The Golden Bowl*, *The Mayor of Casterbridge* are masterpieces or first class works of art—and not because they are or are not A, B, or C.

Yours sincerely,
Leonard Woolf[1]

To Angus Wilson

22/4/62   [Monk's House]

Dear Mr Wilson,

Very many thanks for your letter. We really seem to have much the same view of this particular question. I still think that you may have masterpieces of the pure A class or B class which rule out or ignore the problems or overtones of the C class. Jane Austen refused to consider Fanny's cosmological position in the way in which Tolstoy considers Anna's or Dostoevsky Alyosha's and Ivan's. It is a qualitative difference of content. However, I feel that you would "in principle" say the same. I shall look out for your three talks.[2] I have a blind eye, which I realize is inexcusable, for Stendhal. As regards *Between the Acts*, I deliberately omitted it. I agree that it is exciting, but it is not as clear an example—as pure an example—of what I see the C class of novel to be as *The Waves*. Nor do I think it as good as a novel and

---

1. Wilson replied: ". . . I agree with your assessment of her [VW's] novels, but I am sad that you should leave out *Between the Acts* which for me is really the most exciting experience of all." He argued that LW's C novels were in reality an outstanding version of either A or B; hence if *Pride and Prejudice* was A, he wrote, *Mansfield Park* and *Persuasion* were A+, or LW's C.
2. These were Wilson's Northcliffe Lectures at University College, London, on "Evil in the English Novel." They were broadcast on the BBC Third Programme in December 1962 and subsequently published in the *Listener*.

work of art—though that is again another matter. I am always, too, in some doubt about it; I am never sure that—on its own ground—it really comes off or works out in the end. *The Waves* ends inevitably as the rising and setting of the sun. At the end of *Between the Acts* I am uneasy that there is no end, not because artistically and cosmologically there isn't an end but because perhaps the writer missed it. Though I dont feel at all sure of this.

Yours sincerely
Leonard Woolf

To Edward Albee[1]

Monk's House,
Rodmell, Nr. Lewes, Sussex.

9/8/62

Dear Mr Albee,

Many thanks for your letter and its courtesy in asking my permission. I have no objection to your using my wife's name in the title of your play.

Yours sincerely,
Leonard Woolf

To Jean Love[2]

Monk's House
Rodmell, Lewes, Sussex

21.11.62

Dear Professor Love,

I do not think that Virginia Woolf ever really studied Freud though she must have looked at a good many books which we published. All intelligent people's thinking has been influenced by Freud even though they may not have read his works and she was influenced in that way. She was also greatly impressed by him as a person when we went to see him.

1. Edward Albee (b. 1928), the American playwright, had asked LW's permission to name his latest play "Who's Afraid of Virginia Woolf?" Prior to its staging he sent LW a copy of the manuscript.
2. An American scholar at work on a study of VW's novels.

I am afraid there appears to be no complete copy of *Freshwater* extant.[1]

Yours sincerely
Leonard Woolf

To Jean Guiguet[2]

9/5/63   [Monk's House]

Dear Monsieur Guiguet,

In your book of which we are to publish an English translation [*Virginia Woolf and Her Works*] there is a passage in which you suggest that things have been kept back from the published edition of *A Writer's Diary* because they might show Viriginia Woolf in a poor light as a critic or show her to have been influenced by other writers. I made the selections from the diary and have absolutely no recollection of ever having been influenced or having acted in this way. Would you have any objection to omitting this passage in the English edition? I only ask because as the publisher I might seem to be admitting what you say.

Yours sincerely
Leonard Woolf

To Moses Finley[3]

5/6/63   [Monk's House]

Dear Mr Finley,

I hope that you will not mind my troubling you with a question about the Greeks which has always worried me. My excuse is that I

1. *Freshwater: A Comedy* was a play written by VW in 1923 and rewritten in 1935 for a performance by LW, Vanessa, Julian and Angelica Bell, Duncan Grant, Adrian and Judith Stephen and Eve Younger.
2. Professor of English and American Literature at the University of Aix-en-Provence.
3. (Sir) Moses Finley (1922–1986), fired from Rutgers University for refusing to state whether he had ever been a Communist, went to Cambridge in 1954, where he was later appointed Professor of Ancient History and Master of Darwin College. His book *The Ancient Greeks* had been published by Chatto & Windus.

have read your book just published with great pleasure and admiration and I am fractionally your publisher. What has always puzzled me is how did a person like Socrates live? I have never conceived of him as a landowner or as earning anything professionally. He must have had to buy a certain amount of food and clothing. Could he do that all the year round on what he was paid if he attended the Assembly? And there must have been quite a number of persons who were full citizens economically in the same postion.

Yours sincerely
Leonard Woolf[1]

To Sylvia Townsend Warner

Monk's House
Rodmell, Lewes, Sussex

25/7/63

Dear Sylvia,

Your letter gave me real comfort and pleasure and I had heard from Trekkie that your cat had died at the same time as Troy.[2] What you say about being admitted into a cat's world is true. I have kept many different kinds of animals besides cats and dogs. Each after its kind has its own different kind of world, the dog's differing from the cat's and the cat's from the monkey's and so on. They will all, except the horse, I find, admit you into their world if you go about it the right way and I have never felt any reason for not having an affection for, say, dogs because one has it for cats and so on. But I have never known any animal like Troy.

Leonard

1. Finley replied: ". . . Socrates himself is a special puzzle. He seems twice to have served as a hoplite in the army, which he oughtn't to have done on the evidence of his poverty. He may once actually have worked as a stone-mason, but obviously not in later life, and my guess is that he was supported by friends and disciples, which they could have accomplished at very little cost, given the general standard of living at the time quite apart from Socrates' asceticism. . . ."
2. Troy was a Siamese cat of which LW was deeply fond. Warner had written: "It is the property of cats . . . that they admit one into their godless Saturnine Eden. And when they die, we are cast out of it."

To Sir Henry Lintott[1]

16.10.63

Monk's House
Rodmell, Lewes, Sussex

Dear Harry,

I have been looking at the deeds for this house which I have never looked at since I bought it in 1919; in fact, they have been lying at my solicitors. I find that in 1822 John Glazebrook, who owned the house, married Mercy Ellis. He died in 1829 leaving his property to his widow, Mercy, provided that she did not marry again. However, she did marry Edward Lintott, a carpenter of Brighton, and therefore forfeited Monk's House. In 1849 Mercy died and her husband, Edward Lintott, signed a document saying that he had no claim on the estate of her first husband, John Glazebrook. I think you once told me that your family came from Brighton and I hope Edward Lintott is your ancestor and that you have some blood of Mercy Ellis, who lived in Monk's House. I can trace everyone who lived in Monk's House, together with their sons and daughters in these deeds back to 1707. In the 18th century it was inhabited by a succession of Clears and was always called Clears. It was not called Monk's House until 1919 when the [estate] agent must have invented it. In the 19th century, in fact up to 1919, it was called Glazebrooks.

I hope that the descendant of Mercy Ellis will have a good time in Canada.

Yours
Leonard

To Dorothy and William Humphrey

13/11/63

Monks House
Rodmell

Dearest Dorothy and Bill,

I read *A Voice from the Woods* with immense enjoyment and with great admiration for Bill's powers perfectly controlled. I think Bill gets better and better with the pen or typewriter. There are no pleasures better than what one gets from a story of that kind in so many dimensions, perfectly balanced and sometimes on a razor edge. There are so many things I should like to talk to you about.

1. Sir Henry Lintott (b. 1908), who knew LW through the Apostles, had just been appointed British High Commissioner in Canada.

525

We had a great Fair in the Village Hall here last weekend to raise money to improve the Village Hall's heating. It was opened by Malcolm Muggeridge whom I had never really talked to before and whom I had a prejudice against because of the smartyboots bitterness of his writing.[1] He turned out to be an extremely nice man. As Chairman of the V.H. committee I had to introduce him and so he came along here afterwards and was almost the exact opposite of what I had expected. It is curious how nastily nice people can write. Do nasty people ever write really nicely?

The Fair was an odd affair out of which we made the astonishing sum of £90. Mr. Malagasekara, High Commissioner of Ceylon, and his wife appeared under the tutelage of Kingsley [Martin]. The High Commissioner in an immense diplomatic car over which the Ceylon flag flew; his wife in Sinhalese dress. They were both quite nice and they too came along here afterwards and—Asiatically—when he went off in his vast car he presented me with a pound of the best Ceylon tea and I presented him with a signed copy of my book [*Growing*].

With love to both of you

Your
Leonard

To Trekkie Parsons

27/1/64   [Monk's House]

Dearest,

According to Rita's statement I cannot possibly get a letter to you to Aswan in time so I must send this to Cairo and you wont get it, I'm afraid, until Feb 4.[2] I was very glad to get your wire and hear you had a good journey. I hope your arm didnt worry you.

A lot seems to have happened since you left. There seems to be an animal on heat in every room. Zin shrieks all day in the apple room and I have to put her in the bathroom at night. Bess came on heat on Thursday but does not shriek, I'm glad to say. Coco will be the next, I suppose, and I should think it will be my turn after that. Delos is in great form; he got into the bathroom and pulled yards and yards of

1. Malcolm Muggeridge (b. 1901), journalist and editor of *Punch* 1953–57.
2. Rita Spurdle, Ian Parsons's secretary at Chatto & Windus.

toilet paper off the rolls.[1] I can see him at the moment in the garden; he has taken to spending a lot of time there, chasing birds, I think. . . .

Grim grey weather here, but not really cold. I hope you have the scheduled amount of sun. There is an article by Osbert Lancaster in the *New Statesman* on a journey down the Nile. Rather critical especially of the Pharaohs' idea of art.

I miss you very very much. Love from all animals including your

Leonard

To Dame Peggy Ashcroft

29/1/64

Monk's House
Rodmell, Lewes, Sussex

Dearest Peggy,

I enjoyed Henry enormously.[2] The three together are a wonderful feat, I think, a kind of British Agamemnon, Choephoroe, Eumenides. Your Margaret-Clytemnestra is the most wonderful thing I've ever seen on the stage as she goes from youth to age. I must say I thought that Shakespeare also came extraordinarily well out of it. His passion and at the same time his unblinking icy objective cynicism are terrific.

At one moment I thought that all was lost and I should never get in, because when I got to the theatre I found that they had sent me a ticket for the afternoon performance. There was such an enormous queue that I could not get anywhere near the box office. Two minutes before the performance I at last got hold of a man and found that they had themselves discovered their mistake and waved a ticket for me over the heads of the despairing scrimmaging queue.

I hope we shall see you soon.

Leonard

1. Zin and Delos were LW's cats, Coco his dog; Bess was the Parsons' dog.
2. (Sir) Peter Hall's production of the three parts of Shakespeare's *Henry VI*, in which Dame Peggy had the role of Margaret of Anjou.

To Nancy Bazin[1]

29.1.64

Monk's House
Rodmell, Nr. Lewes   Sussex

Dear Mrs. Bazin,

. . . When she said that music influenced her, Mrs. Woolf meant this in the vaguest way. She was very fond of music and we used to listen to the wireless and gramophone—classical music—practically every night but she had no deep knowledge of its construction. When she said that she thought of her books as music I think that she meant that, for instance, she felt that there were themes in it much in the same way as there are themes in a piece of music. In the same way she was influenced only in the most general way by pictures and the aesthetic theories of people like Roger Fry. She certainly had a great admiration for Cezanne. I don't think she had any belief about non-representational novels. I don't think she was influenced by Baudelaire's ideas. . . .

Yours sincerely
Leonard Woolf

To Nancy Bazin

18.3.64

Monk's House
Rodmell, Nr. Lewes   Sussex

Dear Mrs. Bazin,

Many thanks for your letter of March 7th. I had forgotten the extracts which you quote about nonrepresentational novels and my statements in my letter of the 29th January are obviously too sweeping. But I still think that what she meant by nonrepresentational novels was very different from the views with regard to nonrepresentational pictures and the influence of the aesthetics of Roger Fry upon her was very general. She, certainly in conversation, was very much opposed to many of the theories of Roger Fry with regard to literature.

Yours sincerely
Leonard Woolf

---

1. Bazin was writing a doctoral thesis at Stanford University on "The Aesthetics of Virginia Woolf."

Monk's House
5/4/64   Rodmell, Lewes, Sussex

Dear Sylvia,

You always write the nicest of letters, being one of the nicest of persons—not that that is at all a common collocation. Your letter gave me a great deal of pleasure. If I had stayed in Ceylon, I should never have known you.

Today for the first time for 9 days the sun has shone upon the garden. Why does one live in an east wind under a grey sky; I can only murmur to myself from time to time Ben Jonson's complaint about an even more gloomy side of life, which at least one escapes in the east wind of Rodmell: "What a deal of cold business doth a man mis-spend the better part of life in; in scattering compliments, tendering visits, gathering and venting news, following feasts and plays, making a little winter-love in a dark corner."

Yours ever
Leonard

FROM ANN STEPHEN

June 3rd, 1964

My dear Leonard,
I have just finished vol. 3 of your autobiography [Beginning Again]. *I have enjoyed it tremendously though I am not sure the method of digressions which you have used was a good one. But for me the fascination lies in seeing yet another aspect of all you semi-mythical people who surrounded us when we were young. Of course we saw you all in the streets and squares and even occasionally in houses but that wasn't how we knew you—I mean in the early 1920s—the real you and Virginia and Vanessa, Clive, Duncan, Roger and all of you were a compound of the gossip we picked up in the kitchen from such people as Daisy and her sister Lottie, Mrs Upp and so on.[2] Of course*

1. Having just read *Growing* for a second time, she had written, "I must not be sorry that in May 1911 you sailed for England. If you had not done so I should not have had *Growing* to re-read—reason enough."
2. Daisy and Lottie Hope and Mrs. Uppingham were household help who circulated among the Woolf, Bell and Stephen families.

they only referred to you as Mr W, Mrs B and so on and I can still remember how delighted I was when I first saw through this subterfuge. I saw a compound and this material was compounded with talk from our own parents.

Something seems to have gone wrong, there was always a touch of bitterness when mother [Karin] spoke of the people you include in Bloomsbury and even father [Adrian] sometimes spoke in a tone which I took as a warning not to be deceived into thinking too highly of his family & their Bloomsbury friends. I think Virginia was more or less excluded from the warning but why should I feel it? I also got the impression that there had been some sort of deliberate exclusion of our family from the magic circle and that they were trying to pretend to themselves that it was they who didn't want to be in it.

Anyway, there you all were, larger than life, cracked up by the servants as "great" men and women and played down by my parents as "no more remarkable than anyone else for all they think so highly of themselves" and you were all a bit picturesque and awe-inspiring. I never asked any questions about why there should be this cold feeling. I don't think I really wanted to know the answer; it was bound to be discreditable to someone. I know mother was a bit difficult but surely not so bad as all that in those days. Of course she was soured against art and literature by B. B. and Logan but she admired G. E. Moore as much as anyone and I have always thought psychology was much akin to literature so there was a possible bridge but it was never crossed.[1]

I'm not sure that I want to know the answer now but I thought you might be interested in the question and in how you all looked to us, aged about 6–8 I suppose. . . .

You certainly have awakened a flood of reminiscences—what a mixed metaphor—but I thought you would like to know how much I enjoyed the book. I hope the next volume is well on the way; but one day, I suppose, you will be dealing with people who are still alive and less interesting to me because not part of my childhood mythology. . . .

Yours,
Ann

1. B. B. was Bernard Berenson (1865–1959), the distinguished art historian. Logan Pearsall Smith (1865–1946), member of a remarkable Philadelphia Quaker dynasty, was an aesthete who lived most of his life in England. His sister Mary (Karin's mother) married B. F. Costelloe and, after his death, Berenson.

My dear Ann,

It was very interesting to get your letter, which recalled many things to me almost forgotten. The trouble with Adrian (and later with Karin) was pretty complicated and dated from prehistoric childhood. Some of it is used in James in *To the Lighthouse*. "Had there been an axe handy, a poker, or any weapon that would have gashed a hole in his father's breast and killed him, there and then, James would have seized it." All Thoby's life and after his death his shadow lay over Adrian. Thoby was extraordinarily charming, physically, mentally, and in character. He was the sort of person whom everyone liked and many adored, and he was quite unspoilt by it. His father was one of his adorers; Adrian who was a rather peevish little boy annoyed his father. Adrian as a boy remained short, while Thoby and all other Stephens were magnificently tall. He became his mother's darling and outside the kind of inner circle of the three others. When he was about 14 or 15 he suddenly began to grow to his enormous height and I think this sapped his strength and energy. He came up to Cambridge towards the end of my time there; Thoby, who was immensely popular both in Trinity and Kings, had just gone down and the process of comparing the two, which had done harm in their boyhood, was repeated in Trinity.

When I came back from Ceylon, Thoby was dead and Adrian was living with Virginia in Fitzroy Square. Soon after, she, he, I, Maynard, and Duncan set up a combined household in Brunswick Square. Adrian was extremely lethargic and critical. Unless pushed into it by Virginia or me, he rarely did anything but sit in a large armchair reading. He had a slight grudge against life, one felt, and he remained somewhat aloof and outside our circle which gradually developed into Bloomsbury. Then he fell in love with Noel [Olivier] and became still more passive, inert, depressed, and aloof when he was rejected by her. Then Karin fell in love with him and swept him into marriage. She was the exact opposite of him: full of energy, life, enthusiasm. She loved boisterous parties. She made up her mind that she would revolutionize him into the same kind of ebullient, sociable person as herself. She could not of course succeed, and for a time she was, I think, pretty unhappy. The Bloomsbury mandarins—Vanessa, Virginia, Lytton— shook their heads over it, as you may imagine. They liked Karin, but in their habitual reserved way and with critical reservations. Adrian, as I have explained, had always been outside the inner circle and had resented it. Karin was not the kind of person to be able to bring him into it, and the war—when they went off to live at Radlett (wasn't it?)—increased the separation. After the war when we gradually all returned to Bloomsbury, they remained aloof and the situation you saw as a child developed.

Virginia and I liked you and Judith very much and would have liked to see more of you. But you were extremely elusive. You would suddenly appear on our doorstep in Tavistock Square locked out from your own house and in need of food and shelter or Judith would come to lunch in Rodmell from a camp, but then you would disappear for months. But I must stop this. I hope I shall soon see you.

Yours
Leonard

To Shelton Fernando[1]

Monk's House
Rodmell, Nr. Lewes, Sussex

12.8.64

Dear Mr. Fernando,

Many thanks for your letter. Yes, it is true that the University of Sussex gave me an honorary degree and the *New Statesman* had a paragraph about it which mentioned the words you quote.[2] I will have a copy of the *New Statesman* sent to you.

I was very sorry to see that Sir Francis Tyrrel had died. . . . I told a story about him in my book *Growing* but I altered his name so that people would not recognize that it was he. But, in fact, the story was entirely true and the family also referred to in it—the daughters of the planter—were really the Miss Jowitts.[3]

Kindest regards to you and Mrs. Fernando.

Yours sincerely
Leonard Woolf

1. Shelton Fernando (1907–71), Permanent Secretary to Minister of Home Affairs in Ceylon. LW came to know him during his visit to the island in 1960.
2. "The award of a Litt.D. to Leonard Woolf was an uncommonly imaginative gesture. . . . Woolf, at 83, is probably the most implacable iconoclast in England." The paper also paid tribute to him as "a liberal, a rationalist, a deadly dialectician, a born writer and a born gardener."
3. The story, on pages 149–153 of *Growing*, is about a romance between Sir Francis, who was given the pseudonym Christopher Smith, and Ethel Robinson, whose real surname was Jowitt.

To Sylvia Townsend Warner

4/9/64

Monk's House
Rodmell, Lewes, Sussex

My dear Sylvia,

It is always a delight to get a letter from you for it always contains what could only come from you.[1] I approve of the Mormons' crazy logic, for after all if you believe in Mormonism, baptism, and an afterlife, why not baptise the dead into Mormonism back to Adam? It is unbelievable what the human race can believe. I dont know whether you have ever been to church—I go occasionally to a funeral when some Rodmell villager dies, and really what the Mormons believe is chickenfeed for the gullible compared with what the parson tells us to believe on the authority of savage Semitic tribesmen who wandered about Mount Sinai 3000 years ago and of a Greaculus esuriens called Paul who had some kind of an epileptic seizure 1900 years ago.

I read the following in bed this morning before I got up; it seems to me to have that strange touch of subterranean wisdom which goes with all real humor. In America school children have to write a criticism of books which they use in class. A small girl, in a low class, wrote: "This book tells me more about penguins than I care to know."

Yours
Leonard

To Joanna Richardson[2]

15/10/64

Monk's House
Rodmell near Lewes   Sussex

Dear Miss Richardson,

Many thanks for your letter. I have considered this question of a biography several times during the last few years, but have turned tentative proposals down. It could only be done by a complete turning over and turning out of the diaries and letters. I dont think the moment has quite arrived for that. Otherwise I am sure that you would have been a very good person to do it. Though if the moment came for me

1. She had written: "The Probate Office—so I was told yesterday—is constantly invoked by Mormons who want to trace English forebearers . . . in order to have them baptised as Mormons."
2. Richardson is a prolific biographer.

to change my opinion, I should have to give prior consideration to the possibility of Leon Edel doing it. He told me some time ago that he would like to do it. . . .[1]

> Yours sincerely
> Leonard Woolf

To T. S. Eliot

11/11/64

Monk's House
Rodmell, Lewes, Sussex

Dear Tom,

The day before yesterday I got a letter asking me where the quotation "every sea-girl wreathed with seaweed red and brown" came from. I said T S Eliot and took down Prufrock. The result was that I read it straight through—which I had not done for quite a time. It again gave me great pleasure. What a good poet you are and always have been right back to 50 years ago. There is something very beautiful in Prufrock which had never been said before—completely original and you yourself. Also it has something which very few poets, even the best, attain: you write a poem which never lapses; every line keeps on the heights. That is extremely rare. I believe you were 29 when you published Prufrock. I suppose you must have written much before that which you destroyed and which made Prufrock possible.

> Yours ever
> Leonard

To Quentin Bell

22/11/64

Monk's House
Rodmell near Lewes   Sussex

Dear Quentin,

A surprising and ramshackle number of people approach me from time to time asking me to authorize them to write a life of Virginia which means that I should give them access to the diaries and letters. I usually have to give them lunch and politely say no. Among recent

1. Leon Edel (b. 1907) was then at work on the fifth, and final, volume of his biography of Henry James.

534

applicants have been Leon Edel, the Countess of Huntingdon, and Miss Joanna Richardson. I say no because I have so far myself felt that the time has not yet come for a life, that the aura of Bloomsbury or rather the fog which surrounds it has not yet sufficiently dissipated to give a biography a fair chance with the critics. I dont know what you would think about this. As you and Angelica will get the copyrights on my death, you are concerned and in any case I should like to know what you think.

Of the people who have actually approached me Leon Edel would, I think, be best, though he is somewhat desiccated. I think that far and away the best person to do it, if it is to be done, would be you. What would you feel about this?

Yours
Leonard

FROM QUENTIN BELL

23rd November, 1964

Dear Leonard,

Thank you very much for your letter. I don't know what to say about possible biographers. I should have thought Leon Edel, although Olivia says that the Countess of Huntingdon used to be a sensible, competent girl.

I should have thought that the work better not be done by a member of the family or anybody who knows as little about English literature as I do. I must confess I did vaguely agree to consider a proposal to write something on the novels when I was through with my present Oxford lectures, but this was said in a foolish moment and I don't think I shall do it.[1]

I think that the proper time for publication is probably within the next ten years. I find amongst the very young that the old quarrels about Bloomsbury have become as meaningless as the Phalaris controversy and that they are ready to look to, for instance, Duncan's paintings without the parti-pris which has blinded and distorted the views of previous generations.

1. Bell was Slade Professor of Fine Art at Oxford.

We shall be in Sussex for the New Year and can come over to Rodmell and talk it over.

Yours
Quentin

TO VALERIE ELIOT[1]

Monk's House, Rodmell
Lewes, Sussex

6/1/65

Dear Mrs Eliot,

It was a great shock to hear on Monday night the news of Tom's death, though I realized from the note he wrote to me the other day that he must be ill. We saw little of each other in recent years, but he was always the same to and for me as forty years and more ago. I had the deepest of both admiration and affection for him. To have both genius and such a lovable character as he had has always been extraordinarily rare. Virginia too had the greatest affection for him. On Monday night, just before the 10 oclock news, I happened to be reading her diary for 1920 and an account of Tom's first visit to us here that year.

Yours sincerely
Leonard Woolf

TO EDWARD ALBEE

Monk's House,
Rodmell, Nr. Lewes,   Sussex.

28.1.65

Dear Mr. Albee,

I should like to tell you that I went, with Peggy Ashcroft, on Tuesday to your play and we both enjoyed it immensely. It is so amusing and at the same time moving and is really about the important things in life. Nothing is rarer, at any rate, on the English stage.

I wonder if you have ever read a short story which my wife wrote and is printed in *A Haunted House*? It is called Lappin & Lapinova.

1. In January 1957 T. S. Eliot had married Valerie Fletcher, manager of his office at Faber & Faber.

The details are quite different but the theme is the same as that of the imaginary child in your play.

Yours sincerely
Leonard Woolf

To Dorothy and William Humphrey

31/1/65   [Monk's House]

Dearest Dorothy and Bill,

I am ashamed to think how long it is since I wrote to you, but I fall into a kind of literary—if not general—and certainly an epistolary hibernation at this time of the year. How can one write to two people whom one loves in Alassio or Lexington with a north east wind sweeping on to the croft where they played bowls and a grim grey sky hanging not more than two feet above the elms and rain, sleet, or snow banging on the windows? It has been a long pernicious January.

It was pleasant any way to hear what a success Bill's book [*A Voice from the Woods*] is. I felt in my bones it would be, though whenever a book is as good as it is, I always feel a faint fear. It is only the really bad books that one is *absolutely certain* will sell 25,000.

I have no news except that I have a new gardener and have changed my Esse cooker from coal to oil. Both are revolutionary. I should like to come and see you—you must know that—but uncertainties obstruct and I cannot be certain of what I can do the next month or so. I wish you were here in a perfect spring and summer.

My love to you both

Leonard

To John Rae[1]

                                                                    Monk's House
24.2.65   Rodmell, Lewes, Sussex

Dear Mr. Rae,

I cannot understand how anyone could have thought that the ethical teaching of Moore encouraged anyone to believe that they had no moral obligation to consider the effect of their actions. Surely Moore's teach-

---

1. Rae had written to LW about his doctoral thesis at King's College, London, on conscientious objectors.

ing in his book is the exact opposite and in real life he was so puritanically moral in his teaching that you should consider every effect and every action that we used to laugh at him about it and I remember once telling him that he ought not to take another helping of jam (a) because it would make him fat and therefore unable to do his work and (b) because he was giving way to greediness which was bad. I was not myself a conscientious objector in the 1914 war though I thought it was a bad war and one in which we ought not to enter. In fact the only members of what is called Bloomsbury who were conscientious objectors were Lytton Strachey, Duncan Grant and Clive Bell. Neither Duncan Grant or Clive Bell were really disciples of Moore. Lytton Strachey was and would certainly have said that he considered the effect of refusal of service on the country and other people. It is not really true, despite what Harrod says, that he didn't consider public moral obligations. But like most people before the 1914 war, he was not obsessed by these as we all are to-day.

Yours sincerely,
Leonard Woolf

To Quentin Bell

Monk's House
Rodmell near Lewes   Sussex

10.3.65

Dear Quentin,

I am delighted to hear that you really would consider doing the book.[1] I don't think there is any immediate hurry provided that I could say to the people who bother me that arrangements have already been made for the biography to be written by you. I think that it would probably from your point of view be a pity in the immediate future to stop the kind of writing that you are doing and, of course, if you got [the professorship at] Sussex you would probably for a bit have too much work on your hands to do work on it for two or three years, say, but I should be sorry for the postponement to be more than that. I think 10 years would be too much but if you began to read for it in 3 years at the latest, that would be all right. We ought to have a talk about it in the near future.

Yours
Leonard

1. Bell had come to the conclusion that, having grown up around VW and her family and friends, he had a unique qualification for writing her biography.

To Burlington Willes[1]

2.6.65

Monk's House
Rodmell, Nr. Lewes   Sussex

Dear Sir,

Many thanks for your letter of May 23rd. I am afraid there is no question of Monk's House being made into a literary shrine as I shall leave it to someone else after my death.[2]

Yours faithfully
Leonard Woolf

To Lucio Ruotolo[3]

28.7.65

Monk's House,
Rodmell Nr. Lewes,   Sussex.

Dear Professor Ruotolo,

We, of course, knew Wittgenstein though my wife & I did not know him at all well. He stayed with Maynard Keynes one summer in a house near here and we saw a certain amount of him then. My wife did not go to his lectures nor did I and I don't think many of the older people did. His philosophy is so difficult that it would not influence any but the professional philosopher.

Yours sincerely
Leonard Woolf

1. Willes was an American who offered to buy Monk's House and manage it "as a literary shrine."
2. Apart from bequests to certain members of his own and VW's families, LW left his estate, including Monk's House, to Trekkie Parsons, who donated the property to Sussex University. The house was eventually turned over to the National Trust, which operates it as a literary shrine.
3. Ruotolo, Professor of English at Stanford University, had asked if the Woolfs had known Ludwig Wittgenstein and attended his lecture on "Ethics" to the Cambridge Heretics Society in 1929 or 1930, which paralleled certain of VW's interests at the time.

To Victor Lowe[1]

16/8/65

Monk's House
Rodmell, Lewes, Sussex

Dear Professor Lowe,

I am sorry to say that I shall be up in town only one day this week and that I am completely booked up with engagements. It was through the Apostles that I first met Whitehead. We used to have an annual dinner and he was, I think, at one of the first to which I went. I do not remember him coming to a meeting. My recollection is that Moore did not think very highly of Whitehead as a "philosopher"; Russell often used to come to Moore's room and discuss philosophical questions with him, but I do not remember ever seeing Whitehead there. My generation regarded Whitehead with respect as co-author with Russell [of *Principia Mathematica*], but we thought he went much too "religious" in his later books.

The Whiteheads rather disapproved of my wife and her sister and through them of me, Lytton Strachey, Clive Bell &c. Mrs Whitehead was a friend of my wife's family and was, I think, a rather formidable woman. The rift occurred when my wife and her sister, when very young women, went to a Chelsea fancy dress ball in costumes condemned by Mrs Whitehead as unladylike.[2] But this of course has nothing to do with Whitehead's philosophy.

Yours sincerely
Leonard Woolf

To V. S. Pritchett[3]

15.9.65

Monk's House
Rodmell near Lewes   Sussex

Dear Victor,

I rather thought that there was no real evidence for Bloomsbury turning up its nose at Ford and it amuses me rather that you should

1. Lowe, Professor of Philosophy at Johns Hopkins University, had begun a biography of Alfred North Whitehead.
2. They were modeled on those worn by the native women in Gauguin's Tahitian paintings.
3. (Sir) Victor S. Pritchett (b. 1900), novelist, short-story writer and critic, was one of LW's fellow directors on the board of the *New Statesman*.

have said this.[1] It always seems to me strange that Bloomsbury, whatever that might be, was abused for years by people like Ford and Swinnerton and it really is true, I think, that we never did abuse them or turn up our noses at them.[2] Virginia, for instance, wrote dozens of reviews about her contemporaries and there is not one single case in which she turned up her nose in the slightest degree about anyone. On the contrary, as you will see from a book [*Contemporary Writers*] which I am publishing, she writes the most careful and appreciative reviews of people like Ford. I never met Ford nor did she, and the only one who did know him was Clive who, I think, often saw him in Paris with Violet Hunt but I should be very surprised if there is a single word by any one of us against him and I never heard anyone say anything against him.

Yours
Leonard

To Q. D. Leavis[3]

Monk's House, Rodmell
12/11/65   Lewes, Sussex

Dear Mrs Leavis,

I have been reading your book *Fiction and the Reading Public* with great interest and particularly what you say about my wife's novels. You say that *To the Lighthouse* "is not a popular novel" and that it is "unaccessible to a public whose ancestors have been competent readers of Sterne and Nashe". I do not think that the sales of the book support these statements. The book was published 38 years ago and has sold 253,362 copies in Britain and America since publication. The sales for the last two years were as follows:

	Britain	USA	Total
1963	12,981	10,827	23,808
1964	10,142	13,060	23,202

1. Ford Madox Ford (1873–1939), the author and critic; in 1911 he left his wife for Violet Hunt, a novelist.
2. Frank Swinnerton (1884–1982), novelist and critic.
3. Queenie Dorothy Leavis (1906–1981) and her husband, F. R. Leavis, famous Cambridge literary critics, had generally savaged VW's writing, allowing only *To the Lighthouse* a slight measure of grace.

It depends, of course, upon what one means precisely by "popular", but I should have thought that the figures show that the book is certainly just as "accessible" to readers as Sterne and Nashe.

Yours sincerely
Leonard Woolf

To Dorothy and William Humphrey

25/12/65 [Monk's House]

Dearest Dorothy and Bill,

It is Christmas day. The morning service is going on across the orchard; the bells have been ringing; the gloomy heads of the gloomy congregation have passed above the garden wall on their way up church lane to church; Coco, echoing her master's sentiments, rumbles and grumbles and growls at them. Though it is 11.30 A.M. it is twilight, a wet grey sky hanging a few feet above the church steeple. The sun has not been seen in Rodmell for many days. So you see we are having typical Rodmell weather.

But the wish to wish you all good wishes triggered off at last by the church bells has at last made me begin this letter. The wish has been there the whole time and I am ashamed at my not writing to you before. I have read your letters with the greatest eagerness. With two houses, your roots, I am afraid, will go too deep in the USA to allow us ever to see you again in Rodmell. I see that I shall have to uproot myself and visit you.

Trekkie, I know, has written you what news there is from here and I wont repeat it. I hope for a new book from Bill early in 1966.

Love to you both from

Leonard

To Robert Speaight[1]

Monk's House
Rodmell, Lewes, Sussex

12/1/66

Dear Mr Speaight,

I have just read with great interest your obituary notice of Clemence Dane.[2] I was much amused to learn that she regarded the preface in

---

1. Robert Speaight (1904–1976), actor, author and scholar of the theater.
2. Clemence Dane (1888–1965), playwright and novelist.

my wife's *Orlando* as "an unpardonable piece of snobbery" and as an
example of "the central heating of Bloomsbury". I dont expect that
you have ever read the preface. It is in fact ironical, a skit on the
unpardonable snobbery of so many learned and unlearned writers who
write prefaces spattered with well known people to whom they ladle
out their thanks. It is almost impossible to believe that anyone like
Miss Clemence Dane should not have seen this, but it shows how
blinding prejudice can be and how dangerous it is to be ironical.

Yours sincerely
Leonard Woolf

To Roy Thornton[1]

Monk's House
17.2.66   Rodmell near Lewes   Sussex

Dear Mr. Thornton,
   I had very little to do with Wyndham Lewis. I came across him over
the Second Post-Impressionist Exhibition but had nothing really to do
with him after that. That he was a bilious and cantankerous man is
beyond dispute, as he quarrelled with almost everyone he ever knew
and was practically insane with persecution mania. But I have no
rancour against him because, as I say, I had practically nothing to do
with him and only occasionally saw him at picture galleries or a theatre.
I do not know why you say that what you call the Bloomsburies had
a vendetta against him and "muscled him out". In the first place we
were not a group of critics and in the second place, as far as I know,
no one ever criticized Lewis. He was employed by Roger Fry in the
Omega workshops and I don't think Roger ever wrote anything against
him or indeed about him. I should be very interested to know on what
evidence you say that we did this and "arraigned against anyone not
humbly toeing the Bloomsbury line." And what was the Bloomsbury
line?

Yours sincerely
Leonard Woolf

---

1. Thornton was writing a thesis on Wyndham Lewis (1882–1957), the painter, novelist and
critic who loved to hate Bloomsbury.

To Frank Fish[1]

9.3.66   [Monk's House]

Dear Professor Fish,

With reference to your [letter], I would not have any objection to your writing about my wife's work and illness in the frankest possible way. In fact, it would interest me. I do not think that you could say that the psychiatrist in *Mrs. Dalloway* is Sir George Savage, because my wife didn't take people bodily and put them into her books and it would therefore be unfair to identify the two completely. But of course she was a patient of Savage and knew him extremely well and so there is something of him in the book. Her attitude to mental doctors was, I think, tinged by her mental illness and I always told her so. She would occasionally agree.

                                                    Yours sincerely
                                                    Leonard Woolf

To Roy Thornton

                                                    Monk's House
16.3.66   Rodmell near Lewes   Sussex

Dear Mr. Thornton,

I am much amused by your letter. The evidence appears to be simply statements without any evidence to support them by a single person who was 11 years old at the time of the Second Post-Impressionist Exhibition.[2] The members of the so-called "Bloomsbury" were Roger Fry, E. M. Forster, Vanessa Bell, Virginia Woolf, Duncan Grant, Lytton Strachey, Maynard Keynes, Clive Bell and myself. Only Roger Fry and Clive Bell wrote about pictures. Forster, my wife, Maynard Keynes and I wrote about books. Wyndham Lewis continually made the most

1. Frank Fish (1917–1968) was Professor of Psychiatry at Liverpool University and an expert on schizophrenia. Following a lecture on VW to a women's group, he decided to do a study of her illness but died before finishing it.
2. The reference is to Sir John Rothenstein (b. 1901), Director of the Tate Gallery 1938–64, whose *Modern English Painters* portrayed Bloomsbury as a band of conspirators who sought to destroy anyone who did not follow the group's " 'party line' which varied from month to month in accordance with what their leader considered the most 'significant' trends of opinion prevailing in Paris."

violent attacks upon most of us in print. Can you quote a single instance in which any of us ever wrote anything about Wyndham Lewis? In 1913 to 1915 I do not know of any paper in which we wrote other than *The New Statesman*, in which I wrote about politics from time to time.

In the 1920's I was literary editor of *The Nation*. You can refer to *The Nation* and I should be interested if you could find a single quotation from any article or review by any of us to support what Rothenstein says. I should be still more interested if you would quote a single word in any article or review unsigned which would support what he says.

During the 1920's I employed a considerable number of young and unknown writers in *The Nation* and published books by them in the Hogarth Press. I should be interested to know who the young writers were who were not allowed to write in *The Nation* or be published by the Hogarth Press because of malevolence.

Yours sincerely
Leonard Woolf

To Shelton Fernando

Monk's House
Rodmell, Nr. Lewes   Sussex

25.5.66

Dear Mr. Fernando,

I found your letter here on my return from the United States.

Mrs. Parsons and I much enjoyed our visit to the States and Canada though it was pretty strenuous. We were in New York, South Carolina, Washington and Boston and we stayed for a week with friends in Boston and in their country house which was extremely pleasant. We then had two days with another friend in Canada and we did the whole journey by flying. There are some parts of the United States which are very beautiful and pleasant but it is not a country in which I should like to live.

I hear rather depressing accounts about the conditions in Ceylon but that may be prejudiced. I should very much like to hear some time from you how you think things are going.

Yours sincerely,
Leonard Woolf

To MAN RAY[1]
The Hogarth Press Ltd
40-42 William IV Street

1 June 1966
London WC2

Dear Mr. Ray,

Many years ago we met in Bedford Square and you took a photograph of my wife, which was by far the best one ever taken of her. We are publishing four volumes of her collected essays, and we very much want to use this photograph on the jacket. . . .[2]

Yours sincerely,
Leonard Woolf

To MALCOLM MUGGERIDGE
Monk's House

14/10/66
Rodmell, Lewes, Sussex

Dear Malcolm,

It was infuriating last night. Trekkie was driving her car and after ten miles or so something began going wrong with the oil supply. We struggled on but at Hellingly had to creep into a garage. . . .

We were terribly disappointed not to see Kitty and you and you doubly on TV—my butcher this morning asked me whether I had seen you on the TV last night; you were, he said, so good. Will you tell Kitty how sorry we were?[3]

I had Harold Nicolson and a large pumpkin in the car to give you.[4] I will send back Harold by post—it is a fascinating book; it is extraordinary to be born with your mouth full of silver spoons, to have known all the aristocrats from poor Edward VIII to poor Eddie Sackville West, yet to think that only aristocrats really "do", and yet—yet—to be so very uncertain about yourself.

Yours
Leonard

1. Man Ray (1890–1976), the American artist and photographer.
2. The photograph, one of three taken in November 1934, is that with the right forearm raised and the hand half closed.
3. Kitty was Muggeridge's wife and a niece of Beatrice Webb, of whom she co-authored a biography.
4. The Nicolson was *Diaries and Letters 1930–1939*.

23/10/66   [Monk's House]

Dear Professor Fish,

I was very much interested in the enclosed lecture.[1] It may interest you to know that a Japanese woman doctor sent me a lecture on the same subject a few months ago; she has been asked to expand it into a book, has agreed to do so, and is coming next month to discuss certain questions with me (all the way from Japan!).[2] There are a few points in your lecture:

My wife heard the birds talking Greek not in the 1915 attack, but in the first serious breakdown after her mother's death.

It was the doctors (Craig and two others) who called the unconscious state into which she got in 1915 coma.

I do not think that Leslie Stephen could accurately be described as "insensitive". On the contrary I think he was really hypersensitive, and that Virginia's hypersensitivity was very like his. Things "got on his nerves" very easily and he allowed himself the luxury, like many Victorian old gentlemen of the upper classes, of occasionally "going up in smoke". His daughters were inclined to exaggerate his idiosyncrasies. I dont think that he was critical of Virginia, though he was of Adrian Stephen.

It is quite true that Virginia was normally in ordinary everyday life a happy person, very amusing, and frequently gay.

There was one part of her mind which was tremendously controlled and rational. In considering the effect of her mental state upon her writing, should you not take into consideration her criticism as well as her novels. I do not see how the manic-depressive mind, as described by you, could produce her criticism.

With all humility as an ignorant layman, the difficulty which one feels when confronted with your scientific description and diagnosis of manic-depressive insanity is that (1) the symptoms seem to be only an exaggerated form of the similar symptoms which everyone exhibits in everyday life; (2) the exaggerated symptoms also occur in other forms of insanity—the result being that one specialist can e.g. diagnose schizophrenia where another diagnoses manic-depressive.

Yours sincerely
Leonard Woolf

1. This document cannot be traced.
2. Miyeko Kamiya, Japanese psychiatrist; the lecture was "Virginia Woolf, An Outline of a Study on her Personality, Illness and Work" (published in *Confina psychiatrica*, 1965).

31st October [1966]

Dear Mr. Woolf,

Thank you for your letter of 23rd October. I found your criticisms very helpful.

I am not sure if we are really disagreeing about Leslie Stephen as hypersensitive people are often insensitive to the feelings of others. Nevertheless from what you say it is obvious that Virginia's sensitivity was more likely the result of identification with her father than the effect of an overcritical attitude on his part.

As you suggest I must take into account your wife's criticial essays and reviews. My suggestion that she had a cyclothymic temperament may be wrong as it is possible that her basic temperament was hyperthymic—i.e. she was usually mildly elated and only briefly depressed apart from her illnesses. There is however another explanation. The intelligent cyclothymic can "pull himself together" for a few hours if he is mildly depressed or elated. Intelligent patients can produce reasonable work when suffering from a mild depressive illness. I once had a colleague who was a manic depressive who wrote most of his MD thesis while depressed. . . .

Despite the Japanese opposition I intend to continue my research on the relationship of your wife's personality and her illnesses with her work. Would it be possible for me to see the whole of your wife's diary at some time?. . . .

Yours sincerely,
Frank Fish

To FRANK FISH

4/11/66   [Monk's House]

Dear Professor Fish,

Many thanks for letting me see the enclosed which I found very interesting.[1]

As regards the definition and diagnosis of manic-depressive insanity and the symptoms of depression and elation, "normally" my wife was

1. Unidentified.

no more depressed or elated than the normal, sane person. That is to say that for 24 hours of, say, 350 days in the year she was not more depressed or elated than I was or the "ordinary person". Normally therefore she seemed to be happy, equable, and often gay. But (1) when she was what I called well, she was extremely sensitive to certain things, e.g. noise of various kinds, and would be much more upset by them than the ordinary person. These upsets and depressions were temporary and lasted only at the most a few hours. (2) Whenever she became overtired and the symptoms of headache, sleeplessness, and racing thoughts began, the symptoms of depression and elation began. (3) In (1) and (2) I do not think that anyone would have thought the nature or depth of the depression or elation was irrational or insane, but in the two cases in which, in my experience, the symptoms of headache, sleeplessness, and racing thoughts persisted and ended in what to me seemed insanity, the depression and elation, in nature, content, depth, seemed to become irrational and insane.

I am very sorry not to be able to agree to your reading the unpublished diaries. There is a good deal in them which makes it impossible to publish them during the lifetime of some people. So many people apply to me for permission to read them that I have had to make a rule not to allow them to be read except by my wife's nephew who will write a biography of her.

Yours sincerely
Leonard Woolf

To A. N. L. Munby[1]

Monk's House
Rodmell near Lewes   Sussex

10/12/66

Dear Mr Munby,

I have a MS and book for which I have been offered £350 by an American dealer and I have decided to sell it for that amount. But I have been told that I ought to offer it to King's College for that amount as you might wish to acquire it to add to your T S Eliot books &c. The history of the material is as follows. In October 1928 Eliot told my wife and me that he had written a poem which he would like us to criticize; he would send us a typescript and he hoped that we and Mary Hutchinson would come one evening and criticize it. Some days

---

1. Munby was Librarian of King's College, Cambridge.

after this he sent us the typescript of what later became *Ash Wednes-day*. On the first of the five pages of typescript he has written in ink: "No need to acknowledge this. We look forward to meeting you on the tenth. T." We went after dinner on the 17th (not the 10th) and Mrs Hutchinson and McKnight Kauffer were also there.[1] We each in turn criticized the poem. When *Ash Wednesday* was published, Eliot sent us a copy with the following inscription in it: "For Virginia & Leonard Woolf from T S Eliot. I hope this is better than the first version." There are considerable differences between the typescript and the published version. The American dealer has offered me £350 for the typescript and book together, but I would prefer to sell them to King's for that amount if you wanted them.[2]

Yours sincerely
Leonard Woolf

To Dame Peggy Ashcroft

Monk's House
Rodmell, Lewes, Sussex

27/12/66

Dearest Peggy,

I love hearing your voice any how, where, or when, and you are practically the only person I like to hear reading poetry. (I rather like to hear poets read their own poetry (e.g. Tom Eliot) in that extraor-dinary drone in which I am sure all good poets have read their own poetry since Homer droned in Asia Minor.) So I wont give away the record or the beautiful engraved handkerchiefs. Christmas is passing now in a grey dark day and pouring rain. I had my two Christmas dinners on the 25th. The first was with Lydia [Keynes] and Logan at the White Hart.[3] She has no servants now so could not give the turkey at Tilton, but insisted on my coming to the White Hart. She was all tied up in a multiplicity of shawls out of which looked her bright red face. The White Hart was packed and the other guests looked at us and each other in a wild surmise.

1. Edward McKnight Kauffer (1890–1954), an American artist whose illustrations and de-signs were very popular in Britain, designed one of the wolf's-head devices used by the Hogarth Press.
2. King's did.
3. A Keynes-Woolf Christmas dinner was a tradition going back many decades. Logan Thompson was Lydia's farm manager and chauffeur. The White Hart is an inn in Lewes.

The second dinner was at Juggs with the David family all in great spirits.[1] We talked of you, wishing you were with us. . . .

I wish you had been here, but hope it wont be long before you are.

Love and every good
wish for 1967 from
Leonard

To Nigel Nicolson[2]

Monk's House

2/1/67

Rodmell near Lewes   Sussex

Dear Nigel,

It was really extraordinarily nice to see you here after so many years. If you would ever care to come and lunch here, do suggest it.

As regards your questions, can you describe the printing machine to me? The first machine we bought was a very small hand machine which one stood on a table; it could print only one page demy at a time. We printed *Two Stories* by Virginia and me and *Poems* by Tom Eliot on it. After that we bought a large platen machine worked by a treadle on which one could print 4 crown octavo pages; it was on this that we printed *Waste Land*. Virginia and I did the setting & I always did the machining. Later on in Tavistock Square I got a better platen machine. We printed ourselves all books with the imprint "Printed and Published by Leonard & Virginia Woolf at the Hogarth Press"; books not actually set and machined by us always had the imprint "Published by Leonard and Virginia Woolf at the Hogarth Press" or simply "The Hogarth Press".[3]

The position after my death will be that I shall have left the copyrights in everything to Angelica Garnett and Quentin Bell. Personally I have no feelings against the publication of anything, agreeable or disagreeable about myself or my relations, friends, and acquaintances.

1. The dinner was with Trekkie and Ian Parsons at Juggs Corner, near Kingston. Richard David was head of Cambridge University Press.
2. Nigel Nicolson (b. 1917), author and publisher, had written to inquire whether the printing press in the tower at Sissinghurst Castle since 1930 was the first Hogarth Press machine and what books had been printed on it. He also asked about the publication of VW's letters to his mother, V. Sackville-West.
3. In a subsequent exchange of letters it was confirmed that the press at Sissinghurst was the first platen machine.

Whenever one really knows the facts, one finds that what is accepted by contemporaries or posterity as the truth about them is so distorted or out of focus that it is not worth worrying about. All that one should do is to do nothing to add to the distortion. That is why I have always so far been against publishing Virginia's letters. Unless one can publish them in bulk and letters which she wrote to all sorts of different people, it would give, I feel, a distorted view of her. As I said, so far as she (and I) are concerned, I would not mind what was published. But one cannot publish everything, so long as some people are still alive who would be hurt or damaged. There are still a few, but the time is coming soon when there will be no one who might object.

As regards the editor of the Virginia-Vita correspondence, I think the best editor would be either Quentin Bell or yourself. Quentin is in fact going to write a life of Virginia next year when he will have a sabbatical year. I must, I think, have Vita's letters to Virginia, or at any rate some of them—I am not absolutely sure that she did not destroy some. The fact is I find it extremely difficult to force myself to read old letters and I have continually put off going methodically through the mass which I have here. Let me know some time what you think about it.

> Yours ever
> Leonard

FROM LORD FISHER OF LAMBETH

March 11, 1967

Dear Mr Woolf,

I am a mere 79, hoping soon to be an octogenarian; but may I without impertinence write about your T.V. interview with Malcolm Muggeridge? In fact I only saw and heard the last few minutes of it— but it is about what you said in these last minutes that I want to write. Like Cicero long ago you looked sadly about you and said that beyond all doubt death was the end for everyone. I just wondered why you did not add "Of course, I may be wrong and the Christian right, though I cannot bring myself to believe that." At least it would give you the chance to tell God what you think of him, if he's there!—but you preferred positive disbelief for which there is, I think, no finally convincing evidence—only speculation.

Jesus Christ taught (and taught nothing but) the fact that there is an eternal Kingdom of God, that he came from it and returned to it— and that with or without his aid mortal men can find their way into it now. That is a more exciting belief, I have found, than the negative belief that there is nothing beyond.

I hope you will pardon me for saying so much.

Yours sincerely
FISHER OF LAMBETH

To Lord Fisher of Lambeth

Monk's House,

[March 12, 1967]   Rodmell, nr. Lewes   Sussex.

Dear Lord Fisher,

Many thanks for your letter which interested me a great deal. The trouble about these kind of beliefs is this. I am 7 years older than you are and we were both born towards the end of the 19th century. If we had been born 3000 or 4000 years before that, we should have believed absolutely that God had ordained that we must eat our fathers. If we had been born 2,500 years ago in Canaan, we should have believed absolutely that God had showed his backside to Moses and that an eye for an eye and a tooth for a tooth was a most exciting positive belief. If, at the same time, we had been born in Athens, we should have believed absolutely that God had appeared as the swan and had a child by a girl called Leda. If we had been born 2000 years ago in Palestine, we should have believed that God had never said an eye for an eye or a tooth for a tooth but turned the other cheek. I have lived for 7 years very close to Buddhists, Hindus and Muhammadans and it was my business to understand pretty closely what their beliefs were and how they affected their behaviour. They believed just as intensely as you do in their beliefs and for the same reason but many of them, especially the Hindus horrified me and would horrify you. Of course I agree with you that a positive belief is usually more exciting than a negative belief but what worries me is the truth of a belief. And in all the positive beliefs that we are concerned with here, there is no evidence of their truth other than the belief in them.

Yours sincerely
Leonard Woolf

I think the real difference between us is that you believe that God made man in his image while I believe that man made God in his image. When men thought it right to eat their fathers, God revealed this truth to them; when men believed that it was right to exact an eye for an eye, they made a god on Mount Sinai who revealed this truth to them—and so on.

To H. M. Hastings-Hungerford[1]

15.3.67   [Monk's House]

Dear Mrs Hastings-Hungerford,
    Many thanks for your letter. The fact that it would make one unhappy if one didn't believe does not seem to me any reason for believing and, of course, it does not make life unbearable because there are so many people who dont believe and still enjoy their lives.

                                          Yours sincerely
                                          Leonard Woolf[2]

To J. B. Priestley

15.3.67   [Monk's House]

Dear Jack,
    In the old days long ago sitting next to each other on the *New Statesman* board, we used to call each other by our christian names. I was very glad to hear from you again and interested in what you say. I don't agree that there is a great deal of evidence that the mind can exist apart from the body and that personality can exist after death. The facts, which go under the name of ESP, do not *prove* that we can function outside ordinary time and space; they require a great deal more investigation before we can be certain that we understand exactly what they are and what they imply. I do not, of course, say that it is totally impossible for there to be an afterlife; what I say is

1. She had seen the TV interview and had written that intellectuals were atheistic because, like Satan, they wanted to know more than God.
2. She replied, "You know, if your wife had had some belief, she would never have ended her life as she did."

that there is absolutely no evidence that there is an afterlife and that it is extremely improbable considering the time that man has existed on earth that there would be no evidence if there were an afterlife.

Yours
Leonard

To Stanley Richardson

24/3/67 [Monk's House]

Dear Mr Richardson,

What astonishes me about you religious people is your extraordinary arrogance, rudeness, and uncharitableness. You are like your churches, with their popes, Archbishops, Presbyters, and parsons, who profess to follow and preach Christ, but in practice do and say everything which most horrified him.

You arrogantly tell me I am talking nonsense and then go on to say that you know things which even my cat or my dog would know that you dont or cant know. It is pitiful and humiliating to think that after thousands of years of human history, in which people like Socrates, Christ, Montaigne, and Voltaire have lived and taught, human beings should be so complacently ignorant and uncivilized, so arrogantly uncharitable.

Yours truly
Leonard Woolf

To Alice White[1]

14/4/67 [Monk's House]

Dear Miss White,

Your letter depresses me because of the arrogance and self-complacency with which religious people seem almost always to regard non-believers and the important questions which they raise. Why should you assume that I do not know anything about psychi-

---

1. White was Secretary and Treasurer of the Churches' Fellowship for Psychical and Spiritual Studies.

555

cal research and that I "evidently have not considered the proposition. . . ."[sic]? I knew intimately Mrs Verrall and her daughter Helen, who was secretary of the Psychical Research Society and have talked for hours with them about psychical research. There is no evidence from psychical research that mind can exist apart from matter. I have not only read but have published important works on extra-sensory phenomena. There is no evidence from investigation of what are called extra-sensory phenomena that mind can exist apart from matter.

You not only ignore my arguments, but you do not take the trouble to attend to what I say. I do not say that I know that mind cannot exist apart from matter or body; I do not say that I know that there is no life after death; I do not say that I know that God does not possess a backside which he showed to Moses; I do not say that I know that the universe was or was not created by a God or a Devil. I have never said that I cannot "conceive of life without a physical body." What I said and say is that there is no evidence of any kind for any of these propositions, and I am not prepared to believe in propositions for which there is no evidence other than the fact that in 1967 Miss Alice White (or for that matter I myself) would like them to be true and other than the fact that some anonymous Semite said they were true some 2000 or 3000 years ago.

Of course I agree that the conclusions of Myers, Lodge &c have to be considered and I have considered them and read their books. None of them produced any evidence of life after death or of mind existing apart from matter. Myers (a credulous man) and Barrett were not great men. Conan Doyle wrote admirable detective stories, but did not have an "extraordinary analytical" mind. Lodge was certainly not a great man and his testimony is suspect. Only Faraday was a great man of the five you mention; he furnishes no evidence of an afterlife.

You talk of a "new revelation", but all you seem to be telling me is that if you believe something for which there is no evidence, that is a "new revelation".

Yours sincerely
Leonard Woolf

1/5/67   [Monk's House]

Dear Mrs Kamiya,

I was reading a novel of Jane Austen when something struck me which I thought might be of interest to you in your work on Virginia, though I feel it is rather presumptuous on my part, as a layman, to write to you who are an expert. However the point is this. In *Pride and Prejudice* and in several of the other novels there is a very lively minded young woman—the heroines in *Pride and Prejudice* and in *Emma*, who are completely mistaken about some person and important question, and yet in the end see their mistake, fall in love and are loved, and live happily ever after. I think these characters are unconsciously Jane herself, who obviously from her books and letters, had this kind of lively, critical, and witty and ironical mind. She never married and one can see that she would have frightened off most young men and would have turned down on her side most of them. It seems to me the mistake and ultimate success of her heroines is a kind of compensation daydream for her failure in real life.

I seem to see the same thing in one curious phenomenon in Virginia's books. In real life she had some complex about food. When she was insane she refused to eat altogether and even when well she had a curious complex about food, for it was always difficult to get her to eat enough to keep her well. Yet she really enjoyed food in a perfectly normal way though she would not like to admit this. The curious thing is that food plays a very important part in her books, e.g. the elaborate description of Boeuf en Daube in *To the Lighthouse* and the importance of the lunches in *A Room of One's Own*. Is there not a kind of compensation here too, the admission of the liking for and importance of food in the fiction which was irrationally suppressed or denied in actual life.

I hope you dont mind my suggesting this.

Yours sincerely
Leonard Woolf

24/5/67   [Monk's House]

Sir,

In a review of my book *Downhill All the Way* in your issue of May 12 you wrote that to me

> "observant Jews and the monkeys in the Jerusalem Zoo are comparable and equally contemptible, chiefly because they have long hair."

This is a travesty of what I said. You may not agree with my criticism of the orthodox Jews in Jerusalem, but that is no excuse for ascribing views to me which I have never expressed or held. I did not mention or criticize *observant* Jews. I wrote solely about the sect of orthodox Jews in Jerusalem. I did not criticize them or say that they are contemptible *because* they have long hair—which would have been imbecile on my part. I criticized their political, social, and metaphysical attitude to long hair and far more important things than long hair. It is this attitude, not their hair, which I deplore because of its disastrous political and social effects upon Israel, a state and a country which I admire and respect. This is a question profoundly important not merely to Israel, but to the whole world. For the same kind of political and social theory and action has had terrible effects in the last 50 years in Germany and many other countries. That a serious Jewish paper should not treat it seriously seems to me lamentable.

                                                            Leonard Woolf

To Lucy Norton[1]

                                                        Monk's House,
9/7/67   Rodmell, Lewes, Sussex

Dear Miss Norton,

I feel sure that you will not agree with what I am about to write and I am sure that you may be right. But it is no good not saying exactly what one thinks. I think the letters disappointing and, if I had to decide, I would not publish them. My main reason is that they are

---

1. Lucy Norton, biographer and translator, had received from James Strachey a large batch of letters which her brother, Harry, had written to him and to Lytton between 1905 and 1924. They largely concerned love affairs, particularly James's with Rupert Brooke. Miss Norton had asked LW's advice about publishing them.

so much about intimate psychological small beer that except for the interest in buggery I cannot imagine their being of interest to or even understandable by the ordinary reader. Though I personally knew fairly intimately practically all the personae, I found it often difficult to follow what was happening, and rather boring to have to peer about in the general psychological fog. My second reason is that I think the letters give a very false picture of Harry, and to a lesser extent of the personae to whom or about whom he writes. This is always the case where a few letters of someone to only one person are published— they necessarily give almost always a very one sided view of all concerned. In this case it is terribly one sided, because it is all dominated by the semi-real, semi-unreal personal drama which at that time largely owing to Lytton was imposed upon Cambridge personal relations. There was really much more to Harry—and indeed to them all—than appears in these sometimes very interesting, but often very silly, letters.

I return the letters and hope you will not mind what I say.[1]

Yours sincerely
Leonard Woolf

To Michael Goldman

30.8.67   [Monk's House]

Dear Mr. Goldman,
I don't quite know what the answer to your question is.[2] I think T. S. Eliot was slightly anti-semitic in the sort of vague way which is not uncommon. He would have denied it quite genuinely.

Yours sincerely
Leonard Woolf

1. She accepted LW's advice and deposited the letters in the British Library.
2. Goldman had written to ask "If from your personal knowledge of Eliot, you would consider that he had anti-semitic traits."

559

6 October 1967

My dear Leonard,
  What an excellent review of the Holroyd book on Lytton! . . .[2] It's
puzzling, isn't it, what happens when all the letters & juvenilia are
laid out on the table? It seems to impede, rather than aid, under-
standing. I felt this when I read Christopher Hassall's book on Rupert
Brooke. I felt it again when this summer I was working on a second
edition of Leslie Stephen *& remembered your criticism of my book as*
being too harsh on L. S. & too influenced by Vanessa. . . . I think
perhaps biographers should be warned that letters, & even diaries, do
not necessarily reflect the inner man: that there is no one single inner
man, but lots of characters often in conflict with each other & pre-
senting different faces to different people. I thought you brought this
out wonderfully well in your review about Lytton's nature. You man-
aged to puncture a lot of biographers' shibboleths—especially dear
to them is the notion that if only you dig deep enough you will always
find a man of profound & tragic depth of emotion. . . .

Yours ever
Noël

To Lord Annan

Monk's House
Rodmell, Lewes, Sussex

7/10/67

My dear Noel,
  It was very pleasant to get your letter. I was rather sorry (rather
seems to be a favourite word of mine) that I had consented to review
the book. I had liked Mr Holroyd and had thought that he would
probably write a good book. I tried to say as much as I could in his
favour, but it really is a bad book.

1. Noël Annan (b. 1916), Fellow 1944–56 and Provost 1956–66 of King's College, Cambridge;
Provost of University College, London, 1966–78; Vice-Chancellor of London University
1978–81; created Baron Annan in 1965.
2. In a review in the *New Statesman* of the first volume of Michael Holroyd's biography of
Lytton Strachey, LW praised the author's assiduous scholarship but regretted his failure to
understand his subject, having been taken in by Strachey's epistolary self-dramatization.
"Lytton is always dying of love at the top of his voice in 475 pages."

What you say about biography is very interesting, particularly the fog which seems to spread over masses of letters and juvenilia just laid out on a table or in a book. It is partly the deadness of the dead. All these things dashed off in half a minute by a living hand and mind are served up to us as if they were carved in stone, and the more there are of them the more marmoreal they become. But the main thing is the obvious fact that in letters and diaries people tend (1) much more often to write when they are miserable than when they are happy. Virginia noticed this somewhere in her diaries. (2) to exaggerate and dramatize their miseries. Not only our sweetest songs are those which tell of saddest thoughts, but they are also the sweetest to the singer.

It is a curious fact that Pepys is almost the only intelligent diarist who does not go to his diary only or mainly when he is miserable. His diary is extraordinarily objective and emotionally unbiased.

Yours
Leonard

To John Lehmann

19/10/67   [Monk's House]

Dear John,

I have no objection to your quoting the words from [Virginia Woolf's] *Roger Fry*. I much look forward to your book on the Sitwells [*A Nest of Tigers*]; I hope your use of the word nest in the title means that you are showing what they were—cuckoos in tiger's clothing.

Yours ever
Leonard

To Lyall Wilkes[1]

13/1/68   [Monk's House]

Dear Sir,

My experience is that it is no good trying to find the causes of anti-semitism. The thing is so irrational that a long course of psycho-

1. Wilkes was a Labour MP 1945–51 and a circuit court judge.

analysis alone would uncover its origin in any particular case. I do not know why Tom Eliot was anti-semitic. In conversation and ordinary life he did not, in my presence at any rate, ever show any signs of it. I think we must have discussed it, but I do not remember with what result.

Yours sincerely
Leonard Woolf

To C. P. Snow[1]

17/1/68

Monk's House
Rodmell, Lewes, Sussex

Dear Lord Snow,

I have just read your *Variety of Men* with great interest, particularly your account of Hardy.[2] The episode of his life with R. K. Gaye, to which you do not refer, has always puzzled me, and I have often wondered what effect, if any, it had on his future life. In 1901 when I was an undergraduate at Trinity, Hardy had only recently been made a Fellow. This also applied to Gaye who had been elected to a classical Fellowship. Gaye and Hardy were inseparable and they saw hardly any one except each other and had almost withdrawn from college life. In a curious way I got to know them quite well (so far as that was possible) and saw quite a lot of them. I shared rooms with Saxon Sydney-Turner who subsequently was in the Treasury. Both he and Gaye had been at Westminster and knew each other well. Gaye and Hardy had a passion for every kind of game (and also for collecting railway tickets) and I had the same passion for games (not for tickets) and we induced something of the same in Saxon. We all four used to play cricket for hours in our or their rooms with a walking stick and a tennis ball; we also often played bowls with them on the Fellows bowling green. I used to contrive not to give up my tickets when I travelled by train in order to contribute to their collection.

I never liked Gaye very much, but was very fond of Hardy. The atmosphere which surrounded them was very strange and so therefore was one's relations with them. Hardy was an Apostle as were Saxon

1. Charles Percy Snow (1905–1980), scientist, administrator and novelist, was created a life peer in 1964.
2. G. H. Hardy (1877–1947), the famous mathematician.

and I, but he had cut himself off from the Society. His charm was of course extraordinary, but the two of them seemed to live in a world cut off from that of the rest of us.

Then Gaye committed suicide. I never heard even a conjecture of why he did it, and as it was not very long before I went for seven years to Ceylon, I never saw anything of Hardy after this, and, as I said, I have often wondered what, if any, effect this had on his subsequent life.[1] For instance, you say that he preferred Oxford to Cambridge. I wonder whether deep down within him this was really the case. When I knew him, he was certainly one of the most Cambridge of Cambridge men I have ever known and underneath the surface of his strange existence with Gaye he had, I think, a great attraction to Trinity and Cambridge. Did the tragedy of Gaye cause his "flight" from Cambridge to Oxford?

Yours sincerely
Leonard Woolf

FROM C. P. SNOW

18th January, 1968.

Dear Mr Woolf,
Thank you for your most interesting letter.
Hardy never spoke to me about his relation with Gaye. But I had heard about it from others, and it was, of course, one of the three intense human passions of his life. It may very easily have had a profound effect upon him. He was not very good at identifying what we should now call 'unconscious' reasons for his behaviour. I suppose you have read his Bertrand Russell and Trinity College? *In that he gives the unpleasant atmosphere of Trinity in wartime as one of the major causes of his moving to Oxford. The psychological shock of Gaye's death he probably buried with more intensity than would be possible to most of us. . . .*
What a remarkable group you all were! I have never seen a convincing explanation why Cambridge from, say, the appearance of

---

1. LW's memory failed him; Strachey had written him a long letter in April 1909 explaining that Gaye's suicide was the consequence both of his failure to receive a permanent Trinity fellowship and of Hardy's waning affection.

*Bertrand Russell at Trinity for about forty years attracted more of
the highest talent than any university which has ever existed.*

Yours sincerely
Charles Snow

To Melvin Lasky[1]

14.2.68   [Monk's House]

Dear Mr. Lasky,

Thank you for sending me the proof of Goronwy Rees's article. I
am afraid that I cannot write you anything of any length as I have
already reviewed the book at length for *The New Statesman* and I
cannot repeat myself.

As regards the specific questions which Mr. Rees asks of me: Why
I did not mention the fact that some of my friends were homosexuals,
my answer would be:

(1) not being a homosexual myself it was irrelevant to my relation
to them;

(2) it was irrelevant to the subject treated by me in my autobiography;

(3) when I wrote, it was still unusual to reveal facts which might
be painful to living people unless it was absolutely vital to mention
them.

You may use this as a note or as a letter if you wish to do so but
personally I do not think it is worth your while.

Yours sincerely
Leonard Woolf

---

1. Lasky was Editor of *Encounter*, which was to publish a long review by Goronwy Rees
of both volumes of Holroyd's biography of Lytton Strachey. Rees expressed himself puzzled
that authors such as LW and Harrod had passed over in silence the importance of homosexual
love in the lives of Strachey, Keynes and their friends. Lasky sent LW, Harrod and several
other authors an advance copy of the article with a request for comment. LW alone responded
and the body of his letter was published in the May issue.

To Dame Peggy Ashcroft

29/4/68

Monk's House
Rodmell, Lewes, Sussex

Dearest Peggy,

Many thanks for Mr Wax.[1] I think I shall write to him.

. . . I read *Landscape* and listened to the broadcast.[2] I thought you were wonderful and the whole thing very impressive. It has an air of its own and is not just a stunt which so many things are. I recorded it, but not very successfully and for some reason missed your last sentence. My own doubt about Pinter is his central idea, the chromosome which organizes or should organize every sentence. What exactly is it?

I had a letter from Trekkie this morning from the island [Djerba]. It sounds very beautiful

Your loving
Leonard

To Dan Jacobson[3]

3/6/68

[Monk's House]

Dear Mr Jacobson,

It was very nice of you to send me your review which interests me much. I value your judgment because I read and was impressed by your autobiographical book some time ago. I like criticism and am never distressed by it, and I am sure there is much truth in yours.

As regards my judaism, I know that it is strange that it should have had so little effect upon my life. I have always been conscious of being a Jew, but in the way in which, I imagine, a Catholic is conscious of being a Catholic in England or someone else of being of Huguenot descent, or even perhaps in the way a man is conscious of having been

1. Wax was a literary agent whom LW wished to contact in connection with various proposals to film *Mrs. Dalloway*.
2. Harold Pinter's *Landscape*, banned from the stage by the Lord Chamberlain because of several four-letter words, had been performed on BBC radio.
3. Dan Jacobson (b. 1929), a South African novelist resident in London. In a review of the first three volumes of LW's autobiography in the March 1968 *Commentary*, he had confessed himself perplexed: "In his reticences as in his candor, here and elsewhere, this particular Jew . . . provokes one to declare that the English are simply impenetrable, the most opaque people in the world, sphinxes all."

at Cambridge and not Oxford. I have always been conscious of being primarily British and have lived among people who without question accepted me as such. Of course I have all through my life come up against the common or garden antisemitism, from the Mosley type to "some of my best friends have been Jews." But it has not touched me personally and only very peripherally. I cannot think of a single instance of it having the slightest influence on my career or social life in Ceylon.

I expect that to a certain extent your criticism of me as ignoring the critics is justifiable. Of course I have always been aware of the views of the Leavises &c. But in the first place I have always held that their idea of Bloomsbury as an entity which you can treat as an Aunt Sally and hated or a subject of eulogy and defence is absurd. Also I find the personal vendettas and moral indignations mixed up with all this boring and to enter into it is a waste of time.

I do not think it really true that "I accept Bloomsbury's assumptions about itself." I do not agree that there was any such thing as Bloomsbury in that sense or that "it" had any assumptions. I do not think that I "take for granted the finesse of Lytton Strachey's achievement"—I have never rated his achievement as very high—but he had an effect. I think *The Waves* is probably a very considerable work of art. I do not think that any of my wife's other books come near it. I think *To the Lighthouse* however a remarkable book, and that this is not just personal or "Bloomsbury" prejudice is perhaps shown by the fact that last year, 40 years after it was published, 24,688 copies were sold in Britain and 25,780 in the USA, a total of 50,468.

The one thing that I have always maintained is that I may be wrong—just like every one else.

Yours sincerely
Leonard Woolf

To Patricia Hutchins

Monk's House
Rodmell, Lewes, Sussex

19.6.68

Dear Mrs. Hutchins,

Many thanks for your letter and also for the book [*Ezra Pound's Kensington*] which I shall read with great interest. I was not put off in the least by the subject of Pound though I have never been able to appreciate him. Perhaps after reading your book I shall be able to do so.

The revolt of the young does not disturb me. I think they have been doing the same ever since Cain killed Abel. The only difference from age to age is the amount of violence which is used. We thought in my youth that we were just as much in revolt as people do now but we were against violence and, of course, we had not the same amount of publicity in those times. . . .

Yours sincerely
Leonard Woolf

To Baroness Asquith of Yarnbury[1]

3/7/68   [Monk's House]

Dear Lady Asquith,

I was extremely glad to get your letter and in a sense relieved. I rarely review now and had no desire to review Lady Cynthia's diary.[2] But Karl Miller, who has just taken over the editorship of the *Listener*, is a friend of mine, and when they rang up and asked me to review the book, I said yes. I did not know Lady Cynthia but of course had heard about her from Desmond [MacCarthy] and others and I thought the book might be interesting. When I read it, it did really seem to me appalling, and in any other circumstances I would have sent it back, as there is not much point in reviewing a book which one thoroughly dislikes.

It relieves me to know that you think that I was not unfair to it or to her, for I am fully aware that I am prejudiced against the kind of thing for which it stands. The more I read it, the more extraordinary it seemed to me that those responsible for it (including the publisher) should have put it out as it is. Quite apart from merely the feelings of people still alive, there is at least one most dangerous libel on Diana Cooper (page 112).[3] I cant understand Leslie Hartley's performance.[4]

1. Violet Bonham Carter (1887–1969), daughter of Prime Minister Asquith, had written to praise LW for his review of a book that had "brought pain and shame to the Asquith family."
2. *Diaries 1915–1918*, by Lady Cynthia Asquith (1887–1960), daughter of the Earl of Wemyss and wife of Lady Asquith's brother Herbert.
3. According to the entry, she took chloroform in preparation for a sex orgy.
4. Leslie Hartley (1895–1972), a novelist.

I simply cannot believe that he did not read the book. Is it conceivable that, if you were suddenly given the MS of the most intimate diaries of your intimate friend and read five pages of Lady Cynthia's, you would not have sat down and read every word of it before committing yourself to write an introduction to it? I have never known him well, but I have known him for a terribly long time—indeed, ever since he, David Cecil and a large contingent of Oxford young men used to come out to Garsington on a Sunday afternoon. He always seemed to me a rather gentle and sensible person.

I think it may interest you to know that, after he wrote his second letter in the *Listener*, I wrote him the following private letter (to which he has not replied): "I think it would be absurd to continue our public correspondence, though I think you were singularly unfair in what you said about me in relation to Lady Cynthia's child.[1] I said nothing about those facts for two reasons: first, they were entirely irrelevant to what I wrote about in my review; secondly, for me publicly to discuss what was a private, personal, and painful situation, which in the diary is, of course, not fully explained—would have been both insensitive and impertinent."

Yours sincerely
Leonard Woolf

To William Plomer

Monk's House
Rodmell, Lewes, Sussex

12/8/68

Dear William,

Yes, Friday will be all right and I shall expect you at 1—and much look forward to it.

About the year 1913 I actually began a novel to be called The Empire Builder. It began with a boy of 16 kicking a stone along the towpath at Richmond, imagining how the stone, which had lain for years in one spot, suddenly found itself uprooted to a completely new world 50 yards away. Symbolical? Autobiographical? I think it may have been a good beginning, but it never got any further.

Yours
Leonard

1. The child was autistic.

To S. P. Rosenbaum[1]

14/9/68

Monk's House
Rodmell, Lewes, Sussex

Dear Mr Rosenbaum,

Many thanks for sending me the Leavis articles. They are very interesting. What always causes me mild surprise with regard to Leavis and some of the other hostile critics of my wife's books is that they do not see that the books are about the deepest and most important things in the world, in society—and in the universe. It is perfectly legitimate criticism to say that they fail to deal successfully with these subjects, but to ignore *what they are about* and simply say that they are "vacant" and "pointless" and have no "concern for any appearance of grasp or point" (whatever exactly the Professor of English Literature may mean by that) seems to me just silly.

I hope you will manage somehow to introduce bowls into the University of Toronto and perhaps a degree in bowls, in which case I shall expect an honorary D.B. Toronto.

Yours sincerely
Leonard Woolf

To Richard Church[2]

24/10/68

Monk's House
Rodmell, Lewes, Sussex

Dear Richard,

It was very pleasant to see your handwriting again. We are really getting old though I rather quicker than you. You entered the Civil Service 59 years ago; I left it 57 years ago. I should like to see you again. Could you ever get over here for lunch?

The monks in Monk's House are quite fraudulent, an invention of the agent in 1919. It was lived in by the Cleere family from 1702 to

---

1. Professor of English Literature at the University of Toronto; he had sent LW a review by Q. D. Leavis of *Three Guineas* and one by F. R. Leavis of *Between the Acts*.
2. Richard Church (1893–1972), who had worked in the Customs and Excise Department before becoming a poet and novelist, had written from his address, "The Priest's House, Sissinghurst Castle," to comment on LW's letter in *The Times* about the Civil Service. A P.S. said: "How ironical that you should live in a Monk's House & I in a Priest's House—and both of us so savagely anti-clerical!"

1780 (John Cleere being a carpenter from Rottingdean), and it was always called Cleeres.

Yours
Leonard Woolf

To William Plomer

24/11/68

Monk's House
Rodmell, Lewes, Sussex

Dear William,

It was very pleasant to get your letter. Like you, I was attacked by what they call a virus which attacked me in what they call the intestine. It was not very bad but lasted for a week. I was just on the point of complete recovery when I was attacked by another bug or virus of the influenza type. With a temperature I had to stay in bed, but I am now to all intents and purposes recovered. But I hate not feeling well.

I have been reading Joe [Ackerley]'s account of himself and his father [*My Father and Myself*]. What odd books he wrote, but he was an odd man. After years of friendship he quarrelled with me because, on one of his visits to Lewes, sitting in the garden having tea, we heard a snarling behind us and his dog Queenie and my dog Nigg were having the sort of yapping, snapping, snarling hysterical dust-up which shows the difference between a bitch fight and a dog fight. I took it calmly and in fact separated them without difficulty. Joe did not say anything to me, but he told Trekkie that I had behaved monstrously— my horrible dog had attacked his beloved Queenie and I had paid no attention to this and had not even said that I was sorry. Joe never came near me again.[1]

I hope we shall meet very soon. Thank Charles for his good wishes.

Yours ever
Leonard

1. Queenie, a German shepherd, was the love of Ackerley's life, and his concern for her went to ludicrous extremes. In 1956 he wrote a book about her, *My Dog Tulip*.

To Roberta Rubenstein[1]

                                          Monk's House
14/12/68   Rodmell, Lewes, Sussex

Dear Roberta,

I was glad to get your letter. We much enjoyed your visit and it
would be nice to see you again. Would you come and lunch here on
Friday, January 3? And shall I wait to give you your MS then or shall
I send it to you by post? I have begun to read it and find much of
interest in it. There are one or two things which I should like to discuss
with you. What is your evidence for saying that Virginia had never
read a Russian novel until she read *Crime and Punishment* in 1912?
The translations of Turgenev by Constance Garnett were published
1894 to 1899. I certainly read some of these at Cambridge in 1901 and
I should have thought that she had read some long before 1912. *Anna
Karenina* in Garnett's translation appeared in 1901 and I certainly read
this at Cambridge and I should have thought she did before 1910. In
a list of the greatest writers which Lytton Strachey and I drew up for
our amusement in 1901 (and which I still possess) Tolstoy appears in
the first class. I can hardly believe that Virginia had not read anything
of his by 1901. (I dont think she had read or was at all influenced by
Bergson.)

I am glad you sent me the poems. I liked *Games* very much and I
also liked *Rebirth*. I was not sure about the others. You must go on
writing.

                                          Yours
                                          Leonard Woolf

To Sir Denis Brogan[2]

                                          Monk's House
11/1/69   Rodmell, Lewes, Sussex

Dear Sir Denis Brogan,

I was much interested by your article in the *Spectator* and particularly by what you say about my wife's books. Like so many highbrow

1. An American Fulbright scholar, Rubenstein was writing a doctoral thesis on "Virginia
Woolf's Response to Russian Literature" at the University of London.
2. Sir Denis Brogan (1900–1974) was Professor of Political Science and Fellow of Peterhouse,
Cambridge.

writers, you assume that her reputation has been a casualty of the last war and that people no longer read her. If the sales of her novels are any evidence, the opposite is in fact the case. The sales of all her novels have steadily increased in the last 25 years. In the last three years the sales of *To the Lighthouse* have been over 50,000 per year; the sales of this book in 1967 were 56,653 copies. On an average I think I get four or five letters every year from postgraduates who are writing Ph.D. theses on "The Novels of Virginia Woolf". It is true that I get about the same number of letters from postgraduates writing Ph.D. theses on "The Labour Party's Foreign Policy between the Years 1919 and 1939." Such is fame.

Yours sincerely
Leonard Woolf

To Dame Peggy Ashcroft

Monk's House
Rodmell, Lewes, Sussex

5/2/69

Dearest Peggy,

I have been thinking of you and the *Delicate Balance* continually for the last 24 hours.[1] It and you were really marvellous. It is years since I have seen anything so completely remarkable. I once used to say to myself: "Well, I've seen Sarah, Duse, Réjane, and Ellen Terry," but I now say to myself: "Well, I've seen Sarah, Réjane, Duse, and Peggy Ashcroft." And you beat them all for range.

The supper was a perfect ending. I liked Trevor Nunn very much—what a strange face he has.[2]

Much love
Leonard

I dont think that Réjane
was really as good as the
other three.

1. Edward Albee's play was having its London premier.
2. Trevor Nunn (b. 1940), Associate Director of the Royal Shakespeare Company.

To Bernard Blackstone[1]

10/2/69   [Monk's House]

Dear Professor Blackstone,

. . . Though I think Holroyd's first volume too long and that he takes Lytton too seriously, I think much better of him than he does of me. Perhaps I can say what Voltaire once said in similar circumstances: "Perhaps we are both wrong."

There was, I daresay, a streak of what people call mysticism in Virginia, but not, I think, of religion. She had no more sense of a God than I have.

Yes, I remember our evening on the Acropolis very well and I should much like to visit you. Give my regards and also Mrs Parsons' to your wife.

                                        Yours sincerely
                                        Leonard Woolf

To Norah Smallwood

30/5/69   [Monk's House]

Dear Norah,

I enclose corrected proofs of my book [*The Journey Not the Arrival Matters*]. Would it be possible to get someone to make the index? I dont think I could make a reasonable job of it in my present state.

And could you find out from Harcourt Brace whether or not they want us to send them a set of corrected proofs—or are they going to take sheets?

                                        Yours
                                        Leonard

---

1. An itinerant professor of English literature, with a particular interest in VW, Blackstone was at this time Professor of English Literature at American University of Beirut.

BIOGRAPHICAL
APPENDIX

BELL, ARTHUR CLIVE HEWARD (1881–1964), was LW's contemporary at Trinity College, Cambridge, where he mingled with both the sporting set and the intellectuals, without being fully accepted by the latter. Lytton Strachey's disdain for "that little canary-coloured creature" was shared by LW; the two consequently grieved when Vanessa Stephen agreed to marry him in 1907. Vanessa lost interest in him after several years, and, though they always remained on friendly terms, he thereafter lived with a succession of female companions, chief of whom was Mary Hutchinson. He was an influential critic of the fine arts, published poems, contributed to the *New Statesman* and was a friend of Picasso. Civilization, he maintained in a book by that title, was a product of a leisure class, and he did his best in his own life to prove it. LW disliked him for his early flirtations with VW, resented his central place in his own social circle and frowned on his bohemian life. He painted a hostile portrait of him as Arthur in *The Wise Virgins*.

BELL, JULIAN HEWARD (1908–1937), elder son of Clive and Vanessa Bell, went to King's College, Cambridge, in 1927; he read history but came to have more interest in writing poetry. Following several years during which everything and nothing interested him, he accepted the

575

professorship of English at the University of Wuhan, in China, in 1935. After a year there he found himself bored, homesick and involved in an impossible affair with the wife of a Chinese colleague; he resigned in early 1937 to take part in the Spanish Civil War. Though LW had found him a position with Labour leader Hugh Dalton, and despite the entreaties of his mother and VW, he went to Spain as an ambulance driver and was killed by a shell. LW liked him but was at times exasperated by his egocentricity.

BELL, QUENTIN CLAUDIAN STEPHEN (b. 1910), younger son of Clive and Vanessa Bell, had a deep interest in art from his early years. He studied painting in Paris and for a time had a studio in Rome. In the 1930s he took up pottery making, and this eventually became a primary vocation. After the Second World War he wrote about art and occupied a series of academic posts: Lecturer in Art Education at Newcastle 1952–62; Professor of Fine Arts at Leeds 1962–67; Slade Professor at Oxford 1964–65 and Professor of the History and Theory of Art at Sussex 1967–75. LW's respect for him was such that he chose him to be VW's biographer; the highly acclaimed biography appeared in 1972. In 1952 he married Anne Olivier Popham, who edited VW's diary.

DAVIES, MARGARET CAROLINE LLEWELYN (1861–1944), was the daughter of a distinguished Christian socialist clergyman. After leaving Girton College, Cambridge, in 1883, she devoted herself to advancing the rights and education of women, particularly of the working class. She became General Secretary of the Women's Co-operative Guild in 1889. Assisted by an equally competent companion, Lilian Harris (1866–1949), she had built the Guild from fifty-one branches with 1,800 members to more than 1,000 branches with 52,000 members by the time she retired in 1921. A socialist and pacifist, she became a strong supporter of the League of Nations and of the Labour Party. She welcomed the Russian Revolution and had a lasting and sympathetic interest in the Soviet Union. It was through her that LW became active in Guild activities and feminist causes. Their warm friendship never dimmed. "If she had been a man, her achievements would have filled probably half a page in *Who's Who*; though she lived to be over 70, you will not find the name of Margaret Llewelyn Davies in any edition of it—the kind of fact which made—and makes—feminism the belief or policy of all sensible men" (*Beginning Again*).

DAVIES, CROMPTON LLEWELYN and THEODORE LLEWELYN, two of Margaret's six brothers, were brilliant scholars and Apostles whom LW knew at Cambridge. Theodore went into the Treasury; Crompton became a solicitor.

ELIOT, THOMAS STEARNS (1888–1965), poet and critic, met LW in 1917 or 1918, and they became increasingly good friends. Although the ideological gulf between them was deep, each greatly liked and respected the other. LW was Eliot's sponsor when he took British citizenship in 1927 and the person to whom Eliot turned for counsel when Vivien Heigh-Wood (1888–1947), his first wife, suffered mental problems. LW greatly admired Eliot's poetry and was deeply proud to have been the publisher of *Poems* and *The Waste Land*.

FORSTER, EDWARD MORGAN (1879–1970), went to King's College, Cambridge, where he read classics. LW and Strachey nicknamed him "the taupe" (mole) because of his elusiveness and diffidence. At the conclusion of their Cambridge years, Forster wrote to him: "I know you much less than I like you," and it was only after LW's return from Ceylon that the two became good friends. Although LW regarded him as "a perfect old woman" and was critical of his first novels, he came to have steadily increasing respect for both the person and his writing. It was at Forster's suggestion that LW published his novels with Edward Arnold, Forster's publisher. LW encouraged Forster to complete *A Passage to India* and commissioned several works from him for the Hogarth Press. The two men shared similar views on religion, empire, socialism and civil liberties, and they collaborated in helping writers who were victims of philistine laws and judges.

GARNETT, ANGELICA VANESSA (b. 1918), daughter of Vanessa Bell and Duncan Grant, studied acting and music before taking up painting, decoration and drawing. In 1942 she married David Garnett, literary critic and novelist. Of LW she wrote in her autobiography, *Deceived with Kindness*: "He was made of different material from the rest of us, something which, unlike obsidian, couldn't splinter, and inevitably suggested the rock of ages."

KEYNES, JOHN MAYNARD (1883–1946), arrived in Cambridge a year after LW and had a brilliant academic career at King's College. LW immediately recognized his outstanding intellect—he and Strachey recruited him for the Apostles—but he disliked him, considering him intellectually unscrupulous and a manipulator. To some extent LW's feelings were swayed by VW and Strachey, who at times were deeply antipathetic to him. LW's comments in his autobiography about Keynes are a masterpiece of praising with faint damn. It is sometimes said that Keynes was anti-Semitic and that LW resented him for it; there is no evidence to support either claim. Overtly, relations between the two were always friendly and they worked together amicably on the *Nation*; one of the reasons Keynes gave up the journal in 1930 was LW's decision to resign as literary editor. LW was fond of Keynes's wife, Lydia Lopokova, and she of him.

LEHMANN, JOHN (1907–1987), went to Trinity College, Cambridge, where he developed lifelong literary interests. In 1931 he became apprentice manager of Hogarth Press. After eighteen months, he left and went to Vienna and, later, Berlin, where he became a friend of Christopher Isherwood and other writers. He devoted himself to the literary avant-garde and in 1936 began publishing a series entitled *New Writing*. Two years later he bought VW's share of the Hogarth Press and became general manager. A conscientious and dynamic administrator, he attracted a number of new writers and kept the Press operating efficiently throughout the war. However, with different aims and a difficult temperament, he eventually had strong disagreements with LW and dissolved the partnership. He founded his own publishing house, which closed after seven years, and, later, the *London Magazine*. In 1978 he wrote *Thrown to the Woolfs*, a sometimes distorted account of his years with the Hogarth Press.

MACCARTHY, DESMOND (1877–1952), was at Trinity College several years before LW but met him at meetings of the Apostles. After a period of free-lance writing, he became literary editor of the *New Statesman* in 1920. He founded the literary quarterly *Life and Letters* in 1927 and was senior literary critic of the *Sunday Times* from 1927 until his death. His charm was legendary—and nowhere better conveyed than in *Sowing*—and there were few people of whom LW was as fond. Like other friends, LW regretted MacCarthy's failure to become the great writer that seemed his destiny. MacCarthy's literary work did not go unrecognized; he was knighted in 1951 and received an honorary degree from Cambridge the next year.

MACCARTHY, MARY (MOLLY) WARRE-CORNISH (1882–1953), Desmond's wife, was the daughter of the Vice Provost of Eton and an author. To induce Desmond to write his masterpiece, she tried everything from locking him in a room to moving to the Isle of Wight. With the same aim in mind, in 1919 she founded the Novel Club, which became the Memoir Club the year after. "Her vagueness and fluttering indecision must have been perpetually nourished by a lifetime of waiting for Desmond to return to dinner to which he had forgotten that he had invited several friends" (*Beginning Again*).

MARTIN, BASIL KINGSLEY (1897–1969), after receiving a double first in history at Magdalene College, Cambridge, went on to lecture at the London School of Economics, at which time LW recruited him to review for the *Nation*. Following an apprenticeship at the *Manchester Guardian*, he was offered the editorship of the *New Statesman* when it was amalgamated with the *Nation* in 1931. LW told him: "Take it for seven years. Not for longer, because journalism rots the brain." He stayed for twenty-nine years, became one of the outstanding journalists of his time and made the *New Statesman* the most prestigious of the weeklies. He was a spokesman for the left at a time when the entire intellectual community was on the left. His spectacularly bad political judgment provoked LW's furious disagreement, which in turn drove Martin into frenzies of anguish. After his death, his companion, Dorothy Woodman, wrote to LW: "During my life with Kingsley— over 30 years—you always meant so much to him. In many ways more than anyone else. He loved you even when he disagreed violently with you."

MOORE, GEORGE EDWARD (1873–1958), arrived at Trinity College, Cambridge, in 1892, was Prize Fellow there 1898–1904, University Lecturer in Moral Sciences 1911–25 and Professor of Philosophy 1925– 39. His attack on Hegelianism initiated a revolution in Anglo-American philosophy and made him a dominant influence in it for half a century. He was venerated by undergraduates of LW's generation, and LW considered him the only great man he ever knew. In 1954 Moore was awarded the Order of Merit; LW was shocked that Moore accepted an official honor.

PARSONS, IAN (1906–1980), studied at Winchester and Trinity College, Cambridge, where he took a first in English literature. While still an undergraduate, he decided to become a publisher and joined Chatto & Windus in 1928. After wartime military service with the RAF in France and then in Air Force intelligence, he returned to the firm, and became its chairman in 1954. It was through him that LW arranged to sell John Lehmann's equity in the Hogarth Press to Chatto & Windus

579

in 1946. He and LW were close friends and colleagues for the remainder of LW's life.

PARSONS, TREKKIE, née Ritchie, was born in Natal of British parents, who returned to Britain during the First World War. Her sister, Alice, wrote two novels published by the Hogarth Press; her brother, Patrick, rose to be Air Vice-Marshal in the RAF. She studied painting at the Slade, and in the early 1930s met LW and VW and designed jackets for several Hogarth Press books. She married Ian Parsons in 1934. After working in the intelligence service during the war, she resumed painting and continued to exhibit until 1985. In 1943 she became LW's closest friend; they were neighbors on Victoria Square in London and in Sussex until the end of his life.

SACKVILLE-WEST, VITA (1892–1962), only child of the 3rd Baron Sackville and wife of Harold Nicolson, diplomat and writer, was a poet, novelist and gardener. She met the Woolfs in 1923 and soon fell in love with VW, with whom she had an intimate relationship from 1925 until 1928. The affair does not appear to have damaged LW's genuine and lasting affection for her. She was the first person to whom he wrote to tell of VW's suicide. "Vita was an honest, simple, sentimental, romantic, naïve, and competent writer," was LW's estimate of her as an author. He valued her loyalty to the Hogarth Press, which benefited significantly from several of her novels. Her attitude toward him she expressed to Nicolson in 1938: "I know he is tiresome and wrong-headed and sometimes Jewish but really with his school-boyish love for pets and toys (gadgets) he is irresistibly young and attractive." She was shocked when LW rejected her novel *Grand Canyon* and angered by his refusal to publish VW's letters to her.

STEPHEN FAMILY

STEPHEN, SIR LESLIE, (1832–1904), the distinguished literary critic and author, founding editor of the *Dictionary of National Biography* and holder of honorary degrees from Cambridge, Oxford, Edinburgh and Harvard. He married, as his second wife, *Julia Duckworth* (1846–1895). Each had children by a previous marriage—in Leslie's case, a daughter, *Laura* (1870–1945), who was mentally retarded and lived in a home; in Julia's case, *George*, a public official, *Gerald*, a publisher, and *Stella*. Leslie and Julia had, in addition to ADELINE VIRGINIA (1882–1941), three children.

STEPHEN, ADRIAN LESLIE (1883–1948), youngest of the children, went to Trinity College, where he read law. In 1914 he married *Karin Costelloe* (1889–1953), the most brilliant woman philosophy student of her time at Cambridge. At her initiative the couple took medical degrees and became psychiatrists in 1926. Their marriage was troubled and, in their devotion to their successful practices, they badly neglected their children, *Ann* (b. 1916) and *Judith* (1918–1972). VW was not close to Adrian and did not like Karin; LW tried to help Karin through a bad time in the 1940s by encouraging her to write a biography of Freud and was fond of Ann and Judith. Karin suffered increasingly from manic-depression, probably inherited from her mother, Mary Berenson, and ended her life by suicide.

STEPHEN, JULIAN THOBY PRINSEP (1880–1906), known to LW and his friends as "the Goth" because of his stature and solidity, regarded LW as his closest friend when the two were contemporaries at Trinity College. LW wrote of him: "He had greater personal charm than anyone I have ever known." After leaving Cambridge, Thoby studied law and was called to the bar in Inner Temple in 1904, but before taking up practice, he died of typhoid fever contracted in Greece.

STEPHEN, VANESSA (1879–1961), the noted painter, married Clive Bell in 1907 but soon tired of him. After an affair with Roger Fry, the art critic and painter, she lived and worked until her death with the painter Duncan Grant. Her children were Julian Heward, Quentin Claudian Stephen and Angelica Vanessa.

STRACHEY FAMILY

STRACHEY, LIEUTENANT-GENERAL SIR RICHARD (1817–1908) was a member of one of the great nineteenth-century Anglo-Indian families. A remarkable engineer and scientist, he was twice President of the Royal Geographical Society. He married *Jane Maria Grant* (1840–1928), who was equally adept at argument, poetry and billiards. They had ten children, who were all rich in brains, talent and eccentricity. LW's great fondness for the whole family, collectively and individually, is recorded in his autobiography.

Other family members mentioned in these pages:

STRACHEY, DOROTHY (1865–1960), the eldest of the children, married, to her family's initial distress, a French painter, Simon Bussy, and thereafter lived mostly in France. She was a close friend of Matisse and an intimate of André Gide, whose works she translated.

STRACHEY, GILES LYTTON (1880–1932), an Apostle and LW's closest friend at Trinity College, offered LW entrée into the upper-middle-class intellectual aristocracy. Physically and temperamentally weak, he for many years fell short of all his high ambitions—in the History Tripos (twice), in the Trinity fellowship competition (twice) and in his love affairs (repeatedly). In 1918 his *Eminent Victorians* inaugurated a new mode of biography and made him famous overnight. Although LW outgrew his intimacy with Strachey and did not rate his literary contribution as being great, he remained a devoted friend.

STRACHEY, JAMES BEAUMONT (1887–1967), followed his brother Lytton to Trinity, where he was elected an Apostle but was an academic flop. In 1920 he married *Alix Sargant-Florence* (1892–1973). They spent their honeymoon in Vienna, where they were the first couple to be analyzed by Freud. While maintaining an active analytic practice himself, he was the leading English translator of Freud's psychoanalytical works, culminating in the *Standard Edition of the Complete Psychological Works of Sigmund Freud.*

STRACHEY, JOAN PERNEL (1876–1951), was Vice Principal of Newnham College, Cambridge 1910–23 and Principal 1923–41.

STRACHEY, MARJORIE (1882–1964), was a good teacher and a bad writer, though she was published by the Hogarth Press.

STRACHEY, OLIVER (1874–1960), an accomplished musician and a brilliant mathematician, began his career with the Indian railways but during the two world wars was a cryptographer in the War Office. In 1911 he married *Rachael Costelloe* (1887–1940), elder daughter of Mary Berenson and an active feminist.

STRACHEY, PHILIPPA (1872–1968), known as "Pippa," helped organize the first mass woman-suffrage demonstration, in 1907, and spent the next forty-five years promoting women's rights. "I have never known anyone more profoundly and universally a person of good-will than she was . . ." (*The Journey Not the Arrival Matters*).

S YDNEY - T URNER , S AXON (1880–1962), shared rooms with LW at Trinity College. Although opposites by nature, they remained lifelong friends. With his first-class brain, he was an Apostle and took a double first in classics, but he lacked any drive, imagination or creativity. LW found him profoundly repressed, "physically and mentally . . . ghost-like, shadowy," inclined to long silences. Yet he had an indefinable charm, and what he did not say, some suspected, was probably more interesting than what many others did. He was a linguist of sorts and composed music. An opera devotee and a Wagner addict, he attended more than a hundred performances of *Tristan und Isolde* alone. He had a career in the Treasury but never told anyone what he did. Making a decision—whether to marry or even whether to take a taxi—was beyond him, but the love of his life, Barbara Bagenal, cared for him to the end. He gambled away most of his money on horses and ended his days in a small flat where he watched television on a set purchased by a subscription, to which LW contributed.

W EBB , B EATRICE (1858–1943), and S IDNEY (1859–1947), social re-formers, Fabian socialists, founders of the *New Statesman* and the Fabian Research Bureau, "discovered" LW through an article he wrote for the *New Statesman* on the Women's Co-operative Guild congress in June 1914. In commissioning him to write a study on international order following the outbreak of the First World War, they opened the way for LW into the Fabian Society, the Labour Party, the *New States-man* and his later activities in international affairs. Although LW found the Webbs conservative and conventional in their political and social goals, he retained throughout his life a strong respect and deep affec-tion for them.

WOOLF FAMILY

W OOLF , S OLOMON R EES S YDNEY , always known as "Sidney" (1844–1892), was born in London of a prosperous family—his father owned a number of fashionable shops—and attended boarding school at Kew and University College School, which he left at sixteen to study law. He was called to the bar as a solicitor in 1860, became a barrister four years later and built up the City's leading practice in bankruptcy law. He also engaged in criminal and common-law cases and was the author of two legal treatises. In 1890 he was appointed a queen's counsel. He was clearly on the rise, and a few weeks before his death publicly declared an interest in entering Parliament as a Liberal Unionist. Physically frail, his last years were a constant struggle against ill health. He was a Reformed Jew, and though he scarcely practiced his religion he followed a strict ethic based on the maxim of the Prophet Micah, "What doth the Lord require of thee, but to do justly, and to love mercy, and to walk humbly with thy God?"

WOOLF, MARIE BATHILDE DE JONGH (1850–1939), married Sidney Woolf in 1875. She was the widow of Zacharias W. A. Goldstücker, a fur merchant from Silesia, who had died two years earlier. She was born in Amsterdam, the daughter of a rich diamond merchant who moved to London in the middle of the nineteenth century. The family had a Scandinavian branch through Marie's sister Flora, who married Arnold Abrahamson, a Dane; one of their daughters, Charlotte, a painter, married Otto Mannheimer, a Swedish jurist and parliamentarian. LW found the de Jonghs soft compared to the tough Woolfs, and family correspondence leaves the impression that Marie, called "Lady" by all the family except LW, was an intelligent and warmhearted but demanding and self-pitying matriarch. In October 1900 she wrote to LW: "In some ways we two are very opposite natures, but we must try and meet each other a little more in the future. Only try to understand that I am a very 'love thirsty' soul. . . ."

WOOLF, ARNOLD HERBERT SIDNEY (1879–1949), LW's older brother, became head of the family after Sidney's death. Starting work on the stock exchange at the age of sixteen, he was an immediate success and later founded his own stockjobbing firm, which prospered. He figured vaguely as the father in LW's *The Wise Virgins*.

WOOLF, BELLA SIDNEY (1877–1960), had an early and lifelong penchant for writing and encouraged LW to contribute articles and verses to the *Jewish Chronicle*. She later wrote stories for children's magazines and ultimately published two dozen books, many of them children's stories and travelogues. She visited LW in Ceylon, where she met and in 1910 married Robert Lock (1879–1915), former Fellow of Gonville and Caius College, Cambridge, then Assistant Director of the Colombo Horticulture Gardens. In 1921 she married LW's Colonial Civil Service colleague Wilfrid Thomas Southorn (1879–1957), who became Colonial Secretary in Hong Kong and, after being knighted, Governor and Commander-in-Chief of the Gambia. LW was closer to her than to any other family member, and until his marriage she was the person in whom he most fully confided.

WOOLF, CECIL NATHAN SIDNEY (1887–1917), followed LW to St. Paul's and Trinity, where he gained a First in both parts of the History Tripos. His treatise "Bartolus of Sassoferrato," still authoritative, won him a Trinity fellowship and the Thirwall Prize. He was considered one of the most promising scholars of his generation. Commissioned in the Royal Hussars in 1914, he was sent to France the following year and was killed in the Battle of Cambrai in 1917.

WOOLF, CLARA HENRIETTA SIDNEY (1885–1934), was an active suffragist and during the First World War a volunteer nurse. She liked to travel, visiting Ceylon, Denmark and, in the early 1920s, New York, where, while working at the New York Public Library, she met and married George Walker (1867–1944), an American journalist and expert in mining and metallurgy.

WOOLF, EDGAR SIDNEY (1883–1981), was educated at St. Paul's and Sidney Sussex College, Cambridge, where he took a second in classics. After military service during the First World War, he eventually became a partner in Herbert's firm. Although fond of his sisters, particularly Clara, he had poor relations with Herbert and his other brothers and was prey to what one of them, in a letter to LW, labeled "paranoid tantrums."

WOOLF, FLORA SIDNEY (1886–1975), an active suffragist during her teens, married George Sturgeon, an unambitious schoolmaster who came from a rich family. After his death, she led a nomadic life, mostly in East Africa, remarking to LW in 1952 that she had lived in "60 hotels in two years."

WOOLF, HAROLD BENJAMIN SIDNEY (1882–1967), went to St. Paul's, but instead of going on to Cambridge went into the City, where he was a success on the stock exchange. After serving in the First World War, he made a fortune as a nitrate broker. Retiring while fairly young, he bought and sold property and played the stock market. He wrote to LW of *Sowing*: "It is easier to be truthful of anything but oneself, & you have succeeded."

WOOLF, PHILIP SIDNEY (1889–1962), went to St. Paul's and, failing the exam for Trinity, spent an unhappy period at Sidney Sussex College, Cambridge, and left to study languages to be a Foreign Office interpreter. On being rejected by the Foreign Office, he studied painting. Extremely close to Cecil, he collaborated with him in publishing in 1914 a translation of Stendhal's *De l'amour*, joined the same cavalry regiment at the outbreak of the war, fought by his side in France and was wounded by the same shell that killed Cecil. In LW's view, Philip never recovered from his brother's death. After the war he studied farm management and from 1922 to 1952 was manager of James de Rothschild's Waddesdon Manor estate. After the suicide of his wife, he lived with Bella; after her death, he committed suicide. He was, after Bella, the family member of whom LW was most fond.

WOOLF, SIDNEY JOHN, died at the age of three months in 1878.

INDEX

TO LETTERS

Kankesanturai, 94; Kegalla, 117; Kyats, 77; Mannar, 120, 126–7; Marichchukkaddi, 112; Matara, 70; Pearl Fishery, 93 & n, 94, 112 & n, 113–7, 120; Poonaryn, 100, 102; Pt. Pedro, 101; Tissamaharama, 142; Trincomalee, 103, 104 *see also* Woolf, Leonard, CEYLON YEARS
Cézanne, Paul, 231, 528
Chamberlain, Neville, 407 & n
Charity Organization Society, 179n
Chatto & Windus, publishers, 317, 363
Chekhov, Anton, 281 & n
China, 437 & n, 450 & n
Church, Richard, 569 & n
  letter to, 569–70
  letter from, 569n
Churchill, Winston, 404, 491
Cicero, 552
Clare, John, 289 & n
Clear, John, 525, 569–70
Cleere, John *see* Clear, John
Cleeve, Margaret, 444 & n
  letter to, 444
Clementi, Sir Cecil, 395 & n
Clifford, Sir Hugh, 137n
Clifford, James, 494n
Clifford's Inn, 195 & n, 474, 484n
Cockburn, Claude, 406n
Cole, G. D. H., 382 & n
Cole, Margaret: *The Story of Fabian Socialism*, 447 & n, 448
  letter to, 447–8
Colefax, Lady Sibyl, 231 & n
Collett, Mrs. S. B., 512 & n
Collins, John Churton: LW reviews his book, 38 & n; and Gosse, 508n, 509
Collins, Mr., 489 & n
Colonial Office, 47 & n, 174, 388–9, 393
Colonies, Secretary of State for the, 389
Colonies, Under Secretary of State for the
  letters to, 172, 175
Condorcet, J. A. N. C., 445

Congreve, William, 283–4
Conrad, Joseph, 289
Constable, publishers, 317
Contemporary Review, 224
Cookson, G. M., 70
Cooper, Lady Diana, 567 & n
Co-operative News: LW's article for, 382 & n
Coquelin, Constant-Benoît, 510–11 & n
Corelli, Marie, 23 & n, 278 & n
Cornford, Frances, 356
Cornford, Francis: *Thucydides Mythistoricus*, 132
Cornwall, 17, 18, 20
Cox, Frederick, 501 & n
Cox, Katharine (Ka), 195 & n, 196, 200n, 383
Craig, Maurice: on VW's having children, 181 & n, 182; on VW's recovery, 198; VW not to be alone, 209; and VW's 1915 breakdown, 211, 212, 213, 547; and LW's military exemption, 214–5 & n; VW to rest more, 220
  letter from, 220
Craik, Dinah, *John Halifax, Gentleman*, 75
Cranium (dining club), 302, 514, 515
Crewe, Marquess of, 423 & n
  letter to, 424–5
  letter from, 423–4
Criterion, 282n, 307
Critical Quarterly, 364n
Cromer, Earl of: *Modern Egypt*, 146
Crossland, Anthony, 441 & n
Crossman, Richard, 436 & n
Curtis, Lionel, 444 & n
Curtis Brown, Spencer, 492

Daily Herald, 207n, 281 & n, 414 & n, 415
Dakin, Hugh, 446n
  letter to, 446–7
Dalton, Hugh, 242 & n
Dane, Clemence, 542 & n, 543
Darwin, Charles, 424

for, 536; reading of own poetry, 550; and anti-Semitism, 559, 562; *Ash-Wednesday*, 237–8, 549–50; *Homage to John Dryden*, 364–5 & n; *Poems*, 279 & n, 356, 364, 551; *Prufrock*, 279, 534; *The Waste Land*, 238, 356, 364, 551

 letters to, 227–8, 237–8, 239, 279, 282–3, 297, 298, 487, 495–6, 534

Eliot, Valerie, 536 & n
 letter to, 536
Eliot, Vivien, 227 & n, 228
Elizabeth II, Queen, 329 & n, 359, 452
Ellis, Mercy, 525
Elton, Charles: "Luriana," 488 & n
Ely, Dorothy, 215 & n
Emmott, Lord, 217 & n
Erdman, Charles, 516 & n, 518, 570
Eugénie, Empress, 136 & n, 137
Euphrosne, 100 & n, 101, 132
Euripides, 39 & n, 445
Everest, Louie, 473 & n, 489 & n

Faber & Faber, publishers, 317
Fabian Society, 382 & n, 425n, 432n, 438, 447–8, 452, 473
Faraday, Michael, 424
Farrell, Sophie, 171
Ferenczi, Sandor, 304n
Fergusson, D. J., 223
Fernando, Shelton, 532 & n
 letters to, 532, 545
Fichtl, Paula, 425n
Finley, Moses, 523n
 letter to, 523–4
 letter from, 524n
Fish, Frank: to write on VW's illness, 544 & n; assessment of VW's illness, 548
 letters to, 544, 547, 548–9
 letter from, 548
Fisher, Emmeline (Emmie), 234
Fisher, H. A. L., 216 & n
Fisher of Lambeth, Archbishop Lord: 453 & n; and terrorism in

Middle East, 453–8; and immortality, 552–4
 letters to, 453–8, 553–4
 letter from, 552–3
Fisher of Lambeth, Lady, 453 & n, 455–7
Fitzwilliam Museum, 475 & n
Flaubert, Gustave: *Madame Bovary*, 29, 132–3
Flugel, J. C., 304n
Ford, Ford Madox, 540–41 & n
Forster, Edward Morgan ("the taupe"): biog. note, 577; "querulous & apologetic," 40; depressing, 51; writes to LW, 78, 95; "certain to 'make a name,'" 105; "What a success," 130 & n; muddled idea of reality, 141, 142; at ballet, 166; and *The Wise Virgins*, 197n; and study of VW, 239n; and Potocki de Montalk, 306; and Cavafy, 350n, 351, 353–4; and article for *Show*, 360–61; and Bloomsbury, 497 & n, 544; and VW's letters, 498; solicits advice, 498 & n, 499; ref, 181n; *Letter to Madan Blanchard*, 303–4, 305n; *The Longest Journey*, 37n, 130; *Marianne Thornton*, 498; *Maurice*, 49n; *A Passage to India*, 498n; *A Room with a View*, 49n, 141, 142; *Where Angels Fear to Tread*, 105 & n, 109
 letters to, 303–4, 305, 351, 360–61, 498–9
 letters from, 305n, 498 & n
Fowler, H. W. and F. G.: *The King's English*, 278 & n
France: LW visits, 27; Woolfs visit, 226–7, 232, 239, 241; VW visits, 229–30, 233–5; Vanessa in, 230 & n; and First World War, 383; and Abyssinian crisis, 403–5; and Spanish civil war, 409
Franco, Francisco, 409
Franklin, Mrs. Ernest, 233
Franklin, John, 290 & n

Nowell-Smith, Simon, 501 & n
    letter to, 501
Nunn, Trevor, 572 & n

O'Brien, R. B.: *The Life of Parnell;*
    The Life of Russell, 82
Observer, 256n
    letter to, 356
Olivier, Noel, 531
Oriental Book Society, 326
Osborne, Dorothy, 233 & n, 234

Pain, Barry, 29
Palestine, 393, 428–30, 454–8
Pall Mall Gazette, 21
Palmer, Herbert, 292 & n; *Songs of*
    Salvation Sin and Satire, 292
    letter to, 292–3
Pape, Fred, 229–30 & n
Parnell, Charles Stewart, 79 & n
Parsons, Ian: biog. note, 579–80;
    and Rilke translation, 357; and
    Ackerley's autobiography, 358;
    and sales of Eliot's works, 364
    & n; LW's Christmas with, 551
    & n; ref, 451n, 491
    letters to, 363–5
Parsons, Trekkie: biog. note, 580;
    LW on her painting, 478, 481–2,
    483; LW's affection for, 478,
    479, 480–2, 483, 484–5, 486–7;
    her lithograph of LW, 480 & n;
    her portraits of LW, 518n; in
    Egypt, 526–7; and LW's will,
    539n; with LW to United
    States, 545; Christmas with, 551
    & n; in Tunisia, 565; and
    Ackerley, 570; ref, 510, 542, 573
    letters to, 475–7, 478–82, 483–5,
    486–7, 489–90, 491, 526–7
Partridge, Dora *see* Carrington,
    Dora
Partridge, Ralph, 281 & n, 282n
    letter to, 281
Passfield, Lord *see* Webb, Sidney
Pater, Walter: *Renaissance,* 14 & n
PAX, 398–9

Peace Ballot, 402 & n
Pearsall, C. W., 19 & n
Perham, Margery, 439 & n
    letter to, 439–40
    letter from, 439n
Pericles, 445–6, 478
Perks, Mr., 136 & n
Peterson, Maurice, 405
Pinter, Harold: *Landscape,* 565 & n
Pippett, Aileen: *The Moth and the*
    Star, 494–5 & n, 502
Plato, 13 & n, 36; "a filthy beast,"
    26 & n; *Symposium,* 14;
    Timeus, 20
Plomer, William: "how wise," 238 &
    n; "savage and hubristic," 299;
    leaves Hogarth Press, 315–6;
    his royalties, 318 & n; poetry of,
    356; and van der Post's preface,
    362 & n; praises Woolfs, 505 &
    n; gives LW birthday gift, 516;
    review of *Growing,* 518; ref,
    296; *The Case is Altered,* 318n;
    At Home: Memoirs, 505 & n; *I*
    Speak of Africa, 296, 318n;
    Paper Houses, 299 & n, 318n;
    Sado, 318n; *Turbott Wolfe,*
    291–2, 318n, 362 & n
    letters to, 238, 240, 291–2, 299,
    306, 315–6, 362, 505–6, 516,
    518, 568, 570
Political Quarterly, 242n, 300 & n,
    307, 403n, 426 & n, 427n, 447
    & n
Pollock, John, 166
Poor Law Minority Report, 183
Pope, Alexander, 211 & n
Port Said, 66, 114
Postgate, Raymond, 325 & n; *How*
    to Make a Revolution, 326–7 &
    n; *What to do with the B.B.C.,*
    325 & n, 326 & n
Pound, Ezra, 566–7
Prewett, Frank: *Poems,* 281 & n
Price, Ferdinando Hamlyn, 118 & n,
    126–7, 129
Priestley, J. B., 340 & n, 341
    letter to, 554–5
Pritchett, V. S., 540 & n

602

love affairs of, 108n, 558n;
blackballs Furness, 119 & n; to
Moscow, 203; report on *Moses
and Monotheism*, 336 & n; and
books given to Rodker, 351–2 &
n; and *Standard Edition* of
Freud, 353, 365 & n; death of,
365 & n; and Lytton-VW
letters, 498; ref, 166, 185, 189,
278, 492
Strachey, Joan Pernel: biog. note,
582; 221
Strachey, John, 419 & n, 420, 422
& n
Strachey, Marjorie: biog. note, 582;
183, 211 & n
Strachey, Oliver: biog. note, 582
Strachey, Philippa ("Pippa"): biog.
note, 582; 29n, 38 & n, 125,
488n
Strachey, Rachel Costelloe ("Ray"):
biog. note, 582; 210 & n
Strachey, Lt. Gen. Sir Richard: biog.
note, 581; 34 & n
Strand Magazine, 179 & n
Suez Canal, 66, 440 & n, 441, 455
Sunday Times, 259n, 508
letter to, 258
Sussex, University of, 532, 539n
Sutro, Alfred, 95n
Swanwick, Helena Maria, 412 & n
letter to, 412–3
Sweden, 166–7
Swinnerton, Frank, 541 & n
Swithinbank, Bernard, 128n, 139
Switzerland: as model for Ceylon,
417
Sydney-Turner, Saxon: biog. note,
583; "the King," 13 & n; and
academic exams, 19, 30 & n;
worried by *Timeus*, 20; and
Civil Service, 40, 46 & n;
farewell dinner with LW, 50; a
thin letter from, 95; "purely
wicked?," 98; knows Templer,
99; poetry of, 100 & n, 101; and
Thoby's death, 122–3; "the
billiard marker," 128; and
hangings, 133; sends sestina,

136; mellowing, 138; "made me
laugh," 139; VS marries?, 146,
147, 149; gives LW Spanish
dictionary, 178–9; bored, 183;
his mind rather like God's, 486;
ref, 17, 21, 106, 113, 149, 186,
230, 562
letters to, 15–16, 25, 27, 30, 46,
119, 120–21, 122–3, 125–6,
135–6, 140–41, 150–51, 178–9
Synge, Richard, 243n

Tate, Allen, 487 & n
Tavistock Square, No. 52: Woolfs
leave, 244–5; destroyed by
bombs, 247, 248
Tawney, R. H., 399 & n
Taylor, A. J. P., 448 & n, 449
Temple, Charles, 225 & n, 439–40
Templer, G. D., 99, 103–4
Terry, Ellen, 572
Thomas, J. H., 386 & n
Thomas, Jean, 181n, 184n, 185
Thompson, Logan, 550 & n
Thomson, Marjorie, 282 & n, 286
Thorne, W. J., 387 & n
Thornton, Roy, 543 & n
letters to, 543, 544–5
Thucydides, 478
Thwaites, Margaret
letter to, 485–6
Tiller, Terence, 342 & n, 343–5;
Poems, 342n
Times, The: and VW's death, 253–4
& n; and Suez Canal dispute,
441; whimpering letters to, 443;
and Israeli reprisal raid, 453 &
n; and extermination of old
people, 505
letters to, 453, 505
Times Literary Supplement: LW to
review for, 181 & n; VW's
reviews in 230n; 233n; and
Aldington, 294; VW's unsigned
essays in, 502; ref, 69, 204, 290,
327
Trevelyan, Sir Charles, 448–9
Trevelyan, Charles Philips, 92n

Woolf, Cecil Nathan Sidney: biog.
note, 585; 176, 189, 219 & n,
220, 411
Woolf, Clara Henrietta Sidney: biog.
note, 585
Woolf, Edgar: biog. note, 585; and
LW's wish to marry, 166n;
opinion of LW, 493–4, 509 &
n; ref, 27
letter to, 509–10
letters from, 166n, 493–4
Woolf, Flora Sidney: biog. note,
585; 39, 125n, 484, 490 & n
letter to, 490
letter from, 143
Woolf, Harold Benjamin: biog. note,
585; 27, 493
Woolf, Leonard Sidney
YOUTH AND EDUCATION: reads *Job*,
13 & n; "poets . . . are the
happiest," 15; existential
doubts, 16–17; arouses
antagonism, 19, 33; essay on
mystics, 21n; examinations and
prizes, 21 & n, 28n, 30 & n, 31;
essay on Byron, 24 & n, 25, 26,
27–28 & n; lectured on
paiderastia, 26; letters from
Strachey, 28, 49 & n, 52; vets
Stephen and Keynes, 29 & n;
books read, 29; conversations
with Moore, 32, 37, 38, 52, 176;
visits Strachey family, 34 & n;
"Thoughts" of, 35; and
Principia Ethica, 36, 48; and
Ainsworth, 37–38, 52; and Civil
Service exam, 39 & n, 40–42 &
n, 44; with Keynes in Wales, 42
& n, 43; to be an usher?,
44–49; to be a writer?, 44, 50;
to go to the colonies?, 44–47;
wins Eastern cadetship, 48;
reads "Warren Hastings," 48,
49; chooses Ceylon, 49;
farewells, 50–51; visits Moore in
Edinburgh, 52
CEYLON YEARS: opinion of country,
68, 72, 76, 77, 80, 87, 110, 181;
opinion of colleagues, 68–69,

70, 71–72, 76–77, 78, 80,
81, 83–84, 88–89, 105; to
Jaffna, 70–71; administers
"exemptions," 75–76, 141;
introduces Yenism, 78; opinion
of Tamils, 78, 80, 91, 117, 131–2;
"go for" fame, 79; trial of rape
case, 84–85; takes deposition of
dying man, 86, 101–2; inspects
leaky ship, 90; tries civil case,
92; searches for corpse, 94;
gives tea party, 96; in love with
Vanessa, 98 & n; in love with
Mrs. Lewis, 98; and Governor's
visits, 99–100, 101; makes
sexual debut, 102; uses "the
method," 106 & n; gets typhoid
fever, 108 & n; returns
Strachey's letters, 108–9, 112;
encounters American tourist,
109–10, 111; supervises Pearl
Fishery, 112, 113–7; and ugly
female, 116; "the Arab is
superb," 117; "prepared to
shoot myself," 118; acting AGA
in Mannar, 120, 126; and death
of Thoby Stephen, 122–4, 141;
pleasure of riding, 124; opinion
of colonial rule, 125, 127–8;
witnesses hangings, 125–6, 133;
gambling winnings, 127 & n; in
love with "Gwen," 128 & n, 345
& n; in trouble with "Jaffna
Association," 129; to Kandy, 131
& n; "Lord of ten million
blacks," 131n; in love with
"Rachel," 134 & n; to "vanish
into Italy," 135; attends
Empress Eugénie, 136 & n, 137;
to Hambantota, 137–8; on
circuit, 139, 140–41, 144;
investigates a murder, 141–2;
gives money to family, 143 & n;
advised on marriage, 148; leave
postponed, 150
RELATIONSHIP WITH VIRGINIA: first
encounters, 50n, 98, 166;
encouraged to marry, 145, 147 &
n, 148–50; decides to marry,

Woolf, Leonard Sidney
    PUBLISHING AND EDITING (*cont.*)
    picture book, 507; his selections
    for *A Writer's Diary*, 523; *see*
    also Hogarth Press and
    Lehmann, John
    WRITINGS OF: *After the Deluge*, 243;
    articles and reviews, 38 & n,
    47n, 188 & n, 281 & n, 306–11;
    329 & n, 340 & n, 382 & n,
    403n, 412n, 414 & n, 415 & n,
    423 & n, 424, 427n, 446n, 447 &
    n, 485 & n, 513 & n, 514–5, 560
    & n, 564 & n, 567–8;
    autobiography (general), 363 &
    n, 513, 565 & n; *Barbarians at*
    the Gate, 415 & n, 416 & n, 418
    & n, 419, 420 & n, 421 & n, 422
    & n, 423 & n; *Beginning Again*,
    529–30; *Co-operation and the*
    Future of Industry, 222; in *Does*
    Capitalism Cause War?, 397n;
    Downhill All the Way, 558;
    Empire and Commerce in
    Africa, 439 & n; *Growing*, 518,
    526, 529n, 532; *International*
    Government, 390 & n; *The*
    Journey Not the Arrival
    Matters, 573; poetry, 16, 146,
    151; *Principia Politica*, 13n, 493,
    511; *Quack, Quack!*, 324, 325 &
    n, 407–8 & n; *Socialism and*
    Co-operation, 391; *Sowing*, 512,
    513, 514; *Stories of the East*, 281
    & n; *Two Stories*, 276, 551; *The*
    Village in the Jungle, 91n, 180 &
    n, 181, 192, 195, 197 & n; *The*
    Wise Virgins, 195 & n, 196–7 &
    n, 198, 199 & n, 200 & n, 493
    LITERARY OPINIONS AND COMMENTS:
    Aristotle, 25; *The Brothers*
    Karamazov, 166, 520–21; Lord
    Byron, 23, 24, 25; *Candide*, 132;
    categories of novels, 519–22;
    Crotchet Castle, 521; C. Day
    Lewis, 299, 313–4; Charles
    Dickens, 121, 520–21; *A Doll's*
    House, 32; T. S. Eliot, 237–8,
    534; *Fathers and Children*, 520;

    E. M. Forster, 105, 130, 141, 142;
    The Golden Bowl, 521; Maxim
    Gorky, 22; Horace, 248; *A*
    Rebours, 25; *Jane Eyre*, 521;
    Book of Job, 13 & n; *The King's*
    English, 278; F. R. and Q. D.
    Leavis, 566, 569; "Luriana,"
    488; Archibald MacLeish,
    297; *Madame Bovary*, 29,
    132–3; 520; *The Mayor of*
    Casterbridge, 521; *Le Père*
    Goriot, 22–23; Samuel Pepys,
    561; *Phèdre*, 17, 24; Harold
    Pinter, 565; Plato, 13; Ezra
    Pound, 566–7; *Pride and*
    Prejudice, 520–21; Jean-Paul
    Sartre, 347–8; William
    Shakespeare, 22, 520, 527;
    Lytton Strachey, 132, 280, 566;
    Alfred de Vigny, 82; *War and*
    Peace, 520; *Wuthering Heights*,
    521
    HIS ASSESSMENT OF VW'S WRITINGS:
    Between the Acts, 255–6, 521–2;
    Jacob's Room, 520; *Mrs.*
    Dalloway, 497, 520; *Night and*
    Day, 520; *To the Lighthouse*,
    497, 520, 566; *The Voyage Out*,
    520; *The Waves*, 260, 497,
    520–22, 566; *A Writer's Diary*,
    520; *The Years*, 485, 520
    HIS HANDLING OF VW'S LITERARY
    ESTATE: MS for Sackville-West,
    259–60; disposition of her
    MSS, 475 & n, 499 & n, 500;
    publication of her essays, 484 &
    n, 500 & n, 502; publication of
    her letters, 488, 494–5 & n,
    495–6, 497, 498, 500, 502–3,
    503–4; 551–2; her diaries,
    493–4, 502, 523, 536, 548, 549,
    561; her biography, 513, 533–4,
    534–6, 538; her copyrights, 535,
    551
    POLITICAL ACTIVITIES AND VIEWS:
    women's suffrage, 125, 143;
    Women's Co-Operative Guild,
    201 & n, 203, 208, 209 & n, 215
    & n, 216–9, 224, 381, 382 & n;

military service, 214–5 & n,
497, 538; Nazism, 316, 319, 325;
royal family, 329, 383, 408 & n,
410; attends Fabian summer
school, 382; First World War,
383–4, 385–7, 451, 538; his
study on internationalism, 384
& n, 385; Socialist International
conference, 386n, 387 & n;
Ceylon self-rule, 388–9; Soviet
Union, 389, 409, 414–5, 418 &
n, 419–22, 423n, 436, 438,
440–41; stands for parliament,
390 & n; class wars and
national wars, 390–91; Boxer
Indemnity Committee, 391–2;
intercedes for Salvemini,
392–3; treatment of subject
peoples, 393–4; government of
Kenya, 394–5; British
isolationism, 396; the League
and collective security, 396–7,
400–407, 412–3; war and
capitalism, 397 & n, 398; peace
movement, 398–9; House of
Lords, 399–400; "Labour
party drives me mad," 407;
Spanish civil war, 409–10, 411;
"this king business," 410;
ethnic devolution in Ceylon,
416–7; getting Labour
party commitment, 417–8;
intellectuals in politics, 423–5;
intervenes for Freuds, 425–6;
Baldwin's sins, 426–7; racial
discrimination in Africa, 427–8;
Arabs and Jews in Palestine,
428–30, 454–8; war crimes
trials, 430; German Social
Democrats, 431–2; German
communal psychology, 432–3;
Hungarian show trials, 434–5;
pro-Soviet slant of *New
Statesman*, 434–9, 442–3;
ends and means in politics,
435, 450–51, 453–8; mass
execution of Chinese,
437, 450–51; mistrust of
Balogh, 437–9, 452; economic

imperialism in Africa, 439; Suez
Canal dispute, 440–41, 455;
Hungarian revolt, 442–3; Elgin
Marbles, 443 & n; resigns from
RIIA, 444; liberty in ancient
world, 445–6; self-rule by
African blacks, 446–7; defends
Webbs, 447–8; Nazi atrocities,
448–50; 1964 Italian election,
451; Harold Wilson, 452;
terrorism, 453–8; Zionism,
454–5; muddles about with
Labour and Fabians, 473; debt
owed the Webbs, 477;
conditions in Ceylon, 545

PERSONAL LIFE, VIEWS AND
RELATIONSHIPS: his ethnic
identity as a Jew, 13, 20, 45,
180, 237–8, 454, 565 & n, 566;
acting and actors, 17, 24, 31–2,
510–11, 527, 565, 572; religion,
19, 78, 533, 553–4, 573; sex, 24,
102, 124, 128, 130; immortality,
35, 78, 553–6; Jews, Judaism
and anti-Semitism, 45, 408 & n,
558, 559, 561–2; Jesus Christ,
102, 359, 434, 453–4, 457, 555;
relations with his family, 143 &
n, 178, 195 & n, 196–7, 493–4,
509–10, 511–2; portraits of, 171
& n, 480 & n, 518 & n;
"nothing matters," 222–3;
learns to drive, 229–30; calls
on Freud, 244 & n; Freud's
contribution, 359–60, 515; sees
Vanessa weekly, 473; "one must
. . . defy fate," 475–7;
relationship with Trekkie
Parsons, 478, 479, 480–82, 483,
484–5, 486–7; happiest those
without affections, 478; on
success and failure, 481–2, 519;
to read to Memoir Club, 482–3;
Bloomsbury, 496–7, 503–4,
507, 529–32, 543–5, 566;
advises Forster, 498 & n, 499;
gift of money, 503; proposes
exterminating fat old people,
505; praised by Plomer, 505 &

613

Woolf, Leonard Sidney

calls on Freud, 244 & n; final breakdown and suicide, 250–51 & n, 252–4 & n, 255–6 & n, 257 & n, 258 & n, 259 & n; leaves MS to Sackville-West, 259–61; her mode of writing, 260, 475; and offers from other publishers, 317; attends WCG Congress, 381, better not in parliament, 424; refused an honor, 452; being painted or photographed, 475, 546 & n; disposition of her MSS, 475 & n, 499 & n, 500; and publication of her letters, 488, 494–5 & n, 495–6 & n, 497, 498, 500, 502–3, 503–4; 551–2; parody of her style, 492 & n; revised essays, 494 & n; and Bloomsbury, 497, 503–4, 529–32, 544; her unsigned articles, 500 & n, 502–3; and London Library, 501 & n; her diaries, 493–4, 502, 536, 548, 549, 561; praised by Plomer, 505 & n; offense to Gosse, 508; her copyrights, 535, 551; disapproved of, by Whiteheads, 540 & n; sales of her books, 541, 566, 572; and her father, 547, 548

OPINIONS AND INFLUENCES: Baudelaire, 528; Bergson, 485–6 & n, 571; Cézanne, 528; contemporary writers, 541; Ford Madox Ford, 540–41; Freud and mental doctors, 522, 544; Roger Fry, 528; music, 528; religion, 573; Russian writers, 571; Wittgenstein, 539

HER WRITINGS: articles and essays, 230n, 233n, 494 & n, 499n, 500, 502–3; *Between the Acts*, 250, 255–6 & n, 261 & n, 499n, 521 & n, 522, 569 & n; *The Common Reader*, 228, 259 & n, 260, 499n, 502; *Contemporary Writers*, 541; *Mrs. Dalloway*, 259n, 260, 261, 497 & n, 499n,

520, 544; *Flush*, 229n, 259, 499n; *Freshwater*, 523 & n; "Gas at Abbotsford," 499n; *Granite and Rainbow*, 500n; *Haunted House*, 484 & n, 536; *Jacob's Room*, 499n, 520; "Lapin and Lapinova," 536–7; *To the Lighthouse*, 488, 497, 499n, 520, 531, 541 & n, 542, 557, 566, 572; "The Mark on the Wall," 276; *Monday or Tuesday*, 281 & n; *Night and Day*, 520; *On Being Ill*, 475 & n; *Orlando*, 233 & n, 259n, 260 & n, 542–3; *Roger Fry*, 251n, 499n, 561; *A Room of One's Own*, 237 & n, 557; *Three Guineas*, 499n, 569 & n; *Two Stories*, 276; *The Voyage Out*, 173, 520; *The Waves*, 259n, 260, 485, 497, 499n, 520–22, 566; *A Writer's Diary*, 493–4, 512 & n, 523; *The Years*, 242 & n, 259, 485, 499n, 520

WRITINGS AND COMMENTS ABOUT HER: proposed study, 239 & n, 240; biography, 513, 533–6; by Clemence Dane, 542–3; by Floris Delattre, 485–6 & n; by Jean Guiguet, 523; by Miyeko Kamiya, 547n; by the Leavises, 541–2, 569 & n; by Monique Nathan, 495 & n; by Aileen Pippett, 494–5, 502; by V. Sackville-West, 256 & n

TRAVEL: Bayreuth, 149; Berlin, 235 & n, 236; France, 226–7, 229 & n, 232, 233 & n, 234–5, 241, 496; Greece, 240; Ireland, 241; Italy, 139n, 179–80, 241, 296; Spain, 178–9, 225–7, 439; West Country, 237–8

letters to (chapter 3, *passim*)